CLIMATE CHANGE AND YOUTH MENTAL HEALTH

Climate change is the biggest threat of our century, one that will impact every aspect of children's lives: their physical, emotional, moral, financial, and social health and well-being. The relationship between the climate crisis and mental health in young people is therefore by definition multidisciplinary and multicultural, requiring multiple perspectives on how to understand and guide younger generations. This book provides a unique synthesis of those perspectives – the science, psychology, and social forces that can be brought to bear on supporting young people's psychological well-being. No matter the setting in which an adult may interact with younger people, this book provides the intellectual rigor and tools to ensure those interactions are as helpful and supportive as they can be.

BETH HAASE, MD, is a steering committee member of the Climate Psychiatry Alliance and has chaired the American Psychiatric Association and Group for the Advancement of Psychiatry Climate Committees. Clinical Professor of Psychiatry at the University of Nevada and Psychiatric Chief at Carson Tahoe Hospital, she also produced *Frogs in a Pot*, a film exploring emotional and practical strengths needed by children in a climate-changed world.

KELSEY HUDSON, PHD, chairs the Climate Psychology Alliance North America's Youth Subcommittee. Her clinical work, research, and advocacy focuses on climate-related youth mental health. Her perspectives have been featured by *NPR*, *USA Today*, and the *Boston Globe*.

CLIMATE CHANGE AND YOUTH MENTAL HEALTH

Multidisciplinary Perspectives

EDITED BY

ELIZABETH HAASE
University of Nevada at Reno School of Medicine

KELSEY HUDSON
Climate Psychology Alliance North America

Shaftesbury Road, Cambridge CB2 8EA, United Kingdom

One Liberty Plaza, 20th Floor, New York, NY 10006, USA

477 Williamstown Road, Port Melbourne, VIC 3207, Australia

314–321, 3rd Floor, Plot 3, Splendor Forum, Jasola District Centre, New Delhi – 110025, India

103 Penang Road, #05–06/07, Visioncrest Commercial, Singapore 238467

Cambridge University Press is part of Cambridge University Press & Assessment, a department of the University of Cambridge.

We share the University's mission to contribute to society through the pursuit of education, learning and research at the highest international levels of excellence.

www.cambridge.org
Information on this title: www.cambridge.org/9781009252959

DOI: 10.1017/9781009252904

© Cambridge University Press & Assessment 2024

This publication is in copyright. Subject to statutory exception and to the provisions of relevant collective licensing agreements, no reproduction of any part may take place without the written permission of Cambridge University Press & Assessment.

First published 2024

A catalogue record for this publication is available from the British Library

Library of Congress Cataloging-in-Publication Data
NAMES: Haase, Elizabeth, 1963– editor. | Hudson, Kelsey, editor.
TITLE: Climate change and youth mental health : multidisciplinary perspectives / edited by Elizabeth Haase, MD, University of Nevada at Reno School of Medicine, Kelsey Hudson, PhD, Climate Psychology Alliance North America.
DESCRIPTION: Cambridge, United Kingdom ; New York, NY : Cambridge University Press, 2024. | Includes bibliographical references and index.
IDENTIFIERS: LCCN 2023052221 | ISBN 9781009252959 (hardback) | ISBN 9781009252904 (ebook)
SUBJECTS: LCSH: Climatic changes – Psychological aspects. | Youth – Mental health.
CLASSIFICATION: LCC BF353.5.C55 C55 2024 | DDC 155.9/15–dc23/eng/20240213
LC record available at https://lccn.loc.gov/2023052221

ISBN 978-1-009-25295-9 Hardback
ISBN 978-1-009-25291-1 Paperback

Cambridge University Press & Assessment has no responsibility for the persistence or accuracy of URLs for external or third-party internet websites referred to in this publication and does not guarantee that any content on such websites is, or will remain, accurate or appropriate.

Contents

List of Figures	*page* viii
List of Tables	ix
List of Textboxes	x
List of Contributors	xi
Preface and Introduction	xiii
Considerations	xxi
Acknowledgments	xxii

PART I CONCEPTUAL FOUNDATIONS OF CLIMATE DISTRESS IN YOUNG PEOPLE

1 Climate Distress among Young People: An Overview   3
   Susan Clayton and Tara Crandon

2 Definitions and Conceptualizations of Climate Distress: An International Perspective   21
   Panu Pihkala

3 Psychiatric Perspectives on Youth Climate Distress: Using the Biopsychosocio-environmental Knowledge Base to Understand and Assess for Clinical Level Symptoms   40
   Elizabeth Haase

4 Developmental Perspectives on Understanding and Responding to Mental Health Impacts of Climate Change on Young People   70
   Francis Vergunst and Helen L. Berry

5 Neuropsychiatric Perspectives on the Biology of Anxiety and Youth Climate Distress   93
   Jacob Lee and Anthony Guerrero

Contents

6 Psychoanalytic and Relational Perspectives on Youth Climate Distress 111
Archana Varma Caballero and Janet L. Lewis

7 Understanding the Role of Trauma and Dissociation in Youth Responses to Climate Crises: Eco-Neglect as Institutional Child Abuse 130
Karen Hopenwasser

8 Cognitive Behavioral Principles for Conceptualizing Young People's Eco-Emotions and Eco-Distress 148
Elizabeth Marks and Kelsey Hudson

9 A Research Agenda for Young People's Psychological Response to Climate Change 168
Joshua R. Wortzel

PART II MULTIDISCIPLINARY PERSPECTIVES ON YOUTH CLIMATE DISTRESS

10 Therapists' Perspectives: Psychotherapeutic Techniques with Applicability to Climate Distress 189
Elizabeth Allured and Barbara Easterlin

11 Ecological and Intersectional Perspectives to Reduce Young Adults' Climate Distress: Reflections from a Work That Reconnects Program 210
Aravinda Ananda and Margaret Babbott

12 Pediatricians' Perspectives: Youth Climate Distress in the Pediatric Setting 231
Samantha Ahdoot

13 A Legal Perspective on Judicial Remedies to Respond to Young People's Climate Distress 251
Andrea Rodgers and Kelsey Dunn

14 Coping with Climate Change among Young People: Meaning-Focused Coping and Constructive Hope 269
Maria Ojala and Xiaoxuan Chen

15 Social-Ecological Perspectives and Their Influence on Climate Distress in Young People 287
Tara Crandon, Hannah Thomas, and James Scott

16	Parenting and Grandparenting Our Youth in the Climate Crisis *Judith Van Hoorn, Susie Burke, and Ann Sanson*	309
17	Perspectives on Addressing Young People's Climate Distress in Education *Matt Carmichael*	329
18	Activists' Perspectives: Using Climate Activism to Heal Youth Climate Distress *Jennifer Uchendu and Elizabeth Haase*	347
19	Perspectives from Creative Spaces: Transforming Climate Distress through Creative Practice and Re-storying *Jeppe Graugaard*	367
20	Landback: Climate Justice and Indigenous Youth Mental Health in the Anthropocene *Kyle X. Hill and Lynn Mad Plume*	385
21	Future Directions: Youth Climate Distress and Climate Justice *Sarah Jaquette Ray and Britt Wray*	403

Appendix A: Resource List for Educators   420
Appendix B: Costs and Benefits of Activism Scale   421
Index   423

Figures

3.1	Climate Change Anxiety Scale (CCAS).	page 42
4.1	Pathways and processes linking climatic stressors to increased mental health vulnerability drawn from the empirical literature.	75
4.2	Example of systems approach used to examine the relationship between *one* climatic stressor, drought, and mental health through the environmental degradation of one's home.	81
5.1	Elements of the Behavioral Approach System (BAS) and Behavioral Inhibition System (BIS).	98
5.2	The Stress-Diathesis model.	104
7.1	PTSD symptoms in older children.	137
8.1	Case conceptualization 1: Eco-distress with clinically significant impairment.	157
8.2	Case conceptualization 2: Constructive eco-distress.	158
11.1	The spiral of the Work That Reconnects, as painted by Dori Midnight.	215
12.1	Role of pediatricians in a changing climate.	233
12.2	Pathways of impact.	234
15.1	An example of Bronfenbrenner's social-ecological framework.	289

Tables

2.1	Suggestions of nuanced descriptions of some terms related to climate distress.	*page* 25
3.1	Nonpharmacological interventions used to treat child and adolescent anxiety and depression.	51
5.1	Behavioral Approach System.	99
5.2	Behavioral Inhibition System.	99
6.1	Tasks of grief.	113
6.2	Immature defenses as they relate to climate change.	115
6.3	Eriksonian developmental stages of young people, their resultant virtues, and the implications of climate change.	117
6.4	Types of containment with climate-related examples.	123
10.1	Developmental stages.	193
11.1	Earth Leadership Cohort applicant responses to the question: What do you hope to gain from the experience of being a member of the Earth Leadership Cohort?	214
11.2	The psychological function of each station of the WTR spiral.	216
11.3	Four discoveries explored in the "Seeing with new/ancient eyes" station.	218
15.1	A summary of proposed exacerbating and protective influences on climate distress in young people, and recommendations.	292
17.1	Summary of domains and themes identified from interviews.	341
19.1	Examples of cultural metaphors that guide how we think about our subjectivity.	370

Textboxes

4.1	Key concepts in developmental psychopathology.	73
4.2	Research priorities.	83
5.1	Anxiety versus anxiety disorder, defined.	94
5.2	The *Unheimliche*.	96
12.1	"Can I take my baby outside?"	235
12.2	Pediatricians help pass young athlete heat protection legislation in Virginia.	237
12.3	"Can you help my son's nightmares?"	238
12.4	Psychological first aid: Core actions.	239
12.5	American Academy of Pediatrics (AAP) Council on Children and Disasters.	240
12.6	"They were cooked open on the sand."	241
12.7	New York State Children's Environmental Health Centers (NYSCHECK).	243
12.8	Pediatrician chapter climate advocate program.	243
15.1	Case study: Problems across the individual, micro, and techno-subsystems.	298
15.2	Case study: A mesosystem problem.	300
15.3	Case study: An exosystem problem.	302
15.4	Case study: A macro-system problem.	303
16.1	Moving to refugee camps: Suggestions for parents.	315
18.1	Selected types of activism.	348

Contributors

SAMANTHA AHDOOT, MD, FAAP, University of Virginia School of Medicine

ELIZABETH ALLURED, PSYD, Adelphi University

ARAVINDA ANANDA, MEM, Living Revolution

MARGARET BABBOTT, PHD, Licensed Clinical Psychologist

HELEN L. BERRY, PHD, Macquarie University

SUSIE BURKE, PHD, The University of Queensland

MATT CARMICHAEL, New Collaborative Learning Trust

XIAOXUAN CHEN, MA, University of California, Berkeley

SUSAN CLAYTON, PHD, The College of Wooster

TARA CRANDON, MA, The University of Queensland

KELSEY DUNN, JD-MS, Stanford University

BARBARA EASTERLIN, PHD, Climate Psychology Alliance North America

JEPPE GRAUGAARD, Nordic Center for Regenerative Learning

ANTHONY GUERRERO, MD, University of Hawaiʻi

ELIZABETH HAASE, MD, University of Nevada at Reno School of Medicine

KYLE X. HILL, PHD, MPH, University of Minnesota

KAREN HOPENWASSER, MD, Weill Cornell Medicine

KELSEY HUDSON, PHD, Climate Psychology Alliance North America

JACOB LEE, MD, Climate Psychiatry Alliance

JANET L. LEWIS, MD, University of Rochester

LYNN MAD PLUME, MPH, University of North Dakota

ELIZABETH MARKS, DCLINPSY, University of Bath, Bath Centre for Mindfulness and Community

MARIA OJALA, PHD, Örebro University

PANU PIHKALA, PHD, University of Helsinki

SARAH JAQUETTE RAY, PHD, California State Polytechnic University, Humboldt

ANDREA RODGERS, JD, Our Children's Trust

ANN SANSON, PHD, University of Melbourne

JAMES SCOTT, PHD, The University of Queensland

HANNAH THOMAS, PHD, The University of Queensland

JENNIFER UCHENDU, MA, SustyVibes

JUDITH VAN HOORN, PHD, University of the Pacific

ARCHANA VARMA CABALLERO, MD, Washington Baltimore Center for Psychoanalysis

FRANCIS VERGUNST, DPHIL, University of Oslo

JOSHUA R. WORTZEL, MD, MPHIL, MS(ED), Brown University

BRITT WRAY, PHD, Stanford School of Medicine

Preface and Introduction

Young people growing up today must navigate the challenges of youth while also facing the urgent spiritual, developmental, existential, and safety-related challenges presented by climate change. Given the enormous differences in how youth across the globe experience the impacts of climate change, understanding the complex relationship between the climate emergency and young people's mental health is an inherently multidisciplinary and multicultural endeavor, one that requires us to engage in reflection, creativity, questioning, collaboration, and reimagining. The viewpoints gathered in this volume represent our effort to engage in this way, and to offer a platform that outlines multiple and diverse ways to acknowledge and support young people's right to a safe and livable planet.

This volume is a collection of multidisciplinary perspectives that explores, in this moment of heightened recognition, how climate mental health and adjacent fields currently approach the complex and interacting effects of climate change on young people. This book gathers and unites different voices to advance collaborative scholarship and to encourage future academic, healthcare-related, educational, legal, and community-based efforts aimed at understanding and supporting youth through the planetary emergency.

This volume aims to accomplish three main goals:

1. To demonstrate that the relationship between the climate and environmental emergencies and young people's mental health exists and must be taken seriously as a significant factor impacting young people's psychological well-being.
2. To provide multidisciplinary and multidimensional perspectives on the topic of climate change and youth mental health by placing individuals and communities in conversation to inform, shape, and build off each other's work.

3. To assemble a volume that offers frameworks for understanding how climate change influences youth mental health, and to provide guidance and future directions for a global crisis that will only become more prevalent in young people's lives.

To root us in the complex and interacting ways in which climate change influences young people's well-being, Part I of the volume – Conceptual Foundations of Climate Distress in Young People – provides an in-depth overview of the psychiatric and psychological evidence and theoretical frameworks surrounding the emerging psychological responses associated with the climate crisis. To do this, Part I lays out evidence for climate distress and related syndromes at different ages; provides terminology and definitions to capture the complex psychological responses to climate change; explores psychiatric and developmental considerations; and proposes future research agendas. A variety of theoretical models are offered – including trauma-based, cognitive behavioral, relational, psychoanalytic, neurobiological, and biopsychosocio-environmental understandings of emotional dysregulation – for the purpose of forwarding a more individualized and nuanced understanding of climate distress.

Susan Clayton and Tara Crandon lead Part I with an overview, describing both positive and negative impacts of climate emotions and coping styles on mental health and tracing the development of scales that measure functional impairment related to climate change anxiety. In exploring the downstream complexities of climate emotion, the authors highlight the work of Galway and Beery, which shows that *hope* correlates with *negative* climate emotions such as betrayal, anger, and grief, and that expressing them can facilitate environmental action. Similarly, awareness of climate change can evoke soliphilia and other warm emotions. These are important rebuttals to those who claim fear-mongering when we encourage young people to express climate change feelings. Clayton and Crandon provide an in-depth analysis of the Climate Change Anxiety Scale, which has been able to disaggregate climate anxiety from clinical anxiety and depression across a variety of international populations, despite the role of cultural factors in shaping how climate distress is experienced.

Through an artful analysis of the concept of distress itself, Panu Pihkala provides a definitional framework for the book. He offers interdisciplinary and multicultural definitions and conceptualizations of climate distress, drawing on environmental, psychological, and philosophical perspectives. Pihkala explores the relationship between climate distress and other climate-related terminology, touching on how these terms have been used historically and the ways in which contextual, political, societal, and cultural factors and power dynamics shape our interpretations of these phenomena. He closes by emphasizing the dual character of climate distress as both a potential mental health issue and a fundamentally adaptive response, and offers us a novel, nonpathologizing, and culturally sensitive definition for climate-related psychological distress.

Beth Haase provides an in-depth and comprehensive look at the relationship between climate distress and clinical symptoms from a psychiatric perspective. Haase situates this debate in the historical and sociopolitical foundations from which climate distress is observed, defined, and interpreted as well as the ongoing developmental processes in the young people it affects. She condenses complex questions about the relationship between climate responses and clinical symptoms into digestible lists and action items, and delves into psychiatric understandings of the factors that contribute to adaptive and maladaptive anxiety, depression, and traumatic stress. This chapter reviews the evidence for and against climate distress as a psychopathology, suggests how to assess a young person with significant climate distress for overlapping psychiatric syndromes and risks, and concludes with a series of case studies. This chapter may be a particularly helpful guide for those in the mental health and medical fields.

The developmental theme is developed by Francis Vergunst and Helen Berry. The authors masterfully review a systems thinking and developmental life course perspective, highlighting the many iterative feedback loops affecting development between the growing young person and climate-induced changes in the microsystem, mesosystem, and exosystem. Vergunst and Berry's suggestions for how to assess such complex systems quickly and intervene at points of maximum stress provide much-needed guidance for responding to the multiple intersecting climate risks that impact younger generations.

Youth facing climate change have the thorny task of staying connected to real threats without overwhelming their stress-response systems. Jacob Lee and Anthony Guerrero describe how understanding the neurobiology of anxiety can inform the supports we offer young people with climate distress. They lay out the neuroanatomy of the fear system, highlighting the delicate balance of the opposing behavioral approach and behavioral inhibition systems. Lee and Guerrero conclude that keeping stress levels low enough to promote curiosity and explorations in response to challenges can protect against extreme stress, and suggest that we teach young people skills for emotional regulation and cognitive control.

Archana Varma Caballero and Janet Lewis suggest innovative ways of applying traditional psychodynamic conceptualizations of grief, regression, and Kleinian object relations to understand adaptive and maladaptive climate responses. They offer a novel application of Erik Erikson's psychosocial developmental stages to explain the particular emotional challenges of climate awareness for trust, self-esteem, hope, and engagement. Emphasizing the importance of an adequate emotional "container" for the feelings aroused by such a complex problem, the authors provide a useful categorization of fragmented, rigid, and flexible psychic "containers" for those involved with young people. Varma Caballero and Lewis take a developmental approach to understanding adolescent climate responses by exploring the relationship between climate distress and adolescents' agency development, adult levels of ambivalence, drive regulation, superego development, and intellectual complexity.

Karen Hopenwasser minces no words in calling out our neglect of climate change as a global abuse of our young people. She labels our failure to imagine and care about the future of our children as a neglect of one of the basic imaginative capacities of caregivers safeguarding their young. She then shifts our focus to the dissociative response to trauma, which allows us to more fully comprehend how we neglect to attend to our environment and how numbing ourselves diminishes our imaginative capacity. Finally, she offers embodied cognition (the idea that our minds are not only connected to our bodies but also that our bodies influence our minds) and felt sense (an internal bodily awareness) as modes of human consciousness that will allow us to respond to our youth with greater care and intention.

Elizabeth Marks and Kelsey Hudson explore young people's ecologically related thoughts, emotions, behaviors, and physical sensations in clinical settings, and offer a cognitive behavioral framework for conceptualizing eco-distress with concrete guidance on developing eco-aware case conceptualizations. Two detailed case conceptualizations are provided – one showing impairing eco-distress and one showing constructive eco-distress – with each illustrating different outcomes. They conclude by emphasizing that, although it is not young people's responsibility to "feel better" about or "solve" the climate and environmental emergencies, cognitive behavioral principles can encourage cognitive, emotional, and behavioral flexibility in young people's climate-related responses.

To conclude Part I, Joshua Wortzel provides a map for moving the field forward by proposing a comprehensive future-oriented research agenda to skillfully fill the gaps in our understanding of climate distress in pediatric populations. The agenda is organized into five broad domains: defining climate emotions, assessing their epidemiology, understanding their psychological meanings and consequences, developing interventions, and exploring the biological impacts of climate change on young people's mental health.

Part II – Multidisciplinary Perspectives on Youth Climate Distress – offers a more intimate look into how climate distress manifests in a variety of settings, including schools, families, psychotherapy, and community organizing. The distinct perspectives in Part II offer tools for adults working in a variety of disciplines both to formulate a more comprehensive understanding of how young people experience climate change psychologically and to respond accordingly. The multidisciplinary viewpoints offered throughout Part II challenge the existing narrative promoted by governmental agencies and fossil fuel industries – which privileges, distorts, and overemphasizes the importance of individual actions alone – and emphasize the significance of adults' responsibility and collective action.

Elizabeth Allured and Barbara Easterlin start off Part II by providing detailed examples of the ways that psychotherapeutic skills can be applied to young people suffering from climate distress, with a focus on Acceptance and Commitment Therapy and psychodynamic frameworks. This chapter will be particularly useful to mental health providers wanting to understand the nuances of working with this material in the context of other ongoing clinical concerns.

Aravinda Ananda and Margaret Babbott offer a beautiful narrative of therapeutic processes that can create meaningful engagement and community with young climate activists. They lay out the theoretical and spiritual underpinnings and actual practices of the Work That Reconnects and describe its use with their Earth Leadership Cohorts for young adults aged 18 to 30. True transition to an ecocentric culture that functions without oppression or exploitation demands full attention to its intersectional and justice aspects. Their thoughtful description of the evolution of their work in response to the lived experiences of their cohort members is a good point of entry for others seeking intersectional awareness and justice in climate work.

Samantha Ahdoot provides another clinical chapter, exploring the health and mental health impacts of climate change that present in pediatric settings. Topics discussed in routine visits, such as caring for an infant during a heatwave, can provide opportunities for pediatricians to provide climate health education, show empathy with climate distress, and offer suggestions for local climate engagement. Ahdoot lays out pediatricians' roles as clinicians, educators, and advocates and provides clear guidance on how to take action in each domain.

Andrea Rodgers and Kelsey Dunn from Our Children's Trust offer an exploration on legal remedies for responding to youth climate distress. Correction of the problem through climate justice in the courts can play a critical role in mitigating young people's climate-related physical, psychological, and moral injuries, and can counteract the effects of institutional betrayal. To support this position, Rodgers and Dunn report on young people who are taking their governments to court and provide in-depth descriptions of youth-led climate litigation efforts that use climate science to support claims of human rights violations. This chapter provides a comprehensive review of the obstacles that young people face in seeking and obtaining legal remedies, the human rights that are violated by the climate crisis, and the reasons why access to courts is a crucial aspect of climate distress mitigation.

Maria Ojala and Xiaoxuan Chen review the literature on constructive hope and meaning-focused coping, which are tools that have been found to mitigate the negative emotional effects of climate activism and other climate experiences that cannot be fully solved by problem solving alone. Ojala and Chen discuss the practical implications of these studies, gifting us with specific advice on using and encouraging meaning-focused coping.

Tara Crandon, Hannah Thomas, and James Scott offer a Systems Theory perspective on how young people's development can be impacted by the spheres in which they are embedded: the micro, meso, macro, exo, techno, and chronological matrices of their lives. The chart within their chapter gives a profoundly helpful overview of the exacerbating and protective influences at each level, as well as recommendations for how to help young people at each layer of their experience that are supported by case studies and a deeper exploration of each element of the theory.

Judith Van Hoorn, Susie Burke, and Ann Sanson focus on the experience of parenting young people during the climate and environmental emergencies. Drawing from multidisciplinary research in parenting science, child and youth development, and disasters, they provide guidance on how a wide variety of individuals in parenting and caregiving roles can help young people cope with the direct and indirect effects of climate change, focusing on factors that exacerbate social inequalities. Specific strategies are offered to help children manage climate emotions, foster a sense of agency and hope, and support active engagement.

To address climate distress in schools, educator Matt Carmichael provides a rich supply of examples and resources for individuals in educational settings, which he gleaned from recent in-depth interviews with educators who are incorporating climate emotions into their work with young people. Through thematic analysis of these interviews, Carmichael identifies common themes in this work: Young people clearly experience difficult emotions when learning about climate change, need adults to respond to disturbing truths and to process their own emotions about them, and can benefit from meaningful connection to others and to the outdoors. Young people are less naive and defensive about climate-related topics than adults, and can experience institutional betrayal if the threats to their future are not acknowledged and addressed.

Jennifer Uchendu and Elizabeth Haase focus on youth-led climate activism and organizing from both personal and conceptual perspectives. Jennifer Uchendu, founder of SustyVibes and a leading force of global young climate activist and organizing work, chronicles her personal journey in youth climate organizing through an intimate narrative. Generalizing this experience, Uchendu and Haase outline different types of activism and highlight organizing principles that have been adopted by youth climate activist groups. The authors offer a helpful literature review on the risks and benefits of activism for youth mental health that will be useful for a variety of individuals seeking to support young people currently engaged in, or hoping to engage in, activism and organizing.

Drawing from the work of the Dark Mountain Project, Jeppe Graugaard provides another valuable chapter for those working in the educational setting. This chapter focuses on creative ways that young people can escape the "runaway narrative" of the unsustainable late-capitalist cultural predicament into which they have been born. Graugaard explains that new beliefs, new ways of making meaning, and new narratives about living a good and just life are fundamental to helping the next generation transition away from unsustainable and unjust social structures. Art and the artist become central to this endeavor, as it is through imagination and improvisation that we do something new.

Kyle X. Hill and Lynn Mad Plume guide us in acknowledging the intersecting crises of climate change and Indigenous youth mental health and wellness within the context of the profound social, cultural, and ecological disruptions resulting from settler colonialism. Hill and Mad Plume's narrative examines the disruptions that settler colonialism, White supremacy and capitalism have created for Indigenous belief and knowledge systems and on Indigenous young people and their communities, ultimately disrupting all of our relationships to the land. Throughout the chapter, the authors recognize how appropriate attention to Indigenous Traditional Ecological Knowledge represents a profound opportunity for restorative justice for Indigenous Peoples as well as for global climate adaptation efforts.

Our volume concludes with a commentary by Sarah Jaquette Ray and Britt Wray, two of the leading and most innovative voices in this area. Ray and Wray call out the "mental healthification" and Westernization of climate distress as well as the professionalization of those legitimized to respond to it, focusing on the importance of people-centered approaches to describing and defining climate-related suffering. They encourage us to see emotions as the base of effective climate responses, just as emotions have always been the source of political movements. They foresee great progress ahead through this approach, with emotions like institutional betrayal and moral injury contributing to the development of heightened critical consciousness of our social structure. They identify queer, Indigenous, feminist, posthumanist, and disability lenses (among others) as providing theory, scholarship, and practices that can facilitate challenges to heteropatriarchal and unsustainable models of family, community, and social structure and connection. Their work establishes an important framework for those for whom this book will be a starting point of innovative exploration and program development.

Considerations

The landscape of the climate and environmental emergencies, and how they relate to young people's mental health, is shifting rapidly. We therefore acknowledge that in many ways we are only beginning to understand the true scope of this phenomenon. So while we consider the perspectives shared in this volume to be a valuable reflection of some of the historical and current frameworks for understanding youth climate distress and resilience, we recognize that one volume cannot possibly capture all the perspectives, experiences, and nuances of this global issue. There are many models in mental health and adjacent fields that are not explored in depth here but nonetheless deserve recognition and application; many of these are outlined in Ray and Wray's concluding chapter. Despite these considerations, we hope this volume provides a framework for understanding certain important aspects of young people's climate-related mental health, and spotlights what is worth doing at this critical moment, one in which obstacles like blame-shifting, systemic inequities, diversion, reinterpretation, naive optimism, and indifference can stymie the hope, self-efficacy, and action we so urgently need.

Acknowledgments

We would like to acknowledge first and foremost that this book has emerged from the collective feeling and effort, born of our love for our planet and its creatures, in those young and old who are working ceaselessly to protect its future for those who will inherit it. Among these, we are incredibly grateful for our contributors, who have so generously and freely shared their wisdom, expertise, and time, and give many thanks to Stephen Acerra and Rowan Groat, our editors at Cambridge University Press, for bringing this collaborative project to life.

We owe a special note of gratitude to Dr. Emily Diamond, who researches the traumatic impacts of environmental events on young children and who generously provided us with verbal and written expert feedback at the beginning stages of this volume. Dr. Diamond is one of the few researchers who have included secondary and tertiary stressors – which occur on the heels of extreme weather and natural disasters – in her data. Her studies highlight the multiple traumas that are accumulating with climate stresses, closing down safe emotional avenues for young people to reach their human potential. Adverse childhood events like these carry a lifelong psychological toll, for which adults who fail to prevent climate worsening will be responsible. We credit her with impressing on us the rapid pace of this field, and how much more will need to be done for all of our work to remain relevant to their struggles.

Kelsey is thankful for the Climate Psychology Alliance North America, Climate Psychiatry Alliance, Association of Behavioral and Cognitive Therapies' Climate Change and Psychology Special Interest Group, Moms Clean Air Force, University of Vermont, Louisiana State University Health Sciences Center, Boston University's Center for Anxiety and Related Disorders, Yale School of Public Health's Climate Change and Health Certificate Program, Bread and Butter Farm, the Sierra Club, Bread and Puppet, and the countless nonprofits and organizations focusing on climate change and mental health. Her friends, teachers, colleagues, mentors, and supervisees in these organizations have supported, challenged, and shaped her thinking and priorities. She gives thanks to KB, KW, her friends and family, and her partner for their never-ending curiosity, openness, and sturdiness. She also extends appreciation for the nonhuman beings whose grounding and healing presence connects us to more ecocentric ways of relating to one another. Most importantly, Kelsey wants to acknowledge that this volume would not have happened without Beth Haase, who generously agreed to join as a coeditor and whose knowledge, determination, and curiosity brought this project together in a meaningful way. Beth has written extensively about climate change and mental health, held leadership positions in the climate committees of the American Psychiatric Association and the Group for the Advancement of Psychiatry (GAP), and started her journey in this field with a film, *Frogs in a Pot*, exploring the emotional needs of children in response to climate stress many years before the topic gained significant traction. Beth brought strong dedication and creativity to the coediting process, and Kelsey is immensely grateful for her collaboration.

Beth is grateful particularly to her darling Raindog, who keeps her afloat, and to the leadership of the Carson Tahoe Regional Medical Center, for considering this work important enough to give her the time to do it. She gives thanks to those who have been her guiding stars, her incredible coeditor, Kelsey Hudson, who keeps empathy and positive regard at the center of every interaction, and her daughters, Rennie and Maddie Meyers, as well as all those who have been her teachers in this field: the members of the GAP Climate Committee, the American Psychiatric Association Climate Committee, and the Climate Psychiatry Alliance, the Black Rock Desert, Mount Tamalpais, Berkeley and Sadie, Jessica Haller, Lise Van Susteren, Laurie Nadel, Stacey Wittek, Jonathan Alpert, David Adler, Barnaby, Will Rogers, Alan Tasman, and Wes Sowers, as well as the South Bronx Alliance, Climate Reality Project, Bioneers, the Work That Reconnects, Greening Forward, Spirit Rock, the Burning Man community, Dark Mountain, ecoAmerica, and so many other individuals and organizations.

To our clients: It is a privilege to support you in not only acknowledging the psychological, spiritual, and existential impacts of the climate and environmental emergencies but also in moving towards a more valued, purposeful, and meaningful life in our different communities. We are honored to join you on this journey and thank you for your courage and willingness to share.

Finally, we thank young people across the globe. We commit to acknowledging and validating your experiences and to advocating for your just and safe future.

PART I

Conceptual Foundations of Climate Distress in Young People

CHAPTER 1

Climate Distress among Young People
An Overview

Susan Clayton and Tara Crandon

Introduction

Awareness of climate change is growing. Along with the increasingly definitive and detailed visible evidence that the climate is changing, there is increased recognition of negative impacts on human well-being. The sixth assessment report from the Intergovernmental Panel on Climate Change (IPCC) described the threats, from impacts on physical health through exposure to disasters, heat, poor air quality, and disease vectors; to impacts on food systems and the economy; and to negative effects on social inequity and individual mental health (IPCC, 2022).

This increased awareness brings increasing worry. A 2022 international survey, for example, found that more than nine out of ten respondents in seven countries (among 192 countries and territories surveyed) were worried about climate change. Majorities in most countries expected climate change to harm future generations and to threaten their own country or territory in the next twenty years, although a smaller number expected to be personally harmed (Leiserowitz et al., 2022). In a 2021 survey of 10,000 young people around the world (Hickman et al., 2021), more than half said that they were "extremely" or "very" worried about climate change, and only 5 percent said they were not worried.

In the face of these challenges, worry and anxiety in response to climate change are not surprising. Worry and anxiety can be adaptive when people are faced with a threat. Where worry is the usual reaction to negative news, anxiety is a future-oriented emotional response that tends to focus attention on the need to respond to a problem. In this way it can be associated with appropriate preparations for the imminent threat, such as behavioral modifications that will decrease the threat and/or increase the ability to cope with it. However, extreme levels of anxiety can become overwhelming, associated with the maintenance of unresolved worry and continued focus on a problem. When anxiety is difficult to control or manage, causes difficulty functioning in important domains (e.g., work, family, life), and is accompanied by physical symptoms and severe distress (Barlow, 2000), it could be considered a disorder.

Climate change is beyond the ability of any individual to fully resolve. Indeed, as a "wicked" problem (i.e., an issue that is complex, challenging, or impossible to solve), it is unlikely to be fully resolved in any manner. Instead, it describes an evolving state of affairs whose full impacts cannot be clearly predicted but which is likely to reduce quality of life for almost everyone. Thus, it is reasonable that thinking about climate change would evoke some degree of anxiety. One way for people to respond is through emotion-focused coping, which involves managing their negative emotions, for example by avoiding the issue or by cognitively reframing the issue as not important. This is a maladaptive response as it fails to address the problem, which becomes even larger as we ignore it. But facing the issue may also be problematic if the negative emotions become overwhelming, leaving the anxious individual paralyzed with fear (Lazarus & Folkman, 1984).

As children, adolescents, and young adults face the reality of an altered climate that threatens human well-being, many will experience anxiety and other distressing emotions. This is not a pathological response or de facto evidence of mental illness, but for some the anxiety will reach levels that impair mental health. In order to help those who experience these powerful impacts, it is important to understand the nature, predictors, and consequences of climate change-related distress and anxiety.

Describing Climate Anxiety

In recent years, media and anecdotal reports about "climate anxiety," "climate change anxiety," or "eco-anxiety" have grown substantially. In order to know what climate anxiety is and whether climate anxiety itself is growing, however, there needs to be a consistent definition and a reliable way of assessing it. One key question concerns its intensity and the extent to which it is "practical" or "paralyzing." Many surveys have simply asked about climate worry or concern, which does not necessarily imply a reaction that is intense enough to motivate behavior or to threaten mental health. Based on her experiences talking with children, often in therapeutic settings, Hickman (2020) distinguished multiple levels of eco-anxiety. The "significant" and "severe" levels were associated with emotional distress, with impacts on cognition and behavior. Similarly, in discussing climate anxiety, Pihkala (2022) distinguished between "practical" or "constructive" anxiety, and "paralyzing" anxiety, to acknowledge the different behavioral responses, or lack of response, that may accompany individuals' experiences of anxiety.

A systematic approach to assessing the potential clinical implications was developed by Clayton and Karazsia (2020), who focused on the question of whether climate change anxiety (CCA) might indicate the kind of functional impairment that would make it clinically relevant. Their paper presented a Climate Change Anxiety Scale (CCAS) that was based on established measures of rumination and functional impairment. In two studies based on US samples, the CCAS showed a reliable structure with two components: cognitive/emotional impairment, associated with difficulty concentrating or regulating emotions; and functional impairment, associated with difficulty working, socializing, or having fun. Notably, both components were significantly correlated with having experience of climate change (e.g., experienced a natural weather disaster) and with a short measure of depression and anxiety. Levels of climate anxiety were generally low, with about 3–10 percent of respondents saying they "often or almost always" experienced these symptoms, and as many as 20–25 percent saying they "sometimes" experienced them (Clayton & Karazsia, 2020). A later US study (Schwartz et al., 2022), using separate measures of depression – the Patient Health Questionnaire-8 (PHQ-8) – and anxiety – the General Anxiety Disorder-7 (GAD-7), found that CCAS scores were significantly correlated with both variables. There was no correlation with age in this study, but the range was limited because the sample consisted mostly of undergraduate students.

In the past few years, multiple studies have used the CCAS in other countries. Wullenkord et al. (2021) found that the CCAS was reliable in Germany, though they did not replicate the factor structure of the original study. Levels of climate anxiety were low and did not differ according to age, education, or income, though women reported higher levels of climate anxiety. CCAS scores were positively correlated with anxiety and depression, support for pro-environmental policies, and pro-environmental behavior intentions. In a Polish study (Larionow et al., 2022), women, again, showed higher levels of climate anxiety; age and education were both slightly negatively correlated with CCAS. Subscale scores were related to depression but not anxiety using the PHQ-4. A similar factor structure was reported in Belgium (Mouguiama-Daouda et al., 2022). In a large sample from multiple French-speaking countries, almost 12 percent of the sample reported experiencing anxiety frequently (Heeren et al., 2022). Women and younger adults showed higher climate anxiety, but there were no differences associated with education. In a sample of adolescents from the Philippines (Simon et al., 2022), higher scores on the CCAS again related positively to both experience of climate change and behavioral engagement. Although the samples cannot be directly compared, it is worth noting that scores were higher in the Philippines than in the US studies. In another study from the Philippines, CCAS was negatively correlated with mental health, and positively correlated with psychological distress (Reyes et al., 2021). In samples from India, China, and Japan, as well as the United States, Tam et al. (2023) found that a two-factor structure was reliable across countries, but demographic predictors varied. In sum, these studies suggest the CCAS is a reliable instrument that can discriminate climate anxiety from clinical anxiety and depression across a variety of populations, although further work should explore differences in levels and discrepancies in the factor structures.

Climate change anxiety by no means represents the only emotional response to climate change, or even the only negative emotion. Several researchers have emphasized grief or depression as a response to climate change (Cunsolo & Ellis, 2018; Ojala et al., 2021); this grief or sadness is based on the perceived loss of something valued, such as a healthy environment or specific natural places, and is thus likely to be stronger among people who place a higher value on the natural environment and/or have greater experience with the loss or change of places that hold importance to them (Wang et al., 2018). Many people also experience emotions with a moral judgment component: personal guilt or shame; anger at those who are contributing the most to climate change; or a feeling of betrayal because those who are supposed to be responsible for assuring people's well-being (e.g., parents, governments) are failing to act. Based on a review of the literature, Pihkala (2022) describes a taxonomy of climate emotions, with the most commonly discussed including anxiety, grief, guilt or shame, hope, and anger or frustration. The term "climate distress" may be used to recognize this range of emotions that one may feel in relation to climate change.

Emotional responses are complex, and most people may feel more than one of these emotional responses to climate change, either sequentially or simultaneously. Indeed, Galway and Beery (2022) found that hope was positively correlated with most of the negative emotions (e.g., worry, fear, sadness, anxiety). One implication is that allowing people the opportunity to describe and discuss their own negative emotions will not prohibit their ability to also feel positive emotions. Several studies have suggested the importance of acknowledging the negative emotional response to help people cope with those reactions (Doherty et al., 2022; Ojala, 2015). For young people, it may therefore be important for educational contexts, in which information about climate change is presented, to also allow discussion and validation of emotional responses (Baker et al., 2021; Ojala, 2015).

In studying and describing these emotions, we are concerned about their implications for well-being and for behavior. Is climate anxiety a threat to mental health? Alternatively, if climate anxiety motivates sustainable behavior, could it actually increase well-being? Research shows that emotional responses to climate change, and negative emotions in particular, are important predictors of behavior (Brosch, 2021). However, negative emotions about climate change are also related to insomnia and poorer (self-reported) mental health (Ogunbode et al., 2021; Schwartz et al., 2022).

There is no threshold score on the CCAS above which people are considered to have problematic "climate anxiety," and it is important to acknowledge that climate-related distress is not a diagnosable disorder according to diagnostic classification systems. The significance of a particular emotional response depends on the individual's social context, both because the acceptability of expressing specific emotions will vary across cultures, and because the social support received will help to determine the impact of feeling a specific emotional reaction. Iniguez-Gallardo et al. (2021) remind us that the emotional response to climate change will be affected by cultural factors. In their Ecuadorian sample, powerlessness was a stronger emotional theme than it has been found to be in US samples, presumably because Ecuador has less impact on global policies and global carbon emissions. Powerlessness may also be a particularly significant emotion for some younger people, since most of them are not yet in positions of financial, social, or political influence.

The media frequently comment on declining mental health among young people. Yet media outlets also often describe young people as representing hope for the future because of their willingness to engage in climate change activism. It is important to attend to the levels and correlates of climate anxiety and distress among youth, both for their own health and for them to have, in turn, the resilience to attend to the health of the planet.

Climate Distress in Young People

> As climate change disrupts the environment, children are being forced to grow up in an increasingly dangerous world.
> (UNICEF 2021)

Young people face a future burdened by climate change, and the negative implications are increasingly coming into focus (Sanson et al., 2019). Physically, young people are more susceptible to health risks related to air pollution, heat, infectious diseases, as well as water and food shortages

(Akachi et al., 2009; Helldén et al., 2021). As extreme weather-related disasters increase in severity and frequency, young people are most at risk of injury and death (Bartlett, 2008). Climate change may even pose risks during prenatal development; exposure to increased humidity and natural disasters *in utero* are associated with preterm birth, prenatal complications, and adverse long-term mental health outcomes (Davenport et al., 2017; Rothschild & Haase, 2022; Subramaniam, 2007). As climate change evolves, young people may progressively experience climate-related stressors that can have a profound impact on mental health (e.g., disrupted education, forced displacement, trauma).

Young people are vulnerable not just because of physiological differences but because of their social position in society: less independence means they can experience more indirect and vicarious impacts, for example based on the ways in which parents, caregivers, or teachers are affected by climate change. Their stage of psychological development is also relevant as they may experience a strong emotional reaction to perceived betrayal or neglect of responsibility by those in charge, including governmental authorities, or to the intergenerational inequities that climate change presents (Thiery et al., 2021). For some young people, climate change may disrupt important connections to culture and place.

Youth is a critical life phase spanning from late childhood through to young adulthood, which is typically understood as between the ages of 12 and 25 years. The United Nations defines "youth" as the "transition from the dependence of childhood to adulthood's independence." This phase is marked by rapid changes and maturation across social, emotional, psychological, and physical development; it is a time of growing independence, identity, and responsibility. These transitions can be difficult for young people and the presence of adverse events can greatly impact a young person's long-term well-being (Hardgrove et al., 2014). For current and future younger generations, this period in life is when most may come to learn about climate change and realize the gravity of the situation. When we use terms such as "young people" we are referring to studies that investigate people between the ages of 12 and 25 years. However, even children as young as 8 years old are reporting worries about climate change, with some describing associated bad dreams or impacts on sleeping and eating habits (Atherton, 2020).

> I guess for me it [climate change] became real during the Black Summer bushfires. It was like an apocalypse. I remember seeing all these pictures where the sky was red – the air was thick and smoky. There were all these posts on my feed about how many animals were lost in the fires and how

much vegetation was being destroyed. I remember my friends saying, "this is climate change". Sometimes it feels like we're trying to beat something that feels impossible. It's suffocating. (20-year-old young person, anonymous personal communication, 2022)

Prevalence

There is a plethora of ways in which young people encounter climate change. Some may be spatially and temporally exposed to climate-induced stressors such as extreme weather disasters, erosion, drought, and extreme heat; others may learn of climate change through the media, at school, and through their parents or friends. Irrespective of how a young person is connected to climate change, evidence suggests that a high proportion of young people are concerned about the climate crisis. In their global study, Hickman and colleagues (2021) found that the majority of respondents in each and every country studied reported being moderately to extremely worried.

Research has generally shown that young people report greater concern about and belief in climate change, compared to adults (Clayton & Karazsia, 2020; Lewis et al., 2019). Young people are also more likely to report worry, anger, and guilt, as well as less hope about climate change, than older generations (Swim et al., 2022). This appears to be especially prominent in countries from the Global South, where concern, belief, and willingness to act are generally found to be greater than in countries such as Australia, the United States, and the United Kingdom (Hickman et al., 2021; Lee et al., 2020).

What Does Climate Distress Look Like in Children and Youth?

As with adults, climate distress in young people comprises emotional, cognitive, and behavioral elements. Emotions towards climate change can range in salience, severity, and valence (i.e., pleasant to unpleasant). Young people may respond to or manage these emotions through active (behavior) or intrapersonal (cognitive) means. Some young people may think and act in positive, constructive, and helpful ways; others may be unable to act or think in helpful ways or may use maladaptive coping mechanisms. How these aspects of climate distress manifest will likely differ according to a young person's internal (e.g., one's sense of connection to the environment) and external (e.g., experience of climate change) circumstances (Crandon et al., 2022), as well as personal resilience and psychological style. While experiences of climate distress are unique for each young person, it is useful to consider patterns or themes in the range of emotions, cognitions, and behaviors of young people.

Emotions

> I feel angry that we have to deal with this. I also feel a lot of fear – I don't know how much time we have left to do something and that really scares me. Sometimes I feel hypocritical too, because I haven't always thrown the right thing in the right bin, but I'm also really worried.
>
> (13-year-old young person, anonymous, personal communication, 2022)

Climate distress may involve an array of complex, distressing, and unpleasant emotional experiences, including fear, anger, shame, guilt, and helplessness. In the global survey conducted by Hickman and colleagues (2021), young people reported many negative emotions, but rarely indifference (29 percent). Perhaps the aspect most investigated in young people is the experience of anxiety and concern about climate change, often described with the term climate anxiety. As described above, anxiety can serve an adaptive biological and evolutionary function, prompting one to prepare for anticipated threats, or it can be paralyzing. For young people, a future laden with the uncertainty and threat of climate change is likely to evoke anxiety and fear.

Studies have shown that young people also express confusion, betrayal, and a sense of abandonment in response to adult inaction. Young people, who are most likely to be affected by climate change, generally have less agency and power to create meaningful change compared to adults. For some young people, as they develop increasing independence, choice and responsibility, this may highlight inaction by their peers, family, or community members. Perceiving older generations as failing to protect younger generations or to prepare them for impending harm may evoke generational anger and resentment (Hickman et al., 2021). This distress may be furthered when young people feel silenced, which may be the case when young people are excluded from decision making (e.g., voting) or are criticized by others for demanding action (Crandon et al., 2022). For example, some young people may feel dismissed when characterized by government officials or the media as experiencing "needless anxiety" (Crowe, 2019).

Climate change, and the way one responds to it, can also evoke pleasant emotions such as hope, optimism, connection to others, motivation, a "warm glow" (a feeling one gets when acting in an environmentally friendly way), and "soliphilia" (a feeling of protectiveness, love, and responsibility towards the planet) (Schneider et al., 2021). For young people, these feelings may be evoked when involved in environmental projects (e.g., at home, at school, or in the community), when connecting with their peers on climate change issues (e.g., school projects or climate action marches), or when spending time in nature. To date, there is little evidence on the extent to which young people experience pleasant climate emotions, although some young people have reported feeling optimistic and hopeful (Hickman et al., 2021; Ojala, 2012). Emotions of a pleasant nature may be more likely to motivate people to engage in pro-environmental behavior. Young people who are more hopeful about climate change, for example, may be more likely to report a willingness or greater engagement with pro-environmental action (Ojala, 2011; Stevenson & Peterson, 2016). Another study found that eliciting anticipated pride (e.g., imagining the feelings of pride that may follow engaging in pro-environmental behavior) may lead to higher motivation to act compared to guilt (Schneider et al., 2017).

Cognitions

> Every time I see something about climate change, I just think we're too late to fix it. I think about the ice caps melting. I think that it's gonna keep getting hotter. I think resources will keep getting smaller and everyone will be fighting for one thing. Things will become more in-demand – things that we need on a daily basis.
>
> I think about having kids and I'm worried about their future, what it's gonna be like for them.
>
> (21-year-old young person, Aquino, J., personal communication, 2022)

Evidence suggests that young people may have both positive (e.g., trusting scientists to come up with solutions) and negative (e.g., perceiving humanity as doomed) thoughts about climate change. Whether a young person's thoughts are positive or negative is likely to be driven by their understanding of the situation. Hickman and colleagues (2021), for example, showed that young people reported having more negative thoughts if they also reported feeling betrayed by their governmental response to climate change.

Young people's thoughts can also take the form of cognitive strategies to cope with or influence their feelings about climate change. For example, meaning-based coping involves positively reappraising a threat or finding benefits within adverse events, such as about how others are actively working together to address climate change. Meaning-focused coping has been linked to positive affect (e.g., life satisfaction, optimism) and less negative affect in young people (Ojala, 2012). Other young people may use problem-solving coping, which involves identifying and planning to implement actionable solutions. Both meaning-focused coping and problem-solving coping have been associated with greater environmental engagement in young people (Ojala, 2012).

Another cognitive strategy identified in youth is rumination, a passive and repetitive negative focus on one's distress, its causes, and consequences. For example, an individual may have repetitive negative thoughts about their own emotional distress, or how their behavior might contribute to climate change (Clayton & Karazsia, 2020; Hogg et al., 2021). It has been suggested that rumination may be used when attempting to counterintuitively control or avoid the threat (Ojala, 2012; Stroebe et al., 2007).

Positive or negative thoughts and cognitive strategies do not inherently indicate how adaptive a young person's response to climate change may be. Rather, it could be argued that a young person's adaptation is better reflected by whether their emotions or thoughts lead to meaningful behavioral coping.

Behaviors

> In every choice I make, I see the reaction. Energy consumption, food consumption, transport emissions, waste. I see how I contribute to a growing climate crisis. Though, in these everyday actions I also see how awareness has changed my behaviour. Reducing my plastic waste, composting scraps, eating less meat, catching public transport.
>
> I think for previous generations the threat of "climate change" was easy to ignore, something that's "too far off". For me, it is tangible and too real to ignore.
>
> (24-year-old young person, Lindsay, A.,
personal communication, 2022)

Climate distress may lead to changes in behavior, which may be considered helpful or unhelpful for the individual as well as for climate mitigation efforts. Studies have shown that young people who are distressed, anxious, or concerned about climate change may be more engaged or willing to engage in pro-environmental behavior. One longitudinal study also found that sustained climate worry over time was linked to greater engagement with news and politics (Sciberras & Fernando, 2021). Yet climate change can also lead to functional impairment in young people.

More specifically, climate distress in youth has been associated with difficulties engaging in school or work, as well as spending time with family and friends (Clayton & Karazsia, 2020; Hickman et al., 2021). Climate distress can also impact the life choices and long-term behaviors of young people; some young people have reported hesitancy to have children or to travel due to their feelings about climate change. A survey of Americans aged 13–29 in 2021 found that they expected climate change to affect decisions about where to live, what to buy, what to eat, and whether to have children, and only 15 percent said it would not influence their future decisions (Isaacs-Thomas, 2021).

Moving from Climate Distress to Posttraumatic Growth and Resilience

Young people have the capacity to be leaders in sustainability, influence policy decision-making, communicate about climate change to the public, as well as direct and contribute to efforts that mitigate climate change (Haynes & Tanner, 2015). However, there is a risk of assigning young people an unfair proportion of responsibility for addressing the crisis. There is the potential for young people to become overwhelmed by continuous climate-related triggers over time (e.g., weather disasters, conflict between nations, governmental inaction) (Crandon et al., 2022). Given the ongoing risks that climate change poses for young people, there is an urgent need to support youth to cope with climate change in ways that are protective of their mental health. One way to do this may be in strengthening individual and community psychological resilience.

Resilience has been described as "bouncing back" from adversity; that is, one's capacity to return to psychological equilibrium and functioning following stressful events. Much of the research regarding resilience and climate-related stressors focuses on natural disasters. Following disasters, young people may be more likely than adults to experience high levels of mental health problems such as stress, anxiety, and depression, and less likely to exhibit resilience, when compared to adults (Chen et al., 2020). Although many young people who experience post-disaster distress recover or develop resilience in the year following the disaster (Chen et al., 2020), it is possible that climate distress could become chronic as young people face gradual and long-term climate-related impacts (e.g., changing environments and biodiversity loss over time), as well as stressors that will become more frequent and intense as climate change evolves. Trajectories of resilience versus psychopathology following climate adversities will also be influenced by contextual and systemic factors. For example, post-traumatic stress disorder (PTSD) symptoms in children and young people following bushfire/wildfire disasters may be greater when young people perceive their own life is under threat, or when they are experiencing ongoing loss and disruption (McDermott et al., 2005; Yelland et al., 2010). As another example, young people living in an underresourced or historically disinvested community may also experience different and more intense psychological consequences.

One of the ways in which climate anxiety and distress manifest among young people may be through their decisions about the future. Attempts to promote resilience among youth may need to focus on providing new skills for making decisions under conditions of increasing uncertainty.

Limited empirical evidence explores the effectiveness of interventions that aim to strengthen resilience in children and young people experiencing climate distress. Despite this, there is an established evidence base for programs and interventions that aim to foster potential drivers of resilience, such as the ability to manage emotional distress through meditation, mindfulness, and other techniques, increased engagement in climate advocacy and mitigation, as well as building feelings of hope, agency, and pro-environmental behavior in young people (Haynes & Tanner, 2015).

Importantly, resilience focuses on recovery and maintaining coping long term. This focus may neglect the critical need to challenge and change social-ecological, economic, and political systems to adequately address climate change (Adams et al., 2021; Bahadur & Tanner, 2014). Indeed, some research has shown that psychological resilience to extreme weather events may be associated with a diminished motivation for climate change mitigation (Ogunbode et al., 2019). Several authors have thus suggested a focus on transformational resilience (Doppelt, 2016). This strategy is based on the concept of posttraumatic growth, in which difficult events provide an opportunity for change and realignment of priorities towards greater social connection and spiritual growth. Within the posttraumatic growth model, climate stressors can be catalysts to improve outcomes for the environment, the climate, and human and social well-being (Doppelt, 2016). For young people, this would mean holding uncertainty and despair, whilst also looking to reimagining and building a different future.

A comprehensive view of resilience should acknowledge the interdependent links between human and ecosystem health, so that a shortsighted attempt to emphasize individual mental health does not take priority over working toward a mutually sustainable and healthy environment (Bingley et al., 2022) and instead is based on the recognition that a healthy environment is fundamental to mental health. The goal should not be to eliminate negative emotions in response to climate change but to encourage a healthy understanding of and reaction to those emotions.

Future Directions

Research provides increasing evidence that young people are distressed about climate change; however, there remain wide and far-reaching gaps that research, community-based interventions and public health policy must promptly address to support the coping and mental health of different groups of young people (as discussed by Wortzel in Chapter 9). The various threats surrounding diverse groups of young people (e.g., from different geographical locations, cultures, socioeconomic backgrounds) lead to different threats to mental health as well. The subsequent chapters of this book will use a range of perspectives to bring these complex causal connections into deeper focus.

Vulnerability to climate change, including its emotional impacts, is not evenly distributed (Dooley et al., 2021). There are inequities in exposure to the effects of climate change, in the degree of impact, and in the sources of resilience that are available. Poorer people and countries, for example, are often situated in areas that are more strongly affected by climate change. Within these areas, young people often have fewer resources to protect themselves from those impacts and to recover from them (Hanna & Oliva, 2016; Sanson et al., 2019). Young people living in rural areas may also be more strongly affected by climatic changes that threaten their community's predominant source of food, water, and employment. Indigenous peoples may find that their entire culture and traditional practices continue to be threatened in a way that is less true for other individuals. Indeed, the spiritual and cultural significance of the land for some Indigenous young people is such that its decay may have a profound impact on their psychological health and identity.

Beyond the research community, it is especially important for the adults surrounding young people (e.g., families, educators, and mental health professionals) and particularly those in positions of power (e.g., those in government, policy, the fossil fuel industry) to consider the impacts of climate change on young people and the distress it may evoke. In recognizing and responding to these impacts, it is critical to work alongside and uplift young people as active agents of change and key stakeholders in planetary health, their own physical and mental well-being, as well as the future.

References

Adams, H., Blackburn, S., & Mantovani, N. (2021). Psychological resilience for climate change transformation: Relational, differentiated and situated perspectives. *Current Opinion in Environmental Sustainability*, 50, 303–309. https://doi.org/10.1016/j.cosust.2021.06.011

Akachi, Y., Goodman, D., & Parker, D. (2009). Global climate change and child health: A review of pathways, impacts and measures to improve the evidence base. *Innocenti Discussion Papers*. https://doi.org/10.18356/32199510-en

Atherton, R. (2020). Climate anxiety: Survey for BBC Newsround shows children losing sleep over climate change and the environment. www.bbc.co.uk/newsround/51451737

Bahadur, A., & Tanner, T. (2014). Transformational resilience thinking: Putting people, power and politics at the heart of urban climate resilience. *Environment and Urbanization*, 26(1), 200–214. https://doi.org/10.1177/0956247814522154

Baker, C., Clayton, S., & Bragg, E. (2021). Educating for resilience: Parent and teacher perceptions of children's emotional needs in response to climate change. *Environmental Education Research*, 27(5), 687–705. https://doi.org/10.1080/13504622.2020.1828288

Barlow, D. H. (2000). Unraveling the mysteries of anxiety and its disorders from the perspective of emotion theory. *American Psychologist*, 55(11), 1247–1263. https://doi.org/10.1037//0003-066x.55.11.1247

Bartlett, S. (2008). The implications of climate change for children in lower-income countries. *Children, Youth and Environments*, 18(1), 71–98. www.jstor.org/stable/10.7721/chilyoutenvi.18.1.0071

Bingley, W. J., Tran, A., Boyd, C. P., Gibson, K., Kalokerinos, E. K., Koval, P., … Greenaway, K. H. (2022). A multiple needs framework for climate change anxiety interventions. *American Psychologist*, 77(7), 812. https://doi.org/10.1037/amp0001012

Brosch, T. (2021). Affect and emotions as drivers of climate change perception and action: A review. *Current Opinion in Behavioral Sciences*, 42, 15–21. https://doi.org/10.1016/j.cobeha.2021.02.001

Chen, S., Bagrodia, R., Pfeffer, C. C., Meli, L., & Bonanno, G. A. (2020). Anxiety and resilience in the face of natural disasters associated with climate change: A review and methodological critique. *Journal of Anxiety Disorders*, 76, 102297. https://doi.org/10.1016/j.janxdis.2020.102297

Clayton, S., & Karazsia, B. T. (2020). Development and validation of a measure of climate change anxiety. *Journal of Environmental Psychology*, 69, 101434. https://doi.org/10.1016/j.jenvp.2020.101434

Crandon, T. J., Scott, J. G., Charlson, F. J., & Thomas, H. J. (2022). A social-ecological perspective of climate anxiety in children and adolescents. *Nature Climate Change*, 12, 123–131. https://doi.org/10.1038/s41558-021-01251-y

Crowe, D. (2019). Morrison warns against "needless anxiety" after Thunberg climate speech. *The Sydney Morning Herald*, September 25.

Cunsolo, A., & Ellis, N. R. (2018). Ecological grief as a mental health response to climate change-related loss. *Nature Climate Change*, 8(4), 275–281. https://doi.org/10.1038/s41558-018-0092-2

Davenport, F., Grace, K., Funk, C., & Shukla, S. (2017). Child health outcomes in sub-Saharan Africa: A comparison of changes in climate and socio-economic factors. *Global Environmental Change*, 46, 72–87. https://doi.org/10.1016/j.gloenvcha.2017.04.009

Doherty, T. J., Lykins, A. D., Piotrowski, N. A., Rogers, Z., Sebree Jr, D. D., & White, K. E. (2022). 11.12 – Clinical psychology responses to the climate crisis. In G. J. G. Asmundson (Ed.), *Comprehensive clinical psychology* (2nd ed., Vol. 11, pp. 167–183). Elsevier. https://doi.org/doi:10.1016/B978-0-12-818697-8.00236-3

Dooley, L., Sheats, J., Hamilton, O., Chapman, D., & Karlin, B. (2021). *Climate change and youth mental health: Psychological impacts, resilience resources, and future directions.* See Change Institute.

Doppelt, B. (2016). *Transformational resilience: How building human resilience to climate disruption can safeguard society and increase wellbeing.* Routledge.

Galway, L. P., & Beery, T. (2022). Exploring climate emotions in Canada's provincial north. *Frontiers in Psychology*, 13, 920313. https://doi.org/10.3389/fpsyg.2022.920313

Hanna, R., & Oliva, P. (2016). Implications of climate change for children in developing countries. *The Future of Children*, 26(1), 115–132. www.jstor.org/stable/43755233

Hardgrove, A., Pells, K., Boyden, J., & Dornan, P. (2014). Youth vulnerabilities in life course transitions. UNDP (United Nations Development Programme).

Haynes, K., & Tanner, T. M. (2015). Empowering young people and strengthening resilience: Youth-centred participatory video as a tool for climate change adaptation and disaster risk reduction. *Children's Geographies*, 13(3), 357–371. https://doi.org/10.1080/14733285.2013.848599

Heeren, A., Mouguiama-Daouda, C., & Contreras, A. (2022). On climate anxiety and the threat it may pose to daily life functioning and adaptation: A study among European and African French-speaking participants. *Climatic Change*, 173(1), 15. https://doi.org/10.1007/s10584-022-03402-2

Helldén, D., Andersson, C., Nilsson, M., Ebi, K. L., Friberg, P., & Alfvén, T. (2021). Climate change and child health: A scoping review and an expanded conceptual framework. *The Lancet Planetary Health*, 5(3), e164–e175. https://doi.org/10.1016/S2542-5196(20)30274-6

Hickman, C. (2020). We need to (find a way to) talk about … eco-anxiety. *Journal of Social Work Practice*, 34(4), 411–424. https://doi.org/10.1080/02650533.2020.1844166

Hickman, C., Marks, E., Pihkala, P., Clayton, S., Lewandowski, R. E., Mayall, E. E., … van Susteren, L. (2021). Climate anxiety in children and young people and their beliefs about government responses to climate change: A global survey. *The Lancet Planetary Health*, 5(12), E863–E873. https://doi.org/10.1016/S2542-5196(21)00278-3

Hogg, T., Stanley, S., O'Brien, L., Wilson, M., & Watsford, C. (2021). The Hogg eco-anxiety scale: Development and validation of a multidimensional scale. *Global Environmental Change*, 71, 102391. https://doi.org/10.1016/j.gloenvcha.2021.102391

Iniguez-Gallardo, V., Lenti Boero, D., & Tzanopoulos, J. (2021). Climate change and emotions: Analysis of people's emotional states in southern Ecuador [original research]. *Frontiers in Psychology*, 12. https://doi.org/10.3389/fpsyg.2021.644240

IPCC (2022). *Climate change 2022: Impacts, adaptation, and vulnerability*. Contribution of Working Group II to the Sixth Assessment Report of the Intergovernmental Panel on Climate Change [H.-O. Pörtner, D. C. Roberts, M. Tignor, E. S. Poloczanska, K. Mintenbeck, A. Alegría, M. Craig, S. Langsdorf, S. Löschke, V. Möller, A. Okem, & B. Rama (eds.)]. Cambridge University Press. doi:10.1017/9781009325844.

Isaacs-Thomas, I. (2021). How young people feel about climate change and their future. *PBS News Hour*, November 5. www.pbs.org/newshour/science/young-people-are-optimistic-that-theres-time-to-prevent-the-worst-effects-of-climate-change

Larionow, P., Sołtys, M., Izdebski, P., Mudło-Głagolska, K., Golonka, J., Demski, M., & Rosińska, M. (2022). Climate change anxiety assessment: The psychometric properties of the Polish version of the Climate Anxiety Scale. *Frontiers in Psychology*, 13. https://doi.org/10.3389/fpsyg.2022.870392

Lazarus, R. S., & Folkman, S. (1984). *Stress, appraisal, and coping*. Springer.

Lee, K., Gjersoe, N., O'Neill, S., & Barnett, J. (2020). Youth perceptions of climate change: A narrative synthesis. *WIREs Climate Change*, 11(3), e641. https://doi.org/10.1002/wcc.641

Leiserowitz, A., Carman, J., Buttermore, N., Neyens, L., Rosenthal, S., Marlon, J., Schneider, J., & Mulcahy, K. (2022). International public opinion on climate change, 2022. Yale Program on Climate Change Communication and Data for Good at Meta.

Lewis, G. B., Palm, R., & Feng, B. (2019). Cross-national variation in determinants of climate change concern. *Environmental Politics*, 28(5), 793–821. https://doi.org/10.1080/09644016.2018.1512261

McDermott, B. M., Lee, E. M., Judd, M., & Gibbon, P. (2005). Posttraumatic stress disorder and general psychopathology in children and adolescents following a wildfire disaster. *Canadian Journal of Psychiatry/La Revue canadienne de psychiatrie*, 50(3), 137–143. https://doi.org/10.1177/070674370505000302

Mouguiama-Daouda, C., Blanchard, M. A., Coussement, C., & Heeren, A. (2022). On the measurement of climate change anxiety: French validation of the Climate Anxiety Scale. *Psychologica Belgica*, 62(1), 123–135. https://doi.org/10.5334/pb.1137

Ogunbode, C. A., Böhm, G., Capstick, S. B., Demski, C., Spence, A., & Tausch, N. (2019). The resilience paradox: Flooding experience, coping and climate change mitigation intentions. *Climate Policy*, 19(6), 703–715. https://doi.org/10.1080/14693062.2018.1560242

Ogunbode, C. A., Pallesen, S., Böhm, G., Doran, R., Bhullar, N., Aquino, S., … Lomas, M. J. (2021). Negative emotions about climate change are related to insomnia symptoms and mental health: Cross-sectional evidence from 25 countries. *Current Psychology*, 42, 845–854. https://doi.org/10.1007/s12144-021-01385-4

Ojala, M. (2011). Hope and climate change: The importance of hope for environmental engagement among young people. *Environmental Education Research*, 18(5), 625–642. https://doi.org/10.1080/13504622.2011.637157

Ojala, M. (2012). Regulating worry, promoting hope: How do children, adolescents, and young adults cope with climate change? *International Journal of Environmental and Science Education*, 7(4), 537–561. https://files.eric.ed.gov/fulltext/EJ997146.pdf

Ojala, M. (2015). Hope in the face of climate change: associations with environmental engagement and student perceptions of teachers' emotion communication style and future orientation. *Journal of Environmental Education*, 46(3), 133–148. https://doi.org/10.1080/00958964.2015.1021662

Ojala, M., Cunsolo, A., Ogunbode, C. A., & Middleton, J. (2021). Anxiety, worry, and grief in a time of environmental and climate crisis: A narrative review. *Annual Review of Environment and Resources*, 46(1), 35–58. https://doi.org/10.1146/annurev-environ-012220-022716

Pihkala, P. (2022). Toward a taxonomy of climate emotions. *Frontiers in Climate*, 3. https://doi.org/10.3389/fclim.2021.738154

Reyes, M. E. S., Carmen, B. P. B., Luminarias, M. E. P., Mangulabnan, S. A. N. B., & Ogunbode, C. A. (2021). An investigation into the relationship between climate change anxiety and mental health among Gen Z Filipinos. *Current Psychology*, 42, 7448–7456. https://doi.org/10.1007/s12144-021-02099-3

Rothschild, J., & Haase, E. (2022). The mental health of women and climate change: Direct neuropsychiatric impacts and associated psychological concerns. *International Journal of Gynecology & Obstetrics*, 160(2), 405–413. https://doi.org/10.1002/ijgo.14479

Sanson, A. V., Van Hoorn, J., & Burke, S. E. L. (2019). Responding to the impacts of the climate crisis on children and youth. *Child Development Perspectives*, 13(4), 201–207. https://doi.org/10.1111/cdep.12342

Schneider, C. R., Zaval, L., & Markowitz, E. M. (2021). Positive emotions and climate change. *Current Opinion in Behavioral Sciences*, 42, 114–120. https://doi.org/10.1016/j.cobeha.2021.04.009

Schneider, C. R., Zaval, L., Weber, E. U., & Markowitz, E. M. (2017). The influence of anticipated pride and guilt on pro-environmental decision making. *PLoS One*, 12(11), e0188781. https://doi.org/10.1371/journal.pone.0188781

Schwartz, S. E. O., Benoit, L., Clayton, S., Parnes, M. F., Swenson, L., & Lowe, S. R. (2022). Climate change anxiety and mental health: Environmental activism as buffer. *Current Psychology*, 42, 16708–16721. https://doi.org/10.1007/s12144-022-02735-6

Sciberras, E., & Fernando, J. W. (2021). Climate change-related worry among Australian adolescents: An eight-year longitudinal study. *Child and Adolescent Mental Health*, 27(1), 22–29. https://doi.org/10.1111/camh.12521

Simon, P. D., Pakingan, K. A., & Aruta, J. J. B. R. (2022). Measurement of climate change anxiety and its mediating effect between experience of climate change and mitigation actions of Filipino youth. *Educational and Developmental Psychologist*, 39(1), 17.–27. https://doi.org/10.1080/20590776.2022.2037390

Stevenson, K., & Peterson, N. (2016). Motivating action through fostering climate change hope and concern and avoiding despair among adolescents. *Sustainability*, 8(1), 6. www.mdpi.com/2071-1050/8/1/6

Stroebe, M., Boelen, P. A., van den Hout, M., Stroebe, W., Salemink, E., & van den Bout, J. (2007). Ruminative coping as avoidance. *European Archives of Psychiatry and Clinical Neuroscience*, 257(8), 462–472. https://doi.org/10.1007/s00406-007-0746-y

Subramaniam, V. (2007). Seasonal variation in the incidence of preeclampsia and eclampsia in tropical climatic conditions. *BMC Women's Health*, 7(1), 18. https://doi.org/10.1186/1472-6874-7-18

Swim, J. K., Aviste, R., Lengieza, M. L., & Fasano, C. J. (2022). OK Boomer: A decade of generational differences in feelings about climate change. *Global Environmental Change*, 73, 102479. https://doi.org/10.1016/j.gloenvcha.2022.102479

Tam, K.-P., Chan, H.-W., & Clayton, S. (2023). Climate change anxiety in China, India, Japan, and the United States. *Journal of Environmental Psychology*, in press.

Thiery, W., Lange, S., Rogelj, J., Schleussner, C.-F., Gudmundsson, L., Seneviratne, S. I., … Wada, Y. (2021). Intergenerational inequities in exposure to climate extremes. *Science*, 374(6564), 158–160. https://doi.org/doi:10.1126/science.abi7339

UNICEF (2021, 19 August). The impacts of climate change put almost every child at risk. www.unicef.org/stories/impacts-climate-change-put-almost-every-child-risk

Wang, S., Leviston, Z., Hurlstone, M., Lawrence, C., & Walker, I. (2018). Emotions predict policy support: Why it matters how people feel about climate change. *Global Environmental Change*, 50, 25–40. https://doi.org/10.1016/j.gloenvcha.2018.03.002

Wullenkord, M., Toger, J., Hamann, K. R., Loy, L., & Reese, G. (2021). Anxiety and climate change: A validation of the Climate Anxiety Scale in a German-speaking quota sample and an investigation of psychological correlates. *Climatic Change*, 168(3), 1–23. https://doi.org/10.31234/osf.io/76ez2

Yelland, C., Robinson, P., Lock, C., La Greca, A. M., Kokegei, B., Ridgway, V., & Lai, B. (2010). Bushfire impact on youth. *Journal of Traumatic Stress*, 23(2), 274–277. https://doi.org/10.1002/jts.20521

CHAPTER 2

*Definitions and Conceptualizations
of Climate Distress*
An International Perspective

Panu Pihkala

Introduction

As this volume shows, climate distress is on the rise worldwide. Various concepts are used to describe it. Each concept carries with it a certain historical and interpretive legacy. Furthermore, each concept is stylistically and linguistically different; each offers incentives for slightly different interpretations via its form. Various people may use concepts for various purposes, and there may be battles between interpretations and usages of concepts.

The way in which concepts are used matters for several reasons: communicative, ethical, and therapeutic. Language needs to be able to depict reality as accurately as possible, and important things need attention via communication and conceptualization. Concepts can give recognition to phenomena and the people who experience them; and in this case, people who experience climate distress need recognition and validation for their feelings. As for various ways of reacting to climate distress, different conceptualizations may direct attention towards different kinds of (re)actions. For example, if a concept sounds pathological, responses are more likely to be oriented in that vein. The complexity of climate distress as a phenomenon and its close links with several other issues produces challenges for conceptualizations and communication. For example, how should we pay attention conceptually to both the adaptive and maladaptive forms of climate distress?

In this chapter, definitions and conceptualizations of climate distress are discussed from interdisciplinary environmental studies, psychology, and philosophy perspectives. Climate distress as a concept is given detailed analysis: what exactly does "distress" mean here? It is also discussed in relation to several associated key concepts, most notably climate anxiety. The history of the usage of related terms is also briefly discussed. Furthermore, it is pointed out that contextual factors shape conceptualizations and their interpretations in a complex manner. Examples of related terminology in various languages are provided, and special attention is given to a case example of related dynamics in two Nordic countries: Finland and Sweden. This is, to the author's knowledge, the first time that climate distress as a concept has been analyzed in relation to more exact definitions of distress.

The relationships between key concepts and phenomena will be discussed in more depth below, but certain main issues deserve attention first. Although distress is a widely used concept, its boundaries are not clear (Phillips, 2009), and this definitional obscurity then directly affects how climate distress is used. Climate anxiety is the primary concept used (Cunsolo et al., 2020) (see also Chapter 1 in this volume), and any conceptual analysis of climate distress requires discussion of the relation between these two. Anxiety is also a broad-ranging concept with many different connotations (Barlow, 2004; Kurth, 2018; LeDoux, 2016). A third closely related concept is worry, which once again includes many possible manifestations and interpretations (Ojala et al., 2021). For example, worry can manifest both as negative rumination and as constructive thinking about potential threats. It is evident that, when broadly defined, both climate distress and climate anxiety can include various kinds of worry, and thus these three key concepts include significant overlap.

Previous Research

Research about conceptualizations of climate distress is growing but still relatively scarce. One of the most in-depth analyses has been made by medical anthropologist Wardell (2020) in her article "Naming and Framing Ecological Distress," which analyzes a sample of thirty online articles, blogs, and videos. Wardell's main aim was to study meaning-making processes in the ecological crisis and to analyze the connotations of various concepts. Wardell points out that related concepts may be linked with diagnoses and various views about subjectivity. She argues that care is needed when analyzing how long-standing issues related to medical concepts may influence the interpretations of new terminology around ecological distress. However, it is notable that she does not actually define distress as a term, which is a common feature in writings on this topic.

Wardell's analysis includes many ethical discussions. She notes the pathologizing, individualizing, and universalizing tendencies in many usages of terms related to ecological distress, and she argues for greater care in terminological usage. Wardell asks: "Can care for distressed individuals be framed in a way that acknowledges the structural and ecological context of these times?" (2020, p. 195). She argues for a systemic understanding of various forms of ecological distress, and warns against "over-applying an ethnocentric English-language lexicon" (p. 196). There should be opportunities for people to use localized, contextually sensitive terms for various related phenomena.

Various usages and definitions of eco-anxiety and climate anxiety have also been studied. This author has produced an interdisciplinary analysis of the usages of "eco-anxiety" (Pihkala, 2020a) and discussed anxiety as part of the broad possible spectrum of climate emotions (Pihkala, 2022b). The term "anxiety" can refer to a wide array of phenomena, ranging from strong anxiety states to anxiety emotions. As an emotion, anxiety arises when a person encounters some kind of problematic and potentially threatening uncertainty (Kurth, 2018); however, it is highly important to note that eco-anxiety can have many forms. Together with philosopher Charlie Kurth, this author has argued that eco-anxiety is fundamentally "practical anxiety": it serves an adaptive purpose by drawing people's attention to threats (Kurth & Pihkala, 2022). Thus, this author has joined Wardell in warning against overly pathologizing interpretations of eco-anxiety and ecological distress (Pihkala, 2022a), and has argued that "practical eco-anxiety" needs more attention (Kurth & Pihkala, 2022; Pihkala, 2020a). Broadly, eco-anxiety may result in either distancing reactions or engagement with reacting constructively to the threats. It is also possible to positively influence people's reactions to eco-anxiety, for example via education and communication (Moser, 2019; Pihkala, 2020b).

Coffey and colleagues (2021) have produced a systematic scoping review which operationalizes eco-anxiety in various texts. Their results demonstrate that the concepts of worry and distress are used frequently in these studies and highlight that the relationships between anxiety, worry, and distress are often not carefully differentiated. Although Coffey and colleagues do not engage in their own analysis about what the concepts of anxiety, worry, and distress mean and how they are related to each other, they do point out that there is a lack of clarity in the literature about how to define eco-anxiety and argue that more research is needed, particularly from non-Western contexts.

The way one defines eco-anxiety informs their interpretations of related emotional and mental states. If a definition leans towards the pathological, our understanding of its manifestations will likely also tend towards pathologizing. This is a major concern when applied to an often-cited description of eco-anxiety, "chronic fear of environmental doom" (Clayton et al., 2017), which Coffey and colleagues (2021) argue could be a "consistent definition" because it is commonly mentioned. However, it is not the official definition of the American Psychiatric or American Psychological Associations, although some sources claim it is (cf. Coffey et al., 2021, p. 4), and it is problematic in many ways. Instead of anxiety, it speaks of chronic fear, which is only one possible aspect of eco-anxiety. There is significant scholarship about the differences between fear and anxiety, even though they are both emotional reactions to perceived threats (e.g., Daniel-Watanabe & Fletcher, 2022; Kurth, 2018; LeDoux, 2016). Other problematic elements of this description include the vagueness of "environmental doom" and the pathologizing tone of the word "chronic" (for critique, see Barnwell et al., 2020). The risk of pathologizing eco-anxiety can be reduced by using broader and more exact definitions.[1]

Scholars have further noted that climate distress can be closely related to various emotions and mental states beyond anxiety. For instance, grief can include distress, although it is worth noting that it is not the grief itself that causes the distress, but rather the loss and damage that brought on the grief (Solomon, 2004). Growing research literature about ecological grief and climate grief often includes mentions of distress (Cunsolo Willox & Ellis, 2018; Cunsolo Willox & Landman, 2017). For example, Comtesse and colleagues mention "climate change-induced distress" frequently in their article about climate grief, but they do not define what distress is (Comtesse et al., 2021).

Table 2.1 displays suggestions of nuanced descriptions of some terms related to climate distress; these are not meant to be clinical terms, but instead depictions of emotions, feelings, and mental states. A distinction is made between the broad ecological crisis and then the climate crisis as a major part of it. It is important to note that these phenomena may have various intensities and many of them relate to both the global situation and various particular events. This list of examples focuses on emotional tones around sadness, anxiety, fear, and worry; numerous other emotional tones may naturally be linked with climate distress, such as anger, feeling betrayed, guilt, and confusion (for a wide array of climate emotions, see Pihkala, 2022b; for a creative list of various "Earth Emotions," see Albrecht, 2019).

---

[1] This author has discussed this 2017 definition with Dr. Susan Clayton, the lead author of the report where that description is mentioned. She expressed that the aim was not to give any fundamental definition of eco-anxiety, and she herself has worked later with more exact measures and descriptions of climate change anxiety (see Clayton, 2020; Clayton & Karazsia, 2020; and Chapter 1 in this volume).

Table 2.1 *Suggestions of nuanced descriptions of some terms related to climate distress*

Term	Suggested description
Eco-anxiety	Anxiety-related feelings that are significantly shaped by the ecological crisis
Climate anxiety	Anxiety-related feelings that are significantly shaped by the climate crisis
Eco-fear (ecological fear)	When compared to eco-anxiety, a more explicit expectation of imminent harm because of ecological damage and threats
Climate fear	When compared to climate anxiety, a more explicit expectation of imminent harm because of climate change
Ecological worry	Various manifestations of worry that are related to the condition of ecological systems and habitats
Climate worry	Various manifestations of worry that are related to the climate crisis
Ecological distress	Various kinds of distress that are significantly shaped by the ecological crisis
Climate distress	Various kinds of distress that are significantly shaped by the climate crisis
Ecological grief	Grief because of the ecological crisis
Climate grief	Grief because of the climate crisis
Climate sadness	Various kinds of sadness because of the climate crisis
Solastalgia	Place-related feelings of sadness and longing because of damage to the environment (cf. nostalgia)
Climate depression	Various depressive moods and feelings that are significantly shaped by the climate crisis (I would separate this from clinically defined depression, even though there may be interconnections)
Winter grief	One example of a more specific form of climate grief that may also result in distress: grief because of changes in winter conditions due to climate change
Snow anxiety	Another example of a more specific form of climate anxiety that may also result in distress: anxiety because of desiring snow but not knowing whether it will come this year because of changes in winter conditions due to climate change

Overall, it is difficult to find exact definitions of climate distress from the literature. As will be seen below, this reflects difficulties in defining distress in general.

An Analysis of "Distress"

Scholars of distress – as a general concept – have observed that the term encompasses various formulations, such as distress, psychological distress, and emotional distress.

In psychiatric literature, distress is mentioned often in the diagnostic systems (the Diagnostic and Statistical Manual of Mental Disorders [DSM], and the International Statistical Classification of Diseases and Related Health Problems [ICD]) as part of various psychological issues. Most often, distress is linked with the level of functional impairment in various disorders (Phillips, 2009). However, some scholars have argued that distress is a transient phenomenon, linked with significant stressors; if and when the stressor is removed or people learn to cope with it, distress is removed or reduced (Horwitz, 2007). Thus, distress as a concept may be used in psychiatric literature either as related strongly to long-lasting syndromes or as related to significant transient stress.

Drapeau et al. (2011) provide in-depth explorations of "psychological distress," which is a concept often used in literature about distress. They observe that definitions of psychological distress often include symptoms of anxiety and depression. Sometimes distress is linked with emotional disturbance, sometimes with clinical conditions. Drapeau and colleagues point out that psychological distress seems to be "a medical concern mostly when it is accompanied by other symptoms" (p. 106). They also highlight the importance of taking cultural factors into account, since these factors shape interpretations and expressions of distress. The authors utilize the following working definition of distress: "state of emotional suffering characterized by symptoms of depression and anxiety."

In common use of language, distress often refers to some kind of significant mental disturbance, usually accompanied by somatic manifestations. For example, it is more severe than just being upset about something. In dictionaries, distress is often defined as a feeling of "extreme sorrow, suffering or pain," to quote the *Cambridge Dictionary* as a telling example (https://dictionary.cambridge.org/dictionary/english/distress).[2] The extent to which common people in various cultures and areas interpret distress as either moderate or extreme remains open to interpretation.

The American Psychological Association's (APA) definitions of distress offer various possibilities for applying the concept of distress to climate matters:

---

[2] Dictionaries also mention the formulation "to be in distress," for example a ship that needs help. A side note: this might actually be adopted to use in relation to the climate crisis – "Our Green Boat is in distress." https://dictionary.cambridge.org/dictionary/english/distress

distress:
1. the negative stress response, often involving negative affect and physiological reactivity: a type of stress that results from being overwhelmed by demands, losses, or perceived threats. It has a detrimental effect by generating physical and psychological maladaptation and posing serious health risks for individuals. This generally is the intended meaning of the word stress. Compare eustress.
2. a negative emotional state in which the specific quality of the emotion is unspecified or unidentifiable. (APA Dictionary, https://dictionary.apa.org/distress)

What, then, should be thought about "climate distress?" Certain prominent climate psychologists, such as Rosemary Randall (2019), have argued that climate distress would be a less pathologizing concept than climate anxiety. In certain contexts, this may be so, but the emphasis on impaired function in the above-mentioned broad range of interpretations of distress makes this author cautious about applying this argument across various contexts. It may be that in some contexts, distress is less pathologizing than anxiety, but not necessarily in all of them.

Based on these various definitions of distress, the terms climate distress and climate anxiety share a number of common features:

– Both are often defined as difficult mental states
– Both have links to feeling overwhelmed and worried
– Both are often defined as including various kinds of emotional disturbance, where the exact components are difficult to define but commonly include symptoms of stress, anxiety, and depression
– Both can manifest both as strong symptoms and as milder, coping-related symptoms (see also Chapter 9).

This number of shared features could easily lead to the conclusion that climate anxiety and climate distress can be used interchangeably. But the discussion above points to the need for critical analysis of what various people mean by the term they do use; both terms can be shaped for use with a variety of connotations. Randall (2019) prefers climate distress over climate anxiety because the common manifestations are not just anxiety, but a broader range of phenomena. However, if climate anxiety is used broadly – as it often is – then it also includes other phenomena than strictly or simply defined anxiety.

Furthermore, at least two other issues need definitional attention: the adaptive potential in climate distress and its possible links with depression and grief. Just as we need to define climate anxiety further, various kinds of "climate depression" should be explored, and scholars have indeed started to discuss that concept (Budziszewska & Kałwak, 2022; Pihkala, 2022b). When more exact language is needed, there should be a focus on discriminating between anxiety, depression, and distress, even when these reactions overlap. There should also be clear guidelines for discerning normal but often complex grief from more pathological depression. Budziszewska and Kałwak (2022) observe that, while many people identify with climate depression and find the concept helpful for public recognition, its usage may include stigmatizing and medicalizing tendencies at the same time.

Climate distress also has the potential to be adaptive, rather than harmful (see Chapter 8). Many scholars have argued that experiencing climate anxiety can have a strongly adaptive element because it alerts a person to real threats, which include some kind of uncontrollability and uncertainty (Hogg et al., 2021; Kurth & Pihkala, 2022; Pihkala, 2020a, p. 2; Wullenkord et al., 2021). The interconnections between climate distress and anxiety also highlight adaptive qualities, especially views of distress that emphasize that it is an appropriate response to stressors (Horwitz, 2007).

The adaptive potential of climate distress complicates the definitional issues about its relation with eustress, "a good kind of stress," referring to positive reactions to a stressor (e.g., Nelson & Simmons, 2003). Some dictionaries define distress as opposite of eustress. However, these boundaries are not easy to apply to climate distress, because the negative stress generated by difficult situations may also lead to positive growth and problem-solving. Climate distress may feel worse than clear cases of eustress, but when more carefully analyzed, climate distress has the potential to be a good kind of stress, in addition to its challenging aspects.

History of Climate Distress (and Closely Related Concepts)

Although specific terms for any ecological distress are relatively recent, reading historical sources illustrates that people have felt ecological distress for a long time. A phenomenological history of climate distress – its existence as a phenomenon – dates back at least to mid-twentieth-century, amidst those few climate scientists who already then knew about the dangers of runaway climate change. As climate awareness grew along with the rising temperatures, a growing number of people started to feel climate distress in various forms. "Climate concern" and "climate worry" were discussed (e.g., Ojala, 2007; van der Linden, 2017), but concepts to describe more pressing climate distress only emerged in the 2000s.

The concept of eco-anxiety appears to have first been used in the early 1990s, but it gained more prominence around 2007 (Albrecht, 2019). At the same time, the concept of solastalgia was created by Australian environmental philosopher Glenn Albrecht. This concept refers to a feeling of loss and homesickness because one's environs have been damaged (Albrecht, 2019; Albrecht et al., 2007). Higginbotham and colleagues, including Albrecht, developed a place-oriented "environmental distress scale" in 2006, which included solastalgia (Higginbotham et al., 2006). Some people also used these concepts, eco-anxiety and solastalgia, to refer to climate distress, while others argued that it would be better to have a wider vocabulary for various phenomena and differentiate between terms (e.g., climate anxiety and eco-anxiety) (Pihkala, 2020a). The concepts of climate anxiety and climate change anxiety came into use more frequently at the end of the 2010s, and in 2020 the first proposal for a psychological measurement of "climate change anxiety" was introduced by social psychologist Susan Clayton and her colleague Bryan Karazsia (Clayton & Karazsia, 2020). In the early 2020s, many researchers either tested this Climate Anxiety Scale (see Chapter 1) or developed their own proposals for related scales (Hepp et al., 2022; Hogg et al., 2021; Stewart, 2021).

The youth climate movement represents an important faction of people linked with climate anxiety and climate distress. Some of its proponents – such as one of its prominent leaders Greta Thunberg – have spoken openly about their climate distress (Thunberg et al., 2020), leading the concepts of climate anxiety and distress to gain much more media attention. In the background, there was also scholarly discussion about what terminology would serve the best (e.g., Pihkala, 2020a; Randall, 2019; Wardell, 2020). The older discourses about climate change worry were also continued and linked with the more recent concepts (e.g., Verplanken et al., 2020; for an overview, see Ojala et al., 2021). Stress reaction frameworks were discussed by several scholars and psychologists in relation to climate change (e.g., Budziszewska & Kałwak, 2022; Clayton et al., 2017; Helm et al., 2018).

Concepts, Interpretations, and Power

At the end of the 2010s, the concept of climate anxiety in particular quickly became intertwined with politics and identity politics. Several climate sceptics framed climate distress as neurotic and unfounded (e.g., Prager, 2019). A growing number of research articles about these discourses are now being published. For example, a recent analysis of media discussions about the School Strike for Climate movement in Australia found that concerned student activists were portrayed either as "ignorant zealots," "anxious pawns," "rebellious truants," or "extraordinary heroes" (Mayes & Hartup, 2022). Many climate activists resisted patronizing categorizations and claimed climate distress as their own, saying that it is not pathological but rather a sign of paying attention (e.g., Lawton, 2019; Uchendu, 2022; see also Uchendu and Haase, Chapter 18 in this volume).

As Wardell (2020) points out in her insightful analysis (and as clearly demonstrated above), the uses of climate anxiety concepts include power dynamics that benefit from critical examination and critical pedagogical analysis. It needs to be asked: who wants to use which concepts, in what way(s), and why? As mentioned previously, climate distress and anxiety have been framed quite differently by different groups – for example, by young climate activists and climate sceptics. These different interpretations not only have ethical and political implications, but also mental health implications. For a young person feeling climate distress, it is quite a different experience to be told by their community that they are manifesting a much-needed awareness than to be told that they are experiencing mental health problems.

Recently, eco-anxiety scholar Jennifer Uchendu (2022) has discussed these issues around power dynamics and framings of eco-anxiety. Her research shows that many young people are thinking about these subjects. For example, a young climate activist from the UK reflects insightfully:

> Eco-anxiety has to do with recognizing your own power and how it intersects with privileges. I am in Brighton, I am a white, middle-class citizen and have grown up in that sort of setting, so I have a specific eco-anxiety and it is important to recognize the power relations that have created this eco-anxiety … Eco-anxiety comes in different forms and is dependent on the power relations within which you are situated. I think it is important to be reflective of your positionality. If not, you will not understand the root causes of your eco–anxiety. (Uchendu, 2022, p. 545)

Several agendas relating to power-based usages of climate distress and related concepts can be identified:

- Psychological purposes: controlling the narrative about what people are feeling and experiencing
- Environmental ethical purposes: profiling climate distress in a value-laden way, as beneficial or maladaptive (or both, depending on the case) in relation to action on ecological issues
- Other political and ethical purposes: framing climate distress to support political or ethical arguments

Following from these potential manipulations, the following arguments can also be made about wise and ethical uses of these conceptualizations:

– Psychological definitions should be as accurate as possible, with sensitivity to how the same concept may be understood in different ways by various people and peoples (for example, anxiety interpretations).
– Othering, pathologizing, gaslighting and other unethical uses of power should be resisted in definitions and uses of climate distress.
– While there is a need for unifying concepts that enable public and professional discussion about phenomena, various people should have the right to develop and use concepts as they themselves deem suitable for their experiences. For example, if a group wants to call their climate distress "climate suffering" or "climate enthusiasm," they should have the right to do so in their own speech, as long as others' rights are respected.

Finally, the following general arguments can be made specific to the usage of climate distress as a concept:

– The close connections between distress and many other mental states should be kept in mind. This applies especially to anxiety, worry, stress reactions, and low/depressive moods.
– The manifold possibilities inherent in climate distress as related to coping and adaptation should be taken into account. In other words, there is a need for understanding both the adaptive and maladaptive potentials of climate distress.
– Climate distress felt by children and youth should be recognized and validated by adults (see Hickman et al., 2021; Pihkala, 2020b; Vergunst & Berry, 2021; Verlie, 2022).
– The impacts of different cultures and languages on terminological usage should be considered. This issue will be discussed next in more detail.

Different Cultures and Languages

The roles of culture and language are quite complex in relation to conceptualizations of climate distress. There may be literal translations of key concepts, such as anxiety and distress, but these words may be heard in slightly different tones across various languages and cultures. Moreover, there are many subcultures in any given culture, and these may have their own interpretive biases. For example, the French word *anxiété* has a different connotation than the German *angst*, both in history and in the present (for some reflections on the history of anxiety terminology, see Kurth, 2018; LeDoux, 2016).

In any given language and culture, the following factors are likely to have a role in how climate distress is conceptualized and used linguistically:

– What term was first used in prominent writings and other publications about the topic
– What the interpretative history of various related concepts in a given culture and language has been
– How these various terms are seen in relation to pathology and medical treatment
– Whether there is identity politics around climate distress and if so, what kind
– How the helping professionals in that culture and language are speaking – or not speaking – about various forms of climate distress.[3]

In the following, the general popularity of various terms across cultures is described on the basis of casual internet searches of both scholarly publications and general media. More rigorous research is needed in the future to explore international terminology more fully, including an analysis of whether the persons involved have contributed to the namings of the issues. To this author's knowledge, this is the first preliminary review of their usage.

In French, the most commonly used general concept currently seems to be *éco-anxiété*. *Anxiété climatique* is the other climate-related specific term. Solastalgia is also used in various ways and translated as *la solastalgie*. Other terms have been proposed: for example, ecopsychologist Jean-Pierre Le Danff prefers *souffrance écologique*, directly translated as ecological suffering (in a psychological manner).[4]

In Spanish, *ecoansiedad* seems to be emerging as the general concept, although *ansiedad ecológica* is also used. *La ansiedad climática* is the climate-oriented form.[5] In Italian, *ecoansia* is used by many psychologists.[6]

---

[3] As of now, there is an absence of definitions about these matters in psychiatry. However, certain psychological organizations have actively advocated for a wide-ranging understanding of climate distress, such as the Climate Psychology Alliance especially in Great Britain and MIELI ry in Finland. See www.climatepsychologyalliance.org/, Rintala, 2022, and www.ymparistoahdistus.fi/, accessed December 13, 2022.
[4] See, for example, https://reporterre.net/Deprime-par-la-crise-climatique-Voici-comment-soigner-l-eco-anxiete and www.anxiete.fr/eco-anxiete-detresse-changements-climatiques/, accessed December 13, 2022.
[5] https://es.wikipedia.org/wiki/Ecoansiedad, accessed December 13, 2022.
[6] https://aiacc.it/, accessed April 28, 2023.

In German, the concept of *angst* has a special history because of its close links with existentialist thought, and can be translated as fear, anxiety, fright, anguish, dread, worry, or cowardice. Many terms for eco-anxiety and climate distress include the root *angst* concept and thus the historical link to this philosophical tradition, including *Klima-angst*, *Öko-Ängste*, and *Umweltangst* (see Bronswijk & Hausmann, 2022; Rieken et al., 2021). It is difficult to estimate from outside Germany which of these terms is the most commonly used.

A case example of how these terms are used in two Nordic countries, Finland and Sweden, will be discussed in more depth next, as an example of the many dynamics around conceptualizations of climate distress. The author is himself from Finland and has been an active participant in the public discussions around climate distress in Finland. He also speaks Swedish.

Both of these countries, situated at the north end of Europe, have certain special features regarding discourses of climate distress. The prominent climate activist Greta Thunberg, who has frequently been linked with discussions about climate distress, is from Sweden and started her activism there. There has been significant media discussion about Greta and climate anxiety in Sweden, sometimes in highly polarized connotations (Berglund, 2019). In Finland, the first waves of a national media discussion about eco-anxiety and climate distress had started already in 2017, somewhat earlier than in most countries in the world (for this author's personal reflections on these developments, see Pihkala, 2019).

These two countries – small in population but with international influence which exceeds their size – have interesting differences with regard to climate distress conceptualizations. In Swedish, the whole phenomenon is called by the Swedish equivalent of climate anxiety, *klimatångest* (e.g., Berglund, 2019), while in Finland, a separation has been made between *ympäristöahdistus* – literally "environment-anxiety," referring to eco-anxiety – and *ilmastoahdistus*, which means climate anxiety more specifically (e.g., Hyry, 2019). The Finnish vocabulary thus enables more nuanced description of related phenomena, although some Finns still equate these two. Neither of the two languages has a commonly used word for distress as a concept: for example, in Finnish, the English-shaped technical word *distressi* exists, but it is used only by some psychological and medical professionals, so that for common people, any talk about "ilmastodistressi" – climate distress in a literal form – would sound very unnatural.

The Finnish discourse is also a fascinating example of how contextual factors shape understandings of climate-related concepts. From the beginning of the national discussion in 2017, there has been a strong emphasis on both the nonpathological fundamental quality of eco-anxiety and of the possibility that eco-anxiety may manifest in psychologically challenging ways such as prolonged anxiety. The general discussion started from a technically nonclimate concept, *ympäristöahdistus* (eco-anxiety), even though climate anxiety was also discussed. In Autumn 2018, there was a major rise in climate awareness, and climate anxiety started to be more discussed than before. Public discussions about climate distress became more contested and the various reactions to Greta Thunberg were similarly intense in Finland as in other parts of the world, although not as intense as in Sweden. The views about climate distress became more polarized, which this author believes to be due to identity politics and the psychosocial pressures behind them (cf. Hoggett, 2019).

In 2019, Sitra, the Finnish Innovation Fund, conducted a national survey of climate emotions in Finland, prepared with the help of several scholars, including this author. The results of this survey showed that 25 percent of all respondents thought that climate anxiety, *ilmastoahdistus*, is a suitable term to describe their feelings towards climate change; of the youngest age segment, the number was more than 33 percent. The survey included questions about more debilitating manifestations of anxiety and depression linked with climate change in the respondents' minds, and only between 4 and 10 percent of those endorsing climate anxiety reported these (Hyry, 2019; Sangervo et al., 2022). Thus, in the Finnish discourse, the closest equivalent to climate distress, *ilmastoahdistus* (climate anxiety), was seen by many Finns as not mainly pathological (see also Rintala, 2022).

These examples from a variety of countries show some of the diversity in terminology and interpretations of climate distress. Although data on people's interpretations of related terms is not available for many countries, at least in Finland the contextual equivalent of climate distress is seen by people to include the dual character (i.e., adaptive and maladaptive) that scholars have argued it to have (see Marks and Hudson, Chapter 8 in this volume).

Towards the Future

Inquiry and action around climate distress are invigorated at the moment, in the first half of the 2020s. Scholars manifest a growing awareness of the dual character of climate distress as both a potential challenge for mental health and a potential adaptive reaction based on noticing very real climate problems, with many questions to be answered about possible applications of these understandings.

Various scales and measures for climate change-related psychological impacts are being developed. A few observations about recent scales serve as an example of terminology and interpretations. The research article describing the development of the Hogg Eco-anxiety scale (Hogg et al., 2021) discusses distress, but the final scale items feature anxiety and worry as concepts. In a recent preprint (Hepp et al., 2022), scholars have developed a "climate change distress and impairment" scale, which separates distress from impairment. Hepp and colleagues see climate distress as spanning anxiety, sadness, and anger, thus linking many different climate emotions together. Thus, their preprint joins those voices that see climate distress as fundamentally nonpathological and adaptive. It remains to be seen how climate distress is defined in these measures and what aspects of it are studied – and what are not (see also Clayton and Crandon, Chapter 1 in this volume).

As was noted above, Coffey and colleagues (2021) observe that the definition of eco-anxiety in an EcoAmerica and APA publication (Clayton et al., 2017), "a chronic fear of environmental doom," is referenced in many sources, and thus they think that it "could provide a consistent definition" (p. 4). However, that definition has been criticized for its potential pathologizing interpretations (Barnwell et al., 2020; see also the discussion in Pihkala, 2020a) – and other options do exist. In this author's opinion, merely speaking about climate anxiety and distress as "anxiety and distress which are significantly related to climate change" would serve as basic definitions. That way, the plurality of cultural and emotional meanings of anxiety and distress is given space, and premature pathologizing of any one state of mind avoided.

It remains to be seen what forms of climate distress will manifest and emerge in the coming years. It is clear that there will be many social and ecological changes due to the pressures generated by the climate crisis, but at the same time there is significant unpredictability and there will likely be much variation in local circumstances. Nevertheless, having a wide vocabulary of various climate-related emotions and mental states will help in recognizing and encountering the emerging forms of climate distress.

References

Albrecht, G. (2019). *Earth emotions: New words for a new world*. Cornell University Press.
Albrecht, G., Sartore, G.-M., Connor, L., Higginbotham, N., Freeman, S., Kelly, B., … Pollard, G. (2007). Solastalgia: The distress caused by

environmental change. *Australasian Psychiatry: Bulletin of the Royal Australian and New Zealand College of Psychiatrists*, 15(S1), S95–S98. https://doi.org/10.1080/10398560701701288

Barlow, D. H. (2004). *Anxiety and its disorders: The nature and treatment of anxiety and panic* (2nd ed.). Guilford Press.

Barnwell, G., Stroud, L., & Watson, M. (2020). Critical reflections from South Africa: Using the Power Threat Meaning Framework to place climate-related distress in its socio-political context. *Clinical Psychology Forum*, 332 (August), 7–15.

Berglund, K. (2019). There is no alternative: A symbolic interactionist account of Swedish climate activists. Vol. Master's thesis [Lund University, Department of Sociology]. http://lup.lub.lu.se/student-papers/record/8990902/file/8990903.pdf

Bronswijk, K. van, & Hausmann, C. M. (2022). *Climate emotions: Klimakrise und psychische Gesundheit*. Psychosozial-Verlag. www.beck-shop.de/hausmann-bronswijk-climate-emotions/product/34000720

Budziszewska, M., & Kałwak, W. (2022). Climate depression. Critical analysis of the concept. *Psychiatria Polska*, 56(1), 171–182. https://doi.org/10.12740/PP/127900

Clayton, S. (2020). Climate anxiety: Psychological responses to climate change. *Journal of Anxiety Disorders*, 74, 102263. https://doi.org/10.1016/j.janxdis.2020.102263

Clayton, S., & Karazsia, B. T. (2020). Development and validation of a measure of climate change anxiety. *Journal of Environmental Psychology*, 69, 101434. https://doi.org/10.1016/j.jenvp.2020.101434

Clayton, S., Manning, C. M., Krygsman, K., & Speiser, M. (2017). *Mental health and our changing climate. Impacts, implications, and guidance*. APA & EcoAmerica.

Coffey, Y., Bhullar, N., Durkin, J., Islam, M. S., & Usher, K. (2021). Understanding eco-anxiety: A systematic scoping review of current literature and identified knowledge gaps. *Journal of Climate Change and Health*, 3, 100047. https://doi.org/10.1016/j.joclim.2021.100047

Comtesse, H., Ertl, V., Hengst, S. M. C., Rosner, R., & Smid, G. E. (2021). Ecological grief as a response to environmental change: A mental health risk or functional response? *International Journal of Environmental Research and Public Health*, 18(2), 734. https://doi.org/10.3390/ijerph18020734

Cunsolo, A., Harper, S. L., Minor, K., Hayes, K., Williams, K. G., & Howard, C. (2020). Ecological grief and anxiety: The start of a healthy response to climate change? *The Lancet Planetary Health*, 4(7), e261–e263. https://doi.org/10.1016/S2542-5196(20)30144-3

Cunsolo Willox, A., & Ellis, N. R. (2018). Ecological grief as a mental health response to climate change-related loss. *Nature Climate Change*, 8(4), 275–281.

Cunsolo Willox, A., & Landman, K. (Eds.) (2017). *Mourning nature: Hope at the heart of ecological loss & grief*. McGill-Queen's University Press.

Daniel-Watanabe, L., & Fletcher, P. (2022). Are fear and anxiety truly distinct? *Biological Psychiatry Global Open Science*, 2(4), 341–349.

Drapeau, A., Marchand, A., & Beaulieu-Prévost, D. (2011). Epidemiology of psychological distress. In L. L'Abate (Ed.), *Mental illnesses – Understanding, prediction and control* (pp. 105–133). InTech.

Helm, S. V., Pollitt, A., Barnett, M. A., Curran, M. A., & Craig, Z. R. (2018). Differentiating environmental concern in the context of psychological adaption to climate change. *Global Environmental Change*, 48, 158–167. https://doi.org/10.1016/j.gloenvcha.2017.11.012.

Hepp, J., Klein, S. A., Horsten, L., Urbild, J., & Lane, S. P. (2022). The climate change distress and impairment scale: Introduction of the measure and first findings on pro-environmental behavior. *PsyArXiv*. https://doi.org/10.31234/osf.io/j6pbu

Hickman, C., Marks, E., Pihkala, P., Clayton, S., Lewandowski, R. E., Mayall, E. E., … Susteren, L. van (2021). Climate anxiety in children and young people and their beliefs about government responses to climate change: A global survey. *The Lancet Planetary Health*, 5(12), e863–e873. https://doi.org/10.1016/S2542-5196(21)00278-3

Higginbotham, N., Connor, L., Albrecht, G., Freeman, S., & Agho, K. (2006). Validation of an environmental distress scale. *EcoHealth*, 3, 245–254.

Hogg, T. L., Stanley, S. K., O'Brien, L. V., Wilson, M. S., & Watsford, C. R. (2021). The Hogg Eco-Anxiety Scale: Development and validation of a multidimensional scale. *Global Environmental Change*, 71, 102391. https://doi.org/10.1016/j.gloenvcha.2021.102391

Hoggett, P. (2019). *Climate psychology: On indifference to disaster*. Palgrave Macmillan. https://doi.org/10.1007/978-3-030-11741-2

Horwitz, A. V. (2007). Distinguishing distress from disorder as psychological outcomes of stressful social arrangements. *Health*, 11(3), 273–289. https://doi.org/10.1177/1363459307077541

Hyry, J. (2019). *Kansalaiskysely ilmastonmuutoksesta ja tunteista [National survey on climate change and emotions]*. Sitra, the Finnish Innovation Fund. https://media.sitra.fi/2019/08/21153439/ilmastotunteet-2019-kyselytutkimuksen-tulokset.pdf & https://media.sitra.fi/2019/11/29131052/sitraclimate-emotions-report-2019.pdf

Kurth, C. (2018). *The anxious mind: An investigation into the varieties and virtues of anxiety*. MIT Press.

Kurth, C., & Pihkala, P. (2022). Eco-anxiety: What it is and why it matters. *Frontiers in Psychology*, 13. https://doi.org/10.3389/fpsyg.2022.981814

Lawton, G. (2019). I have eco-anxiety but that's normal. *New Scientist*, 244(3251), 22. https://doi.org/10.1016/S0262-4079(19)31914-1

LeDoux, J. (2016). *Anxious: Using the brain to understand and treat fear and anxiety*. Penguin Books.

Mayes, E., & Hartup, M. E. (2022). News coverage of the School Strike for Climate movement in Australia: The politics of representing young strikers' emotions. *Journal of Youth Studies*, 25(7), 994–1016. https://doi.org/10.1080/13676261.2021.1929887

Moser, S. C. (2019). Not for the faint of heart: Tasks of climate change communication in the context of societal transformation. In G. Feola, H. Geoghegan, &

A. Arnall (Eds.), *Climate and culture: Multidisciplinary perspectives of knowing, being and doing in a climate change world* (pp. 141–167). Cambridge University Press.

Nelson, D. L., & Simmons, B. L. (2003). Eustress: An elusive construct, an engaging pursuit. In P. L. Perrewe & D. C. Ganster (Eds.), *Emotional and physiological processes and positive intervention strategies* (Vol. 3, pp. 265–322). Emerald Group. https://doi.org/10.1016/S1479-3555(03)03007-5

Ojala, M. (2007). *Hope and worry: Exploring young people's values, emotions, and behavior regarding global environmental problems*. Örebro University, Universitetsbiblioteket.

Ojala, M., Cunsolo, A., Ogunbode, C. A., & Middleton, J. (2021). Anxiety, worry, and grief in a time of environmental and climate crisis: A narrative review. *Annual Review of Environment and Resources*, 46(1). https://doi.org/10.1146/annurev-environ-012220-022716

Phillips, M. R. (2009). Is distress a symptom of mental disorders, a marker of impairment, both or neither? *World Psychiatry*, 8(2), 91–92.

Pihkala, P. (2019). Eco-anxiety and hope (a blog by Panu Pihkala). https://ecoanxietyandhope.blogspot.com/2019/11/eco-anxiety-in-finland-tale-of-national.html

Pihkala, P. (2020a). Anxiety and the ecological crisis: An analysis of eco-anxiety and climate anxiety. *Sustainability*, 12(19), 7836. https://doi.org/10.3390/su12197836

Pihkala, P. (2020b). Eco-anxiety and environmental education. *Sustainability*, 12(23), 10149. https://doi.org/10.3390/su122310149

Pihkala, P. (2022a). Commentary: Three tasks for eco-anxiety research – a commentary on Thompson et al. (2021). *Child and Adolescent Mental Health*, 27(1), 92–93. https://doi.org/10.1111/camh.12529

Pihkala, P. (2022b). Toward a taxonomy of climate emotions. *Frontiers in Climate*, 3. https://doi.org/10.3389/fclim.2021.738154

Prager, D. (2019). If you can't sell your hysteria to adults, try kids. *National Review*, 24, 9. www.nationalreview.com/2019/09/american-left-climate-change-hysteria-kids/

Randall, R. (2019). Climate anxiety or climate distress? Coping with the pain of the climate emergency. *Online Discussion Forum/Blogs*. https://rorandall.org/2019/10/19/climate-anxiety-or-climate-distress-coping-with-the-pain-of-the-climate-emergency/

Rieken, B., Popp, R., & Raile, P. (2021). *Eco-anxiety – Zukunftsangst und Klimawandel: Interdisziplinäre Zugänge* (1st ed.). Waxmann.

Rintala, H. (2022). Support for distress associated with climate change in Finland – "The mind of eco-anxiety." Climate Adapt (EU). https://climate-adapt.eea.europa.eu/en/metadata/case-studies/support-for-distress-associated-with-climate-change-in-finland-2013-201cthe-mind-of-eco-anxiety201d

Sangervo, J., Jylhä, K. M., & Pihkala, P. (2022). Climate anxiety: Conceptual considerations, and connections with climate hope and action. *Global Environmental Change*, 76, 102569. https://doi.org/10.1016/j.gloenvcha.2022.102569

Solomon, R. C. (2004). On grief and gratitude. In R. C. Solomon (Ed.), *In defense of sentimentality* (pp. 75–107). Oxford University Press. https://doi.org/10.1093/019514550X.003.0004

Stewart, A. E. (2021). Psychometric properties of the Climate Change Worry Scale. *International Journal of Environmental Research and Public Health*, 18(2), 494. https://doi.org/10.3390/ijerph18020494

Thunberg, G., Thunberg, S., Ernman, M., & Ernman, B. (2020). *Our house is on fire: Scenes of a family and a planet in crisis*. Penguin Random House.

Uchendu, J. O. (2022). Eco-anxiety and its divergent power holds: A youth climate activist's perspective. *South African Journal of Psychology*, 52(4), 545–547. https://doi.org/10.1177/00812463221130586

van der Linden, S. (2017). Determinants and measurement of climate change risk perception, worry, and concern. In M. C. Nisbet, S. S. Ho, E. Markowitz, S. O'Neill, M. S. Schäfer, & J. Thaker (Eds.), *The Oxford encyclopedia of climate change communication*. Oxford University Press.

Vergunst, F., & Berry, H. L. (2021). Climate change and children's mental health: A developmental perspective. *Clinical Psychological Science*, 10(4). https://doi.org/10.1177/21677026211040787

Verlie, B. (2022). *Learning to live with climate change: From anxiety to transformation*. Routledge.

Verplanken, B., Marks, E., & Dobromir, A. I. (2020). On the nature of eco-anxiety: How constructive or unconstructive is habitual worry about global warming? *Journal of Environmental Psychology*, 72, 101528. https://doi.org/10.1016/j.jenvp.2020.101528

Wardell, S. (2020). Naming and framing ecological distress. *Medicine Anthropology Theory*, 7(2), 187–201. https://doi.org/10/17157/mat.7.2.769

Wullenkord, M., Tröger, J., Hamann, K., Loy, L., & Reese, G. (2021). Anxiety and climate change: A validation of the Climate Anxiety Scale in a German-speaking quota sample and an investigation of psychological correlates. *Climatic Change*, 168(20). https://doi.org/10.1007/s10584-021-03234-6

CHAPTER 3

Psychiatric Perspectives on Youth Climate Distress
Using the Biopsychosocio-environmental Knowledge Base to Understand and Assess for Clinical Level Symptoms

Elizabeth Haase

Introduction: A History of the Relationship Between Climate Distress and Clinical Symptoms

As youth distress about climate change has risen around the world, political forces have sought to delegitimize and polarize the way it is viewed, claiming it either as a mass hysteria inflicted on young people by doomscrolling climate zealots or as a sickness, a pathology akin to other anxiety disorders. On the other side of this political battle, those who understand the climate emergency have wholeheartedly validated youth distress, but with lesser consideration of the trait and state anxiety, depressive symptoms, familial conflicts, and developmental and social forces that may be manifesting through or influencing its expression, as with any other psychological focal point of a young person's concerns. The impact of climate stress – both direct and psychological – on brain development has also not been explored, nor has its relationship with the youth mental health crisis that has occurred in parallel with its rise (Centers for Disease Control and Prevention [CDC], 2023). These are fundamentally psychiatric issues: the need to distinguish illness from a range of normal reactions; explore etiological influences; and the need to protect everyone, including young people, against stigma and misuse of science in ways that may cause mental harm or worsening of symptoms. There are also interesting questions about toxic positivity, denial of misuse and abuse of children (as well as their weaponization), the relationship between suffering, sanity, and transcendence, and other psychospiritual and existential questions embedded within this debate. This chapter reviews the evidence for and against climate distress as a psychopathology, considers what needs to be further determined to answer this question, and suggests how to assess a young person with significant climate distress for overlapping psychiatric syndromes and risks.

Although it has been expressed for decades, climate distress as a mass phenomenon came to significant media and academic attention only in the latter half of the 2010s, with significant academic study of its features taking hold by 2023. Until that point, it had been defined loosely and evaluated mostly through large opinion polls using terms such as climate stress, worry, concern, anxiety, or sadness and did not particularly differentiate these terms from each other (American Psychological Association, 2018; Leiserowitz et al., 2018). While these polls did ask about intensity of distress, they did not assess or measure coincident psychiatric conditions or symptoms. A small number of studies included some measure of psychological characteristics associated with climate distress (reviewed in Ramadan et al., 2023). These studies suggested that younger age groups and being female (Henker et al., 1995; Sundblad et al., 2007; Searle & Gow, 2010), altruistic and pro-environmental beliefs (Schultz, 2001), connection to nature (Ojala, 2005), problem-focused coping (Ojala, 2012), knowledge of climate change and its health effects (Sundblad et al., 2007), and positive traits of imagination and appreciation for new ideas (Verplanken & Roy, 2013) were among the associations with climate distress per se, as distinguished from pro-environmental attitudes or actions.

Qualitative studies of young people (MacDonald et al., 2015) found more negative emotions associated with environmental change, and high levels of worry have also been found by Hickman et al. (2021), particularly in those who are poor, more directly impacted by climate change, and living in the Global South. Agho et al. (2010) found that climate worry was associated with overall higher global psychological distress, and Searle and Gow (2010) found coincident elevated scores on a scale of depression and anxiety in about 20 percent of those with more climate worry, although these numbers are not particularly different than population norms. Significant levels of difficulty tolerating uncertainty and future worry were also found more often in their climate-worried group.

In the absence of a validated climate distress scale, most early studies worked by expert consensus to develop questions about climate-related feelings (Searle & Gow, 2010; Reser et al., 2014; Hickman et al., 2021). While survey questions on climate anxiety had shown internal reliability and consensus validity, until 2020 the only validated scales that had been used included an Environmental Identity Scale (Clayton et al., 2021) and the Nature Relatedness Scale (Nisbet et al., 2009), neither of which asks about distress.

In 2020, Clayton and Karazsia published a Climate Change Anxiety Scale (CCAS) (Figure 3.1) which was validated in two US samples totaling

> Please rate how often the following statements are true of you.
>
> | 1 | 2 | 3 | 4 | 5 |
> |---|---|---|---|---|
> | Never | Rarely | Sometimes | Often | Almost always |
>
> 1. Thinking about climate change makes it difficult for me to concentrate
> 2. Thinking about climate change makes it difficult for me to sleep
> 3. I have nightmares about climate change
> 4. I find myself crying because of climate change
> 5. I think, "why can't I handle climate change better?"
> 6. I go away by myself and think about why I feel this way about climate change
> 7. I write down my thoughts about climate change and analyze them
> 8. I think, "why do I react to climate change this way?"
> 9. My concerns about climate change make it hard for me to have fun with my family or friends
> 10. I have problems balancing my concerns about sustainability with the needs of my family
> 11. My concerns about climate change interfere with my ability to get work or school assignments done
> 12. My concerns about climate change undermine my ability to work to my potential
> 13. My friends say I think about climate change too much
>
> Note: items 1-8 form the cognitive impairment subscale; items 9-13 are the functional impairment subscale.

Figure 3.1 Climate Change Anxiety Scale (CCAS).

337 participants. This scale developed items about environmental emotions from blog and other available reports, focusing on anxiety, which it refers to as concern, and then assessed both functional and cognitive/emotional impact through items from the Weiss Functional Impairment Scale (Weiss et al., 2018), Ruminative Responses Scale (Treynor et al., 2003) and Drive for Muscularity Scale (McCreary, 2007). Other scales, such as the Hogg Eco-Anxiety Scale (Hogg et al., 2021), are now elaborating on this work by asking more specific research questions targeting behavioral symptoms associated with worry about one's impact on the planet, for example.

The CCAS includes many items associated with depression (sleep impairment, concentration difficulties, sadness, anhedonia, self-doubt, guilt, and rumination) while also assessing for a level of "climate concern" (the term used for anxiety) that is functionally impairing from a variety of angles. It has subsequently been used in a number of ongoing studies (detailed in Chapter 1) which show a pattern of overlapping anxiety and depressive symptoms in respondents as well as different patterns of cognitive emotional (versus functional) impairment in the different groups studied. Results of these studies, which have included both adults and younger people, support the validity of the subscales of the CCAS.

Climate distress generally refers to a broad range of feelings, including sadness, fear, anger, guilt, betrayal, and others. In this chapter, climate distress refers particularly to depressed and anxious reactions to climate change. This focus allows for an exploration of the interplay of these two climate emotions with pediatric anxiety and depressive disorders – the most relevant psychiatric syndromes with which they are likely to overlap. While there have been cases of climate distress associated with obsessive compulsive symptoms, most notably in Greta Thunberg (Farmer, 2019) and psychosis in a child (Wolf & Salo, 2008), these are less common and less reported phenomena.

Clinical Questions about Climate Distress in Young People

Despite the progress in research on climate anxiety described above, as of 2022, there remained no studies delineating climate distress from and understanding its overlap with other internationally recognized psychological and psychiatric syndromes, including diagnosable pediatric anxiety and depressive disorders. Many fundamental questions about the relationship between clinical and nonclinical anxious and depressive responses to climate change in young people thus remain to be explored from an objective, data-driven scientific perspective. These include:

1. Are the levels of climate-related impairment seen in recent research at a level that should invite professional mental health support?
2. Do nonpathological climate emotions in young people exist on a continuum with pathological emotions, or are they discrete in nature?
3. Are there any psychological or psychopathological elements that are prevalent in *all* presentations of youth climate distress, regardless of whether it rises to clinical/pathological levels?
4. When clinical conditions are found in young people with climate distress, what is the nature of that relationship – causal or correlational?
5. What are the similarities and differences between climate anxiety and other forms of anxiety in young people?
6. What factors contribute to youth climate distress evolving into a clinically impairing condition, assuming it can be a stressor contributing to this progression?
7. How do symptoms and syndromes of anxiety, depression, and PTSD that are linked to direct trauma from climate disasters influence our description of climate distress syndromes that emerge without such direct experience?
8. Is youth climate distress found more commonly in young people and/or in family with greater – or lesser – mental health morbidity?

9. Does the social validation of youth climate distress and its source improve or worsen coping capacities?
10. What role does social messaging play in youth climate distress?
11. What mental schemas, biases, and defenses for interpreting reality are used by youth who do *not* have climate anxiety, youth who do, and youth with clinical anxiety disorders?
12. Does the currently recommended response to youth distress – encouraging meaning-based connection to like-minded groups and collective action – in fact improve psychological outcomes and protect the brain from the impacts of chronic stress? If so, at what points in development or emotional moments would its application be most protective?
13. What neurological and psychobehavioral outcomes should we measure in this group, given that climate distress may also be a sign of, and perhaps even contribute to, psychic health?

While questioning these relationships could be taken as undermining and invalidating the clearly reality-based climate concerns of young people, it is critical we ask these questions to avoid repeating the errors of psychiatric history, which is replete with examples of well-meaning individuals defining conditions and treatments in ways which later prove to be a disservice to those so labelled – from the naming of witches, phrenological traits, and penis envy to the pathologizing of homosexuality, gender discordance, and other conditions, to name a few. Psychiatric fads similarly have come and gone, with surges in diagnostic prevalence that in some cases – for example, hysteria, borderline personality disorder, and recall of childhood sexual abuse – have been iatrogenic, meaning, at least partly, a result of the activity of the profession or the professional (Overholzer, 2014). It therefore matters that these questions be asked critically and with a neutral scientific eye. Particularly given that a number of studies have suggested no adverse mental health effects – and, moreover, positive adaptive traits (Verplanken & Roy, 2013; Berry & Peel, 2015; Helm et al., 2018) – in those who are concerned about climate change, we owe it to our young people to get them the mental health support they will need to face the climate emergency.

As beautifully explored elsewhere in this volume by Pihkala (Chapter 2), Clayton (Chapter 1) and others, climate distress involves a range of emotions, including anxiety, worry, fear, shame, sadness, anger, guilt, and others (Hickman et al., 2021; Kurth & Pihkala, 2022). Climate distress also encompasses a range of attitudes about the relationship between the self and external conditions, including issues of identity, self-esteem, possibility and capacity, connectedness, acceptance, generativity, existential meaning, and hope. These qualities of the self clearly overlap with the most important developmental tasks of young people, and are also understood differently in different cultures (Wardell, 2020; see also Chapters 2, 11, 18, and 21 in this volume). All this must be considered in formulating the role of climate distress in the developing self of the young person for a full psychological and psychiatric understanding of its function and importance.

Distinguishing Adaptive from Maladaptive Sadness and Anxiety

As noted above, existing research on climate anxiety does not reliably distinguish anxious and depressive responses. Kurth and Pihkala (2022) have divided climate distress responses into anxiety-like responses (nervous, afraid, scared, worried), self-reflective responses (shame and guilt), and grief-oriented responses, (upset, depressed, distressed). In Chapter 2, here, however, Pihkala concludes that climate distress and climate anxiety can be used relatively interchangeably, based on their shared features of being difficult mental states in which one is overwhelmed and worried, associated with various kinds of emotional disturbance across a spectrum of severity, and encompassing stress, anxiety, and depression. Psychiatric perspectives on anxiety and depression can perhaps contribute here.

Generally, anxiety is the response to a threat and, in most circumstances, is adaptive. This is as true for healthy anxiety about climate change as it is for healthy anxiety about any other challenge. In regards to climate anxiety, Kurth and Pihkala (2022) have described "practical anxiety" as that which motivates pro-environmental action.

Healthy anxiety is characterized by the following features:

1. The distress is appropriate to the scale of threat or risk of an external problem.
2. The distress does not overwhelm the individual's ability to function.
3. The distress serves adaptive functions including motivation, drive, information-gathering, and problem solving.
4. The distress leads to risk minimization.
5. Goal-setting in response to the distress aims to solve the problem rather than reduce the upsetting feelings.
6. The distress ends when the precipitating event or problem is over.

In contrast to healthy anxiety the unhealthy anxiety of clinical pediatric disorders has these notable features:

1. It is delineated from nonclinical anxiety by significant impairment of function.
2. It is not necessarily adaptive – that is, it does not necessarily motivate thought and behavior that solve the problem or increase survival.
3. Activity is focused on an avoidant response to the physiological manifestations of anxiety and stress – trying to get rid of uncomfortable body sensations and get away from the thing causing anxiety – rather than reducing how dangerous it is to the person per se.
4. Anxiety is typically disproportionate to the danger of the fearful stimulus.
5. Anxiety persists well beyond the duration of the threat or occurs well in advance.

In contrast to anxiety, the positive role of sadness has less robust research support. Sadness is an emotional response to pain, usually due to loss or emotional injury. It has positive functions (Lomas, 2018) which include:

1. Improving memory and attention to detail, which improves accuracy and judgment.
2. Decreasing risky independent behavior, lessening energy expenditure and therefore increased proximity to the safety of the group.
3. Evoking protection and connection, through compassion and generosity from others and yourself.
4. Contributing to moral development and psychological awareness.
5. Motivating reparative or transformative action through love, longing, and care.

When carried to extremes, the losses and social hurts that cause us to feel sad and provoke these benefits can contribute to its unhealthy cousin, clinical depression. Features that make depression maladaptive include:

1. Neurovegetative symptoms: This psychiatric term refers to negative changes in sleep, appetite, physical energy, and drive, and ability to concentrate and remember.
2. Extremes in negative views, including self-hate, helplessness, hopelessness, excess guilt, and suicidal ideation.

The Psychiatric Understanding of Pediatric Anxiety and Depression

In order to understand whether a young person's climate anxiety and sadness is clinically significant, we must first situate ourselves in the foundations of pediatric anxiety and depression more generally. To understand what leads to clinical levels of anxiety and depression in a given patient, or to the development of a psychiatric condition more generally, psychiatrists and other mental health professionals rely on the biopsychosocial model developed by George Engel (1977). This model understands clinical states in the individual to be the result or sum of biological predispositions such as genetics, hormones, brain development, and so on; of psychological history, including traumas, relationships, and other cognitive and emotional influences; and of social conditions, which are broadly interpreted to include not only community, schooling, friendships, work, nationality, and other relationships outside the nuclear family, but also external influences such as environmental toxins and habitat. Many working in the area of climate health, however, feel that this model should be renamed the "biopsychosocio-*environmental*" model, to place greater emphasis on non-human interactions and the external natural world as an influence on the symptoms expressed in a particular situation.

Pediatric depression has been associated with a long list of the biopsychosocial influences above and others, including social risks of early severe losses, disaster and trauma exposure, poverty, racism, poor school or family function, poor health habits including excess sugar consumption, gaming and internet time, substance use, obesity and lack of exercise, LGBTQ+ status, bullying and other abuse, early puberty, and genetic risks of family depression and serotonin, dopamine, and monamine oxidase polymorphisms. Family genetics plays the largest role in this list (Selph & McDonagh, 2019). For adolescents, peer rejection also plays a very significant role (Platt et al., 2013). All of these factors may contribute to the intersectional distress of climate change. Adverse social determinants of health that contribute to depression occur significantly more often in areas more subject to environmental injustice and adverse climate impacts, which themselves have adverse effects on the brain (as described later in this chapter). Psychologically, the kinds of losses that contribute to clinical depression can emerge from climate-related losses in nature, including the loss of beloved animals and experiences associated with attachment, such as time in nature with parents. Negative peer responses to a young person's climate distress might also be expected to significantly increase depressive risk.

Anxiety is often conceptually divided into "state" and "trait" anxiety. Whereas state anxiety is a transient response to an adverse event, "trait anxiety" refers to the sum of the biological and psychological factors that make one more susceptible to anxiety and has been shown to increase risk for clinical anxiety and depressive disorders. Recent studies suggest that state anxiety operates through different brain circuits than trait anxiety (Saviola et al., 2020), supporting the biological plausibility that climate anxiety could operate through different neural pathways than more pathology-associated trait anxiety concerns.

Chief among the characteristics of those with high trait anxiety is greater anxiety sensitivity. Anxiety sensitivity is a concept describing an individual's higher sensitivity to body sensations, a greater tendency to interpret body sensations as evidence that something is wrong, and greater physiological stress response in response to the threat-related thoughts. For example, for most people, a temporary tightness in the chest after exercising may not even be noticed, while a person with anxiety sensitivity will interpret this chest tightness as a sign of an impending asthma or heart attack, and blood pressure, heart rate, galvanic skin response (the electric conductance of skin) cortisol levels, and other markers of autonomic distress will spike higher than population averages. This exaggerated physical anxiety response then becomes even further misinterpreted as a sign that something is *really, really* wrong, leading to a vicious cycle of increasing anxious distress (Sadock & Sadock, 2005, p. 1726). People with high trait anxiety are often in a state of hyperarousal, and are also more likely to show neuroticism, negative interpretations of events, difficulty letting go of their fears, and difficulties paying attention and learning, even in situations that are generally considered to be safe (Knowles & Olantunji, 2020).

Behavioral inhibition is another premorbid (meaning before the onset of) characteristic of young people who go on to develop clinical anxiety disorders. Behavioral inhibition is similar to anxiety sensitivity in that the individual has an exaggerated physiological response to an anxiety trigger, but in this case, the trigger is an unfamiliar *external* situation rather than an internal physical sensation, similar to but more all-encompassing than, for example, stranger anxiety in infants. Behavioral inhibition is likely an inherited temperamental characteristic and is associated with later clinically significant social anxiety in up to one-third of the children who show this trait early in life (Sadock & Sadock, 2005, pp. 1726–1727).

Parental and genetic input can also modulate children's anxiety levels. Children whose parents have an anxiety disorder are almost four times as likely to develop one themselves (Micco et al., 2013), and genetics correlations of *trait* anxiety in monozygotic twins, who share 100 percent of their genes, are quite high. At the same time, the *total* genetic heritability of clinical anxiety disorders is thought to be reasonably low, as shown in children-of-twins studies (Eley et al., 2015) which demonstrate that total environment, which encompasses both the overlapping genetics and environmental interactions between an anxious child and their anxious parent, plays the most significant role compared with children adopted into other families, where both genetics and rearing differ. Parents with anxious children tend to be more overprotective and less warm, and parents with anxiety disorders tend to also be more overprotective, intrusive, anxious, rejecting, and negative in how they respond to the anxiety of their children than other parents (Ginsberg et al., 2004), mostly because these parents are likely to be more distressed by their child's distress than parents with a more relaxed style. Parents of children who develop anxiety disorders are also more likely to model fear and avoidance of things that cause anxiety, rather than teaching the child to cope with the threat. Literature has also shown that parents who become highly focused on an aspect of a child's life, whether it be bodily functions such as urination, safety, social disapproval, or school performance, increase children's anxiety (Sadock & Sadock, 2005, p. 1727). Most readers can intuitively understand these research findings if they imagine how a child is trained to feel by a parent who becomes terrified and tense when the child is on a jungle gym versus one who encourages the child to swing, fall, pick themselves up without worry and try again. The latter style encourages the child to develop an internal locus of control, which refers to the child's perception that they are in charge of what happens to them through a cause-and-effect relationship between their behavior and its outcomes. Those with high internal locus of control generally have lower mental health morbidity of all kinds, although with some variability by age and across the literature (Groth et al., 2019).

In terms of parenting styles that may be more helpful to young people with distress, parenting studies have traditionally examined two main parental qualities: Demandingness, referring to how much a parent supervises, expects, exerts power over, and controls what a child is doing, and Responsiveness, referring to emotional warmth, acceptance, support, and willingness to reason with a child. Based on combinations of these two traits, several common styles of parenting have been identified:

1. Authoritative parenting: High warmth, high demandingness
2. Authoritarian parenting: Low warmth, high demandingness
3. Permitting: High warmth, low demandingness
4. Neglecting: Low warmth, low demandingness

The most successful style of parenting is authoritative, which provides the right amount of guidance and adequate expectations for children but also warmly supports their increasing independence. In contrast, authoritarian parenting is associated with lower academic and social achievement and competence, poor coping in stressful situations, and more internalizing and externalizing behavior problems, including delinquency and substance abuse. Permitting parenting is thought not to offer adequate structure to support young peoples' development, and neglectful parenting leads to obvious deficits in what children can feel and achieve (Merlin et al., 2013).

All of these findings have important ramifications for youth climate anxiety, in particular how adults model an appropriate fear response to the climate crisis. On the one hand, this research-based knowledge highlights the capacity and possibility that intrusive adult overfocus on climate in a child's life experience might generate clinical levels of distress in children. They also suggest that anxiety about climate change in adults who do not have anxiety disorders is unlikely to be significant enough to "cause" pathological anxiety disorders in children, as suggested by those who fear-monger the idea of adults causing mass hysteria. Additionally, young people with high levels of trait anxiety and behavioral inhibition or parents with anxiety disorders may be more in need of therapeutic support for their climate distress. For a comprehensive list of nonpharmacological interventions used to treat child and adolescent anxiety and depression, see Table 3.1.

Taken in sum, the literature reviewed above also guides us to strive for the following when responding to young people who have anxiety about climate change, particularly those with high trait anxiety:

1. Accept their anxieties without criticism or judgment
2. Minimize hyperarousal and catastrophic responses in ourselves and in them
3. Encourage children to stand up to their fears courageously and actively find solutions
4. Allow children to take risks by responding to things that make them anxious without our involvement
5. Be available as an authoritative figure to debate, support, and provide guidelines and boundaries for what they want to do without setting rigid rules
6. Help them to look actively for and attend to markers that a situation is safe, not just to signs of danger
7. Help them avoid overexposure and overdedication, appropriately limit exposure to anxiety-producing information, and provide skills for switching cognitive attention when they become overabsorbed.

Table 3.1 *Nonpharmacological interventions used to treat child and adolescent anxiety and depression. Adapted from https://effectivehealthcare.ahrq.gov/products/childhood-depression/protocol*

Intervention type	Interventions
Psychological/psychosocial	Cognitive behavioral therapies, rational emotive behavior therapy, behavioral activation, other behavioral therapy, interpersonal therapy, directive counseling, Katathym-imaginative Psychotherapy, family therapy, parent education, self-help groups, problem-solving therapy, autonomic training, combined-modality therapy, psychological adaptation therapies
Lifestyle	Exercise (physical activity), diet therapy, mindfulness (including mindfulness-based stress reduction), meditation (including mindfulness mediation), relaxation therapy, massage therapy, music therapy, art therapy, integrative restoration, visualization, tai-chi, yoga, spirituality, acupuncture
Supplements	St. John's Wort, SAMe, fish oil, melatonin, L-tryptophan, folic acid, 5-HTP, zinc, chromium, gingko biloba, vitamin E, omega-3 fatty acids, hypericum, inositol, selenium
Other	Electroconvulsive therapy, transcranial magnetic stimulation, light therapy (phototherapy), hypnotherapy (including self-hypnotherapy), neurofeedback, deep brain stimulation, biofeedback

We must consider the important caveat here that while the worries of young people with anxiety disorders are generally considered irrational or disproportionate, even if they have been triggered by a real exposure or a grain of truth, the line between irrational and rational climate worry remains undefined because of the unpredictable, complex, potentially existential, and evolving nature of the climate problem. This leaves room for reasonable people on both sides of the aisle to disagree as to whether a young person's climate fears are excessive. Therefore, climate uncertainty means that we must not minimize some young individuals' fears about life-threatening realities as hysteria even if they seem irrational to us. It also means it is rational to reflect on whether, in attending to a young person's climate anxiety, we could contribute to hysterical exaggeration of the likely risks or collude with a child to avoid fully exploring other developmental fears, such as what will happen when the child becomes an adult, for which climate risks have become a substitute focus. Finally, even in worst case scenarios where death is possible or even certain, climate uncertainty guides us to model realistic forms of hope and support young people's capacity for grit and courage under any conditions. Many of the chapters elsewhere in this book (e.g., Chapters 6 and 14) offer techniques for bringing these tensions into helpful union.

Overlapping Features of Psychiatric Syndromes and Youth Climate Distress

Anxieties in young people that have been conceptualized as clinical anxiety disorders include separation anxiety, specific phobias, generalized anxiety disorder (GAD), social anxiety disorder, agoraphobia, panic disorder, and selective mutism. Obsessive compulsive disorder (OCD) and trauma-and stressor-related disorders, which are separate categories in the fifth edition of the *Diagnostic and Statistical Manual of Mental Disorders* (*DSM-5*), are also considered to have important links to anxiety. Pediatric depressive disorders include persistent depressive disorder (PDD, previously dysthymia), major depressive disorder (MDD), and disruptive mood dysregulation disorder (American Psychiatric Association, 2013).

In addition to the core diagnostic features of functional impairment and avoidance of fearful situations/changes in mood, clinical pediatric anxiety and depressive disorders can be organized by certain common features, which may also help us look for their coexistence with climate anxiety and sadness:

1. The disorder is characterized by heightened sensitivity to, preoccupation with and rumination about specific aspects of reality (GAD, OCD, specific phobias, MDD, PDD, climate change).
2. The disorder is characterized by concern about attachment and connection to others (separation anxiety, social anxiety, isolation and preoccupation with social rejection in depression, connection to the natural world).
3. The distress is characterized by withdrawal and avoidance (specific phobias, selective mutism, agoraphobia, depressive disorders).
4. The disorder is triggered by real and frightening event(s) (PTSD, some panic disorder, and some specific phobias, climate-related extreme weather and other climate effects).
5. The disorder is characterized by overfocus on worst-case events (OCD, separation anxiety, negative cognitive framing in depression, preoccupation with mass extinction).
6. Risk of developing/having the disorder is associated with early life adversity, including abuse, domestic violence, deprivation, natural

disaster, injury, or death of a family member (PTSD, MDD, PDD, DMDD, disproportionate burden of climate distress on marginalized populations).
7. The disorder is characterized by recurrent and persistent distress despite resolution of the inciting stressor (OCD, specific phobias, separation anxiety, social anxiety).
8. The disorder impairs sleep, eating, thinking and energy (MDD, PDD, GAD).
9. The disorder is characterized by irritability and rage (depressive disorders, GAD, anger about climate betrayals and lack of progress).
10. The disorder is characterized by extreme sadness (MDD, PDD, climate grief, solastalgia, climate nihilism, climate-related suicide).

Tabulating the qualities of a young person's response to climate change in terms of the features identified above may also help us consider what *kind* of climate distress a young person is experiencing and how to respond to it effectively. For example, a young person who is intensely worried their parents will be killed in a typhoon may be manifesting separation anxiety and should be approached with sensitivity to separation concerns, whereas a youth who ritualistically cannot leave the house without sorting the garbage into precise recycling categories for fear the plastic will kill polar bears might be developing obsessive compulsive symptoms, or just need an approach and outlets for their climate distress appropriate to someone with a more obsessive style.

Young people are also in the process of developing a self, which includes building self-esteem, defining who they are and what will comprise a meaningful life, developing skills and resolving existential questions to move towards life goals, solidifying moral values, and learning to manage social and societal relationships independently. Many are negotiating emerging sexuality, decisions about substance use, and dealing with the complexities of bullying, peer pressures, violence, and crises such as COVID-19 (see CDC, 2023). Adolescence is a particularly fertile time for these developmental tasks, as well as a time when a young person may begin to grasp the scale and implications of the climate emergency for their future.

We must therefore add the psychological developmental issues that are manifested in a young person's presentation to the tabulation of their climate distress:

1. Identity: How is the young person's climate response shaping their identity or self-concept and vice versa?

2. Self-esteem: How is the young person's climate response impacting their self-esteem and sense of empowerment?
3. Role maturation: How is the young person's climate response allowing them to gain maturational capacities such as leadership, social skills, and problem-solving abilities?
4. Life goals: How is the young person's climate response affecting their capacity to achieve life goals such as having a career and family?
5. Thriving: How is the young person's climate response allowing them to function and thrive?
6. Existentialism: How is the young person's climate response serving to help them resolve universal human existential questions and fears?
7. Social relations: What relationship between self and society is being solidified by the relationship between the young person and others around them through their climate distress?

Psychiatric Pathology and the Adolescent Brain

Psychiatrists are mental health professionals who provide psychotherapy, prescribe medications and treat neurological disorders with behavioral and emotional symptoms. A psychiatric assessment of youth climate distress must, then, also consider the biological impact of both climate change and adolescence on the human brain.

The adolescent brain is currently an active research priority, with two large longitudinal studies, the ABCD (Adolescent Brain Development Study), and HBCD (Healthy Brain and Child Development) studies underway to refine what has been an underfunded area of neurobiological and sociopsychological understanding (Volkow et al., 2020). Earlier emphasis on the problematic aspects of adolescent cognition and risk taking has given way to an appreciation for the tremendous cognitive and emotional wisdom that is gained through adolescent trial-and-error learning and enrichment of social networks. Rather than being viewed as it has been traditionally – as a problem of underactive frontal lobe function that leads to near-delusional omnipotence, impulsivity, and poor judgment – adolescent brains are now known to actively restructure neural circuits in a way that improves their efficiency and "supports coordinated neural processing underlying executive function" (Baum et al., 2020). This process includes a 100 percent increase in brain myelination, which coats developing nerves with a protective fatty sheath, as well as extensive pruning of brain areas and capacities that are not stimulated to develop (Arain et al., 2013).

At the same time, there is a very high degree of individual difference in the development of these capacities, such that some adolescents will be very strong, and others very weak, in the gains in mental flexibility, reasoning, memory, inhibitory control, and motor speed. Gender differences also exist, with pubertal sex steroids including Dehydroepiandrosterone (DHEA), testosterone, and estradiol all having roles in development of the amygdala, a brain area associated with negative emotion, and frontal lobes, which are associated with executive function. This means that there will be differences between genders, and differences among individuals, in the capacity to process climate stresses. Both GABA-ergic systems, important for relaxation and inhibitory control, and serotonin activity, which differs in adolescents due to decreased 5HT1A binding and increased serotonin transporter expression (reviewed in Cousins & Goodyer, 2015), are less functionally important in adolescents than in adults. In contrast, glutaminergic circuits, responsible for brain activity and excitability, are relatively more dominant (see Arhain et al., 2013). In the ventral striatum, increased dopamine levels likely improve adolescents' capacity to remember and to learn when learning is rewarded (i.e., feedback-learning). These increased dopamine levels also increase motivation for social participation and value-based "updating" of existing judgments. Both give adolescents improved intellectual control as these circuits integrate with and strengthen other circuits in the hippocampus and prefrontal cortex (summarized from review, Galvan, 2021). This implies that implementing new social structures and teaching climate resilience can have greater impact during this period, but also that adolescents may be turned away from sustainable ways of living or suffer more emotional damage in social milieus where such concerns are negatively reinforced.

Important for work with climate distress, adolescent risk-taking has been shown to be greater under stress and under conditions of potential loss or heightened emotionality. This risk-taking behavior can be mitigated by greater ventral striatal activity, which can also mitigate depressive symptoms in adolescents who show the greatest distress over societal circumstances (Tashjian & Galvan, 2018). Ventral striatal activity can be enhanced by a variety of factors, including prosocial activity, feedback learning, and strong stable friendships. This suggests that the current recommended strategy for coping effectively with climate distress in young people – pro-environmental activity in friendly communities that often involves rapid learning of new sustainable solutions to problems – is likely to have substantial emotional and cognitive benefits for teens. These benefits would be predicted to include reduction in depression and anxiety but also, to some, risk of increased symptoms if there was not adequate reward for their efforts through climate progress. It is also likely that those with additional emotional stressors from poor social determinants of health or trauma may have difficulty capturing these benefits, as discussed below. These and other concerns have been helpfully reviewed by UNICEF (2017).

Furthermore, adolescence is a time when appreciation for fairness, trust, cooperation, and the capacity to mentalize the thoughts and feelings of other people expands. This ability to read the intentions, thoughts, and feelings of others means that adolescents pay more attention to how adults are handling the world, which can contribute to both their upset as well as to their growth. Given that social exclusion and social reward strongly shape adolescent decisions, it is important that young people with climate distress feel included and valued in their efforts by those on whom they are modelling themselves, to hold on to the value-based growth that is occurring.

Prior to adolescence, young people may have not developed the mature cognitive and emotional structures (Koss & Gunnar, 2018) that can allow them to understand the complexity and uncertainty in how planetary systems may respond to global warming as well as the possibility of multistep and multiparticipant solutions that evolve over time. Younger children may therefore be more literal, egocentric, black and white, and emotionally dysregulated in their climate distress when poor climate predictions or news arise.

Chronic Stress and Adolescent Brain Development

Young people who are continually overstressed by climate change are at risk of direct negative developmental impacts on brain health as a result of this distress. Adolescence (broadly defined as 10 to 25 years) is already a time when psychiatric illnesses emerge, with the peak age of onset for any mental disorder being 14 years (Kessler et al., 2005), and sustained threats have been shown to increase depression, anxiety, and other problems (Grant et al., 2004). Some parts of the brain are more sensitive to stress hormones than at other periods of development (Koss & Gunnar, 2018). Regions of the brain that "extinguish" (i.e., reduce or eliminate) fears are less capable of change, implying that recovery from stress encountered during these years *in particular* is more difficult (Pattwell et al., 2012). Cumulative life stress in adolescents is also associated with lower executive function and smaller volumes of some brain areas, and is associated with more anhedonia (inability to experience pleasure), major depressive disorder, and substance use disorders (Sheth et al., 2017). Toxic stress from alcohol, nicotine, and other drugs of abuse also play a role (Arain et al., 2013). These and other biological and psychiatric impacts are likely to be significantly higher in groups experiencing racial and ethnic discrimination (Adam et al., 2020), although these systemic factors are significantly understudied, as are the impacts of climate change on these systems overall.

At the same time, inadequate stress levels are also associated with poor development and psychopathology (see Koss & Gunnar, 2018 for a discussion). This underlies the psychiatric concepts of optimal levels of stress providing stress inoculation, meaning the ability to cope with later challenges. By providing teens with challenging experiences coupled with adequate support, we can increase their courage and resilience to face climate challenges.

The Direct Influence of Climate Change on Adolescent Brain Health

As we consider the hardwired biology that may influence how climate distress impacts younger brains, the direct impacts of climate change itself on brain physiology must also be borne in mind. Children's physiology is different than that of adults. Their ability to tolerate heat based on body surface area, nutritional requirements, ability to process medications and toxins in the liver, and susceptibility to new infectious diseases all contribute to greater mental and physical vulnerability to climate-related changes in heat, air pollution, food availability and vector-borne illnesses (Landrigan et al., 2004). Air pollution, more than 80 percent of which is caused by the greenhouse gases that cause global warming (World Energy Council, 2013) has numerous deleterious effects on developing brains. Children raised in areas with high air pollution levels have more behavioral problems, ADHD, learning disorders, lower IQs (Perera, 2017), psychotic symptoms and depression (Manczak et al., 2022) than their peers. High temperatures are associated with irritability and poor school performance (Goodman et al., 2018). Food scarcity and micronutrient deficiencies in iron, zinc, and protein also lead to intellectual stunting and more negative emotions of all kinds in children, as well as behavioral problems (Shankar et al., 2017). While the impact of air pollution and higher temperatures on suicides and suicidal ideation in adolescents in particular has not been studied, suicidal acts and feelings have been clearly demonstrated to increase with these conditions in the population as a whole (Dumont et al., 2020). A young person struggling with climate distress may also manifest the impacts of these neurobiological adversities and show behavioral problems, difficulties with cognitive processing of the complexities and scale of climate change, and suicidal thoughts and actions. Consideration of these biological impacts should therefore form part of our response to their distress, including how they might be mitigated through improved air quality (e.g., plants in the bedroom, air filters with air conditioning, improved shade for urban heat islands) and nutrition (e.g., school lunch programs, parental education).

Assessment and Presentation of Psychiatric Disorders within Youth Climate Distress

Taken together, these factors should be incorporated into a full psychiatric assessment of a young person with climate distress in the following ways:

1. State aspects of their current distress (i.e., their emotional reaction to the climate situation) and how they are coping with it
2. Trait anxiety and its impacts on their distress
3. Nonclimate-related stressors in the young person's life, including parental anxiety in particular, as well as parental mental health issues, parenting style, peer relationships and responses, and social, ecological, and intersectional determinants of health
4. The roles of identity formation and adolescent brain development on the way they are presenting with and manifesting climate distress
5. Neurobiological impacts on symptoms due to climate change itself
6. The presence or absence of a clinical anxiety or depressive disorder, with particular focus on the potential overlap between the kinds of worries and grief about climate change and the kinds found in clinical psychiatric disorders
7. Individual and community-based strengths, such as innate gifts, family and community strengths, and capacity for resilience in both the young person and their environment

With all of these influences, it would be natural to ask how significant the psychiatric impacts of youth climate distress might be for rates of anxiety and depression. Although this relationship requires further scientific study, epidemiological studies show that the rates of anxiety disorders are low and the rates of climate distress high, which allows us to reasonably conclude that we would not usually expect to see clinical symptoms of anxiety or depression in those with climate distress. Climate distress surveys have generally shown moderate to severe anxiety about climate change in over 65 percent of adult respondents (American Psychiatric Association,

2020) and 80 percent of young people (Hickman et al., 2021). In contrast, approximately 20 percent of children meet criteria for an anxiety disorder, with approximate prevalence rates from most to least common being 3.5 percent for social phobia and separation anxiety disorder, 2.4 percent for specific phobia, 1.5–4 percent for generalized anxiety disorder, and less than 1 percent for OCD and panic disorder respectively (Sadock & Sadock, 2005, p. 3281). Taking these prevalence rates and climate anxiety surveys at face value, a person working with climate-distressed young people would not expect to find any type of clinically impairing anxiety disorder in more than a third of children with moderate to severe climate distress, and any specific anxiety disorder meeting full criteria in more than one in twenty. These expectations are somewhat consistent with the initial results from the validation of the CCAS, with approximately 3–10 percent reporting functionally impairing symptoms "often or almost always" and 20–25 percent reporting symptoms "sometimes" (Clayton et al., 2021).

Similarly, the 80 percent rates of climate anxiety in young people globally (Hickman et al., 2021) are substantially higher than the cumulative 15–25 percent rates of depressive disorders in young people which rise slowly across the adolescent years, starting particularly around age 16–17 and peaking around age 25 (Sadock & Sadock, 2005, p. 3263). While we should be reassured that most youth with climate distress do not appear to have clinical level need, suicidal thoughts, plans, and attempts have also increased steadily in recent decades, with up to 20 percent of adolescents reporting serious suicidal thinking (CDC, 2023). While suicide in young people continues to be relatively rare – between 1 and 10 per 100,000 – it also remains the number two cause of death in this group (CDC, 2023). The lack of any data about depressive and suicidal symptoms in teens with high climate distress is an area of urgent need.

Putting It All Together: Climate Distress and Psychiatric Symptoms

We will now examine a series of fabricated cases in order to illustrate how clinically significant psychiatric symptoms in young climate-distressed people may be intertwined with their concern.

Case Presentations

Case 1: Annie
Annie, age 10, became increasingly preoccupied with climate change after her home was damaged by flash floods in their narrow river valley.

She is highly anxious about the drive to school, particularly the part that involves driving over a cracked bridge. For several hours before these trips, she checks the weather, looks at the road repair notifications posted by the town, and packs and repacks her backpack with different flashlights, stuffed animals, hats, and water bottles. She is so exhausted that she often falls asleep in her early morning classes. Whenever she sees something in the news about climate change, she reads it quickly. She can speak in great detail about climate facts, and frequently argues with her parents about wanting to move.

Annie has a number of symptoms of generalized anxiety disorder, including worry that consumes excess time, irritability, muscle tension, and fatigue. The amount and severity of her symptoms meet clinical criteria, in that she is spending time unproductively (spending excess hours failing to resolve her worries into clear solutions) and has impairments in her school functions and relationships. Her distress was triggered by a traumatic event and is associated with some hypervigilance, but does not meet criteria for PTSD. At the same time, Annie shows features of adaptive anxiety by informing herself about the threat, reducing future threats through her preparations, adapting her behavior to new circumstances, and attempting to build a responsive community with her parents to enact reality-based threat mitigation. Annie's case shows the way clinical and nonclinical climate anxiety symptoms can overlap. Psychotherapy work with Annie may resolve the clinical levels of her distress if it includes validating her concerns; directing her interest in emergency planning into trainings, local volunteer opportunities, and connections to peers with similar experiences; and helping her parents respond to Annie by informing themselves and making plans with her – perhaps to move or rebuild more safely – while also helping her understand the financial and interpersonal losses of a precipitous move that must be accounted for to avoid a panicked response.

Case 2: Jayden
Jayden, age 13, has a strong attachment to the natural world. Since early childhood, he has shown a strong connection to animals and plants, playing with wild rabbits, taming squirrels and birds, and identifying plants on family hikes. Since reading a news article on a recent climate report, he has become increasingly depressed, telling his parents that he does not care what happens in school, will probably not live long enough to graduate college, and will never have a girlfriend or be a father. When his parents try to cheer him up, he just points out the changes to the nearby woods – the alarming decrease in birds and rabbits, dry rotting trees, and increasing

presence of bear and coyotes who have moved closer to human populations. At times he sobs, panicking at all the rabbits that will now be killed. He will no longer go out with his father, causing him to miss valuable time in nature and with his parent, and at times says he's not sure how long he can stand to watch this decline.

Jayden is experiencing a fair degree of depression. He increasingly sees only the negative aspects of the world around him, feels hopeless and helpless, and has anhedonia for previously valued activities. He is also experiencing ecological grief and sadness over all that is being lost in the world and in his future, as well as solastalgia, the missing of and longing for the natural landscapes he grew up with. Jayden needs to be assessed for self-harm and suicide risk, which can increase when individuals become defeated or despairing about climate impacts. His climate-related depression has severe negative developmental impacts; at a time when most teens are beginning to have trial relationships, develop the intellectual skills that are necessary for further education and career growth, identify with and look to adults they admire as they experiment with possible future roles for themselves, and build athletic skills and strengths that will sustain physical health through their adult lives, he has withdrawn from these developmental activities. While it is possible that Jayden will recover and reconnect to the things he loves – particularly if he can establish peer connections around these interests – it is also possible that he may need more mental health care. Given Jayden's concerns, it would be critical for his mental health provider to acknowledge and validate his climate-related sadness during treatment and avoid marginalizing or dismissing his experiences. Other factors, such as separation anxieties or emerging social anxiety related to leaving his home base to attend high school, might also contribute to Jayden's distress. Jayden's comfort in this new "outdoor" world with new peers could be facilitated by drawing on his secure attachment to nature to find new connections to peers and explore novel environments. To help Jayden hold hope and hopelessness – as well as climate and social realities – side by side, he could be empowered to create change locally and strengthen his dialectical thinking skills. These strategies may create reality-based and meaning-based positive spaces for Jayden to engage without disavowing the realities he is accepting. Issues of attachment, to both human and other living beings, should be important considerations in this treatment.

Case 3: Rita*
*The inclusion of Rita in this case series may trouble some readers. It has been provided for several reasons:

1. Eco-terrorism is increasingly seen as a viable response to the far greater magnitude of deaths that result from fossil fuel company inaction (Tremblay, 2012).
2. Clinicians and educators may increasingly encounter students like Rita.
3. Clinicians must be prepared to respond both empathically as well as intervene to prevent violence against others in these situations.

Rita, age 16, is a star student who is dedicated to ocean activism. As a child, she loved the water; however, after developing a phobia of sharks she began to avoid the beach and cry and run away when she saw images of sharks in movies or on television. She was able to overcome this phobia by exposure therapy, which involved visiting many aquariums and tidepools and falling in love with marine life in the process. Since her first exposure to climate change, she has learned everything she possibly can about changes in ocean acidity, temperature, coral composition, and fish populations. She is a regular at local beach clean-ups, and volunteered for "The Great Pacific Garbage Patch" clean-up charity.

Rita recently told her parents that she will not apply to college, and instead plans to work for Greenpeace on missions sabotaging ships carrying fossil fuels. In the ensuing family conflict, Rita's parents are surprised by the intensity of her rage. She begins to have panic attacks when they question her about her summer plans. As high school graduation approaches, they notice that her hands are increasingly red and raw, and that she washes them repeatedly every time she comes up from the "chemistry lab" she has had since childhood in the basement. Worried about OCD and what she may be using to wash her hands, they search downstairs, where they are alarmed to find both rudimentary bomb supplies and an ongoing experiment with plastic-digesting bacteria.

Rita's climate-related anxiety probably meets psychiatric criteria for specific phobia, panic disorder, and possibly OCD. At the same time, her unconventional course should not be viewed as clearly pathological. She embodies a trend in younger people, who are forgoing more traditional models of building a future by imagining new self-stories to connect themselves to moral and sustainable lives. Her early specific phobia, common in children, is easily overcome. In psychodynamic therapy, her love of oceans would be seen as a healthy reaction formation, turning her fear of sharks into its opposite through sublimation and mastery, both healthy defenses. Her healthy response to distress about the oceans leads her to community, solution-focused action, and creative solutions to environmental challenges that decrease the threat. Until she approaches high school graduation, and the conflict between her parents' values and her own reaches a crisis point, her climate anxiety does not appear to take a toll on her function. Her consideration of eco-terrorism demonstrates the intensity of her commitment and feelings of betrayal as well as her realistic assessment of the dire and threatening nature of the climate crises, and is considered ethical in circles which consider it the only remaining moral response to the genocide wrought on vulnerable populations by the passive social response to the fossil fuel industry. At the same time, Rita is at risk of overdedication and obsessive-compulsive symptoms focused on undoing a threatening thought, here perhaps associated with detonating a bomb. She would need to be assessed for paranoid symptoms, anxiety and mood symptoms, and OCD. Specific attention would need to be paid to the function of her eco-terrorism-related thoughts and behaviors, including an assessment of homicidal ideation and a clear understanding of the context(s) in which these thoughts and behaviors occur (e.g., within the context of OCD, as a response to feelings of anger and moral outrage, etc.).

Psychotherapeutic intervention would need to take an accepting, non-judgmental response to Rita's belief that eco-terrorism is the best and/or only course of action, acknowledging that the therapist is immersed in the same climate emergency and ethical dilemmas, but without the sense of existential and moral despair and powerlessness Rita is experiencing as a young person. Building confidence that adults working in this area and therapists will not placate or immediately dismiss rage is an essential piece of a good alliance with young people, who may otherwise throw these supportive adults into the basket of disinterested or corruptible caretakers. Acknowledging the extreme fear that exists alongside Rita's anger and emphasizing the number of people working on the climate problem, recent progress, and the inherent uncertainties in how complex climate systems will evolve may create space for Rita to take normal developmental steps in relationships and education in addition to her activism, reducing her level of anxiety from a symptomatic crisis to a healthy level that will get her "unstuck" from the ruminative repetitive actions she is engaged in now. As part of these discussions, the therapist might explore Rita's values, the existential meaning behind her beliefs, coping strategies to manage burnout and allow Rita to engage with valued action over the long term, and possibly perspective taking (e.g., acknowledging potential safety and legal consequences of various types of violent and nonviolent direct action) to enhance her sense of efficacy and choice rather than acting primarily from intense emotions. In this case, climate anxiety exists on a continuum with healthy anxiety despite the flair of discrete symptoms from time to time, and can be worked with to reduce anxiety into a form that can be dealt with through action when it becomes paralyzing or manifests in irrational solutions or symptoms.

Conclusion

These cases illustrate several ways that climate distress and clinical levels of anxiety and depression may overlap, and how psychiatrists and others working with climate feelings in young people can begin to tease them apart and respond. As the examples of anxious distress illustrate, all anxiety is shaped by the qualities of the individual. Some disorders are based in experience (PTSD) while others occur out of the blue (panic disorder). Climate anxiety also can arise from both direct and imagined climate exposure. Some young people will only develop concern after a concrete personal threat such as a hurricane or a drought. Others will begin to ruminate on the future impacts of climate change after reading about it. For some, these experiences will lead to clinical levels of symptoms; for others, they will be transformative existential moments furthering lifelong growth. Many therapeutic questions about how to protect our young people from the adverse impacts of their distress and climate change itself remain. Therapies such as ACT (acceptance and commitment therapy), DBT (dialectical behavioral therapy), CBT (cognitive behavioral therapy), existential therapy, and others have not been fully mined for the wisdom they can offer to young people struggling to balance a host of current and future, interpersonal and social concerns. Suicidal, psychotic, and violent ideas and behaviors merit clinical intervention, as in any circumstance, but must also be considered from a values-based perspective to find and empathize with the emotional sanity and integrity reflected therein. The core qualities of a therapeutic alliance that are valuable to young people and with which we should respond now have always been – and still include – a relationship that is flexible, warm, and more friendly and less formal that adult therapy, with a person who is judged to be genuine, accepting, trustworthy, respectful, interested, and supportive, and who is able to attend to moments where adolescents experience a severe loss of hope or trust (Stige et al., 2021). We can use this relationship, as well as the science of psychiatric syndromes, their biopsychosocio-environmental origins, and their effective interventions, to devise responses appropriate to the symptoms and experiences of young people as they face this challenging future, while also continuing progress on the rapid decarbonization that is essential for their long-term mental health.

References

Adam, E. K., Hittner, E. F., Thomas, S. E., Villaume S. C., & Nwafor, E. E. (2020). Racial discrimination and ethnic racial identity in adolescence as modulators of HPA axis activity. *Development and Psychopathology*, 32(5), 1669–1684. https://doi.org/10.1017/S095457942000111X

Agho, K., Stevens, G., Taylor, M., Barr, M., & Raphael, B. (2010). Population risk perceptions of global warming in Australia. *Environmental Research*, 110(8), 756–763. https://doi.org/10.1016/j.envres.2010.09.007

American Psychiatric Association (2013). *Diagnostic and statistical manual of mental disorders* (5th ed.). Arlington, VA: American Psychiatric Publishing.

American Psychiatric Association (2020). Opinion Poll, Annual Meeting.

American Psychological Association (2018). Stress in America: Generation Z. Stress in AmericaTM survey.

Arain, M., Haque, M., Johal, L., Mathur, P., Nel, W., Rais, A., Sandhu, R., & Sharma, S. (2013). Maturation of the adolescent brain. *Neuropsychiatric Disease and Treatment*, 9, 449–461. https://doi.org/10.2147/NDT.S39776

Baum G. L., Cui, Z., Roalf, D. R., Ciric, R., Betzel, R. F., Larsen, B., … Satterthwaite, T. D. (2020). Development of structure–function coupling in human brain networks during youth. *Proceedings of the National Academy of Sciences – PNAS*, 117(1), 771–778. https://doi.org/10.1073/pnas.1912034117

Berry, H., & Peel, D. (2015). Worrying about climate change: Is it responsible to promote public debate? *BJPsych International*, 12(2), 31–32. https://doi.org/10.1192/S2056474000000234

Centers for Disease Control and Prevention (2023). Youth risk behavior survey data. www.cdc.gov/yrbs, accessed April 30, 2023.

Clayton S., Czellar, S., Nartova-Bochaver, S., Skibins, J. C., Salazar, G., Tseng, Y.-C., Irkhin, B., & Monge-Rodriguez, F. S. (2021). Cross-cultural validation of a revised environmental identity scale. *Sustainability*, 13(4), 2387. https://doi.org/10.3390/su13042387

Clayton, S., & Karazsia, B. (2020). Development and validation of a measure of climate change anxiety. *Journal of Environmental Psychology*, 69. https://doi.org/10.1016/j.jenvp.2020.101434

Cousins, L., & Goodyer, I. M. (2015). Antidepressants and the adolescent brain. *Journal of Psychopharmacology*, 29(5), 545–555. https://doi.org/10.1177/0269881115573542

Dumont, C., Haase, E., Dolber, T., Lewis, J., & Coverdale, J. (2020). Climate change and risk of completed suicide. *Journal of Nervous and Mental Disease*, 208(7), 559–565. https://doi.org/10.1097/NMD.0000000000001162

Eley T. C., McAdams, T. A., Rijsdijk, F. V., Lichtenstein, P., Narusyte, J., Reiss, D., … Neiderhiser, J. M. (2015). The intergenerational transmission of anxiety: A children-of-twins study. *American Journal of Psychiatry*, 172(7), 630–637. https://doi.org/10.1176/appi.ajp.2015.14070818

Engel, G. (1977). The need for a new medical model: A challenge for biomedicine. *Science*, 196, 129–136.

Farmer, S. (2019). How Greta Thunberg's autism helped make her the world's most important person in 2020. https://thehill.com/changing-america/well-being/468091-opinion-activist-greta-thunbergs-autism-doesnt-hold-her-back/
Galván, A. (2021). Adolescent brain development and contextual influences: A decade in review. *Journal of Research on Adolescence*, 31(4), 843–869. https://doi.org/10.1111/jora.12687
Ginsburg, G. S., Siqueland, L., Masia-Warner, C., & Hedtke, K. A. (2004). Anxiety disorders in children: Family matters. *Cognitive and Behavioral Practice*, 11(1), 28–43. https://doi.org/10.1016/S1077-7229(04)80005-1
Goodman, J., Hurwitz, M., Park, J., & Smith, J. (2018). Heat and learning (NBER Working Paper No. 24639). Cambridge, MA: National Bureau of Economic Research. Retrieved from https://ideas.repec.org/p/ecl/harjfk/rwp18-014.html
Grant, K. E., Compas B. E., Thurm A. E., McMahon S. D., & Gipson P. Y. (2004). Stressors and child and adolescent psychopathology: Measurement issues and prospective effects. *Journal of Clinical Child and Adolescent Psychology*, 33(2): 412–425.
Groth, N., Schnyder, N., Kaess, M., Markovic, A., Rietschel, L., Moser, S., ... Schmidt, S. J. (2019). Coping as a mediator between locus of control, competence beliefs, and mental health: A systematic review and structural equation modelling meta-analysis. *Behaviour Research and Therapy*, 121, 103442. https://doi.org/10.1016/j.brat.2019.103442
Helm, S. V., Pollitt, A., Barnett, M. A., Curran, M. A., & Craig, Z. R. (2018). Differentiating environmental concern in the context of psychological adaption to climate change. *Global Environmental Change*, 48, 158–167. https://doi.org/10.1016/j.gloenvcha.2017.11.012
Henker, B., Whalen, C. K., & O'Neil, R. (1995). Worldly and workaday worries: Contemporary concerns of children and young adolescents. *Journal of Abnormal Child Psychology*, 23(6), 685–702. https://doi.org/ 10.1007/BF01447472
Hickman, C., Marks, E., Pihkala, P., Clayton, S., Lewandowski, R. E., Mayall, E. E., ... van Susteren, L. (2021). Climate anxiety in children and young people and their beliefs about government responses to climate change: A global survey. *The Lancet Planetary Health*, 5(12), e863–e873.
Hogg, S. K., O'Brien, L. V., Wilson, M. S., & Watsford, C. R. (2021). The Hogg Eco-Anxiety Scale: Development and validation of a multidimensional scale. *Global Environmental Change*, 71, 102391. https://doi.org/10.1016/j.gloenvcha.2021.102391
Kessler, R. C., Berglund, P., Demler, O., Jin, R., Merikangas, K. R., & Walters, E. E. (2005). Lifetime prevalence and age-of-onset distributions of DSM-IV disorders in the National Comorbidity Survey replication. *Archives of General Psychiatry*, 62(6), 593–602.
Knowles, K. A., & Olatunji, B. O. (2020). Specificity of trait anxiety in anxiety and depression: Meta-analysis of the State-Trait Anxiety Inventory. *Clinical Psychology Review*, 82, 101928. https://doi.org/10.1016/j.cpr.2020.101928
Koss, K. J., & Gunnar, M. R. (2018). Annual research review: Early adversity, the hypothalamic–pituitary–adrenocortical axis, and child psychopathology.

Journal of Child Psychology and Psychiatry, 59(4), 327–346. https://doi.org/10.1111/jcpp.12784

Kurth, C., & Pihkala, P. (2022). Eco-anxiety: What it is and why it matters. *Frontiers in Psychology*, 13, 981814. https://doi.org/10.3389/fpsyg.2022.981814

Landrigan P. J., Kimmel, C. A., Correa, A., & Eskenazi, B. (2004). Children's health and the environment: Public health issues and challenges for risk assessment. *Environmental Health Perspectives*, 112(2), 257–265. https://doi.org/10.1289/ehp.6115

Leiserowitz, A., Maibach, E., Rosenthal, S., Kotcher, J., Ballew, M., Goldberg, M., & Gustafson, A. (2018). *Climate change in the American mind: December 2018*. Yale Program on Climate Change Communication and George Mason University Center for Climate Change Communication.

Lomas, T. (2018). The quiet virtues of sadness: A selective theoretical and interpretative appreciation of its potential contribution to wellbeing. *New Ideas in Psychology*, 49, 18–26. https://doi.org/10.1016/j.newideapsych.2018.01.002

MacDonald, J. P., Willox, A. C., Ford, J. D., Shiwak, I., Wood, M., Government, R. I. C., & Team, I. (2015). Protective factors for mental health and well-being in a changing climate: Perspectives from Inuit youth in Nunatsiavut, Labrador. *Social Science and Medicine*, 141, 133–141. https://doi.org/10.1016/j.socscimed.2015.07.017

Manczak, E. M., Miller, J. G., & Gotlib, I. H. (2022). Census tract ambient ozone predicts trajectories of depressive symptoms in adolescents. *Developmental Psychology*, 58(3), 485–492. https://doi.org/10.1037/dev0001310

McCreary, D. R. (2007). The Drive for Muscularity Scale: Description, psychometrics, and research findings. In J. K. Thompson & G. Cafri (Eds.), *The muscular ideal: Psychological, social, and medical perspectives* (pp. 87–106). American Psychological Association. https://doi.org/10.1037/11581-004

Merlin, C., Okerson, J. R., & Hess, P. (2013). How parenting style influences children: A review of controlling, guiding, and permitting parenting styles on children's behavior, risk-taking, mental health, and academic achievement. *William and Mary Educational Review*, 2(1), 32–43.

Micco, J. A., Henin, A., Mick, E., Kim, S., Hopkins, C. A., Biederman, J., & Hirshfeld-Becker, D. R. (2009). Anxiety and depressive disorders in offspring at high risk for anxiety: A meta-analysis. *Journal of Anxiety Disorders*, 23, 1158–1164.

Newbury, J. B., Arseneault, L., Beevers, S., Kitwiroon, N., Roberts, S., Pariante, C. M., Kelly, F., & Fisher, H. L. (2019). Association of air pollution exposure with psychotic experiences during adolescence. *JAMA Psychiatry*, 76(6), 614–623. https://doi.org/10.1001/jamapsychiatry.2019.0056

Nisbet, E. K. L., Zelenski, J. M., & Murphy, S. A. (2009). The Nature Relatedness Scale: Linking individuals' connection with nature to environmental concern and behaviour. *Environment and Behavior*, 41, 715–740.

Ojala, M. (2005). Adolescents' worries about environmental risks: Subjective well-being, values, and existential dimensions. *Journal of Youth Studies*, 8(3), 331–347. https://doi.org/10.1080/13676260500261934

Ojala, M. (2012). How do children cope with global climate change? Coping strategies, engagement, and well-being. *Journal of Environmental Psychology*, 32(3), 225–233. https://doi.org/10.1016/j.jenvp.2012.02.004

Overholser, J. C., (2014). Chasing the latest fad: Confronting recent and historical innovations in mental illness. *Journal of Contemporary Psychotherapy*, 44(1), 53–61. https://doi.org/10.1007/s10879-013-9250-z

Pattwell, S. S., Duhoux, S., Hartley, C. A., Johnson, D. C., Jing, D., Elliott, M. D., ... Lee, F. S. (2012). Altered fear learning across development in both mouse and human. *Proceedings of the National Academy of Sciences USA*, 109(40), 16318–16323.

Perera, F. P. (2017). Multiple threats to child health from fossil fuel combustion: Impacts of air pollution and climate change. *Environmental Health Perspectives*, 125, 141–148.

Platt, B., Kadosh, K. C., & Lau, J. Y. F. (2013). The role of peer rejection in adolescent depression. *Depression and Anxiety*, 30(9), 809–821. https://doi.org/10.1002/da.22120

Ramadan, R. A., Lavoie, S., Gao, C. X., Manrique, P. C., Anderson, R., McDowell, C., & Zbukvic, I. (2023). Empirical evidence for climate concerns, negative emotions and climate-related mental ill-health in young people: A scoping review. *Early Intervention in Psychiatry*. https://doi.org/10.1111/eip.13374

Reser, J. P., Bradley, G. L., & Ellul, M. C., (2014). Public risk perceptions, understandings and responses to climate change. In J. P. Palutikof, S. L. Boulter, J. Barnett, & D. Rissik (Eds.), *Applied studies in climate adaptation* (pp. 43–50), John Wiley & Sons.

Sadock, B. J., & Sadock, V. A. (2005). *Kaplan & Sadock's comprehensive textbook of psychiatry* (8th ed.). Lippincott Williams & Wilkinson (Vol I: 1726–27, 3262–3).

Saviola, F., Pappaianni, E., Monti, A., Grecucci, A., Jovicich, J., & De Pisapia, N. (2020). Trait and state anxiety are mapped differently in the human brain. *Nature, Scientific Reports*, 10(1), 11112. https://doi.org/10.1038/s41598-020-68008-z

Schultz, W. (2001). The structure of environmental concern: Concern for self, other people, and the biosphere. *Journal of Environmental Psychology*, 21(4), 327–339. https://doi.org/10.1006/jevp.2001.0227

Searle, K., & Gow, K. (2010). Do concerns about climate change lead to distress? *International Journal of Climate Change Strategies and Management*, 2(4), 362–379. https://doi.org/10.1108/17568691011089891

Selph, S. S., & McDonagh, M. S. (2019). Depression in children and adolescents: Evaluation and treatment. *American Family Physician*, 100(10), 609–617.

Shankar, P., Chung, R., & Frank, D. A. (2017). Association of food insecurity with children's behavioral, emotional, and academic outcomes: A systematic review. *Journal of Developmental and Behavioral Pediatrics*, 38(2), 135–150.

Sheth, C., McGlade, E., & Yurgelun-Todd, D. (2017). Chronic stress in adolescents and its neurobiological and psychopathological consequences: An RDoC perspective. *Chronic Stress*, 1, 247054701771564. https://doi.org/10.1177/2470547017715645

Stige, S. H., Barca, T., Lavik, K. O., & Moltu, C. (2021). Barriers and facilitators in adolescent psychotherapy initiated by adults-experiences that differentiate adolescents' trajectories through mental health care. *Frontiers in Psychology*, 12, 633663. https://doi.org/10.3389/fpsyg.2021.633663

Sundblad, E. L., Biel, A., & Gärling, T. (2007). Cognitive and affective risk judgements related to climate change. *Journal of Environmental Psychology*, 27(2), 97–106. https://doi.org/10.1016/j.jenvp.2007.01.003

Tashjian, S. M., & Galvan, A. (2018). The role of mesolimbic circuitry in buffering election-related distress. *Journal of Neuroscience*, 38, 2887–2898. https://doi.org/10.1523/JNEUROSCI.2470-17.2018

Thompson, T., Lloyd, A., Joseph, A., & Weiss, M. (2017). The Weiss functional impairment rating scale-parent form for assessing ADHD: Evaluating diagnostic accuracy and determining optimal thresholds using ROC analysis. *Quality of Life Research*, 26(7), 1879–1885. doi: 10.1007/s11136-017-1514-8.

Tremblay, H. (2012). Eco-terrorists facing armageddon: The defence of necessity and legal normativity in the context of environmental crisis. *McGill Law Journal*, 58(2), 321–364. https://doi.org/10.7202/1017517ar

Treynor, W., Gonzalez, R., & Nolen-Hoeksema, S. (2003). Rumination reconsidered: A psychometric analysis. *Cognitive Therapy and Research*, 27(3), 247–259. https://doi.org/10.1023/A:1023910315561

UNICEF Office of Research – Innocenti (2017). *The adolescent brain: A second window of opportunity*. UNICEF Office of Research – Innocenti, Florence.

Verplanken, B., & Roy, D. (2013). "My worries are rational, climate change is not": Habitual ecological worrying is an adaptive response. *PloS One*, 8(9), e74708. https://doi.org/10.1371/journal.pone.0074708

Volkow, N. D., Gordon, J. A., Koob, G. F., Birnbaum, L. S., Clayton, J. A., Koroshetz, W. J., … Croyle, R. T. (2020). An examination of child and adolescent neurodevelopment through national institutes of health studies. *Public Health Reports*, 135(2), 169–172. https://doi.org/10.1177/0033354919900889

Wardell, S. (2020). Naming and framing ecological distress. *Medicine Anthropology Theory*, 7(2), 187–201. https://doi.org/10.17157/mat.7.2.768

Weiss, M. D., McBride, N. M., Craig, S., & Jensen, P. (2018). Conceptual review of measuring functional impairment: Findings from the Weiss Functional Impairment Rating Scale, *BMJ Mental Health 2018*, 21, 155–164, scale available at www.caddra.ca/wp-content/uploads/WFIRS-S.pdf

Wolf, J., & Salo, R. (2008). Water, water, everywhere, nor any drop to drink: Climate change delusion. *Australasian Psychiatry: Bulletin of the Royal Australian and New Zealand College of Psychiatrists*, 42(4), 350–350. https://doi.org/10.1080/00048670701881603

World Energy Council (2013). *World energy resources 2013 survey: Summary*. World Energy Council.

World Population Review (2023). Suicide rate by country, 2023, https://worldpopulationreview.com/country-rankings/suicide-rate-by-country, accessed April 30, 2023

Zaleski, Z. (1996). Future anxiety: Concept, measurement, and preliminary research. *Personality and Individual Differences*, 21(2), 165–174.

CHAPTER 4

Developmental Perspectives on Understanding and Responding to Mental Health Impacts of Climate Change on Young People

Francis Vergunst and Helen L. Berry

Climate Change and the Mental Health of Young People

As climate change alters the environments that human life, and all life, have evolved to survive in, many of its effects are now irreversible. Changes to land, oceans, and the atmosphere will persist for thousands of years, causing major disruptions to ecosystems and human societies. These changes are occasionally benign. But, mostly, they make the world a more stressful and dangerous place to grow up, and an emerging body of research shows that they are harming the mental health of young people. Much attention has focused on the question of how young people are responding psychologically to the threat of climate change – including the emotional states it elicits, such as feelings of fear, anxiety, anger, frustration, and guilt. Questions about the broader effects of climate change on youth mental health, which begin before birth and extend across the life course, remain under-studied. In this chapter, we argue that a holistic view that draws on a developmental life course perspective can help us appreciate the full dimensions and scope of the climate change burden, and thus better adapt and respond to the mental health challenges it brings.

The effects of climate change are now widely observable. Heatwaves, storms, droughts, floods, and wildfires are becoming more frequent, intense, unpredictable, and severe. Across most of the world, they are aggravating drought, food insecurity, infectious disease, biodiversity loss, displacement, and forced migration (Ebi et al., 2021; Romanello et al., 2021). But beyond geophysics, climate change and its effects are not easily defined or categorized. In this chapter, we refer to *climatic stressors*. These are the consequences of climate change that we observe and experience, such as severe weather events. Climatic stressors result in *exposures* to harm, which can range from mild to severe (Ebi et al., 2021). Exposures, in turn, have *impacts*, defined as tangible consequences for mental health and well-being. These are also distributed along a continuum from mild to severe.

Similar challenges are raised by attempts to define the dimensions of mental health and illness. Here, we take a broad view of mental health that is not confined to the presence or absence of psychiatric diagnoses. It also includes states of healthy emotional, behavioral, and cognitive functioning, as well as states of psychological resilience and well-being. We thus view mental health as a general adaptive capacity (or vulnerability) that enables (or hinders) the flexible regulation of emotional, behavioral, and cognitive states in the face of life's day-to-day ups and downs (Hayes et al., 2018; Herrman, 2001).

While general and scientific awareness of the link between climate change and mental health is no longer new, the impacts on young people, especially when viewed across the life course, have been only rarely considered. This long-term perspective matters because mental health represents precious human capital – that is, the capacity to reach one's potential and participate fully in society. To the extent that climate change undermines mental health, it will also undermine the future capital of society. Indeed, the costs of poor mental health are well documented, especially for the young: mental health problems disrupt education, undermine employment, increase stigma, discrimination, and social isolation, and are associated with a higher incidence of lifetime health morbidities, including increased suicide risk and earlier death (WHO, 2021). Climate change is already increasing this burden, and it is therefore critical to better understand how this occurs so that effective adaptive and preventive action may be taken.

Young people represent a large and psychologically vulnerable population. People aged 0 to 24 years make up 41.0 percent of the global population, with 25.5 percent aged 0–14 and 15.5 percent aged 15–24 (UN, 2022). The peak age of onset for any mental disorder is 14.5 years and around two-thirds of all disorders are established by age 24 years (Solmi et al., 2021). In high-income countries, roughly one in eight children have mental disorders that cause symptoms and impairment at any given time (Barican et al., 2022). While reliable estimates from low- and middle-income countries are more difficult to obtain, a systematic review of six countries in sub-Saharan Africa reported that 14.3 percent of children aged 0–16 years had some psychopathology and around one in ten met criteria for a specific psychiatric disorder (Cortina et al., 2012). Furthermore, this burden is expected to rise as low- and middle-income countries follow the sociodemographic trends of increasing living standards and better health already observed in high-income countries across the twentieth century (Baranne & Falissard, 2018).

The United Nations Children's Fund estimates that half of the world's 2.2 billion children are at "extremely high risk" from climate change due to disruptions to healthcare, education, food security, and other key resources (UNICEF, 2021). Children are also highly vulnerable to the physical health burden of climate change, including noncommunicable disease risks. Physical and mental health interact in important ways, and physical health and illness influence psychopathology risk (Firth et al., 2019). Compared to adults, young people, especially very young children, have less effective heat adaptation capacities, higher exposure to toxins per unit of body weight (e.g., water, air, and food-borne), and greater vulnerability to insect-borne vectors (Colón-González et al., 2021; Garcia & Sheehan, 2016). All of these are expected to increase with climate change. Furthermore, it is estimated that 89.3 percent of the world's young people aged 0–24 years live in low- and middle-income countries (UN, 2022), which are predominantly located in regions identified as being most vulnerable to the effects of climate change (Thiery et al., 2021).

Climate stressors are multiple, complex, interconnected, and ongoing. Weather-related extreme events, interacting with ongoing changes to underlying local climates (e.g., increasingly hotter summers), can harm a child's development from the start of life onwards, having additive, interactive, and cumulative effects on mental health vulnerability. Compared to older generations, young people also have more life years ahead in which to be exposed to the current and worsening impacts of climate change. Thus, by taking a developmental life course approach, it is possible to properly consider the effects of climate change that set young people on developmental trajectories that cascade across the life course and shape their mental health and illness. Indeed, a key reason for adopting such an approach is that it emphasizes the importance of early detection and prevention: the ideal point at which to intervene to mitigate risks and improve long-term outcomes, and to do so cost-effectively. It is towards this developmental perspective, as applied to mental health and illness, that we now turn.

Developmental Psychopathology

Developmental psychopathology is a conceptual framework for understanding and studying the development of mental health and illness using a life course perspective. The concept gained prominence in psychiatric

> **Textbox 4.1 Key concepts in developmental psychopathology**
> - Development is the product of genetic, physiological, social, emotional, cognitive, behavioral, and cultural factors which change across time and in response to one another
> - The timing, frequency, and intensity of early stressors can set children on developmental trajectories that can do lifelong harm to mental health and illness
> - Development is nonlinear and early exposures can operate with additive, interactive, and cumulative effects to increase vulnerability across the life course
> - Psychological development occurs within multiple nested contexts (e.g., individuals, within families, communities, and societies); and the interaction between these contexts
> - Development is a process of adaptation, and what is adaptive in one context may not be adaptive in another context

research in the 1970s (Achenbach, 1974), and developed rapidly in the 1980s and 1990s to become an interdisciplinary field with broad applications in child development, clinical psychology, psychiatry, public health, and international development (Jaffee, 2019; Rutter, 1988). The approach emphasises the value of both normal and abnormal developmental processes in explaining the emergence of psychopathology and, importantly, views mental health problems as quantitative dimensions rather than qualitative categories (Martin et al., 2018) (Textbox 4.1).

A core assumption of the approach is that development is shaped by the dynamic interplay between physiological, genetic, cognitive, emotional, social, and environmental factors. Furthermore, the timing and sequence of exposure to early adversity and traumas (e.g., abuse, poverty, weather disasters) can have additive, interactive, and cumulative effects on development and set children on trajectories that increase mental health vulnerability across the life course (Beauchaine et al., 2018). More broadly, development is understood as an ongoing adaptive process that involves repeated transitions into new life phases. In other words, psychopathology emerges not as "a static set of diagnostic entities but rather as the product of the failure to obtain core developmental competences [and, we would add, resources], leading to a progressive veering from normal developmental trajectories and an accumulation of behavior patterns considered maladaptive in most contexts, even though at least some of these behaviors may have been adaptive in the context of deprived or harsh early environments" (Hinshaw, 2017).

Developmental psychopathology emphasizes relationships between biological, psychological, and social contexts that characterize human development. Ecological models have been used to describe the dynamic interacting nature of these processes (Noffsinger et al., 2012), to which we would stress the importance of adding built, natural and political environments (Berry et al., 2018). In the context of climate change, climatic stressors – such as storms, floods, droughts, and wildfires – could disrupt healthy development at multiple levels: the biological (e.g., stress-induced changes in DNA methylation and alteration of the body's stress-response system), the microsystem (e.g., increased family conflict), the mesosystem (e.g., disruptions to community social support and functioning), the exosystem (e.g., reduced access to key services), and the macrosystem (e.g., civil unrest, displacement). Importantly, these systems do not operate in isolation and are likely to interact in complex ways to increase vulnerability with additive, interactive and cumulative effects across development (Masten & Cicchetti, 2010) and, in turn, to contribute substantively to the multiple environments in which other children are also developing. This life course approach to development is being increasingly applied to physical health development as well.

To illustrate the relationship between climatic stressors and mental health across the early life course, it is helpful to consider several examples. Figure 4.1 shows how climatic stressors, which are becoming more frequent and severe with climate change, lead to direct and indirect exposures that can derail healthy physical and psychological development. For convenience, development is divided into four periods – (1) prenatal, (2) early childhood, (3) middle childhood, and (4) adolescence – based on both biological boundaries (e.g., birth, puberty) and socially defined transitions, such as entry into formal education. While exposure to climatic stressors can occur at any point along the developmental timeline, those that occur early, or are more severe and protracted, can set in motion developmental trajectories that cascade across the life course, particularly if both are the case. To better understand the vulnerabilities of each period, it is useful to consider several examples from each developmental period illustrated in the figure (Vergunst & Berry, 2021).

Prenatal Period

The prenatal period is characterized by extremely high developmental vulnerability. An extensive literature describes the effects of exposure to stressors on embryonic and fetal development and subsequent

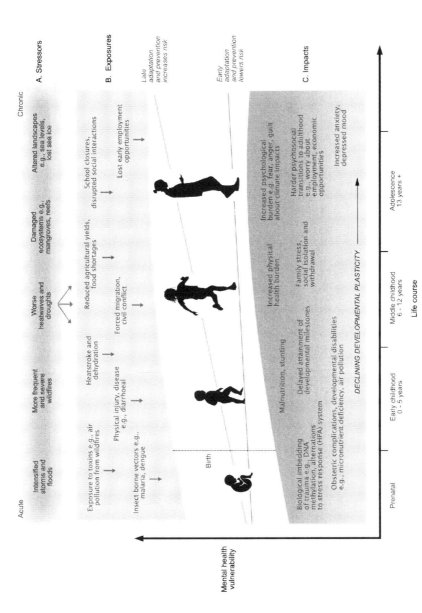

Figure 4.1 Pathways and processes linking climatic stressors to increased mental health vulnerability drawn from the empirical literature.

adverse developmental outcomes, including increased risk of neurodevelopmental and psychiatric disorders. In the context of climate change, climatic stressors can lead to direct and indirect exposures to trauma that harm the developing fetus (Figure 4.1). Exposures occurring during this period operate primarily through biological pathways that alter healthy neuropsychological development while psychosocial stressors occurring in other systems (e.g., mesosystem or macrosystems) are mediated by maternal and household factors such as family functioning.

One intuitive and well-studied prenatal risk factor is heat. Hotter average temperatures, and more severe and protracted heatwaves, are among the most well-documented consequences of global climate change. Heatwaves and hotter average temperatures increase the risk of obstetric complications, preterm birth, low birth weight, and still birth (McElroy et al., 2022; Samuels et al., 2022). Perinatal birth complications are a well-established risk factor for neurodevelopmental and psychiatric disorders such as attention deficit hyperactivity disorder, schizophrenia, mood disorders, and suicidal behaviors (Abel et al., 2010; Anderson et al., 2021; Orri et al., 2021). Another set of well-studied climatic stressors are severe weather events such as tropical storms, floods, droughts, and wildfires. These events can directly harm individuals, damage and destroy property and livelihoods, disrupt access to education and healthcare services, and reduce access to essential services. Exposures to acute stressors during pregnancy can trigger stress responses that alter embryonic and fetal development in ways that lead to dysregulation of the child's hypothalamic pituitary adrenal axis stress response system (Faravelli et al., 2012). Even if early stress doesn't lead to an increase in psychiatric disorders, it can contribute to delays in the attainment of developmental milestones, including language and cognitive development, which carry costs of their own, and are known to covary with mental health vulnerability (Evans, 2019; Laplante et al., 2004).

Climate change can also impact healthy psychological development through more indirect and slow-moving stressors – such as drought, food insecurity, displacement, and forced migration – which directly affect the mother, thus undermining pregnancy outcomes (Olson & Metz, 2020), and have longer-term effects on development after birth (see Figure 4.1). These stressors are initially mediated by parental factors, such as material and psychosocial resources, but increasingly have direct impacts, via the family (mesosytem), education (mesosystem), and community (exosystem) that the child inhabits.

Early Childhood

Early childhood, from 0 to 5 years, is a period of high vulnerability due to physiological immaturity, rapid neuropsychological development, and susceptibility to disease. Children establish strong emotional bonds with caregivers in the first years, followed by rapid language and cognitive development and growing social and emotional skills development. Threats from heat exposure, malnutrition, insect-borne vectors (e.g., malaria), and air-, water- and foodborne toxins are significant (Mangus & Canares, 2019; Sheffield & Landrigan, 2011). Early exposures directly alter healthy brain development through biological pathways (e.g., stress) and through increased physical health problems that delay the attainment of health development and increase lifetime psychopathology risk (Firth et al., 2019). Once established, maladaptive developmental trajectories lead to the accumulation of negative life events, such as low academic attainment, school incompletion, and unemployment (Butler et al., 2014), which increase stress, erode psychological resilience, and undermine the accumulation of human capital for individuals and societies (Caspi et al., 1998; Mani et al., 2013).

Indirect and slow-moving climatic stressors – such as food shortages, civil unrest, displacement, and forced migration – can contribute to stressors that tax the resources and resilience of families and communities and drive poor health behaviors (e.g., inadequate diet and physical activity), which directly harm the child or undermine the quality of childrearing that can be offered (Smith & Pollak, 2020). These stressors can themselves increase other long-term impacts on children, such as child neglect and maltreatment, which are well-established risk factors for psychiatric disorders (McCrory et al., 2022).

Middle Childhood

Middle childhood, from 6 to 12 years, remains a period of high developmental vulnerability. In addition to exposures that may have accrued during the prenatal or early childhood periods, middle childhood is characterized by new risks arising from growing psychosocial independence, including the formation of social relationships with peers, teachers, and the wider community, which are vulnerable to disruption. Acute disasters – such as storms, floods, and wildfires – are a principal pathway through which climate change will initially impact the mental health of young people and are associated with increased incidence of sleep problems, PTSD, substance use, depression, and anxiety symptoms and disorders (Clemens et al., 2020; Noffsinger et al., 2012). Epidemiological studies show that prevalence rates for PTSD for children exposed to disasters range from 15–30 percent, and around half of those remain traumatized and symptomatic 18 months later (Alisic et al., 2014; McDermott et al., 2014). Furthermore, reviews of the disaster literature have found that children experience higher rates of severe mental health impairments compared to adults (29.6 percent vs 18.3 percent) and may be more vulnerable than are adults to storm-related PTSD (Norris et al., 2002; Stanke et al., 2012).

In addition to effects of direct climatic stressors, subacute and chronic stressors – such as drought, food insecurity, and economic precarity – can have downstream effects that disrupt the child's education, leisure activities, and social support networks (Carnie et al., 2011). These experiences, especially when coupled with vulnerabilities caused by early adversities, can delay attainment of developmental milestones, disrupt the healthy transition to adolescence, and increase mental health vulnerability (Akresh, 2016; Garcia & Sheehan, 2016). During the middle childhood period, fears of catastrophe and loss and worry about climate change and its anticipated effects are likely to increase.

Adolescence

The adolescent period, which runs from age 13 into early adulthood, is characterized by major physiological, emotional, and behavioral changes, and the onset of new psychiatric disorders peaks at this time (Paus et al., 2008). These changes are complemented by increasing psychosocial independence including the formation of a more stable personal identity, peer groups, independent interests, leisure activities, and increasing self-reliance. Vulnerability to the impacts of acute weather events remains high. Hotter average temperatures and heatwaves pose significant and ongoing threats across multiple functional domains: They erode sleep quality, reduce physical activity, increase aggressive behaviors, amplify depressive emotional sentiment, disrupt learning and cognitive test performance, and reduce high school graduation rates – even when the historically high temperatures cease to be socially remarkable (Minor et al., 2022). These events can interfere with education completion and delay the attainment of economic and social goals, such as employment, creating additional stress in the lives of young people.

Adolescents are more likely to be aware of, and to worry about, the impacts of climate change compared to other age groups. International surveys show that adolescents and young people are highly concerned about the impacts of climate change (Hickman et al., 2021). A growing research literature shows that climate change elicits strong emotional responses including feelings of fear, anxiety, anger, frustration, and guilt, hopelessness, and despair (Ojala et al., 2021). Although there is no evidence yet that these states have a causal effect on rates of mental disorders, it is at least plausible that they interact with and exacerbate symptoms for already-existing disorders, and further work is needed to examine these relationships.

In summary, the literature reviewed above shows that a series of complex, interconnected, and interacting stressors, driven by climate change, are increasing mental health vulnerability of young people at every developmental phase from the start of life onwards. Impacts that occur early, or are severe, repetitive, or protracted, can and have cascading effects on development of mental health and well-being across the life course. Developmental approaches taken together, particularly when analyzed as complex systems, provide a framework for conceptualizing these relationships and guiding research development and can assist with response planning and policy development. In the following section, we draw on the developmental life course approach, with an emphasis on longitudinal studies, to highlight conceptual and methodological challenges on the road ahead.

Measuring and Responding to Climate Change

Measurement Challenges

The question of how to conceptualize and measure how climate change influences mental health poses unique challenges. For a start, the mismatch between timescales of climate change and human lifespans mean that most studies focus on the link between weather-related stressors and climate variability, rather than climate change per se (Massazza et al., 2022). Second, geophysics can only offer an estimate of the likelihood of climate change being responsible for any particular extreme event, such as a specific wildfire or flood. Nevertheless, attribution studies are increasingly convincing (Ebi et al., 2020), as is people's lived experience of their local weather patterns. Third, mental health problems are the product of long, interconnected causal chains that begin before birth, often interacting with the environment in complex ways to create feedback loops that cascade across development to deliver final outcomes. This picture is further complicated by the fact that, in addition to direct impacts, climatic stressors frequently have indirect downstream effects that alter environments and human societies in myriad ways to increase mental health vulnerability, creating uncertainty about both pathways and mechanisms. One way to conceptualize the relationship between climatic stressors and the many domains of mental health that can be impacted is to apply a 'systems thinking' approach (Berry et al., 2018).

Systems thinking is a conceptual approach that considers causes and effects as interconnected, mutually reciprocal components of a system, nested within or overlapping other complex systems. The approach has particular appeal in the context of climate change because it can help to elucidate the complex interplay between climatic stressors, exposures, vulnerability, and mental health outcomes, and their reciprocal effects on the system in which they are embedded (Berry et al., 2018). Recent reviews show that the systems approach can be successfully applied to mapping the complex, multidimensional ways in which climate change shapes mental health (Gousse-Lessard et al., 2022; Hayward & Ayeb-Karlsson, 2021). Systems thinking can, equally, be used to map the relationships between climatic stressors and children's present and future mental health and wellbeing (see Figure 4.2).

Although efforts to **map** how climate change shapes mental health are already underway, a stronger developmentally sensitive approach is required. This means defining the key climatic stressors for different developmental periods, the regions in which impacts occur (e.g., locally, nationally, globally), and the populations that are most at risk – all under multiple climate change scenarios. It is vital to understand that children grow up in specific physical places; predictive analyses of the likely prevalence and course of mental health, and interventions that will work in the real world, must therefore be localized to be relevant and helpful. Such information will be essential for policy development and response planning in the short and long term. Interactions between mental and physical health should also be tracked and modeled, especially in low- and middle-income countries where children already carry a high health burden, and will increasingly do so, as climate changes advance (Firth et al., 2019). Mapping exercises should define and consider the multiple domains of mental health that climate change will shape for specific places. Consideration must include subclinical psychological distress, psychiatric disorders, hospital admissions, self-harm, and suicidal behaviors. Substance use problems, which are most prevalent among young people, and frequently co-occur and interact with mental health problems, should

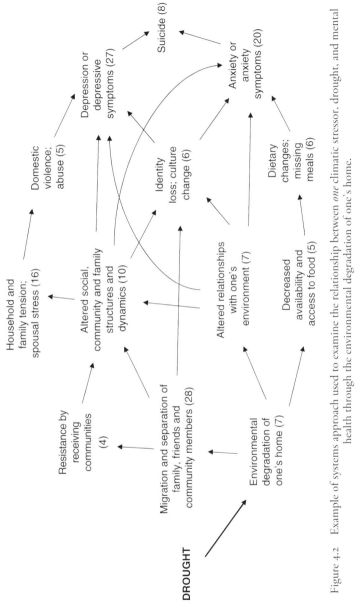

Figure 4.2 Example of systems approach used to examine the relationship between *one* climatic stressor, drought, and mental health through the environmental degradation of one's home.

be monitored and tracked as a key dimension of young people's mental health and well-being (Vergunst et al., 2022). So too should maladaptive behaviors that are harmful to others, such as interpersonal violence and terrorism.

Throughout this chapter we have emphasized the process of ongoing adaptation across the life course that characterizes mental health and illness. This implies a need for **long-term studies** that track normal and abnormal psychological process in response to climate change and its stressors across development (Nissan et al., 2021). We have previously argued for the use of birth cohort studies and long-term population registry data because they are already available and can be quickly leveraged through linkages with administrative data – for example, meteorological, health, genetic, education, and tax return data – to monitor development over long time periods (Vergunst & Berry, 2021). These methods should be further complemented with mixed methods, qualitive designs (e.g., to better understand young people's psychological responses to climate change), survey data, quasi experiments, and so on (see Textbox 4.2).

Another important piece of the response planning puzzle is to understand the **mechanisms** through which climatic stressors affect psychological development. Currently, evidence from both human and animal studies demonstrates a robust link between adverse early life experiences and negative developmental outcomes, but the physiological and neurocognitive process that underlie these effects are not well understood (Smith & Pollak, 2020). One suggestion is that attention should also be focused on questions about intensity, severity, chronicity, and developmental timing of climate change-related stressors. For instance, while prior research has focused on the 'first 1,000 days' as a period of especially high developmental vulnerability, more recent studies have challenged this measurement period, showing that adverse experiences in adolescence may have even larger negative effects on developmental outcomes, including mental health, when compared with equivalent experiences that occur in the early childhood periods (Huei-Jong et al., 2021; Woodard & Pollak, 2020). Addressing these unresolved questions would help to clarify key periods for targeted prevention efforts and inform climate adaptation policy development – and here again, specificity (who, what, when, *and where*) will be important. In summary, the arguments presented here, in conjunction with recent reviews of quantitative studies of climate change and mental health, show that conceptual and methodological innovation are needed to understand and measure the impacts of climate change on the psychological health and well-being of young people (Massazza et al., 2022).

> **Textbox 4.2 Research priorities**
>
> - Conduct impact-targeted systematic reviews of the scientific and grey literatures on the effects of climate change-related events on healthy psychological development across the life course
> - Support interdisciplinary research on the effects of acute (e.g., wildfires, floods), subacute (e.g., heatwaves), and chronic (e.g., drought, food shortages) stressors on the cognitive, social, and emotional development of children across the world
> - Examine how the intensity, severity, chronicity, and developmental timing of exposures influence the healthy psychological development of children (including additive, interactive, and cumulative effects)
> - Clarify the mechanisms through which climate change-related stressors increase mental health vulnerability (e.g., disrupted sleep, lost education)
> - Conduct cross-cultural studies on how children are adapting psychologically to climate change (e.g., fear, anxiety, guilt) and what they are doing to cope
> - Evaluate how resilience can be promoted and vulnerability reduced at the individual and group levels so that children are equipped to live with climate change
> - Identify existing and new research designs, analytic approaches, and data sources that can help address these questions in the immediate and long term (Vergunst & Berry, 2021)

Responses to Improve Youth Mental Health

Climate change is part of all future scenarios and young people today will not know a world without it. Adaptation will require deep changes that become so embedded in everyday 'healthy living' that they are no longer linked to the climate crisis. But getting there will be psychologically taxing; accepting what previous generations have done to the planet and what it means for our collective futures, and indeed the future of all sentient life, can generate powerful emotions. Much more work is needed to understand these processes in young people of all ages so that psychologically healthy adaptive processes can be realized. At a minimum, this will require recognizing these reactions as normal and healthy responses to events that are, in nearly every way, a predictable and preventable tragedy.

The most important responses to climate change, by far, will be the *collective* national and international responses to reduce greenhouse gas emissions, including the planning and implementation of effective adaptive strategies (Buse et al., 2022). Unfortunately, a recent review of the evidence on human adaptation to climate change reported that adaptations are "largely fragmented, local and incremental, with limited evidence of transformational adaptation and negligible evidence of risk reduction outcomes" (Berrang-Ford et al., 2021, p. 989). Within the healthcare sector, nearly two-thirds of countries worldwide do not have adequate national health emergency frameworks and are unprepared to respond to climate-related health emergencies (Romanello et al., 2021). Furthermore, mental disorders already affect around 1 billion people worldwide – including around one in six children – and cost the global economy more than US$1 trillion per year, yet account for just 2.1 percent of national healthcare expenditure (WHO, 2022). In short, substantial investment in response planning and mental health services are required to meet the mental health challenges faced by children.

At the levels of **individual and local community action**, more work is needed to understand how children and young people can most effectively adapt to living with climate change. This may not be achieved by constant bombardment of climate change-related news – which could, for vulnerable individuals, elevate the risk of posttraumatic stress symptoms (Dick et al., 2021) – and it is critical to engage young people in conceptualizing responses. Further work is also needed to establish age-appropriate "best practice" for improving young people's engagement with climate change (Mah et al., 2020); employing a "**collective causes** and **collective solutions**" framing is more effective at generating proactive engagement than is a framing that emphasizes individual responsibility (Obradovich & Guenther, 2016). Some evidence indicates that young people who engage in climate change mitigative and adaptive efforts experience a mental health boost, and further study of these associations is warranted. Crucially, adults must facilitate and support young people's efforts to engage and respond to climate change. This will mean learning how to help them participate in making and implementing decisions that will, after all, affect them most. Scaling up climate change education in school settings – for teachers as well as children – could be an effective strategy. Indeed, a recent review called for "the development of new forms of climate change education that directly involve young people in responding to the scientific, social, ethical, and political complexities of climate change" (Rousell & Cutter-Mackenzie-Knowles, 2020).

The **virtuous cycle** between effective responses to climate change and enhanced psychological well-being have yet to be fully realized. This means setting in motion responses and adaptive actions that have dual and mutually reinforcing benefits for climate change and mental health and well-being, such as promoting more active transport like walking and cycling over motor vehicles, eating more plant-based diets rather than animal products, and so on. More broadly, we have argued elsewhere that we strongly favor community-based responses because they shift the onus from primarily the individual to primarily the group. We endorse a model of 'preventive psychiatry' that prioritizes investment in universal public health approaches targeting the social determinants of mental disorders (Braveman & Gottlieb, 2014; Fusar-Poli et al., 2021). This requires increased investment in education, employment, social support, housing, criminal justice, poverty alleviation, community development, greenspace, environmental protection, and immigration reform. The approach is strongly supportive of the global mental health and sustainable development goals which seek to improve global mental health while simultaneously tackling climate change and protecting the environment (Patel et al., 2018).

The **global injustice** of climate change has been repeatedly noted but is worth restating, partly because of the pernicious effect that climate change-related injustice itself has on mental health (Berry, 2022). Currently, around 89.3 percent of the world's young people aged 0–24 years live in low- and middle-income countries, which are overwhelmingly located in equatorial regions that have been identified as being most at risk from climate change (UN, 2022). People living in these regions are currently and historically least responsible for causing climate change and are amongst the least resourced to adapt to the short-term shocks and enduring harm generated by climatic stressors. The global reach of climate change means that no country can fully insulate itself from its effects, especially in the long term (e.g., food shortages, forced migration). Effective global strategies to mitigate the worst harms (e.g., through rapid adaption and prevention) are a rational necessity, to say nothing of the moral imperative. In practice, this means doing much more to support populations living in vulnerable regions, especially those currently and historically most disadvantaged, by buffering their response and adaptation capabilities. It should also be noted that inequality gradients exist within as well as between nations, and those living with complex disadvantage and marginalization in wealthier nations also require and merit effective support. Within this, the needed investment in adapting public health services for climate change must include developing and scaling up mental and general health services for young people (McGorry et al., 2022).

In planning policy activities and health interventions, we must remember that nearly all formal scientific knowledge about how climate change affects health has been generated by wealthy countries using data drawn from samples in their own nations – and is therefore not representative of the global majority (Henrich et al., 2010). Nor is it representative of marginalized groups in wealthy nations. These within- and between-nations inequities must be acknowledged by those who inform, make, and implement decisions (e.g., governments, nongovernmental organizations, health agencies, researchers) so that more locally adapted, culturally informed measurement and mitigation strategies may be pursued (Zhang et al., 2021). Indeed, we must go beyond this to actively enable representative participation in decision-making about what to do and how to fund and implement decisions. These people, especially young people, have a moral right as well as a practical need to sit at the world's decision-making tables.

Summary and Conclusions

Climate change presents major challenges to the mental health and well-being of young people. Its effects are already being observed across the world and are expected to accelerate as climate change advances. Even with swift and effective adaptive action, the reversal of important and hard-won human development goals now appears unavoidable, with disastrous consequences for health and well-being. We have shown that taking a developmental life course perspective offers a practical framework for understanding the pathways and processes through which this might occur, and can inform the development of age-appropriate, targeted harm prevention and health promotion strategies. The threat we face is overwhelming and urgent. But decision-making that is inclusive, just, well-informed and intellectually rigorous can lead not only to excellence in adaptive action but to changing the world for the better.

References

Abel, K. M., Wicks, S., Susser, E. S., Dalman, C., Pedersen, M. G., Mortensen, P. B., & Webb, R. T. (2010). Birth weight, schizophrenia, and adult mental disorder: Is risk confined to the smallest babies? *Archives of General Psychiatry*, 67(9), 923–930. https://doi.org/10.1001/archgenpsychiatry.2010.100

Achenbach, T. M. (1974). *Developmental psychopathology*. Ronald Press.

Akresh, R. (2016). Climate change, conflict, and children. *The Future of Children*, 26(1), 51–71.

Alisic, E., Zalta, A. K., van Wesel, F., Larsen, S. E., Hafstad, G. S., Hassanpour, K., & Smid, G. E. (2014). Rates of post-traumatic stress disorder in trauma-exposed children and adolescents: Meta-analysis. *British Journal of Psychiatry: The Journal of Mental Science*, 204, 335–340. https://doi.org/10.1192/bjp.bp.113.131227

Anderson, P. J., de Miranda, D. M., Albuquerque, M. R., Indredavik, M. S., Evensen, K. A. I., Van Lieshout, R., … Doyle, L. W. (2021). Psychiatric disorders in individuals born very preterm / very low-birth weight: An individual participant data (IPD) meta-analysis. *EClinicalMedicine*, 42, 101216. https://doi.org/10.1016/j.eclinm.2021.101216

Baranne, M. L., & Falissard, B. (2018). Global burden of mental disorders among children aged 5–14 years. *Child and Adolescent Psychiatry and Mental Health*, 12(1), 19. https://doi.org/10.1186/s13034-018-0225-4

Barican, J. L., Yung, D., Schwartz, C., Zheng, Y., Georgiades, K., & Waddell, C. (2022). Prevalence of childhood mental disorders in high-income countries: A systematic review and meta-analysis to inform policymaking. *Evidence-Based Mental Health*, 25(1), 36–44. https://doi.org/10.1136/ebmental-2021-300277

Beauchaine, T. P., Constantino, J. N., & Hayden, E. P. (2018). Psychiatry and developmental psychopathology: Unifying themes and future directions. *Comprehensive Psychiatry*, 87, 143–152. https://doi.org/10.1016/j.comppsych.2018.10.014

Berrang-Ford, L., Siders, A. R., Lesnikowski, A., Fischer, A. P., Callaghan, M. W., Haddaway, N. R., … Abu, T. Z. (2021). A systematic global stocktake of evidence on human adaptation to climate change. *Nature Climate Change*, 11(11), 989–1000.

Berry, H. (2022). Global warming is people knowingly harming other people. *BMJ*, 378, o2132. https://doi.org/10.1136/bmj.o2132

Berry, H., Waite, T., Dear, K., Capon, A., & Murray, V. (2018). The case for systems thinking about climate change and mental health. *Nature Climate Change*, 8(4), 282–290. https://doi.org/10.1038/s41558-018-0102-4

Braveman, P., & Gottlieb, L. (2014). The social determinants of health: It's time to consider the causes of the causes. *Public Health Reports*, 129(Suppl 2), 19–31.

Buse, K., Bhaumik, S., Miranda, J. J., Hunnisett, C., Batz, C. S., & Feeny, E. (2022). Individual responsibility: A red herring that lets the fossil fuel industry off the climate catastrophe hook. *BMJ*, 378, o1656. https://doi.org/10.1136/bmj.o1656

Butler, C., Bowles, D., McIver, L., & Page, L. (2014). *Mental health, cognition and the challenge of climate change*. CABI Publishing. https://openresearch-repository.anu.edu.au/handle/1885/36206

Carnie, T.-L., Berry, H., Blinkhorn, S. A., & Hart, C. R. (2011). In their own words: Young people's mental health in drought-affected rural and remote NSW. *Australian Journal of Rural Health*, 19(5), 244–248. https://doi.org/10.1111/j.1440-1584.2011.01224.x

Caspi, A., Wright, B. R. E., Moffitt, T. E., & Silva, P. A. (1998). Early failure in the labor market: Childhood and adolescent predictors of unemployment in the transition to adulthood. *American Sociological Review*, 63, 424–451.

Clemens, V., von Hirschhausen, E., & Fegert, J. M. (2020). Report of the intergovernmental panel on climate change: Implications for the mental health policy of children and adolescents in Europe – A scoping review. *European Child & Adolescent Psychiatry*. https://doi.org/10.1007/s00787-020-01615-3

Colón-González, F. J., Sewe, M. O., Tompkins, A. M., Sjödin, H., Casallas, A., Rocklöv, J., Caminade, C., & Lowe, R. (2021). Projecting the risk of mosquito-borne diseases in a warmer and more populated world: A multi-model, multi-scenario intercomparison modelling study. *The Lancet Planetary Health*, 5(7), e404–e414. https://doi.org/10.1016/S2542-5196(21)00132-7

Cortina, M. A., Sodha, A., Fazel, M., & Ramchandani, P. G. (2012). Prevalence of child mental health problems in sub-Saharan Africa: A systematic review. *Archives of Pediatrics & Adolescent Medicine*, 166(3), 276–281. https://doi.org/10.1001/archpediatrics.2011.592

Dick, A. S., Silva, K., Gonzalez, R., Sutherland, M. T., Laird, A. R., Thompson, W. K., … Comer, J. S. (2021). Neural vulnerability and hurricane-related media are associated with post-traumatic stress in youth. *Nature Human Behaviour*, 5, 1578–1589. https://doi.org/10.1038/s41562-021-01216-3

Ebi, K. L., Åström, C., Boyer, C. J., Harrington, L. J., Hess, J. J., Honda, Y., … Otto, F. E. L. (2020). Using detection and attribution to quantify how climate change is affecting health. *Health Affairs*, 39(12), 2168–2174. https://doi.org/10.1377/hlthaff.2020.01004

Ebi, K. L., Vanos, J., Baldwin, J. W., Bell, J. E., Hondula, D. M., Errett, N. A., … Berry, P. (2021). Extreme weather and climate change: Population health and health system implications. *Annual Review of Public Health*, 42(1), 293–315. https://doi.org/10.1146/annurev-publhealth-012420-105026

Evans, G. W. (2019). Projected behavioral impacts of global climate change. *Annual Review of Psychology*, 70, 449–474. https://doi.org/10.1146/annurev-psych-010418-103023

Faravelli, C., Lo Sauro, C., Godini, L., Lelli, L., Benni, L., Pietrini, F., … Ricca, V. (2012). Childhood stressful events, HPA axis and anxiety disorders. *World Journal of Psychiatry*, 2(1), 13–25. https://doi.org/10.5498/wjp.v2.i1.13

Firth, J., Siddiqi, N., Koyanagi, A., Siskind, D., Rosenbaum, S., Galletly, C., … Stubbs, B. (2019). The Lancet Psychiatry Commission: A blueprint for protecting physical health in people with mental illness. *The Lancet Psychiatry*, 6(8), 675–712. https://doi.org/10.1016/S2215-0366(19)30132-4

Fusar-Poli, P., Correll, C. U., Arango, C., Berk, M., Patel, V., & Ioannidis, J. P. A. (2021). Preventive psychiatry: A blueprint for improving the mental health of young people. *World Psychiatry*, 20(2), 200–221. https://doi.org/10.1002/wps.20869

Garcia, D. M., & Sheehan, M. C. (2016). Extreme weather-driven disasters and children's health. *International Journal of Health Services: Planning, Administration, Evaluation*, 46(1), 79–105. https://doi.org/10.1177/0020731415625254

Gousse-Lessard, A.-S., Gachon, P., Lessard, L., Vermeulen, V., Boivin, M., Maltais, D., … Le Beller, J. (2022). Intersectoral approaches: The key to mitigating psychosocial and health consequences of disasters and systemic risks. *Disaster Prevention and Management: An International Journal*, ahead of print.

Hayes, K., Blashki, G., Wiseman, J., Burke, S., & Reifels, L. (2018). Climate change and mental health: Risks, impacts and priority actions. *International Journal of Mental Health Systems*, 12. https://doi.org/10.1186/s13033-018-0210-6

Hayward, G., & Ayeb-Karlsson, S. (2021). "Seeing with empty eyes": A systems approach to understand climate change and mental health in Bangladesh. *Climatic Change*, 165(1), 29. https://doi.org/10.1007/s10584-021-03053-9

Henrich, J., Heine, S. J., & Norenzayan, A. (2010). Most people are not WEIRD. *Nature*, 466, 29. https://doi.org/10.1038/466029a

Herrman, H. (2001). The need for mental health promotion. *The Australian and New Zealand Journal of Psychiatry*, 35(6), 709–715. https://doi.org/10.1046/j.1440-1614.2001.00947.x

Hickman, C., Marks, E., Pihkala, P., Clayton, S., Lewandowski, R. E., Mayall, E. E., ... Susteren, L. van. (2021). Climate anxiety in children and young people and their beliefs about government responses to climate change: A global survey. *The Lancet Planetary Health*, 5(12), e863–e873. https://doi.org/10.1016/S2542-5196(21)00278-3

Hinshaw (2017). Developmental psychopathology as a scientific discipline. In T. P. Beauchaine & S. Hinshaw (Eds.), *Child and adolescent psychopathology* (3rd ed., pp. 3–32). Wiley. https://contentstore.cla.co.uk/secure/link?id=3497bc43-22a5-e711-80cb-005056af4099

Huei-Jong, G., Biroli, P., & Belsky, D. (2021). Critical periods in child development and the transition to adulthood. *JAMA Network Open*. https://doi.org/doi:10.1001/jamanetworkopen.2020.33359

Jaffee, S. R. (2019). Editorial: The rise and rise of developmental perspectives in child psychology and psychiatry. *Journal of Child Psychology and Psychiatry*, 60(4), 329–332. https://doi.org/10.1111/jcpp.13055

Laplante, D. P., Barr, R. G., Brunet, A., Galbaud du Fort, G., Meaney, M. L., Saucier, J.-F., Zelazo, P. R., & King, S. (2004). Stress during pregnancy affects general intellectual and language functioning in human toddlers. *Pediatric Research*, 56(3), 400–410. https://doi.org/10.1203/01.PDR.0000136281.34035.44

Mah, A. Y. J., Chapman, D. A., Markowitz, E. M., & Lickel, B. (2020). Coping with climate change: Three insights for research, intervention, and communication to promote adaptive coping to climate change. *Journal of Anxiety Disorders*, 75, 102282. https://doi.org/10.1016/j.janxdis.2020.102282

Mangus, C. W., & Canares, T. L. (2019). Heat-related illness in children in an era of extreme temperatures. *Pediatrics in Review*, 40(3), 97–107. https://doi.org/10.1542/pir.2017-0322

Mani, A., Mullainathan, S., Shafir, E., & Zhao, J. (2013). Poverty impedes cognitive function. *Science*, 341(6149), 976–980. https://doi.org/10.1126/science.1238041

Martin, J., Taylor, M. J., & Lichtenstein, P. (2018). Assessing the evidence for shared genetic risks across psychiatric disorders and traits. *Psychological Medicine*, 48(11), 1759–1774. https://doi.org/10.1017/S0033291717003440

Massazza, A., Teyton, A., Charlson, F., Benmarhnia, T., & Augustinavicius, J. L. (2022). Quantitative methods for climate change and mental health research: Current trends and future directions. *The Lancet Planetary Health*, 6(7), e613–e627. https://doi.org/10.1016/S2542-5196(22)00120-6

Masten, A. S., & Cicchetti, D. (2010). Developmental cascades. *Development and Psychopathology*, 22(3), 491–495. https://doi.org/10.1017/S0954579410000222

McCrory, E., Foulkes, L., & Viding, E. (2022). Social thinning and stress generation after childhood maltreatment: A neurocognitive social transactional model of psychiatric vulnerability. *The Lancet Psychiatry*, 9(10), 828–837. https://doi.org/10.1016/S2215-0366(22)00202-4

McDermott, B., Cobham, V., Berry, H., & Kim, B. (2014). Correlates of persisting posttraumatic symptoms in children and adolescents 18 months after a cyclone disaster. *The Australian and New Zealand Journal of Psychiatry*, 48(1), 80–86. https://doi.org/10.1177/0004867413500349

McElroy, S., Ilango, S., Dimitrova, A., Gershunov, A., & Benmarhnia, T. (2022). Extreme heat, preterm birth, and stillbirth: A global analysis across 14 lower-middle income countries. *Environment International*, 158, 106902. https://doi.org/10.1016/j.envint.2021.106902

McGorry, P. D., Mei, C., Chanen, A., Hodges, C., Alvarez-Jimenez, M., & Killackey, E. (2022). Designing and scaling up integrated youth mental health care. *World Psychiatry*, 21(1), 61–76. https://doi.org/10.1002/wps.20938

Minor, K., Bjerre-Nielsen, A., Jonasdottir, S. S., Lehmann, S., & Obradovich, N. (2022). Rising temperatures erode human sleep globally. *One Earth*, 5(5), 534–549. https://doi.org/10.1016/j.oneear.2022.04.008

Nissan, H., Diggle, P., & Fronterre, C. (2021). *Combining climate and health data: Challenges and opportunities for longitudinal population studies*. Wellcome. https://wellcome.org/reports/combining-climate-and-health-data-challenges-and-opportunities-longitudinal-population

Noffsinger, M. A., Pfefferbaum, B., Pfefferbaum, R. L., Sherrieb, K., & Norris, F. H. (2012). The burden of disaster: Part I. Challenges and opportunities within a child's social ecology. *International Journal of Emergency Mental Health*, 14(1), 3–13.

Norris, F. H., Friedman, M. J., Watson, P. J., Byrne, C. M., Diaz, E., & Kaniasty, K. (2002). 60,000 disaster victims speak: Part I. An empirical review of the empirical literature, 1981–2001. *Psychiatry*, 65(3), 207–239.

Obradovich, N., & Guenther, S. M. (2016). Collective responsibility amplifies mitigation behaviors. *Climatic Change*, 137(1), 307–319. https://doi.org/10.1007/s10584-016-1670-9

Ojala, M., Cunsolo, A., Ogunbode, C. A., & Middleton, J. (2021). Anxiety, worry, and grief in a time of environmental and climate crisis: A narrative review. *Annual Review of Environment and Resources*, 46(1), 35–58. https://doi.org/10.1146/annurev-environ-012220-022716

Olson, D. M., & Metz, G. A. S. (2020). Climate change is a major stressor causing poor pregnancy outcomes and child development. *F1000Research*, 9. https://doi.org/10.12688/f1000research.27157.1

Orri, M., Vergunst, F., Turecki, G., Galera, C., Latimer, E., Bouchard, S., … Côté, S. M. (2021). Long-term economic and social outcomes of youth suicide attempts. *British Journal of Psychiatry*, 1–7. https://doi.org/10.1192/bjp.2021.133

Patel, V., Saxena, S., Lund, C., Thornicroft, G., Baingana, F., Bolton, P., … UnÜtzer, J. (2018). The Lancet Commission on global mental health and sustainable development. *The Lancet*, 392(10157), 1553–1598. https://doi.org/10.1016/S0140-6736(18)31612-X

Paus, T., Keshavan, M., & Giedd, J. N. (2008). Why do many psychiatric disorders emerge during adolescence? *Nature Reviews. Neuroscience*, 9(12), 947–957. https://doi.org/10.1038/nrn2513

Romanello, M., McGushin, A., Napoli, C. D., Drummond, P., Hughes, N., Jamart, L., … Hamilton, I. (2021). The 2021 report of the Lancet Countdown on health and climate change: Code red for a healthy future. *The Lancet*, 398(10311), 1619–1662. https://doi.org/10.1016/S0140-6736(21)01787-6

Rousell, D., & Cutter-Mackenzie-Knowles, A. (2020). A systematic review of climate change education: Giving children and young people a "voice" and a "hand" in redressing climate change. *Children's Geographies*, 18(2), 191–208. https://doi.org/10.1080/14733285.2019.1614532

Rutter, M. (1988). Epidemiological approaches to developmental psychopathology. *Archives of General Psychiatry*, 45(5), 486–495. https://doi.org/10.1001/archpsyc.1988.01800290106013

Samuels, L., Nakstad, B., Roos, N., Bonell, A., Chersich, M., Havenith, G., … Kovats, S. (2022). Physiological mechanisms of the impact of heat during pregnancy and the clinical implications: Review of the evidence from an expert group meeting. *International Journal of Biometeorology*, 66(8), 1505–1513. https://doi.org/10.1007/s00484-022-02301-6

Sheffield, P. E., & Landrigan, P. J. (2011). Global climate change and children's health: Threats and strategies for prevention. *Environmental Health Perspectives*, 119(3), 291–298. https://doi.org/10.1289/ehp.1002233

Smith, K. E., & Pollak, S. D. (2020). Rethinking concepts and categories for understanding the neurodevelopmental effects of childhood adversity. *Perspectives on Psychological Science*, 16(1), 1745691620920725. https://doi.org/10.1177/1745691620920725

Solmi, M., Radua, J., Olivola, M., Croce, E., Soardo, L., Salazar de Pablo, G., … Fusar-Poli, P. (2021). Age at onset of mental disorders worldwide: Large-scale meta-analysis of 192 epidemiological studies. *Molecular Psychiatry*, 1–15. https://doi.org/10.1038/s41380-021-01161-7

Stanke, C., Murray, V., Amlôt, R., Nurse, J., & Williams, R. (2012). The effects of flooding on mental health: Outcomes and recommendations from a review of the literature. *PLOS Currents Disasters*. https://doi.org/10.1371/4f9f1fa9c3cae

Thiery, B. W., Lange, S., Rogelj, J., Schleussner, C.-F., Gudmundsson, L., Seneviratne, S. I., … Wada, Y. (2021). Intergenerational inequities in exposure to climate extremes. *Science*, 374(6564), eabi7339. https://doi.org/10.1126/science.abi7339

UN (2022). World Population Prospects 2022. Department of Economic and Social Affairs Population Division, United Nations. https://population.un.org/wpp/Download/Standard/Population/

UNICEF (2021). The climate crisis is a child rights crisis: Introducing the Children's Climate Risk Index. www.unicef.org/reports/climate-crisis-child-rights-crisis

Vergunst, F., & Berry, H. L. (2021). Climate change and children's mental health: A developmental perspective. *Clinical Psychological Science*, 10(4), https://doi.org/10.1177/21677026211040787

Vergunst, F., Berry, H. L., Minor, K., & Chadi, N. (2022). Climate change and substance-use behaviors: A risk-pathways framework. *Perspectives on Psychological Science: A Journal of the Association for Psychological Science*, 18(4), 17456916221132740. https://doi.org/10.1177/17456916221132739

Vins, H., Bell, J., Saha, S., & Hess, J. J. (2015). The mental health outcomes of drought: A systematic review and causal process diagram. *International Journal of Environmental Research and Public Health*, 12(10), 13251–13275. https://doi.org/10.3390/ijerph121013251

WHO (2021). *Mental health atlas 2020*. World Health Organization. www.who.int/publications/i/item/9789240036703

WHO (2022). *Mental health and climate change: Policy brief*. World Health Organization. www.who.int/publications/i/item/9789240045125

Woodard, K., & Pollak, S. D. (2020). Is there evidence for sensitive periods in emotional development? *Current Opinion in Behavioral Sciences*, 36, 1–6. https://doi.org/10.1016/j.cobeha.2020.05.004

Zhang, S., Braithwaite, I., Bhavsar, V., & Das-Munshi, J. (2021). Unequal effects of climate change and pre-existing inequalities on the mental health of global populations. *BJPsych Bulletin*, 1–5. https://doi.org/10.1192/bjb.2021.26

CHAPTER 5

Neuropsychiatric Perspectives on the Biology of Anxiety and Youth Climate Distress

Jacob Lee and Anthony Guerrero

Introduction

The more we discuss climate change with young people, the more we come to understand their growing worry. While young people report grief, despair, guilt, shame, powerlessness, sadness, or anger in response to climate change, reports of anxiety are among the most common emotional responses reported worldwide (Stanley et al., 2021; Stewart, 2021; Wu et al., 2020). This **climate anxiety**, which describes the feeling of concern regarding the present or future of our planet, has also become a source of debate in the media and culture. Many times this debate mistakenly conflates anxiety, which describes tension and worried thoughts, and anxiety disorders, a group of psychiatric disorders which involve a pattern of excess anxiety that interferes with normal functioning.

Anxiety itself is often a logical and protective state generated by the brain in response to danger, as the associated changes in thoughts and behaviors can help steer us towards safety. But the anxiety response comes with trade-offs, increasing the heart rate, blood pressure, and modifying the activity of countless life-sustaining biological and neurological processes. The level of anxiety an individual experiences is a product of both personality and the stressfulness of the situation. We describe the tendency to become anxious as "trait anxiety" and the act of feeling anxious as "state anxiety." Those with higher trait anxiety are more likely to experience an anxious state in a given situation.

Anxiety disorders include conditions such as generalized anxiety disorder, panic disorder, phobias, and social anxiety disorder. Some lists also include obsessive-compulsive disorder (OCD) and trauma-related conditions such as posttraumatic stress disorder (PTSD). Anxiety becomes pathologic when sensitivity to it is too great, triggering perseveration and rumination, which inhibit its resolution. Anxiety disorders often develop when we are exposed to severe stress or stress experienced over a long

> **Textbox 5.1 Anxiety versus anxiety disorder, defined**
>
> Anxiety: According to the *American Psychiatric Association* (2022), anxiety is a normal response to stress and can even be beneficial in some situations; for example, when worrying about an exam makes a teen extra studious.
>
> Anxiety disorder: Anxiety of excessive intensity or duration, which causes difficulty in life functioning. Some lists include trauma-related and obsessive conditions under anxiety disorders, while the APA (2022) considers them a separate but related category.

period of time. The prevalence of anxiety disorders is higher in young people than in adults, and anxiety disorders are the single most common mental health challenge for youth. In a classroom of ten students, one or two will likely have a diagnosable anxiety disorder (Clayton, 2020a; Kenwood & Kalin, 2021; Peris & Galván, 2021; Perino et al., 2021).

Stress is any perceived or real stimulus in which a situation demands more than we can comfortably give. The body has evolved numerous systems throughout the central and peripheral tissues to both promote and suppress stress response (Conrad, 2011; Schneiderman et al., 2005). The body produces neurotransmitters, peptides, and hormones specifically to protect against stress. Those exposed to chronic stress experience several consequences of damage to and from these systems, including compromised immune systems, long-lasting cardiovascular disease, or problems with healthy development.

The emotional responses to climate change sit at an interesting cross-section between anxiety and anxiety disorder (see Textbox 5.1), with psychiatrists and behavioral health experts openly debating how to categorize this growing phenomenon. Some psychiatrists believe climate anxiety should be a psychiatric diagnosis in the *Diagnostic and Statistical Manual of Mental Disorders* (*DSM-5*), while others vehemently disagree, seeing this as the over-pathologizing of a normal fear response. These psychiatrists view climate anxiety as a rational, widespread phenomenon of appropriate worry in young people, but one which may be severe enough to impair functioning (Verplanken & Roy, 2013) and can overlap with known psychiatric illnesses, possibly responding to their same treatments.

Acute and Chronic Climate-Related Anxiety

Climate change can increase anxiety in those exposed to climate-related disasters, but also in those who learn about them and anticipate future eco-catastrophe. This may be particularly true in individuals with high trait anxiety. The severity and closeness of exposure to climate disruption appears to impact outcome, as does the degree of damage, time course, inability to collect possessions, and perception of the threat of loss (Agyapong et al., 2018; Madakasira & O'Brien, 1987). To provide real-world context to these statements and their associated neurobiological impairments, the following material describes three examples of young people impacted by climate change, emphasizing the diversity of anxious responses we observe in this population.

Vignette 1: Acute Severe Traumatic Stress
Malia, a 14-year-old female living in coastal Florida, is being seen by her pediatrician. She is withdrawn and upset and is wearing a cast on her left leg. During previous visits, Malia was brought in by her mother or father, but today she is accompanied by her aunt, who tells the pediatrician that both of Malia's parents were killed in the recent hurricane, which was unusually fierce and occurred outside of the typical hurricane season. Malia was also injured by the partial collapse of her family home. The aunt describes Malia as "in a daze" since the hurricane three weeks ago. With some difficulty, the pediatrician is able to get Malia to describe the nightmares and flashbacks she has had since the storm and her new distrust of the sea.

Vignette 2: Chronic Traumatic Stress
Luis is a 17-year-old who comes from a farming family living in California. Luis presents to clinic with increasing concern over a record-setting drought, saying that his family may need to abandon farming entirely. Already the droughts have caused his family significant hardship, contributing to his father's high blood pressure and leading Luis to consider leaving the profession his family has worked in for generations. His grades at school have dropped, and he can't sleep well.

Vignette 3: Exacerbation of Existing Anxiety Disorder
Gayathri is a 15-year-old female with obsessive-compulsive disorder who has been seen for years by a child and adolescent psychiatrist. She has previously suffered from obsessions about infection, and after reading on the *Centers for Disease Control* and Prevention (CDC, n.d.) website that climate change is increasing the risk for pandemic disease, she worries that her family members will die if she does not clean every surface in her house daily.

Our changing climate can cause both acute and chronic anxiety in previously healthy young people, and can exacerbate preexisting psychiatric conditions. In an **acute** sense, extreme events can bring extreme trauma.

Young people might lose their homes or primary caregivers, and face significant disruption to their routines. **Chronic** anxieties can result from large-scale social and community disruption.

The Function of Anxiety

When we describe someone as experiencing anxiety, what do we mean in terms of their brain activity? What changes occur in the conscious and unconscious mind (see Textbox 5.2), and how can we expect these changes to alter behavior?

It can be helpful to start by evaluating the evolutionary purpose of the anxious response. Organisms that are insufficiently suited to their current environment are at a disadvantage in passing on their genes. Natural selection increases fitness, including neural and psychic fitness, by optimizing survival-relevant behaviors (Mobbs et al., 2015). If an individual's anxiety about a real danger keeps them out of harm's reach, that individual will be more likely to pass on their genes. The human stress response is an evolutionary adaptation providing benefits to vigilance, arousal, and reaction speed (Conrad, 2011).

At the simplest level, the nervous system is a tool that analyzes and responds to external threats. The human brain is a particularly complex system that has evolved to richly model possible outcomes (Kapeller & Jäger, 2020) with a goal of reducing surprise and optimizing safety. We engage our powerful imagination to consider possible futures, simulating potential encounters with threats. Our brains can produce complex predictions involving simulation, detailed analysis, compensation for pre-existing biases, and logical reasoning. The human capacity for modeling future threats likely exceeds that of any other species (Mobbs et al., 2015).

Our imagination arises from an ever-evolving web of communication and signaling pathways between multiple regions of our brain. The

---

Textbox 5.2 The *Unheimliche*

Perhaps the most famous psychiatrist of all, Sigmund Freud, believed that the experience of anxiety relied on an element he called the *Unheimliche*, translated as "un-homelike" or "uncanny." Writing in 1919, he argued that seeing familiar objects or environments become unfamiliar was deeply unsettling, and could sometimes challenge one's beliefs about themselves. This theory provides a classical psychoanalytic framework for climate-related anxiety, particularly that concerning changes in our landscapes and the natural world (Freud, 1919).

fundamental unit in this process is the **neuron**, the brain's signaling cell. Along with our brain's connections, the neurons themselves are continually changed in a lifelong tweaking process called **neuroplasticity**. Our brain is constantly comparing our mental image of a situation with the eventual real thing and adjusting our biases and thinking accordingly (Fitzgerald et al., 2021; Mobbs et al., 2015).

Humans can use social language to further develop our threat understanding, known as **social learning**. It is reasonable to consider that communicating about historical and upcoming threats increases risk for anxiety by introducing remote or abstract threats into our imagination, although such contemplation may also serve a soothing function (Mobbs et al., 2015). Imagining dangerous future scenarios thus risks exposing us to excessive stress yet allows the human mind to develop complex risk-reduction strategies. In other words, anticipatory anxiety about a situation can often be the first step towards avoiding or improving it.

Two Systems in Balance

If anxiety can protect us from danger at the risk of causing excessive stress, how does the brain find the proper balance? Which neural systems are involved in that process?

Studies of human and animal brains find that certain brain regions are more intimately involved in anxious, stress, and fear responses. The most illustrative studies use functional magnetic resonance imaging (fMRI) imaging, in which brain regions "light up" based on their level of activation. Across many species and stages of development, the amygdala, hippocampus, hypothalamus, and frontal cortex are most often involved in anxiety and fear responses. As you can see in Figure 5.1, there's significant overlap between the brain regions most involved in these circuits, and understanding these circuits is as important as understanding the regions involved.

Most relevant are the two competing systems that influence our safety-related thoughts and actions, the **Behavioral Approach System** (BAS) and the **Behavioral Inhibition System** (BIS). These systems oppose each other, modifying behavior in both systems based on the brain's current risk assessment.

Let's begin by discussing the BAS, an important circuit in human reward-seeking, motivation, and exploration. This system affects behaviors we think of as crucial parts of human personality and mood. BAS activation leads to extraverted and explorative behavior, which occurs when the

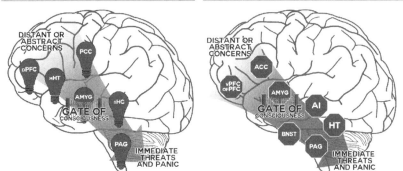

Figure 5.1   Elements of the Behavioral Approach System (BAS) and Behavioral Inhibition System (BIS).

brain finds risks to be distant. When this system is activated, the brain works to identify solutions to anxiety-producing stimuli. When the anxious stimulus is perceived as manageable, BIS activation is shortened or resolved, allowing BAS signaling to dominate (Kapeller & Jäger, 2020). This is anxiety at its most productive, allowing a young person to recognize a threat and adapt appropriately. As the BAS matures, adolescents can engage in healthy risk taking, allowing them to explore and learn from their environment (Clayton, 2020b; Perino et al., 2021).

Anatomically speaking, the BAS is composed of six major parts. At their most basic level, these brain regions react on a spectrum ranging from mere awareness of a distant or abstract threat to a full panic response in the face of immediate threat at the opposite extreme. Charles Darwin proposed that fear can be described as a gradient from casual attention to extreme terror, and that animals are more active when they perceive no danger (Mobbs et al., 2015).

A closer look at the BAS and BIS anatomy can be found in Tables 5.1 and 5.2. Please note that all brain regions have multiple functions in addition to those listed. Tasks are commonly worked on by multiple brain regions at once.

Of course, not all risks young people take are a good idea. Adolescence is a time of increased risk for substance abuse, unwanted pregnancies, drunk driving, and other dangerous behaviors (Gruber, 2009). To limit exposure to excessive risk, the brain uses the BIS, the brain's major anxiety circuit. Activity in this pathway generates anxious arousal, leading to avoidant behaviors to distract or distance oneself from the situation. The closer the

Table 5.1 *Behavioral Approach System (Fitzgerald et al., 2021; Kenwood & Kalin, 2021; Mobbs et al., 2015)*

Brain area	Functional role
Dorsal Prefrontal Cortex (DPFC)	This region performs our baseline evaluation of risk, and stimulates openness to activation/exploration
Posterior Cingulate Cortex (PCC)	This part of the cortex is responsible for rumination
Septo-Hippocampal region (SHC)	This region of the hippocampus is responsible for cognitive awareness of worry
Amygdala (AMYG)	Activates the sense of fear/anxious arousal, opens the gate to subjective anxiety
Medial Hypothalamus (MHT)	This brain region performs active risk assessment and signals the body to produce stress hormones if risk is detected
Periaqueductal gray matter (PAG)	This ancient brain region is shared with our oldest evolutionary relatives, and generates the fight/flight/freeze response, as well as panic

Table 5.2 *Behavioral Inhibition System (Dulcan, 2021; Fitzgerald et al., 2021; Gifford, 2011; Hammack et al., 2015; Kenwood & Kalin, 2021; Mobbs et al., 2015; Namkung et al., 2018)*

Brain area	Functional role
Ventral Prefrontal Cortex (VPFC) Orbitofrontal Prefrontal Cortex (OFPFC)	Involved in complex anxieties, interpreting sights and sounds for danger, producing anticipatory anxiety, and performing the baseline evaluation of risk
Anterior Cingulate Cortex (ACC)	Kicks off sympathetic excitation, causing tachycardia, hypertension and pupil dilation, involved in anxious obsessive thoughts
Amygdala (AMGY)	Activates the sense of fear/anxious arousal, opens the gate to subjective anxiety
Bed nucleus of the stria terminalis (BNST)	Most of the amygdala's output passes through this pathway, which monitors for sustained threats and activates the HPA hormonal stress response
Anterior Insula (AI)	Involved in initiation of motor actions in response to subjective feelings such as anxiety, and regulates autonomic response to worry
Hypothalamus (HT)	Generates escape-seeking desire
Periaqueductal gray matter (PAG)	This ancient brain region is shared with our oldest evolutionary relatives, and generates the fight/flight/freeze response as well as panic

brain anticipates the danger to be, the more it increases these avoidant behaviors, pumping the brakes on positive exploratory behaviors which might be less crucial for immediate survival. In the youngest children, excessive activation of the BIS might contribute to a failure to thrive, while older children and adolescents might experience mood changes and excessive worry. Those with anxiety disorders experience heightened sensitivity to risk and negative outcomes, leading to changes in their behaviors (Perino et al., 2021; Yook et al., 2010).

The anatomy of the BIS and BAS have significant overlap, at least at a quick glance. In many cases, the difference between BIS and BAS signaling involves activation of slightly different regions within a brain structure, or of signaling to different structures altogether.

The **amygdala** is a major contributor to this circuit, with increased activity seen in most studies of brain changes in pediatric anxiety disorders. The amygdala serves as a gate, preventing minor worries from reaching our conscious thought while allowing more serious anxieties to become part of our subjective experience. It also has a role in healthy anxiety (Fitzgerald et al., 2021: Kenwood & Kalin, 2021: Mobbs et al., 2015). Stress not only activates this brain region, it also drives changes within the amygdala's very structure, which becomes physically larger with short- or long-term overuse. Increasingly, studies show that these structural changes can remain for a long time, even with a prolonged stress-free period. Perhaps more important than these changes in baseline function is the reinforcement of the amygdala's connections to partnered brain regions (Nooner et al., 2013). In addition to the signals the amygdala sends to the brain, it also communicates with the body's key hormonal stress system, the hypothalamic-pituitary-adrenal (HPA) stress axis.

At the end of this circuit lies the **periaqueductal gray matter**, which remains as one of our oldest brain regions, part of the so-called "lizard brain." Just like a lizard on the sidewalk running from your shadow, this part of our brain handles immediate fight, flight, freeze, and panic responses. The freeze response, in particular, represents the maximum BIS response, pausing nearly all activities and prioritizing safety.

Through a process called extinction, a brain can reduce how strongly it responds to threatening or anxiety-provoking stimulus. This can be observed in a person exposed to two surprises within a short window; the second response may not be as strong. The process of extinction requires healthy function of the amygdala and prefrontal cortex (Gerhard et al., 2021).

The balance between the BIS and BAS gives an incomplete picture of the extent of the anxious response in a given situation. As described earlier, misperceptions of risk (both underestimates and overestimates) can have major ramifications for the experience of anxiety. A pattern of risk overestimation may lead to behavioral inhibition, a temperament trait which can emerge early in life and is a risk factor for the development of anxiety and anxiety disorders.

The balance between these brain circuits is complex and is impacted by differing rates of development of relevant brain regions. For that reason, the developmental stage is an important consideration when looking at climate-related anxiety in young people. For example, the brains of an elementary school student and a high schooler demonstrate significant differences in how they respond to threats. Young children lack the brain mechanisms to independently evaluate complex threats, and instead look to their caregivers to model an appropriate level of concern. Secure attachment to a guardian is required to develop a sense of security, and to develop a healthy balance between risk and anxiety. As described earlier, adolescents may underestimate risks (Gerhard et al., 2021; Kenwood & Kalin, 2021; Sullivan & Opendak, 2021).

Sometimes coping mechanisms which were previously adaptive can become problematic. Imagine a young woman who begins journaling to better understand her feelings about climate change. At first, the journal helps her better understand the emotions she feels. Over time, she becomes consumed by the climate crisis in her journaling. Her entries become fixated on the negative, leading her to feel increasingly anxious and depressed. She begins to isolate herself, spending hours writing and reading about climate disasters, which heightens her eco-anxiety instead of alleviating it. Avoidance, a critical feature of anxiety disorders, frequently becomes excessive as the flight response reinforces future avoidance. For instance, an individual with social anxiety may avoid social situations due to fear of embarrassment or judgment. If avoidance successfully prevents uncomfortable feelings in these situations, it reinforces the belief that avoidance is an effective coping strategy, leading to increased avoidance behavior in the future (Afifi et al., 2012; Gifford, 2011; Jones & Davison, 2021).

Anxious responses also impact young people's behavior. This influence is particularly relevant for engaging in pro-environmental actions, which are ultimately necessary for adapting to and mitigating the climate and environmental crises. These actions begin with a personal choice to contribute to the protection and preservation of the environment. The relationship between eco-anxiety and pro-environmental behavior is complex, with some studies showing increases in eco-anxiety with more pro-environmental behavior and others showing decreases. An increase in eco-anxiety does not inherently lead to increased pro-environmental behavioral. Pro-environmental intention is likely with more exposure to information about climate change risks. But given that stress is defined as any stimulus that demands more than we can comfortably give, exposure to more risk information than a person can handle can also reinforce climate skepticism. People generally tend to avoid engagement with threats over which they feel they have no control, a behavior that is influenced by the BIS. In this way, defeatist messaging about climate change perils may reinforce inaction or avoidance in some by enhancing BIS signaling (Kapeller & Jäger, 2020; Venhoeven et al., 2013). Some refer to this phenomenon as **ecoparalysis** – the inability to act due to a perception that the problem is too big to address (Albrecht, 2011).

Most young people are more stressed by threats where the risks are vague or ambiguous. Just as negative messaging can tilt the balance towards the BIS, appropriately positive messaging can increase BAS activation, promoting resilience against excessive worry and encouraging solution-seeking. Clinical experience shows that behavioral activation can be enhanced through community environmental action, which allows our brain's risk assessment tools to accurately consider the planet's many protective factors, including environmentalists, activists, and other helpers. Social learning of this kind can introduce us to new ways to live sustainably and help us identify ways that individuals and communities can manage climate adversity (Peris & Galván, 2021).

Building Resilience in a Young Brain

When we study the brains of anxious young people, we find that increased attention to threats increases anxious thoughts (Perino et al., 2021). Anxious youth devote more brainpower to worrying about threats, reducing their ability to attend to other information. We can train young people to focus more on nonthreatening stimuli through talk therapy or self-soothing. By focusing on specific goals, affirmations, character strengths, or positive visualizations, young people can reduce their innate overassessment of risk (Perino et al., 2021).

One important area of brain functioning is called cognitive control – the brain's ability to flexibly change its thoughts and behaviors, resist automatic urges, tolerate fear responses from systems such as the BIS, and move on to other thoughts and behaviors that might be more productive (Fitzgerald et al., 2021). Healthy development involves acquiring and training these cognitive control skills, which are often underdeveloped in people diagnosed with anxiety disorders, and a growing body of research suggests that talk therapy and/or medications may improve this functioning (Fitzgerald et al., 2021). There are also experimental approaches requiring further study, such as using specialized videogames to train cognitive control. Youth experiencing climate-related anxiety (even if it does not reach the level of an anxiety disorder), might benefit from these therapies.

As mentioned earlier, young brains are more "neuroplastic," or adaptable, than mature brains. The ability to rapidly restructure the brain might partially explain why anxiety and anxiety disorders peak during adolescence. Stresses or challenges during this important development period can have an outsized impact on how an individual perceives and responds to threats throughout their life (Gerhard et al., 2021). Because the brains of young people are particularly adaptable, they might also be more receptive to interventions which "rewire" the brain to reduce anxiety. Research using functional brain imaging shows a significant ability to modify the BIS, BAS, and other anxiety-related brain circuits using these therapies (Fitzgerald et al., 2021). In this way, young people have additional vulnerability to climate-related anxiety, but also benefit from a greater potential for recovery.

Cognitive and Emotional Factors That Modulate the Climate Stress Response

Anxiety affects not only cognitive control but also young peoples' views of self and the ways they hear and see the world. Children and adolescents with anxiety disorders have been found to have less development of the **Default Mode Network**, an important brain circuit involved in self-esteem, identity, and future planning (Dulcan, 2021). This circuit, which involves the PFC and PCC, is perhaps unsurprisingly tied closely to the behavioral approach circuits. This network likely plays a role in shaping a young person's inner narratives about their personal values, environmental beliefs, and long-term goals in the context of climate change.

Similarly, the **Salience Network**, which filters out background noise and brings crucial information to our attention, is found to have altered activity in young people with anxiety disorders. This network, which uses adrenaline, stress hormones, and acetylcholine to signal, connects the amygdala, ACC, PFC, and other brain regions. This network likely plays a role in a young person's understanding of the significance of climate change to them individually. It may contribute to recognizing environmental

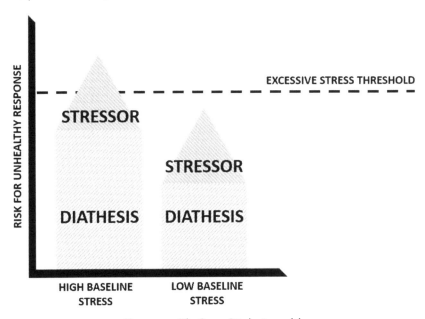

Figure 5.2 The Stress-Diathesis model.

threats, prioritizing climate-related goals, and finding motivation to take action to mitigate climate change.

These characteristics of young people with anxiety disorders mean that some youth literally see the world differently, as well as their place within it, and may partially explain why some young people are more vulnerable to climate-related stress and anxiety. Even individuals exposed to the same stressor may have different outcomes based on their medical history, socioeconomic factors, and other risk factors. This relationship between stressful experiences, personal and genetic factors, and total stress outcomes is described in the **Stress-Diathesis model** (Figure 5.2). This model suggests that individuals have varying levels of vulnerability (diathesis) to stress-related outcomes and are more likely to exceed the threshold of stress they can manage comfortably. In the context of climate change, this model implies that some people may be more susceptible to experiencing negative psychological effects due to climate-related stressors, such as increased anxiety or depression (Berry et al., 2010; Schneiderman et al., 2005).

The importance of this model is reflected in changes to the diagnostic manual that mental health professionals use, which now considers both exposure and the subjective response to the exposure to be important for the outcomes of traumatic experiences (APA, 2022; Canino et al., 1990; Neria et al., 2007). Other potential risk factors for anxiety disorders include a family history of anxiety disorder, adverse childhood events, exposure to high stress at a young age, or a natural attention bias towards threat-related stimuli, which can be detected through specialized testing (Amstadter et al., 2010; Dulcan, 2021; Yook et al., 2010). Youth who experience natural disasters before age five are at increased risk for anxiety disorders, and we know from studies of trauma and adverse childhood events that earlier exposure confers a higher level of risk (Maclean et al., 2016). Finally, while anxiety disorders per se have not been shown to vary with temperature or air pollution, these climatic exposures do correlate with more negative affect, which is likely to contribute to climate distress (Wang et al., 2020).

Applying Neurobiological Insights to Help Youth Navigate Climate Distress

There are a number of neurobiological considerations that can inform how we think about and support young people who are increasingly understandably anxious about the world they are set to inherit. As increasing natural disasters increase in frequency and severity, we can expect rates of anxiety and anxiety disorders to increase across the population. The extent of this increase will depend on how much young people's stress response systems are overactivated, impairing their hormonal systems, cognitive abilities, and the ability to regulate the fear response. Youth with anxiety disorders – or who are more vulnerable to anxiety disorders by virtue of overattending to risks and feared situations – experience more exaggerated physiological responses to threats and therefore will be particularly vulnerable. Training all children in threat management strategies will be helpful, with particular attention to those more at risk. Such training may include tools to reduce physiological hyperarousal when anxious, to decrease exposure to triggers to anxiety, and to retain cognitive control and focus under high-threat situations such as natural disasters.

As behavioral health services are often overwhelmed following disasters, this preparation might involve training primary care providers to carry out psychiatric triage following disasters or enhancing community resilience through future-oriented coping or adaptive behaviors classes for groups (Bassilios et al., 2012; Climate Change's Toll on Mental Health, 2017; Karlsson, 2011). Whether post-disaster or in the course of routine outpatient follow up, environmentally competent behavioral health professionals can assist young people in understanding and expressing their emotional responses to climate change through active listening and validating concerns.

If you work with or are a parent to young people, you can discuss what they are hearing about climate change and provide factual, nonalarmist information appropriate to their age and developmental level. If a youth is consuming excessive media about climate change, you can work with them to set appropriate boundaries surrounding news consumption. You can empower young people to transition from behavioral inhibition to behavioral activation by encouraging solutions-minded thinking, encouraging pursuit of personal goals, and avoiding hopelessness or defeatism (Kapeller & Jäger, 2020; Venhoeven et al., 2013). Evaluate their beliefs about their ability to enact positive change in their local environment and help connect them with groups or individuals who are taking action to restore and greenify their communities. Given that developing and maintaining social networks protects against impairing levels of trauma and anxiety, social interaction should be highly encouraged (APA, 2022; Weintrobe, 2021).

Community leaders can help prepare their residents to take regionally appropriate preparedness measures based on geographic risks (e.g., sea rise, disasters, heat etc.), help community members register for evacuation, or encourage the preparation of "Go Bags" with essential supplies (Watts et al., 2021). Physicians and members of healthcare teams can connect patients with disaster readiness resources and supplies, which is an evidence-based approach to improve outcomes for children and adolescents (Lazarov & Bar-Haim, 2021). While individual clinics and healthcare facilities can take steps to prepare for acute post-disaster surges, enhanced utilization of services may occur for over a year, often requiring broader support and funding from the government (Adebäck et al., 2018; Hrabok et al., 2020; Spittlehouse et al., 2014). Increased funding for mental healthcare will be essential at both the national and international levels. Involving everyone, including children and traditionally underrepresented populations, in efforts to address climate change and promote climate justice holds the potential for significant mental health benefits. By including diverse perspectives, voices, and experiences, we can foster a sense of empowerment, agency, and belonging among individuals who have often been marginalized. Directly engaging children equips them with the knowledge, skills, and motivation to become informed advocates for the planet's well-being and for their own mental health. By centering the voices of underrepresented communities, we acknowledge and address the disproportionate impacts of climate change on their psychological health. Together, we can create a more inclusive, equitable, and resilient society, where climate action and mental health advocacy go hand in hand for a sustainable and healthier future for all.

References

Adebäck, P., Schulman, A., & Nilsson, D. (2018). Children exposed to a natural disaster: Psychological consequences eight years after 2004 tsunami. *Nordic Journal of Psychiatry*, 72(1), 75–81. https://doi.org/10.1080/08039488.2017.1382569.

Afifi, W. A., Felix, E. D., & Afifi, T. D. (2012). The impact of uncertainty and communal coping on mental health following natural disasters. *Anxiety Stress and Coping*, 25(3), 329–347. https://doi.org/10.1080/10615806.2011.603048.

Agyapong, V. I. O., Hrabok, M., Juhás, M., Omeje, J., Denga, E., Nwaka, B., ... Li, X. (2018). Prevalence rates and predictors of Generalized Anxiety Disorder symptoms in residents of Fort McMurray six months after a wildfire. *Frontiers in Psychiatry*, 9. https://doi.org/10.3389/fpsyt.2018.00345

Albrecht, G. (2011). Chronic environmental change: Emerging "psychoterratic" syndromes. In *International and cultural psychology series* (pp. 43–56). Springer Nature. https://doi.org/10.1007/978-1-4419-9742-5_3

American Psychiatric Association (2022). *Diagnostic and statistical manual of mental disorders* (5th ed., text rev.). https://doi.org/10.1176/appi.books.9780890425787

Amstadter, A. B., Koenen, K. C., Ruggiero, K. J., Acierno, R., Galea, M. D., Kilpatrick, D. G., & Gelernter, J. (2010). NPY moderates the relation between hurricane exposure and generalized anxiety disorder in an epidemiologic sample of hurricane-exposed adults. *Depression and Anxiety*, 27(3), 270–275. https://doi.org/10.1002/da.20648

Bassilios, B., Reifels, L., & Pirkis, J. (2012). Enhanced primary mental health services in response to disaster. *Psychiatric Services*, 63(9), 868–874. https://doi.org/10.1176/appi.ps.201100534.

Berry, H. L., Bowen, K., & Kjellstrom, T. (2010). Climate change and mental health: A causal pathways framework. *International Journal of Public Health*, 55(2), 123–132. https://doi.org/10.1007/s00038-009-0112-0

Canino, G. J., Bravo, M., Rubio-Stipec, M., & Woodbury, M. (1990). The impact of disaster on mental health: Prospective and retrospective analyses. *International Journal of Mental Health*, 19(1), 51–69. https://doi.org/10.1080/00207411.1990.11449153

Centers for Disease Control and Prevention (n.d.). *Climate change and infectious diseases*. www.cdc.gov/ncezid/what-we-do/climate-change-and-infectious-diseases/index.html

Clayton, S. (2020a). Climate anxiety: Psychological responses to climate change. *Journal of Anxiety Disorders*, 74, 102263. https://doi.org/10.1016/j.janxdis.2020.102263

Clayton, S. (2020b). The insidious impacts of climate change: Mood, mental health, and psychosocial well-being. *One Earth*, 2(6), 530–531. https://doi.org/10.1016/j.oneear.2020.05.019

Climate Change's Toll on Mental Health (2017). www.apa.org, Press release, March 29. www.apa.org/news/press/releases/2017/03/climate-mental-health

Conrad, C. D. (2011). *The handbook of stress: Neuropsychological effects on the brain*. John Wiley &Sons.

Dulcan, M. K. (2021). *Dulcan's textbook of child and adolescent psychiatry* (3rd ed.). AmericanPsychiatric Pub.

Fitzgerald, K. D., Schroder, H. S., & Marsh, R. (2021). Cognitive control in pediatric obsessive-compulsive and anxiety disorders: Brain-behavioral targets for early intervention. *Biological Psychiatry*, 89(7), 697–706. https://doi.org/10.1016/j.biopsych.2020.11.012

Freud, S. (1919). The "Uncanny." In *The complete psychological works* (Vol. XVII, pp. 217–56). Hogarth Press, 1955.

Gerhard, D. M., Meyer, H. C., & Lee, F. S. (2021). An adolescent sensitive period for threat responding: Impacts of stress and sex. *Biological Psychiatry*, 89(7), 651–658. https://doi.org/10.1016/j.biopsych.2020.10.003

Gifford, R. (2011). The dragons of inaction: Psychological barriers that limit climate change mitigation and adaptation. *American Psychologist*, 66(4): 290–302. https://doi.org/10.1037/a0023566

Gruber, J. (2009). Introduction, in J. Gruber (Ed.), *Risky behavior among youths: An economic analysis* (pp. 5–12). University of Chicago Press.

Hammack S. E., Todd, T. P., Kocho-Schellenberg, M., & Bouton, M. E. (2015). Role of the bed nucleus of the stria terminalis in the acquisition of contextual fear at long or short context-shock intervals. *Behavioral Neuroscience*, 129(5), 673–678. doi: 10.1037/bne0000088

Hrabok, M., Delorme, A., & Agyapong, V. I. (2020). Threats to mental health and well-being associated with climate change. *Journal of Anxiety Disorders*, 76, 102295. https://doi.org/10.1016/j.janxdis.2020.102295

Jones, C. A., & Davison, A. (2021). Disempowering emotions: The role of educational experiences in social responses to climate change. *Geoforum*, 118, 190–200. https://doi.org/10.1016/j.geoforum.2020.11.006.

Kapeller, M. L., & Jäger, G. (2020). Threat and anxiety in the climate debate: An agent-based model to investigate climate scepticism and pro-environmental behavior. *Sustainability*, 12(5), 1823. https://doi.org/10.3390/su12051823

Karlsson, L. (2011). *Vermont climate change health effects adaptation [White paper]*. Vermont Department of Health. https://anr.vermont.gov/sites/anr/files/specialtopics/climate/documents/VTCCwhitepapers/VTCCAdaptHealthEffects%20.pdf

Kenwood, M. M., & Kalin, N. H. (2021). Nonhuman primate models to explore mechanisms underlying early-life temperamental anxiety. *Biological Psychiatry*, 89(7), 659–671. https://doi.org/10.1016/j.biopsych.2020.08.028

Lazarov, A., & Bar-Haim, Y. (2021). Emerging domain-based treatments for pediatric anxiety disorders. *Biological Psychiatry*, 89(7), 716–725. https://doi.org/10.1016/j.biopsych.2020.08.030

Maclean, J. C., Popovici, I., & French, M. T. (2016). Are natural disasters in early childhood associated with mental health and substance use disorders as an adult? *Social Science & Medicine*, 151, 78–91. https://doi.org/10.1016/j.socscimed.2016.01.006.

Madakasira, S. & O'Brien, K.F. (1987). Post-traumatic stress disorder following disasters: A systematic review. *Journal of Nervous and Mental Disease*, 175, 286–290. https://doi.org/10.1097/00005053-198705000-00008

Mobbs, D., Hagan, C. C., Dalgleish, T., Silston, B., & Pravost, C. (2015). The ecology of human fear: Survival optimization and the nervous system. *Frontiers in Neuroscience*, 9. https://doi.org/10.3389/fnins.2015.00055

Namkung, H., Kim, S., & Sawa, A. (2018). The insula: An underestimated brain area in clinical neuroscience, psychiatry, and neurology. *Trends in Neurosciences*, 41(8), 551–554. https://doi.org/10.1016/j.tins.2018.05.004

Neria, Y., Nandi, A., & Galea, S. (2007). Post-traumatic stress disorder following disasters: A systematic review. *Psychological Medicine*, 38(4), 467–480. https://doi.org/10.1017/s0033291707001353

Nooner, K. B., Mennes, M., Brown, S., Castellanos, F. X., Leventhal, B., Milham, M. P., & Colcombe, S. J. (2013). Relationship of trauma symptoms to amygdala-based functional brain changes in adolescents. *Journal of Traumatic Stress*, 26(6), 784–787. https://doi.org/10.1002/jts.21873

Perino, M. T., Yu, Q., Myers, M. J., Harper, J. C., Baumel, W. T., Petersen, S. E., … Sylvester, C. M. (2021). Attention alterations in pediatric anxiety: Evidence from behavior and neuroimaging. *Biological Psychiatry*, 89(7), 726–734. https://doi.org/10.1016/j.biopsych.2020.07.016

Peris, T. S., & Galván, A. (2021). Brain and behavior correlates of risk taking in pediatric anxiety disorders. *Biological Psychiatry*, 89(7), 707–715. https://doi.org/10.1016/j.biopsych.2020.11.003

Schneiderman, N., Ironson, G., & Siegel, S. D. (2005). Stress and health: Psychological, behavioral, and biological determinants. *Annual Review of Clinical Psychology*, 1(1), 607–628. https://doi.org/10.1146/annurev.clinpsy.1.102803.144141

Spittlehouse, J. K., Joyce, P. R., Vierck, E., Schluter, P. J., & Pearson, J. F. (2014). Ongoing adverse mental health impact of the earthquake sequence in Christchurch, New Zealand. *Australian and New Zealand Journal of Psychiatry*, 48(8), 756–763. https://doi.org/10.1177/0004867414527522.

Stanley, S. K., Hogg, T. L., Leviston, Z., & Walker, I. S. (2021). From anger to action: Differential impacts of eco-anxiety, eco-depression, and eco-anger on climate action and wellbeing. *Journal of Climate Change and Health*, 1, 100003. https://doi.org/10.1016/j.joclim.2021.100003

Stewart, A. E. (2021). Psychometric properties of the climate change worry scale. *International Journal of Environmental Research and Public Health*, 18, 494. doi: 10.3390/ijerph18020494

Sullivan, R. M., & Opendak, M. (2021). Neurobiology of infant fear and anxiety: Impacts of delayed amygdala development and attachment figure quality. *Biological Psychiatry*, 89(7), 641–650. https://doi.org/10.1016/j.biopsych.2020.08.020

Venhoeven, L. A., Bolderdijk, J. W., & Steg, L. (2013). Explaining the paradox: How pro-environmental behaviour can both thwart and foster well-being. *Sustainability*, 5(4), 1372–1386. https://doi.org/10.3390/su5041372

Verplanken, B., & Roy, D. (2013). "My worries are rational, climate change is not": Habitual ecological worrying is an adaptive response. *PLoS One*, 8(9), e74708. https://doi.org/10.1371/journal.pone.0074708.

Wang, J., Obradovich, N., & Zheng, S. (2020). A 43-million-person investigation into weather and expressed sentiment in a changing climate. *One Earth*, 2(6), 568–577. https://doi.org/10.1016/j.oneear.2020.05.016

Watts, N., Amann, M., Arnell, N. W., Ayeb-Karlsson, S., Beagley, J., Belesova, K., … Costello, A. J. (2021). The 2020 report of The Lancet countdown on health and climate change: Responding to converging crises. *The Lancet*, 397(10269), 129–170. https://doi.org/10.1016/s0140-6736(20)32290-x

Weintrobe, S. (2021). *Psychological roots of the climate crisis: Neoliberal exceptionalism and the culture of uncare.* Bloomsbury Academic.

Wu, J. Z., Snell, G., & Samji, H. (2020). Climate anxiety in young people: A call to action. *The Lancet Planetary Health*, 4(10), E435–36. https://doi.org/10.1016/S2542-5196(20)30223-0

Yook, K., Kim, K. H., Suh, S. Y., & Lee, K. (2010). Intolerance of uncertainty, worry, and rumination in major depressive disorder and generalized anxiety disorder. *Journal of Anxiety Disorders*, 24(6), 623–628. https://doi.org/10.1016/j.janxdis.2010.04.003

CHAPTER 6

Psychoanalytic and Relational Perspectives on Youth Climate Distress

Archana Varma Caballero and Janet L. Lewis

Introduction

Psychoanalytic theory, which originated from the work of Sigmund Freud (1888), highlights key developmental stages in childhood and unconscious mental content and processes that are powerful drivers in our lives. As such, psychoanalytic theory traditionally examined the dynamics of one's internal conflicts, not sociopolitical dilemmas such as climate change. Despite this history, psychoanalytic thought offers valuable insights into the climate crisis.

Young people today face not only a storm of their own intense conscious and unconscious feelings and impulses, but also catastrophic circumstances including climate change that can impede daily living. As we will emphasize throughout this chapter, we adults need to understand and face our own distress – put on our own oxygen masks first – to help young people bear their distress and face their circumstances.

Psychoanalytic Perspectives on the Ongoing Ecological Crisis: Understanding "Disavowal" in Our Failure to Appreciate and Act on Environmental Loss

To be in the best position to help ourselves and young people, we can look through a psychoanalytic lens to understand the role of the unconscious in perpetuating the climate crisis. While ambivalence or mixed feelings about acknowledging climate change is normal and universal (Lertzmann, 2012), the unconscious defense mechanism of disavowal can leave us feeling paralyzed, with diminished power to affect change. Disavowal is simultaneous knowing and not-knowing of painful realities, where the mind unconsciously avoids processing the magnitude of its grief and terror (Weintrobe, 2013). Disavowal leads us to accept our participation in climate change on a detached, intellectual level without feeling or acting proportionally to the magnitude of its implications. The following anecdote illustrates climate-related ambivalence and disavowal at work.

Jill rewards herself for a difficult work year by booking a much-anticipated safari. She longs for a change of scenery from her monotonous desk job and longs to see wild animals up close. Her friends think the trip is a wonderful idea. After such a hard year, Jill feels entitled to this dream vacation and doesn't want to give any thought to the long airplane flight and its destructive environmental impact. When Jill reaches her destination, she sees the airport runway cut through the savannah and feels the uncomfortable onset of a tension headache. Jill is ambivalent about her responsibilities to the environment. On the one hand, she feels nature is precious; on the other hand, she doesn't want to see herself as destructive in her own impact on the environment. The full extent of her conflicting feelings is disavowed, not fully conscious, giving her a vague feeling of tension and anxiety that she can't place.

Like Jill, we all have various levels of ambivalence and disavowal regarding climate change. From a psychoanalytic perspective, we will discuss various sources of disavowal of climate change including: (1) the unconscious effects of societal pressures, (2) our incomplete mourning of losses, (3) our minds' tendencies to regress to immature defense mechanisms in order to avoid anxiety, and (4) the challenge of processing environmental betrayal.

Unconscious Effects of Societal Pressures
Social patterns can have a hypnotic effect on us, termed *the consensus trance* (Tart, 1986) or *automaton conformity* (Fromm, 1941), whereby we collectively turn away from the harrowing realities in front of us. We unconsciously follow the crowd to bury our heads in the sand, or are distracted by propaganda or marketing pressuring us to ignore our intuition that something is wrong. This social-psychological process has been described in relation to numerous atrocities. Unconscious responses to such societal pressures contribute to seemingly widespread apathy towards the environmental crisis. Underneath paralysis and disavowal, we have more complicated feelings as we will describe later.

Unprocessed Grief
The extent of the losses facing us due to climate change are emotionally overwhelming, so we feel intimidated by the prospect of processing them (Lertzmann, 2012). Rosemary Randall (2009) sums up the tasks of grieving climate change, building on the work of Worden's (1983) *Grief Counseling and Grief Therapy* (Table 6.1). All of these tasks of grief and their pitfalls

Table 6.1 *Tasks of grief*

Tasks of grief	Maladaptive responses
Accepting the reality of loss, first cognitively, then emotionally	Denial of the: -facts of the loss -meaning of the loss -irreversibility of the loss
Working through the painful emotions of grief (despair, fear, guilt, anger, shame, sadness, yearning, disorganization)	Shutting off all emotion, idealizing what is lost, bargaining, numbing the pain through alcohol, drugs, or manic activity
Adjusting to the new environment/ acquiring new skills/developing a new sense of self	Not adapting, becoming helpless, bitter, angry, depressed, withdrawing
Reinvesting emotional energy	Refusing to love, turning away from life

are relevant to both losses of our natural environment and losses created by accompanying social disruptions and tragedies.

From a psychoanalytic perspective, to process grief we need adequate "containment" – supportive others whom we can rely on to tolerate our difficult emotions and facilitate our abilities to think during anxiety-provoking moments (Bion, 1962). The mother provides containment to her wailing baby when she takes in the baby's distress, does not flood the baby with her own reactive anxiety, and interacts with the baby in a co-created soothing "conversation" (verbal and nonverbal; conscious and unconscious). Containment paves the way for us to bear what is difficult to bear.

Grieving the natural world is complicated. Our complicity in this catastrophic environmental loss complicates our grief, and due to climate destruction, the soothing backdrop of the natural world is less available to help us process our grief (Saint Amour, 2020). Even this complicated reality can nonetheless be processed when, as per the tasks of grief in Table 6.1, we accept the situation's painful implications and undertake the necessary work with others to develop a new sense of ourselves. This new sense of ourselves, consistent with both the losses and the positive aspects of our potential futures, will allow us to reinvest our energy into our changing world.

Regression to Immature Defenses
Yet another way to explain our perpetuation of the climate crisis despite its destructive impact on us is our psychological regression to infantile defenses. In infancy, unconscious conflicts begin between love and hate, dependence and envy; from a psychoanalytic point of view, we are ravenous for mother's care, entirely at her mercy, and cannot tolerate that she

has separate needs of her own. Unable to fathom mother's separateness, we behave as though she continues to function as a womb, existing only for our sustenance. We similarly treat the natural world as a "breast and toilet mother" (Keene, 2012), there only to satisfy our needs for food and waste disposal. This is a psychologically regressed position, in which, like an infant, we lack the ability to curb our impulses for gratification or consider Mother Earth's separate needs. This regression arises for multiple reasons. We are anxious and conflicted about our dependence on the Earth. Additionally, the unconscious deprivation we feel from living in an unstable and detached society creates in us an unconscious desire for limitless supplies from the Earth, as if this could compensate for other nurturance we lack (Weintrobe, 2013).

As psychoanalyst Melanie Klein (1946) described, the infant experiences ravenous hunger and dependent feelings when separated from the nurturing womb. In this "paranoid-schizoid" state, the infant uses "splitting" and "projection" to make sense of its reality. In its mind, the infant separates itself and others into all-good (loving, "good breast") and all-bad (persecuting, "bad breast") parts, and attributes or "projects" intolerable parts of itself, its own fear or rage, onto the mother or caregiver. Those who maintain extreme positions on climate change might also employ splitting and projection by denying their own feelings of inadequacy and guilt and projecting them onto another group of either climate change deniers, or climate change activists (see Table 6.2).

To cope with fears, the infant also makes use of what Klein refers to as the manic defense (Klein, 1940). Manic defenses are overinflated and grandiose ways of thinking and behaving that keep our helpless, sad, and guilty feelings at bay. We unconsciously resist awareness of feeling small by instead feeling triumphant and powerful. Manic defenses underlie our determination to continue charging forward with our current socioeconomic systems while ignoring the dangers to humanity and the environment, as though we will not be harmed by our own systems and behavior (see Table 6.2).

We can learn from the more mature "depressive position," which Klein theorized that the infant develops in the middle of the first year of life when it begins to understand that the mother is a separate person. The infant begins to feel sadness about its mother's separateness, and guilt about its rage towards its mother. Like infants, we all vacillate in and out of the depressive and the paranoid-schizoid positions, and anxiety-provoking situations may cause us to regress to the paranoid-schizoid position. While we avoid sadness and mourning by avoiding the depressive position, being able

Table 6.2 *Immature defenses as they relate to climate change*

Type of defense	Dialogue revealing such defense at work
Manic defense Denying vulnerability and guilt, feeling omnipotent instead	"We don't need to be concerned about climate change. Humans in the future will come up with some kind of technology to save us. We might even find a way to live on the moon."
Splitting and projection Injecting parts of ourselves that feel helpless and incompetent into others and denying them in ourselves	"Those propagandists talking about climate change are uninformed and wasting their breath."

to move to the depressive position and process our grief can then lead to new skills, a new sense of self, and the ability to invest in a reality-based life. For the purposes of this chapter, we invite you to consider the depressive position as a "depressive-accepting" position: accepting the realistic limits of our natural world and our relationships, and mourning our part in damaging them while productively engaging with these imperfect figures.

The Challenge of Processing Environmental Betrayal

Another factor contributing to our collective disavowal of the climate crisis is difficulty processing betrayal, or painful relational trauma. The psychoanalytic concept of trauma is specifically concerned with serious threats to significant attachments (Szajnberg, 2022). Young people in particular describe climate-related feelings of betrayal. A landmark study by Hickman and colleagues (2021), which surveyed the climate emotions of 10,000 young people, highlighted the prominence of their experiences of betrayal, specifically by governments (58.5 percent), undergirded by other beliefs such as: "People have failed to take care of the planet" (82.6 percent) and "The future is frightening" (75.5 percent). Young people not only feel betrayed by the government but also by older adults (Jones & Davison, 2021).

Climate-related emotions such as anxiety and grief are not as intimately experienced as betrayal. A 16-year-old quoted by Hickman (2019) said: "I think it's different for young people. For us the destruction of the planet is personal." A personal experience of betrayal is intensely experienced within a particular relationship or set of relationships; suddenly, abstract ideas about climate change morph into tangible, deep feelings. With betrayal one can feel "torn apart," losing a feeling of being "mutually carried" by those on whom one depends (Bach, 2018, p. 561).

The seriousness of a betrayal is determined by "an interaction between the significance and depth of the trusting bond" on the one hand, and "the magnitude of the harm caused" on the other (Rachman, 2010, p. 305). By this calculation, the betrayal involving climate change is of a stunning magnitude for young people in their relationship with their societies and adults. For all of us, the betrayal is also exceedingly stark as we all feel disappointed and unprotected by ourselves, our leaders, and the Earth.

*A Psychoanalytic Developmental Perspective:
Understanding the Psychological and Social Tasks of
Young People Relative to Climate Change*

Particular Developmental Stages and Climate Change
Thinking about climate change psychoanalytically requires us to think not only about what goes on within individuals' minds, but also about how those minds interact with larger social and environmental circumstances. Many psychoanalytic theorists (Horney, Adler, and those in relational and feminist traditions) take social and historical circumstances into account. We focus here on the work of Erik Erikson, which we find particularly accessible and useful for thinking about life stages; however, while Erikson's writing indicates deep reflection on issues of culture, race, ethnicity, and historical trauma (Syed & Fish, 2018), the universal applicability of any developmental framework across cultures is open to further investigation. Erikson developed a theory of psychosocial development that outlined stages from infancy through old age, describing the mental, social, and functional tasks of each stage. Each stage involves a "crisis," or the need to grapple with and master a particular psychosocial experience. Developmentally, it is common and appropriate that all these developmental tasks are revisited later in life, requiring or allowing for improved mastery of a particular stage. Table 6.3 describes the Eriksonian stages and our proposed implications of climate change within each stage.

The Particular Importance of the First Developmental Stage
The first of these crises in infancy, trust versus mistrust, is particularly relevant to climate change. Feelings of climate betrayal re-evoke this core tension of trust/mistrust, returning both young people and adults to the infantile topics of fear and hope (and the Kleinian paranoid-schizoid and depressive positions). When greater resilience is achieved at this level, it strengthens our potential for the entire stairway of development, supporting our abilities for effective functioning within the world.

Table 6.3 Eriksonian developmental stages of young people, their resultant virtues, and the implications of climate change (Erikson, 1950; Erikson, 1968; Newman & Newman, 2001)

Conflict or crisis	Age at negotiation	Virtues or vital strengths from sufficient mastery	Implications of the psychosocial stressor of climate change
Basic trust/ Mistrust	Infancy	Hope	For infants, climate-caused trauma can disrupt the reliable caretaking that they need to negotiate the stage. Revisiting the stage – occurs when climate-related betrayal is experienced or when one notices one's own naivete about the climate crisis. Basic questions arise as to what is trustworthy and where we can find meaning. Hope can be restored by the exercise of reasonable hope, radical hope, and meaning-focused coping, all best facilitated by socially supportive environments. Hope, and sufficient trust in oneself and others, is required for negotiation of all subsequent stages.
Autonomy/ Shame and doubt	Toddlerhood	Will	For toddlers, climate-caused trauma can disrupt caretakers' abilities to moderate sources of frustration and support opportunities for autonomy. Revisiting the stage – occurs as we face needing to act in new, unfamiliar ways in response to climate challenges. We have to choose new, radical and imperfect ways to live and adapt and tolerate our shame and doubt about these choices. A sense of will is reclaimed as we negotiate these choices.
Initiative/ Guilt	Preschool	Purpose	For preschoolers, climate-caused environmental traumas can interfere with caregivers' abilities to support initiative and the appropriate regulation of guilt. The child may experience excess personal guilt inappropriately for environmental problems, losses, and traumas. Revisiting the stage – occurs as we grapple with climate guilt. We can reclaim purpose by allowing ourselves to experience the new hope available within our new responsibilities and the pleasure and agency involved in confronting problems.
Industry/ Inferiority	School age	Competence	For school age children, caregivers' and teachers' climate anxiety or demoralization can interfere with promoting a realistic appreciation for work and persistence within the child. Revisiting the stage – occurs as we struggle to maintain faith in our skills to navigate the environmental crisis. A sense of competence is reclaimed as we savor the pleasure arising from diligence in our work and collaboration with others.

Table 6.3 (*cont.*)

Conflict or crisis	Age at negotiation	Virtues or vital strengths from sufficient mastery	Implications of the psychosocial stressor of climate change
Group identity/ Alienation [Stage added by Barbara Newman and Phillip Newman (2001)]	Early teens	Affiliation	For the early adolescent, traumatic climate disruptions can interfere with group affiliations. Additionally, the necessary experience of being able to be loyal to a group can be compromised by a lack of shared attitudes toward the environmental crisis, leading to a sense of personal social inadequacy. Revisiting the stage – occurs as we feel alienated in familiar groups not sharing our level of climate concern or engagement. We reclaim our sense of affiliation when we consciously search for those who share our values and interests, savor the sense of "we" that exists, and do our part in maintaining the group.
Identity/ Role diffusion	Adolescence	Fidelity	For the adolescent, climate-caused environmental trauma and society's climate inaction can thwart the young person's developmental search for a clear ideological outlook and plans for an adult future, interfering with a sense of identity and capacity to be faithful to values. Revisiting the stage – occurs when we feel apathetic or cynical. A sense of core identity and fidelity to values is reclaimed when we reassert social values as a matter of identity or discover new sustainable ways of acting based on those core personal values.
Intimacy/ Isolation	Young adulthood	Love	For the young adult, the overwhelm of social crises can result in avoidance of contact with people and activities that require commitment, thwarting the essential functions of love and work. A sense of betrayal by adults can lead to cynicism about adult roles. Revisiting the stage – occurs as we isolate from reality, as it becomes clear that being in an intimate relationship with anyone or anything in this world now requires fresh commitments to protect them and it. We reclaim our capacity for love when we take these necessary new commitments seriously. In our capacity for intimacy with nature, revisiting this stage occurs when we notice we have lost track of the impact of our actions on the beings with whom we cohabit the planet and must now take them seriously, claiming new professional and personal identities.

Interactions of Climate Concerns with Other Developmental Issues

Young people need and want optimal containment and safety during key developmental periods, both from the familial homebase and from peer groups and institutions. However, in confronting climate change, they must instead deal with many external instabilities and even traumas, in addition to living through their own inevitable developmental instability. *With climate change, they are experiencing developmental instability within environmental/social instability, and at times even developmental trauma within social or environmental trauma.* Their reactions to these instabilities can vary but may include feeling a sense of betrayal (Hickman et al., 2021) and taking self-destructive action (Bodnar, 2008). Importantly, this climate distress may coexist with other mood and developmental issues, as illustrated by the following vignette.

> Zeke is a 19-year-old Hispanic American college student with chronic depression and anxiety. He experienced relational trauma in his childhood when his father had a string of affairs and his mother placed him in the middle of explosive marital arguments. Experiencing this upheaval from the ages of 8–12, when children are highly motivated by external approval (corresponding to the Eriksonian stage of industry vs inferiority), Zeke grew desperate to please his parents. He excelled in school and hid his angry feelings from others. Zeke is now trying to make sense of the role he wants to play in the adult world, which he feels is cold and bleak. He feels demoralized living in an unstable society in which climate change goes largely unchecked and he lacks motivation for occupational success and community engagement. His early experience of not feeling cared for by his parents is magnified and re-experienced now due to the climate crisis, as he feels his needs have not been kept in mind by older generations who were focused on their own gratification. Zeke's unresolved and reactivated childhood feelings of powerlessness keep him from progressing developmentally and "launching" forward.

Climate change, and the inadequate societal response thus far, can evoke for any of us the terrifying feeling of there being "no parents home" keeping our needs in mind (Haseley, 2019). Possibly worse could be a feeling that the parents *are* home but are destructive and self-absorbed; as with Zeke, youth who feel their parents were too self-involved may be particularly sensitive to our collective neglect of the natural world. Their concern for climate change must be recognized as legitimate in its own right, while we can also understand the relational triggers that may intensify their reactions to climate change.

Recommendations

Important psychoanalytic principles to keep in mind when helping young people are healthy attachment, the maintenance of a secure sense of self, and the process and functions of containment. These recommendations can also help adults appreciate and work with our own vulnerable feelings evoked by climate change. At any age, we unconsciously hold inside younger parts of ourselves that remember feeling small and powerless.

Promote Healthy Attachment to the Natural World

Promoting healthy attachment to the natural world is one way to help children with climate distress. As we develop, we internalize how healthy or unhealthy our important relationships are and keep these experiences alive in our minds. Like our relationships with parents or siblings, the natural, or more-than-human, world, is an important "figure" in our development, and it remains so, unconsciously if not consciously (Bodnar, 2008). Young children feel quite connected to the natural world. The childhood landscape is rich with images and books depicting mischievous and sweet animals to whom we feel a deep connection. "For instance, a five-year-old girl I know sent her first Valentine's card to the dog in the family," describes psychoanalyst Sally Weintrobe (Turner, 2021).

Using language and images with children that highlight our loving relationship to nature and our growing knowledge about how to be better stewards of this relationship promotes healthy attachment to the natural world. Albrecht (2020) and Pihkala (2022) emphasize the importance of using language that can capture and elicit positive feelings in relation to climate change. Similar to the concept of saying "survivor" rather than "victim" with regards to trauma, Albrecht suggests we speak of the Symbiocene (a new era valuing our interdependence with the natural world) rather than the Anthropocene (an era irreversibly marked by our damage to the environment) (Albrecht, 2020). It is important to bear in mind, however, that there are those for whom contact with natural environments is associated with personal or cultural historical trauma, complicating the envisioning of a loving relationship with nature. This has been particularly described for African American communities (Dooley et al., 2021), which carry the historical trauma of forced labor on the land, lynchings in the woods, and the more recent experiences as marginalized communities intimate with environmental degradations. From a psychoanalytic point of view, all conflicting aspects of one's experience with the natural world can be explored while working towards healthy attachment.

Promote Healthy Kinds of Hope
In order to navigate feelings about climate change, it is crucial to maintain a stable sense of self that balances trust and mistrust, creating healthy hope. Research on young adolescents shows that meaning-focused coping, or optimism for creative solutions not only for climate change but also for achieving one's own goals in life, is an important way of maintaining psychological resilience (Ojala, 2012a, 2012b). Weingarten (2010) outlines a framework for maintaining "reasonable hope" in the face of devastation, recognizing hope as a verb that one "does" by creating goals and adjusting them when obstacles are confronted. In this way of thinking, sometimes abandoning a particular goal is heartbreaking, but one continues to "do" hope by persevering. Lear (2006) advocates for "radical hope" using the example of the Crow nation, which faced the dramatic loss of its land, resources, and way of life in the late nineteenth century. "What makes this hope *radical* is that it is directed toward a future goodness that transcends the current ability to understand what it is" (Lear, 2006).

Promote Alignment with Values in Response to the Problem
We are able to restabilize our sense of self when we act in ways that are consistent both with reality and with our values. As a society we are already feeling the impacts of climate change in extreme natural disasters, disruptions of supply chains, and forced migration. Bendell's (2018) Deep Adaptation model acknowledges the magnitude of disruptions that await us and suggests that we actively define our values in the following areas:

- *Resilience:* what do we most value that we want to keep, and how?
- *Relinquishment:* what do we need to let go of so we don't make matters worse?
- *Restoration:* what could we bring back to help us with these difficult times?
- *Reconciliation:* with what and whom shall we make peace as we awaken to our mutual mortality?

In promoting these means of stability, we assist young people to both recognize experiences of doubt and despair *and* cultivate the practice of welcoming joy by accepting small measures of success and actively living in a way that aligns with values.

Become Good-Enough, Flexible Containers

As we grapple with frightening realities, the concept of containment is particularly relevant to helping young people develop and maintain a secure sense of identity amidst so much that is destabilized. As we discussed in reference to grief, containment allows us to bear what is difficult to bear and have the mental space to think and be engaged. The young person needs containment-providing relationships with adults, institutions, and peer groups. These relationships are particularly vital at present when innovative thinking and novel engagements are required of all of us in the evolving climate crisis.

An oft-quoted concept in psychoanalytic literature is the "good-enough" parent who is imperfect and yet allows the child to experience an appropriate balance of frustration and gratification (Winnicott, 1953). This concept is illustrated by the following account from Sally Weintrobe:

> I was very moved by the sight of a mother holding her teenage daughter as her daughter wept uncontrollably at a moment on Westminster bridge during the Extinction Rebellion occupation in autumn 2018. I was not only moved but impressed by the mother who rather than trying to avoid the pain was there to help by sharing and being a witness to the situation and her daughter's pain and offering comfort. (Turner, 2021)

In Table 6.4, we detail three different types of containers as kinds of parental responses (Ben Asher & Goren, 2006). These are three different states of mind that might be exhibited by those who are responding in climate-related interactions with young people; the flexible container provides adequate containment and space to think for the young person distressed by climate change.

Crucial Considerations with Younger Children

Younger children have patterns of thinking that can distort reality, leaving them vulnerable to anxiety or dissociation (blocking things out of consciousness) in response to the overwhelming threat of climate change. Their immature unconscious defense mechanisms and other psychological characteristics include a propensity towards:

- projection (feeling a threat coming from outside of oneself that is actually inside of oneself)

Table 6.4 *Types of containment with climate-related examples*

Type of container	Description	Example of dialogue
Fragmented container	The content (i.e., the young person's feelings, thoughts and behavior) floods the container with anxiety, which the container (i.e., the other person, group, or institution) is not able to tolerate	"Your school needs to stop scaring you about climate change. If they don't stop, I'm going to have to pull you out and send you to another school. How are we supposed to deal with this?"
Rigid container	The rigidity of the container does not enable outside content to penetrate it (i.e., the container cannot let in any of the emotional implications of what the young person is presenting).	"Let's focus on the positive and not worry about these big things that we can't control. I'm sure everything will be fine."
Flexible container	The container takes in the contained's contents (i.e., the other is able to take in the young person's thoughts without being overwhelmed) and in turn tolerates and shapes it into something bearable that is offered back to the young person.	"Yes, I understand your worry; it is scary that the climate is changing. Do you want to talk or read more about it together?"

- introjection (experiencing something as inside of oneself that was outside of oneself)
- feeling very close to and identified with other living things
- legendary imaginations through "magical thinking"
- endless curiosity without yet having all the faculties of logic to make sense of information
- inner worlds that they may not share with trusted adults.

Because of concerns about overwhelming young children, some advocate for restraint in discussing disturbing topics with them such as climate change. Within education, on the one hand some subscribe to the dictum *no tragedies before the fourth grade* (Sobel, 1996), while on the other hand, others question that tenet (Armstrong, 2010). While children are perceptive about what is taking place around them, the explanations they concoct can be surprising. A child's distorted understanding can produce anxiety and even functional impairment. Erikson, for example, reportedly cured a young boy of severe constipation by explaining to him how childbirth works (Erikson, 1950). Using euphemistic language, drawing a lady elephant with her "inner compartments" and "two exits" (ibid., p. 55) he relieved the boy of the fear that he might drop a baby into the toilet while defecating. Erikson first had to patiently play with and listen to that child as a receptive and flexible container to uncover his unconscious anxieties.

In the above example, the boy's parents may not have discussed childbirth with him, even though he was most likely seeing pregnant women and hearing about babies in tummies. Similarly, children are ultimately exposed to information about climate change through media, allusions in conversation, and fragments of disturbing information or experience. Without adult guidance and conversations attending to what the child is hearing and thinking, the child's imagination and distortions go to work, surmising that what is happening must be too big and scary to even be thought about, let alone spoken about or acted upon. Trusted adults should be curious about what is going on inside of children's minds and be prepared to address the "elephant in the room" of climate change.

Drawing upon understandings of how climate anxieties arise developmentally (Weintrobe, 2013), here are particularly important sources of climate-related anxiety and fear in young children:

– *Early abandonment fears:* fear that they will be alone in a dangerous world.
– *Fears of annihilation:* fears that they will be physically maimed or destroyed. Caregivers being able to discuss children's fears and taking their own thoughtful environmental actions helps the child see there are capable people in charge.
– *Fear of destroying what they depend on:* Because of their ego-centric worldview (feeling that the world revolves around them), young children can tend to feel more responsible for climate change and may have an exaggerated sense of guilt and responsibility. Broadening responsibility to the whole community in how we talk to children and letting them see collective action is important.
– *Fear of unfamiliar aspects of nature*: This is similar to stranger anxiety. As discussed above, it is important to help children feel connected to nature rather than afraid of it when possible.
– *Fear of being powerless/loss of control*: We can help children maintain "reasonable hope" by setting goals, identifying pathways to those goals, and revising them. This creates a "hope process" regardless of the success or lack of success of each action.

Keeping these anxieties in mind, the young child's parent has important roles in preventing and mitigating climate anxiety and distress.

Other adults also contribute to these tasks by:

- creating an anchor where openness thrives so that the child can discuss their feelings and thoughts
- being present to the child empathically, and noticing the child's fear
- cultivating courage by keeping in mind and being able to convey that "difficult" is not the same as "bad"
- trusting that the child can make it through difficulties rather than feeling we should protect them from everything
- inviting learning, courage, and wisdom.

Crucial Considerations with Adolescents

Adolescents deserve particular attention in our psychoanalytic understanding of young people and climate change. Studies describe an "adolescent dip" where environmental attitudes and behavior reach a low point from ages 14 to 18 (Lee et al., 2020; Otto et al., 2019). Experts speculate that the dip can be partially attributed to avoidance by the adolescent, who must now deal with more difficult decisions around their own environmental impacts, compared to the younger child who faces fewer decisions (Lee et al., 2020). Feelings of powerlessness among young people, including feeling stuck participating in destructive economic, transportation and other systems, may lead to disengagement as a means of coping with this decisional complexity (Ojala, 2012a, 2012b). It has also been suggested that adolescents are less interested in the natural world. Certainly, it is a time of heightened concern and anxieties regarding peer relationships. Whether or not this "adolescent dip" in environmental attitude and behavior will shift is yet to be seen, as societal pressures related to climate change mount and there are now quite active youth movements (Lee et al., 2020).

Adolescence is a time prone to psychological trauma. Their minds have a fluidity that leaves them vulnerable as they go back and forth between attachment and autonomy, trying on new roles (Levy-Warren, 2000). Adolescent developmental tasks include *drive and affect regulation*, or learning to modulate intense drives and emotions, and *superego integration*, or developing a clear sense of conscience (Sugarman, 2017). These processes in adolescence go back and forth between progression and regression.

From a psychoanalytic perspective, adolescents must learn to tolerate powerful aggressive and sexual feelings that become conscious during this period. Not only is there new hormonal influence on these drives, but also from a psychoanalytic point of view adolescence echoes toddlerhood as the young person experiences substantial new internal and external expectations without enough experience to have competence in meeting them. Those who struggle with the task of tolerating and modulating their aggressive and sexual drives, as many adolescents do during this phase, may unconsciously feel their minds to be unalterably "polluted" and can feel resigned to the world's pollution also (Searles, 1972), which is overwhelmingly reflected in so many arenas including but not limited to climate change – for example, mass shootings, discriminatory violence, and a rise in authoritarian governments. Yet, the opportunity to think about climate change can provide a useful opportunity for adolescents to think consciously about their own aggressive impulses, and how to cope with them meaningfully in solidarity with others.

Keeping the adolescent's vulnerabilities in mind, the caretaking or mentoring adult has important roles. While an adolescent may seem to be separating from parents, the situation is more usefully conceptualized as the adolescent pivoting away, with the parents' attitudes and behavior lodged firmly in the back of the adolescent's mind. Parents should allow and foster ambiguities and "both/and thinking": for example, recognizing the inconvenience for the adolescent in reevaluating social utilization of single-use plastics, while also appreciating that being thoughtful about one's choices brings a sense of personal agency to one's life. Holding in mind such dialectics, or seemingly opposing experiences and concepts, and increasing the adolescent's acceptance and tolerance of multiple aspects of reality are especially important. These opposing feelings/concepts may include, among others, certainty and uncertainty, hope and hopelessness, and "nature as comfort" and "nature as threat" (Lewis et al., 2020): all are simultaneously true aspects of our experiences.

Concluding Comments

Our own unconscious motivations can be pitfalls. Young people are particularly vulnerable to the impacts of climate change and we all have a responsibility to support them as they deal with and process climate realities. However, we should also be aware of two problematic, less conscious motivations that may lurk in our minds as we undertake these efforts.

First, by focusing on another generation, we may skip over our own ongoing processing and our need to form spaces with others (e.g., other parents, teachers, therapists) to discuss our own feelings about climate change. If we do not contain one another as peers and are not bearing our own grief, guilt, and feelings of betrayal, then we won't be good-enough flexible containers for young people.

Secondly, we may consciously or unconsciously hope that young people will step up to save us. This attitude belies an inappropriate sense of personal helplessness, denying our *own* agency. Our own helpless feelings end up unconsciously transmitted to the very young people whom we seek to help. Stepping up with ourselves and also with young people, with faith in ourselves as well as in them, is the appropriate attitude for us to maintain. Many unconscious factors, as described throughout this chapter, interfere with our maintenance of this attitude, so we must work intentionally, and continually, to cultivate this mindset.

References

Albrecht, G. A. (2020). Negating solastalgia: An emotional revolution from the Anthropocene to the Symbiocene. *American Imago*, 77(1), 9–30.

Armstrong, C. L. (2010). *No tragedies before grade four? Expert opinion on teaching climate change to children*. (Doctoral dissertation, Royal Roads University).

Bach, S. (2018). Some thoughts on trust and betrayal. *Psychoanalytic Dialogues*, 28(5), 557–568.

Ben-Asher, S., & Goren, N. (2006). Projective identification as a defense mechanism when facing the threat of an ecological hazard. *Psychoanalysis, Culture & Society*, 11, 17–35. https://doi.org/10.1057/palgrave.pcs.2100057

Bendell, J. (2018). Deep adaptation: A map for navigating climate tragedy. *IFLAS Occasional Paper*. https://lifeworth.com/deepadaptation.pdf

Bion, W. R. (1962; reprinted 1984). *Learning from experience*. Karnac.

Bodnar, S. (2008). Wasted and bombed: Clinical enactments of a changing relationship to the earth. *Psychoanalytic Dialogues*, 18(4), 484–512.

Dooley, L., Sheats, J., Hamilton, O., Chapman, D., & Karlin, B. (2021). *Climate change and youth mental health: Psychological impacts, resilience resources, and future directions*. See Change Institute.

Erikson, E. H. (1950). *Childhood and society*. W. W. Norton & Co.

Erikson, E. H. (1968). *Identity: Youth and crisis (No. 7)*. W. W. Norton & Co.

Freud, S. (1888). Hysteria. In J. Strachey (Ed.), *The standard edition of the complete psychological works of Sigmund Freud* (vol. 1, pp. 37–59). Hogarth Press.

Fromm, E. (1941). *Escape from freedom*. Farrar and Rinehart.

Haseley, D. (2019). Climate change: Clinical considerations. *International Journal of Applied Psychoanalytic Studies*, 16(2), 109–115.

Hickman, C. (2019). Children and climate change: Exploring children's feelings about climate change using free association narrative interview methodology. In P. Hoggett (Ed.), *Climate psychology: On indifference to disaster. Studies in the psychosocial* (pp. 41–59). Palgrave Macmillan.

Hickman, C., Marks, E., Pihkala, P., Clayton, S., Lewandowski, R. E., Mayall, E. E., … van Susteren, L. (2021). Climate anxiety in children and young people and their beliefs about government responses to climate change: A global survey. *The Lancet Planetary Health*, 5(12), e863–e873.

Jones, C. A., & Davison, A. (2021). Disempowering emotions: The role of educational experiences in social responses to climate change. *Geoforum*, 118, 190–200.

Keene, J. (2012). Unconscious obstacles to caring for the planet: Facing up to human nature. In S. Weintrobe (Ed.), *Engaging with climate change: Psychoanalytic and interdisciplinary perspectives* (pp. 144–159). Routledge.

Klein, M. (1940). Mourning and its relation to manic-depressive states. *International Journal of Psychoanalysis*, 21, 125–153.

Klein, M. (1946). Notes on some schizoid mechanisms. In *The Writings of Melanie Klein* (vol. III, pp. 1–24). Hogarth Press, 1975. Originally published in *International Journal of Psychoanalysis*, 27.

Lear, J. (2006). *Radical hope: Ethics in the face of cultural devastation*. Harvard University Press.

Lee, K., Gjersoe, N., O'Neill, S., & Barnett, J. (2020). Youth perceptions of climate change: A narrative synthesis. *Wiley Interdisciplinary Reviews: Climate Change*, 11(3), e641.

Lertzman, R. A. (2012). The myth of apathy: Psychoanalytic explorations of environmental subjectivity. In S. Weintrobe (Ed.), *Engaging with climate change: Psychoanalytic and interdisciplinary perspectives* (pp. 117–133). Routledge.

Levy-Warren, M. (2000). *The adolescent journey*. Jason Aronson.

Lewis, J. L., Haase, E., & Trope, A. (2020). Climate dialectics in psychotherapy: Holding open the space between abyss and advance. *Psychodynamic Psychiatry*, 48(3), 271–294.

Newman, B. M., & Newman, P. R. (2001). Group identity and alienation: Giving the we its due. *Journal of Youth and Adolescence*, 30(5), 515–538.

Ojala, M. (2012a). Regulating worry, promoting hope: How do children, adolescents, and young adults cope with climate change? *International Journal of Environmental and Science Education*, 7(4), 537–561.

Ojala, M. (2012b). How do children cope with global climate change? Coping strategies, engagement, and well-being. *Journal of Environmental Psychology*, 32(3), 225–233.

Otto, S., Evans, C. W., Moon, M. J., & Kaiser, F. G. (2019). The development of children's environmental attitude and behavior. *Global Environmental Change*.

Pihkala, P. (2022). Toward a taxonomy of climate emotions. *Frontiers in Climate*, 199.

Rachman, S. (2010). Betrayal: A psychological analysis. *Behaviour Research and Therapy*, 4(4), 304–311.

Randall, R. (2009). Loss and climate change: The cost of parallel narratives. *Ecopsychology*, September, 118–129.

Saint-Amour, P. K. (2020). There is grief of a tree. *American Imago*, 77(1), 137–155.

Searles, H. F. (1972). Unconscious processes in relation to the environmental crisis. *Psychoanalytic Review*, 59(3), 361–74.

Sobel, D. (1996). *Beyond ecophobia: Reclaiming the heart in nature education*. Orion Society.

Sugarman, A. (2017). The transitional phenomena functions of smartphones for adolescents. *Psychoanalytic Study of the Child*, 70, 135–150.

Syed, M. & Fish, J. (2018). Revisiting Erik Erikson's legacy on culture, race, and ethnicity. *Identity*, 18(4), 274–283.

Szajnberg, N. M. (2022). Response to Abram's "On Winnicott's Concept of Trauma." *International Journal of Psychoanalysis*, 103, 381–382.

Tart, C. T. (1986). *Waking up: Overcoming the obstacles to human potential*. iUniverse.com.

Turner, J. (2021). Interview with Sally Weintrobe. Association of Child Psychotherapists, September 9. https://childpsychotherapy.org.uk/interview-sally-weintrobe

Weingarten, K. (2010). Reasonable hope: Construct, clinical applications, and supports. *Family Process*, 49(1), 5–25.

Weintrobe, S. (2013). The difficult problem of anxiety in thinking about climate change. In S. Weintrobe (Ed.), *Engaging with climate change: Psychoanalytic and interdisciplinary perspectives* (pp. 33–47). Routledge.

Winnicott, D. W. (1953). Transitional objects and transitional phenomena: A study of the first not-me possession. *International Journal of Psychoanalysis*, 34, 89–97.

CHAPTER 7

Understanding the Role of Trauma and Dissociation in Youth Responses to Climate Crises
Eco-Neglect as Institutional Abuse Child Abuse

Karen Hopenwasser

An hour or more before a thunderstorm arrives, my dog Raffi begins to tremble and refuses to go out for a walk. She senses the barometric pressure change or feels a vibrational energy from afar. She is "tuned" into her surrounding environment. While her consciousness is in part cognitive, it is deeply weighted toward embodied awareness. When a storm approaches, she manifests a physiological fear response shared by generations of her ancestral dog family. I have never succeeded in teaching her to disregard the power of the rumbling sky.

Embodied awareness is an emergent property of brain, mind, and body. It is dependent upon a multitude of connections between our brains and our bodies, contributing to a sense of self in the world. In humans, our evolved cognitive capacity makes embodied awareness a more complex process than it is in my canine companion, a process that is understood as emergent. *Emergence* refers to "what parts of a system do together that they would not do alone" (https://necsi.edu/emergence). I am capable of thinking about my fear response to storms. I can decide when and how to take shelter. There are days when I run home with Raffi because each thunderclap accentuates my fear being out under the trees. There are other days when I know that we have plenty of time. When I am contemplating whether to walk leisurely, or instead to sprint home, I am using my mind and body in a highly integrated way to process information. I am experiencing sentience.

Humans are not the only species capable of this level of integration. Research about cognition and consciousness in animals (particularly cephalopods, elephants, birds, dogs, and dolphins) challenges the philosophical view of *human exceptionalism*, a belief that humans are intrinsically of greater value than other life on the planet, a belief that fails to recognize the profound interdependence of all life on earth. There is little doubt, though, that we distinguish ourselves from other species in being exceptionally dangerous animals, solely responsible for industrialization, colonization, production of fossil fuel energy, and deforestation of the planet. Humans can manifest an indifference and cruelty that is difficult to comprehend.

In this chapter, which focuses on the relationship between trauma and youth climate change distress, I present some of the consequences of indifference and the serious mental health challenges it poses for youth on a global scale. Lessons learned from the treatment of severely traumatized individuals can help us to understand indifference as a state of mind, and that our capacity to shift states of mind is a unique function of the human ability to dissociate. *Dissociation*, in response to trauma, is a psychological and neurobiological process that allows individuals to manage unbearable pain. A dissociative response can result in a sense of disconnection, such as feeling unreal or feeling numb, and can lead to compartmentalized states of mind or to the separation of the felt sense of mind and body. Brain imaging studies have identified that there are changes in brain network functional connectivity as a result of emotional trauma (Lebois et al., 2021).

Recognition of dissociative adaptation can facilitate our understanding of how humans in industrialized societies are becoming increasingly disconnected from the natural world.

Biological rhythms that were once attuned to natural cycles, such as sunrise and sunset, or seasonal crop changes, are increasingly out of sync.

The psychological processing of climate change is most often framed in the context of denial – either denial that it is happening or denial that it is a threat. George Marshall suggests that our brains are wired to ignore the threat of climate change, that "the most pervasive narrative of all is the one that is not voiced: the collective, social norm of silence" (Marshall, 2014, p. 3). The metaphor of the comet in the film *Don't Look Up* (McKay, 2021) is not just a scream to notice what is so obvious, but a call to **notice how we do not notice**. If we shift from talking about denial to studying how we do not notice, then we might better understand our ability to neglect this environment that our children will inherit.

From adults who were mistreated as children we have learned much about adaptation to fear, pain, and suffering, including how dissociation allows one to maintain functioning. In traumatized children, dissociation supports survival by allowing for continued growth and development despite significant suffering. Once I learned to recognize the signs and symptoms of dissociation, I began to appreciate that it is possible to simultaneously know and not know that an experience is life threatening.

Knowing and not knowing is a paradox. When we do not know about looming danger, such as climate change, we are managing anxiety while ultimately risking longer-term survival. Indifference to our environment is a level of dissociation that is highly maladaptive. When we fail to imagine the future of our children, that failure becomes a traumatic neglect, a form of child abuse.

Writer, historian, and activist Rebecca Solnit stated so clearly that climate change is industrial-scale violence:

> If you're poor, the only way you're likely to injure someone is the old traditional way: artisanal violence, we could call it – by hands, by knife, by club, or maybe modern hands-on violence, by gun or by car. But if you're tremendously wealthy, you can practice industrial-scale violence without any manual labor on your own part. You can, say, build a sweatshop factory that will collapse in Bangladesh and kill more people than any hands-on mass murderer ever did, or you can calculate risk and benefit about putting poisons or unsafe machines into the world, as manufacturers do every day.
> (Solnit, 2018, p. 83)

A variation on industrial-scale violence is institutional abuse – abuse perpetrated by or within institutions or organizations outside of the family. When parents fail to make home environments safe for their children, we call that neglect. When empowered leaders of society fail to make the environment safe for our children, we must also call that neglect.

Noticing neglect requires a mindful and embodied awareness of a felt sense, a concept introduced by Eugene Gendlin in *Focusing Therapy* and further developed by Peter Levine in *Somatic Experiencing Therapy* (Gendlin, 1982; Levine, 1997). This felt sense can be described with words but does not require words to be known. "The 'felt sense' is, rather, the sense of the whole of a situation. The felt sense can *include* thoughts, feelings and intuitions, but a felt sense is somehow more than all that" (https://focusing.org/felt-sense/what-focusing). The concepts of felt sense and embodied awareness emerged from an integration of philosophy, psychology, and neuroscience.

Phenomenology, as a philosophy of the lived experience of human beings in the world, describes awareness in a relational context – person to person, individual to group, individual and group to environment. In addition, embodied awareness can be best understood through the lens of complex, nonlinear systems theory. While a full explanation of nonlinear systems theory is outside the scope of this chapter, a statement by David Krakauer, the president of the Santa Fe Institute, might be helpful here: "There are … on this planet, phenomena that are hidden in plain sight.

These are the phenomena that we study as complex systems: the convoluted exhibitions of the adaptive world – from cells to societies. Examples of these complex systems include cities, economies, civilizations, the nervous system, the Internet, and ecosystems" (https://santafe.edu/what-is-complex-systems-science). One philosophical takeaway is that there is an interconnectedness of all that exists on our planet, which some have called the web of life (Capra, 1997).

Industrialized and digitalized societies are becoming increasingly dissociative, with diminishing embodied awareness of a rhythmic attunement to the planet (Lifton, 1993; Sapiains et al., 2015; Worthy, 2008). With the loss of rhythmic attunement comes a loss of connection.

Intellectually, we get it. We do seem to appreciate the role that feeling and being connected plays in thriving. But we do not translate this knowledge into action. This is one of many paradoxes shaping climate change awareness. The increasing dichotomy between intellectual knowledge and embodied awareness highlights a profound loss of Indigenous scientific literacy. Indigenous sciences incorporate traditional ecological knowledge, such as the "concepts of stewardship and caretaking … in which humans approach the world with the attitude of respectful partners in genealogical relationships of interconnected humans, non-human beings, entities and collectives who have reciprocal responsibilities to one another" (Whyte et al., 2015, p. 1). Indigenous traditional ecological knowledge expresses that we lay down a path in walking (Machado, 2003; Varela et al., 1993), that we cocreate the world in which we live.

Psychoanalyst Sally Weintrobe links neoliberal exceptionalism with the lethality of an uncaring, narcissistic mentality, a state of mind quite opposite to the concept of stewardship. Neoliberal exceptionalism is based upon a belief that wealthy individuals have a right to grow their wealth through a free market unregulated by government. This helps to explain perpetration by greedy, powerful corporations and indifference within wealthy Global North societies (Weintrobe, 2021). But what about everyone else? Why are parents and grandparents from every corner of the earth not screaming on the streets about environmental conditions that will cause extreme hardship and will kill their progeny?

Knowing about Child Neglect

The history of child abuse and neglect is a disturbing topic, and most people would rather not think about it. For hundreds of years, in many societies children were considered the property of their fathers, subject to infanticide, physical abuse, sexual abuse, and neglect (Thomas, 1972). In nineteenth-century Europe and the United States, before the advent of labor laws, poor children suffered cruelty while laboring long hours in factories and mills (Mason, 1996). Prior to 1875, there were no organized nongovernment agencies established to protect children in need in the United States. Following a famous child abuse case in 1875, the New York Society for the Prevention of Cruelty to Children – a charitable, nongovernmental organization (Meyers, 2008) – was established. In the United States, the oversight of child welfare remained in the domain of nongovernmental agencies until 1935, when the Aid to Dependent Children was established through the Social Security Act (Meyers, 2008). However, public attention to the mistreatment of children remained minimal and sporadic. Then, in 1962, a group of pediatricians published an article, "The Battered Child Syndrome," which stirred wider awareness about the physical mistreatment of children (Kemp et al., 1984).

There have been significant changes in social attitudes about child welfare with codification of the rights of children to be protected from neglect and abuse, though these protections too often do not translate into well-being for children. The exposure of structural racism within child welfare systems (Roberts, 2022; Burton & Montaban, 2021) must be considered as we explore the tension between individual rights and protection of children.

More global attention to child protection rights emerged with the League of Nations in 1924. Then, in 1959, the United Nations adopted The Declaration of the Rights of the Child, although it took another thirty years – not until 1989 – for the General Assembly to vote on the Convention of the Rights of the Child (CRC). Within the CRC is Article 3: that the best interests of the child must be a top priority in all things that affect children. As mentioned, though, the best interests of the child are subject to both cultural and social determinants that need to be carefully considered.

The CRC was the most rapidly ratified treaty in history, yet the United States remains the only member nation that has, to date, failed to ratify it. Signed in 1995 by the US Ambassador to the United Nations, Madeleine Albright, no US president has ever sent the treaty to Congress for approval. Some speculate that the US legislature would perceive these human rights rules as an interference with the authority of individual parents over their children.

These individualistic, antigovernment beliefs, long embedded in US history, are manifest in other profoundly important social issues such as gun control. Here is another paradox. Statistical evidence demonstrates that we further endanger the lives of our children by prioritizing the protection of an individual right to bear arms. With increasing gun violence has come increasing anticipation of violence, so that now we are stressing the emotional well-being of our children as we teach them to anticipate a shooter in school. One study of social media postings following active school shooting drills found that students reported a 42 percent increase in stress and anxiety and an almost 39 percent increase in depression during the ninety days following active shooter drills, compared with the ninety days before the drills (El Sherief et al., 2021). These drills can activate profound emotional responses, including confusion about whether there is an actual shooter in the school. The American Academy of Pediatrics addressed this in a position paper published in 2020. They state:

> Active shooter drills are often planned and conducted without guidance from those familiar with the unique needs and vulnerabilities of individual or groups of children, which is critical to inform best practices. The unique needs of young children (e.g., those in early care and education settings), children who suffered traumatic events in the past, and those with physical, intellectual, and neurodevelopmental disabilities are rarely considered and addressed in live exercise planning. (Schonfeld et al., 2020)

These drills are scheduled, even though we do not know if recurrent active shooter drills will put some children at risk for posttraumatic stress symptoms (PTSS). Similar to climate change neglect, the failure to address gun control in the United States is disembodied from science. "Disciplinary separation, reductionism and the disassociation of humans from nature have left science and society ill-prepared for current issues that demand interdisciplinary collaboration and the integration of humans and nature" (Bradshaw & Bekoff, 2001, p. 461).

Neglect Is Abuse

Language about climate inaction as a form of child neglect is increasingly evident in public media discourse. For example, the *San Francisco Chronicle* recently published an article with the headline "Inaction on climate is child abuse" (Cook-Shonkoff, 2022). Unsurprisingly, supporters of the fossil fuel industries have objected to these statements. When individuals and activists begin to name abuse, those responsible for perpetration frequently respond by attacking the victimized. Psychologist and trauma expert Jennifer Freyd describes this as DARVO – Deny, Accuse,

Reverse Victim and Offender (Freyd, 1997, 2003). Some politicians have counter-attacked with the accusation that youth climate activists are being used (and thereby abused) by adults with an agenda. The young climate activist Anjali Sharma responded with an opinion piece in the *Guardian* newspaper: "Dear politicians, young climate activists are not abuse victims, we are children who read news" (Sharma, 2022). While youth engaged in climate change issues do not see themselves as victims of abuse, they do belong to a generation that is experiencing neglect. Their actions – fighting for their right to live and survive on this planet – are a source of hope and evidence of a resilience that will be addressed later in this chapter.

Around the globe, legal actions are being taken to fight back against this neglect, to secure the legal rights of youth to a healthier and safer climate. Some of these legal efforts are described by Rodgers and Dunn in Chapter 13 of this book. The expectation that there could be legal recourse and increased government oversight is consistent with the emergence of child protection laws regarding abuse and neglect at home and in the workplace.

PTSD in Children

As I write about the traumatic impact of climate warming on future generations of all species, I struggle. I did not imagine how difficult this would be. For forty years I have worked clinically with individuals who were brutally mistreated as children by adults who themselves were mistreated or were mentally unwell. But I rarely felt defeated and hopeless. The consequences of interpersonal trauma are treatable. Awareness of intergenerational transmission of trauma can lead to social transformation. Today, as I focus on society's failure to even know about the trauma of climate change, I struggle to manage my own feelings of helplessness and rage. There are so many individuals who have experienced climate-related natural disasters, including refugees struggling to survive in the context of diminished community and diminished social support. The physical and mental health consequences of their struggle go unnoticed by the rest of the world. As W. H. Auden wrote in his poem "Musée des Beaux Arts," suffering takes place "While someone else is eating or opening a window or just walking dully along" (Auden, 1979, p. 79).

Most of what we understand about PTSD (see Figure 7.1) in children and adolescents comes from studying the direct impact of interpersonal violence and natural disasters. The National Center for PTSD (US Department of Veterans Affairs) states:

> **Posttraumatic symptoms in older children include:**
>
> - Reliving the event over and over in thought or in play
> - Nightmares and sleep problems
> - Becoming very upset when something causes memories of the event
> - Lack of positive emotions
> - Becoming very upset when something causes memories of the event
> - Lack of positive emotions
> - Intense ongoing fear or sadness
> - Irritability and angry outbursts
> - Constantly looking for possible threats, being easily startled
> - Acting helpless, hopeless or withdrawn
> - Denying that the event happened or feeling numb
> - Avoiding places or people associated with the event

Figure 7.1 PTSD symptoms in older children.

> Children and teens could have PTSD if they have lived through an event that could have caused them or someone else to be killed or badly hurt. Such events include sexual or physical abuse or other violent crimes. Disasters such as floods, school shootings, car crashes, or fires might also cause PTSD. Other events that can cause PTSD are war, a friend's suicide, or seeing violence in the area they live. (www.ptsd.va.gov/understand/common/common_children_teens.asp)

In younger children, symptoms often present as physical complaints, such as stomachache or headache, or a restlessness frequently misdiagnosed as attention deficit disorders.

In addition to suffering the direct consequences of environmental adversity, children experience obstacles to healthy psychological development when their caretakers are struggling to survive.

> Young children have no direct control over the environment they live in. They cannot control the quality of the air they breathe, the fluids they drink, the food they eat, or their exposure to contaminants or infectious diseases. Children are therefore far more vulnerable to climate-related disasters, and their care and protection from harm is more complicated. The onus is on adults to provide the protection and safety that children need. (Stanberry, et al., 2018, p. 1)

Thus, when adults are themselves overwhelmed by environmental stresses, children can suffer not only the direct dangers of environmental disasters but also increased anxiety caused by parental helplessness.

In certain regions that are hit the hardest by environmental changes, forced migration and violent conflict increases the risk of both sexual and labor trafficking of children. "Evidence suggests that climate change and biodiversity loss aggravate all types of gender-based violence against women and girls" (Reem, 2022, p. 7).

In the first half of this chapter, I have connected the history of child neglect with our understanding of posttraumatic dissociation as it now becomes increasingly relevant to the long-term consequences of a climate change crisis. The key points are:

- Humans have evolved as a species with unique intellectual and cognitive capabilities to destroy the world in which they inhabit.
- This ability to destroy is a function of a loss of embodied wisdom (intelligence), or a failure to integrate cognitive and embodied knowledge of complex systems. This reflects a Western ignorance and bias against Indigenous science and has contributed to profound social injustice.
- One way in which knowledge is lost is through a process of dissociation – not knowing about something in a consciously integrated way.
- Dissociation is a psychobiological adaptation to intense stress, fear, and helplessness.
- Our failure to see and comprehend the human contributions to climate change is tantamount to neglect of our children and is a form of child abuse.
- Globally, there has evolved an increasing awareness that children have the human right to be protected by those with greater power. In the past century there have been numerous court decisions and legislative actions to protect children from harm, though we understand that both implicit and explicit racism can bias individuals and agencies enacting these protections.
- We are slowly recognizing that inaction about climate change is a failure to protect our children.
- Ultimately, acting on the threat of environmental collapse (famine, drought, air pollution, etc.) will require a mindful awareness of our dissociative disconnection from what we know but do not acknowledge.

As we view global climate warming through a trauma informed lens, we are talking about large-scale traumas, such as floods, drought, hurricanes, and wildfires, as well as small traumas, the cumulative experiences in which the changing environment hinders social and economic well-being. For some children, the psychological impact of cumulative small traumas – many of which are caused by interpersonal stressors – will cause lifelong injury. Chronic economic distress secondary to loss of resources is associated with increased interpersonal violence, substance abuse and dependency, depression, and exacerbation of psychiatric illness (Doherty & Clayton, 2011; Clayton et al., 2017). This has profound consequences throughout a child's life, from early development of attachment style to school performance issues to adolescent risks of depression, anxiety, and substance use.

In very young children trauma may increase anxiety about separation from caregivers, cause nightmares, contribute to fussy eating, and increase crying. As children get older, they may express feelings of shame, have difficulty concentrating in school, and experience difficulty sleeping. Adolescents may report depression and suicidal feelings, development of eating disorders, abuse of substances, risky sexual behavior, and poor attendance in school.

Research and Treatment

Considerable peer-reviewed research on the impact of trauma upon children's mental health and brain development informs our clinical work. Whether we are examining the effects of interpersonal trauma or the consequences of larger-scale disaster, this research explores:

1. How trauma disrupts the balance of the sympathetic and parasympathetic nervous system (van der Kolk, 2014; Porges, 1995)
2. How mistreatment in childhood shapes brain development (Perry, 2001; Perry & Pollard, 1998)
3. The emergent relationship between brain development and personal identity (Putnam, 1997; Teicher & Samson, 2016; Schore, 2013), and
4. The influence of environmental stress on gene expression (Yehuda et al., 2014; Bowers & Yehuda, 2016)

The influence of environmental stress on gene expression, or epigenetic changes, become the legacy of trauma on future generations. Numerous mental health clinicians (e.g., Levine, 1997; Ogden et al., 2006; Menakem, 2017) have applied research findings to therapeutic process, developing unique somatic psychotherapeutic approaches to treatment.

Adverse Childhood Events (ACEs)

As stated in a report by the National Scientific Council on the Developing Child (2005, 2014):

> The future of any society depends on its ability to foster the healthy development of the next generation. Extensive research on the biology of stress now shows that healthy development can be derailed by excessive or prolonged activation of stress response systems in the body and the brain, with damaging effects on learning, behavior, and health across the lifespan. Yet policies that affect young children generally do not address or even reflect awareness of the degree to which very early exposure to stressful experiences and environments can affect the architecture of the brain, the body's stress response systems, and a host of health outcomes later in life.

The increasing immediate traumas of environmental disasters are the most obvious consequences of climate change. But we are also seeing an increase in the anticipation of negative consequences, including preoccupation with anticipated extinction. Of 10,000 children and youth recently surveyed in a global study, "75% said that they think the future is frightening and 83% said that they think people have failed to take care of the planet" (Hickman et al., 2021). Look through the eyes of these young people and you will see neglect and feel fear.

Fear has a profound impact upon the nervous system, causing immediate and chronic symptoms as well as longer-term health problems. Children who suffer both acute and chronic trauma from climate-related change are suffering adverse childhood experiences (ACEs) that will likely affect their future mental and physical health. The most noted examples of ACEs include abuse within the family, witnessing violence, parental loss, serious mental health problems in the family, suicide of a family member, incarceration of a parent, poverty, and racism. For children now experiencing climate related disasters – especially those who have lost caretakers, lost their homes, and lost their communities – we must categorize these climate-mediated traumas as adverse childhood events with lifelong consequences.

> A large and growing body of research indicates that the underlying mechanism by which ACEs are associated with health outcomes is through the development of toxic stress, a chronic activation of the stress response system. Toxic stress results in dysregulation of the limbic-hypothalamic-pituitary-adrenal axis, elevating levels of catecholamines ("fight or flight" response), cortisol, and proinflammatory cytokines, leading to cascading effects on the nervous, endocrine, and immune systems. These changes can affect attention and other executive functioning, impulsive behavior, brain reward systems, decision-making, and response to stress throughout the life span. (Jones et al., 2020, p. 25)

Children experiencing chronic climate change adversity face compounding adverse experiences – trauma from acute natural disaster and increased incidence of interpersonal trauma triggered by extreme stress. Research supports these interacting forces. For example, rising temperatures correlate with increased hostility and violence (Anderson, 2001). "Floods bring mourning, displacement, and psychosocial stress due to loss of lives and belongings, as a direct outcome of the disaster or of its consequences. All these are risk factors for PTSD, depression, and anxiety…." (Cianconi et al., 2020).

The impact of climate change-related disasters looms larger in our awareness than the impact of neglect. While some children manifest anxiety clearly connected to concerns about climate change, others will take the path of psychic numbing. Here is another paradox – we need to feel our feelings to foster sustainable resilience. Antonio Damasio, head of the University of Southern California's Brain and Creativity Institute, has researched and written extensively about the neurobiological pathways that integrate awareness of feelings and how this integration influences our ability to make good decisions. Based upon research conducted with individuals who have suffered loss of function in certain brain regions, he has demonstrated that we need to feel our feelings **in our bodies** to wisely make use of our ability to be sentient (Damasio, 1999).

When adaptation to stress facilitates dissociation, we may suffer less in the moment, but at the cost of planning for future environmental challenges. Many mental health professionals and educators are not trained to notice psychic numbing. Instead, we are vulnerable to making judgments about youth who seem indifferent. It would be helpful to shift from criticizing young people for tuning out to understanding that disconnection can be an adaptation to stress. We now must urgently work on building the necessary resilience that would allow children and youth to safely feel feelings in the face of increasingly rapid environmental changes.

The Complexity of Resilience

The spark for scientific inquiry is creativity, a state of mind dependent upon imagination. It is imagination that allows humans to consider the possibilities of what is yet not known. When institutions "regard nature as a mere inanimate resource and a target of opportunity … it is a failure of imagination. Failures of compassion and charity are failures of imagination" (Snyder, 1995, p. 61). In resilient youth, trauma can cause suffering but will also foster growth and wisdom. Youth engaged in climate activism are inspirational examples of resilience embodied.

As I have been describing, the ability to witness danger and simultaneously not see it is a capacity to dissociate and compartmentalize information. Again, this is not simply psychological denial. This is a neurophysiological process (Frewen & Lanius, 2006) which has been studied through brain imaging in individuals who have experienced abuse. Sometimes not remembering one's own experience of trauma is functional, adaptive, and seemingly resilient. This is described by Laub and Auerhahn (1993) in their seminal paper "Knowing and Not Knowing Massive Psychic Trauma: Forms of Traumatic Memory." Some of the most dramatic stories of forgetting (i.e., dissociating) horrendous trauma have been told by individuals who have experienced the atrocities of the Holocaust, or the Cambodian, Armenian, and Rwandan genocides. These individuals, in remembering horrors happening to others, but not to themselves, are managing what would otherwise be unbearable memories.

Some posttraumatic reactions can be treated through careful exposure to the traumatizing triggers or memories, but often it is counter therapeutic to force a frightened person to face their fear. Therapeutic treatment is a slow process of learning how to bear the unbearable. In relation to past events, this process often depends upon one essential ingredient: imagining a future. If the trauma itself is a vision of no future, then retreating into "not knowing" understandably feels like the only option.

> Possibly the most common misinterpretation of resilience is "bouncing back." Resilience is in fact the ability to adapt and change, to reorganize, while coping with disturbance. It is all about changing in order not to be changed. A resilient system … does not bounce back to look and behave exactly like it did before. Resilient systems are learning systems. (Walker, 2020)

Based upon this understanding of social-ecological resilience, the dissociation of knowing about climate change as gross neglect (of planet and progeny) can be considered a negative form of resilience – believing everything is OK, no need to feel stressed – short-term adaptation at the expense of long-term survival. In the long-term therapeutic work of healing from trauma, one of the greatest challenges is to acknowledge and accept that the trauma happened, that it cannot be undone, and that some of the consequences are irreversible. The felt sense that the irreparable cannot be fixed can trigger profound grief, which in some vulnerable individuals leads to depression. In the most vulnerable this can trigger suicidal feelings. Grief about irreparable damage to our planet is yet another mental health paradox. While it can contribute to depression and in some cases increase suicidality, it can also motivate activism, creativity, and dedication to fight for change. So much conversation about climate change is specifically focused on predicting disaster in the future. It is crucial to remind ourselves and our children that what we do now will have an impact upon the future even though we cannot clearly see it. The challenge is to remember that we lay down the path in walking, together. I have observed in my work with adolescents and adults traumatized as children how feeling connected to a community fosters this resilience and eases pain.

Importantly, awareness alone is not sufficient. More and more essays, books, articles, webinars, and workshops are pushing for increased awareness of climate distress, while most communities are not prepared to manage that awareness. So many people do not know what to do about how they feel. Increased awareness of the dangers of climate change without an increased ability to manage that awareness will contribute to the experience of extreme stress and potentially increase mental health problems. Rising awareness coupled with helplessness exacerbates anxiety, despair, and maladaptive coping strategies.

In addition, we cannot separate the many social justice issues in the world from the climate change challenge. At any one moment the felt sense of cruelty, hatred, and indifference is overwhelming and can easily trigger hopelessness. But as author and researcher Britt Wray so wisely says, "Dread is a resource floating freely in the air, and it's this generation's job to capture it. In order to do that, the first thing we must do is find a container for our overwhelming emotions" (Wray 2022, p. 73). The hard work of containing and regulating overwhelming emotions without denying, dissociating, or collapsing into despair is similar to the work therapists have been doing for decades addressing the impact of other traumas. My traumatized patients need me to bear witness and validate their experiences in the safe space of a therapeutic relationship. Youth who are emerging into awareness of climate change dangers need to get that kind of support as well from trauma-informed professionals and educators.

Collective trauma (whether single natural disasters, racial discrimination, poverty, famine, or intergenerational transmission of trauma) can be countered by supporting creative expression within a community. Throughout human history, individuals have participated in singing and dancing, drumming and storytelling, and creating in rhythm together, solidifying social connections and fortifying group strength. Programs such as the Common Threads Project, in which small groups of women who have experienced interpersonal violence and displacement create "story cloths" together, lessens shame and fosters resilience (https://

commonthreadsproject.org/). Other programs are developing in response to climate disasters. In Butte County California, the Camp Fire tragedy caused massive destruction and left thousands of people traumatized. Nearby, California State University at Chico has developed an Ecotherapy program for those in their community impacted by this disaster. The goal of the program "is to promote the well-being of both people and the land through guided therapeutic and restorative activities in local natural environments" (www.csuchico.edu/basic-needs/ecotherapy-program.shtml). These kinds of programs foster healing and resilience in a group therapeutic process. Descriptions of other programs can be found in Chapters 11 and 19 of this book.

Creative expression in a communal context facilitates the holding of unbearable information and decreases the individual need to dissociate knowing about the pain. Mental health professionals and educators have an opportunity to validate what youth already know, but to do so we must recognize that the trauma is shared.

While writing this chapter I kept a copy of *All We Can Save: Truth, Courage, and Solutions for the Climate Crisis* (Johnson & Wilkinson, 2020) next to me on my desk. Intermittently I would pick it up and randomly read a brief essay, or poem or story, giving to myself a sense of connection with others doing the work of knowing about climate change. This connection fortified my own will to stay focused and keep working. Every step of the way forward must be appreciated in the context of connection – to each other, to life on the planet, to the life of the planet.

References

Anderson, C. (2001). Heat and violence. *Current Directions in Psychological Science*, 10(1), 33–38.
Auden, W. H. (1979). Musée des Beaux Arts. In E. Mendelson (Ed.), *Collected poems: W. H. Auden*. Vintage Books, Random House.
Bowers, M. E., & Yehuda, R. (2016). Intergenerational transmission of stress in humans. *Neuropsychopharmacology*, 41(1), 232–244. doi:10.1038/npp.2015.247.
Bradshaw, G. A., & Bekoff, M. (2001). Ecology and social responsibility: The re-embodiment of science. *Trends in Ecology & Evolution*, 16, 460–465. https://doi.org/10.1016/S0169-5347(01)02204-2
Burton, A. O., & Montauban, A. (2021). Toward community control of child welfare funding: Repeal the child abuse prevention and treatment act and delink child protection from family well-being. *Columbia Journal of Race and Law*, 11(3). Available at SSRN: https://ssrn.com/abstract=3905041
Capra, F. (1997). *The web of life: A new scientific understanding of living systems*. Anchor.

Cianconi P., Betrò S., & Janiri L. (2020). The impact of climate change on mental health: A systematic descriptive review. *Frontiers in Psychiatry*, 11. doi: 10.3389/fpsyt.2020.00074.

Clayton, S., Manning, C. M., Krygsman, K., & Speiser, M. (2017). *Mental health and our changing climate: Impacts, implications, and guidance.* American Psychological Association, and ecoAmerica.

Cook-Shonkoff, A. (2022). Inaction on climate is child abuse. *San Francisco Chronicle*, August 2.

Damasio, A. (1999). *The feeling of what happens: Body and emotion in the making of Consciousness.* Harcourt.

De Bellis, M. D., & Zisk, A. (2014). The biological effects of childhood trauma. *Child and Adolescent Psychiatric Clinics of North America*, 23(2), 185–222.

Doherty, T. J., & Clayton, S. (2011). The psychological impacts of global climate change. *American Psychologist*, May–June, 66(4), 265–276. doi: 10.1037/a0023141

El Sherief, M., Saha, K., Gupta, P., Mishra, S., Seybolt, J., Xie, J., … De Choudhury, M. (2021). Impacts of school shooter drills on the psychological well-being of American K-12 school communities: A social media study. *Humanities and Social Sciences Communications*, 8, 315. https://doi.org/10.1057/s41599-021-00993-6

Frewen, P. A., & Lanius, R. A. (2006). Neurobiology of dissociation: Unity and disunity in mind-body-brain. *Psychiatric Clinics of North America*, 29(1), 113–128. https://doi.org/10.1016/j.psc.2005.10.016

Freyd, J. J. (1997). Violations of power, adaptive blindness and betrayal trauma theory. *Feminism & Psychology*, 7(1), 22–32. https://doi.org/10.1177/0959353597071004

Freyd, J. J. (2003). What is DARVO? http://dynamic.uoregon.edu/~jjf/defineDARVO.html.

Gendlin, E. T. (1982). *Focusing.* Bantam.

Hickman, C., Marks, E., Pihkala, P., Clayton, S., Leandowski, R. E., Mayal, E. E., … van Susteren, L. (2021). Climate anxiety in children and young people and their beliefs about government responses to climate change: A global survey. *The Lancet Planetary Health*, 5(12). https://doi.org/10.1016/S2542-5196(21)00278-3

Johnson, A. E., & Wilkinson, K. K. (2020). *All we can save: Truth, courage, and solutions for the climate crisis.* One World.

Jones, C. M., Merrick, M. T., & Houry, D. E. (2020). Identifying and preventing adverse childhood experiences. *JAMA*, 232(1), 25–26. doi: 10.1001/jama.2019.18499

Kemp, C. H., Silverman, F. M., Steele, B. F., Droegemueller, W., & Silver, H. K. (1984). The Battered Child Syndrome. *JAMA*, 251(24), 3288–3294. doi:10.1001/jama.1984.03340480070033

Krakauer, D. (2019). *Worlds in plain sight.* SFI Press. https://santafe.edu/what-is-complex-systems-science

Laub, D., & Auerhahn, N. (1993). Knowing and not knowing massive psychic trauma: Forms of traumatic memory. *International Journal of Psychoanalysis*, 74, 287–302.

Lebois, L. A. M., Li, M., Baker, J. T., Wolff, J. D., Wang, D., Lambros, A. M., … Kaufman, M. L. (2021). Large-scale functional brain network architecture changes associated with trauma-related dissociation. *American Journal of Psychiatry*, 178(2), 165–173. doi:10.1176/appi.ajp.2020.19060647.

Levine, P. (1997). *Waking the tiger*. North Atlantic Books.

Lifton, R. J. (1993). *The protean self: Human resilience in an age of fragmentation*. Basic Books.

Machado, A. (2003). *There is no road* (trans. D. Malone & M. Berg). White Pine Press (original work published 1912).

Markel, H. (2009). Case shined first light on abuse of children. New York Times, December 13.

Marshall, G. (2014). *Don't even think about it: Why our brains are wired to ignore climate change*. Bloomsbury.

Mason, M. A. (1996). *From father's property to children's rights: The history of child custody in the United States*. Columbia University Press.

McKay, A. [Director]. (2021). *Don't Look Up* [Film]. Hyperobject Industries and Bluegrass Films.

Menakem, R. (2017). *My grandmother's hands*. Central Recovery Press.

Meyers, J. (2008). A short history of child protection in America. *Family Law Quarterly*, 42(3), 449–463.

National Scientific Council on the Developing Child (2005/2014). Excessive stress disrupts the architecture of the brain developing brain. Working paper 3. Updated edition. www.developingchild.harvard.edu

New England Complex Systems Institute. https://necsi.edu

Ogden, P., Minton, K., & Pain, C. (2006). *Trauma and the body*. Norton Professional Books.

Perry, B. D. (2001). The neurodevelopmental impact of violence in childhood. In D. Schetky & E. P. Benedek (Eds.), *Textbook of child and adolescent forensic psychiatry* (pp. 221–238). American Psychiatric Press.

Perry, B. D. & Pollard, R. (1998). Homeostasis, stress, trauma and adaptation: A neurodevelopmental view of childhood trauma. *Child and Adolescent Psychiatric Clinics of North America*, 7(1), 33–51.

Porges, S. W. (2011). *The polyvagal theory: Neurophysiological foundations of emotions, attachment, communication, and self-regulation*. Norton.

Putnam, F. (1997). *Dissociation in children and adolescents: A developmental approach*. Guilford Press.

Reem, A. (2022). Report of the Special Rapporteur on violence against women and girls, its causes and consequences; Violence against women and girls in the context of the climate crisis, including environmental degradation and related disaster risk mitigation and response, Seventy-seventh General Assembly of the United Nations.

Roberts, D. (2022). *Torn apart*. Basic Books.

Sapiains, R., Beeton, R. J. S., & Walker, I. A. (2015). The dissociative experience: Mediating the tension between people's awareness of environmental problems and their inadequate behavioral responses. *Ecopsychology*, 7(1), 38–47.

Schonfeld, D. J., Melzer-Lange, M., Hashikawa, A. N., & Gorski, P. A. (2020). Participation of children and adolescents in live crisis drills and exercises. *Pediatrics*, 146(3), e2020015503.

Schore, A. (2013). Relational trauma, brain development, and dissociation. In J. Ford & C. Courtois (Eds.), *Treating complex traumatic stress disorders in adolescents and children*. Guilford Press.

Sharma, A. (2022). Dear politicians young climate activists are not abuse victims we are children who read news. The Guardian, April 27.

Snyder, G. (1995). Earth day and the war against the imagination. In G. A. Snyder, *Place in space* (pp. 56–64). Counterpoint.

Solnit, R. (2018). Climate change is violence. In R. Solnit, *Call them by their true names: American crises (and essays)* (pp. 83–87). Haymarket Books.

Stanberry, L. R., Thomson, M. C., & James, W., (2018). Prioritizing the needs of children in a changing climate. *PLoS Med*, 15(7): e1002627.

Teicher, M. H., & Samson, J. A. (2016). Annual research review: Enduring neurobiological effects of childhood abuse and neglect. *Journal of Child Psychology and Psychiatry* 57(3), 241–266.

Thomas, M. P., (1972). Child abuse and neglect part I – Historical overview, legal matrix, and social perspectives. North Carolina Law Review, 50, 293.

UNICEF (2021). *The climate crisis is a child rights crisis: Introducing the children's climate risk index*. United Nations Children's Fund.

Van der Kolk, B. (2014). *The body keeps the score*. Viking Press.

Varela, F. J., Thompson, E., & Rosch, E. (1993). *The embodied mind: Cognitive science and human experience*. MIT Press.

Walker, B. (2020). Resilience: What it is and is not. *Ecology and Society*, 25(2), 11. https://doi.org/10.5751/ES-11647-250211

Weintrobe, S. (2021). *Psychological roots of climate consciousness: Neoliberal exceptionalism and the culture of uncare*. Bloomsbury Academic.

Whyte, K. P. Brewer, J. P., & Johnson, J. T. (2015). Weaving Indigenous science, protocols and sustainability science. *Sustainability Science*, published online. http://link.springer.com/article/10.1007%2Fs11625-015-0296-6

Worthy, K. (2008). Modern institutions, phenomenal dissociations, and destructiveness toward humans and the environment. *Organization & Environment*, 21(2), 148–170.

Wray, B. (2022). *Generation dread: Finding purpose in an age of climate crisis*. Alfred A. Knopf.

Yehuda, R., Daskalakis, N. P., Lehrner, A., Desarnaud, F., Bader, H. N., Makotkine, I., … Meaney, M. J. (2014). Influences of maternal and paternal PTSD on epigenetic regulation of the glucocorticoid receptor gene in Holocaust survivor offspring. *American Journal of Psychiatry*, 171, 872–880.

CHAPTER 8

Cognitive Behavioral Principles for Conceptualizing Young People's Eco-Emotions and Eco-Distress

Elizabeth Marks and Kelsey Hudson

Overview

This chapter illustrates how to create a psychological "map" of a young person experiencing distress related to what we will call the Climate and Ecological Emergencies (CEE). The map provides the client and clinician a way to organize how the client comes to think, feel, and act the way they do. Various theoretical frameworks are used to understand the information clients bring so that the clinician can respond effectively and compassionately. In the mental health field, this process is called "formulation" or "case conceptualization." We begin by defining case conceptualizations and providing suggestions on how to create ecologically aware case conceptualizations for young people. We then provide an overview of cognitive behavioral (CB) theory and show how it can provide insight into what may exacerbate and ameliorate unhelpful levels of distress. By offering two examples of case conceptualizations – one showing impairing eco-distress and one showing constructive eco-distress – we argue that CB frameworks can be useful for understanding varying levels of distress in young people. This in turn might support young people in becoming more flexible in their cognitions, emotions, and behaviors so that they are less likely to feel overwhelmed by eco-distress.

Terminology

Throughout this chapter we refer to "eco-distress" and "eco-emotions" when discussing young people's psychological responses to climate change and planetary health. Although there are many terms in the literature (e.g., climate anxiety, eco-anxiety, ecological grief, solastalgia), we opted for terms that can encompass a wide range of thoughts and feelings relevant to young people.

- "Eco" (rather than "climate") was chosen based on new research illustrating that climate concerns often arise alongside broader ecological concerns relating to issues such as pollution and biodiversity loss (Hogg et al., 2021) and the consumerist, carbon-intensive cultures of many modern societies. Humanity and nature are inseparable, and many young people are aware that the CEE threaten multiple ecosystems, and therefore us.
- We refer to the Climate and Ecological Emergencies (CEE) as a broad term encompassing the range of severe threats currently facing our planet.
- "Distress" emphasizes our nonpathologizing approach and avoids terms such as "anxiety," which are easily conflated with specific diagnoses. "Distress" encapsulates the rich variety of emotions reported across the literature (e.g., anxiety, grief, sadness, anger, shame, guilt), as well as associated functional impairment. Furthermore, people with lived experience use this term themselves, making it client-centered and personally meaningful.
- "Eco-emotions" is a term we use more broadly to emphasize that concerns about planetary health involve more than distress; they also include positively valenced feelings such as hope, inspiration, and empowerment that would be lost if we focused solely on 'distress'.

What Are Case Conceptualizations?

Case conceptualization describes a clinical process that provides a systematic framework or 'formulation' for understanding a client's experiences. Case conceptualizations based on cognitive behavioral (CB) theory identify an individual's thoughts, emotions, physical sensations, and behaviors, and explore how these factors interact. By delineating these components and situating them within the individual's broader social-ecological context (i.e., developmental, personal, familial, societal, global), the client can better understand what predisposed, precipitated, and maintains their distress. Case conceptualization is a collaborative process that also highlights a client's strengths and protective factors (Kuyken et al., 2009). A strong case conceptualization lays a foundation from which clinicians and clients collaboratively develop hypotheses about existing psychological challenges. It subsequently informs treatment goals and guides interventions that are tailored to each client. Clinicians usually formulate an initial case conceptualization from the information obtained during the clinical intake and assessment process, but conceptualizations are adapted and revised throughout treatment in light of new information, themes, and changes within the client (Persons, 2022).

Case conceptualization requires gathering, synthesizing, and organizing multiple pieces of information to better understand an individual within their personal and broader contexts. It identifies how a presenting problem (i.e., why someone is seeking professional help) manifests in the person's life through psychological, physical, and behavioral changes. It also identifies any functional impacts on their life (e.g., social, familial, occupational, educational, cultural). The conceptualization includes relevant factors affecting the presenting problem, including an individual's historical experiences, their underlying beliefs, relationships, family, and cultural expectations. Attempts made to respond to or cope with the problems are identified, along with their effectiveness and any resistance to such attempts (both internal and external). The interaction(s) between these experiences and the person's broader sociocultural contexts are explored. Together, this information is used to formulate a case conceptualization: a comprehensive understanding of which elements of a young person's life can exacerbate and ameliorate their distress, including strengths and protective factors. The conceptualization is used to make hypotheses about what changes might be beneficial to the young person and offers a "road map" for therapy. As therapy progresses and more information becomes available, the conceptualization can be refined and developed.

Eco-Aware Case Conceptualization

Young people's ecologically related thoughts, emotions, behaviors, and physical sensations contribute to, interact with, and are influenced by factors from their internal and external environments. An eco-aware case conceptualization based on CB theory should unpack these factors and use them to "integrate how the client's current clinical presentation synergizes with climate-related threats to further elucidate the client's psychological concerns" (Doherty et al., 2022, p. 177). There are various ways to conceptualize eco-distress, and depending on a practitioner's orientation, other frameworks may be used (see Chapter 10 by Allured & Easterlin for examples). We have chosen case conceptualization based on CB theory because it offers a clear and accessible way to understand how key processes affect psychological distress. This approach is offered with the recognition that the CEE are a real, existential threat and that it is healthy and rational for young people to be distressed in response.

Incorporating Context, Sociocultural Factors, and Environmental Identity

Any understanding of suffering and resilience must be culturally informed and take the following factors into account: individual and cultural identities, beliefs, attitudes, and practices; age and developmental stage; systemic inequities; and positions of power and privilege (Sperry, 2022). A comprehensive case conceptualization should situate a young person's problems within their broader sociocultural contexts, which influence how eco-emotions and distress are experienced and expressed (Crandon et al., 2022). A comprehensive review of factors influencing young people's eco-related development is found in Chapter 15 (Crandon et al.), and Chapter 4 (Vergunst & Berry). Briefly, important contextual factors include developmental stage (e.g., young child, older adolescent); geographical location (e.g., living in an area with historical or ongoing climate-related disasters); mental health status (e.g., related mental health challenges, traumatic life events); institutional and structural inequalities (e.g., racial discrimination); and interpersonal and family factors (e.g., family beliefs) (Dummet, 2010).

Several frameworks exist to guide socioculturally informed conceptualizations. The Social GGRRAAACCEEESSS (also called the "Social Graces") (Burnham, 1992, 1993; Roper-Hall, 1998) framework offers a structure for critically exploring issues of social difference, power, and diversity in therapeutic settings and encompasses fifteen areas, including gender, geography, race, religion, age, ability, appearance, class, culture, ethnicity, education, employment, sexuality, sexual orientation, and spirituality (Burnham, 2012). The ADDRESSING framework (Hays, 2016) similarly considers various forms of social identity, including Indigenous heritage and national origin (Hays, 2016). The DSM-5 Cultural Formulation Interview offers a brief, semistructured interview protocol to examine the cultural dimensions of illness (American Psychiatric Association [APA], 2013). It uses open questions to assess an individual's cultural definition of their experience, such as "What troubles you most about your problem?"; "What do you think caused this problem?"; and "People deal with their problems in different ways. What do *you* do to cope?"

Environmental identity, defined as "one's self concept and sense of relations with nature and the natural world, including other species, settings, and places" (Doherty et al., 2022, p. 171), is relevant to eco-aware conceptualization because it can interact with other forms of identity. For many young people, the existential depth and moral implications of the CEE, including the implications for the natural world, have a spiritual or philosophical element and raise questions about meaning, mortality, and responsibility (Pihkala, 2022). These questions are particularly relevant for adolescents, whose identity development is more fluid than in adults and who commonly experience existential concerns during this critical developmental stage (Berman et al., 2006).

Reflexivity and Clinician Context

Clinicians must be able to reflect upon how their positionality shapes their interpretation of clients' reports and functioning. Providers with greater awareness of the CEE, its psychological impacts, and its interaction with broader context(s) will be better equipped to create informed conceptualizations of a young person's concerns and respond to them compassionately (Fenley et al., 2022). For example, a provider with little climate awareness may misinterpret (or even dismiss) young people's climate distress, perhaps regarding it as unrealistic or irrelevant. In contrast, a provider with awareness of climate concerns and their potential impacts on mental health would likely take a more validating approach.

An Overview of Cognitive Behavioral Theory

Classic CB theory claims that the impact of external events upon an individual is shaped by the perception and interpretation of the events. The simplest CB model, "ABC," describes this as an Activating event (A), which leads to Beliefs (B) (i.e., thoughts/cognitions) about the event and its meaning, and results in emotional, behavioral, and physiological Consequences (C) (Ellis, 1991). Over time, the way people interpret events can become habitual. In clinical conditions such as anxiety or depression, people exhibit automatic, negatively biased patterns of thinking, with accompanying negative consequences. Clinical conditions are frequently characterized by a thinking style that is repetitive, negative, and often unconstructive, such as worry or rumination (Watkins, 2000).

According to CB theory, an individual's emotional reaction to a situation depends on how the situation is interpreted. Interpretations of threat lead to fear and anxiety; interpretations of loss lead to sadness; interpretations of personal inadequacy lead to guilt, shame, and depressed mood; and those of injustice lead to anger. All emotions have a physiological correlate; for example, anxiety tends to cause physiological arousal with uncomfortable bodily sensations such as tension or breathlessness. Both the emotional and concomitant physiological responses may then be further interpreted negatively, generating a positive feedback loop of increasing distress. These interpretations shape the actions taken in response to a perceived problem, which often include avoidance, monitoring of or hypervigilance towards a situation of concern, and seeking reassurance. In models of clinical anxiety, avoidance and hypervigilance arise in response to situations that are inaccurately appraised as dangerous and are termed 'Safety Seeking Behaviors.' Although these behaviors are attempts to create safety, they paradoxically increase focus on the negative thoughts and emotions that elicited them, further fueling vicious cycles of distress. For example, if a young person avoids a feared situation because they perceive it as highly dangerous (although it is in fact unlikely to cause harm), they cannot determine what *actually* happens when they approach (vs avoid) the situation. Continued avoidance prevents them from testing out what happens when they face their fear, which increases avoidance behaviors and further strengthens beliefs about what is dangerous. This can even lead to the development of more negative beliefs about emotions and body sensations being dangerous or intolerable. Of course, for situations that are realistically dangerous (e.g., gun violence, abuse), avoidance and hypervigilance may be appropriate protective responses, particularly if other forms of agency are not accessible. An important part of case conceptualization is to identify when these reactions are functional or protective and when they are unhelpful.

Increased focus on perceived threats increases the salience of threat-related information. This attentional bias distorts perception and makes the worst outcomes seem more likely, further reinforcing negative cognitions and distress (Cisler & Koster, 2010). Other behaviors that unintentionally maintain or exacerbate distress include attempts to avoid, suppress, or deny emotion, which has been linked with higher levels of internalizing and externalizing symptoms in children and adolescents (Compas et al., 2017). These CB factors have been formulated as a "vicious flower" in clinical disorders for young people (e.g., Haig-Ferguson et al., 2021) and can be adapted for application to climate distress. Regardless of a young person's specific mental health challenges, the vicious flower formulation demonstrates the importance of CB factors in distress maintenance (Mansell et al., 2009).

CB theory maintains that distress arises from a misinterpretation of reality as more threatening or negative than others might perceive. This relationship underpins cognitive behavioral therapy (CBT), which focuses on identifying and changing unhelpful thoughts by challenging thought content (e.g., classic CBT) or adjusting how an individual *relates* to thinking (e.g., third wave approaches such as mindfulness-based cognitive therapy, Acceptance and Commitment Therapy, or Compassion Focused Therapy).

Meaning is central to CB theory, which suggests that core beliefs – our deeply held, central ideas about ourselves, others, and the world – act as a lens through which we perceive our experiences. Negative core beliefs usually lead to negative thoughts and painful emotions (e.g., guilt, sadness), whereas neutral and realistic core beliefs typically lead to more balanced reactions. Many core beliefs are developed in childhood and are shaped by life events including early experiences, relationships, and attachments. Young people who experience difficulties in these areas may be vulnerable to developing negatively toned core beliefs; for example, a child who experiences bullying may develop core beliefs about being unlovable or unworthy, which in turn increases vulnerability to anxiety, low mood, or depression (e.g., Dozois & Beck, 2008). Core beliefs tend to be long-standing, but with practice they can change to become more flexible, realistic, and balanced.

Important Considerations When Applying CB Theory to Eco-Distress

Three key assumptions underpinning CB theory require scrutiny when applied to nonclinical experiences such as eco-distress. The first assumption of clinical disorders is that "negative" emotions and distress arise because the cognitions are unrealistic and/or irrational. As this book powerfully demonstrates across multiple disciplines, this is not the case for eco-distress, where concern arises from a realistic understanding of the severity of the CEE, the existential threat and uncertainty faced by humanity and other species, and the intersection of the CEE with global injustice. Although eco-distress may be painful, most of the thoughts and beliefs expressed are both realistic and rational. Still, some elements may be unrealistic or unconstructive (Moorey, 1996), which we explore below.

The second assumption is that negatively valenced emotions are unhelpful, unwanted, and maladaptive. This is particularly true for "second-wave" cognitive behavioral therapies, which highlight how the *content* of thoughts and beliefs affects behaviors and emotions (Dobson & Dozois, 2021).

This assumption is challenged by research showing that there are positive relationships between distressing eco-emotions (anxiety, depression, anger) and the pro-environmental behaviors needed to mitigate the worst outcomes of the CEE (Stanley et al., 2021; Verplanken et al., 2020). Furthermore, eco-distress is often valued by those reporting it as an indication of their compassion for the world and its connection with their identity and morality, suggesting that is not wholly negative. For adolescents, sharing eco-emotions can foster social connection and feelings of belonging to wider networks of care. Case conceptualizations for young people with eco-distress must acknowledge that emotions (including negatively valenced ones) are natural, necessary, and "tell us important things about what is going on in our lives" (Ehrenreich-May, 2018, p. 92). In general, therapeutic and community-based interventions should recognize that eco-distress is painful and also that simply trying to remove eco-emotions is inappropriate unless they become functionally impairing (Hickman, 2020).

The third assumption of clinical disorders is that "negative" emotions are associated with an underlying meaning (i.e., core belief) that is self-referential, unhelpful, and negatively toned. Because young people's core beliefs are still developing and are influenced by the actions and beliefs of significant others (particularly caregivers in childhood and peer groups in adolescence), we argue that "negative" emotions related to eco-distress are less tied to such negative core beliefs. In support of this argument, there is evidence that eco-distress shows only small correlations with measures of psychopathology, whilst also showing significant positive associations with positive and valued core beliefs about ecological identity (Verplanken et al., 2020) and attitudes (Verplanken & Roy, 2013). Similarly, individuals who are more culturally or personally connected to nature, including Indigenous Peoples or earth scientists, may be more vulnerable to developing eco-distress (Coffey et al., 2021). Here, the CEE can threaten essential and usually protective core beliefs relating to the deep sense of meaning that culture, religion, and spirituality bring to human lives. Cultural, religious, and spiritual beliefs, which are vital sources of strength and succor, can feel imperiled by the CEE. Psychological conceptualizations must explore deeper meanings within eco-distress, as they may be an anchor in the face of existential threats.

Across various developmental stages, it is reasonable to expect that exposure to the CEE shapes young people's developing core beliefs, particularly those around safety, justice, and fairness. Young people are forced to bear witness to continued dependence on fossil fuels alongside chronic climate inaction by adults and governmental bodies. How might this affect beliefs about personal agency, reliability of others, safety, or the benevolence of the wider world? We need to examine whether eco-distress affects the development of core beliefs and to research how particular cultural or spiritual beliefs influence or protect against distress.

It is also important to recognize that, without careful cultural adaptations, CB concepts may not feel acceptable to individuals from diverse backgrounds and could even conflict with cultural and spiritual beliefs (Rathod et al., 2019). Although there have been recent shifts towards decolonizing psychotherapy practices and broadening representation in the provision of mental healthcare, CB frameworks are underpinned by a Western, individualistic understanding of mental health and illness, and much of the research has focused on white, European American, and relatively well-resourced individuals (Naeem, 2019). There is good evidence that CB approaches can be effectively adapted for individuals and groups from various cultures and subcultures, including those navigating unrelenting and chronic stressors such as refugees and asylees (King & Said, 2019) and girls experiencing homelessness (Castaños-Cervantes, 2019). But while evidence-based guidelines for adapting CB conceptualizations and therapies exist (Rathod et al., 2019), experts in this area agree that significant work is required to improve access to evidence-based mental health care (Naeem, 2019) that is adapted for different developmental and cultural situations such as caregiver dynamics and social expectations.

With these caveats, we offer a transdiagnostic (i.e., applicable to various types of mental health challenges and levels of distress) CB framework for understanding, formulating, and responding to young people's eco-distress. The first approach describes the types of experiences relevant to someone reporting severe or *impairing eco-distress* (Figure 8.1) and involves significant functional impairment. The second describes more balanced or *constructive eco-distress* (Figure 8.2) (Verplanken et al., 2020; Pihkala, 2020), which recognizes the motivational and constructive nature of emotions such as anxiety and highlights eco-care (i.e., people feel like this *because they care about* other beings). Constructive eco-distress involves experiencing negatively valenced emotions, which are painful, yet also motivate adaptive, valued behaviors. In this model, positively valenced emotions (hope, inspiration, etc.) can also be present and there is a respectful relationship towards the distress, which is seen as an important reflection of one's core values and moral code, and which should be honored and cared for. We argue that the aim of the case conceptualization and

Cognitive Behavioral Principles

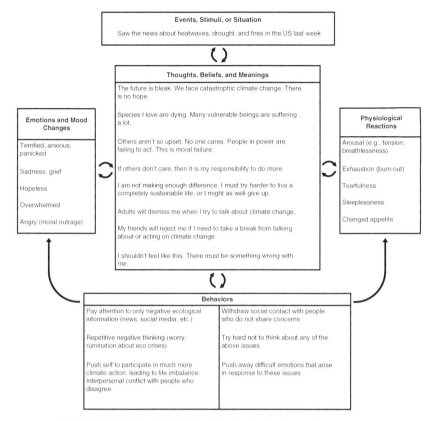

Figure 8.1 Case conceptualization 1: Eco-distress with clinically significant impairment.

subsequent therapeutic work with eco-distress is not to remove it, but to instead help people move from the first model (impairing) to the second (constructive). For example, an individual may begin with thoughts such as "Since others don't care, it's my responsibility to do more" and shift to "I am doing what I can to make a difference. Although individual action alone is insufficient, I know I am one part of a larger system that cares." The only way eco-distress will ever be "cured" is if our society transforms to one that is sustainable, just, carbon-neutral, and respectful of biodiversity and vulnerable populations. Both the impairing and constructive models include *existential eco-distress*, as questions of meaning and existence often arise in response to the CEE (Pihkala, 2022).

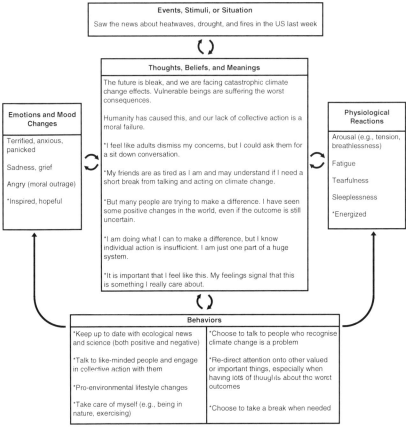

Figure 8.2   Case conceptualization 2: Constructive eco-distress.

Case Conceptualizations for Eco-Distress

In each of these conceptualizations, the hypothesized "situation" that elicits distress is a common experience: seeing news about extreme weather (heat, drought, wildfires). The responses shown in the diagrams, or "flowers," are composites of reports of eco-distress based on the literature, the authors' clinical experiences with young people and adults, and a qualitative study with nine adults of varying ages conducted by the first author (Zevallos Labarthe & Marks, 2024). As such, these conceptualizations may be more aligned with adolescents' experiences, and more collaborative research with younger children is required to explore differences. Although it is possible that one person would report several of the common thoughts placed in the middle of each flower, it is more likely that only a few would be reported. We included a wide range of possible interpretations here to illustrate how case conceptualization can apply to a broad audience and to indicate the types of emotional, behavioral, and physiological consequences to look out for (details for each diagrammatic formulation follow in the text). Importantly, conceptualizations occurring post-disaster or involving other direct climate impacts would likely differ, as young people may need more immediate, trauma-informed care (e.g., Psychological First Aid).

Impairing Eco-Distress

Impairing Eco-Distress Processes

Impairing eco-distress is often characterized by negatively valenced thoughts about the CEE which are fundamentally accurate but skewed towards catastrophic, repetitive negative thinking styles (e.g., unconstructive worry, rumination). According to CB theory, an individual might be prone to experiencing these thoughts and thinking styles due to core beliefs shaped by earlier experiences, which are often observable in other life domains as well (e.g., strong beliefs around personal responsibility, perfectionism, or self-criticism). There may also be an intolerance of uncertainty or being out of control.

Although these thoughts and beliefs might motivate pro-environmental behavior, the skew towards powerful and repetitive negative thinking can elicit intense or more extreme actions (e.g., overengagement in news, becoming overly consumed with activism or volunteering). This unsustainable behavioral approach can lead to burnout and exhaustion, particularly for young people who struggle to find the motivation or time to take care of themselves, or who might be in a social circle where they feel an expectation from others (such as similarly active peers) that it is not acceptable to take a break. Other behaviors driven by thoughts and emotions might include hypervigilance to climate-related news and social media, particularly the negative stories. These behaviors lead to a confirmation bias that the worst is happening, which increases distress. In our clinical, research, and community experiences, young people commonly have relationships with people who they perceive as less concerned, which is often managed either through avoidance or having conflictual conversations. Both avoidance and conflict tend to perpetuate distress and preoccupation, which can reduce meaningful social connection and lower mood. Feeling personally responsible for societal transformation, particularly without synchronous engagement with a like-minded community, can create a sense of aloneness and powerlessness, making efforts feel futile and positive outcomes unachievable. The bodily consequences of impairing eco-distress may include physiological arousal and impaired energy, motivation, sleep, and appetite, and the stress connected with impairing eco-distress can also make it harder for young people to cope with other common stressors. The impairing eco-distress model aligns with a "problem focused coping" style, which is associated with increased behavioral engagement and self-efficacy in adolescents, as well as with negative affect (Ojala, 2015).

In addition to thoughts about the CEE, individuals often hold beliefs about their abilities and expectations around managing and coping with difficulties in general. For example, someone with high self-standards, the need to not feel certain emotions, and low self-efficacy might be more negative and self-critical about having "failed" to make a difference in the world. They may also judge themselves or feel overwhelmed for having certain feelings, which may result in attempts to control or prevent them. The harder they try to suppress their feelings, the more they paradoxically exacerbate the problem and exhaust themselves.

The CEE have been conceptualized as a type of systemic trauma which puts young people at risk of experiencing moral distress and moral injury (Hickman et al., 2021 Zevallos Labarthe & Marks, 2024). Moral injury arises from being part of a system where the powerful have failed to act quickly enough to prevent loss and catastrophe. It causes extensive harm, leaving young people feeling abandoned, betrayed, belittled, anguished, and angry about their unwanted complicity in this damage (Hickman et al., 2021). The moral aspects of the CEE highlight the importance of gaining a deeper understanding of what the CEE *means* to each individual and how this relates to their personal history.

Impairing Eco-Distress Outcome

The initial result of the impairing eco-distress cycle may not appear problematic at first, as it may initially lead to increases in energy and engagement, boosted by physiological arousal and the motivating forces of anxiety and anger. It could also lead to the development of a stronger sense of self-efficacy and significant personal transformation focused on pro-environmental and pro-social behaviors, which in turn could enhance a sense of belonging and purpose with like-minded peers, if this is available to the individual. However, risk factors highlighted here (e.g., emotional avoidance, negative self-referential beliefs, repetitive negative thinking styles) may maintain or increase distress. In the longer term, ongoing distress could prevent sustained engagement with environmental issues, which may explain why problem-focused coping alone increases negative affect (Ojala, 2015). Without protective coping factors such as finding meaning in distress, prioritizing self-care, participating in community-based action, and taking respite, arousal and distress will grow and lead to exhaustion, burnout, and even disengagement with environmental care. This cycle may increase vulnerability to other clinical issues in the longer term, although more research is needed on the relationship between eco-distress and psychopathology.

Constructive Eco-Distress

Constructive Eco-Distress Processes

Similar to impairing eco-distress, constructive eco-distress recognizes the dire reality of the crises. However, this realization exists alongside hope and is grounded in sustainable action. Recognizing the meaning underlying their distress allows young people to value the eco-emotions themselves. In the constructive eco-distress model, negative thoughts about catastrophe are still present but they are less repetitive or consistently focused on the most catastrophic outcomes. The positive effect of identifying meaning in one's distress aligns with findings that meaning-focused coping in adolescents was linked to pro-environmental engagement and efficacy as well as life satisfaction, positive affect, and reduced negative affect (Ojala, 2012). Meaning-focused coping aligns with a cognitive approach where a situation is reframed more positively but still realistically (Ojala, 2012), and the resulting shift in emotions helps the individual work with a stressor constructively even if it cannot be removed (Folkman, 2008).

In the constructive eco-distress cycle, the young person still recognizes the catastrophic implications of the CEE, but their thoughts include broader viewpoints and place the CEE in deeper perspectives of time and place. For example, a young person may consider that although threat is present, many actual outcomes are still unknown because interactions between human and natural systems are complex and unpredictable.

This viewpoint allows room to imagine positive outcomes, such as social transformations arising from unexpected large-scale shifts in society in the form of positive social tipping points (Lenton et al., 2022), large-scale social movements, global cooperation, and scientific advances. It is worth bearing in mind that the cognitive shift from immediate to long-term consequences is quite complex and often requires the ability to think abstractly. Depending on a child's age and developmental stage, their brain may not yet be able to digest such cognitively complex and abstract concepts (e.g., Blakemore & Choudhury, 2006), and younger children may need support in developing broader perspectives on the CEE. For example, they might instead find hope in admired scientists or other societal figures or notice positive changes in their local community.

Constructive eco-distress could also facilitate maturation in larger personal and identity development, such as revising life goals and exploring philosophical, existential, or spiritual questions (Ojala, 2012). Broader perspectives allow for more mixed emotional responses in which painful and positive emotions are held together. Seeing that individual action has limited impact means that responsibility is disseminated across humanity. This perspective can reduce young people's perfectionistic or overdemanding expectations of themselves and reduce the sense of personal failure- or futility-based thoughts in response to negative ecological news. Instead, the young person can continue to engage in pro-environmental behaviors which are driven by deeper values such as the desire to help or protect human and nonhuman beings from harm.

Although there might be similarities in the behavioral responses seen in individuals with impairing and constructive eco-distress, the *how* and the *why* behind the behaviors differ. For example, a young person might continue to engage purposefully with the CEE by staying informed; however, they may feel less overwhelmed because they have learned to engage with the news in a mindful and purposeful way, from trusted sources with a range of perspectives. Socially, the young person may join a community with shared environmental concerns and benefit from the newfound strength, solidarity, and connection from those relationships. Exploring and sharing CEE concerns and the importance of self-care with like-minded others could increase young people's capacity to not only manage adverse reactions to those whom they perceive as less concerned but also to take a step back and take care of their well-being when necessary. Some young people might engage in community or lifestyle changes aimed at increasing safety or lessening impact; for example, a child and their family could advocate for their school to reduce reliance on carbon-based infrastructure, or a young adult may write to local politicians about their concerns.

An important part of moving from impairing to constructive eco-distress includes seeing the distress itself not as unwanted but as a natural, human response with intrinsic value that demonstrates care for the world and other beings. Accepting the existence of difficult thoughts and feelings, without judging or fighting them, is an important part of psychological health (Ford et al., 2018) and is central to many third wave CB approaches such as Acceptance and Commitment Therapy, Compassion Focused Therapy, and mindfulness-based cognitive therapy. Learning to allow eco-emotions to arise and pass, without fighting them, is likely easier if eco-distress can be reframed as an understandable response to the CEE, related to core environmental, spiritual, and cultural concerns and identities. Strengthening abilities in dialectical thinking may also facilitate the move from impairing to constructive eco-distress.

Adopting a less judgmental, more compassionate stance enables young people to engage in behaviors that support well-being and resilience. Responding to emotional distress with compassion rather than judgment promotes adaptive coping skills (such as self-care or taking a break vs pushing beyond personal limits), both acutely and longer term. Enhancing compassion for oneself and for others may also help young people deepen their understanding of feelings such as anger, guilt, and shame. A compassionate response makes burnout and exhaustion less likely while still supporting purposeful, sustainable pro-environmental engagement. By making time for rest and repair, physiological arousal will be reduced, and focusing on feelings of hope, compassion, and inspiration will be energizing rather than draining.

Constructive Eco-Distress Outcome

In the constructive eco-distress cycle, appraisals of the CEE as catastrophic are appropriate and realistic. However, in contrast to impairing eco-distress, balancing this with an appreciation of uncertainty and reducing personal expectations generates more variable emotions, physiological sensations, and behaviors, and offers more opportunities to choose how to respond rather than being motivated only by intense and difficult emotions. This approach may also better support individuals to act together towards collective societal transformation by decreasing hopelessness.

Impairing versus Constructive Eco-Distress: Conclusions and Future Directions

The case conceptualizations above showcase how impairing and constructive eco-distress, although based on similar concerns about the CEE, can lead to very different outcomes. Constructive eco-distress allows young people to experience more balanced responses and remain engaged in the face of the CEE. Impairing eco-distress is likely to lead to hopelessness, potential disengagement from needed action, and even a vulnerability to clinical distress. Conceptualizing eco-distress this way has implications for processes that might help young people find more constructive and less painful ways of living with the CEE. Existing guidelines within CB therapeutic frameworks offer ways in which young people could make changes that will help them move from impairing to constructive eco-distress. These include learning skills in cognitive flexibility, emotion regulation and mindfulness, self-care strategies, and values-based action. CB frameworks may also create room to explore the reframing of negative beliefs about the self and how one feels about the CEE, if this is relevant to an individual's impairing eco-distress. Future research should specifically investigate how CB approaches to eco-distress could be adapted in culturally, geographically, developmentally, and identity-sensitive ways. We end by emphasizing that, although we believe that CB conceptualizations and treatment approaches offer one possible route to reducing the suffering young people experience in response to the CEE, *it is not the responsibility of young people to find a way to feel "better" about this situation, nor is it their responsibility to solve it*. Responsibility for this lies with adults – particularly those in positions of power – to shift the structural, political, and economic systems that maintain climate inaction and continue global dependency on fossil fuels.

Contribution Statement

Kelsey Hudson prepared the sections on case conceptualizations and sociocultural and contextual factors. Elizabeth Marks provided the theoretical background and figures and prepared all other sections on CB theory as applied to eco-distress.

References

American Psychiatric Association (2013). Cultural formulation interview (CFI). In *Diagnostic and statistical manual of mental disorders* (5th ed.). APA.

Bandura, A., & Cherry, L. (2019). Enlisting the power of youth for climate change. *American Psychologist*, 75(7), 945–951. https://doi.org/10.1037/amp0000512

Berman, S. L., Weems, C. F., & Stickle, T. R. (2006). Existential anxiety in adolescents: Prevalence, structure, association with psychological symptoms and identity development. *Journal of Youth and Adolescence*, 35(3), 285–292. https://doi.org/10.1007/s10964-006-9032-y

Blakemore, S. J., & Choudhury, S. (2006). Development of the adolescent brain: Implications for executive function and social cognition. *Journal of Child Psychology and Psychiatry*, 47(3–4), 296–312. doi:10.1111/j.1469-7610.2006.01611.x.

Burnham, J. (1992). Approach–method–technique: Making distinctions and creating connections. *Human Systems*, 3(1), 3–27.

Burnham, J. (1993). Systemic supervision: The evolution of reflexivity in the context of the supervisory relationship. *Human Systems*, 4(3), 349–381.

Burnham, J. (2012). Developments in Social GRRRAAACCEEESSS: Visible-invisible and voiced-unvoiced. In I. B. Krause (Ed.), *Culture and reflexivity in systemic psychotherapy: Mutual perspectives* (pp. 139–160). Karnac Books.

Castaños-Cervantes, S. (2019). Brief CBT group therapy for Mexican homeless girls. *The Cognitive Behaviour Therapist*, 12. https://doi.org/10.1017/S1754470X18000272

Cisler, J. M., & Koster, E. H. (2010). Mechanisms of attentional biases towards threat in anxiety disorders: An integrative review. *Clinical Psychology Review*, 30(2), 203–216. https://doi.org/10.1016/j.cpr.2009.11.003

Coffey, Y., Bhullar, N., Durkin, J., Islam, M. S., & Usher, K. (2021). Understanding eco-anxiety: A systematic scoping review of current literature and identified knowledge gaps. *Journal of Climate Change and Health*, 3, 100047. https://doi.org/10.1016/j.joclim.2021.100047

Compas, B. E., Jaser, S. S., Bettis, A. H., Watson, K. H., Gruhn, M. A., Dunbar, J. P., Williams, E., & Thigpen, J. C. (2017). Coping, emotion regulation, and psychopathology in childhood and adolescence: A meta-analysis and narrative review. *Psychological Bulletin*, 143(9), 939–991. https://doi.org/10.1037/bul0000110

Crandon, T. J., Scott, J. G., Charlson, F. J., & Thomas, H. J. (2022). A social–ecological perspective on climate anxiety in children and adolescents. *Nature Climate Change*, 12(2), 123–131. https://doi.org/10.1038/s41558-021-01251-y

Daniels, J., & Loades, M. E. (2017). A novel approach to treating CFS and co-morbid health anxiety: A case study. *Clinical Psychology & Psychotherapy*, 24(3), 727–736. doi:10.1002/cpp.2042.

Dobson, K. S., & Dozois, D. J. (2021). *Handbook of cognitive-behavioral therapies*. Guilford Press.

Doherty, T. J., Lykins, A. D., Piotrowski, N. A., Rogers, Z., Sebree Jr., D. D., & White, K. E. (2022). Clinical psychology responses to the climate crisis. In G. J. G. Asmundson (Ed.), *Comprehensive clinical psychology* (2nd ed., vol. 11, pp. 167–183). Elsevier. https://dx.doi.org/10.1016/B978-0-12-818697-8.00236-3.

Dozois, D. J. A., & Beck, A. T. (2008). Cognitive schemas, beliefs and assumptions. In K. S. Dobson & D. J. A. Dozois (Eds.), *Risk factors in depression* (pp. 121–143). Elsevier Academic Press. https://doi.org/10.1016/B978-0-08-045078-0.00006-X

Dummett, N. (2010). Cognitive–behavioural therapy with children, young people and families: From individual to systemic therapy. *Advances in Psychiatric Treatment*, 16(1), 23–36. doi:10.1192/APT.BP.107.004259

Ehrenreich-May, J. (2018). *Unified protocol for transdiagnostic treatment of emotional disorders in adolescents: Workbook*. Oxford University Press.

Ellis, A. (1991). The revised ABC's of rational-emotive therapy (RET). *Journal of Rational-emotive and Cognitive-behavior Therapy*, 9(3), 139–172.

Fenley, A. R., Sanchez, A., Pincus, D. B., Hudson, K., Farley, A., & Merson, R. (2022). What to do when worries ring true: How CBT clinicians can address realistic worries among youth with anxiety during our challenging times [Clinical round table]. Association for Behavioral and Cognitive Therapies Convention, New York, November 17–20. www.abct.org/2022-convention/

Folkman, S. (2008). The case for positive emotions in the stress process. *Anxiety, Stress, and Coping*, 21(1), 3–14. doi.org/10.1080/10615800701740457

Ford, B. Q., Lam, P., John, O. P., & Mauss, I. B. (2018). The psychological health benefits of accepting negative emotions and thoughts: Laboratory, diary, and longitudinal evidence. *Journal of Personality and Social Psychology*, 115(6), 1075. doi:10.1037/pspp0000157

Haig-Ferguson, A., Cooper, K., Cartwright, E., Loades, M. E., & Daniels, J. (2021). Practitioner review: Health anxiety in children and young people in the context of the COVID-19 pandemic. *Behavioural and Cognitive Psychotherapy*, 49(2), 129–143. doi:10.1017/S1352465820000636

Hays, P. A. (2016). *Addressing cultural complexities in practice: Assessment, diagnosis, and therapy* (3rd ed.). American Psychological Association. https://doi.org/10.1037/14801-000

Hickman, C. (2020). We need to (find a way to) talk about … eco-anxiety. *Journal of Social Work Practice*, 34(4), 411–424. https://doi.org/10.1080/02650533.2020.1844166

Hickman, C., Marks, E., Pihkala, P., Clayton, S., Lewandowski, R. E., Mayall, E. E., … van Susteren, L. (2021). Climate anxiety in children and young people and their beliefs about government responses to climate change: A global survey. *The Lancet Planetary Health*, 5(12), e863–e873. doi:10.1016/S2542-5196(21)00278-3

Hogg, T. L., Stanley, S. K., O'Brien, L. V., Wilson, M. S., & Watsford, C. R. (2021). The Hogg Eco-Anxiety Scale: Development and validation of a multidimensional scale. *Global Environmental Change*, 71, 102391. https://doi.org/10.1016/j.gloenvcha.2021.102391

King, D., & Said, G. (2019). Working with unaccompanied asylum-seeking young people: Cultural considerations and acceptability of a cognitive behavioural group approach. *The Cognitive Behaviour Therapist*, 12, E11. doi:10.1017/S1754470X18000260

Kuyken, W., Padesky, C. A., & Dudley, R. (2009). *Collaborative case conceptualization*. Guilford Press.

Lenton, T. M., Benson, S., Smith, T., Ewer, T., Lanel, V., Petykowski, E., … Sharpe, S. (2022). Operationalising positive tipping points towards global sustainability. *Global Sustainability*, 5, E1. doi:10.1017/sus.2021.30

Mansell, W., Harvey, A., Watkins, E. D., & Shafran, R. (2009). Conceptual foundations of the transdiagnostic approach to CBT. *Journal of Cognitive Psychotherapy*, 23(1), 6–19. https://doi.org/10.1891/0889-8391.23.1.6

Moorey, S. (1996). When bad things happen to rational people: Cognitive therapy in adverse life circumstances. *Frontiers of Cognitive Therapy*, 450–469.

Naeem, F. (2019). Cultural adaptations of CBT: A summary and discussion of the Special Issue on Cultural Adaptation of CBT. *The Cognitive Behaviour Therapist*, 12, E40. doi:10.1017/S1754470X19000278

Ojala, M. (2012). How do children cope with global climate change? Coping strategies, engagement, and well-being. *Journal of Environmental Psychology*, 32(3), 225–233. https://doi.org/10.1016/j.jenvp.2012.02.004

Ojala, M. (2015). Hope in the face of climate change: Associations with environmental engagement and student perceptions of teachers' emotion communication style and future orientation. *Journal of Environmental Education*, 46(3), 133–148. http://dx.doi. org/10.1080/00958964.2015.1021662

Persons, J. B. (2022). Case formulation. *Cognitive and Behavioral Practice*, 29(3), 537–540. https://doi.org/10.1016/j.cbpra.2022.02.014

Pihkala, P. (2020). Eco-anxiety and environmental education. *Sustainability*, 12, 10149. doi:10.3390/su122310149

Pihkala, P. (2022). Eco-anxiety and pastoral care: Theoretical considerations and practical suggestions. *Religions*, 13(3), 192. https://doi.org/10.3390/rel13030192

Rathod, S., Phiri, P., & Naeem, F. (2019). An evidence-based framework to culturally adapt cognitive behaviour therapy. *The Cognitive Behaviour Therapist*, 12, E10. doi:10.1017/S1754470X18000247

Roper-Hall, A. (1998). Working systemically with older people and their families who have come to grief. In P. Sutcliffe, G. Tufnell, & U. Cornish (Eds.), *Working with the dying and bereaved: Systemic approaches to therapeutic work* (pp. 177–206). Macmillan.

Sperry, L. (2022). *Highly effective therapy: Developing essential clinical competencies in counseling and psychotherapy*. Routledge. https://doi.org/10.4324/9780203869963

Stanley, S. K., Hogg, T. L., Leviston, Z., & Walker, I. (2021). From anger to action: Differential impacts of eco-anxiety, eco-depression, and eco-anger on climate action and wellbeing. *Journal of Climate Change and Health*, 1, 100003. doi:10.1016/J.JOCLIM.2021.100003

Verplanken, B., Marks, E., & Dobromir, A. I. (2020). On the nature of eco-anxiety: How constructive or unconstructive is habitual worry about global warming? *Journal of Environmental Psychology*, 72, 101528. https://doi.org/10.1016/j.jenvp.2020.101528

Verplanken, B., & Roy, D. (2013). "My worries are rational, climate change is not": Habitual ecological worrying is an adaptive response. *PLoS ONE*, 8(9). https://doi.org/10.1371/journal.pone.0074708

Watkins, E. R. (2008). Constructive and unconstructive repetitive thought. *Psychological Bulletin*, 134(2), 163. doi: 10.1037/0033-2909.134.2.163

Zevallos Labarthe, I. & Marks, E. (2024) "The complete opposite of what you morally believe": (In)action on climate change by State authorities and powerful bodies drives moral injury and eco-distress in UK young people. *The Cognitive Behavioural Therapist (in press)*

CHAPTER 9

A Research Agenda for Young People's Psychological Response to Climate Change

Joshua R. Wortzel

The preceding chapters of this book have detailed what is known about the phenomenology, biological and psychological underpinnings, developmental and cultural considerations, and definitional distinctions of the effects of climate change on young people's mental health. Much still remains unknown. In a literature review conducted in August 2021, my colleagues and I identified only forty peer-reviewed research articles in pediatric mental health and climate change (Wortzel, Lee et al., 2022). Of the authors interviewed, 75 percent reported researching in this space for the past five years or less, and 80 percent were under the age of 50. This is a field that is small and in its nascency.

The goal of this concluding chapter of Part I is to propose a comprehensive research agenda to fill in the many gaps in what we know about climate distress in pediatric populations. As a research agenda, it strives to identify research priorities in the decade ahead, note potential pitfalls of this research, and recommend questions and projects that would particularly help push this field forward. It will touch upon and briefly summarize many of the topics discussed in greater depth in the preceding chapters with the intent of providing an overarching map for what is needed to move the field forward. The reader is encouraged to refer back to prior chapters for their discussions of more granular research questions, as well as to consider others' published research agendas for the field of climate mental health outside of pediatric populations (Hwong et al., 2022).

This research agenda is subdivided into five domains: (1) delineating types of climate emotion symptoms and syndromes, (2) assessing their epidemiology, (3) understanding their psychological meaning and sequelae, (4) developing interventions for them, and (5) exploring the biological impacts of climate change on children's psychological responses. It concludes with considerations for how the research community and funding bodies can adjust to help support such a research agenda.

Delineating Types of Climate Emotion Symptoms and Syndromes

Most types of climate distress that have been studied pertain to anxiety. This is likely because anxiety disorders comprise the largest proportion of mental health conditions among children and adolescents (31.9 percent) and have the earliest age of onset (Merikangas et al., 2010). Fundamental to understanding children's anxious responses to climate change is the concept of trait versus state anxiety. *Trait anxiety* refers to characterological factors that predispose people to heightened worry in response to stimuli, whereas *state anxiety* describes individuals' physiological and psychological responses to adverse situations (Leal et al., 2017). This parsing of anxiety symptoms is only starting to be applied to climate anxiety (Materia, 2016). While nonpersonality factors, such as socioeconomic status, profession, and geographic location, predispose certain individuals to more climate distress than others, developing a better psychological understanding of who is most affected by this distress through the lens of trait versus state anxiety is critical to identify and delineate types of climate anxiety (Pihkala, 2020).

Relatedly, the terms used to describe aspects of climate anxiety are often inconsistently delineated and have considerable overlap. Examples include *solastalgia*, distress in response to environmental changes to one's home, *eco-anxiety*, a dread associated with degradation of the environment more generally, *eco-paralysis*, an inability to engage in actions to reduce climate change due to their perceived futility, and *eco-nostalgia*, the perception that the environment was better prior to climate change (Albrecht, 2011; Clayton, 2020). While these terms are helpful in conceptualizing the myriad ways that climate change can contribute to anxiety symptoms, they have limited utility in research settings if they are not more stringently defined and if we lack tools to distinguish them both from each other and from other psychological responses (Coffey et al., 2021; Pihkala, 2020).

The issue of whether these terms are being used to denote clinical syndromes with pathological implications or healthy responses to the stress of climate change is also important. Most scholars and practitioners in this field agree that a certain degree of anxiety and discomfort about addressing climate change is appropriate – it is a healthy, mature response to the global climate catastrophe – and it can be a motivating force for climate action. However, anxiety about climate change can become clinically significant too if, for example, it starts affecting individuals' ability to sleep, work, or socialize, and it can also comanifest with other diagnosable psychiatric conditions such as generalized anxiety disorder (Clayton, 2020). Within the concept of *eco-anxiety*, more research is needed to help distinguish between healthy responses to climate change and those responses that require clinical intervention. It is also important to expand our understanding and delineation of other emotional responses to climate change, including depression, anger, and grief. For example, what cognitive schemas about climate change or underlying state versus trait depressive factors lead to the development of these alternative emotional responses among young people? The methods and considerations used to investigate climate anxiety might be applicable to studying these other emotions as well.

Climate distress has also been understood in terms of traumatic stress, grouped into acute, chronic, posttraumatic, and pretraumatic phenomenologies. Some of the most robust data we currently have regarding climate distress have looked at the short-term and long-term psychological impacts of natural disasters on children's mental health (Kousky, 2016). However, as climate change progresses, many communities will face repeated extreme weather events. There is less literature providing insights into the psychology of communities responding to these repeated natural disasters, and the responses of these communities will likely be different from communities recovering from only one (Hahn et al., 2022). The concept of chronic traumatic stress developed in research of refugees and survivors of torture may offer relevant, parallel insights into the psychological impact of repeated natural disasters (Fondacaro & Mazulla, 2018). As the anticipatory threat of natural disasters becomes more pervasive, some individuals may also develop pretraumatic stress syndromes, a phenomenon thus far primarily studied in predeployed soldiers (Kaplan, 2020). These individuals can experience "flash-forward" events, panic attacks, and phobias related to the traumatic events they anticipate experiencing (Berntsen & Rubin, 2014). The identification and treatment of this condition also needs to be researched as it might be an area where preventive interventions could be particularly effective.

Researching the Epidemiology of Climate Emotion Symptoms and Syndromes

It is currently difficult to know how many young people experience distress about climate change, though preliminary worldwide data suggest that over half of 16- to 25-year-olds are very worried or extremely worried about it (Hickman et al., 2021). Robust quantitative data on younger children is even more lacking. This lack of clarity on the prevalence of climate distress is partly because the field has not had validated scales to measure climate distress until recently; however, there are now at least four published, validated climate change anxiety measures (Clayton & Karazsia, 2020; Helm et al., 2018; Hogg et al., 2021; Stanley et al., 2021), and there are likely others in development. These surveys are limited in that they have been validated in primarily white, Anglo-European cultures and depend upon self-report of psychological symptoms. It is essential to utilize these scales in larger, more diverse populations of young people to see which children are most affected and most vulnerable. It will also be helpful to validate these surveys against more objective measures of psychiatric symptoms than self-report. For example, surveying children presenting for other mental health concerns in outpatient and inpatient settings may help explore how climate distress is contributing to their psychiatric symptoms, which can be measured empirically by clinical providers. It will also be important to age-adjust the questions we pose to younger children, as qualitative data suggest that children process aspects of climate distress in ways that are consistent with their stages of psychological development (Benoit, 2022; Thomas et al., 2022).

Identifying demographic factors that are associated with increased vulnerability to climate distress is a broad area of research that will require several approaches. For example, there is some evidence that youths living in previously and currently colonized countries tend to express more worry about climate change compared to young people in more affluent, geopolitically dominant countries (Hickman et al., 2021). Surveys of eco-anxiety show that women also tend to report more anxiety about climate change than men (Coffey et al., 2021). Research has so far generally failed to address the effects on people of other genders. Further identification of which groups are most vulnerable to climate change distress and how that varies by setting and sociocultural factors will be important for identifying the etiology of this process and developing and triaging interventions for affected young people.

Parental mental health and parenting practices likely also impact children's psychological vulnerabilities to climate change. Severe maternal stress during pregnancy can also significantly alter the hypothalamic–pituitary–adrenal axis and epigenetics of the developing fetus (Vergunst & Berry, 2021), as well as the long-term anxiety profiles of these children (Davis & Sandman, 2012). Postnatally, children are also affected by how environmental stressors impact adults' psychological resources for parenting, such as the time and emotional reserve that parents have to provide Winnicottian "good enough" caretaking and positive regard for their children's healthy psychological development (Winnicott, 1963; Xerxa et al., 2021). Research is needed to specifically explore these aspects of family function in the context of short- and long-term climate change and familial responses to climate stress.

Related to these predisposing vulnerabilities to climate change distress are the concepts of co-occurring traumas and intersectionality, the idea that societal factors such as race, gender, and class are interconnected and compounding. For example, women and children are disproportionately affected by domestic violence, and there is evidence that climate stressors exacerbate domestic violence (Adams et al., 2021; Schumacher et al., 2010). Many individuals, particularly BIPOC (Black, Indigenous, and people of color) communities, may be more vulnerable to the psychological effects of climate change because of other co-occurring adversities they face (Kaijser & Kronsell, 2014; McMullen & Dow, 2022). Given that some groups, particularly Black Americans, have been and continue to be both deprived of and targeted in outdoor spaces, the relationships that young people of different sociocultural communities have with the natural world, environmental degradation, and the outdoor spaces they find most therapeutic, may also differ (Doherty et al., 2022). These communities need to be surveyed, and the impacts of greenspace on the well-being of these communities should continue to be studied (South et al., 2018). Research is needed to understand the impacts of these co-occurring, intersectional factors on climate distress, guided by community leaders and those knowledgeable about environmental justice. Conceiving of climate change and its sequelae as adverse childhood experiences (ACEs) may be a useful paradigm in general, and research methodologies used to study ACEs might be applied to intersectional climate stressors as well.

Understanding the Psychological Meaning and Sequelae of Climate Change in Young People

There are numerous psychological impacts of climate change on child development, and we are just in the initial stages of identifying them. These involve self-states, psychodynamics, and thought distortions. For example, self-efficacy and self-agency are aspects of psychological function that are formed during childhood and adolescence, and youths raised in an era of rapid climate change may suffer impairments in these areas of psychological development when they are left feeling hopeless and powerless to do anything about it (Nice et al., 2022). This disempowerment can result in *moral disengagement*, a process by which young people learn to suspend their moral outrage at a societal problem (Bandura, 2016). Young people who have disengaged from moral concern about climate change can continue to feel positive regard for their elders and function in a society where their lifestyles actively contribute to the problem. Thus, moral disengagement to preserve one's self-concept can contribute to climate denialism, and research is needed to study how best to promote moral reengagement and support ongoing moral development in these individuals.

There are other psychodynamic aspects of young people's responses to climate change that can be similarly maladaptive and require study and intervention. Climate change has been defined as a *hyperobject*, a process so vast and integrated into the fabric of society that it is difficult for the human mind to grasp and approach it (Morton, 2013). To cope with a problem that is intractable on a personal level, individuals can engage in psychological splitting and other psychological defenses such as projection, displacement, dissociation, and repression, which avoid addressing climate change and can fuel other conflicts, such as political extremism and bigotry. There is a need to help individuals manage their anxieties to hold together a variety of difficult dialectics, including individual agency and collective agency in addressing climate change, hope and hopelessness about the future, and nature as a source of comfort which requires our protection versus nature as a threat to human health and safety as climates become less hospitable (Lewis et al., 2020). Research is needed to validate these dialectics and develop therapeutic tools to help young people maintain them. Efforts that have utilized dialectical behavioral therapy (DBT) to address other hyperobjects such as racism may offer key insights into developing therapeutic DBT approaches for climate change that can be studied empirically (Pierson et al., 2022).

Cognitive distortions and worldviews that impede adaptation to climate change, such as denial of humanity's contribution to global warming or belief in a fully technological solution to climate change, also need to be studied. Existing therapeutic paradigms for addressing real existential threats, such as health anxiety during the COVID-19 pandemic, may be useful when designing social strategies to address cognitive biases with respect to climate change (Kini et al., 2020). Assessing behavioral and future-oriented responses to climate distress, such as youth reporting hesitancy about childbearing due to climate change (Hickman et al., 2021), should also be studied. A short survey in clinical settings where female-bodied individuals are offered birth control might be administered to assess whether climate concerns play a role in their decision.

Developing Interventions for Climate Emotion Symptoms and Syndromes

The corollary research question that arises from research on psychological responses to climate change is what to do about these responses. While psychological first-aid programs have been developed as part of post-disaster protocols (Everly & Lating, 2022), in general, proactive interventions to increase communities' mental health services around climate change are lacking, especially in countries expected to be most imminently affected. A few countries, including Thailand and Myanmar, have invested resources to develop community mental health infrastructures to support the immediate and long-term needs of communities affected by natural disasters (Roudini et al., 2017). Research on the effectiveness of these programs will be important for iteration and improvement of these interventions and to motivate other countries to follow suit. Studying telehealth implementations will also be essential to reach psychiatrically underserved areas during climate stressors (Augusterfer et al., 2018). Beyond services for disaster settings, there is a growing need for nondisaster-related climate distress interventions, which we will focus on here.

The goal of most current approaches to reducing climate distress is not to pathologize or "treat away" people's psychological responses, except in those instances where it contributes to clinical levels of impairment. Rather, the goal is to transmute climate distress into *eco-action* – behavioral engagement to address climate change. There is some evidence that distress about climate change may predict behavioral engagement and adaptation (Clayton, 2020; Ojala, 2015). Other emotions, such as anger and depression about climate change, may also be motivating (Stanley et al., 2021). For some individuals, however, emotions about climate change can be so overwhelming and options for action so numerous and inchoate that they remain stuck in a position of inaction (i.e., *eco-paralysis*) (Ágoston et al., 2022). Researching interventions to move people from eco-paralysis to eco-action is an important next step for the field.

Promoting helpful coping paradigms around climate change is an active area of research. Three fundamental forms of coping have been identified: problem-focused coping, which involves behavioral engagement in climate action or activism, emotion-focused coping, which involves use of cognitive reframing to de-emphasize the threat of climate change, and meaning-focused coping, which draws on a person's beliefs, values, and goals to foster positive affect toward the stress of climate change (overviewed in Clayton, 2020). Only preliminary work has been done to determine how these coping strategies can be fostered and which appear most salutary and effective in motivating climate action (Ojala & Bengtsson, 2019). Additional research in larger, more diverse samples is needed.

Psychological resilience, posttraumatic growth, and transformational resilience are all concepts for improved coping after climate distress. *Resilience* refers to a person's ability to cope with an emotional crisis and return to precrisis levels of psychological function, and *posttraumatic growth* refers to the process by which an individual can achieve better psychological health compared to their precrisis function (Adams et al., 2021). *Transformational resilience* refers to the process of achieving posttraumatic growth by making positive, adaptive changes to how individuals and society think and function (Doppelt, 2017). There have been developments about how to foster resilience around climate change, such as The Race to Resilience, an initiative of the United Nations that aims to build a programmatic infrastructure by 2030 to support the basic physical and psychological resilience of four billion of the most climate-vulnerable individuals (Belkin, 2022). It will be important for the field to achieve the relatively harder task of developing programs to foster posttraumatic growth and transformational resilience as well.

Based on these treatment paradigms, a number of interventions are under development. Educating children, their parents, and their medical providers about climate distress is one large category of interventions. Schools offer a unique environment where children can learn about the science of climate change, be provided with opportunities for eco-action, and be socialized into problem- and meaning-focused coping with climate distress (Baker et al., 2021). While some school interventions have been evaluated for their effectiveness in managing eco-anxiety in children, further research that engages students in age-appropriate, achievable interventions and in more diverse student populations would be beneficial.

Interventions to teach parents to recognize and manage their own climate distress are needed. Parental and caretaker psychological awareness and emotional stance toward climate change have been shown to directly influence children's coping strategies toward climate change (Ojala & Bengtsson, 2019). It is also important for parents to learn how to talk to their children about these issues. Resources have been created to help parents navigate these discussions (DeMocker, 2020; Wortzel, Champlin et al., 2022), but there is a need to empirically test the effectiveness of these interventions, particularly across cultures.

Pediatric mental health providers comprise another important group to target for education about climate mental health, as they can help their patients and patients' families process and address climate distress. Currently, a minority of psychiatry trainees learn about climate mental health (Wortzel, Haase et al., 2022). While curricula on climate change are being created at many institutions, there is currently little consensus on what these curricula should include, and their effectiveness as learning tools has not been studied. Psychiatry trainees should also receive instruction and mentorship in more ecologically sustainable clinical practices (Wortzel, Guerrero et al., 2022), and the psychological impact of this more sustainable practice on physicians and their patients should be studied. Additionally, helping mental health providers access and process their own climate distress is important in enabling them to be available and informed to discuss these issues with their patients (Lewis et al., 2020).

Psychoeducation is another class of interventions to help young people process and cope with climate distress, and these are some of the most studied interventions for climate distress to date (Wortzel, Lee et al., 2022). Children, especially young children, can lack the words to describe their climate distress, and psychoeducation can help improve their ability to identify and express their emotions and thoughts. Children may also benefit from education about what their parents and communities are already doing to address climate change, which can help them feel less alone and angry that adults are not taking care of them (Vergunst & Berry, 2021). Psychoeducation can be more accessible to disseminate in community or school settings compared to psychotherapeutic interventions requiring mental health and medical personnel, and studies of these types of interventions are promising for further research and development.

Aside from education interventions, many established psychotherapies are applicable to climate distress, though all require further development and testing to assess their effectiveness. Acceptance and commitment therapy, psychodynamic and object relations work, dialectical behavioral therapy, cognitive behavioral therapy (CBT), and psychological first aid have all been suggested as useful approaches (Baudon & Jachens, 2021; Doherty et al., 2022; Lewis et al., 2020; Randall, 2009). Group therapy is another treatment modality that is being explored (Baudon & Jachens, 2021). These group interventions have been conducted in mostly community contexts, and very few have been studied empirically for their effectiveness in managing climate distress. Such research is needed for their further development.

Means of studying the effectiveness of psychotherapeutic interventions in children are numerous (Weisz & Kazdin, 2010), and these methods can be applied to therapies for climate distress. For example, to study the effectiveness of manualized therapies, one might adapt a self-directed CBT phone application to provide interventions for commonly held cognitions contributing to climate distress. Data on changes in self-reported climate distress could be collected over the course of this application's use. For therapies that require interpersonal, real-time interventions, one could recruit providers and their pediatric patients from the Climate-Aware Therapists Directory (Climate Psychology Alliance North America, 2022). Providers could receive trainings in multiple climate therapy modalities, and changes in patients' climate distress could be measured to compare the relative effectiveness of these therapies. Similarly, comparing outcomes of different group therapy models to address climate distress could be conducted, as has been published for other indications (Burlingame et al., 2003).

There are a number of other novel interventions that also merit attention and investigation. Activism as therapy is the concept that engaging in activities to address climate change can help inoculate against or improve climate distress (Schwartz et al., 2022). Some evidence suggests that individual actions, such as eating less meat and making one's home more fuel efficient, or collective activism, such as engaging with groups of like-minded people to take local political action, may have both positive and negative effects on mental health (Boehnke & Wong, 2011; Chen & Gorski, 2015; Ojala, 2012). Green exposure interventions to increase connectedness to nature and lower climate distress levels are also under study (Baudon & Jachens, 2021; Doherty et al., 2022).

Exploring the Biological Impacts of Climate Change on Children's Psychological Responses

The biology of how climate change affects children's psychology is an area of research that is essentially unstudied; however, from literature in animal models and adults, there is a growing appreciation that changes in climate may have direct biological impacts on mental health. For example, in adults, heatwaves are associated with increased negative emotions (Noelke et al., 2016), worsening mental health (Obradovich et al., 2018), and increased rates of suicide and episodes of violence (Carleton et al., 2016). There is preliminary evidence that this relationship exists in adolescent populations as well (Akkaya-Kalayci et al., 2017). Hotter temperatures are also associated with exacerbations and increased hospitalizations of a number of psychiatric conditions (Thompson et al., 2018). Mechanisms of action for the relationship between temperature and mental health outcomes remain unclear, though they may have to do with the effects of ambient heat on serotonin (Raison et al., 2015) and other neurotransmitters (Machado-Moreira et al., 2012). It is unknown how ambient temperatures may impact young people's anxieties and other affective responses to climate change through molecular and epigenetic mechanisms. Neurofunctional studies of how climate distress may be similar to or differ from other mental health conditions have also not been conducted.

There are other direct and indirect effects of climate change that likely have biological impacts on mental health. For example, there is a now well-established correlation between exposure to airborne pollutants and neurodevelopmental disorders in children (Perera, 2017). Increases in atmospheric concentrations of carbon dioxide decrease macro- and micronutrient concentrations, such as iron and zinc, in many staple crops (Beach et al., 2019), which have been associated with the increased prevalence of multiple mental health conditions, including depression, bipolar disorder, autism, and neurocognitive disorders (Chen, Su et al., 2013; Swardfager et al., 2013). Currently, there is little to no understanding of how these indirect impacts of climate change are impacting the neurophysiology of young people, which will likely impact their psychological, emotional, and cognitive function.

Conclusion

This chapter has explored the state of research on pediatric psychological responses to climate change and the strengths and limitations of our knowledge to date. This research agenda can be grouped into five domains. First, it discussed the importance of delineating existing definitions of climate distress, which includes distinguishing between normal and pathological stress responses to climate change and integrating concepts from existing anxiety and trauma literature, such as state versus trait anxiety and pre- versus posttraumatic stress responses. Second, regarding studying the epidemiology of climate distress, it reviewed the importance of developing and validating scales to measure aspects of climate emotion symptoms and syndromes, identifying who is most vulnerable and resilient to this stress, and considering the effects of parental mental health and parenting practices on the epidemiology of young people's psychological responses to climate change. Third, it reviewed the need to explore the psychological meaning and sequelae of climate change, including concepts of moral disengagement, dialectics of climate distress, and cognitive distortions.

Fourth, it discussed a number of conventional and novel interventions to address climate distress, which have been conceptualized and preliminarily tested but require further investigation. Finally, it briefly reviewed several ways in which climate change, both directly and indirectly, may impact young people biologically and discussed the need to study the impact of these changes on their psychological responses to the climate crisis.

Several issues must be addressed if the global research community is to achieve these research goals:

1. We need to ensure that this research is not overly colored by political persuasion and preconceived notions that climate change *must* be bad for mental health. Historical reflections on science, particularly in mental health, reveal many times when humanity has believed a phenomenon to be true only to find inadequate evidence. Investigations into climate distress so far have largely been descriptive and uncontrolled. While these types of methodologies have been helpful, larger, blinded quantitative studies with clear hypotheses will be critical moving forward.
2. While medical specialization offers an excellent means of treating and studying disorders with discrete, primarily biological etiologies, it has been far less effective in approaching transdiagnostic, socioenvironmental conditions spanning multiple disciplines (Detsky et al., 2012). Research in pediatric mental health and climate change requires overcoming these tendencies to silo to better address the multidimensional and biopsychosocial problems that climate change poses.
3. Issues with research funding must be addressed. Current funding structures primarily promote an individualistic research approach (Utzerath & Fernández, 2017) that is less effective in addressing systemic issues such as climate change. A more communal, collaborative funding structure could propel research of climate mental health. Currently, the interdisciplinary nature of climate mental health research appears to be less attractive to funders, a finding corroborated by the literature (Bromham et al., 2016). A specific call for grants on climate and mental health is also essential (Hayes et al., 2018).

In sum, there is exciting research being conducted in this field of climate emotion symptoms and syndromes in young people, with more to be done and obstacles to overcome. This chapter proposes starting points to hopefully promote this action.

References

Adams, H., Blackburn, S., & Mantovani, N. (2021). Psychological resilience for climate change transformation: relational, differentiated and situated perspectives. *Current Opinion in Environmental Sustainability*, 50, 303–309. https://doi.org/10.1016/j.cosust.2021.06.011

Ágoston, C., Csaba, B., Nagy, B., Kőváry, Z., Dúll, A., Rácz, J., & Demetrovics, Z. (2022). Identifying types of eco-anxiety, eco-guilt, eco-grief, and eco-coping in a climate-sensitive population: A qualitative study. *International Journal of Environmental Research and Public Health*, 19(4), 2461. www.mdpi.com/1660-4601/19/4/2461

Akkaya-Kalayci, T., Vyssoki, B., Winkler, D., Willeit, M., Kapusta, N. D., Dorffner, G., & Özlü-Erkilic, Z. (2017). The effect of seasonal changes and climatic factors on suicide attempts of young people. *BMC Psychiatry*, 17(1), 365. doi:10.1186/s12888-017-1532-7

Albrecht, G. (2011). Chronic environmental change: Emerging "psychoterratic" syndromes. In I. Weissbecker (Ed.), *Climate change and human well-being: Global challenges and opportunities* (pp. 43–56). Springer New York.

Augusterfer, E. F., Mollica, R. F., & Lavelle, J. (2018). Leveraging technology in post-disaster settings: The role of digital health/telemental health. *Current Psychiatry Reports*, 20(10), 88. doi:10.1007/s11920-018-0953-4

Baker, C., Clayton, S., & Bragg, E. (2021). Educating for resilience: Parent and teacher perceptions of children's emotional needs in response to climate change. *Environmental Education Research*, 27(5), 687–705. doi:10.1080/13504622.2020.1828288

Bandura, A. (2016). *Moral disengagement: How people do harm and live with themselves*. Worth.

Baudon, P., & Jachens, L. (2021). A scoping review of interventions for the treatment of eco-anxiety. *International Journal of Environmental Research and Public Health*, 18(18). doi:10.3390/ijerph18189636

Beach, R. H., Sulser, T. B., Crimmins, A., Cenacchi, N., Cole, J., Fukagawa, N. K.,... & Ziska, L. H. (2019). Combining the effects of increased atmospheric carbon dioxide on protein, iron, and zinc availability and projected climate change on global diets: A modelling study. *The Lancet Planetary Health*, 3(7), e307–e317. https://doi.org/10.1016/S2542-5196(19)30094-4

Belkin, G. (2022). The race is on to nurture resilient people for a resilient planet. *Psychiatric Times.* www.psychiatrictimes.com/view/the-race-is-on-to-nurture-resilient-people-for-a-resilient-planet

Benoit, L. (2022). Understanding youths' concerns about climate change: a cross-cultural qualitative study of a generation's ecological burden and resilience. Paper presented at the 69th Annual Meeting of the American Acadamy of Child and Adolescent Psychiatry, Toronto, Canada.

Berntsen, D., & Rubin, D. C. (2014). Pretraumatic stress reactions in soldiers deployed to Afghanistan. *Clinical Psychological Science*, 3(5), 663–674. doi:10.1177/2167702614551766

Boehnke, K., & Wong, B. (2011). Adolescent political activism and long-term happiness: A 21-year longitudinal study on the development of micro- and macrosocial worries. *Personality and Social Psychology Bulletin*, 37(3), 435–447. doi:10.1177/0146167210397553

Bromham, L., Dinnage, R., & Hua, X. (2016). Interdisciplinary research has consistently lower funding success. *Nature*, 534(7609), 684–687. doi:10.1038/nature18315

Burlingame, G. M., Fuhriman, A., & Mosier, J. (2003). The differential effectiveness of group psychotherapy: A meta-analytic perspective. *Group Dynamics: Theory, Research, and Practice*, 7(1), 3.

Carleton, T., Hsiang, S. M., & Burke, M. (2016). Conflict in a changing climate. *The European Physical Journal Special Topics*, 225(3), 489–511. doi:10.1140/epjst/e2015-50100-5

Chen, C. W., & Gorski, P. C. (2015). Burnout in social justice and human rights activists: Symptoms, causes and implications. *Journal of Human Rights Practice*, 7(3), 366–390. doi:10.1093/jhuman/huv011

Chen, M. H., Su, T. P., Chen, Y. S., Hsu, J. W., Huang, K. L., Chang, W. H., … & Bai, Y. M. (2013). Association between psychiatric disorders and iron deficiency anemia among children and adolescents: A nationwide population-based study. *BMC Psychiatry*, 13(1), 161. doi:10.1186/1471-244X-13-161

Clayton, S. (2020). Climate anxiety: Psychological responses to climate change. *Journal of Anxiety Disorders*, 74, 102263. https://doi.org/10.1016/j.janxdis.2020.102263

Clayton, S., & Karazsia, B. T. (2020). Development and validation of a measure of climate change anxiety. *Journal of Environmental Psychology*, 69, 101434. https://doi.org/10.1016/j.jenvp.2020.101434

Climate Psychology Alliance North America (2022). Climate-aware therapist directory. www.climatepsychology.us/climate-therapists

Coffey, Y., Bhullar, N., Durkin, J., Islam, M. S., & Usher, K. (2021). Understanding eco-anxiety: A systematic scoping review of current literature and identified knowledge gaps. *Journal of Climate Change and Health*, 3, 100047. https://doi.org/10.1016/j.joclim.2021.100047

Davis, E. P., & Sandman, C. A. (2012). Prenatal psychobiological predictors of anxiety risk in preadolescent children. *Psychoneuroendocrinology*, 37(8), 1224–1233. doi:10.1016/j.psyneuen.2011.12.016

DeMocker, M. (2020). So your kids are stressed out about the climate crisis. www.sierraclub.org/sierra/so-your-kids-are-stressed-out-about-climate-crisis

Detsky, A. S., Gauthier, S. R., & Fuchs, V. R. (2012). Specialization in medicine: How much is appropriate? *JAMA*, 307(5), 463–464. doi:10.1001/jama.2012.44

Doherty, T., Lykins, A., Piotrowski, N., Rogers, Z., Sebree, D., & White, K. (2022). Clinical psychology responses to the climate crisis. In G. J. G. Asmundson (Ed.), *Comprehensive clinical psychology*. Elsevier.

Doppelt, B. (2017). *Transformational resilience: How building human resilience to climate disruption can safeguard society and increase wellbeing*. Routledge.

Everly Jr, G. S., & Lating, J. M. (2022). *The Johns Hopkins guide to psychological first aid*. Johns Hopkins University Press.

Fondacaro, K., & Mazulla, E. (2018). The Chronic Traumatic Stress Framework: A conceptual model to guide empirical investigation and mental health treatment for refugees and survivors of torture. *Torture Journal*, 28(1). https://doi.org/10.7146/torture.v28i1.105477

Hahn, M. B., Van Wyck, R., Lessard, L., & Fried, R. (2022). Compounding effects of social vulnerability and recurring natural disasters on mental and physical health. *Disaster Medicine and Public Health Preparedness*, 16(3), 1013–1021. doi:10.1017/dmp.2020.476

Hayes, K., Blashki, G., Wiseman, J., Burke, S., & Reifels, L. (2018). Climate change and mental health: Risks, impacts and priority actions. *International Journal of Mental Health Systems*, 12(1), 28. doi:10.1186/s13033-018-0210-6

Helm, S. V., Pollitt, A., Barnett, M. A., Curran, M. A., & Craig, Z. R. (2018). Differentiating environmental concern in the context of psychological adaption to climate change. *Global Environmental Change*, 48, 158–167. https://doi.org/10.1016/j.gloenvcha.2017.11.012

Hickman, C., Marks, E., Pihkala, P., Clayton, S., Lewandowski, R. E., Mayall, E. E., … & van Susteren, L. (2021). Climate anxiety in children and young people and their beliefs about government responses to climate change: A global survey. *The Lancet Planetary Health*, 5(12), e863-e873. https://doi.org/10.1016/S2542-5196(21)00278-3

Hogg, T. L., Stanley, S. K., O'Brien, L. V., Wilson, M. S., & Watsford, C. R. (2021). The Hogg Eco-Anxiety Scale: Development and validation of a multidimensional scale. *Global Environmental Change*, 71, 102391. https://doi.org/10.1016/j.gloenvcha.2021.102391

Hwong, A. R., Wang, M., Khan, H., Chagwedera, D. N., Grzenda, A., Doty, B., … & Compton, W. M. (2022). Climate change and mental health research methods, gaps, and priorities: A scoping review. *The Lancet Planetary Health*, 6(3), e281-e291. https://doi.org/10.1016/S2542-5196(22)00012-2

Kaijser, A., & Kronsell, A. (2014). Climate change through the lens of intersectionality. *Environmental Politics*, 23(3), 417–433. doi:10.1080/09644016.2013.835203

Kaplan, E. A. (2020). Is climate-related pre-traumatic stress syndrome a real condition? *American Imago*, 77(1), 81–104.

Kini, G., Karkal, R., & Bhargava, M. (2020). All's not well with the "worried well": Understanding health anxiety due to COVID-19. *Journal of Preventive Medicine and Hygiene*, 61(3), e321–e323. doi:10.15167/2421-4248/jpmh2020.61.3.1605

Kousky, C. (2016). Impacts of natural disasters on children. *The Future of Children*, 26(1), 73–92. www.jstor.org/stable/43755231

Leal, P. C., Goes, T. C., da Silva, L. C. F., & Teixeira-Silva, F. (2017). Trait vs. state anxiety in different threatening situations. *Trends in Psychiatry and Psychotherapy*, 39, 147–157.

Lewis, J. L., Haase, E., & Trope, A. (2020). Climate dialectics in psychotherapy: Holding open the space between abyss and advance. *Psychodynamic Psychiatry*, 48(3), 271–294.

Machado-Moreira, C. A., McLennan, P. L., Lillioja, S., van Dijk, W., Caldwell, J. N., & Taylor, N. A. S. (2012). The cholinergic blockade of both thermally and non-thermally induced human eccrine sweating. *Experimental Physiology*, 97(8), 930–942. https://doi.org/10.1113/expphysiol.2012.065037

Materia, C. J. (2016). *Climate state anxiety and connectedness to nature in rural Tasmania*. University of Tasmania, https://eprints.utas.edu.au/23089/

McMullen, H., & Dow, K. (2022). Ringing the existential alarm: Exploring BirthStrike for Climate. *Medical Anthropology*, 41(6–7), 659–673. doi:10.1080/01459740.2022.2083510

Merikangas, K. R., He, J.-p., Burstein, M., Swanson, S. A., Avenevoli, S., Cui, L., ... Swendsen, J. (2010). Lifetime prevalence of mental disorders in U.S. adolescents: Results from the National Comorbidity Survey Replication–Adolescent Supplement (NCS-A). *Journal of the American Academy of Child & Adolescent Psychiatry*, 49(10), 980–989. https://doi.org/10.1016/j.jaac.2010.05.017

Morton, T. (2013). *Hyperobjects: Philosophy and ecology after the end of the world*. University of Minnesota Press.

Nice, M. L., Forziat-Pytel, K., Benoit, C., & Sturm, D. C. (2022). School counselor and environmental educator partnerships: Reducing eco-anxiety from climate change, increasing self-efficacy, and enhancing youth advocacy. *Professional School Counseling*, 26(1), 2156759X221090525. doi:10.1177/2156759X221090525

Noelke, C., McGovern, M., Corsi, D. J., Jimenez, M. P., Stern, A., Wing, I. S., & Berkman, L. (2016). Increasing ambient temperature reduces emotional well-being. *Environmental Research*, 151, 124–129. https://doi.org/10.1016/j.envres.2016.06.045

Obradovich, N., Migliorini, R., Paulus, M. P., & Rahwan, I. (2018). Empirical evidence of mental health risks posed by climate change. *Proceedings of the National Academy of Sciences*, 115(43), 10953–10958. doi:10.1073/pnas.1801528115

Ojala, M. (2012). How do children cope with global climate change? Coping strategies, engagement, and well-being. *Journal of Environmental Psychology*, 32(3), 225–233. https://doi.org/10.1016/j.jenvp.2012.02.004

Ojala, M. (2015). Hope in the face of climate change: Associations with environmental engagement and student perceptions of teachers' emotion communication style and future orientation. *Journal of Environmental Education*, 46(3), 133–148. doi:10.1080/00958964.2015.1021662

Ojala, M., & Bengtsson, H. (2019). Young people's coping strategies concerning climate change: Relations to perceived communication with parents and friends and proenvironmental behavior. *Environment and Behavior*, 51(8), 907–935. doi:10.1177/0013916518763894

Perera, F. (2017). Multiple threats to child health from fossil fuel combustion: Impacts of air pollution and climate change. *Environmental Health Perspectives*, 125(2), 141–148. doi:10.1289/EHP299

Pierson, A. M., Arunagiri, V., & Bond, D. M. (2022). "You didn't cause racism, and you have to solve it anyways": Antiracist adaptations to dialectical behavior therapy for white therapists. *Cognitive and Behavioral Practice*, 29(4), 796–815. https://doi.org/10.1016/j.cbpra.2021.11.001

Pihkala, P. (2020). Anxiety and the ecological crisis: An analysis of eco-anxiety and climate anxiety. *Sustainability*, 12(19). doi:10.3390/su12197836

Raison, C., Hale, M., Williams, L., Wager, T., & Lowry, C. (2015). Somatic influences on subjective well-being and affective disorders: The convergence of thermosensory and central serotonergic systems. *Frontiers in Psychology*, 5, 1580. doi:10.3389/fpsyg.2014.01580

Randall, R. (2009). Loss and climate change: The cost of parallel narratives. *Ecopsychology*, 1(3), 118–129. doi:10.1089/eco.2009.0034

Roudini, J., Khankeh, H. R., & Witruk, E. (2017). Disaster mental health preparedness in the community: A systematic review study. *Health Psychology Open*, 4(1), 2055102917711307. doi:10.1177/2055102917711307

Schumacher, J. A., Coffey, S. F., Norris, F. H., Tracy, M., Clements, K., & Galea, S. (2010). Intimate partner violence and Hurricane Katrina: Predictors and associated mental health outcomes. *Violence and Victims*, 25(5), 588–603. doi:10.1891/0886-6708.25.5.588

Schwartz, S. E. O., Benoit, L., Clayton, S., Parnes, M. F., Swenson, L., & Lowe, S. R. (2022). Climate change anxiety and mental health: Environmental activism as buffer. *Current Psychology*. doi:10.1007/s12144-022-02735-6

South, E. C., Hohl, B. C., Kondo, M. C., MacDonald, J. M., & Branas, C. C. (2018). Effect of greening vacant land on mental health of community-dwelling adults: A cluster randomized trial. *JAMA Network Open*, 1(3), e180298. doi:10.1001/jamanetworkopen.2018.0298

Stanley, S. K., Hogg, T. L., Leviston, Z., & Walker, I. (2021). From anger to action: Differential impacts of eco-anxiety, eco-depression, and eco-anger on climate action and wellbeing. *Journal of Climate Change and Health*, 1, 100003. https://doi.org/10.1016/j.joclim.2021.100003

Swardfager, W., Herrmann, N., Mazereeuw, G., Goldberger, K., Harimoto, T., & Lanctôt, K. L. (2013). Zinc in depression: A meta-analysis. *Biological Psychiatry*, 74(12), 872–878. https://doi.org/10.1016/j.biopsych.2013.05.008

Thomas, I., Martin, A., Wicker, A., & Benoit, L. (2022). Understanding youths' concerns about climate change: A cross-cultural qualitative study of a generation's ecological burden and resilience. https://doi.org/10.21203/rs.3.rs-2188446/v1

Thompson, R., Hornigold, R., Page, L., & Waite, T. (2018). Associations between high ambient temperatures and heat waves with mental health outcomes: A systematic review. *Public Health*, 161, 171–191. https://doi.org/10.1016/j.puhe.2018.06.008

Utzerath, C., & Fernández, G. (2017). Shaping science for increasing interdependence and specialization. *Trends in Neurosciences*, 40(3), 121–124. https://doi.org/10.1016/j.tins.2016.12.005

Vergunst, F., & Berry, H. L. (2021). Climate change and children's mental health: A developmental perspective. *Clinical Psychological Science*, 10(4), 767–785. doi:10.1177/21677026211040787

Weisz, J. R., & Kazdin, A. E. (2010). *Evidence-based psychotherapies for children and adolescents*. Guilford Press.

Winnicott, D. W. (1963). From dependence towards independence in the development of the individual. In *The Maturational Processes and the Facilitating Environment* (pp. 83–92). Hogarth Press.

Wortzel, J. D., Champlin, L. K., Wortzel, J. R., Lewis, J., Haase, E., & Mark, B. (2022). Reframing climate change: Using children's literature as a residency training tool to address climate anxiety and model innovation. *Academic Psychiatry*, 46(5), 584–585. doi:10.1007/s40596-022-01651-y

Wortzel, J. R., Guerrero, A. P. S., Aggarwal, R., Coverdale, J., & Brenner, A. M. (2022). Climate change and the professional obligation to socialize physicians and trainees into an environmentally sustainable medical culture. *Academic Psychiatry*, 46(5), 556–561. doi:10.1007/s40596-022-01688-z

Wortzel, J. R., Haase, E., Mark, B., Stashevsky, A., & Lewis, J. (2022). Teaching to our time: A survey study of current opinions and didactics about climate mental health training in US psychiatry residency and fellowship programs. *Academic Psychiatry*. doi:10.1007/s40596-022-01680-7

Wortzel, J. R., Lee, J., Benoit, L., Rubano, A., & Pinsky, E. G. (2022). Perspectives on climate change and pediatric mental health: A qualitative analysis of interviews with researchers in the field. *Academic Psychiatry*, 46(5), 562–568. doi:10.1007/s40596-022-01707-z

Xerxa, Y., Delaney, S. W., Rescorla, L. A., Hillegers, M. H. J., White, T., Verhulst, F. C., … & Tiemeier, H. (2021). Association of poor family functioning from pregnancy onward with preadolescent behavior and subcortical brain development. *JAMA Psychiatry*, 78(1), 29–37. doi:10.1001/jamapsychiatry.2020.286

PART II

*Multidisciplinary Perspectives
on Youth Climate Distress*

CHAPTER 10

Therapists' Perspectives
Psychotherapeutic Techniques with Applicability to Climate Distress

Elizabeth Allured and Barbara Easterlin

This chapter is authored by clinicians Elizabeth Allured, PsyD (EA) and Barbara Easterlin, PhD (BE), both experienced in working with climate distressed[1] youth clients. The focus of this chapter is on therapeutic perspectives and techniques. All client names used in the vignettes are pseudonyms.

Introduction: Hearing the Voices of Children and Parents

Emma, 7: "Is the whole world going to be destroyed?"

Jason, 17: "The first world will escape it with technology but people in the third world and animals are done for!"

Parent: "My 10-year-old said we only have 12 years left to live because of climate change. What should I tell her?"

Therapist Defense Against Their Own Climate Distress

What happens when we read these children's words? Does hearing these concerns set off too much anxiety of our own? It is hard to imagine a more tragic situation than the deaths of children due to a disaster that is unfolding because grown people, especially those controlling governments and businesses, will not adequately protect them. Hearing children's fears may increase clinicians' own anxiety, guilt, sadness, helplessness, rage, and other conflicting emotions tied to the climate emergency. Anxiety in particular is a response to losing important aspects of one's sense of self or community and signals that something

---

[1] Climate distress is the phrase we will use in this chapter to encompass all dysphoric climate emotions such as climate-related anxiety, anger, and depressive feelings.

is amiss, that danger or losses lie ahead from an upcoming decision. If there is too little anxiety, dangers might be ignored. But if anxiety is too high, a kind of "emotional paralysis" can set in. Clinicians are not immune to this, nor are parents.

When we have brought up the climate crisis with parents, some of them have said, "It's too much. I just try not to think about it." This discomfort is not only quite noticeable to children but can also significantly impact adults' ability to hear children's attempts to discuss the topic.

Starting in earliest infancy, we are continually "reading" and "sending" emotional and social signals to those in close proximity (Beebe & Lachman, 2013). Even infants a few months old react strongly to their caregivers' emotional states. Our emotional energy is felt, even if we are silent or saying something quite different. This is partly because much of our communication is nonverbal; for example, our body language might convey tension or calmness, curiosity or disinterest, acceptance or rejection. Likewise, our voice tone, gestures, length of conversation, and distance or proximity to a child convey our intentions to deepen a conversation or to close it down. Messages to children are more often accepted and taken seriously when adults' verbal and nonverbal messages are congruent. If we tell our children that we care about the ecosystem we are leaving them, yet do not take any actions toward protecting it, they may interpret our statement with mistrust.

For all these reasons, preparing to talk with youth about the climate crisis involves understanding our own feelings and thoughts. Our words must convey our honest, complex reactions in a digestible form without withholding the truth or trying to inappropriately reassure young people. Just as each child needs a listener to help them think about this challenging environmental situation, clinicians too need support in building awareness of their responses to this great threat to humanity and to children in particular. Expressing reactions to friends, colleagues, or family members can help clinicians listen to youth without bumping into unprocessed feelings of their own.

> "There are those who listen, and those who hear." (Whis.stem.men.knee, Nuu-chah-nulth elder from Vancouver Island, B.C., 1987)

Clinicians who welcome climate conversations provide young people with a sense of stability as they sort through their varied reactions, which in turn establishes the therapist as a safe source of information, guidance, and community.

The Therapist as a Role Model for Managing Climate Distress

When children develop typically, they expect that adults will protect them and teach them how to recognize and react to dangers, both practically and emotionally. Currently, many children find that their parents and other authority figures are not useful role models for taking the climate crisis seriously because these adult figures are not acting as if their lives depended upon swift action. Mental health clinicians can step into this needed role by modeling an awareness of climate-related danger and risks, respect for related emotions, and willingness to consider climate change as a factor in life decisions. In line with research showing that tolerating uncertainty about climate change leads to greater engagement with the topic in adolescents (Ojala, 2015), clinicians can also model living with real uncertainty about whether action will be taken in time to avert the worst of the crises. Clinicians can reveal environmentally engaged aspects of themselves without "proselytizing" directly or indirectly by including sustainability themes in the waiting room or by offering play therapy materials that might engage environmental feelings. Young people are attracted to learning from and following Greta Thunberg, who models a life based on a reduced carbon impact and speaking the scientific truth about the problem. In a similar and therapeutically helpful way, clinicians can model an "environmentally examined" life, a life that is abreast of the climate science and bases decisions upon this new reality.

When Is Treatment Indicated for Climate Distress?

Not all climate distress requires treatment. Consulo et al. (2020) and others suggest that ecological threats are a cause for reasonable concern and possibly anxiety, but not necessarily a mental health problem requiring intervention. With support, validation, and encouragement of values-driven action, many people are able to manage their climate distress without psychological intervention. However, in our clinical experience, climate-informed therapy may be indicated when climate distress amplifies subthreshold or comorbid mental health vulnerabilities such as addiction, mood disorders, anxiety disorders, past trauma, and other psychiatric disorders. These conditions may also be exacerbated by extreme weather events or disasters, in which case treatment should be considered.

*How Does Climate Distress Manifest in Children,
Adolescents, and Young People?*

Given that young children are less equipped with a vocabulary to describe their inner experience, symbolic expressions of distress are sometimes seen through play behaviors, enactments, and artwork. Although there is limited research demonstrating how climate distress may present in young people across various developmental stages and cultures, we hear anecdotes from climate-informed clinicians that the same patterns seen in other mental health conditions hold true. As with adults, climate distress may result in changes in young clients' patterns of sleep, appetite, and ability to concentrate, and result in headaches, stomachaches, and muscle aches (American Psychiatric Association, 2022). Children may regress in various other areas of development, such as becoming more anxious about separation from caregivers or showing less independence in normal daily routines. Behavioral acting out at home or at school may escalate as unprocessed agitation increases.

In addition, the impact of climate and weather education in the classroom without social-emotional support may have an unwanted effect on children who are vulnerable to anxiety (see Carmichael, Chapter 17 in this volume), and at times upon children who are not. Allured (2014) wrote, "Our school systems educate [students] in sustainable practices, but may be making them more anxious in the process. Some children fear failure of the biospheric holding environment, leading to anxiety and various forms of defense. They no longer see the world as predictably sustaining, but rather as potentially toxic" (pp. 35–36).

Climate-Informed Therapy Issues Specific to Children and Youth

*Developmental Tasks and Their implications
within Clinical Climate Distress Work*

Developmental level should be a primary consideration in climate-informed therapy. For preadolescent children, treatment goals might focus on providing a sense of safety, especially where there has been prior trauma. For children with preexisting (i.e., before climate concerns surfaced) mental challenges such as ADHD, depression, or anxiety, focusing on the reality of the climate crisis before enhancing self-efficacy and emotional regulation skills may be counterproductive. In these cases, priority should be given to understanding the child's external support system, strengths, and general life stressors. Therapy with the goal of understanding feelings about larger world dysfunctions is generally more relevant for adolescents, and climate work is no exception.

To illustrate possible developmental considerations in climate-aware care, Piaget's developmental stages and their implications for climate distress work are presented in Table 10.1.

Table 10.1 *Developmental stages (Piaget, 1971)*

Age (approximate)	Stage	Developmental tasks	Implications within climate distress work
Birth to 2 years	Sensorimotor	Attachment to caregivers and the natural world; expectations and perceptions of safety within both; tolerance of disruptions	Conduct therapy with caregivers present. Focus on strengthening attachment relationships; develop ways of repairing disruptions related to caregivers or environment. Provide self-care strategies to caregivers undergoing challenging adjustments to mitigate impacts of their stress on offspring.
2 to 7 years	Preoperational	Movement toward autonomy and mastery in environment; practicing meaningful interactions with others	Encourage connection with the natural world to promote security (e.g., planting, harvesting, learning about animals, noticing the weather). Support parents in helping children process exposure to climate crisis events/news or to direct disaster impacts with concrete play and drawing materials. Provide containment and space for thoughts and feelings.
7 to 11 years	Concrete operations	Developing an understanding of interrelated parts, and the perspectives of others	Employ concrete play materials to further encourage a connection with nature. Discuss how components of ecosystems interact and how we can be helpful parts of our own. Allow for feelings of loss, fear, anger, and uncertainty in words and through materials.

Table 10.1 (*cont.*)

Age (approximate)	Stage	Developmental tasks	Implications within climate distress work
12 years and older	Formal operations	Use of abstract concepts: learning about larger systems such as government, economics, and cultures; understand inner factors such as motivations, habits, and avoidances	Focus on finding peers supportive of client's interests. Encourage connection with nature and place. Explore values and career choices based upon changing ecosystems and social conditions. Explore possible intergenerational conflicts/differences.

Note: For the purpose of this discussion, Piaget's four stages of development were employed. Other developmental models that might be considered include, among others, Mahler, Erikson, and social constructivist theories.

Intergenerational Differences in the Experience of the Climate Crisis

While previous generations have experienced similar existential threats of war, nuclear annihilation, widespread famine, and other calamities, at no other time in history has civilization been threatened by global climate collapse and human extinction. The collective denial and ignorance of present and past generations contributed to systemic circumstances that, at best, are a failure to fathom the impact of exceptionalism and neo-liberalism (Weintrobe, 2021) and at worst, leave a world that may not sustain human life. Our youth have every reason to feel let down, pessimistic, and even victimized by the indifference of generations who benefited from unjust systems built on colonization, oppression, patriarchy, and unfair resource distribution. These compounded factors contribute to an overall feeling of lost control, fatalism, lowered agency, and hopelessness among our young clients, sometimes giving rise to lower motivation to pursue interests and education. As one of our young adult clients said: "Why should I finish my college degree when there won't be fish in the ocean in 30 years?"

In an international climate anxiety survey, Hickman et al. (2021) found that 56 percent of 10,000 young people aged 16–24 feel humanity is "doomed." Adults may even gaslight or shame children for their accurate perceptions of the climate situation, discouraging further communication. In a recent study of youth mental health and climate change commissioned by the Oregon State Office of Public Health (Sifuentes et al., 2022), youth reported feeling "dismissed by adults and the older generation." This sentiment makes seeking trust and care from adults difficult and may make young people feel at odds with older generations. There is evidence that this mistrust can extend to governments and policymakers and whether they will take corrective action on behalf of young people; in the Hickman et al. (2021) global survey, more than 80 percent report feeling "betrayed" by the government.

Working within a Framework of an Uncertain Future

Adolescents and young adults in our practices report that uncertainty about the future is a central problem driving their climate distress. Tolerating uncertainty is also challenging for many of us clinicians. In addition, closure – in the psychotherapeutic sense – may be difficult simply because the source of distress does not allow for closure since it is ongoing and increasing in intensity. These factors present therapeutic conundrums for child and adolescent therapists. As much as our clinical instincts may drive us to offer a neat end point of treatment, the goal instead is to hold the uncertainty and to help our young clients develop confidence that they can face and cope with this crisis in meaningful ways, in part by using their own inner resources. We do this by validating their negative emotions, and when they are ready, by communicating with them in a future-oriented, open-minded, and solutions-based style (Ojala, 2015). In addition to their inner resources, "safety" can be experienced within consistent, caring human attachment relationships that will follow them throughout childhood and adolescence, regardless of outer turmoil and climate dysregulation. As an example, while transgenerational transmission of trauma multiplies the stresses experienced from the climate crisis, BIPOC communities have been experiencing ongoing existential threats since long before the onset of the climate crisis and have remained resilient.

Intersectional Factors

Children have had no say in the development of a system that oppresses others and relegates communities of color, Indigenous Peoples, and others penalized for their sexuality, gender, or unlucky geography to more economic stressors, strife, and degrading living conditions. Climate distress contains many overlapping and intersectional social and environmental injustices that contribute to a Gordian Knot of emotion, outrage, and concern. The goal of climate-aware therapy is not just symptom reduction, but also to bear witness to and respond in the context of the extraordinary situation that today's youth are growing up within.

Climate-Aware Intake and Assessment

Clayton and Karazsia (2020) have published a validated climate anxiety research scale for adults; however, there are currently no validated measures of climate-related feelings for children for use in therapeutic settings. Without such scales, we advocate adding an item or two regarding the future to our diagnostic interviews conducted in the very beginning phases of therapy. An open-ended question such as "what are your concerns about the future?" can let our young clients know that we are open to the conversation about climate change or other social or cultural crises. The therapist may want also to enquire about the young person's relationship with nature and animals, their understanding of climate impacts, pro-environmental behaviors, familial attitudes towards climate change and adaptation, and intersectional vulnerability and resilience to climate threats.

Core Components of Climate-Informed Therapy

Dooley and colleagues (2021) provide a cross-disciplinary, climate-informed therapeutic approach for young people, which is synthesized from their review of existing literature and resources, as well as insights from subject matter experts. They identified seven "core components" that have the potential to promote coping and emotional resilience in the face of climate distress: (1) acknowledging and validating feelings, (2) emotional coping tools, (3) social connection, (4) connecting with nature, (5) climate action, (6) self-care, and (7) climate justice awareness. We define resilience as the capacity to prepare for, recover from, and adapt in the face of trauma, challenge, and adversity. As shown in the vignettes later in this chapter, many of these components can be used with young children and adolescents.

In addition, environmental psychology research supports encouraging a relationship with nature as well as taking climate action to increase well-being and effectiveness. Both correlational and experimental research have shown that interacting and connecting with nature have cognitive benefits (Schertz & Berman, 2019) and even limited contact with natural environments improves well-being (Bratman et al., 2019). A comprehensive review shows a strong correlation between time spent in green spaces and children's overall health, attention, and mood (Fyfe Johnson et al., 2021). Anxiety about the climate crisis is shown to increase some types of pro-environmental behaviors, especially among youth (Whitmarsh et al., 2022). We assume that all of these components are applicable and important to our therapeutic work with children.

Therapeutic Components of Two Major Schools of Psychotherapy with Children

Cognitive Behavioral Therapy and Acceptance and Commitment Therapy

Cognitive behavioral therapy (CBT) relies on skill-building strategies based on age-appropriate psychoeducation, recognition, and management of somatic correlates, cognitive restructuring techniques, and gradual exposure to and desensitization of feared situations or patterns of thought with the goal of extinguishing (Albano & Kendall, 2002) and allowing new learning about the feared situation (Craske et al., 2008). CBT aims to challenge or eradicate unwanted or unhelpful thoughts, emotions, and behaviors. Feeling states are often externalized in treatment, meaning that they are separated from the individual's experience of self for the purpose of examination.

Third-wave cognitive behavioral modalities, such as acceptance and commitment therapy (ACT), dialectical behavior therapy (DBT), and mindfulness based cognitive therapy (MBCT) incorporate mindfulness, self-compassion, and acceptance. ACT includes these features, typically noted as the six processes of change, which have significant applicability to climate distress (Hayes et al., 2006). The six core processes of ACT are described below; despite the certain progression of climate difficulties, there are many possibilities and ways to be effective within each area of impact. Thus, helping clients become flexible in their thoughts about what is possible in the climate response is important.

1. Helping the client develop an *accepting and flexible* relationship to unwanted experiences and thoughts and identify and move toward what matters to them (i.e., their values). In the case of climate distress, values might include care for nature, activism oriented at preserving nature, environmental justice, or sustainable practices.
2. *Cognitive defusion* from "stuck" thoughts and feelings by using mindfulness to monitor and allow the arising of thoughts, sensations, and feelings (experiential acceptance), rather than trying

to change, control, or get rid of them (experiential avoidance). In the case of climate distress, the goal is to open oneself to the range of cognitions and feelings associated with climate change rather than suppressing those experiences.

3. ACT uses *present moment awareness and mindfulness* to increase psychological flexibility with respect to difficult feelings. Psychological flexibility means contacting the present moment as fully as possible and orienting toward expanding behavioral choices, rather than striving to control or avoid unwanted thoughts and feelings.

4. Flexibility and perspective (*self as context*) can be cultivated by helping young clients develop awareness of the range of their emotions and internal storytelling, and also by teaching specific skills for managing internal experience, reducing avoidance, recruiting other trusted adults to help develop agency, and separating sense of self from the feeling state. This is especially important since feelings, when fused with the child's sense of self, may feel unapproachable and overwhelming. When fearful thoughts and experiences are defused from the self and seen as states that come and go, the young client can learn to feel more grounded. Thus, externalization of uncomfortable thoughts and feelings about disasters and climate change can be quite helpful.

5. *Values development* in ACT can involve overarching values areas such as safety, friendships, engagement in social issues, education, or career, or about qualities of action such as acting courageously or responding to one's fear with kindness and understanding. Teenagers' idealism easily enables values development conversations about environmentalism, and even young children can often articulate what is important to them.

6. Supporting clients in taking *committed action* to build patterns of change. The central goal of ACT is taking action in small steps towards what we want our lives to be, based on deeply held personal values. Eco-anxiety as experienced by children, especially with its accompanying frightening and possibly catastrophic thoughts and feelings, is a good target for small therapeutic steps using the aforementioned externalization, mindfulness, cognitive defusion, and values clarification.

Case Vignette: Environmental Disaster Fears and ACT

In the following vignette, elements of an ACT therapy orientation, as well as Dooley and colleagues' (2021) seven-point formulation, described earlier in this section, were used with Cassidy, an 8-year-old white, cisgender girl who had endured a wildfire near her Northern California home, which she later learned might have been related to climate change.

Case History and Symptomology

Cassidy had no previous history of trauma or other psychiatric symptoms. After the fire in a group of homes adjacent to her own neighborhood, she began exhibiting mild symptoms of PTSD including sleep onset difficulty, rehearsing and replaying what she knew or imagined about the wildfire, and distractibility. Primarily, she was preoccupied with the worry that global warming meant another wildfire might occur. At intake with Barbara Easterlin (BE), her parents felt Cassidy's worries were contributing to separation anxiety and to sleep and attention problems, which also impacted her ability to learn and retain information in school. On a fear hierarchy, Cassidy rated her own fear of wildfire at an "8 or 9" out of 10. She was given a DSM-5 diagnosis of Adjustment Disorder with Anxiety. In Cassidy's words: "I get scared at night after my mom leaves me alone. Sometimes I think about the animals in the forest who had to run from the fire. I think about the fire a lot and my parent's friends whose house burned."

Therapeutic Process: Developing Acceptance, Mindfulness, Perspective Taking, and Capacity for Cognitive Defusion

Taking into consideration Piaget's developmental framework presented earlier in this chapter, BE expected Cassidy, as a normally developing child in the operational stage, to possess some degree of the following: capacity for insight; ability to express feelings, thoughts, and perspective taking; and ability to make connections between those phenomenological experiences. These skills are key to the core processes of ACT.

The first treatment stage for Cassidy required gathering the presenting problems as she saw them, offering validation, and helping her to relate to them mindfully and with acceptance. For both Cassidy and her parents, it was important to not only identify and validate her fear but also to assure her parents that her avoidance behaviors had an important function so that they would not become overly frustrated with Cassidy (i.e., her distracted and preoccupied thoughts, wanting her mom to sleep with her, checking behaviors, and demands for reassurance). Involving parents for several sessions of psychoeducation and helping them to model mindfulness and acceptance is a key part of ACT therapy at this early age, as is encouraging an attitude of curiosity and exploration. An ACT case formulation required understanding the function of Cassidy's behaviors and helping her build tolerance for the unwanted feelings and fears. Given her age, drawing, role playing, and play were part of symbolizing and relating to these uncomfortable feelings.

To increase defusion from her fear, Cassidy was encouraged to draw a picture of the fire and to name it (i.e., externalization). She called it "Feroshio" and drew a fiery stick figure that wielded balls of fire. When asked what Feroshio might say to scare her, she replied he said things such as: "You can never be safe" and "Your mom and dad can't protect you." Creating a character to represent Cassidy's inner dialog helped her to disentangle herself from her unconscious fears and beliefs, creating space to safely explore their origins and veracity. With an older child, the ACT therapist may also attempt to move into *self-as-context* here by inquiring: "Who is having these thoughts and feelings here and now?" or "What part of you is looking at these thoughts and feelings?" This is done to foster a self-perspective that is stable and vast, and which can contain all kinds of thoughts and feelings.

Cassidy was encouraged to say aloud the frightening statements or taunts Feroshio might say as BE wrote them down. This was done with some humor, as a little levity normalized them but also illuminated their relative absurdity. Getting frightening thoughts out into the open is the first step in defusing from them. Over several sessions, which also included other topics of concern and play activities to build rapport and trust, Cassidy became better able to direct her awareness to her thoughts and feelings and even to more subtle beliefs about her own efficacy. Using her "strong" inner voice, she learned she could tell Feroshio that she didn't believe him but understood his protective function.

Values Development and Committed Action

Connection with values, even for a young child, can help stabilize the motivation for enduring difficult feelings. When a child feels a sense of meaning and alignment with values regarding the environment, they may be more likely to access uncomfortable emotions because they are part of or in service of the child's own mission. Increased flexibility gives the client space to move in valued life directions. Since part of child psychotherapy involves parent coaching for reinforcing new behaviors and strengths, BE guided conversations between Cassidy and her parents about concrete ways they could make their home and neighborhood more fire safe. For example, they removed flammable plants next to their home, covered some of the intake vents with a finer screen to discourage embers, participated in a neighborhood text alert system, and made sure their interior fire sprinklers were in good working order.

Cassidy's therapy included ways to not only stay safe and be courageous, but also to identify actions in alignment with her values of being a helper to nature and animals. In working on her values, she partnered with her parents and targeted "three things we can do to make the environment better," including being careful about how much water they used and making their yard a "friendly place for the butterflies and bees" by planting drought tolerant flowering plants.

Older children and adolescents can benefit from the ACT therapists' guidance to feel inspired by the idea that they can play a meaningful part in fighting climate change.

Psychodynamic and Psychoanalytic Therapies

Research has shown that seven common factors underlie psychodynamic and psychoanalytic psychotherapy (Shedler, 2010):

1. **Psychodynamic treatments focus on expressing affect and verbalizing feelings**. In the context of climate distress, treatment would focus on identifying emotions that are problematic for the child to express in other settings. Treatment would also identify conflicting feelings, such as sadness along with anger, and work to make these conflicting feelings more conscious and open for recognition and discussion.
2. **Treatment aims to bring to awareness to how individuals try to avoid troubling feelings and thoughts**, whether these are expressed through behaviors or through psychological defenses such as denial, disavowal, or dissociation. With climate distress, the clinician might notice behaviors such as clients bringing up the topic but quickly dismissing it or using humor as a defense.
3. **Treatment helps the client understand repetitive themes woven through their relationships** and other aspects of their lives. For example, if the client begins to see how they use obsessive thought in response to anxiety, they may be open to understanding how obsessive thoughts about apocalyptic themes are part of their generalized style and recognize that their anxiety will likely decrease when underlying conflicts or fears are understood.

4. **Treatment focuses on understanding early childhood relationships**, and how patterns established in these attachment relationships continue to influence one's choice of relationship partners and the way one interacts and expects to be treated within current relationships. Adolescents can learn how their attachment relationships have prepared them to face the current climate reality, and whether they are effective.
5. **Relationships play a key role in mental health**, and any relationship difficulties we experience can impact our abilities to meet our emotional needs. Children and adolescents can be encouraged to pursue supportive peer relations and learn conflict management strategies. These relationships can allow for more functional communication of emotional needs and conflicts regarding external problems, including the climate crisis.
6. **The therapy relationship is a focus at times**, with the intention to reveal the client's repetitive relational patterns as they are expressed within the therapy dyad. For instance, the therapist can be a target for the client's anger regarding the climate crisis, a target that does not retaliate the way other adults might. The therapist can allow new relational experiences (e.g., assertiveness, vulnerability, and curiosity about the larger world/political systems) "in vivo" that are useful in other settings, such as school or home.
7. **Psychodynamic treatments place value on the exploration of the client's fantasy world**. Some of this fantasy life becomes known through the client's dreams and daydreams, and for children, in their play (Gil, 1991; Santostefano, 2004). This fantasy life is seen as bypassing the more rigid defenses that keep troubling feelings and thoughts from conscious awareness. For young children who express fears about the future or recollect prior extreme weather events, play figures of human and animal models as well as toy buildings and vehicles could be offered. For adolescents, curiosity about their dreams, during sleep as well as daytime fantasies, may reveal not only fears but resolutions and solutions as well.

Case Vignette: Psychodynamically Informed Therapy for Climate Distress

In the following vignette, several psychodynamic features above are noted, along with other therapy techniques.

Case History and Symptomatology

Jennifer, a 16-year-old female Asian student, entered treatment with EA for high anxiety regarding socializing outside of her home. At 3 years of age, Jennifer was hospitalized for asthma from severe seasonal and environmental allergies, after which she was often avoidant of going outdoors and to peers' homes due to fears of an asthma attack occurring without her parents around. Her therapy, which had begun a few years prior, had focused upon verbalizing her feelings regarding her vulnerability to illness, and on becoming assertive regarding her needs for protection (from allergens) in her peers' homes. Overall, Jennifer's presentation was one of anxious adjustment due to the sequelae of an ongoing medical condition. As this treatment was in progress, Jennifer arrived for a session with obsessive thoughts, looking very anxious.

Therapeutic Process: The Expression of Affect and the Verbalization of Feelings

Jennifer: "My science teacher told us in 20 years this climate change will be irreversible. And that we'll all be doomed. Kids asked him if people were doing enough to try to stop it, and he said 'no.' So, you know, all my other problems seemed like little problems! And that's good! But this bigger problem is terrible! I can't stop thinking about it!"

She continued: "Someone else asked the teacher if he had solar panels on his roof and he said he thought they were ugly. Well … DUH! So us kids are supposed to solve this problem! I'm really scared."

As Jennifer was comfortable expressing her fears verbally, EA moved toward her anger about children like herself being expected to solve this crisis, allying with her sense of outrage about being abandoned by the "adults in charge."

EA: "I don't think you kids are responsible to solve this."

In this statement, EA hoped Jennifer would sense that her feelings would not be discounted, and that EA acknowledged the seriousness of this environmental crisis.

Therapeutic Process: The Key Role of Early Attachment Relationships

Jennifer: "Are my parents sane? They don't seem to be worried about this. They just said that my generation will fix it when we get older."

Jennifer was very securely attached to her parents, and their mental and physical health greatly impacted her.

EA: "What are you most afraid of?"

Jennifer: "Well, it would be bad enough if me and my family were going to die. But I don't want EVERYBODY to die." She paused. "Do you think we're doomed?"

EA: "It depends. I think there are many good solutions for most of the problems we're facing."

Although this avoided exploring Jennifer's fear of extinction, EA wanted to offer a balanced perspective about the problem at this point due to the obsessive nature of Jennifer's thoughts.

Immediately, Jennifer said, "But are people going to fix things?"

Therapeutic Process: The Normalization of Affect

EA: "I … hope so. More people are worried about it than ever before. About 60% now here in the U.S."

Jennifer: "That's more than half."

EA: "Yes. And there's a Senate committee just about the climate crisis, Republicans and Democrats."

Jennifer: "Really?"

Sharing information about the solutions to the climate crisis is akin to sharing possible treatment recommendations to an adolescent facing a cancer diagnosis. Knowing the extent of the disease, first of all, is crucial; knowing that there are treatments, secondly, is essential; knowing what the treatments would involve is the next step towards confronting the illness.

Therapeutic Process: Exploring the Client's Fantasy World

In the following session, Jennifer still exhibited significant anxiety, which was discovered through a dream she shared:

Jennifer: "We were at your apartment, at the beach, or something, talking about global warming. You were pregnant." When asked what the dream brought to mind, she said, "I've been afraid of global warming, whether I want to bring a child into the world … I really want a child. I have this horrible fear I might not be able to have a child. Our science teacher said, 'I would be afraid for your kids.' Do you think it's gonna be okay to have a baby?"

Sadness filled EA as she imagined being Jennifer, tenderly holding the dream of loving her unborn child, partly herself, contained within the protective womb of her therapist's body. EA wished she could allow Jennifer to realistically hope for a safe, life-sustaining world for a child born several years from now. It's likely Jennifer noticed the therapist's sadness, as she asked again:

"Do you think it's gonna be okay?"

EA: "I … hope so, but it will depend on many things changing."

EA's empathic grief for Jennifer in the countertransference validated Jennifer's own feelings of loss. It also encouraged Jennifer to continue to take the issue seriously despite the emotional pain and the lack of support in her family and educational settings.

Therapeutic Process: Psychoeducation and Family Intervention

In the following session, the therapist gave Jennifer a book about climate crisis solutions (Hawken, 2017). She and her parents read the book at home. Afterwards, her parents became more interested in the topic, and in trying to see how they could help. Jennifer felt more effective and confident in speaking up with others. She became more interested in politics and the larger world in which decisions about her future were being made. For the first time, she ventured on a weekend trip away from her home and family with three high school friends, and her anxiety was minor and manageable.

Use of the Outdoor Environment as an Aspect of Treatment

Although Jennifer was previously unable to be outdoors by herself, she began to walk alone on a nearby beach. This became one of her favorite pastimes during the subsequent Covid-19 pandemic. EA saw this practice of walking outside as a way of feeling safer, more connected, and confident in the outdoor world, and Jennifer concurred.

In this treatment, Jennifer's eco-anxiety resolved as she eventually accepted both the risks and the potential progress in the future, and successfully increased her ability to assertively follow her social and other interests in the present. She consolidated this learning through her anchoring relationships with her parents, the natural world, and the therapist.

The Use of Emotions in the Therapy Relationship in Working with Climate Distress

Allowing ourselves to experience fear and sadness for our young clients enables us to become more aware of their needs for protection, empowerment, and the right to a viable ecosystem. This can strengthen the therapeutic alliance and our attachment bonds to these youth. The therapeutic relationship can become a valued resource and grounding "anchor" within a society undergoing climate dysregulation, especially if clients cannot express their feelings of fear, anger, or despair in other settings.

Sociopolitical Discussion in Therapy

Sociopolitical factors significantly influence mental health (Hoggett, 2013; Samuels, 2017; Weintrobe, 2021) and are worthy of discussion in the therapy office. For instance, addressing the mental health needs of child immigrant refugees would seem inadequate without processing feelings about abandoned homelands, treatment by immigration officials, and their cultural identity in a new place. Discussing sociopolitical impacts in therapy is particularly important with adolescents, as these experiences are interrelated with the climate crisis and can impact emotional health, identity formation, and maturation toward responsible adulthood.

Likewise, concerns about social and environmental injustice can be distressing to youth and can be processed through to a productive resolution. A high school-aged adolescent in treatment with EA explored his fears and anger about the unequal impacts of the climate crisis on peoples and ecosystems in the northern versus southern hemispheres. He eventually pursued this interest by attending a summer program focused on international conflict resolution, and is eagerly pursuing a college degree in a related field (Allured, 2019). As Samuels (2017) noted, the development of a political self can be crucial in a growing sense of agency.

When we, as well as our clients, can face the damage done by our exploitative colonization of others, or as Orange (2017) puts it, to "hold the ungrievables," there is the possibility for deeper change for everyone.

The Role of Hope

We can encourage hope with young clients while simultaneously acknowledging uncertainty about outcomes. Hope can be cultivated precisely *because* outcomes have not yet been determined for this crisis. Working within uncertainty parallels the general work of psychotherapy: Outcomes are not known at the beginning of treatment and depend on the hard work of raising awareness of the hidden etiology of problems that are creating havoc or dysfunction. Therapists are generally reluctant to predict an outcome in therapy; in a similar way, therapists need to refrain from predicting a specific outcome related to the environmental crisis when young clients bring this up. Instead, therapists can lean on definitions of hope that do not imply success of a specific action or actions. Vaclev Havel wrote:

> Hope is not the same thing as optimism. It is not the conviction that something will turn out well, but the certainty that something makes sense, regardless of how it turns out. (Havel, 1990)

Psychological maturity requires an acceptance of challenges, of disappointments, and even of mortality, held within secure attachment relationships. We can provide one such anchoring relationship as our young clients move toward this capability in uncertain times.

References

Albano, A. M., & Kendall, P. C. (2002). Cognitive behavioural therapy for children and adolescents with anxiety disorders: Clinical research advances. *International Review of Psychiatry*, 14, 129–134. https://psycnet.apa.org/doi/10.1080/09540260220132644

Allured, E. (2014). Blind spot in the analytic lens: Our failure to address environmental uncertainty. In B. Willock, R. Coleman Curtis, & L. Bohm (Eds.), *Understanding and coping with failure: Psychoanalytic perspectives*. Routledge.

Allured, E. (2019). The illusion of a future: Adolescents face smoke and mirrors with a good-enough and bad-enough eco-analyst. Manhattan Institute Conference: Climate Change, Inside and Outside the Consulting Room, December 12, 2020. Unpublished manuscript.

American Psychiatric Association (2022). *Diagnostic and statistical manual of psychiatric disorders* (5th ed., text rev.). APA. https://doi.org/10.1176/appi.books.9780890425787htt

Beebe, B., & Lachman, F. (2013). *The origins of attachment: Infant research and adult treatment*. Routledge.

Bratman, G. N., Anderson, C., Berman, M., Cochran, B., & Devries, S. (2019). Nature and mental health: An ecosystem service perspective. *Science Advances*, 5(7) doi: 10.1126/sciadv.aax090

Clayton, S., & Karazsia, B (2020). Development and validation of a measure of climate anxiety. *Journal of Environmental Psychology*, 69, 101434. https://doi.org/10.1016/j.jenvp.2020.101434

Consulo, A., Harper, S. L., Minor, K., Hayes, K., Williams, K. G., & Howard, C. (2020). Comment: Ecological grief and anxiety: The start of a healthy response to climate change? *The Lancet Planetary Health*, 4(7), E261–E263. https://doi.org/10.1016/S2542-5196(20)30144-3

Craske, M. G., Kircanski, K., Zelikowsky, M., Mystkowski, J., Chowdhury, N., & Baker, A. (2008). Optimizing inhibitory learning during exposure therapy. *Behaviour Research and Therapy*, 46(1), 5–27. https://doi.org/10.1016/j.brat.2007.10.003

Dooley, L., Sheats, J., Hamilton, O., Chapman, D., & Karlin, B. (2021). *Climate change and youth mental health: Psychological impacts, resilience resources, and future directions*. See Change Institute.

Fyfe Johnson, A. L., Hazlehurst, M. F., Perrins, S. P., Bratman, G. N., Thomas, R., Garrett, K. A., ... & Tandon, P. S. (2021). Nature and children's health: A systematic review. *Pediatrics*, 148(4), e2020049155. https://doi.org/10.1542/peds.2020-049155

Gil, E. (1991). *The healing power of play: Working with abused children*. Guilford Press.

Havel, V. (1990). *Disturbing the peace*. Knopf Publishing, pp. 181–182.

Hawken, P. (2017). *Drawdown: The most comprehensive plan ever proposed to reverse global warming*. Penguin Books.

Hayes, S., Luoma, B., Bond, F., Masuda, A., & Lillis, J. (2006). Acceptance and commitment therapy: Model, processes and outcomes. *Behaviour Research and Therapy*, 44(1), 1–25. https://doi.org/10.1016/j.brat.2005.06.006

Hickman, C., Marks, E., Pihkala, P., Clayton, S., Lewandowski, R. E., Mayall, E. E., ... & van Susteren, L. (2021). Climate anxiety in children and young people and their beliefs about government responses to climate change: A global survey. *The Lancet Planetary Health*, 5(12), e863–e873. doi:10.1016/S2542-5196(21)00278-3

Hoggett, P. (2013). Climate change in a perverse culture. In S. Weintrobe (Ed.), *Engaging with climate change: Psychoanalytic and interdisciplinary perspectives*. Routledge.

Klein, M. (1997). *The psychoanalysis of children*. Vintage.

Lifton, R. (2017). *The climate swerve*. The New Press.

Ojala, M. (2015). Hope in the face of climate change: Associations with environmental engagement and student perceptions of teachers' emotion communication style and future orientation. *Journal of Environmental Education*, 46(3), 133–148. http://dx.doi.org/10.1080/00958964.2015.1021662

Orange, D. (2017). *Climate crisis, psychoanalysis, and radical ethics*. Routledge.

Piaget, J. (1971). The theory of stages in cognitive development. In D. Ross, M. P. Ford, & G. B. Flamer Green (Eds.), *Measurement and Piaget*. McGraw-Hill.

Samuels, A. (2017). The "activist client": Social responsibility, the political self, and clinical practice in psychotherapy and psychoanalysis. *Psychoanalytic Dialogues*, 27, 678–694. https://doi.org/10.1080/10481885.2017.1379324

Santostefano, S. (2004). *Child therapy in the great outdoors: A relational view*. Routledge.

Schertz, K., & Berman, M. (2019). Understanding nature and its cognitive benefits. *Current Directions in Psychological Science*, 28(5). https://doi.org/10.1177/0963721419854100

Shedler, J. (2010). The efficacy of psychodynamic psychotherapy. *American Psychologist*, 65(2), 98–109. https://psycnet.apa.org/doi/10.1037/a0018378

Sifuentes, J. E., York, E. A., & Thomas, J. R.(2022). Climate change and youth mental health. Oregon Health Authority, May. https://sharedsystems.dhsoha.state.or.us/DHSForms/Served/le4212.pdf

Sullivan, H. (1954). *The psychiatric interview: The technique of the personal inquiry; A valuable guide for the psychiatrist, social worker, personnel manager and counsellor.* Norton and Co.

Weintrobe, S. (2021). *Psychological roots of the climate crisis: Neoliberal exceptionalism and the culture of uncare.* Bloomsbury.

Whis.stem.men.knee (1987, February) Open Center Workshop, New York.

Whitmarsh, L., Player, L., Jiongco, A., James, M., Williams, M. O., Marks, E., & Kennedy-Williams, P. (2022). Climate anxiety: What predicts it and how is it related to climate action? *Journal of Environmental Psychology*, 83, 101866. https://doi.org/10.1016/j.jenvp.2022.101866

Winnicott, D. (1985). *The maturational processes and the facilitating environment: Studies in the theory of emotional development.* Hogarth Press.

CHAPTER 11

Ecological and Intersectional Perspectives to Reduce Young Adults' Climate Distress
Reflections from a Work That Reconnects Program

Aravinda Ananda and Margaret Babbott

A reckoning with our climate crisis, in both its sociopolitical and ecological impacts, is central to young adults' coming of age in the twenty-first century. Its impact differs depending on geography, proximity to direct and indirect threats, social location, social-emotional capacities, developmental stage, and other biophysical factors. In this chapter, we explore the role of intentional peer spaces that support young adults to express their feelings about the climate crisis, be heard with mutual respect, connect with something greater than themselves and replenish themselves for contributing to a better world.

Many young people engage in various forms of activism in response to the social and ecological impacts of the climate crisis. Climate activism has occurred in many forms for decades, although these efforts have often not been recognized by dominant cultures. Climate activism is not, therefore, new in the twentieth and twenty-first centuries. What is new is its expansion into the mainstream and the growing recognition by adults and governments in positions of power. Climate activism presents potential risk and reward to the well-being of young activists. Benefits include a sense of agency, belonging, empowerment, existential meaning-making, sense of duty and ethical integrity, hope, stress-regulation, and development of an environmental self. In addition, participation in various actions can be highly energizing and galvanize emotions into embodied collective exuberance. In contrast, risks include physical and emotional depletion, hopelessness, despair, disillusionment, powerlessness, overwork and burnout, conflicts within and between peer groups, and vulnerability to mental health issues as covered elsewhere in this volume (Budziszewska & Głód, 2021; Fisher, 2016; Ojala, 2012; Schwartz et al., 2022). As such, young adults engaged in climate activism can use support to help restore and sustain them.

Studies demonstrate that youth climate activists associate the climate crisis with the harm perpetuated by colonialism and capitalism, including Indigenous genocide and displacement, systemic racism, femicide, and separation from direct connection with the earth. They seek to address climate issues from an intersectional perspective and process: "They want power to be shared differently, and to challenge institutional politics itself" (Bowman & Pickard, 2021, p. 506). One example is Godden et al.'s (2021) collaboration among Western Australian young people, Aboriginal and non-Aboriginal academics, activists, and practitioners, notable for its inclusion of multiple points of view in research on these concerns. The authors recommend that facilitators "normalize caring; normalize collective action; normalize the conversation about colonialism, capitalism, and climate change and normalize the truth of the climate crisis. They ask us to join them in action" (pp. 1762–1763). Broadening climate conversations to address these other social ills makes explicit the complexity of intersecting systems; opening a dialogue with peers provides young adults an opportunity for a shared, explicit exploration of an often-unnamed fear – that their actions could unintentionally perpetuate the exploitative systems that they are hoping to change.

Because the climate crisis has different impacts on different generations, young people want and need the older generation to listen to their perspectives. Our program, the Earth Leadership Cohort (ELC), is one of many developed to address the social and emotional needs of young adults who are concerned about the climate crisis. A similar program, the Youth Leading Environmental Change program (YLEC), is a multinational environmental engagement initiative for youth (Harré, 2016; Hickman et al., 2016). The program views emerging adults as ripe for civic engagement due to their openness to change, identity formation in flux, optimism, and fresh perspective. Specifically, the YLEC model identifies four central ingredients: (1) fostering systems thinking, (2) encouraging personal reflection, (3) building action competence, and (4) providing role modeling and support. YLEC leaders recommend that youth engaged in environmental action need to understand the complex, global nature of climate change, their connection to and interdependence with the natural world, and the experiences of people currently most impacted by environmental degradation. Programs for young activists must be as complex and comprehensive as the issue itself (Hickman et al., 2016, pp. 168–169).

Our program, an adaptation of the Work That Reconnects (WTR), was not a climate justice "training" program, but it attracted many young activists who felt called to be in service to the complex matrix of demands of these planetary times. Likewise, our program was not intentionally psychotherapeutic, but its core relationally based approaches were reparative: focus on reconnecting within the self, reconnecting with others in intentional community and reconnecting with the natural world. The foundation of the program was the central importance of belonging, literally, *the work that reconnects* – both human to human and humans to their natural world. The program offered opportunities to disrupt feelings of isolation and helplessness as well as address the false split between humans and nature. Within the holding environment of the program's frame, the group itself provided vitality, spirit, mystery, and sustenance to the experience. Out of this emerged a kind of active hope – hope not in the sense of something you have, but something you do through engagement (Macy & Johnstone, 2022).

In the remainder of this chapter, we offer an overview of the WTR and our adaptation for young adults (particularly late Millennial and Generation Z 18–30-year-olds from the United States who fall into the overlapping developmental stages of emerging [ages 18–25] and young adulthood [ages 25–30]). Then we discuss two features we have found to be essential when working with young adults in the context of climate justice issues. First, paradigms must shift from anthropocentric to ecocentric. Second, we must meet the generational demand for an intersectional approach. The climate crisis continues to reveal historical inequities, violence, and stressors disproportionately experienced by nondominant cultures and groups. For Westernized mental health practitioners working with young adults, it is thus essential to continually examine and address these assumptions embedded in healthcare theory, technique, and practice. In this chapter, we offer an example of one such attempt, albeit imperfect.

The Work That Reconnects and the Earth Leadership Cohort Program

The Work That Reconnects

The Work That Reconnects (WTR) (Macy, 2007; Macy & Brown, 2014; Macy & Johnstone, 2022) is a body of theory and experiential practices that originated in the late 1970s by antinuclear activists who contemplated distressing psychological and emotional topics such as the possibility of global nuclear holocaust. Over time, activists found that speaking with others about their feelings left them feeling enlivened rather than stuck in despair. For this reason, the WTR was originally called "Despair and Empowerment Work." Since the 1980s Joanna Macy, as root teacher, has most prominently developed, facilitated, and infused the work with her scholarship in three areas: systems thinking, deep ecology, and engaged Buddhism. In addition, hundreds of people across the globe have contributed and continue to contribute to this open-sourced body of group practices and theory.

In 2014, Kirstin Edelglass, an experienced WTR facilitator, conceived of the first "Earth Leadership Cohort," an adaptation of the WTR for young adults. She aimed to expand beyond its traditional *Baby Boomer* population to offer young adults a foundation in the WTR.

Earth Leadership Cohort

Between 2014 and 2019, we offered five annual Earth Leadership Cohort (ELC) programs. Each program provided an immersive, residential group experience for young adults aged 18–30 concerned about the state of the world. The program convened over the course of several long weekends, and strove to provide restoration, rejuvenation, and resourcing through connection with caring humans and the outdoors. The retreats offered:

1. Participation in forming and developing intentional community
2. Experiential and contemplative practices that welcomed emotional exploration and validated the inherent complexity and dissonance of these times through multimodal, integrative, small, and large group activities
3. Theoretical scaffolding (e.g., models of ecopsychology, applied systems theory, intersectionality, neuroscience of mind/body activation)
4. Structured and unstructured nature-based experiences.

The authors of this chapter were on the cofacilitation team for all five cohorts. Each ELC program averaged twelve participants – mostly college-educated, employed 18- to 30-year-olds, with an approximate median age of 26. We convened at retreat centers in rural locations with abundant access to the outdoors, a prominent part of the ecological immersive experience. For one of the weekends per cohort, participants joined a larger intergenerational WTR workshop.

Participants completed an application and phone interview. To provide a sense of what these young adults were seeking, we offer a sampling of responses to the application question: "What do you hope to gain from the experience of being a member of the Earth Leadership Cohort?" Table 11.1 shows a sample of responses that we have loosely divided into four overlapping thematic categories: Facilitation/Leadership skills, Self-skills, Restoration and Community.

Table 11.1 *Earth Leadership Cohort applicant responses to the question: What do you hope to gain from the experience of being a member of the Earth Leadership Cohort?*

Thematic category	Participant responses
Facilitation/leadership skills	• I hope to ground myself more in the WTR so that I can do my climate justice organizing from a place of love, peace and fulfillment as opposed to one of anger, sadness, and resentment. And maybe I can learn how to pass on this work to others to keep this wheel going… • I hope to experience tools and practices that build my skills of facing the wall of grief that often keeps people like me with racial and other privileges from confronting what is happening.
Self-skills	• I hope to experience space to feel hurt and sadness for the world's devastation and to release and transform some of the feelings I have been carrying. • Waves of hope vacillate between waves of fear for the future. I want to be part of a community confronting these emotions, wrestling with them, and ultimately emerging with a foundation to help others do the same.
Restoration	• I deeply hope to gain a renewed sense of passion and motivation which seems to have dwindled after so many experiences of feeling ignored or written off as an activist and feeling discouraged after failed attempts to create the community I long for.
Community	• Coming out of college, I can say that it is very rare to find youth-centered spaces that embody self and community-care and where people are supported to be honest with their concerns and hopes. • I want to find a community of practice to support me in this mission, to inspire me. I'd like to find other young people who share my passions. This can be a lonely path.

While each participant was drawn to ELC for different reasons, one shared impulse was to be engaged on behalf of something larger than themselves. Consistent with the literature cited earlier about the psychological toll of climate activism on young people, some of our ELC participants arrived with classic signs of burnout including fatigue, depressed mood, anxiety, dulled spirit, disillusionment, sleep/appetite disruptions, social withdrawal, anger, sense of helplessness, and work/activism/play imbalance.

The Spiral

Although every WTR program is different, each follows the same four stations of "the spiral": Gratitude, Honoring our pain for the world, Seeing with new/ancient eyes, and Going forth (see Figure 11.1). In our program,

Ecological and Intersectional Perspectives

Figure 11.1 The spiral of the Work That Reconnects, as painted by Dori Midnight.

we introduced the spiral in the beginning and referred to it throughout to provide a map that scaffolded the content, process, and intention of the workshop. Within each station, there are numerous practices that facilitate experiential and integrative opportunities. Conceptually, the spiral (an ancient symbol of transformation) reflects a dynamic, continual, and ever-evolving flow. The four stations, similar to the four seasons or four directions, invite psychological complexity of layered emotional experiences. Not unique to the WTR, these transpersonal concepts are found in Indigenous cultures, mythology, world religions, and various therapies.

The WTR spiral has endured across time, location, and constituencies, in part because of its foundation in sound psychological principles. First, it provides a map which offers form, predictability, and a shared understanding of what lies ahead. Second, the four stations introduce the inherent psychological complexity of the human experience and the importance of facing more difficult, painful emotions. Third, consistent with trauma-informed work, the sequence begins with Gratitude, which is based in a secure attachment – love – for some aspect of the living earth system

Table 11.2 *The psychological function of each station of the WTR spiral*

Spiral station	Nature of the station	Psychological function
Gratitude	Orient towards gratitude, awe, and love for life	Helps to ground people and settle nervous systems, resources the capacity to be present with more difficult emotions. Initiates group formation.
Honoring our pain for the world	Allow feelings of fear, anger, sadness, numbness, and shame to arise	Expands capacity to experience and express a wide range of difficult emotions within self and with others. Often this release allows for embodied integration, and can feel cathartic, although the purpose is not to purge feelings, just to be present with them. Sometimes in allowing the feelings to flow, the intensity of them can shift or lessen. Helps to connect people with others thereby reducing alienation and isolation.
Seeing with new/ ancient eyes	Explore insights into the interconnectedness of life and the wider web of connections available to us	Offers refreshing insights, connects participants with something wider than themselves, offers a reframe and empowering stance.
Going forth	Prepare ourselves to contribute towards the healing needed in the living world	Moves people into empowered action by discovering new possibilities, setting intentions, and preparing to enact them.

before moving to areas of insecure, avoidant, or traumatic attachment experiences. And fourth, the spiral offers WTR facilitators a flexible rather than rigid balance between form and freedom, structure, and spontaneity; for each of the four stations, there are numerous options for practices and rituals (individual, small group, large group; cognitive, embodied, contemplative, creative, playful; indoors and outdoors; right brain/ left brain; raucous and solemn). Table 11.2 summarizes the psychological functions of each station of the WTR spiral.

The first station, "Gratitude," grounds the process of the retreat in the gifts of life and invites wonder and awe. In a practice called "open sentences," participants complete a sentence fragment such as "A place that was magical to me as a child was ..." while someone else listens to them without interruption before switching turns. Gratitude practices such as these help to settle the nervous system by eliciting positive affect and by offering individual and group connection.

In the second spiral station, "Honoring our pain for the world," participants are supported through teachings, meditations, practices, and group rituals to be present with painful emotions – fear, anger, sorrow, outrage, despair, futility, guilt, shame – about what is happening in and to our world. In systems theory, open feedback loops are markers of health, using output as input for further growth and activity. When participants express and witness these emotions in this supportive context, many find an expanded sense of connectedness and reduced sense of isolation. Because we only mourn the loss of that which we love, the shared expression and witnessing of these feelings can create a bridge to an energetic collective caring for the world.

These feelings of wider interconnectedness can open people into the third station of the spiral, originally called "Seeing with new eyes." In their book, *Active Hope: How to Face the Mess We're in with Unexpected Resilience and Creative Power* (2022), Macy and Johnstone identify four empowering shifts in perception they call "the four discoveries": a wider sense of self, a different kind of power, a richer experience of community, and a larger view of time (refer to Table 11.3). The focus of this station is to explore paradigmatic shifts counter to dominant culture to help participants make these discoveries of their interconnectedness with the living world, with ancestors and future beings, and with a more diverse understanding of each other.

Influenced by Patricia St. Onge's (2014) contributions to the WTR, many WTR facilitators have expanded the title of this station to "Seeing with new/ancient eyes." Shaped by her Mohawk heritage, St. Onge rightly reminds us that ecocentric and intersectional theories are more ancient than new for most of human history and inherent in Indigenous peoples' lived experiences, wisdom traditions, science, and care of the earth (Charles & Cajete, 2020). By exploring both "new" and "ancient" ideas, we address who is being centered and who is being excluded; this furthers our commitment to discernment regarding cultural appropriation and assumptions.

The spiral, although not linear, concludes with "Going forth." In this last station, participants explore and prepare for how they might like to contribute to the healing needed in the world. This station invites expanded imagination, collective feedback, realistic assessment of current internal and external resources, and intention. Many participants have experienced considerable rejuvenation through expanding their sense of self and agency and by finding hope through engaged and committed action.

Within each retreat, the ELC program followed the WTR spiral structure adapted to each cohort. Over the five years, the facilitators

Table 11.3 *Four discoveries explored in the "Seeing with new/ancient eyes" station (Macy & Johnstone, 2022, p. 81)*

Discovery	Nature of the discovery	Dominant Western culture norm(s) it counters
Wider sense of self	View the self as connected parts of a larger whole. Self-interest is expanded, and self is rooted in wider circles of kinship.	View the self as a separate entity; hyper-individualism, you are alone and must go it alone.
Different kind of power	Power is conceived of as power-with and can be win-win and emergent when people work together. Because power is built through connectedness with others, safety and well-being are achieved through the strength of those connections.	Power is conceived of as power-over and is a win-lose proposition. Domination and coercion are used to achieve safety otherwise you will lose out.
Richer experience of community	Fellowship and diverse community are forms of wealth that enrich our lives, strengthen our security, and give us a more stable foundation from which to act. Interdependence and mutual aid networks can meet many of our needs and be enjoyable.	Self-sufficiency is idealized; it is weak or dangerous to rely on anyone; all our needs can be met through higher productivity which allows us to be secure through better and more material "stuff." Thus, the primary objective is to fix dissatisfaction with consumerism.
Enlarged view of time	Time is circular; humans exist in a long unbroken chain of those who came before and those who will come after present generations. We can draw on the strength of ancestors and be guided by the interests of generations yet to come (encompasses nonhuman beings as well).	Time is linear, the past is in the past and the future which hasn't happened yet is likewise inaccessible. Disproportionate focus on the short-term driven by capitalist economies.

incorporated feedback and increasingly paid attention to group process enactments of sociocultural positions and power. Group dynamics inevitably followed Tuckman's (1965) stages of forming, storming, norming, performing, and adjourning that loosely coincide with the spiral stations. We have experimented with new practices and have integrated other theories into our program including trauma-informed neuroscience concepts, such as Siegel's hand model of the Triune Brain and Window of Tolerance (Siegel, 2020) and intersectionality theory (Nahar, 2017). Simultaneous with the larger national and global reckoning by white dominant institutions with embedded racism, intersectionality emerged as a new/ancient way of seeing within our ELC program.

Ecocentric Approaches in the Work That Reconnects

Foundational to the WTR is the shift away from an anthropocentric paradigm, which places humans as separate from and superior to all other beings, towards an ecocentric paradigm, in which humans are viewed as embedded in the web of life. For example, in contrast to such traditional characterizations as "Man vs Nature," we struggled with how to avoid reinforcing this false separation by referring to "time in nature." In reality, humans *are* nature, are living beings composed of earth, sea, and air inextricably linked with our environments. Instead, we attempted to use the designation of "time outdoors," but were woefully inconsistent. At times, we have used the terminology, "more-than-human" world, coined by Abram (1997) to replace "nonhuman" in order to counter the anthropocentric bias.

Within psychology, the relatively new field of ecopsychology emerged in the 1980s in response to Western psychology's anthropocentric bias. It distinguishes itself from the established environmental and conservation psychologies by its focus on the "equal" and reciprocal relational health of humans and the earth system of which humans are a relatively new and small part (Roszak et al., 1995). It is a broad discipline that explores the human-nature relationship through an ecological lens; there are three central tenets of ecopsychology that ground WTR and specifically, our ELC program:

1. The interconnected interdependence of all living things based on ecology and systems theory
2. The reciprocal relationship between and among the human species and all other species such that as one suffers or thrives so does the other
3. Diversity as foundational to evolution and healthy systems.

Viewing human health through an ecocentric lens promotes well-being on many levels, and the benefits of connection with the more-than-human world have been well established and form the basis of ecotherapy (Buzzell & Chalquist, 2009; Jordan & Hinds, 2016; Robbins, 2020). Contemplative practice or time in the natural world cultivates embodied place-based attunement and recalibrates the human nervous system to tune in to that of the larger earth's living system. Humans feel less distracted or dissociated when their animal body is fully present and oriented to place, time, context via sensory input, breath exchange, temperature, light, and barometric pressure, all of which contributes to feeling that one is part of the larger whole. Specifically, many of the practices that we offer in ELC are consistent with what Doherty (2016) identifies as "environmentalist therapy": "… individual therapeutic experiences to resolve the cultural-level split from wild nature in developed societies that is seen to impact health and identity and to drive ecologically destructive behaviours" (p. 15).

While pretraumatic, or anticipatory stress (Van Susteren, 2018) is considered a healthy response to the social and ecological threats of climate change, it is nonetheless future oriented. Young adults are still in the process of building capacities for braiding together past, present, and future orientations and the respective emotional valences of each. Climate activists can become stuck in fears for the future, forgoing tangible experiences of beauty, joy, awe, and delight. Nature-based connection helps resource and root from a known present rather than an anticipated future. Some of the experiential outdoors practices we have offered include the mirror walk, the evolutionary walk, the soil/soul sustainability practice and sit spots, as described below.

The Mirror Walk (Gratitude)
The Mirror Walk is a multisensorial, embodied pair activity in which one partner leads a second partner, whose eyes are closed, through an outdoor setting. The guiding partner quietly offers sensory experiences such as the texture of stone, the scent of grass, the sound of birds, the taste of wind and allows the guided partner time to explore and savor the sensory experiences. At several points during this "sensory tour," the guiding partner will focus their partner's gaze and say, "Open your eyes and look in the mirror," inviting the guided partner to see the wider world as part of their larger ecological self (Macy & Brown, 2014). WTR practices such as the Mirror Walk help participants open up to the felt experience of interconnectedness with the wider living world and break down mental walls of false separation. This can often lead to a sense of wonder, interconnectedness, enlivenment, and interdependence for participants.

The Evolutionary Walk (Seeing with New/Ancient Eyes)
In the WTR, the concept of "deep time" expands our sense of the contracted 24/7 technology blitz and places the notion in the broader scope

of generational and evolutionary time. For example, one of our cofacilitators, Joseph Rotella, created a walk for ELC that paced out the 13.7 billion years of evolution of the known universe over a third of a mile. Drawing on Swimme and Berry's (1992) work, key evolutionary developments of the universe were named as participants walked. With one step representing 68.5 million years, one walks a long time before Earth is even formed. Humans appear only within the last step of the third of a mile walk. The practice helps participants to have a more embodied sense of the immensity of time in the history of the known universe and can often enliven and empower participants by opening them to wonder at the vastness of existence.

Soil/Soul Sustainability Practice (Going Forth)
Babbott created a Soil/Soul Sustainability Practice which offers another example of an ecopsychologically informed practice offered during the "Going forth" section of the spiral. The exercise illustrates an integrative approach to earth body/human body reciprocity, comparing the needs of soil to our own needs for a sustainable emotional "soil" in which to grow and thrive. The practice begins with three open sentences completed in pairs: (1) A time when I felt burnt out by my activism was…; (2) The ways that I know (body, mind, spirit) that I am feeling burnt out are…; (3) Some things that help sustain me are…. In the second part of the practice, the facilitator collects on newsprint group responses to what healthy soil needs to grow food sustainably (e.g., clean water, sun, pollinators, night, companion planting, rotation). The metaphor of the participant's body as the earth's body invites playfulness and deepens the notion of reciprocal relations. For example, we might ask, "What does lying fallow look like for humans, for you?" or "How about worms? What do you need to aerate your soul?" The final part of the practice is a solo journal practice to identify one's individual soil/soul needs and potential action plan for healthy sustainability.

Sit Spots
For some of the ELCs, we introduced "sit spots," a nature-based relational practice (Young, 2012, 2020). Individuals choose a place outdoors that they return to on a regular basis for a multisensorial experience of a place over time. The simple task is to sit and notice self and nature, self-in-nature, nature-in-self. Over the course of the retreats, these relationships grow as the nervous systems of human and earth sync up. It is a place-based solitude practice that further develops the experience of an ecological self. Often participants have shared that they have established sit spots upon returning home.

Rituals

The WTR utilizes rituals to integrate, mark, and transform experiences. Rituals can be embedded in formal and/or informal religious or spiritual practices, and can be practiced at cultural, communal, and individual levels. One shared feature of rituals is the intentional demarcation of time and space. Most rituals have a beginning, a middle, and an end that includes a shared understanding of its purpose. Marking developmental transitions with rituals supports the development of experiential maps of the self.

For young people overwhelmed by climate emotions, rituals can offer a safe container for complex feelings, meaning-making, and transpersonal experiences. ELC aims to build capacities to tolerate the wide range and varying intensities of emotional responses inherent in the climate crisis. Rituals can offer an integrative mind/body/spirit experience alone or within a community. Participants can experience catharsis (tears, ecstasy) and tap into new realms of imagination and vitality. Rituals are distinct from other WTR practices in that rituals invite participants to speak archetypally as part of a "larger sacred whole" in ways that might seem odd outside of the ritual space, but within it become vehicles for creative transformation (Macy & Brown, 2014). In addition, rituals provide an antidote to perceived isolation when others speak universally on your behalf.

Within ELC, we shared informal rituals such as communal meals (e.g., circling up before eating to pause and express gratitude for the food and its contributors) as well as formal rituals within the program as described in the following two examples. The first is a Circle of Intentions that occurs on the opening evening of the program. After various icebreakers, we facilitate a sharing circle with clear instructions and time boundaries. We begin with a meditative settling of the body and mind, light a central candle, invite each person to take a few minutes to share one of their intentions for our time together, and close with a statement of gratitude as we extinguish the candle. This serves as an introduction to communal ritual-making and welcomes each voice into the community. Over the years, we have experimented with a variety of forms, prompts, council formats, centerpieces, openings, and closings.

Rituals can both help to unlock the numbness that can set in when overwhelmed by painful climate emotions and contain the swell of emotions through a collective process. The Cairn of Mourning is a WTR grief ritual we introduce during the spiral station, "Honoring our pain for the world." "By choosing to honor the pain of loss rather than discounting it, we break the spell that numbs us to the dismantling of our world" (Macy & Brown, 2014, pp. 117–118). We invite people to spend time outside quietly contemplating things that have been lost or are disappearing in this planetary time. Losses can range from the person to the collective, from the tangible to intangible. With our ecocentric-intersectional approach, we have expanded this ritual to emphasize the intersectional impact of both social as well as ecological losses, for example mass incarceration, safe drinking water, collapse of coral reefs, addiction, sexual violence. We ask people to find an object (stone, stick, fallen leaves) to symbolize what they are grieving and bring it with them when we reconvene in a circle. Next, each person takes a turn, when so moved, to place their object in the center of the circle and if they would like, speak about the loss. The group bears witness to each loss, spoken and unspoken, and may acknowledge the offering by vocalization, instrument, or a simple phrase, "We hear you." The end of the ritual can be marked by movement or song.

The capacity to bear grief and mourn inevitable losses in the presence of supportive community expands our sense of interconnectedness. In dominant Western culture, people are often admonished to "get over it and move on" rather than learn how to honor and carry that which has been lost. Feeling "pain for the world" occurs because we allow ourselves to feel the connection. When grief for and from the world flows through us, we open ourselves not only to pain but also to power. In contrast to some climate activism spaces, ELC participants expressed relief that they were able to bring all their emotions, and that there was room for spirituality in its many forms.

The Young Adult Demand for an Intersectional Approach

Overview of the History of Environmental Justice

While the 1960s saw heightened civil rights activism, and the 1970s saw heightened climate activism, the two were not integrated and thus, a predominantly white and middle-class demographic within the environmental movement did not adequately address systemic racism. As such, environmental gains and protections were enacted in largely white communities. This gave rise in the 1980s to an Environmental Justice movement led predominantly by people of color (Thomas, 2022).

With the previous decade, there has been a resurgence of social justice activism with the establishment of Black Lives Matter, the growth of the Indigenous movement for LANDBACK, the MeToo movement, Stop Asian Hate, and LGBTQIA activism. There has also been a growth in youth-led climate activism such as Youth Strike for Climate (also known as Fridays for the Future) started by Greta Thunberg and the US-based Sunrise Movement. Influenced by the social justice movements of the last decade, these youth-led climate movements increasingly embrace an intersectional approach, viewing climate justice and social justice as inextricably interconnected both in root causes and in solutions.

Climate activists with an analysis and worldview that regard colonialism and oppression as causes of the climate crisis seek to dismantle systems of human oppression in tandem with climate action. From this perspective, climate justice and social justice are intertwined, and effective attempts to address one need to address the mindset and behaviors that give rise to both. For example, the youth-led Sunrise Movement defines collective liberation as central to their climate activism.

> We honor and continue the work of movements that came before us. We are fighting to become the generation that turns the tide against racism and the institutions built upon it. We unlearn oppressive attitudes and fearlessly confront a status quo that divides us based on our skin color, the money in our pockets, where we live, who we love and who we are. [Eleventh principle of the Sunrise Movement]

It is increasingly unacceptable for systems of human oppression to play out unchecked in climate movement spaces, and there is disillusionment with climate strategies that replicate the same systems of domination and exploitation that are root drivers of the climate crisis. One inspiring example of addressing human systems of oppression within actions for the climate occurred at Namewog, a Line 3 (oil pipeline) resistance camp in northern Minnesota. Their leadership was held by Indigenous women and two-spirits and one of the camp agreements was to dismantle all of the "isms." Many of the activists who visited the resistance camp were young folks (including some ELC alumni) who also hold a core belief that collective liberation is central to the struggle for a livable climate and future.

As with many environmental organizations in the United States, there has been growing attention within the WTR facilitation community focused on the need to reexamine assumptions and implicit biases embedded in the theory, practice, and facilitation of the WTR and these fruitful, painful, liberating conversations are ongoing and increasingly foregrounded.

Earth Leadership Cohort and Intersectionality

While the cohort experience was deeply transformational for some participants, it was harmful to others. Notably, during the first cohort (ELC-1), the only participant who identified as a person of color withdrew after the first meeting. While some of the reasons for withdrawing were personal, a significant reason was how white-dominant the space was in terms of demographics – this participant was the only person in the room of 80 people who visibly appeared as a person of color. Another reason for withdrawing was how white-dominant the programming was in terms of culture. One example of this is a practice called Harvesting the Gifts of the Ancestors, which is a journey through the human experience since the beginning of the evolution of humans. An earlier version of this practice (as was shared during the first cohort) was framed in a way that centered on heterosexual European-descended peoples, thereby writing out other people's experiences.

The participant of color's abrupt departure prompted increased awareness, concern, and attention that has since significantly shaped how we conducted future cohorts. We became more sensitive to Eurocentric biases embedded in the practices and the absence (exclusion/erasure) of people of color's lived experience. This shone a light on the false split between the environment and social justice movements that has been prevalent for decades in historically white-dominant environmental and climate movements (with the notable exception of the environmental justice movement) and the need to attend to white supremacy operating in many environmental and climate spaces such as WTR.

Just as it is important for therapists to be culturally competent and work to avoid perpetuating microaggressions against their clients, climate movement spaces must work against perpetuating oppressive harms (Sue et al., 2007). In these ways, among others, the ELC seeks to facilitate mutual learning experiences in which facilitators and participants co-create and evolve.

Application of Intersectionality in ELC

Content

Shifts toward intersectionality have also occurred within a concept central to WTR teaching known as "The Great Turning" (Macy & Brown, 2014). The Great Turning describes an epochal shift to life-sustaining human societies. While its outcome is uncertain, The Great Turning is viewed as underway and happening in three dimensions: holding actions to slow down the damage; creation of alternative structures and ways of doing and being; and shifts in consciousness (Macy & Brown, 2014, pp. 6–18; Macy & Johnstone, 2022, pp. 26–34).

The three dimensions of The Great Turning were historically taught as separate spheres with the belief that one need not divide time equally between the three, but rather devote energy in line with one's greatest passions, recognizing that some will be drawn more to holding actions, others to building new structures, and others to supporting a shift in consciousness. We now appreciate that attending to one dimension while ignoring others can not only limit one's power but may also cause harm. The potential for harm is evident when, for example, a switch to so-called renewable energies such as solar panels is made without recognizing that the materials are made with rare earth metals and mined with exploitative labor practices. In this instance, no shift in consciousness has occurred, and detrimental long-term effects result. As Anne Symens-Bucher (2016) teaches, the most powerful actions are those where all three dimensions of The Great Turning overlap.

Practices, actions, or structures that fail to embrace justice and intersectionality are likely to replicate the same hierarchical structures of domination that are a root cause of today's crises. Not only will they not be effective in the long run, but they also run the risk of alienating marginalized peoples along the way, which does further harm and undermines the movement. When teaching the three dimensions of The Great Turning in ELC programs, we now emphasize the importance of holding actions and of new structures embodying a shift in consciousness that reflects a commitment to justice and intersectionality. Too many ELC participants had been part of holding actions or new structures that had not addressed how racism, sexism, classism, and other 'isms were showing up in social interactions and dynamics, and this undermines the strength of this work.

Process

Over the course of the five programs, ELC facilitators increasingly emphasized community process in equal measure to program content to build a more intersectional approach. Time and care were taken to set up a "community container," within which we agreed on norms and behaviors that could facilitate an anti-oppressive space. A significant amount of time was spent when the group first convened exploring people's social location and identity; we discussed how these may contribute to self and group dynamics with respect to systems of oppression. Many steps can be taken to avoid harm from systems of oppression, and when it inevitably occurs, it is important to be willing to pause and explore its complexity and avenues for possible repair. While the work is ever-ongoing to address how systems of oppression operate in climate justice spaces, these initial steps help participants develop greater trust in the safety of the space and feelings of authentic belonging – something that today's young adults crave in an ever-complex world where such concerns may have been dismissed.

Discussion

The ELC version of the WTR has evolved to meet many of the recommendations cited earlier in this chapter: it provides space, time, facilitation for peers and adults to experience caring, collective action, and conversations about colonialism, capitalism, and the climate crisis (Godden et al., 2021). We deliberately amplified activism protective factors and tended to the risk factors. We aimed to help young adults build capacities individually and collectively that might serve, support, and sustain them as they continue to live with the realities of this planetary time. We have integrated nervous system awareness and activation. Collectively, we foregrounded group process and the co-creation of norms and values.

In their verbal and written feedback, many participants reported that ELC was a profound life-changing experience where they felt held, seen, and validated in an intentional community. Throughout the retreats, many participants moved from disillusioned isolation to empowered connection with peers and the living earth, regenerating their care and commitment to present and future justice. The opportunity to be authentic, caring, and vulnerable can be invaluable in modern society, which can often feel isolating.

In addition, the ecocentric approach underlying the WTR provides an antidote to Western culture's relationship to time and urgency. Intentional time outdoors invites re-membering, literally returning participants to the animal body in the present moment. Many ELC participants described feeling overwhelmed and exhausted by the unrelenting urgency of social and ecological threats caused by the climate crisis. While ELC addressed serious issues, it was imbued with spontaneity, play, and creativity. Along with a range of emotional states such as gratitude, anger, grief, confusion, shame, guilt, we continue to re-envision "work" and welcome creative emergence and open-hearted hilarity. We supported what adrienne maree brown (2019) describes as "pleasure activism." ELC programs prioritize radical rest, respite, and reflection in which "being is a form of doing" that explicitly runs counter to the dominant Western culture of achievement.

Limitations and Future Directions

We recognize the inherent limitations of our recommendations due to our small sample size, the specificity of ELC as one particular application of the WTR, the common demographics of many of the ELC participants and facilitators, and that participants self-selected to this particular approach.

As such, caution is warranted with generalizing our recommendations to the young adult population since the reflections offered may not be transferable to groups with a different demographic makeup or function. The reflections in this chapter are offered from the facilitators' viewpoint and would become more three-dimensional and benefit from participants' perspectives. Finally, we are aware that it is hard to capture the essence of an experiential program out of context (i.e., *You just had to be there* ...).

We envision a future in which young people have access to climate justice communities and programs that are informed by ecocentric and intersectional principles. Qualitative and quantitative research of these emerging programs could contribute valuable credibility and exposure on behalf of best practices. These two lenses can be applied across settings such as mental health, education, parent resources, and community organizations. Realistically dismantling the knot of deep-rooted systemic oppressions will take generations. However, the climate crisis may be catalyzing those who have yet to be on the front lines to join those who have been building, sustaining, and thriving, in spite of centuries of apocalyptic-like conditions. As facilitators, ELC has transformed our dread into purpose, isolation into community, and overwhelm into a mysterious form of unfolding active hope.

Acknowledgments

The authors are grateful to each Earth Leadership Cohort (ELC) participant for breathing life into these programs, to cofacilitators Joseph Rotella and Kirstin Edelglass, to Joanna Macy and others who have contributed so much to the development of the Work That Reconnects, and for offering it as an open source so that so many people can benefit from it. In addition, we thank Sarah Pirtle and Patricia Harney for their feedback on earlier versions of the chapter, Satyena Ananda at the Starseed Healing Sanctuary where numerous ELC retreats took place, and all beings in the living systems that made these programs possible.

References

Abram, D. (1997). *The spell of the sensuous: Perception and language in a more-than-human world*. Vintage.

Bowman, B., & Pickard, S. (2021). Peace, protest and precarity: Making conceptual sense of young people's non-violent dissent in a period of intersecting crises. *Journal of Applied Youth Studies*, 4(5), 493–510. https://doi.org/10.1007/s43151-021-00067-z

brown, a.m. (2019). *Pleasure activism: The politics of feeling good*. AK Press.
Budziszewska, M., & Głód, Z. (2021). "These are the very small things that lead us to that goal": Youth climate strike organizers talk about activism empowering and taxing experiences. *Sustainability*, 13(19), 11119. https://doi.org/10.3390/su131911119
Buzzell, L., & Chalquist, C. (Eds.) (2009). *Ecotherapy: Healing with nature in mind*. Sierra Club Books.
Charles, C., & Cajete, G. A. (2020). Wisdom traditions, science and care for the earth: Pathways to responsible action. *Ecopsychology*, 12(2), 65–70. https://doi.org/10.1089/eco.2020.0020
Doherty, T. J. (2016). Theoretical and empirical foundations for ecotherapy. In M. Jordan & J. Hinds (Eds.), *Ecotherapy: Theory, research & practice* (pp. 12–31). Palgrave. https://link.springer.com/10.1057/978-1-137-48688-2_2
Fisher, S. R. (2016). Life trajectories of youth committing to climate activism. *Environmental Education Research*, 22(2), 229–247. https://doi.org/10.1080/13504622.2015.1007337
Godden, N. J., Farrant, B. M., Farrant, J. Y., Heyink, E., Collins, E. C., Burgemeister, B., ... Cooper, T. (2021). Climate change, activism, and supporting the mental health of children and young people: Perspectives from Western Australia. *Journal of Paediatrics and Child Health*, 57, 1759–1764. https://doi.org/10.1111/jpc.15649
Harré, N. (2016). Commentary on the special issue: Youth leading environmental change. *Ecopsychology*, 8(3), 202–205. https://doi.org/10.1089/eco.2016.0030
Hickman, G., Riemer, M., & YLEC Collaborative. (2016). A theory of engagement for fostering collective action in youth leading environmental change. *Ecopsychology*, 8(3), 167–173. https://doi.org/10.1089/eco.2016.0024
Jordan, M., & Hinds, J. (2016). *Ecotherapy: Theory, research & practice*. Palgrave.
Macy, J. (2007). *World as lover, world as self: Courage for global justice and ecological renewal*. Parallax Press.
Macy, J., & Brown, M. (2014). *Coming back to life: The updated guide to the work that reconnects* (rev. ed.). New Society Publishers.
Macy, J., & Johnstone, C. (2022). *Active hope: How to face the mess we're in with unexpected resilience and creative power*. New World Library.
Nahar, S. (2017). Intersectionalization of the work that reconnects. *Deep Times: A Journal of the Work That Reconnects*, 2(5). https://journal.workthatreconnects.org/2017/08/29/intersectionalization-of-the-work-that-reconnects/
Ojala, M. (2012). How do children cope with global climate change? Coping strategies, engagement, and well-being. *Journal of Environmental Psychology*, 32(3), 225–233. https://doi.org/10.1016/j.jenvp.2012.02.004
Robbins, J. (2020). Ecopsychology: How immersion in nature benefits your health. *Yale Environment*, 360, January 9. https://e360.yale.edu/features/ecopsychology-how-immersion-in-nature-benefits-your-health
Roszak, T., Gomes, M. E., & Kanner, A. D. (1995). *Ecopsychology: Restoring the earth, healing the mind*. Sierra Club Books.

Schwartz, S. E. O., Benoit, L., Clayton, S., Parnes, M. F., Swenson, L., & Lowe, S. R. (2022). Climate change anxiety and mental health: Environmental activism as buffer. *Current Psychology*, 42, 16708–16721. https://doi.org/10.1007/s12144-022-02735-6

Siegel, D. J. (2020). *The developing mind* (3rd ed.). Guilford Press.

St. Onge, P. (2014). Learning with communities of color. In J. Macy & M. Brown (Eds.), *Coming back to life: The updated guide to the work that reconnects* (pp. 255–264).

Sue, D. W., Capodilupo, C. M., Torino, G. C., Bucceri, J. M., Holder, A. M. B., Nadal, K. L., & Esquilin, M. (2007). Racial microaggressions in everyday life: Implications for clinical practice. *American Psychologist*, 62(4), 271–286. https://doi.org/10.1037/0003-066X.62.4.271

Sunrise Movement (online). Retrieved December 13, 2022. www.sunrisemovement.org/principles/?ms=Sunrise%27sPrinciples

Swimme, B., & Berry, T. (1992). *The universe story: From the primordial flaring forth to the Ecozoic Era: A celebration of the unfolding of the cosmos*. HarperOne.

Symens-Bucher, A. (2016). An emergent version of the three dimensions of the Great Turning. *Deep Times: A Journal of the Work That Reconnects*, 1(1), 28–31.

Thomas, L. (2022). *The intersectional environmentalist: How to dismantle systems of oppression to protect people + planet*. Voracious/Little Brown and Company.

Tuckman, B. W. (1965). Developmental sequence in small groups. *Psychological Bulletin*, 63(6), 384–399. https://doi.org/10.1037/h0022100

Van Susteren, L. (2018). The psychological impacts of the climate crisis. *British Journal of Psychiatry International*, 15(2), 25–26. https://doi.org/10.1192%2Fbji.2017.40

Young, J. (2012). *What the robin knows: How birds reveal the secrets of the natural world*. Houghton Mifflin Harcourt.

Young, J. (2020). *Repairing emotional isolation by reawakening deep nature connection* [Video]. TED Conferences, April. www.youtube.com/watch?v=QMWSvUpoCYk

CHAPTER 12

Pediatricians' Perspectives
Youth Climate Distress in the Pediatric Setting

Samantha Ahdoot

Introduction

The work of pediatricians has changed dramatically since the founding of modern pediatrics in the late nineteenth century. Infectious diseases, the leading cause of child morbidity and mortality last century (Shulman, 2004), are definitively being replaced by noncommunicable diseases, including mental health conditions, as leading threats to child health in the United States and globally. In 2019, self-harm (including suicide), depressive and anxiety disorders, and interpersonal violence were four of the top ten leading causes of global disability-adjusted life years in young people aged 10–24 years (GBD 2019 Diseases and Injuries Collaborators, 2020). Persistent feelings of sadness or hopelessness and suicidal thinking in American high school students rose between 2011 and 2021, to over one in three and one in five students, respectively (Centers for Disease Control and Prevention, 2022).

This rise of mental health disorders in young people has presented a tremendous societal challenge which is exacerbated by the significant deficit in trained mental health professionals to provide care. In communities with limited resources, the lack of access to mental health services is profound (Becker & Kleinman, 2013). This disparity between need and access to mental health professionals has led to efforts to train primary care providers, including pediatricians, in the provision of mental health treatment. The American Academy of Pediatrics (AAP) has endorsed the role of primary care pediatricians in managing mild and moderate mental health disorders (Walter et al., 2021) and has developed core competencies for delivery of this care (Committee on Psychosocial Aspects of Child and Family Health and Task Force on Mental Health, 2009). Programs and resources have been developed in order to support provision of mental health care in the pediatric primary care setting (Romba & Ballard, 2020).

Pediatricians are uniquely positioned to support mental health in young people. We develop relationships with families over long periods of time and have opportunities to observe our patients as they develop over years. We are often aware of a family's broader social context, have engendered trust through care over time, and have a perspective that is highly valued (O'Brien et al., 2016). Approximately half of pediatric office visits involve developmental, educational, behavioral, emotional, and/or psychosocial concerns (Martini et al., 2012).

Pediatricians therefore have an opportunity to identify and address emerging mental health challenges early in their onset. In addition, pediatricians are well trained in preventative care that can prevent future health problems (Hagan et al., 2017).

As pediatricians assume greater responsibility for prevention and treatment of youth mental health challenges, there is a need to incorporate the role of environmental threats into our care of patients. While "decreasing exposure to environmental toxins and stressors" has been identified as a mental health competency, and "children displaced by disasters" have been identified as a special population of concern (Committee on Psychosocial Aspects of Child and Family Health and Task Force on Mental Health, 2009), climate change is not well appreciated by pediatricians as a mental health risk.

Pediatricians in the United States are already caring for children whose health is affected by climate change. The role of climate change on these health conditions, however, often goes unrecognized. For example, pediatricians caring for children affected by extreme weather events may see events as isolated emergencies rather than connected to the broader problem of climate change. Even pediatricians who embrace the "public health" perspective with regards to child mental health and well-being (Foy & Perrin, 2010) may not yet consider climate change within this broader framework.

There is a rapidly increasing body of literature on the intersections between climate change and the mental health of young people. As reviewed in depth in the other chapters of this book, climate change influences the mental health of young people at every stage of development, from birth through young adulthood. The psychological well-being of young people is affected by climate change today through diverse pathways that can be direct and immediate, indirect and gradual, or vicarious through overarching awareness (Hayes et al., 2018). Children in regions that are more vulnerable by virtue of geography, socioeconomic factors or racism and discrimination are often more susceptible to these effects

Figure 12.1 Role of pediatricians in a changing climate.

(Burke et al., 2018). As climate change impacts continue to mount, the mental health toll can be expected to rise even further.

The need to educate pediatricians regarding the impacts of climate change on child health has been recognized for over a decade. The AAP was the first medical organization in the United States to recognize the health consequences of climate change with its publication of their Policy Statement (Committee on Environmental Health, 2007) and Technical Report (Shea, 2007) on Global Climate Change and Children's Health in 2007. These documents, and the AAP's updated reports in 2015 (Ahdoot et al., 2015), marked a pivotal moment in medicine, whereby a leading medical society acknowledged that its members must care for the planet to care for patients.

Pediatricians serve numerous roles as we seek to promote the mental and physical health of our patients in a changing climate. Figure 12.1 depicts the roles of pediatricians in a changing climate as clinician, educator, and advocate.

As clinicians, pediatricians provide care to young people suffering from climate-related health harms. This work extends beyond the office encounter to the implementation of practical, protective policies that protect against these effects. For example, pediatricians can be instrumental

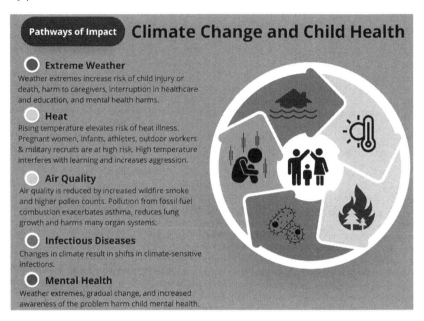

Figure 12.2 Pathways of impact.

in the creation and implementation of heat illness prevention protocols, emergency response systems that include child specific care, and protective strategies against climate sensitive infectious diseases, including vaccination programs.

Pediatricians can serve as educators on the intersections of climate change and health. This work includes working within our institutions to advance a climate and health curriculum for trainees and practicing professionals. Working through our medical societies and within our communities, pediatricians can educate policymakers and the public on climate health risks and protective strategies. These pathways of impact are depicted in Figure 12.2.

Lastly, pediatricians have a unique opportunity to advocate for solutions that reduce further warming. Climate solutions, as advanced by schools, cities, states, and nations, provide a foundation for child physical health. Policies that reduce air pollution and carbon emissions simultaneously help address common child health conditions including asthma, obesity, and hypertension. What is good for the climate is generally good for children. Child health benefits such as active transportation, plant-rich diets, and protection and engagement with natural places, present

> **Textbox 12.1 "Can I take my baby outside?"**
>
> It is July in Texas, and it is very, very hot. Hotter, in fact, than any previous July in the state. Both the nighttime lows and daytime highs have reached record levels, with average temperature 5 °F above average. (NOAA National Centers for Environmental information, 2022) As a pediatrician in an air-conditioned office, you go into an exam room to see four-month-old girl Camille and her mother for a well-baby visit.
>
> As you discuss what to expect in the months ahead, you notice that Camille's mother seems flat. She shares that she is feeling isolated, rarely leaves the house, and sees no one other than her husband in the evening. She asks if it is okay to bring Camille to the park or to indoor events at a local library.
>
> You know that extreme heat is particularly dangerous to infants. You therefore advise that it is not safe to go outside with the baby during the daytime due to the extreme heat. You discuss taking her on walks in the morning and the evening, and bringing her to indoor events during the day, always cooling the car first. You discuss the importance of never leaving Camille unattended in the car.
>
> You review how temperatures are rising due to climate change, so protecting Camille from heat is very important. You share that Texas is leading the nation in wind energy production, generating over one quarter of the nation's wind energy (US Energy Information Administration, 2022), and that clean energy helps protect against warming. You tell her about a group of Texas mothers working for climate change solutions and share their information.

opportunities for pediatricians to promote climate solutions that are also core to our preventative care work with children and families.

The work of pediatricians and their deliberate engagement with young people for climate solutions is vital, not only for protecting children and families, but for promoting hope and resilience. As described by Macy and Johnstone (2022), active hope is a practice whereby a problem is acknowledged, the desired outcome is identified and activities are initiated to help achieve that goal. Working collaboratively towards a shared goal can be mutually beneficial for both young people and pediatricians who may be experiencing climate-related mental health challenges.

In this chapter, I will discuss typical patients (deidentified for confidentiality) that present with climate change-related mental health harms in the pediatric setting. I will discuss the pediatrician's role as clinician, educator, and advocate as we work to address these concerns. In each instance, I will tell the stories of pediatricians who are enacting these solutions across the United States (Textbox 12.1).

A Pediatrician's Approach to Climate Change and Mental Health

Rising Heat in the Pediatrician's Office

Rising heat presents one of the most direct health threats of climate change to child health. The human body is able to cope with temperature within a certain range through thermoregulation, a process that includes behavioral and physiologic responses. This range varies with location, with people in hotter climates generally adapted to cope with higher temperatures (Guo et al., 2014). Heat above this temperature range, however, can lead to heat-related illness (HRI). HRI includes a continuum of illness ranging from mild to potentially fatal heat stroke.

Children compose almost half of those affected by HRI (Mangus & Canares, 2019). Infants are at higher risk to extreme heat due to their higher metabolic rate, smaller blood volume, immature thermoregulation and inability to self-care in response to heat stress (Son et al., 2017; Xu et al., 2012). Adolescents who exercise outdoors in the summer months are also at increased risk, particularly football players (Kerr et al., 2020), young military recruits (Armed Forces Health Surveillance Branch, 2019) and child agricultural workers (Arcury et al., 2019).

Heat poses risks to children outside of HRI beginning in the prenatal period. Numerous studies have found increased adverse birth outcomes including preterm birth and low birth weight as a result of maternal exposure to high temperature (Bekkar et al., 2020). In older children, exposure to higher temperature poses indirect risks including reduced cognitive function (Cedeño Laurent et al., 2018; Wetsel, 2011) and educational achievement (Park et al., 2021). High ambient temperatures have been associated with increased use of emergency mental health services, suicide (Thompson et al., 2018) and aggression (Clayton et al., 2021).

Temperatures are generally higher in urban compared to rural regions. This is attributed to the replacement of vegetation with impervious surfaces and is referred to as the "urban heat island effect" (Ziter et al., 2019). Even within a single urban region, however, variations in the amount of artificial versus natural surfaces can cause temperatures to vary by as much as 10 °C (Shandas et al., 2019). The hottest urban areas are often those inhabited by residents with limited resources and those affected by the historically racist housing policy of redlining (Hoffman et al., 2020).

In response to the rising risk of heat to child health and well-being, pediatricians can play numerous roles. As clinicians, we can include heat awareness and protection strategies in our anticipatory guidance. We protect

> **Textbox 12.2 Pediatricians help pass young athlete heat protection legislation in Virginia**
>
> In Virginia, pediatricians learned that sports safety policy in their state, including prevention of exertional heat stroke, lagged behind other states (Adams et al., 2017). The Virginia Chapter of the American Academy of Pediatrics worked with state legislators to develop a policy to correct this deficiency and provide stronger protection for young athletes. The resulting bill directed the Department of Education to develop guidelines on policies to inform and educate coaches, athletes, parents, and guardians on the nature and risk of heat-related illness. Pediatricians supported this bill which passed during Virginia's 2022 General Assembly.

the most vulnerable children when we review heat protection with new or expecting parents and active young people during the summer months.

As educators, pediatricians can work within our institutions to ensure that heat illness is included in medical education, including information about vulnerable groups and inequitable exposures. Pediatricians can collaborate with community partners to implement heat education and prevention programs. For example, pediatricians can support local groups that provide energy efficiency upgrades for low-income families, or support organizations that plant trees in areas affected by decades of underinvestment.

Pediatricians have an important role to play as advocates for child heat illness prevention policies. Such policies have proven highly effective at reducing heat illness in young athletes (Kerr et al., 2019). Working with school districts, athletic associations and state medical societies, pediatricians can help advance programs that incorporate best practices. The work of pediatricians in Virginia, as described in Textbox 12.2, provides an example of successful advocacy for protection of young athletes from heat (Textbox 12.3).

Climate Disasters in the Pediatrician's Office

Climate-related disasters are life-altering events for children that exact incalculable physical and mental health harms (Orengo-Aguayo et al., 2019). Physical health harms can be immediate, including injuries, drownings, and poisoning. These risks are higher in low-resource communities and nations (Uddin et al., 2021).

Delayed harms include mold exposure and outbreaks of waterborne diseases in the weeks and months after flooding events (Erickson et al., 2019; Flores et al., 2020; Olds et al., 2018). Infectious disease outbreaks may

> **Textbox 12.3 "Can you help my son's nightmares?"**
>
> It is January 2019, and on the daily schedule for your pediatric office in North Carolina is a new patient, Robert, a 10-year-old boy with chief complaint of "nightmares" and no other medical records.
>
> In the room you see Robert in a chair next to his father, who is in a wheelchair. You learn that Robert, his 5-year-old sister, and their father moved to North Carolina about 2 months ago after their home and community in Florida were destroyed by Hurricane Michael.
>
> The family had hoped to ride out the storm in their home, but called for help when they heard on the radio that it would reach Category Five. They were evacuated to a local shelter amidst howling winds and torrential rain. After staying there for days, they returned to the site of their home to find it had become a pile of rubble. Their doctor's office was likewise destroyed.
>
> Robert has been waking up in the night with nightmares about the evacuation. He panics whenever he hears thunder, so he wears headphones when it rains. He is having trouble paying attention during classes in his new school and is often anxious and irritable.
>
> You suspect that Robert has posttraumatic stress disorder (PTSD). You learn that his family is working with a social worker. You contact her and learn that her organization has counselors trained in PTSD. They arrange for an evaluation of Robert.
>
> A few months later you see Robert. He is receiving therapy, is having fewer nightmares and is adjusting to his new school. You share with him that many children had trouble after the storm, and that Florida set up a special program to help kids with psychological problems resulting from Hurricane Michael (Abbott, 2019). You let them know that extreme storms are an increasing concern with climate change, but that North Carolina's Governor is working hard to address the problem (Cooper, 2018).

affect children displaced to crowded shelters (Liu et al., 2019). Violence also presents a risk to displaced children, particularly in families struggling to provide basic necessities (Seddighi et al., 2021). Access to healthcare services, including vaccinations, can be disrupted (Boyd et al., 2017).

Exposure to climate disasters can cause significant mental health harms. Loss of treasured homes, objects, pets, and even family members as well as community devastation can result in psychological trauma in affected children (Clayton et al., 2021; Laor & Wolmer, 2018). Children may suffer from posttraumatic stress disorder (Brown et al., 2019), internalizing (e.g., anxiety, depression) and externalizing (e.g., aggression) mental health disorders (Rubens et al., 2018), and decreased academic performance (Gibbs et al., 2019). Children's post-disaster functioning

> **Textbox 12.4 Psychological first aid: Core actions**
>
> 1. Contact and Engagement – establish a human connection in a non-intrusive, compassionate manner.
> 2. Safety and Comfort – enhance immediate and ongoing safety, provide physical and emotional comfort.
> 3. Stabilization (if needed) – calm and orient overwhelmed or distraught survivors.
> 4. Gather Information on Immediate Needs and Concerns – tailor interventions to identified needs.
> 5. Practical Assistance – offer practical help in addressing needs and concerns.
> 6. Connection with Social Supports – help establish contact with networks including family, friends and community resources.
> 7. Information on Coping – provide information on stress reactions and effective coping.
> 8. Linkage with Collaborative Services – link survivors to available services needed immediately or in the future. (Brymer et al., 2006)

is also affected indirectly by the mental health impacts on caregivers (Pfefferbaum et al., 2016). These events represent significant trauma that, in the absence of supportive caregivers, can contribute to toxic stress. This may lead to a range of negative psychosocial and physical health effects that can extend into adulthood (Ataullahjan et al., 2020; Shonkoff & Garner, 2012).

Given the rise in climate-related disasters (Centre for Research on the Epidemiology of Disasters & UN Office for Disaster Risk Reduction, 2020), pediatricians will increasingly care for affected children. Providing optimal care to these children includes implementing our roles as clinicians, educators, and advocates.

As clinicians, pediatricians must recognize the unique physical and mental health risks children face following disasters. We must be familiar with our community networks and where families can access resources specific to their challenges. To protect children from future disasters, pediatricians can keep immunizations up to date and maintain accessible electronic medical records. We can engage in community disaster planning to ensure that the specific needs of children, including Psychological First Aid immediately following disasters, are addressed. Pediatric offices themselves need disaster management plans, including strategies to protect vaccines in the case of power outages (Textbox 12.4).

> **Textbox 12.5 American Academy of Pediatrics (AAP) Council on Children and Disasters**
>
> In 2019, the AAP launched this new Council and appointed its Executive Committee. The Council on Children and Disasters is dedicated to ensuring that the specific needs of children are considered and addressed in all aspects of disaster planning. One of their activities is the creation of brief videos for pediatric health providers, including videos on preparation for wildfires, hurricanes, and the role of climate change. At the AAP annual meeting in 2021, the Council held programming on protecting the medical home in disasters. The emerging focus on disasters within the AAP is vital to preparing pediatricians to meet the needs of children and serve as child advocates for local, state, and national disaster planning.

As educators, pediatricians can increase medical educational opportunities on climate disasters to ensure practicing and training physicians are prepared. Pediatric offices are also an excellent place for provision of education to families regarding child specific emergency planning information. This is of particular importance for families in underresourced communities with limited access to resources for preparation and response. In Miami Dade County, for example, a Disaster Relief Team was created by medical students to provide medical disaster relief to those most affected by poverty and oppression (Dade County Street Response Disaster Relief Team, 2018).

Pediatricians also must make the connection between individual extreme events and the broader climate-change problem. We can then serve as advocates for our patients by supporting local, state, and national climate solution policies that protect against further harm. In addition, through support of youth climate advocacy initiatives, we can promote active hope in ourselves and our patients (Textboxes 12.5 and 12.6).

Climate-Change Awareness in the Pediatrician's Office

Young people are increasingly exposed to information about climate change. Broadcast television coverage of climate change tripled from 2020 to 2021 (Macdonald, 2022). Adolescents report reliance on social media and television as primary news sources, and large numbers follow topics where are they are likely to hear about climate change. Nearly 80 percent of American adolescents hear their science teachers talk about climate change, at least sometimes (Roser-Renouf et al. 2020).

For children, rising awareness of climate change, independent of experience of personal harm or trauma, can manifest in varied adverse psychological

> **Textbox 12.6 "They were cooked open on the sand"**
>
> In the midst of a busy August day at your Virginia pediatric clinic you see a new 15-year-old patient, Cassie, who recently moved from Washington State. On review of her record, you see she has a history of asthma for which she takes several medications. You prepare to speak to her about an asthma action plan for her new school.
>
> Cassie is cheerful and upbeat, with pink hair and sparkly clothing, and her mother is engaging and supportive. You discuss her asthma and the forms she will need for school. As you prepare to start your exam, you casually ask Cassie how she likes Virginia, noting that it is hotter than Washington.
>
> Cassie's demeanor changes, becoming solemn. She tells you that it wasn't cool in Washington, it was terribly hot. Washington had an unprecedented heat wave, with temperatures above 100 degrees. Her family went to their favorite beach and while walking they saw shellfish cooked open on the sand. This made her very sad.
>
> Seeing Cassie's expression, you acknowledge and validate her feelings. You recognize how deeply connected she must feel to that beach and its animals, and the sadness she must have felt at seeing them suffer. You acknowledge that extreme heat is getter worse due to climate change and that this is making some adolescents anxious, sad, and even angry. You tell her how Virginia recently passed laws that are accelerating our transition to clean energy that protects the climate and wildlife. You tell her that Virginia pediatricians supported these bills in order to protect kids. Lastly, you share information about a youth climate group in Virginia that she could join.

effects. In a large, international survey of young people, a large proportion reported emotional distress regarding climate change. More than three in four surveyed American children expressed that people have failed to care for the planet, and one third expressed that the government is failing young people and they are frightened of the future (Hickman et al., 2021).

Many children feel strong connections to natural landscapes and wildlife. Harm to treasured places and animals can bring feelings of loss and grief, a distress that has been described as "solastalgia" (Albrecht et al., 2007). Absent significant emissions reductions, environmental changes associated with warming will continue to mount, resulting in greater senses of loss. Children among Native American groups whose cultural and spiritual heritage is closely connected to the natural world may suffer particular distress due to climate-change associated ecosystem change and loss (Coffey et al., 2021). This risk is heightened by the targeting of Native American lands for weapons-testing facilities, dump sites, and resource extraction (Vickery & Hunter, 2016).

Pediatricians have been caring for children in an ongoing mental health crisis that was significantly worsened by the COVID-19 pandemic (Leeb et al., 2020). In the midst of competing challenges, pediatricians must recognize climate-change awareness as contributing to mental health suffering in children. Pediatricians need strategies to best support our young patients in the face of this rising threat to their mental health.

The role of the pediatrician begins in the examination room. Pediatricians need to differentiate between appropriate responses and more persistent, pathologic responses as reviewed elsewhere in this volume. Distress about climate change is a normal response to a real problem but can lead to debilitating anxiety/depression, and other mental health concerns in some people (Léger-Goodes et al., 2022). Additionally, preexisting mental health conditions may also be triggered or exacerbated by climate change (Hayes et al., 2018). Pediatricians should be aware of these varied responses and become familiar with climate-aware mental health providers in their region who can help children with significant suffering.

As educators, pediatricians can provide simple, evidence-based climate information in the context of the patient encounter. We can place posters and brochures in our offices regarding local climate and health risks and protection strategies. Pediatricians can also use preventative care guidance as a framework for discussing climate change solutions, a strategy that has been shown to be well received by patients (Lewandowski et al., 2021).

As community leaders and role models, pediatricians can promote opportunities for youth climate education within our own networks, such as through fellowship opportunities, participation in research projects or collaboration on advocacy projects. Pediatricians can collaborate with health trainees as power agents for inclusion of climate change in medical education (Gutschow et al., 2021; Philipsborn et al., 2021; Rabin et al., 2020) (Textbox 12.7).

As we recognize psychological impacts of climate change in our patients, paediatricians can serve as models for hopeful action by working as advocates for climate within our offices and hospitals as well as at the state, national, and international level. Pediatricians across the United States are already serving as climate advocates within their state AAP chapters or as leaders of state clinician climate advocate groups.

Proactive engagement of young people in this work can promote faith in the promise of solutions. Perceived self-efficacy has been shown to be a key determinant of engagement and behavior change in young people with regard to environmental problems (Corner et al., 2015). A focus on hopeful solutions and social engagement has been shown to both bring solace as well as motivate environmental action in young people (Ojala, 2012) (Textbox 12.8).

Textbox 12.7 New York State Children's Environmental Health Centers (NYSCHECK)

The NYSCHECK Summer Student Academy is a practical and foundational program in children's environmental health and public health. It is designed for students from a diverse range of educational backgrounds spanning from high school to medical school. Initially piloted in 2021, the Summer Academy is an opportunity to dovetail into existing summer programs within the NYSCHECK network. During an immersive eight weeks, students of all levels are introduced to the activities of collaborating centers and participate in a course grounded in the principles of environmental health communications. Students explore:

- Foundational principles of public health and children's environmental health
- Leadership in an advocacy project to develop effective and efficient modes of communication in environmental health
- The importance of interprofessional teamwork and academic community partnership collaborations.

The 2022 program included thirty-six students across New York State who engaged in scholarly advocacy projects focused on the health impacts of climate change. Working in small groups, students addressed the ways in which climate change impacts health through the three main routes of environmental exposures: ingestion/dietary exposures, inhalation/respiratory exposures, and contact/dermal (skin) exposures. Equipped with critical thinking and creativity, students in all three subgroups developed unique and novel advocacy projects designed to link the health effects at the individual level to the larger picture of climate change.

Textbox 12.8 Pediatrician chapter climate advocate program

State chapters of the AAP have recognized that climate change is a growing concern among their members and patients. Across the country, pediatricians are elevating their climate-related advocacy in response.

In 2020, the AAP Council on Environmental Health and Climate Change, working with pediatricians concerned about climate change across the country, launched a Chapter Climate Advocates program. By 2022, every chapter in the country had at least one advocate participating in the program. Twenty-six AAP chapters have developed climate change committees, and twenty-one have adopted a policy statement or resolution that addresses how climate change impacts child and family health. Nineteen have added climate change to their websites or their legislative priorities.

The chapter climate advocates meet every month virtually to discuss efforts to advance climate action. Many advocates are working to bring climate curricula to medical school and residency training as well as continuing education for practicing pediatricians. For example, advocates created a Maintenance of Certification module for the American Board of Pediatrics titled "Impact of Climate Change on Pediatric Health Care."

Climate advocates have collaborated with diverse student and community groups including Girl Scouts, art and science museums, municipalities, and universities in order to advance climate action. In addition to their work with the AAP, several advocates have formed Clinicians for Climate Action groups in their states in order to collaborate with clinicians and trainees from other specialties (Byron, 2022).

Conclusion

Pediatricians are at the forefront of the youth mental health crisis. As we care for our young patients, it is vital that we incorporate an understanding of climate change into our practice. This includes a recognition of the pathways through which climate change contributes to child physical and mental health harms. Additionally, pediatric medicine in our changing climate requires unique approaches that go beyond traditional counseling and medical therapy. Pediatricians can promote the mental health of children through our active participation in the societal transition to systems that promote health and preserve a prosperous world. As clinicians, educators, and advocates, pediatricians are uniquely positioned to generate trust, positive engagement, and hope amongst our patients and ourselves.

References

Abbott, D. (2019). First Lady Casey DeSantis announces Florida's first disaster recovery mental health coordinator has been hired and will be deployed to Northwest Florida. *States News Service*, October 16. www.flgov.com/2019/10/16/first-lady-casey-desantis-announces-floridas-first-disaster-recovery-mental-health-coordinator-has-been-hired-and-will-be-deployed-to-northwest-florida/

Adams, W. M., Scarneo, S. E., & Casa, D. J. (2017). State-level implementation of health and safety policies to prevent sudden death and catastrophic injuries within secondary school athletics. *Orthopaedic Journal of Sports Medicine*, 5(9), 2325967117727262. https://doi.org/10.1177/2325967117727262

Ahdoot, S., Pacheco, S. E., & Council on Environmental Health (2015). Global climate change and children's health. *Pediatrics*, 136(5), 1468.

Albrecht, G., Sartore, G., Connor, L., Higginbotham, N., Freeman, S., Kelly, B., ... Pollard, G. (2007). Solastalgia: The distress caused by environmental change. *Australasian Psychiatry*, 15(1_suppl), S95–S98. https://doi.org/10.1080/10398560701701288

Arcury, T. A., Arnold, T. J., Quandt, S. A., Chen, H., Kearney, G. D., Sandberg, J. C., … Daniel, S. S. (2019). Health and occupational injury experienced by Latinx child farmworkers in North Carolina, USA. *International Journal of Environmental Research and Public Health*, 17(1), 248. https://doi.org/10.3390/ijerph17010248

Armed Forces Health Surveillance Branch (2019). Update: Heat illness, active component, U.S. Armed Forces, 2018. *Medical Surveillance Monthly Report*, 26(4), 15–20. www.health.mil/News/Articles/2019/04/01/Update-Heat-Illness

Ataullahjan, A., Samara, M., Betancourt, T. S., & Bhutta, Z. A. (2020). *Mitigating toxic stress in children affected by conflict and displacement*. BMJ, 371, m2876. https://doi.org/10.1136/bmj.m2876

Becker, A. E., & Kleinman, A. (2013). Mental health and the global agenda. *New England Journal of Medicine*, 369(1), 66–73. https://doi.org/10.1056/NEJMra1110827

Bekkar, B., Pacheco, S., Basu, R., & DeNicola, N. (2020). Association of air pollution and heat exposure with preterm birth, low birth weight, and stillbirth in the US: A systematic review. *JAMA Network Open*, 3(6), e208243. https://doi.org/10.1001/jamanetworkopen.2020.8243

Boyd, A. T., Cookson, S. T., Anderson, M., Bilukha, O. O., Brennan, M., Handzel, T., … Gerber, M. (2017). Centers for Disease Control and Prevention public health response to humanitarian emergencies, 2007–2016. *Emerging Infectious Diseases*, 23(13), S196–S202. https://doi.org/10.3201/eid2313.170473

Brown, M. R. G., Agyapong, V., Greenshaw, A. J., Cribben, I., Brett-MacLean, P., Drolet, J., … Silverstone, P. H. (2019). Significant PTSD and other mental health effects present 18 months after the Fort McMurray wildfire: Findings from 3,070 grades 7–12 students. *Frontiers in Psychiatry*, 10, 623. https://doi.org/10.3389/fpsyt.2019.00623

Brymer, M., Jacobs, A., Layne, C., Pynoos, R., Ruzek, J., Steinberg, A., … Watson P. (2006). *Psychological first aid: Field operations guide* (2nd ed.). www.nctsn.org/treatments-and-practices/psychological-first-aid-and-skills-for-psychological-recovery/about-pfa

Burke, S., Sanson, A., & Van Hoorn, J. (2018). The psychological effects of climate change on children. *Current Psychiatry Reports*, 20(5), 1–8. https://doi.org/10.1007/s11920-018-0896-9

Byron, L. G. (2022). Concern for climate drives advocates' activities. *AAP News*, February 1. https://publications.aap.org/aapnews/news/19412/Concern-for-climate-drives-advocates-activities?searchresult=1

Cedeño Laurent, J. G., Williams, A., Oulhote, Y., Zanobetti, A., Allen, J. G., & Spengler, J. D. (2018). Reduced cognitive function during a heat wave among residents of non-air-conditioned buildings: An observational study of young adults in the summer of 2016. *PLoS Medicine*, 15(7), e1002605. https://doi.org/10.1371/journal.pmed.1002605

Centers for Disease Control and Prevention (2022). Youth risk behavior survey data summary and trends report: 2011–2021. www.cdc.gov/yrbs

Centre for Research on the Epidemiology of Disasters, & UN Office for Disaster Risk Reduction (2020). *Human cost of disasters: An overview of the last 20 years (2000–2019)*. CRED, UNDRR. http://hdl.handle.net/2078.1/236410

Clayton, S., Manning, C. M., Speiser, M., & Hill, A. N. (2021). *Mental health and our changing climate: Impacts, inequities, responses.* American Psychological Association and ecoAmerica. https://ecoamerica.org/wp-content/uploads/2021/11/mental-health-climate-change-2021-ea-apa.pdf

Coffey, Y., Bhullar, N., Durkin, J., Islam, M. S., & Usher, K. (2021). Understanding eco-anxiety: A systematic scoping review of current literature and identified knowledge gaps. *Journal of Climate Change and Health*, 3, 100047. https://doi.org/10.1016/j.joclim.2021.100047

Committee on Environmental Health (2007). Global climate change and children's health. *Pediatrics*, 120(5), 1149–1152. https://doi.org/10.1542/peds.2007-2645

Committee on Psychosocial Aspects of Child and Family Health and Task Force on Mental Health (2009). The future of pediatrics: Mental health competencies for pediatric primary care. *Pediatrics (Evanston)*, 124(1), 410–421. https://doi.org/10.1542/peds.2009-1061

Cooper, R. (2018). Executive Order No. 80. North Carolina's Commitment to Address Climate Change and Transition to a Clean Energy Economy.

Corner, A., Roberts, O., Chiari, S., Völler, S., Mayrhuber, E. S., Mandl, S., & Monson, K. (2015). How do young people engage with climate change? The role of knowledge, values, message framing, and trusted communicators. *Wiley Interdisciplinary Reviews. Climate Change*, 6(5), 523–534. https://doi.org/10.1002/wcc.353

Dade County Street Response Disaster Relief Team (2018). www.southfldisasterrelief.org/home, accessed November 14, 2022.

Erickson, T. B., Brooks, J., Nilles, E. J., Pham, P. N., & Vinck, P. (2019). Environmental health effects attributed to toxic and infectious agents following hurricanes, cyclones, flash floods and major hydrometeorological events. *Journal of Toxicology and Environmental Health*. Part B, *Critical Reviews*, 22(5–6), 157–171. https://doi.org/10.1080/10937404.2019.1654422

Flores, A. B., Collins, T. W., Grineski, S. E., & Chakraborty, J. (2020). Disparities in health effects and access to health care among Houston area residents after Hurricane Harvey. *Public Health Reports*, 135(4), 511–523. https://doi.org/10.1177/0033354920930133

Foy, J. M., & Perrin, J. (2010). Enhancing pediatric mental health care: Strategies for preparing a community. *Pediatrics (Evanston)*, 125(Suppl. 3), S75–S86. https://doi.org/10.1542/peds.2010-0788D

GBD 2019 Diseases and Injuries Collaborators (2020). Global burden of 369 diseases and injuries in 204 countries and territories, 1990–2019: A systematic analysis for the Global Burden of Disease Study 2019. *Lancet*, 396, 1204–1222. https://doi.org/10.1016/S0140-6736(20)30925-9

Gibbs, L., Nursey, J., Cook, J., Ireton, G., Alkemade, N., Roberts, M., ... Forbes, D. (2019). Delayed disaster impacts on academic performance of primary school children. *Child Development*, 90(4), 1402–1412. https://doi.org/10.1111/cdev.13200

Guo, Y., Gasparrini, A., Armstrong, B., Li, S., Tawatsupa, B., Tobias, A., … Williams, G. (2014). Global variation in the effects of ambient temperature on mortality: A systematic evaluation. *Epidemiology*, 25(6), 781–789. https://doi.org/10.1097/EDE.0000000000000165

Gutschow, B., Gray, B., Ragavan, M. I., Sheffield, P. E., Philipsborn, R. P., & Jee, S. H. (2021). The intersection of pediatrics, climate change, and structural racism: Ensuring health equity through climate justice. *Current Problems in Pediatric and Adolescent Health Care*, 51(6), 101028. https://doi.org/10.1016/j.cppeds.2021.101028

Hagan, J. F., Shaw, J. S., & Duncan, P. M. (2017). *Bright futures: Guidelines for health supervision of infants, children, and adolescents* (4th ed.). American Academy of Pediatrics.

Hayes, K., Blashki, G., Wiseman, J., Burke, S., & Reifels, L. (2018). Climate change and mental health: Risks, impacts and priority actions. *International Journal of Mental Health Systems*, 12(1), 28. https://doi.org/10.1186/s13033-018-0210-6

Hickman, C., Marks, E., Pihkala, P., Clayton, S., Lewandowski, R. E., Mayall, E. E., … van Susteren, L. (2021). Climate anxiety in children and young people and their beliefs about government responses to climate change: A global survey. *The Lancet Planetary Health*, 5(12), e863–e873. https://doi.org/10.1016/S2542-5196(21)00278-3

Hoffman, J. S., Shandas, V., & Pendleton, N. (2020). The effects of historical housing policies on resident exposure to intra-urban heat: A study of 108 US urban areas. *Climate*, 8(1), 12. https://doi.org/10.3390/cli8010012

Kerr, Z. Y., Register-Mihalik, J. K., Pryor, R. R., Pierpoint, L. A., Scarneo, S. E., Adams, W. M., … Marshall, S. W. (2019). The association between mandated preseason heat acclimatization guidelines and exertional heat illness during preseason high school American football practices. *Environmental Health Perspectives*, 127(4), 47003. https://doi.org/10.1289/EHP4163

Kerr, Z. Y., Yeargin, S. W., Hosokawa, Y., Hirschhorn, R. M., Pierpoint, L. A., & Casa, D. J. (2020). The epidemiology and management of exertional heat illnesses in high school sports during the 2012/2013–2016/2017 academic years. *Journal of Sport Rehabilitation*, 29(3), 332–338. https://doi.org/10.1123/jsr.2018-0364

Laor, N., & Wolmer, L. (2018). Children exposed to mass emergency and disaster: The role of the mental health professionals. In A. Martin, M. Bloch & F. Volkmar (Eds.), *Lewis's child and adolescent psychiatry: A comprehensive textbook*. Lippincott Williams and Wilkins.

Leeb, R. T., Bitsko, R. H., Radhakrishnan, L., Martinez, P., Njai, R., & Holland, K. M. (2020). Mental health-related emergency department visits among children aged <18 years during the COVID-19 pandemic – United States, January 1–October 17, 2020. *Morbidity and Mortality Weekly Report*, 69(45), 1675–1680. http://dx.doi.org/10.15585/mmwr.mm6945a3

Léger-Goodes, T., Malboeuf-Hurtubise, C., Mastine, T., Généreux, M., Paradis, P. O., & Camden, C. (2022). Eco-anxiety in children: A scoping review of the mental health impacts of the awareness of climate change. *Frontiers in Psychology*, 13, 872544. https://doi.org/10.3389/fpsyg.2022.872544

Lewandowski, A. A., Sheffield, P. E., Ahdoot, S., & Maibach, E. W. (2021). Patients value climate change counseling provided by their pediatrician: The experience in one Wisconsin pediatric clinic. *Journal of Climate Change and Health*, 4, 100053. https://doi.org/10.1016/j.joclim.2021.100053

Liu, L., Haynie, A., Jin, S., Zangeneh, A., Bakota, E., Hornstein, B. D., … Shah, U. A. (2019). Influenza A (H3) outbreak at a Hurricane Harvey megashelter in Harris County, Texas: Successes and challenges in disease identification and control measure implementation. *Disaster Medicine and Public Health Preparedness*, 13(1), 97–101. https://doi.org/10.1017/dmp.2018.159

Macdonald, T. (2022). *How broadcast TV networks covered climate change in 2021.* www.mediamatters.org/broadcast-networks/how-broadcast-tv-networks-covered-climate-change-2021, accessed July 11, 2022.

Macy, J., & Johnstone, C. (2022). *Active hope: How to face the mess we're in with unexpected resilience & creative power* (2nd ed.). New World Library.

Mangus, C. W., & Canares, T. L. (2019). Heat-related illness in children in an era of extreme temperatures. *Pediatrics in Review*, 40(3), 97–107. https://doi.org/10.1542/pir.2017-0322

Martini, R., Hilt, R., Marx, L., Chenven, M., Naylor, M., Sarvet, B., & Ptakowski, K. K. (2012). *Best principles for integration of child psychiatry into the pediatric health home.* www.aacap.org/App_Themes/AACAP/docs/clinical_practice_center/systems_of_care/best_principles_for_integration_of_child_psychiatry_into_the_pediatric_health_home_2012.pdf

NOAA National Centers for Environmental information (2022). *Climate at a glance: Statewide mapping, average temperature.* www.ncdc.noaa.gov/cag/, accessed August 29, 2022.

O'Brien, D., Harvey, K., Howse, J., Reardon, T., & Creswell, C. (2016). Barriers to managing child and adolescent mental health problems: A systematic review of primary care practitioners' perceptions. *British Journal of General Practice*, 66(651), e693–e707. https://doi.org/10.3399/bjgp16X687061

Ojala, M. (2012). How do children cope with global climate change? Coping strategies, engagement, and well-being. *Journal of Environmental Psychology*, 32(3), 225–233. https://doi.org/10.1016/j.jenvp.2012.02.004

Olds, H. T., Corsi, S. R., Dila, D. K., Halmo, K. M., Bootsma, M. J., & McLellan, S. L. (2018). High levels of sewage contamination released from urban areas after storm events: A quantitative survey with sewage specific bacterial indicators. *PLoS Medicine*, 15(7), e1002614. https://doi.org/10.1371/journal.pmed.1002614

Orengo-Aguayo, R., Stewart, R. W., de Arellano, M. A., Suárez-Kindy, J. L., & Young, J. (2019). Disaster exposure and mental health among Puerto Rican youths after Hurricane Maria. *JAMA Network Open*, 2(4), e192619. https://doi.org/10.1001/jamanetworkopen.2019.2619

Park, R. J., Behrer, A. P., & Goodman, J. (2021). Learning is inhibited by heat exposure, both internationally and within the United States. *Nature Human Behaviour*, 5(1), 19–27. https://doi.org/10.1038/s41562-020-00959-9

Pfefferbaum, B., Jacobs, A. K., Van Horn, R. L., & Houston, J. B. (2016). Effects of displacement in children exposed to disasters. *Current Psychiatry Reports*, 18(8), 71. https://doi.org/10.1007/s11920-016-0714-1

Philipsborn, R. P., Cowenhoven, J., Bole, A., Balk, S. J., & Bernstein, A. (2021). A pediatrician's guide to climate change-informed primary care. *Current Problems in Pediatric and Adolescent Health Care*, 51(6), 101027. https://doi.org/10.1016/j.cppeds.2021.101027

Rabin, B. M., Laney, E. B., & Philipsborn, R. P. (2020). The unique role of medical students in catalyzing climate change education. *Journal of Medical Education and Curricular Development*, 7, 1–7. https://journals.sagepub.com/doi/10.1177/2382120520957653

Romba, C., & Ballard, R. (2020). Models of mental health consultation and collaboration in primary care pediatrics. *Pediatric Annals*, 49(10), e416–e420. https://doi.org/10.3928/19382359-20200920-01

Roser-Renouf, C., Maibach, E., & Myers, T. (2020). *American adolescents' knowledge, attitudes and sources of information on climate change*. George Mason University. doi:10.13021/z9by-xp87. www.climatechangecommunication.org/all/nasa_teens2020_1/

Rubens, S. L., Felix, E. D., & Hambrick, E. P. (2018). A meta-analysis of the impact of natural disasters on internalizing and externalizing problems in youth. *Journal of Traumatic Stress*, 31(3), 332–341. https://doi.org/10.1002/jts.22292

Seddighi, H., Salmani, I., Javadi, M. H., & Seddighi, S. (2021). Child abuse in natural disasters and conflicts: A systematic review. *Trauma, Violence & Abuse*, 22(1), 176–185. https://doi.org/10.1177/1524838019835973

Shandas, V., Voelkel, J., Williams, J., & Hoffman, J. (2019). Integrating satellite and ground measurements for predicting locations of extreme urban heat. *Climate*, 7(1), 5. https://doi.org/10.3390/cli7010005

Shea, K. M. (2007). Global climate change and children's health. *Pediatrics*, 120(5), e1359–e1367. https://doi.org/10.1542/peds.2007-2646

Shonkoff, J. P., & Garner, A. S. (2012). The lifelong effects of early childhood adversity and toxic stress. *Pediatrics*, 129(1), e232–e246. https://doi.org/10.1542/peds.2011-2663

Shulman, S. T. (2004). The history of pediatric infectious diseases. *Pediatric Research*, 55(1), 163–176. https://doi.org/10.1203/01.PDR.0000101756.93542.09

Son, J., Lee, J., & Bell, M. L. (2017). Is ambient temperature associated with risk of infant mortality? A multi-city study in Korea. *Environmental Research*, 158, 748–752. https://doi.org/10.1016/j.envres.2017.07.034

Thompson, R., Hornigold, R., Page, L., & Waite, T. (2018). Associations between high ambient temperatures and heat waves with mental health outcomes: A systematic review. *Public Health*, 161, 171–191. https://doi.org/10.1016/j.puhe.2018.06.008

Uddin, R., Philipsborn, R., Smith, D., Mutic, A., & Thompson, L. M. (2021). A global child health perspective on climate change, migration and human rights.

Current Problems in Pediatric and Adolescent Health Care, 51(6), 101029. https://doi.org/10.1016/j.cppeds.2021.101029

US Energy Information Administration. (2022). *Texas State energy profile*. www.eia.gov/state/print.php?sid=TX, accessed August 29, 2022

Vickery, J., & Hunter, L. M. (2016). Native Americans: Where in environmental justice research? *Society & Natural Resources*, 29(1), 36–52. https://doi.org/10.1080/08941920.2015.1045644

Walter, H. J., Vernacchio, L., Correa, E. T., Bromberg, J., Goodman, E., Barton, J., … Focht, G. (2021). *Five-phase replication of behavioral health integration in pediatric primary care*. American Academy of Pediatrics (AAP). https://doi.org/10.1542/peds.2020-001073

Wetsel, W. C. (2011). Hyperthermic effects on behavior. *International Journal of Hyperthermia*, 27(4), 353–373. https://doi.org/10.3109/02656736.2010.550905

Xu, Z., Etzel, R. A., Su, H., Huang, C., Guo, Y., & Tong, S. (2012). Impact of ambient temperature on children's health: A systematic review. *Environmental Research*, 117, 120–131. https://doi.org/10.1016/j.envres.2012.07.002

Ziter, C. D., Pedersen, E. J., Kucharik, C. J., & Turner, M. G. (2019). Scale-dependent interactions between tree canopy cover and impervious surfaces reduce daytime urban heat during summer. *Proceedings of the National Academy of Sciences – PNAS*, 116(15), 7575–7580. https://doi.org/10.1073/pnas.1817561116

CHAPTER 13

A Legal Perspective on Judicial Remedies to Respond to Young People's Climate Distress

Andrea Rodgers and Kelsey Dunn

> It is critical that information about the climate crisis' impact on youth comes from us. Too often, I've witnessed adults speculating at how we may feel, and forming conclusions for us, without ever thinking to simply ask us themselves ... Our grief is legitimate, and hearing excuses can lead to more feelings of guilt and disillusionment.
>
> Lauren Wright, youth plaintiff in *La Rose* v. *Her Majesty the Queen*
> (Wright & Rodgers, 2022, pp. 82–83)

From catastrophic flooding to deadly heatwaves, raging wildfires, and a resulting mental health crisis, young people are growing up in an unprecedented and daunting world. The last time global atmospheric carbon dioxide levels were where they are today, global mean sea level was up to 60 feet higher and spruce trees grew on the shores of the Arctic Ocean (Dutton et al., 2015; Dowsett et al., 2016). Currently, the United States is emitting carbon into the atmosphere at roughly the same rate (Jurikova et al., 2020; Cui et al., 2021) that resulted in the extinction of 95 percent of marine species at the end of the Permian era 251.9 million years ago (Foster et al., 2018). It did not have to be this way. For decades, governments have overwhelmingly encouraged fossil fuel use; as described by the Ninth Circuit Court of Appeals' majority opinion in the groundbreaking, youth-led climate change case, *Juliana* v. *United States* (2020), "A substantial evidentiary record documents the federal government has long promoted fossil fuel use despite knowing that it can cause catastrophic climate change, and that failure to change existing policy may hasten an environmental apocalypse."

The burdens knowingly being placed on young people by governments, well-documented in the scientific literature, inevitably raise the question of how legal policy should respond to young people's victimization in the context of their climate distress. This chapter explores that question by presenting stories from young people who are seeking to protect themselves by taking their governments to court. They are charging the government with violating their human right to a safe climate and the cascade of associated rights, including the rights to life, liberty, property, personal security, safety, health, privacy, and cultural and family autonomy. Youth-led climate litigation efforts that are using climate science to support claims of human rights violations illustrate that swift access to justice can help protect young people's human rights and well-being.

The Impact of Climate Change on Young People's Mental Health, in Their Own Words

The climate harms to young people's physical and mental well-being manifest in various forms. Often, they arise from direct exposure to climate-related disasters. For instance, Lauren, a young plaintiff in a suit against the federal government of Canada, *La Rose* v. *Her Majesty the Queen*, has Raynaud's Syndrome, which affects her ability to circulate blood and is painfully worsened by extreme temperatures. Because access to nature is important to her mental health, increasingly frequent extreme weather events that prevent her from going outside exacerbate her depression and physical discomfort (Wright & Rodgers, 2022, p. 82).

Raine, another young plaintiff in the same lawsuit, reports how their Lyme disease and asthma become more severe due to the heatwaves and wildfire smoke that have plagued their home province of British Columbia in recent years. In the fall of 2021, a climate change-induced extreme precipitation event flooded Raine's community, inundating neighboring farms and killing thousands of farm animals. The flooding closed the roads to Raine's house, so they were trapped at home, trying to save their neighbor's animals from drowning, and unable to go to work or get food. Raine experiences anxiety and bouts of depression when thinking about how climate change is impacting their life. Raine's anxiety and depressive symptoms have increased in correlation with the increasing severity of climate-related impacts they experience (Statement of Sierra Raine Robinson, 2022).

Many young people are exposed to recurrent climate-related events which can compound feelings of loss and trauma. Reflecting on a severe flood event she experienced in Calgary at age 7, and which recurred several years later, Sadie, a young plaintiff, wrote that she "can see the effects of the climate crisis right in front of" her and that as she becomes more knowledgeable about the role of climate change in her life, she becomes "incredibly scared" (Sadie, personal communication, 2022).

Some young people, like Albert, a *La Rose* plaintiff, feel a sense of stress and powerlessness as they observe particularly vulnerable people undergo climate harms. Albert's distress brings him to routinely question the value of attending school, pursuing a career, owning a home, and having children. Albert comprehends the dire projections that illustrate what will occur if emissions are not reduced consistent with what scientists say is necessary. This understanding contributes to Albert's increasing mental and psychological pain and is part of the reason Albert took his government to court (Statement of Albert Jérôme Lalonde, 2022).

Young people recognize the threat that climate change poses to their lives and attribute the problem's persistence in part to older generations, the fossil fuel industry, and governments (Hickman et al., 2021). A survey of 2,000 young people aged 8–16 showed that 73 percent are worried about the current state of the planet, 19 percent have nightmares about climate change, and 41 percent have no trust that adults will fix the crisis (Atherton, 2020). Another survey of 10,000 young people aged 16–25 from forty-two countries conducted in twenty-six languages confirmed that climate anxiety affects young people's everyday lives, and observed a positive relationship between climate anxiety and young people's perceptions of their government's role in causing the climate catastrophe (Hickman et al., 2021). As the climate crisis intensifies, and governments continue to disregard the science in favor of continued fossil fuel production, young people's mental health injuries inevitably worsen (Oregon Health Authority, 2022). Experts report that these harms are legitimate and should not be pathologized or seen as "wrong," but should be listened to, treated, and seen as justifying a legal remedy (Van Susteren, 2018a).

The Importance of Science in Responding to Young People's Climate Distress and Protecting Their Human Rights

A common plea from young people seeking to protect themselves from climate harms is to ask decision-makers to listen to the science (Milman & Smith, 2019; Statement of Albert Jérôme Lalonde, 2022). Many commonly internationally recognized legal principles support the use of the best available climate science to protect young people's substantive human rights and fundamental freedoms. The duty of care that ensures protection of these substantive rights is considered the "prime responsibility" of government.[1] Further, there are procedural rights recognized in the American Convention on Human Rights, the Universal Declaration of Human Rights, the International Covenant on Civil and Political Rights, and the International Covenant on Economic, Social and Cultural Rights, such as the right to access information, right to know, and right to benefit from scientific progress that are protected under international law and should inform the development and judicial enforceability of climate and energy legal policy (Orellana, 2021). Other human rights principles that are relevant to the protection of young people in the context of climate change, enshrined in some countries' domestic laws, include the duty to do no harm, the principle of intergenerational justice, the right to access justice, the best interests of the child, and the duty to provide fully informed consent (Legal Response Initiative, 2012; Nguyen, 2020; Access to Justice, n.d.; Humanium, n.d.; Office of the United Nations High Commissioner for Human Rights, 2011). Many national constitutions have provisions that explicitly protect the rights of young people, many of which protect the right to education and to be free from harm (Preda, 2015). For example, Article 227 of Brazil's Constitution explicitly recognizes the duty of government to protect young people's rights to life, health, food, education, leisure, culture, dignity, respect, liberty, and freedom from neglect, discrimination, cruelty, and oppression.

It is imperative that courts honor and enforce human rights obligations to promote and protect young people's substantive rights. Fundamentally, granting young people access to courts to present the best available climate science, and using that science to craft appropriate legal remedies, is a commitment to being truthful with young people, and using that truth to inform the greatest protective actions possible. Young people value the truth and when they hear scientists prescribing one thing (e.g., reduce greenhouse gas emissions), and their governments doing something vastly different (e.g., authorizing increased fossil fuel production), the distress and anxiety they feel is justified, appropriate, and deserving of access to courts for a legal remedy.

---

[1] This duty is explicitly outlined in Article 2 of the 1998 United Nations Declaration on the Right and Responsibility of Individuals, Groups and Organs of Society to Promote and Protect Universally Recognized Human Rights and Fundamental Freedoms (Article 2(1): "Each State has a prime responsibility and duty to protect, promote and implement all human rights and fundamental freedoms, inter alia, by adopting such steps as may be necessary to create all conditions necessary in the social, economic, political and other fields, as well as the legal guarantees required to ensure that all persons under its jurisdiction, individually and in association with others, are able to enjoy all those rights and freedoms in practice."; Article 2(2): "Each State shall adopt such legislative, administrative and other steps as may be necessary to ensure that the rights and freedoms referred to in the present Declaration are effectively guaranteed.").

In the United States, climate change skyrocketed as a key campaign issue during the 2020 Democratic presidential primary (Kurtzleben, 2019). Propelled by youth voices on climate change, the large field of Democratic presidential candidates clamored to present strong climate plans (Tamari, 2019). In one notable debate, then-Vice President Joe Biden promised to end new oil and gas leases on federal lands and offshore waters, stating unambiguously that such leases had to end, "period" (Washington Free Beacon, 2020). In 2021, the Biden administration broke that promise by approving more drilling permits than President Trump had in his own first year as president (Center for Biological Diversity, 2022). Similarly, in 2019, the government of Canada declared a national climate emergency the day before Prime Minister Justin Trudeau approved the Trans Mountain pipeline expansion, authorizing the transport of approximately 600,000 barrels of oil per day from Alberta to British Columbia (Mabee, 2019).

Many leaders at every level of the government around the world exhibit this behavior, which can lead to young people's sense of "institutional betrayal" (Smith & Freyd, 2014). When a disaster happens, people, including young people, search for the cause (Van Susteren, 2018a, p. 15). Institutional betrayal is implicated both when a trusted institution creates the harm and when it fails to take protective action; it is "uniquely harmful because it involves a betrayal of trust in a relationship in which the individual depends on the institution" (Van Susteren, 2018a, p. 16). Human-created crises, known as "technological disasters," may be more harmful to mental health than "natural disasters," even when they create comparable magnitudes of harm, because they represent something that was done by one group of humans to others (Van Susteren, 2018a, p. 16).

Dr. Lise Van Susteren, a forensic psychiatrist and expert on the physical and mental health effects of climate change, is an expert witness in the case *Juliana* v. *United States*, one of the world's first human rights-based climate change cases brought against a government, and in *Held* v. *State of Montana*, the first youth climate change case to go to trial in the United States. Dr. Van Susteren explains institutional betrayal using the analogy of a barn burning down. If your barn burns down due to an unpredictable accident, such as a lightning strike, the psychological impacts will likely be less severe than if it burns down because your neighbor deliberately set a fire close by (Van Susteren, 2018a). Dr. Van Susteren further highlights that in most contexts the US legal system also recognizes this idea – "the greater degree of intentionality with which a harmful act is judged to have been committed, the greater the cost to make the person 'whole,' and, for a criminal act, the harsher the punishment" (Van Susteren, 2018a, p. 17).

As the predicted multifold losses from extreme climate events come to pass, young people's resulting experiences of anger and betrayal will "greatly encumber[] the grieving process, making any recovery that much more difficult" (Van Susteren, 2018a, p. 17).

Perhaps the most widespread act of government-sponsored betrayal in the climate change context is the oft-repeated message that the Paris Agreement (2015) goal of "[h]olding the increase in the global average temperature to well below 2 °C above pre-industrial levels and pursuing efforts to limit the temperature increase to 1.5 °C above pre-industrial levels" will fulfill governments' duty to care for young people and future generations. In fact, the science says otherwise. Climate change is fundamentally the result of an imbalance in Earth's energy system due to more energy being absorbed by Earth than is released back out to space (Our Children's Trust, 2022). To restore Earth's energy imbalance, the scientific consensus is that global carbon dioxide concentrations must be reduced from approximately 416 ppm today to 350 ppm by the end of the century, which would keep levels to well below 1.5 °C of heating (Hansen et al., 2008; Von Schuckmann et al., 2016; Lidji, 2020; Hoegh-Guldberg, 2018; Lindsey, 2022).

Achieving the Paris Agreement goal, on the other hand, would not restore Earth's energy imbalance and would result in heating that would be catastrophic for current and future generations. The Intergovernmental Panel on Climate Change (IPCC) has found that warming of 1.5 °C "[i]s not considered 'safe' for most nations, communities, ecosystems, and sectors and poses significant risks to natural and human systems as compared to current warming of 1 °C..." (Intergovernmental Panel on Climate Change, 2018). At 1.5 °C of heating, 70–90 percent of the world's coral reefs, which feed over 500 million people, will disappear (Hoegh-Guldberg et al., 2018, p. 1), and worldwide glacier melt will result in multi-meter sea level rise, which would inundate coastal cities (Pörtner et al., 2022, p. 61). Scientists have shown "that even the Paris Agreement goal … is not safe as 1.5 °C and above risks crossing multiple tipping points," which occur when parts of the climate system "become self-perpetuating beyond a warming threshold" (Armstrong McKay et al., 2022). Legal policies or judicial remedies that equate the protection of young people's rights with achieving the Paris Agreement represent the highest order of institutional betrayal because they reflect intentional governmental action allowing for harmful levels of warming that demonstrably impair the fundamental rights of young people. As Hawai'i Supreme Court Justice Mike Wilson stated: "We are facing a sui generis climate emergency. The lives of our children and future generations are at stake. With the destruction of our life-sustaining biosphere underway, the State of Hawaiʻi is constitutionally mandated to urgently reduce its greenhouse gas emissions in order to reduce atmospheric CO_2 concentrations to below 350 ppm." (In re: Hawaiʻi Elec. Light Co., 2023).

Institutional betrayal contributes to young people's sense that they must act to protect themselves, which is a tremendous burden to take on in childhood. Dr. Van Susteren explains that some young people have "feelings of frustration towards adults who praise them for their actions instead of taking more actions themselves" (Van Susteren, 2018a, p. 20). Those feelings are especially strong when "directed at the federal government for the abject injustice of being abandoned to a ferociously uncertain future" (Van Susteren, 2018a, p. 20). In 2015, the American Academy of Pediatrics issued a statement alongside a technical report finding that the "specter of far-reaching unchecked climate change" threatens the "social foundations of children's mental and physical health" (American Academy of Pediatrics, 2015). The American Psychological Association, which has been working on climate change issues for over a decade, has stated that "[r]esponding to the climate crisis is an essential task for the current generation and many generations to come" (American Psychological Association, 2022). As we stumble closer to the future that scientists have warned government officials of for decades, young people will know more, not less, about governments' failure to protect them.

In the context of this institutional and judicial betrayal, allowing young people to access their courts in pursuit of rulings that are consistent with scientific knowledge and that ensure government accountability in protecting human rights could have an immediate positive impact on young people's mental health (Van Susteren, 2018b). Luisa Neubauer, a young plaintiff who prevailed in her climate change case against government, poignantly observed that "[t]his can change so much, not just for us here in Germany but for activists worldwide" (Treisman, 2021). André Oliveira, a young plaintiff from Portugal who filed a case against 33 countries in the European Court of Rights said, "It gives me a lot of hope to know that the judges in the European court of human rights recognize the urgency of our case. But what I'd like the most would be for European governments to immediately do what the scientists say is necessary to protect our future" (Watts, 2020).

Access to the Courts Is Vital to Protect Young People's Mental Health

Courts are critical to protecting young people's human rights. The US Supreme Court has developed jurisprudence that favors treating young people as a special class entitled to special protection when state action threatens their constitutional rights (Smith, 2018). While US courts, unlike other nations, have not widely embraced the legal principle of "best interests of the child" outside the family law context, the application of heightened standards of review when judging governmental conduct that uniquely harms young people has a similar effect (Schiratzki, 2013).

For example, in *Brown* v. *Board of Education*, the Court overturned the "separate but equal" principle that allowed for school segregation by focusing on the long-term harms, specifically stigmatic and psychological harms, that racial segregation has on Black and white young people (Smith, 2018). In the context of education rights for undocumented immigrant children, in *Plyler* v. *Doe*, the Court "characterized the education of immigrant children as an 'area of special constitutional sensitivity'" worthy of heightened scrutiny by the courts (Smith, 2018, p. 28). Courts find several factors relevant in applying heightened scrutiny when reviewing government policies that harm children, including the dangers of targeting young people for their age, over which they have no control, the related importance of protecting young people from economic and psychological harm, and the large scale of government systems, which allows them to impose a lifetime of hardship on children if misused (Smith, 2018).

All but three countries (including the United States) have ratified and incorporated the United Nations Convention on the Rights of the Child (Child Rights International Network [CRIN], 2018). The use of the Convention in domestic courts has expanded greatly over the past three decades, with more than 350 cases in over 100 countries (CRIN, 2018). Many cases either directly use or refer to interpretative guidance on the Convention's enshrined principles of the need for special protection of young people, including the best interests of the child, the right to be heard and to access justice, and the right against deprivation of liberty (CRIN, 2018). Regional human rights courts offer similar heightened protection. For example, the European Court of Human Rights and other regional European judicial bodies have extensive protective jurisprudence on the rights of the child (European Union Agency for Fundamental Rights & Council of Europe, 2015).

Justice Delayed Is Justice Denied: *Juliana* v. *United States*

In 2015, twenty-one young plaintiffs sued the United States, challenging the government's affirmative actions and policies that contributed to ongoing climate change, on the basis that such conduct violated the young plaintiffs' constitutional substantive due process rights to life, liberty, and property, as well as their public trust rights (*Juliana* v. *United States*, 2016, pp. 94–95).

As of 2024, young people still had not had their day in court, despite many substantive victories. In November 2016, District Judge Ann Aiken denied the government's and fossil fuel industry intervenors' motions to dismiss and issued a decision recognizing, for the first time, that the US Constitution protects a fundamental right to a safe climate. Specifically:

> Exercising my "reasoned judgment," I have no doubt that the right to a climate system capable of sustaining human life is fundamental to a free and ordered society. Just as marriage is the "foundation of the family," a stable climate system is quite literally the foundation "of society, without which there would be neither civilization nor progress." (*Juliana* v. *United States*, 2016, p. 1250).

The trial date was originally set for February 2018, then delayed until October 2018, before ultimately being stayed by the US Supreme Court ten days before trial (Our Children's Trust, n.d., Juliana).

After the US Department of Justice used a series of unprecedented and extraordinary litigation tactics to delay the case, the case went up to the Ninth Circuit Court of Appeals, where a panel of three judges agreed with many of the young plaintiffs' rights-based claims, including that the young people were suffering concrete injuries at the hand of their government (*Juliana* v. *United States*, 2020, p. 1164). However, despite the "plaintiffs' impressive case for redress" (*Juliana* v. *United States*, 2020, p. 1164), two of the judges on the panel denied the young people the ability to access the courts for a remedy. Instead, the judges urged the young plaintiffs to appeal directly to the executive and legislative branches to redress their human rights violations, even though few of them could vote and the court had already acknowledged that the political branches of government had breached their duty of care (Our Children's Trust, 2020). Judge Josephine Staton dissented, arguing it was the role of the court to hear the case. Judge Staton concluded her opinion (*Juliana* v. *United States*, 2020):

> Where is the hope in today's decision? Plaintiffs' claims are based on science, specifically, an impending point of no return. If plaintiffs' fears, backed by the government's *own studies*, prove true, history will not judge us kindly. When the seas envelop our coastal cities fires and droughts haunt our interiors, and storms ravage everything in between, those remaining will ask: Why did so many do so little? (p. 1191).

The young plaintiffs have filed a motion to amend their complaint with the district court, which was granted, and could put them back on the track to trial. Regardless, a new trial date cannot obscure the reality that these young people have already waited over *eight years* to be heard; for some of the young plaintiffs, that is nearly half of their lives, all while the government's conduct continues to exacerbate the climate crisis.

Justice Granted Is Hope Achieved: *Held* v. *State of Montana*

In 2020, sixteen young residents of Montana challenged their state government's policies promoting the development of fossil fuels, alleging that such actions violated their rights to life, liberty, property, and a clean and healthy environment under the Montana Constitution. Young people in Montana are experiencing climate change impacts that include severe wildfire smoke, flooding, decreased stream flows, and destruction of treasured places such as Glacier and Yellowstone National Parks (Held v. State of Montana, 2020). Judge Kathy Seeley ruled that the young plaintiffs have a right to access their courts to obtain declarations of their constitutional rights, and subsequently set a date for trial in June 2023. The case was the first of its kind to go to trial in the United States.

Judge Seeley's decision provided much-needed optimism and validation to young people around the world. Grace Gibson-Snyder, a plaintiff in the case, explained that young people's "voices are actually being heard by the courts, the government, the people who serve to protect [them] as citizens, and Montana's youth" which makes her "feel hopeful that finally [her] government may begin to serve [her] best interest" (Corbett, 2022). In August 2023 Judge Seeley ruled entirely in favor of the youth, recognizing that "[c]hildren are uniquely vulnerable to the consequences of climate change" and "face lifelong hardships resulting from climate change." Judge Seeley held that the state violated the Youth Plaintiffs' "fundamental constitutional right to a clean and healthful environment, which includes climate as part of the environmental life-support system." (Findings of Fact, Conclusions of Law and Order, Held v. State of Montana, 2023).

The Encouraging Trend towards Youth Access to Courts for Climate Justice

In recent years, young people around the world have been successful in holding their governments accountable for violating their human rights. For example, young people in Belgium, Canada, Colombia, France, Germany, Ireland, and Norway have all been granted access to courts where they could present arguments and evidence that their governments were violating their fundamental rights. While most courts have not yet ordered governments to protect young people's rights in line with best available science (i.e., restoring Earth's energy imbalance), courts have recognized that there is a fundamental right to a life-sustaining climate (e.g., *Juliana* v. *United States*, 2020; *In re: Hawai'i Electric Light Co.*, 2023), acknowledged that "it is indisputable" that climate change exposes youth to "an increased risk of death and an increased risk to the security of the person" (e.g., Mathur v. Ontario, 2023), have required governments to comply with political commitments to address climate change (e.g., *State of the Netherlands* v. *Urgenda Foundation*, 2020) and recognized that the burden to address climate change cannot be placed disproportionately on young people (e.g., *Neubauer* v. *Germany*, 2021). While young people being heard is a victory, the call for a science-based remedy that bends downward the global curve of greenhouse gas emissions remains unanswered.

In the United States, judges have begun to directly question the slow progress towards climate justice in the courts in recent dissenting opinions. The canonization of dissents is the elevation of a once minority viewpoint to a "constitutional stature far superior to that accorded most majority opinions in other cases" (Krishnakumar, 2000, pp. 782, 788). Today, dissents play a powerful role in shaping the future of the law in two major ways. First, dissents serve as a warning to current and future courts to be wary of its own biases and readings of the Constitution (Krishnakumar, 2000). Second, dissents can serve to pave the way for expanding constitutional protections beyond the majority opinion (Krishnakumar, 2000). Such dissents are usually less controversial because they extend rights and liberties without necessarily overturning past majority decisions (Krishnakumar, 2000). As US Supreme Court Justice Charles Evans Hughes wrote, a dissent "is an appeal to the brooding spirit of the law, to the intelligence of a future day, when a later decision may possibly correct the error into which the dissenting judge believes the court to have been betrayed" (Hughes, 1936).

Judge Staton's powerful dissenting opinion in *Juliana* serves to develop climate rights jurisprudence because her admonition of the Ninth Circuit's "judicial restraint" calls on future courts to consider that the majority opinion was wrong in denying young people injured by the harmful climate actions of their own government redress through their courts (*Juliana* v. *United States*, 2020). Judge Staton's dissent also lays the groundwork for future rights expansion by connecting the young plaintiffs' claims to a longer history of jurisprudence correcting social injustices and stating in no uncertain terms that, based on the science, their claims establish real and redressable violations of the rights to life and liberty (Our Children's Trust, 2020).

Other dissenting judges in the United States have already heeded Judge Staton's call. Dissenting to a Washington State Supreme Court order denying young people access to the court, Chief Justice Steven Gonzalez and Justice Helen Whitener highlighted the hypocrisy of "recit[ing] we believe children are our future" then leaving them "no mechanism to assert their rights or the rights of the natural world," concluding that "[t]he court should not avoid its constitutional obligations that protect not only the rights of these youths but all future generations who will suffer from the consequences of climate change" (*Aji P.* v. *State of Washington*, 2021). Justices Peter Maassen and Susan Carney, dissenting in a youth climate change case before the Alaska Supreme Court, explicitly recognized a constitutional right to a livable climate – arguably the bare minimum when it comes to the inherent human rights to which the Alaska Constitution is dedicated (*Sagoonick* v. *State of Alaska*, 2022).

Historically, there is a lag between a powerful dissent and its ultimate adoption as the majority viewpoint. It took Brown v. Board of Education (1954) nearly sixty years to overturn Plessy v. Ferguson (1896). In the context of climate change, however, the scientific reality does not afford the courts the luxury of time. It is thus imperative that courts be accessible and accept their role in defining young people's rights to protection.

While young people are gaining access to courts to protect their human rights in certain parts of the world, concerning trends and obstacles to justice remain. Governments' legal defense strategy, often engineered by political appointees, can be designed to restrict court access, even when there is a recognized rights-based injury. For instance, in the summer of 2022, over 50,000 organizations and individuals signed a petition asking the US Department of Justice to end its opposition to young people's access to the courts in the *Juliana* case and allow them to proceed to trial (Our Children's Trust, n.d., Sign the Petition), showing how the public has been stepping up to support youth access to courts for climate justice. Another challenge to court access is the increasing politicization of courts, with harmful consequences for the protection of individual rights and the rule of law. In Montana, for example, the election for one seat on the state Supreme Court became a hot button issue, largely because of a political divide about the court's role in allowing access to courts for constitutional rights claims (Brulliard, 2022). In the past, judicial elections and selection processes have received little attention, but they are a crucial aspect of democratic systems because it is often judges who are called upon to declare and protect fundamental rights.

Overcoming these obstacles requires the strengthening, and at times rebuilding, of fundamental principles of democratic institutions. For young people, many of whom do not have suffrage rights, seeking access to courts is the sole means available to pursue protection of their rights. It is important for adults to support these young people in taking on the burden of securing climate justice in the courts. To do so, lawyers can begin building avenues for law students and young lawyers to gain litigation experience in the climate context, or by showing up for young people in court at hearings or by filing amicus curiae briefs, so that judges and government attorneys can see that young people have a broad base of community, legal, and political support (Our Children's Trust, n.d., Law Library). Other professionals can work to further advance the scientific record that supports young people's claims and can provide expertise in the form of expert testimony or by educating, organizing, and mobilizing their communities of practice. The American Psychological Association, for example, established a Task Force on Climate Change because "Psychologists have conducted valuable work on the climate crisis and can make even greater contributions to understanding the crisis, mitigating and adapting to climate change, and achieving climate justice" (American Psychological Association, 2022). The media can cover these cases and the young people leading them, making sure to center young people in their stories and ensuring that climate science is accurately reported. Teachers can use the stories of these young people in their classrooms and educate young people about human rights and climate science. Authors, publishers, and filmmakers can write and publish books and films about youth climate change cases, such as the book *As the World Burns* by investigative reporter Lee van der voo, or the film *Youth v. Gov*, directed, produced, and written by filmmaker Christi Cooper. Elected officials can highlight the efforts of these young people and use their influence to bolster the democratic systems needed to protect youth facing a climate emergency. Members of the public can work to ensure the appointment and election of judges who respect the rule of law and open access to justice. A binding, science-based remedy is what will truly respond to young people's climate distress, and supporting young people in their quest for such a remedy is more important now than ever before.

Conclusion

Young people are experiencing undeniable mental health harms due to climate change and government actions that directly contradict scientific consensus and prioritize the use of fossil fuels over young people's futures and well-being. Courts play a vital role in mitigating young people's injuries by counteracting the effects of institutional betrayal through considered review of the science and young people's claims, and by issuing enforceable remedies. Moving forward, legal policy that respects the human rights and fundamental freedoms of young people requires listening to the experts and the young people themselves, both inside and outside of the courtroom. Already, favorable decisions in countries around the world, the US Supreme Court's evolution on expanding young people's rights, and the powerful dissenting opinions from judges in the United States have paved the way to a more just future for young people, but there is still much further to go as Earth's energy imbalance grows and the climate crisis deepens.

References

Access to Justice (n.d.). United Nations and the rule of law. www.un.org/ruleoflaw/thematic-areas/access-to-justice-and-rule-of-law-institutions/access-to-justice/

Aji P. v. State of Washington, 497 P.3d 350, 351, 353 (2021).

American Academy of Pediatrics (2015). Global climate change and children's health: Policy statement. *Pediatrics*, 136(5).

American Psychological Association (2022). *Addressing the climate crisis: An action plan for psychologists.* www.apa.org/science/about/publications/climate-crisis-action-plan.pdf

Armstrong McKay, D. I., Staal, A., Abrams, J. F., Winkelmann, R., Sakschewski, B., Loriani, S., ... Lenton, T. M. (2022). Exceeding 1.5°C global warming could trigger multiple climate tipping points. *Science*, 377(6611). https://doi.org/10.1126/science.abn7950

Atherton, R. (2020). Climate anxiety: Survey for BBC Newsround shows children losing sleep over climate change and the environment. *British Broadcasting Company*. www.bbc.co.uk/newsround/51451737

Brown v. Board of Education of Topeka (1954). 347 U.S. 483.

Brulliard, K. (2022). A little-watched Montana race has become a contentious abortion fight. *The Washington Post*, October 12. www.washingtonpost.com/nation/2022/10/12/montana-supreme-court-abortion/

Center for Biological Diversity (2022). Press release: Legal protests target Biden's plans to resume oil, gas leasing on public lands. https://biologicaldiversity.org/w/news/press-releases/legal-protests-target-bidens-plans-to-resume-oil-gas-leasing-on-public-lands-2022-05-18/

Child Rights International Network (2018). Realising rights? The UN Convention on the Rights of the Child in Court. https://archive.crin.org/sites/default/files/uncrc_in_court.pdf

Corbett, J. (2022). Montana plaintiffs announce first children's climate trial in US history. *Common Dreams*, February 7. www.commondreams.org/news/2022/02/07/montana-plaintiffs-announce-first-childrens-climate-trial-us-history

Cui, Y., Li, M., van Soelen, E. E., Peterse, F., & Kürschner, W. M. (2021). Massive and rapid predominately volcanic CO_2 emission during the end-Permian mass extinction. *PNAS*, 118(37), e2014701118. https://doi.org/10.1073/pnas.2014701118

Dowsett, H., Dolan, A., Rowley, D., Moucha, R., Forte, A. M., Mitrovica, J. X., … Haywood, A. (2016). The PRISM4 (Mid-Piacenzian) paleoenvironmental reconstruction. *Climate Past*, 12(7), 1519–1538. https://doi.org/10.5194/cp-12-1519-2016

Dutton, A., Carlson, A. E., Long, A. J., Milne, G. A., Clark, P. U., Deconto, R., … Raymo, M. E. (2015). Sea-level rise due to polar ice-sheet mass loss during past warm periods. *Science*, 349(6244), aaa4019. https://doi.org/10.1126/science.aaa4019

European Union Agency for Fundamental Rights & Council of Europe (2015). *Handbook on European law relating to the rights of the child.* https://fra.europa.eu/sites/default/files/fra_uploads/fra-ecthr-2015-handbook-european-law-rights-of-the-child_en.pdf

Foster, G., Hull, P., Lunt, D. J., & Zachos, J. C. (2018). Placing our current "hyperthermal" in the context of rapid climate change in our geological past. *Philosophical Transactions of the Royal Society*, 376(3). https://doi.org/10.1098/rsta.2017.0086

Hansen, J., Sato, M., Kharecha, P., Beerling, D., Berner, R., Masson-Delmotte, V., … Zachos, J. C. (2008). Target atmospheric CO_2: Where should humanity aim? *The Open Atmospheric Science Journal*, 2(217).

Held v. State of Montana (2020). No. CDV-2020-307, (Mont. 1st Dist. Ct.) (Complaint). https://static1.squarespace.com/static/571d109b04426270152febe0/t/6210037f5cbf9b34dc9abb84/1645216660046/Held+v+Montana+Complaint.pdf

Held v. State of Montana (2023). No. CDV-2020-307, (Mont. 1st Dist. Ct.). (Findings of Fact, Conclusions of Law and Order), August 14.

Hickman, C., Marks, E., Pihkala, P., Clayton, S., Lewandowski, R. E., Mayall, E. E., … van Susteren, L. (2021). Climate anxiety in children and young people and their beliefs about government responses to climate change: A global survey. *The Lancet Planetary Health*, 5(12). https://doi.org/10.1016/S2542-5196(21)00278-3

Hoegh-Guldberg, O. (2018). Expert report in *Juliana* v. *United States*, No. 15-cv-01517.

Hoegh-Guldberg, O., Jacob, D., Taylor, M., Bindi, M., Brown, S., Camilloni, I., … Zhou, G. (2018). Chapter 3: Impacts of 1.5ºC global warming on natural and human system. In IPCC Special Report, *Global warming of 1.5ºC* (pp. 175–312). Cambridge University Press. www.ipcc.ch/sr15/chapter/chapter-3/

Hughes, C. E. (1936). *The Supreme Court of the United States: Its foundation, methods, and achievements: An interpretation.* Columbia University Press.

Humanium (n.d.). The principle of "the best interest of the child." www.humanium.org/en/the-principle-of-the-best-interest-of-the-child/

In re: Hawaiʻi Elec. Light Co., 526 P.3d 329 (Hawaiʻi Supreme Court 2023).

Intergovernmental Panel on Climate Change (2018). Summary for policymakers. In IPCC Special Report, *Global warming of 1.5ºC* (pp. 3–24). Cambridge University Press. https://doi.org/10.1017/9781009157940.001

Juliana v. United States, 217 F. Supp. 3d 1224 (D. Or. 2016).

Juliana v. United States, 947 F.3d 1159 (9th Cir. 2020).

Jurikova, H., Gutjahr, M., Wallmann, K., Flögel, S., Liebetrau, V., Posenato, R., … Eisenhauer, A. (2020). Permian-Triassic mass extinction pulses driven by major marine carbon cycle perturbations. *Nature Geoscience*, 13, 745–750. https://doi.org/10.1038/s41561-020-00646-4

Krishnakumar, A. S. (2000). On the evolution of the canonical dissent. *Rutgers Law Review*, 52, 781–826.

Kurtzleben, D. (2019). Climate issues: Where 2020 Democrats stand on the Green New Deal and more. *National Public Radio*, September 11. www.npr.org/2019/09/11/758173003/climate-issues-where-2020-democrats-stand-on-the-green-new-deal-and-more

La Rose v. Her Majesty the Queen, No. 1750–19 (Federal Court of Canada) (Statement of Claim to the Defendants) (filed October 25, 2019), appeal docketed 2021 Federal Court of Appeal A-289-20.

Legal Response Initiative (2012). "No-harm rule" and climate change. https://legalresponse.org/wp-content/uploads/2013/07/BP42E-Briefing-Paper-No-Harm-Rule-and-Climate-Change-24-July-2012.pdf

Lidji, A. (Host). (2020). Sir David King, founder & chair, Centre for Climate Repair at Cambridge University [Audio podcast episode]. *Do One Better with Alberto Lidji*, October 4. www.lidji.org/sir-david-king

Lindsey, R. (2022). Climate change: Atmospheric carbon dioxide. *National Oceanic and Atmospheric Association*, May 12. www.climate.gov/news-features/understanding-climate/climate-change-atmospheric-carbon-dioxide

Mabee, W. (2019). Cognitive dissonance: Canada declares a national climate emergency and approves a pipeline. *The Conversation*, June 20. https://theconversation.com/cognitive-dissonance-canada-declares-a-national-climate-emergency-and-approves-a-pipeline-119151

Mathur v. Ontario (2023) ONSC 2316, No. CV-19-00631627-0000 (Ontario Superior Court of Justice) (Reasons for Judgment), April 14.

Milman, O., & Smith, D. (2019). "Listen to the scientists": Greta Thunberg urges Congress to take action. *The Guardian*, September 18. www.theguardian.com/us-news/2019/sep/18/greta-thunberg-testimony-congress-climate-change-action

Neubaue v. Germany (2021). Bundesverfassungsgericht [Federal Constitutional Court], April 9.

Nguyen, J. M. (2020). Intergenerational justice and the Paris Agreement. *E-International Relations*, May 11. www.e-ir.info/pdf/84091

Office of the United Nations High Commissioner for Human Rights (2011). Basic principles of human rights monitoring. In *Manual on human rights monitoring*. United Nations. www.ohchr.org/sites/default/files/Documents/Publications/Chapter02-MHRM.pdf

Oregon Health Authority (2022). Climate change and youth mental health. https://sharedsystems.dhsoha.state.or.us/DHSForms/Served/le4212.pdf

Orellana, M. (2021). Right to science in the context of toxic substances: Report of the Special Rapporteur on the Implications for human rights of the environmentally sound management and disposal of hazardous substances and wastes. *United Nations Digital Library*. https://digitallibrary.un.org/record/3936864?ln=en#record-files-collapse-header

Our Children's Trust (2020). Decision of divided Ninth Circuit Court of Appeals finds primarily for *Juliana* plaintiffs, but holds Federal Judiciary can do nothing to stop the U.S. government in causing climate change and harming children. Press release, January 17. https://static1.squarespace.com/static/571d109b04426270152febe0/t/5e22508873d1bc4c30fad90d/1579307146820/Juliana+Press+Release+1-17-20.pdf

Our Children's Trust (2022). Government climate & energy policies must target <350 ppm atmospheric CO$_2$ by 2100 to protect children & future generations. https://static1.squarespace.com/static/571d109b04426270152febe0/t/62b22f95e407a85914583c12/1655844778728/2022.04.21.Government+Climate+and+Energy+Policies+Must+Target+350+ppm+Atmospheric+CO2+by+2100%5B53%5D.pdf

Our Children's Trust (n.d.). Juliana. www.ourchildrenstrust.org/juliana-v-us

Our Children's Trust (n.d.). Law Library. www.ourchildrenstrust.org/lawlibrary

Our Children's Trust (n.d.). Sign the Petition: Tell Attorney General Garland to end opposition to youth climate justice. https://actionnetwork.org/petitions/sign-the-petition-tell-attorney-general-garland-to-end-opposition-to-youth-climate-justice/?referrer=group-our-childrens-trust-2&source=direct_link

Paris Agreement (2015). United Nations Framework Convention on Climate Change. https://unfccc.int/sites/default/files/english_paris_agreement.pdf

Plessy v. Ferguson (1896). 163 U.S. 537.

Pörtner, H.-O., Roberts, D. C., Adams, H., Adelekan, I., Adler, C., Adrian, R., … Zaiton Ibrahim, Z. (2022). Technical summary. In *Climate change 2022: Impacts, adaptation and vulnerability. Contribution of Working Group II to the Sixth Assessment Report of the Intergovernmental Panel on Climate Change* (pp. 37–118). Cambridge University Press. https://doi.org/10.1017/9781009325844.002

Preda, C. F. (2015). The inclusion of children's rights in national constitutions as an essential component of effective national child policies. https://pace.coe.int/en/files/21757/html

Sagoonick v. State of Alaska (2022). 503 P.3d 777 (Alaska).

Schiratzki, J. (2013). Best interest of the child. *Oxford Bibliographies*. www.oxfordbibliographies.com/view/document/obo-9780199791231/obo-9780199791231-0109.xml

Smith, C. (2018). Expert Report in Juliana v. United States, No. 15-cv-01517.

Smith, C. P. & Freyd, J. J. (2014). Institutional betrayal. *American Psychologist*, 69(6), 575–587. https://doi.org/10.1037/a0037564

Smith, C. P., Gómez, J. M., & Freyd, J. J. (2014). The psychology of judicial betrayal. *Roger Williams University Law Review*, 119, 451–475.

State of the Netherlands v. Urgenda Foundation (2020). 114 Am. J. Int'l L. 729, 730.

Statement of Albert Jérôme Lalonde (2022). La Rose v. Her Majesty the Queen, No. T-1750-19.

Statement of Sierra Raine Robinson (2022). La Rose v. Her Majesty the Queen, No. T-1750-19.

Tamari, J. (2019). How climate change became a Democratic litmus test in the 2020 campaign. *The Philadelphia Inquirer*, May 23. www.register-herald.com/2020/how-climate-change-became-a-democratic-litmus-test-in-the-2020-campaign/article_53f80814-80c2-11e9-8b89-4b712f9429dd.html

Treisman, R. (2021). German court orders revisions to climate law, citing "major burdens" on youth. *NPR*, April 29. www.npr.org/2021/04/29/992073429/german-court-orders-revisions-to-climate-law-citing-major-burdens-on-youth

United Nations (1998). General Assembly resolution 53/144: Declaration on the Right and Responsibility of Individuals, Groups and Organs of Society to Promote and Protect Universally Recognized Human Rights and Fundamental Freedoms. www.ohchr.org/en/instruments-mechanisms/instruments/declaration-right-and-responsibility-individuals-groups-and

Van Susteren, L. (2018a). Expert Report in Juliana v. United States, No. 15-cv-01517 (9th Cir.).

Van Susteren, L. (2018b). Expert Report in Held v. Montana, No. CDV-2020-307 (Mont. 1st Dist. Ct.).

Von Schuckmann, K., Palmer, M. D., Trenberth, K. E., Cazenave, A., Chambers, D., Champollion, N., ... Wild, M. (2016). An imperative to monitor Earth's energy imbalance. *Nature Climate Change*, 6, 138–144. https://doi.org/10.1038/nclimate2876

Washington Free Beacon (2020). Biden calls for banning oil companies from drilling. *YouTube*, March 15. www.youtube.com/watch?v=_M_kMDSdISQ

Watts, J. (2020). European states ordered to respond to youth activists' climate lawsuit. *The Guardian*, November 30. www.theguardian.com/environment/2020/nov/30/european-states-ordered-respond-youth-activists-climate-lawsuit

Wright, L., & Rodgers, A. (2022). Debate: Climate impacts on mental health – a youth perspective. *Child and Adolescent Mental Health*, 27(1), 82–83. https://doi.org/10.1111/camh.12541

CHAPTER 14

Coping with Climate Change among Young People
Meaning-Focused Coping and Constructive Hope

Maria Ojala and Xiaoxuan Chen

Global climate change is not only an imminent threat to the environment and society, but also a psychological risk (Reser & Swim, 2011). Facing the climate threat fully can lead to hopelessness and decreased mental well-being. Young people may be particularly vulnerable to psychological consequences of climate change as they may lack both the material and the psychological resources to deal constructively with the negative emotions that this problem arouses (Crandon et al., 2022; Fritze et al., 2008).

In a review of adolescent coping, Frydenberg (2008) identified societal problems, for example climate change, as one of the main concerns reported by adolescents. Recent research conducted in several countries around the world also shows that young people are very concerned and worried about climate change (Hickman et al., 2021). This worry can be triggered not only by personal experiences with this problem, but also indirectly through school and media (Flöttum et al., 2016). The question then arises: Is this worry a positive motivational force for engagement, or is it related to poor mental well-being – or perhaps both?

Aim of the Chapter

In this chapter, we argue that the way in which young people *cope* with climate worry plays an important role in how worry impacts their actions and wellbeing (see Ojala, 2012a, 2012b). We focus specifically on one way of coping, namely meaning-focused coping. We also emphasize the importance of positive emotions such as constructive hope in the coping process (Folkman, 2008; Park & Folkman, 1997). In addition, we will discuss how these ways of coping can be promoted among young people, with a focus on early adolescence (ages 11–12) to emerging/young adulthood (ages 19–29).

The chapter is organized as follows: First, we review research about coping with climate change and argue that it is vital to consider positive emotions in the coping process. Thereafter, we describe the importance of constructive hope. Next, we discuss the importance of meaning-focused coping in activating hope and promoting positive emotions. We then review studies of meaning-focused coping and hope in the context of climate change and elaborate on the different meaning-focused strategies young people use. We also show how this coping strategy is related to engagement with climate change and well-being, as well as to communication patterns with teachers and parents. We conclude the chapter by discussing different ways in which teachers, parents, and others can help in promoting meaning-focused coping and constructive hope among young people.

Coping, Positive Emotions, and Hope

Coping with Climate Change: From Negative Emotions to Positive Emotions

Coping research often focuses on how people use different strategies to defuse negative emotions. The transactional theory of coping, for example, distinguishes between two main ways of dealing with negative emotions: (1) emotion-focused coping, where the goal is to get rid of, or lessen, negative emotions evoked by a stressor, for example, through distancing and denial-like strategies; and (2) problem-focused coping, where people try to find ways to solve the problem, such as talking with others and searching for information, thereby also indirectly regulating negative emotions (Lazarus & Folkman, 1984).

Research concerning climate change has found that problem-focused coping is positively related to climate-change engagement in all age groups, making it a helpful strategy for all societal actors to get involved in mitigation efforts (Homburg & Stolberg, 2006; Ojala, 2012a, 2013; Ojala & Bengtsson, 2019; Van Zomeren et al., 2010). In contrast, emotion-focused strategies, such as denial of responsibility and deemphasizing the climate threat, are negatively related to engagement. However, among a group of children and a group of teenagers, studies have found a positive relationship between problem-focused coping and one aspect of low subjective well-being, namely general negative affect (Ojala, 2012a, 2013). These findings are in line with the general coping research, which has found that problem-focused coping can lead to lower well-being and more distress when trying to find solutions for stressors that are not fully under one's control (Clarke, 2006; Hallis & Slone, 1999). One could therefore ask if there is another way of coping that could complement problem-focused coping to promote engagement without reducing well-being.

The answer to this question may lie in studies of how people proactively cope with stressors (Frydenberg, 2008). In this area of research, the focus shifts from how people avoid negative states to how people strive for goals and meet challenges under adverse circumstances (Frydenberg, 2008). In proactive coping, future-oriented strategies are used to build resources and to promote an active stance towards a stressor, that is, dealing with the problem in a constructive way (Greenglass, 2002). As such, it is worthwhile to take a closer look at positive emotional-cognitive proactive strategies, such as hope, and the role they play in coping (see also Folkman, 2008).

The Role of Hope and Positive Emotions

Hope is one of the most-discussed concepts in climate psychology and one of few positive emotions that the literature has focused on (for a review, see Ojala, 2023b). Hope consists of both positive expectations about the future (cognitions) and positive feeling states (emotions), and therefore could be seen as a positive emotional-cognitive concept (Snyder et al., 2001). Because climate change is an existential problem involving the future survival of humanity, it can be argued that hope is an absolute necessity for a person to be able to face this enormous threat in an active way while maintaining mental well-being (Hicks, 2014; Ojala, 2012b).

Positive emotions such as hope may co-occur with negative emotions in stressful circumstances (Folkman & Moskowitz, 2000). They do not abolish distress, but instead buffer against the adverse physiological and psychological consequences of stress while broadening people's perception of reality; this, in turn, can help individuals find solutions to the problem (Fredrickson, 2001). According to Larsen et al.'s (2003) coactivation model of coping, feeling positive emotions may help people work through and learn from negative emotions. Folkman (1997) also reasoned that a functional relationship exists between positive and negative emotions in the coping process: Negative feelings may motivate people to search for meaning and positive feelings to get relief, and positive emotions, in turn, can help people appraise the situation as more manageable and bolster problem-focused efforts. Positive emotions, however, do not always arise naturally and often need to be actively cultivated, and a sense of meaning may play an important role in that process. Therefore, the importance of general meaning and purpose, as well as meaning-focused coping, will be described in the next section.

Meaning-Focused Coping

On the Importance of Finding Meaning

Finding meaning and a purpose in life that includes caring for oneself, others, and society can buffer young people from psychological ill-being and a sense of hopelessness (Damon, 2008). For example, Seligman (2002) – a pioneer of positive psychology – argued that the highest form of happiness is to live a meaningful life. This kind of happiness leads to more long-term well-being than happiness related to more simple pleasures, such as consumption and having fun. Thus, finding purpose and meaning in life is vital for young people's healthy development.

In the context of coping, two types of meaning – global and situational meaning – are relevant (Park & Folkman, 1997). Global meaning consists of finding a purpose in life and integrating diverse experiences into a meaningful whole. Situational meaning is an interaction between one's global meaning structure and one's cognitive appraisal of a specific situation. Park and Folkman argued that in stressful situations that are not fully under one's control it is vital to supplement problem-focused coping with strategies aimed at creating meaning. For instance, after experiencing a war with many fatalities, to support their sense of global meaning people may strive to find situational meaning by focusing on the sense of social solidarity that was increased by the war. Creating situational meaning can help people bear and constructively deal with negative emotions (Folkman, 1997).

What Is Meaning-Focused Coping?

Meaning-focused coping could be seen as a form of situational meaning. This form of coping involves strategies to evoke positive feelings that can coexist with worry and other negative emotions and can help people face the difficult situation and manage the stressor constructively (Folkman, 2008). Meaning-focused coping includes strategies such as positive reappraisal, in which an individual acknowledges the stressor but is able to reframe their perspective on it (Folkman, 1997; see also Chapter 8 by Marks and Hudson and Chapter 10 by Allured and Easterlin for examples of cognitive reappraisal). Other meaning-focused strategies include finding benefits in a difficult situation, revising goals, and attending to spiritual beliefs (Folkman, 2008). Coping experts have argued that meaning-focused coping is especially important when a problem cannot be solved at once (or at all) but still demands active involvement, such as dealing with a chronic disease, caring for a terminally ill partner (Folkman, 2008; Folkman & Moskowitz, 2000), or dealing with a societal problem such as climate change (Ojala, 2012a, 2012b). The positive emotions evoked by meaning-focused coping can help people face stressors and build resources. Therefore, meaning-focused coping is thought to promote not only mental well-being but also an active stance toward a problem (Folkman, 2008; Park & Folkman, 1997).

Climate Change, Meaning-Focused Coping, and Constructive Hope

Defiant Hope, Positive Reappraisal, and Trust

Several seminal qualitative studies have been conducted to investigate how young people in different age groups cope with climate change through meaning-focused strategies (Ojala, 2007, 2012b; Pettersson, 2014). In these studies, meaning-focused coping was captured by identifying sources of "constructive hope," that is, hope that in later research has been found to be associated with active engagement concerning climate change and that is not related to denial (Ojala, 2012b, 2015).

Three main meaning-focused strategies were identified through these studies. First, young people who use meaning-focused coping have the capability to switch perspective between acknowledging the grim problem and seeing positive aspects, such as the fact that at least more and more people are becoming aware of the climate problem, that humanity has solved difficult problems before in history, and so on (Ojala, 2007, 2012b; Pettersson, 2014). Similar strategies have been identified in research conducted in different cultural contexts focusing on constructive hope in both youth and adults (see Ojala, 2015; Renouf, 2021; Thomas et al., 2022). Second, these young people tended to place trust in different societal actors such as scientists, technological development, humanity at large, the climate movement, and at least some politicians who take this problem seriously. In this regard, studies with people from different cultural contexts also show that constructive climate change hope is related to similar sources of trust (Geiger et al., 2021; see also Renouf, 2021; Vandaele & Stålhammar, 2022). More recent studies demonstrate that young people quite often emphasize that, in contrast to older generations, they can trust the younger generation, who they believe will fight to solve the climate problem (Joelsson, 2021; Thomas et al., 2022). Third, some young people are quite pessimistic but are determined to be hopeful as an assertion of will, arguing, for example, that without hope there is no reason to do anything (Ojala, 2012b; Vandaele & Stålhammar, 2022). This could be seen as coping through defiant hope in which young people refuse to give in to feelings of hopelessness (see Ojala, 2023b). These three sources of hope together make up meaning-focused coping.

Additional Aspects of Meaning-Focused Coping

Most of the studies that first identified different meaning-focused coping strategies in relation to climate change were conducted in a Northern European context. However, more recent research in other cultural contexts has replicated and extended earlier results.

Several new meaning-focused strategies were identified through an interview study with youth climate-justice activists between the ages of 14 and 18 in the San Francisco Bay Area (Chen, 2021). Participants came from a diversity of racial/ethnic and socioeconomic backgrounds, although most were white or Asian, and all but one were cisgender women. This study used semistructured, in-depth interviews and thematic analysis to identify the rewards and challenges of youth climate activism, as well as the coping strategies with which youths cope with both the climate-change problem and the challenges of being collectively engaged. The novel meaning-focused strategies identified in the study were often used in conjunction with other meaning-focused strategies to cope not only with climate distress but also with the challenges that activism may bring, such as stress, burnout, and potential backlash from those who oppose their cause. In general, these meaning-focused strategies were helpful in promoting positive emotions, increasing resilience, and making long-term action sustainable.

One strategy the youths employed was reminding themselves of their motivation for activism and connecting to a larger purpose, which helped them sustain long-term action (Chen, 2021). Motivations included a love for animals and nature, religious faith, a moral calling for justice, and a desire to protect one's own community. The desire to protect community was particularly prevalent in youths from frontline communities most vulnerable to climate change.

A second strategy concerned engaging in mindfulness and spiritual practices to activate positive emotions, including hiking, yoga, medication, journaling, prayer, and participating in organized religion. One activist, for example, drew on mindfulness practices to focus on the present moment instead of worrying about the future.

A third strategy was to accept the existential uncertainty caused by climate change, and to recognize that, despite their best efforts, it is possible that worldwide catastrophe may still occur. Even though this uncertainty can be a source of intense anxiety and distress, a mindful acceptance stance can help youths cope and can increase their positive emotions overall while sustaining action. For several participants, realizing that the future is uncertain actually allowed them to focus on the present moment and to reprioritize their life according to their values – for example, by giving themselves permission to engage in other activities besides activism once in a while, and to enjoy the fun parts of their youth (see also Folkman, 2008). These activities in turn can increase positive emotions and allow youth activists to replenish their psychological resources for sustainable activism.

Meaning and Hope through Collective Climate Engagement

Young people can also seek to find hope and meaning through collective action. Prior research on youth civic engagement supports the hypothesis that engaging in collective action, such as youth activism, is an adaptive way of responding to macrosocial concerns (Ballard & Ozer, 2016). Specifically, activism can improve youth mental health by reducing young people's feelings of helplessness, increasing their sense of empowerment, and helping them build social capital (Ballard & Ozer, 2016). Youth activism may also lead to changes in policies that improve community health, as well as an increased sense of social trust and community cohesion, which in turn improve the health of youths themselves (Ballard & Syme, 2016). Furthermore, grassroots community organizing and service-learning projects with a high level of youth ownership provides youths with formative learning experiences that support sociopolitical and personal/intellectual development (Nicholas et al., 2019; Christens & Dolan, 2011; Morgan & Streb, 2001), which is associated with increased perceived control over one's sociopolitical environment (Speer et al., 2021). In turn, perceived control over one's sociopolitical environment is positively correlated with other indicators of well-being such as self-esteem, perceived school importance, and sense of community, and negatively correlated with risk behaviors such as bullying, violence, and substance use (Christens & Peterson, 2012; Christens et al., 2015). Additionally, activism is associated with increased youth resilience, as youths who get involved in activism in the face of a perceived sociopolitical threat have lower risks for long-term mental health issues than youths who do not (Boehnke & Wong, 2011).

Some studies have shown that environmental activism can also increase young people's sense of hope and meaning (Chen, 2021; Ojala, 2007; Thomas et al., 2022). For example, Ojala (2007) interviewed young volunteers aged 17 through 25 involved in three environmental or global justice organizations and found that taking collective action allowed them to meet friends who share their values, build an increased sense of self-efficacy, live in accordance with their conscience, and learn more about environmental issues. These rewards elicited positive emotions such as hope, joy, and pride, as well as an increase in perceived global existential meaning (Ojala, 2007). Engaging in climate justice activism can also help youths to clarify their more universal values and find purpose in life, and can even influence them to choose environment- or social-justice-related career goals (Chen, 2021). Additionally, research with young adults has found that collective climate-change engagement buffered the positive relation between climate-change anxiety and depression symptoms, such that the positive correlation between climate-change anxiety and symptoms of anxiety and depression were attenuated with engagement in collective action (Schwartz et al., 2022).

Although the benefits of collective action are clear, youth activism can also come with a number of challenges. Youth activists may face increased exposure to criticism and discrimination, experience increased feelings of anger, and become disillusioned and burnt out (Ballard & Ozer, 2016). These risks are increased in settings in which change is difficult and youth voices are tokenized and not taken seriously (Ballard & Ozer, 2016). Furthermore, these negative effects may be particularly amplified for youths from marginalized communities, given their increased exposure to discrimination and other life stressors (Ballard & Ozer, 2016), as well as the burden that minority communities disproportionately bear in fighting for a more just society (Miller et al., 2021).

Given that climate change is an imminent existential threat to young people, climate activism, in particular, may lead to additional challenges or heightened stress. Youth climate activists themselves have identified several challenges, including more exposure to scarier climate-related news, increased frustration with the lack of governmental and societal progress, difficulty in balancing self-care with activism (see also Ojala, 2007), and tensions in their personal relationships with family or friends who do not share their values (Chen, 2021). Young activists may also experience anger or disappointment towards adults and older generations, especially when they adopt a patronizing attitude towards youth activists. Finally, learning to navigate the social dynamics concerning power and privilege within activist spaces can be stressful, especially initially. Therefore, even for youths engaged with collective action, the meaning-focused strategies mentioned above are important for them to maintain psychological well-being (see Ojala, 2007).

Meaning-Focused Coping, Subjective Well-Being, and Climate Engagement

Quantitative studies have investigated how meaning-focused coping is related to both subjective well-being and climate engagement. In studies with children aged 11 and 12 (Ojala, 2012a) and teenagers (Ojala, 2013), meaning-focused coping was associated with all three aspects of subjective well-being: higher life satisfaction, higher general positive affect, and lower general negative affect.

In addition, in the study with children, meaning-focused coping was particularly important for young people who used a high degree of problem-focused coping, as meaning-focused coping buffered the positive relation between problem-focused coping and general negative affect (Ojala, 2012a). In addition, young people's meaning-focused coping in three studies was positively associated with optimism concerning climate change (Ojala, 2012a, 2013; Wullenkord & Ojala, submitted).

Regarding climate-change engagement, meaning-focused coping has been found to be positively related to both perceived efficacy to be able to fight the climate problem and self-reported climate-friendly behavior in everyday life (Ojala, 2012a, 2013; Ojala & Bengtsson, 2019). Meaning-focused coping foremost has an indirect effect on climate engagement through the use of problem-focused coping; that is, studies support the theoretical idea that meaning-focused coping helps people to use problem-focused strategies to cope with climate change, which then leads to taking action to fight the problem (Ojala & Bengtsson, 2019; Wullenkord & Ojala, submitted). Thus, meaning-focused coping serves a number of roles: motivating problem-focused coping, buffering its negative effects, and ultimately seeming to have positive associations overall with both mental well-being and climate engagement (Wullenkord & Ojala, 2023).

Meaning-Focused Coping and Communication with Parents, Friends, and Teachers

How parents and friends communicate and react to their children's negative emotions can influence whether the child will be able to cope in a constructive way. Eisenberg et al. (1998) found that if parents are aware of their children's negative emotions, accept them, see them as opportunities for learning, help their children to verbalize their emotions, and support them in problem-solving efforts, their children tend to be more successful at coping.

In agreement with general coping research, using meaning-focused coping regarding climate change has been found to be positively associated with having parents and peers that communicate in a supportive and solution-oriented way (Ojala & Bengtsson, 2019). In addition, studies performed in Sweden and England show that the more young people report experiencing constructive hope, the more inclined they are to report that they have teachers who accept their negative emotions such as climate-change worry, who discuss future related issues in the classroom, and who focus not only on the problems but also on positive climate-related trends and what individuals can do (Finnegan, 2022; Ojala, 2015). A quasi-experimental study performed with US college students supports these results by showing that a message about climate change with a cautious, hopeful tone was more likely to lead to meaning-focused coping than other coping strategies, while a message with an alarming tone was more likely to lead young people to deemphasize the seriousness of the climate problem (Park & Vasishth, 2021).

Practical Implications

What, then, are the practical implications of the research reviewed in this chapter? Although research is ongoing, intervention studies in this field are still rare, and in a strict scientific sense, evidence-based interventions are not yet available. However, as other chapters in this book show – for example, Chapter 16 by Van Hoorn and colleagues on parenting, and Chapter 17 by Carmichael on education – it is still important, based on the research that does exist, to provide guidance on how to communicate with young people about climate change and support constructive coping. Below we present some suggested practical implications.

Acknowledge and Verbalize Negative Emotions

This chapter has illustrated that teachers' and parents' perceived reactions to young people's emotions about climate change and other societal problems are related to how young people cope (Ojala, 2015; Ojala & Bengtsson 2019). Given these findings, and based on studies about general emotion regulation, we argue that it is important to validate and help young people verbalize their emotions about climate change. For instance, parents showing interest in and acknowledging their children's feelings have been found to help children regulate their emotions in a constructive way (Eisenberg et al., 1998). Research also demonstrates that acknowledging and validating people's negative emotions prevents them from thinking that it is strange to be feeling what they are feeling, which could increase the risk of poorer psychological well-being (Edlund et al., 2015).

There is also support for the idea that expressing emotions by talking with others or writing about them helps people gain some control over them. An increased sense of control helps people to better solve the problem at hand, leads to increased well-being and protection from poorer mental well-being and apathy (Niederhoffer & Pennebaker, 2009). Discussing emotions with other people can also lead to a better understanding of the problem (Stanton & Low, 2012). This is especially important for global environmental problems, since dialogue can be a way to verbalize important moral and political issues that are not yet articulated (see Ojala, 2023a).

Promote Positive Reappraisal and Discuss Sustainable Futures

To promote positive reappraisal, which is part of meaning-focused coping strategies, insights from general psychological research about how to promote flexible thinking and embrace complexity could be helpful when working with young people expressing negative emotional states. After negative emotions have been acknowledged and discussed, it is vital to identify how young people cope with these emotions (Cunningham et al., 2002; Gillham & Reivich, 2004). Labeling their coping styles and strategies helps young people evaluate their constructiveness and effectiveness. For example, if a young person tends to emphasize only the negative aspects of a situation, one can help them challenge this thinking by asking if there are any other ways of looking at the problem, whether they can identify areas of progress in fighting climate change, and so on. Discussing and exploring different ways of looking at a situation with others can help young people to see that there are a multitude of ways to cope besides the two extremes of getting stuck only in the negative or to deny the seriousness of the climate problem (see Lewis et al., 2020).

Exploring and reimagining what a sustainable future (see Graugaard, Chapter 19 in this volume) might look like can enhance flexible thinking, cultivate hope, and encourage meaning-focused coping. One way to cultivate realistic hope is to encourage young people to talk about the global future in school, for example (Hicks, 2014). When talking about the global future, it is vital to let young people first talk about a *probable* global future, which can often bring up negative emotions and contain dystopian themes. However, it is important not to get stuck there and to then ask the students to imagine a *preferable* future and allow them to be creative and even utopian in this process. What might a sustainable global future look like? After this, students can be encouraged to be more realistic and find pathways – both at an individual and a collective level – to reach a *possible* future (see Hicks, 2014).

Cultivating Trust in Oneself and Trust in Others

Finding pathways to a possible global future involves promoting trust in oneself and other actors, since constructive climate change coping consists of both trusting that one can contribute (problem-focused coping) and that other actors are doing their part (meaning-focused coping) (Ojala, 2012b). Adults can help young people build agency by helping them identify different ways to contribute to mitigate climate change. This approach is also in accordance with pathway thinking in Snyder's well-known hope theory (Snyder et al., 2001). According to Snyder, who connects hope strongly to action, a hopeful person can find different ways to reach a goal or to fight a problem. In the context of climate change, it is critical to show young people that there are a variety of ways to mitigate the problem so that they can build agency and a sense of purpose while engaging in actions that matter to them. Besides being collectively engaged, there are a number of actions that young people and their families can take in everyday life, such as choosing more climate-friendly food or flying less. Additionally, children and teenagers can influence others in school, think about what to study in the future so that they can work with climate-change issues as an adult, and influence people through their hobbies – for example, art and music can be used to influence others to take climate change more seriously.

According to Snyder and colleagues (2001), taking more individual and collective action should be accompanied by agency thinking, which involves finding the motivation to use these identified pathways to a better future. Regarding climate-change engagement, young people will encounter different kinds of conflicts with both collective engagement (Chen, 2021) and everyday actions (see Ojala, 2023a). When faced with these challenges and obstacles, young people may be particularly vulnerable to black-and-white thinking (see Ojala, 2023a); for example, many young people argue that "there is no point in me doing anything if not everyone is acting climate friendly." However, there are also alternative ways of coping with internal and external conflicts. For instance, a young person who believes it is important to eat climate friendly but also feels that their individual actions do not really matter, could think more flexibly by introducing a third element, such as claiming "I can at least be a role model." This kind of dialectical thinking can be seen as a form of postformal thinking and can be promoted in school through, for example, problem-based learning, where students work with real-world problems (Wynn et al., 2019). For more ideas on how to promote dialectical thinking see Lewis et al. (2020).

Promoting trust in other actors is an essential part of meaning-focused coping. Young people need to be introduced to different kinds of organizations and individuals that are working to fight climate change and that can serve as role models for how to continue being active despite the significant difficulties and challenges involved. Participatory processes where young people work together with adults to fight climate change could be a particularly beneficial way to promote trust, constructive hope, and a feeling of efficacy among young people (Bessaha et al., 2022). However, it is important for adults to avoid tokenizing youth voices and instead give young people true power in participatory politics.

Promoting Transformative Learning: Critical Emotional Awareness

Finally, although considering climate change emotions from a mental health perspective is crucial – especially for young people already struggling with their mental health and young people who have experienced climate-related catastrophes firsthand – it is not enough. Critical social theories, such as the concept of critical hopefulness, are also vital frameworks for understanding climate-related emotions within an individual's broader sociocultural context (Christensen et al., 2018). Critical hopefulness involves combining hopefulness about the future with a critical understanding of the specific power relationships and injustices that exist in relation to the problems one faces.

Ojala (2023a) has introduced a concept she calls "critical emotional awareness" as a framework for looking at young people's climate emotions within their systemic and sociocultural contexts. A core element of critical emotional awareness is the acknowledgment that emotions and coping are not solely individual experiences but are also influenced by cultural emotion norms, gender norms, and power. For example, across many cultures worry expressed by a girl or a woman is interpreted differently than worry expressed by a boy or a man (see Conway et al., 2003). Another example is that some politicians encourage us to worry about a specific societal problem while others instead claim that we are being irrational when we worry about the same matter, which could be seen as a political game. To be able to deal with climate change and other global and societal problems in a truly democratic way, that is, to avoid being manipulated by different interest groups, young people need to be taught to critically investigate their emotions and coping in relation to climate change. This can be accomplished by asking questions about why they feel certain emotions and not others, why they use some coping strategies over others, and which power processes and emotion norms could be influencing or exploiting their experience (see also Amsler, 2011).

Acknowledgment

The writing of this article was partly supported by the Swedish Research Council VR under Grant 2021-04607 to Maria Ojala.

References

Amsler, S. (2011). From "therapeutic" to political education: The centrality of affective sensibility in critical pedagogy. *Critical Studies in Education*, 52(1), 47–63. https://doi.org/10.1080/17508487.2011.536512

Ballard, P. J., & Ozer, E. J. (2016). The implications of youth activism for health and well-being. In J. Connor & S. M. Rosen (Eds.), *Contemporary Youth Activism: Advancing Social Justice in the United States* (pp. 223–243). ABC-CLIO.

Ballard, P. J., & Syme, S. L. (2016). Engaging youth in communities: A framework for promoting adolescent and community health. *Journal of Epidemiology and Community Health*, 70(2), 202–206.

Bessaha, M., Hayward, R. A., & Gatanas, K. (2022). A scoping review of youth and young adults' roles in natural disaster mitigation and response: considerations for youth wellbeing during a global ecological crisis. *Child and Adolescent Mental Health*, 27(1), 14–21.

Boehnke, K., & Wong, B. (2011). Adolescent political activism and long-term happiness: A 21-year longitudinal study on the development of micro-and macrosocial worries. *Personality and Social Psychology Bulletin*, 37(3), 435–447.

Chen, X. (2021). Psychological challenges and coping strategies for youth climate activists. Unpublished Master's thesis, University of California, Berkeley.

Christens, B. D., Byrd, K., Peterson, N. A., & Lardier Jr, D. T. (2018). Critical hopefulness among urban high school students. *Journal of Youth and Adolescence*, 47, 1649–1662.

Christens, B. D., & Dolan, T. (2011). Interweaving youth development, community development, and social change through youth organizing. *Youth & Society*, 43(2), 528–548.

Christens, B. D., & Peterson, N. A. (2012). The role of empowerment in youth development: A study of sociopolitical control as mediator of ecological systems' influence on developmental outcomes. *Journal of Youth and Adolescence*, 41(5), 623–635.

Christens, B. D., Peterson, N. A., Reid, R. J., & Garcia-Reid, P. (2015). Adolescents' perceived control in the sociopolitical domain: A latent class analysis. *Youth & Society*, 47(4), 443–461.

Clarke, A. T. (2006). Coping with interpersonal stress and psychosocial health among children and adolescents: A meta analysis. *Journal of Youth and Adolescence*, 35(1), 11–24.

Conway, M., Wood, W.-J., Dugas, M., & Pushkar, D. (2003). Are women perceived as engaging in more maladaptive worry than men? A status interpretation. *Sex Roles*, 49(1/2), 1–10. https://doi.org/10.1023/A:1023901417591

Crandon, T. J., Scott, J. G., Charlson, F. J., & Thomas, H. J. (2022). A social-ecological perspective on climate anxiety in children and adolescents. *Nature Climate Change*, 12, 123–131.

Cunningham, E. G., Brandon, C. M., & Frydenberg, E. (2002). Enhancing coping resources in early adolescence through a school-based program teaching optimistic thinking skills. *Anxiety, Stress, and Coping*, 15(4), 369–381.

Damon, W. (2008). *The path to purpose: How young people find their calling in life*. Free Press.

Edlund, S. M., Carlsson, M. L., Linton, S. J., Fruzzetti, A. E., & Tillfors, M. (2015). I see you're in pain: The effects of partner validation on emotions in people with chronic pain. *Scandinavian Journal of Pain*, 6(1), 16–21. https://doi.org/10.1016/j.sjpain.2014.07.003

Eisenberg, N., Cumberland, A., & Spinrad, T. L. (1998). Parental socialization of emotion. *Psychological Inquiry*, 4, 241–273.

Finnegan, W. (2022). Educating for hope and action competence: A study of secondary school students and teachers in England. *Environmental Education Research*, 29(11), 1617–1636. https:// doi.org/10.1080/13504622.2022.2120963

Fløttum, K., Dahl, T., & Rivenes, V. (2016). Young Norwegians and their views on climate change and the future: Findings from a climate concerned and oil-rich nation. *Journal of Youth Studies*, 19(8), 1128–1143.

Folkman, S. (1997). Positive psychological states and coping with severe stress. *Social Science & Medicine*, (45)8, 1207–1221.

Folkman, S. (2008). The case for positive emotions in the stress process. *Anxiety, Stress & Coping: An International Journal*, 21(1), 3–14.

Folkman, S., & Moskowitz, J. T. (2000). Positive affect and the other side of coping. *American Psychologist*, 55(6), 647–654.

Fredrickson, B. (2001). The role of positive emotions in positive psychology: The broaden-and-build theory of positive emotions. *American Psychologist*, 56(3), 218–226.

Fritze, J. G., Blashki, G. A., Burke, S., & Wiseman, J. (2008). Hope, despair and transformation: Climate change and the promotion of metal health and wellbeing. *International Journal of Mental Health Systems*, 7(2), 2–13.

Frydenberg, E. (2008). *Adolescent coping: Advances in theory, research, and practice.* Routledge.

Geiger, N., Gore, A., Squire, C. V., & Attari, S. Z. (2021). Investigating similarities and differences in individual reactions to the COVID-19 pandemic and the climate crisis. *Climatic Change*, 167, 1–2, https://doi.org/10.1007/s10584-021-03143-8

Gillham, J., & Reivich, K. (2004). Cultivating optimism in childhood and adolescence. *Annals of the American Academy of Political and Social Science*, 591, 146–163.

Greenglass, E. R (2002). Proactive coping and quality of life management. In E. Frydenberg (Ed.), *Beyond coping: meeting goals, visions, and challenges* (pp. 39–62). Oxford University Press.

Hallis, D., & Slone, M. (1999). Coping strategies and locus of control as mediating variables in the relation between exposure to political life events and psychological adjustment in Israeli children. *International Journal of Stress Management*, 6, 105–123.

Hickman, C., Marks, E., Pihkala, P., Clayton, S., Lewandowski, R. E., Mayall, E. E., ... van Susteren, L. (2021). Climate anxiety in children and young people and their beliefs about government responses to climate change: A global survey. *The Lancet Planetary Health*, 5, e863–e873, https://doi.org/10.1016/S2542-5196(21)00278-3

Hicks, D. (2014). *Educating for hope in troubled times. Climate change and the transition to a post-carbon future.* Trentham Books.

Homburg, A., & Stolberg, A. (2006). Explaining pro-environmental behavior with a cognitive theory of stress. *Journal of Environmental Psychology*, 26, 1–14.

Homburg, A., Stolberg, A., & Wagner, U. (2007). Coping with global environmental problems development and first validation of scales. *Environment and Behavior*, 39, 754–778.

Joelsson, K. (2021). "Look to the young": A study on climate change coping, emotion, and hope among emerging adults. Unpublished Master's thesis, Uppsala University, Sweden.

Larsen, J. T., Hemenover, S. H., Norris, C. J., & Cacioppo, J. T. (2003). Turning adversity to advantage: On the virtues of the coactivation of positive and negative emotions. In L. G. Aspinwall & U. M. Staudinger (Eds.), *A psychology of human strengths: Fundamental questions and future directions for a positive psychology* (pp. 211–226). American Psychological Association.

Lazarus, R. S., & Folkman, S. (1984). *Stress, appraisal, and coping.* Springer.

Lewis, J. L., Haase, E., & Trope, A. (2020). Climate dialectics in psychotherapy: Holding open the space between abyss and advance. *Psychodynamic Psychiatry*, 48(3), 271–294. https://doi.org/10.1521/pdps.2020.48.3.271

Miller, K. K., Shramko, M., Brown, C., & Svetaz, M. V. (2021). The election is over, now what? Youth civic engagement as a path to critical consciousness. *Journal of Adolescent Health*, 68(2), 233–235.

Morgan, W., & Streb, M. (2001). Building citizenship: How student voice in service-learning develops civic values. *Social Science Quarterly*, 82(1), 154–169.

Nicholas, C., Eastman-Mueller, H., & Barbich, N. (2019). Empowering change agents: Youth organizing groups as sites for sociopolitical development. *American Journal of Community Psychology*, 63(1–2), 46–60.

Niederhoffer, K. G., & Pennebaker, J. W. (2009). Sharing one's story: On the benefits of writing or talking about emotional experience. In S. J. Lopez & C. R. Snyder (Eds.), *Oxford handbook of positive psychology* (pp. 621–632). Oxford University Press.

Ojala, M. (2007). Confronting macrosocial worries. Worry about environmental problems and proactive coping among a group of young volunteers. *Futures*, 39(6), 729–745.

Ojala, M. (2012a). How do children cope with global climate change? Coping strategies, engagement, and well-being. *Journal of Environmental Psychology*, 32, 225–233.

Ojala, M. (2012b). Regulating worry, promoting hope: How do children, adolescents, and young adults cope with climate change? *International Journal of Environmental and Science Education*, 7(4), 537–561.

Ojala, M. (2013). Coping with climate change among adolescents: Implications for subjective well-being and environmental engagement. *Sustainability. Special issue on Psychological and Behavioral Aspects of Sustainability*, 5(5): 2191–2209.

Ojala, M. (2015). Hope in the face of climate change: Associations with environmental engagement and student perceptions of teachers' emotion communication style and future orientation. *Journal of Environmental Education*, 46(3), 133–148.

Ojala, M. (2023a). Climate-change education and critical emotional awareness (CEA): Implications for teacher education. *Educational Philosophy and Theory*, 55(11), 1109–1120. https://doi.org/10.1080/00131857.2022.2081150

Ojala, M. (2023b). Hope and climate-change engagement from a psychological perspective. *Current Opinion in Psychology*, 49, 101514. https://doi.org/10.1016/j.copsyc.2022.101514

Ojala, M., & Bengtsson, H. (2019). Young people's coping strategies concerning climate change: Relations to perceived communication with parents and friends and pro-environmental behavior. *Environment and Behavior*, 51(8), 907–935. https://doi.org/10.1177/0013916518763894

Park, A., & Vasishth, A. (2021). Exploring how the tone of written climate change communication influences coping strategies. *Journal of Student Research*, 10(3). https://doi.org/10.47611/jsrhs.v10i3.2141

Park, C. L., & Folkman, S. (1997). Meaning in the context of stress and coping, *Review of General Psychology*, 1(2), 115–144.

Pettersson, A. (2014). De som inte kan simma kommer nog att dö!: En studie om barns tankar och känslor rörande klimatförändringarna. Unpublished licentiate thesis, Uppsala University, Sweden.

Renouf, J. S. (2021). Making sense of climate change – the lived experience of experts. *Climatic Change*, 164, 14. https://doi.org/10.1007/s10584-021-02986-5

Reser, J. P., & Swim, J. K. (2011). Adapting to and coping with the threat and impacts of climate change. *American Psychologist*, 66(4), 277–289.

Schwartz, S. E. O., Benoit, L., Clayton, S., Parnes, M. F., Swenson, L., & Lowe, S. R. (2022). Climate change anxiety and mental health: Environmental activism as buffer. *Current Psychology*, 42, 16708–16721. https://doi.org/10.1007/s12144-022-02735-6

Seligman, M. E. P. (2002). *Authentic happiness: Using the new positive psychology to realize your potential for lasting fulfillment*. Free Press.

Simon, P. D., Pakingan, K. A., & Benzon R. Aruta, J. J. (2022). Measurement of climate change anxiety and its mediating effect between experience of climate change and mitigation actions of Filipino youth. *Educational and Developmental Psychologist*, 39(1), 17–27. https://doi.org/10.1080/20590776.2022.2037390

Snyder, C. R., Rand, K. L., & Sigmon, D. R. (2001). Hope theory. A member of the positive psychology family. In C. R. Snyder & S. J. Lopez (Eds.), *Handbook of positive psychology* (pp. 257–275). Oxford University Press.

Speer, P. W., Christens, B. D., & Peterson, N. A. (2021). Participation in community organizing: Cross-sectional and longitudinal analyses of impacts on sociopolitical development. *Journal of Community Psychology*, 49(8), 3194–3214.

Stanton, A. L., & Low, C. A. (2012). Expressing emotions in stressful contexts: Benefits, moderators, and mechanisms. *Current Directions in Psychological Science*, 21, 124–128.

Thomas, I., Martin, A., Wicker, A., & Benoit, L. (2022). Understanding youths' concerns about climate change: a binational qualitative study of ecological burden and resilience. *Child and Adolescent Psychiatry and Mental Health*, 16(110). https://doi.org/10.1186/s13034-022-00551-1

Vandaele, M., & Stålhammar, S. (2022). "Hope dies, action begins?" The role of hope for proactive sustainability engagement among university students. *International Journal of Sustainability in Higher Education*, 23, 272–289, https://doi.org/10.1108/IJSHE-11-2021-0463

Van Zomeren, M., Spears, R., & Leach, C. W. (2010). Experimental evidence for a dual pathway model analysis of coping with the climate crises. *Journal of Environmental Psychology*, 30(4), 339–346.

Wullenkord, M., & Ojala, M. (2023). Climate-change worry among two cohorts of late adolescents: Exploring macro and micro worries, coping, and relations to engagement and wellbeing. *Journal of Environmental Psychology*, 90, 102093, doi.org/10.1016/j.jenvp.2023.102093

Wynn, C. T., Ray, H., & Liu, L. (2019). The relationship between metacognitive reflection, PBL, and postformal thinking among first-year learning community students. *Learning Communities Research and Practice*, 7(2), Article 3.

CHAPTER 15

Social-Ecological Perspectives and Their Influence on Climate Distress in Young People

Tara Crandon, Hannah Thomas, and James Scott

Introduction

Climate distress (often referred to as climate anxiety) describes a range of emotional experiences felt in relation to the climate crisis. Common experiences may include anxiety, grief and loss, shame, sadness, anger, guilt, and hopelessness (Hickman, 2020). These experiences may range in severity (e.g., mild to severe) and adaptivity (from unhelpful and debilitating distress to distress that leads to helpful and productive coping) (Hickman, 2020). Although experiences are heterogeneous, young people are more likely than adults to endorse climate distress (Clayton & Karazsia, 2020). There is a need to consider the interplay of systemic factors that differentially impact the experience of climate distress in young people. Systems theory provides a framework of understanding how a young person's interactions with their surrounding environments can shape how they feel about and cope with climate change (Crandon et al., 2022).

Systems Theory

Systems theory is a transdisciplinary field of study that examines and explains the behavior of complex systems. From a systems perspective, human and environmental systems are intertwined and interconnected. These systems are made up of living organisms, whether humans, animals, or biospheres. Such complex interactions produce, influence, and maintain the patterns of systems over time. Systems thinking describes the act of adopting such a perspective (Whitchurch & Constantine, 1993).

Systems theory was formulated in response to simplistic and traditional scientific approaches to the studies of living organisms and has been applied to climate change and mental health. As a relatively new and rapidly evolving field, much of the research exploring climate change and mental health examines direct associations between factors. For example, how natural disasters may be associated with increases in climate distress, or how distress and pro-environmental behavior are linked. Yet the ways that climate change may impact the mental health of humans, as well as how humans impact climate change, are multifaceted. As one example, rising heat is likely to have a negative effect on physical and psychological well-being. This can affect work/study, or time spent outside or socializing, which in turn further impacts health and well-being. Spending more time indoors (to escape extreme temperature) may mean young people are more socially isolated or unable to engage in their enjoyed activities (e.g., sports). This may influence their social, physical, and emotional health.

Systems theory and its branches (e.g., Family Systems Theory) can provide useful frameworks when understanding the complex relationship between climate change and mental health (Crandon et al., 2022).

Social-Ecological Perspectives and Young People

Drawing from systems theory, social-ecological models are used to understand problems related to physical, psychological, social, and economic health. When conceptualizing health problems, social-ecological models consider the complex interplay between systems. This is often visually depicted as overlapping layers, whereby the factors within one system influence and have a ripple effect on other systems.

Bronfenbrenner's social-ecological theory applies a systems perspective to child development, positing that a child is nested within a complex system of relationships between the child and their surrounding environments (see Figure 15.1). These systemic contexts span from the child's immediate family and peer networks to their broader societal and cultural backdrops (Bronfenbrenner, 1979; Klichowski, 2017). As the child grows, their experiences, views, emotions, and behavioral responses will be shaped by: the young person; the techno-subsystem; the microsystem; the mesosystem; the exosystem; the macrosystem; and the chronosystem. At the center of the systems is the individual *young person*. The young person's unique biological, developmental, and psychological history are considered influential. This includes characteristics such as age, temperament, gender, and geographic location, as well as physical or mental health history.

The *microsystem* refers to the young person's immediate surrounding social and ecological environments with which they directly interact. This layer may include physical spaces that the young person most frequently operates within (e.g., home, garden) as well as the social circles closest to the child (e.g., parents and caregivers, peers, teachers). The influence of

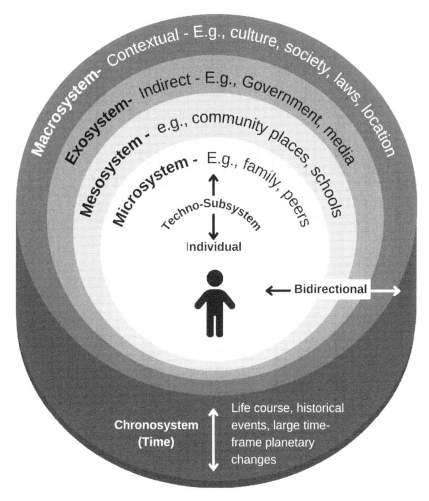

Figure 15.1 An example of Bronfenbrenner's social-ecological framework.

these immediate structures may shift as the young person ages. For example, family may be the child's predominant social influence in adolescence, while peers may become more influential in late adolescence into early adulthood. It should be noted that developmental progression may differ according to culture.

The *techno-subsystem* is a dimension of the microsystem, added in recognition of the increasing role that technology plays in the development of young people. The techno-subsystem captures how young people interact with the world through phones, television, computers, and the Internet. This system is proposed to mediate between a child and the microsystem. That is, technology is often the tool through which a young person interacts with their immediate environments such as their family, friends, and school (Klichowski, 2017), and likely also the outer social-ecological systems.

The mesosystem encompasses the child's community, including their local environments such as their neighborhood, schools, and public places. The mesosystem may include both community places (e.g., buildings) and the local natural environment (e.g., local parks or green spaces). Through the mesosystem, the child's microsystemic social structures intersect, including their parents and caregivers, their peers, teachers, and neighbors.

The *exosystem* layer includes environments that influence a young person's development, despite the young person not necessarily having direct experience or involvement. This system deals with structures such as governmental agencies, healthcare or social services, economic systems, the educational curriculum, or mass media. The exosystem may also include broader environmental landscapes, nationally or internationally.

The *macrosystem* relates to broader collections of influences on a young person which provide a cultural, societal, spiritual, or political contextual background. The history, traditions, values and beliefs, ethnicity, laws, geographic location (e.g., quality of the landscape, vulnerability to weather) and socioeconomic standing of societies and cultures provide a framework for a child's beliefs, perceptions, and experiences.

The *chronosystem* is the overarching layer of time. Over time, events that occur will affect a young person and the systems within which they live, as well as how they interact with or experience these environments. Events may include life transitions (e.g., moving out of home), experiences unique to the young person (e.g., the birth of a new sibling), or historical events (e.g., the evolving impacts of climate change).

Systems thinking and climate distress. Systems thinking has been emphasized in climate science as a useful way to understand the broad range of climate change impacts and adaptation efforts needed (Ballew et al., 2019). Experiences within a system can profoundly shape how climate change impacts population mental health and outcomes (e.g., access to healthcare, policies that address climate change). This calls for whole-population adaptation and intervention, rather than individually focused interventions (Berry et al., 2018). An emerging perspective is that climate distress occurs as a result of the complex interactions between a young person and their surrounding environments (Crandon et al., 2022; Ma et al., 2022;

Vergunst & Berry, 2021). These influences frame how a young person perceives the threats of climate change and shape their emotional, cognitive, and behavioral responses. Thus, psychological support for young people dealing with climate distress must consider systemic-level interventions.

Bidirectional influences. It is also important to note that these influences are bidirectional in nature, whereby a child or young person may mutually shape their surrounding environmental contexts. For example, a young person has the ability to influence their parents' and caregivers' views on climate change, their school's engagement in pro-environmental behavior, and their government's decision-making regarding policies addressing climate change.

Table 15.1 summarizes the positive and negative influences in each system and the associated recommendations and considerations.

Social-Ecological Influences on Young People's Climate Distress

Individual

Exacerbating Influences

Across the globe, young people will experience climate change in vastly different ways. Geographic location may particularly shape the perceptions they hold about the threats brought by climatic changes. Young people living in areas vulnerable to the impacts of climate change may view the climate crisis as more threatening and salient. For example, young people living in the Global South (countries such as Africa, Latin America, the Pacific Islands, and developing countries in Asia) will be disproportionately affected (Vergunst & Berry, 2021). Within these regions, climate change may aggravate preexisting vulnerabilities within their social-ecological system (e.g., famine, poverty). Ocean level rise and other water-related climatic hazards threaten the habitability of areas such as the Pacific Islands and the Philippines, forcing residents to leave their homes and seek refuge elsewhere (Berchin et al., 2017). Climatic changes may also greatly impact agricultural livelihoods (e.g., fishery, farming), which many countries in the Global South depend on economically. This myriad of potential stressors can significantly compromise the physical and psychological health and safety of those living in the Global South, where approximately 85 percent of young people reside (Sanson et al., 2019).

In the Global North (e.g., North America, Europe, and Australia), environmental catastrophes such as wildfires could become more extreme and frequent due to climate change. Young people living in lower socioeconomic areas may be particularly affected. For example, reduced access to

Table 15.1 A summary of proposed exacerbating and protective influences on climate distress in young people, and recommendations

System level	Exacerbating influences	Protective influences	Recommendations
Individual	• Geographic location • Socio-economic background • Neurodevelopment • Early climate and life adversity • Characteristics of the young person	• Adaptive coping behaviors • Level of hope or trust in others • Connection to nature • Pro-environmental beliefs • Personal resilience/characteristics	• Tailor support to a young person's individual needs • For those directly impacted, facilitate access to food, shelter, safety, and healthcare • Provide individualized mental health support • Draw on coping mechanisms and build resilience
Microsystem	• Parents and caregivers modeling distress/coping • Apathy, dismissal, or distancing on the issue • Families undergoing climate-related adversity • Discussing climate change in overly negative ways • Pressure from peers or differing viewpoints • Concern for others experiencing climate adversity	• Parents, caregivers or peers modeling hope, resilience, agency, and pro-environmental engagement • Social support • Time in nature	• Equip families with adequate support, information, and resources • Facilitate effective family communication and engagement with climate mitigation • Engage young people with other young people in discussions or projects
Techno-subsystem	• Immediacy, intimacy of unregulated and unrestricted access to climate-related content • Online misinformation about climate change • Tech algorithms that increase the frequency of potentially triggering information • Reduced connection to nature due to screen time	• Convenience and immediacy of information about climate change and mitigation • Social media as a space for connection between young people, and platform to organize climate-mitigation projects • Increased access to education and mental health support	• Regulate climate-related content • Support and supervise young people to use technology in developmentally appropriate ways • Support young people in connecting with others on climate mitigation

Mesosystem	- Failure to provide a safe space to discuss climate change in school or communities
- Limited/lack of teacher training or restricting teaching or discussing climate change
- Communities experiencing climate diversity and communal distress	- Communal recovery following climate adversity and losses
- Community preparation for future climate adversity
- Collective climate action and social support	- Provide opportunities for young people to connect with others and engage in mitigation strategies and collective action
- Consider development of school curriculum on climate change
- Develop community or peer-based support programs and anticipatory training
- Provide support and training for teachers
Exosystem	- Governments failing to sufficiently address climate change and resulting social divide
- Governments silencing or dismissing young people
- Failing to carefully aid climate policy transitions
- Inadequate disaster-response planning and training	- Governments upholding climate justice and protecting young people through law and policy
- Governments supporting population well-being and access to resources
- Local government initiatives such as urban green spaces
- National public health messaging that educates the public on risks and action	- Develop climate policies that are sensitive to protecting youth well-being
- Decrease global reliance on fossil fuels
- Enable and facilitate population level implementation of climate policies
- Consider the needs of different groups when undertaking climate policy transitions
- Engage young people in discussions and action plans as key stakeholders
Macrosystem	- Cultural values being at odds with ongoing devaluing and destruction of nature
- Environmental change leading to severed attachments to places that hold meaning
- Loss of spiritually and culturally important places
- Loss of culture, identity and disruption to land-based activities that are important to cultures	- Culture, religion, and belief systems driving pro-environmental behavior and collective action
- Communities drawing on and passing down cultural traditions and knowledge to protect the environment
- Faith and support from religion	- Research how loss of place and culture may influence climate distress in young people
- Consider long-term impacts of unavoidable environmental losses on young people
- Facilitate connection to culture, religion, belief systems or places of importance
- Provide communities with resources needed to participate in prevention, preparation, and restoration projects

safe shelters and healthcare during climate-related weather events (e.g., heat waves, natural disasters such as typhoons) can increase risks to mortality, injury, disease, and psychological trauma.

Climate change may also impact the neurodevelopment of young people. Neural biomarkers and heightened neural reactivity are associated with increased risk of mental health problems (e.g., symptoms of anxiety, depression) following hurricanes (Ma et al., 2022). Heatwaves and air pollution, which are projected to increase due to climate change, can lead to obstetric and biological complications in young people, which are known risk factors for neurodevelopmental disorders (Vergunst & Berry, 2021). Even *in utero*, exposure to climate events increases later risk of climate distress (Nomura et al., 2022). These various effects are particularly concerning when considering that young people may have long-term exposure to these neurological risk factors over the lifespan.

As climate-related stressors intensify and become more frequent over time, climate-related adversity may also become more common in early life. Persistent stressors in childhood increase the risk for developing mental health problems (Kessler et al., 2010). Characteristics of the young person (e.g., temperament, self-esteem, tolerance for uncertainty, preexisting mental health concerns) may play a role in their climate risk perception. Trait anxiety (the tendency to perceive stressful events as threatening) for example, has been shown to predict anxiety and posttraumatic stress symptoms in young people following Hurricane Katrina.

Protective Influences
Young people may engage in coping mechanisms that reduce the negative impact of climate distress on well-being and functioning. Cognitively, young people may focus on attempting to problem-solve actions that can address climate change, which has been found to mitigate anxiety symptoms for young people (Ojala, 2011). Additionally, meaning-focused coping (e.g., finding meaning and hope) has been linked to greater well-being and actively engaging in environmental issues (Ojala, 2011).

Behaviorally, a young person may actively attempt to reduce their carbon footprint, or engage in political action (e.g., youth representation forums, protesting). They may alternatively cope by expressing their feelings (e.g., creatively or by connecting with support systems) or using strategies that help regulate their emotions (e.g., listening to music, exercising). Other protective characteristics that can enhance adaptive coping may be a young person's level of hope or trust in others (e.g., climate scientists) and personal identification or connection with nature.

Recommendations and Considerations
Young people are a diverse group with varying circumstances. There is a need to consider this variability and tailor support to individual needs. The priority for young people who are experiencing direct impacts of climate change (e.g., physical vulnerabilities, geographic location) may be in facilitating access to food, shelter, and safety or healthcare for themselves and their families. Young people with preexisting mental health concerns, or who may be particularly impacted by climate distress, may need targeted and individualized mental health support. Young people, parents and caregivers, and professionals may consider drawing upon helpful coping mechanisms already at play, such as listening to music or leading climate action.

Microsystemic Influences

Exacerbating Influences
Bowen's Family Systems Theory recognizes the family unit as a system in which the interactions between family members influence the emotions and behaviors of one another (both within one's family of origin as well as intergenerationally) (Bowen, 1978; Calatrava et al., 2022). Parents and caregivers particularly play a key role in socializing and modeling emotional responses and coping in young people, yet also have a difficult task in raising children in a state of increasing harm and vulnerability attributable to climate change (Gaziulusoy, 2020). Parents and caregivers are reckoning with their own feelings about climate change, with one study showing that parents reported feelings of sadness, hopelessness, anxiety, guilt and disempowerment about their child's future (Gaziulusoy, 2020). Modeling and conveying these emotions could magnify or reduce the distress felt by young people. Conversely, parents may be apathetic, distanced, or dismissive of the issue, or they may have more immediate and salient stressors (Sanson et al., 2018). Young people distressed about climate change may in turn feel resentful, silenced, unsupported, and unsure of how to cope.

Climate distress could be exacerbated when parents and caregivers are undergoing climate-related adversity (e.g., lack of access to healthcare, food, and shelter due to climate-related environmental events). How parents and caregivers communicate and teach their children about climate change and these associated stressors is also a powerful agent of influence. One study found that when young people perceived their parents as talking about climate change in an overly negative way (e.g., "doom and gloom" language) or dismissing their emotional responses, they were more likely to use an emotion-focused coping strategy (e.g., trying to get rid of or escape the feelings). This style of emotional coping is thought to be less effective than other types of coping strategies such as problem-solving or meaning-focused coping (Ojala & Bengtsson, 2018).

As young people grow older, their friends and peers may become the predominant sources of informal learning (Stevenson et al., 2019). Peers inform attitudinal and behavioral norms, leading other young people to mirror emotional (e.g., distress) and behavioral (e.g., climate activism) responses. This can become problematic when young people feel pressured by peers, or when conflict, ostracizing, or even bullying arises due to differing viewpoints. Climate distress may also be exacerbated if young people are feeling concerned about friends overwhelmed by or experiencing climate-related adversity.

Protective Influences
Through modeling and communication, parents and caregivers can foster hope, resilience, agency, and pro-environmental engagement in their children (Sanson et al., 2018; Stevenson et al., 2019). Support from parents and caregivers may also be protective of youth well-being (Ojala & Bengtsson, 2018). Peers can solidify norms and act as role models for how to proactively cope with climate distress, whereby young people could be encouraged to collaboratively engage in pro-environmental projects and discussions (Stevenson et al., 2019). This may amplify a sense of shared responsibility and social support, potentially buffering against poor mental health.

Recommendations and Considerations
It is critical for parents and caregivers to be equipped with adequate support, information, and appropriate resources that they can use to manage and model coping with the threat of climate change. There are several existing resources available to parents and caregivers that provide suggestions for how to communicate and engage young people with the issue of climate change in developmentally appropriate ways (DeMocker, 2018). Peers also provide social support and informal learning. Parents, caregivers, and professionals should consider encouraging opportunities where young people can discuss and work together to address climate change.

The Techno-Subsystem

Exacerbating Influences
The digital world (e.g., the Internet, television) has transformed educational and social spaces that young people occupy (Hollis et al., 2020). The Internet particularly provides innovative opportunities for young people to rapidly learn and interact with others. Yet the immediacy, intimacy,

and often unrestricted access or unregulated content on the Internet can also be risk factors for a young person's mental health (Hollis et al., 2020).

Information about climate change or media coverage may not always be regulated or made appropriate for younger audiences (Gislason et al., 2021). Some young people may have unrestricted access to online misinformation about climate change as well as potentially highly distressing climate-related content (e.g., footage of extreme weather disasters). Furthermore, liking, reacting, or subscribing to receive this type of content on social media may configure media algorithms to continue showing this content to young people (Crandon et al., 2022) and may trigger/retrigger climate distress, impacting overall mental health.

Young people can spend more time using technology than they spend outside, which may reduce their sense of connection to nature (Larson et al., 2018). High levels of "screen time" is associated with poor psychological outcomes in young people, such as poorer cognitive functioning, reduced happiness, and poorer academic outcomes (Oswald et al., 2020). Conversely, time in nature has been associated with reductions in depressed affect, stress, and peer problems, as well as improved cognitive, social, emotional, and language development in young people (Oswald et al., 2020). These opportunities are lost when young people spend time occupying digital rather than natural environments.

Protective Influences. It should be acknowledged that the convenience and immediacy of content and social interactions could have potential benefits for young people (Hollis et al., 2020). Young people can quickly and comprehensively access information about climate change and learn about ways to aid climate mitigation (Crandon et al., 2022; Taber & Taylor, 2009). Social media might connect young people with others who share similar values and can be used as a platform through which young people can organize climate-related projects, as well as support groups. Continued education and mental health support can also be more accessible for young people living in rural places or for those displaced due to climate change. Young people or their families may access self-help information regarding mental health and coping, which is particularly useful for those unable to access mental health support due to socioeconomic constraints.

Recommendations and Considerations

Digital media can be a powerful tool to connect young people to supports and provide information that can help them cope with climate distress. It is critical for policymakers, media professionals, parents and caregivers, and teachers to carefully regulate young people's exposure to climate-related content (Textbox 15.1).

> **Textbox 15.1 Case study: Problems across the individual, micro, and techno-subsystems**
>
> Cameron, a 14-year-old with a history of generalized anxiety, has intrusive thoughts and images about climate change (e.g., thoughts of biodiversity loss). He feels distressed and overwhelmed when he sees things that remind him of climate change, such as pollution and extreme weather events happening around the world. His parents and friends rarely talk about climate change. In an attempt to better understand the issues, he spends increasing time online viewing information on how human activities negatively impact the planet (e.g., overfishing). He feels like there is nothing he can do about climate change. He has started withdrawing from his friends and family.
>
> ### FORMULATION
>
> There are several overlapping systems at play, leading Cameron to feeling overwhelmed. Cameron has an emotionally avoidant family system and disengaged peer system, leading to little opportunity for him to express his climate distress with others. Because of this, he may perceive that others do not feel concerned about the issue. In response to the lack of support from family and peers, Cameron becomes increasingly reliant on technological systems. This exposure may further isolate him, particularly if he views that those around him are harming the planet. His preexisting anxiety may also exacerbate his distress or impact his ability to regulate these feelings.
>
> ### RESPONDING
>
> Cameron may benefit from discussing his concerns in a nonjudgmental environment (e.g., through peer-based support, supervised by a therapist). Cameron's parents and school could benefit from resources and training around the benefits of discussing climate change and engaging in environmentally sustainable activities with him. Cameron's parents might, for example, learn to identify family environmental values and actions that can be implemented in the house. Cameron's parents could support appropriate engagement with technology, be available to discuss and critique the content that he is viewing, and support Cameron to spend time offline in other activities with friends and family.
>
> Cameron and his peers may benefit from forming community groups that young people can join to connect with others, spend time in nature (e.g., nature walks, scouts) and protect the environment (community gardens, restoring green spaces).
>
> Cameron may find it useful to learn strategies that can help him to regulate his emotions such that he does not feel as overwhelmed (e.g., deep breathing, spending time in nature). He may also benefit from targeted intervention with a mental health professional to support him to manage intrusive thoughts.

Mesosystemic Influences

Exacerbating Influences

Schools and communities are instrumental in educating young people about climate change and adaptation. However, classrooms and communities can isolate young people when they do not provide a safe place to discuss climate change (Chawla, 2020). Schools or even local/national governments often hold power over educational curriculum, and power or political dynamics can influence a teacher's academic freedom or willingness to discuss climate change with students. Other teachers may refrain from discussing climate change due to their personal views (Ho & Seow, 2015). Without collaborative discussion and conversation about climate change, communities and schools may convey indifference and futility in climate mitigation.

Accurate information about climate science and the importance of psychological adaptation is important for young people to build self-efficacy and agency (Taber & Taylor, 2009). Yet limited or lack of teacher training can lead to misinformation about climate change and confusion in students (Wise, 2010). Indeed, while educational curriculum may educate young people on the consequences of climate change, they may not necessarily provide young people with tangible adaptation strategies to mitigate risk that they can easily implement.

As climate change evolves, communities will collectively undergo adversity and heightened distress (e.g., floods disrupting a community's access to food, water, shelter, healthcare). Young people may also be impacted by communal level distress; that is, the shared distress felt by a community impacted by short-term (e.g., weather events) or long-term (e.g., deforestation) climatic impacts. Researchers suggest that during events such as natural or weather disasters, survival is a socially shared rather than individual experience. For example, survivors of the 2016–2017 central Italy earthquakes reported intrusive memories about fellow community members, such as witnessing their neighbor experiencing distress or learning of their death (Massazza et al., 2022). Communal distress may be particularly profound for remote/rural or Indigenous communities, where culture, identity, livelihoods, and resources are closely connected to the landscape (e.g., droughts in rural areas affecting agriculture and employment) (Gibson et al., 2019).

Protective Influences

Young people may collectively work with their community to prepare for or recover from physical, financial, and social losses (Matsuyama et al., 2016). (See Textbox 15.2 for a case study example.) Community

> **Textbox 15.2 Case study: A mesosystem problem**
>
> Ruby is a 16-year-old living in an area prone to high temperatures, with an older electric grid and no green spaces. The types of problems she is vulnerable to include distress relating to reduced time in nature, potentially reduced ability to engage in environmental projects, and economic and communal challenges in transitioning to sustainable energy practices. Ruby's community should aim to provide practical support and foster social cohesion (e.g., discussions, communal projects) to help reduce distress in young people and enhance communal well-being. For example, Ruby could benefit from school-based projects to establish green spaces (e.g., planting trees around her school can improve air quality, and provide shelter and shade during extreme temperatures) or engage in other ways with nature (e.g., bird watching).

preparation for future climate-related events can reduce potential physical and psychological harm to young people. For example, community efforts to maintain mangroves which reduce storm surges providing flood preparedness may help to protect young people otherwise vulnerable to flooding. Collective action allows for the burden of climate change to be shared, minimizing isolation and disconnection. School environmental programs can increase climate awareness, feelings of empowerment, self and collective efficacy, and pro-environmental behavior in young people (Crandon et al., 2022). Additionally, community social support may help individuals cope with distress related to environmental change or disasters (Matsuyama et al., 2016).

Recommendations and Considerations
There are numerous avenues for schools and communities to provide opportunities where young people can connect with others and meaningfully engage in individual as well as collective action. Teachers should have access to support and professional training around teaching and discussing climate change effectively in the classroom. There is a need for greater focus on developing and evaluating the long-term effectiveness on community and peer-based programs that could help young people psychologically cope with climate distress and mitigate potential harm.

Exosystemic Influences

Exacerbating Influences
There is general agreement that global coordinated action is urgently needed to respond to climate change. Governments who fail to sufficiently

address climate change will leave young people at a heightened vulnerability to harm and distress. Understandably, some young people living under governments who silence and dismiss their concerns, or fail to implement environmental policies, may experience a sense of hopelessness, betrayal and disempowerment (Hickman et al., 2021). Ineffectual climate mitigation at the governmental level may also create social divides between nations, socioeconomic groups, and generations, such as young people feeling resentful towards older generations for having caused and contributed to the climate crisis. Conversely, climate mitigation policies may have short-term or unjust impacts for families when governments do not carefully aid these transitions (e.g., insufficient resources to adopt energy efficient means). Failure to adequately and appropriately implement policies that address climate change and its impacts can create a myriad of potential stressors for young people.

Protective Influences
Exo-systems can define human rights, where legal and policy action (e.g., resistance to fossil fuels, funding community efforts) can help to uphold climate justice and protect young people. Governments can enact policies that systematically address climate change as well as potential barriers to population health and well-being (Hunt, 2012). Supporting the population with climate preparedness and policy transition may be profoundly protective of population well-being and resilience (Keim, 2008). (See Textbox 15.3 for a case study example.) Urban green spaces (e.g., parks) built as part of local government initiatives, have been associated with improved physical, social, and emotional well-being (Wood et al., 2017). National public health campaigns that simplify and reframe scientific messages about climate change could help to influence population level behavior change and educate the public on risks and protective measures. In turn, this could help reduce young people's vulnerability and distress (Keim, 2008).

Recommendations and Considerations
It is critical for policymakers to develop climate policies that actively protect youth well-being. Decreasing governmental and global reliance on fossil fuels is especially critical in protecting young people. Of further importance is to enable and facilitate population level implementation of environmentally sustainable policies, whereby careful consideration should be given to the needs of different groups in undertaking these transitions. Governments may consider using public health campaigns as a means of educating and supporting adaptation. Furthermore, governments should

> **Textbox 15.3 Case study: An exosystem problem**
>
> Maria is an 18-year-old living in a small community in a rural coastal town, where fishing is the predominant source of livelihood. Her geographic area is vulnerable to typhoons, the most recent of which has had a devastating impact on the community's building infrastructure and fishing sector. Maria is vulnerable to danger from extreme weather, lack of access to food, shelter, and other financial resources. She and her community are vulnerable to distress. Aid from local government is imperative to support Maria and her community in recovering and rebuilding, as well as helping to prepare for future weather events. It is important that Maria has the opportunity to engage in collective community action. Critically, governmental systems around the globe hold a responsibility to implement climate policies and decrease fossil fuels, to mitigate the impact that climate change is having on Maria's community.

engage with young people both in discussing and implementing climate policies, particularly given that young people are key stakeholders in a sustainable future.

Macrosystemic Influences

Exacerbating Influences

Nature is valued by many cultures, religions, and belief-systems around the world. Distress can arise when a young person's ethical, spiritual, moral, or cultural values are at odds with worldwide devaluing and destruction of nature that contributes to climate change. Environmental and climatic changes may sever attachments between young people and places that hold meaning and importance for them (e.g., home, community, lands) (Crandon et al., 2022). Grief may be especially profound when young people are spiritually and culturally connected to such places (e.g., many nature and animistic religions, such as Shinto, believe that natural places possess a spiritual presence or are the embodiment of divinity). Dene Tha' youth from Canada experienced severed connections to meaningful land due to forestry and industrial development occurring over time (MacKay et al., 2020). Loss of culture, identity, and disruption to land-based activities (e.g., hunting, fishing, foraging) due to climatic changes was reported by First Nations individuals in Rigolet (Nunatsiavut, Canada) as negatively impacting their mental health (Cunsolo Willox et al., 2013). These studies highlight that for some young people, climate change threatens to erase homelands and deepen disconnections from cultural traditions and knowledge.

> **Textbox 15.4 Case study: A macro-system problem**
>
> Vidya is a 13-year-old whose core belief systems (culturally and spiritually) are around ecological conservation and nature worship. Her community values rivers and groves as sacred. Vidya has become distressed after reading about significant loss of forestry in some parts of the world, due to climate change. Natural places considered sacred to Vidya's community should be protected through local and governmental laws and dedicated to cultural purposes. Vidya may benefit from collectively engaging in enhancing the conversation and protection efforts of these sacred places which can, in turn, act as an important climate mitigation strategy.

Protective Influences

Cultural, religious, and ethical belief systems might conversely drive a young person to value, protect and restore the environment. Confucian culture, for example, which teaches "harmony between heaven, earth and man," and treating all living beings in the world with kindness, has been found to predict environmental awareness and pro-environmental behavior in Chinese residents (Zhang et al., 2020). Many communities already draw upon and pass down cultural traditions and knowledge to protect and restore the lands on which they live (e.g., the Skolt Sámi in the European Arctic restoring the Vainosjoki River) (Brattland & Mustonen, 2018). These efforts can help reconnect young people with their culture and land (see Textbox 15.4 for a case study example). Spirituality and faith may also provide strong avenues of support for young people. In the Polynesian nation of Tuvalu, community members reported that faith and support from the community's church helped them to cope with distress (Gibson et al., 2019).

Recommendations and/or Considerations

There is little research investigating how loss of place and culture may mediate climate distress in young people. Given that increased connection to nature is often endorsed as a useful coping strategy, there is a need to consider how unavoidable losses to the environment will impact the well-being of young people long term. Practitioners and communities might consider helping young people to continue their connections to culture and place amidst climate change. The impacts of community responses on young people also points to the importance of providing communities with the resources needed to be able to participate and bring prevention, preparation, and restoration projects to fruition.

Systems Adaptivity and the Chronosystem

As mentioned, systemic influences are bidirectional and implementing interventions at any level can have ripple effects that shape youth mental health. Several authors suggest that identifying "vicious cycles" and moving towards establishing "virtuous" cycles at multisystemic levels is critical to reaching long-term beneficial outcomes for human and planetary health (Tidball et al., 2018). From a social-ecological perspective, cycles relate to how systems create and maintain patterns of behavior through feedback loops. Virtuous cycles are considered feedback loops that positively benefit and reinforce the well-being of systems. Vicious cycles, however, are catalyzed by destruction, neglect, and ill-health (Tidball et al., 2018). In the chrono-system, these cycles strengthen and compound over time (e.g., unmitigated climate change events progressively accumulating versus mitigation and restoration efforts across time). From a systems perspective, there is a need to challenge and adapt existing systems to promote optimal child development and resilience (Doppelt, 2016).

For example, virtuous cycles could be established through pro-environmentally focused programs at school, which feeds benefits back into nature, young people, and teachers. As young people conserve, restore, and protect these natural environments, the benefits for environmental and human health become reinforced and strengthened. Further research may look to developing causal loop diagrams aimed at identifying potential systemic feedback cycles that may be impacting youth mental health. Importantly, taking this multilevel approach considers the complexity of systemic interactions, providing the opportunity to intervene early and potentially prevent negative impacts on young people. Furthermore, identifying areas where virtuous cycles can be established might provide guidance for the development, evaluation, and scaling of interventions that are aimed at supporting the mental health of young people.

Conclusions

This chapter provided an overview of how environments can shape a young person's experiences, as well as their views and emotions towards climate change. Using a systems perspective to understand climate distress in young people points to a range of systemic interventions needed, including for family, peer, community, policy, and at the public health level (see Textbox 15.1 for a case example). These interventions should focus on how best to create environments that allow young people to express and harness their climate distress, connect with others, and engage in tangible activities aimed at mitigating climate change in a way that also supports their mental health. Psychological intervention can then focus on those who most need support due to the most severe climate distress that may result from uncontrollable exacerbating factors at various systems levels.

References

Ballew, M. T., Goldberg, M. H., Rosenthal, S. A., Gustafson, A., & Leiserowitz, A. (2019). Systems thinking as a pathway to global warming beliefs and attitudes through an ecological worldview. *Proceedings of the National Academy of Sciences*, 116(17), 8214–8219. https://doi.org/doi:10.1073/pnas.1819310116

Berchin, I. I., Valduga, I. B., Garcia, J., & de Andrade Guerra, J. B. S. O. (2017). Climate change and forced migrations: An effort towards recognizing climate refugees. *Geoforum*, 84, 147–150. https://doi.org/10.1016/j.geoforum.2017.06.022

Berry, H. L., Waite, T. D., Dear, K. B. G., Capon, A. G., & Murray, V. (2018). The case for systems thinking about climate change and mental health. *Nature Climate Change*, 8(4), 282–290. https://doi.org/10.1038/s41558-018-0102-4

Bowen, M. (1978). *Family therapy in clinical practice*. Jason Aronson.

Brattland, C., & Mustonen, T. (2018). How traditional knowledge comes to matter in Atlantic Salmon Governance in Norway and Finland. *Arctic*, 71(4), 375–392. www.jstor.org/stable/26567068

Bronfenbrenner, U. (1979). *The ecology of human development: Experiments by nature and design*. Harvard University Press. https://books.google.com.au/books?id=OCmbzWka6xUC

Calatrava, M., Martins, M. V., Schweer-Collins, M., Duch-Ceballos, C., & Rodríguez-González, M. (2022). Differentiation of self: A scoping review of Bowen Family Systems Theory's core construct. *Clinical Psychology Review*, 91, 102101. https://doi.org/10.1016/j.cpr.2021.102101

Chawla, L. (2020). Helping students cope with environmental change and take constructive civic action. *Green Schools Catalyst Quarterly*, 7(1), 44–57.

Clayton, S., & Karazsia, B. T. (2020). Development and validation of a measure of climate change anxiety. *Journal of Environmental Psychology*, 69, 101434. https://doi.org/10.1016/j.jenvp.2020.101434

Crandon, T. J., Scott, J. G., Charlson, F. J., & Thomas, H. J. (2022). A social-ecological perspective of climate anxiety in children and adolescents. *Nature Climate Change*, 12, 123–131. https://doi.org/10.1038/s41558-021-01251-y

Cunsolo Willox, A., Harper, S. L., Ford, J. D., Edge, V. L., Landman, K., Houle, K., Blake, S., & Wolfrey, C. (2013). Climate change and mental health: An exploratory case study from Rigolet, Nunatsiavut, Canada. *Climatic Change*, 121(2), 255–270. https://doi.org/10.1007/s10584-013-0875-4

DeMocker, M. (2018). *The parent's guide to climate revolution*. New World Library.

Doppelt, B. (2016). *Transformational resilience: How building human resilience to climate disruption can safeguard society and increase wellbeing*. Routledge.

Gaziulusoy, A. İ. (2020). The experiences of parents raising children in times of climate change: Towards a caring research agenda. *Current Research in Environmental Sustainability*, 2, 100017. https://doi.org/10.1016/j.crsust.2020.100017

Gibson, K., Haslam, N., & Kaplan, I. (2019). Distressing encounters in the context of climate change: Idioms of distress, determinants, and responses to distress in Tuvalu. *Transcult Psychiatry*, 56(4), 667–696. https://doi.org/10.1177/1363461519847057

Gislason, M. K., Kennedy, A. M., & Witham, S. M. (2021). The interplay between social and ecological determinants of mental health for children and youth in the climate crisis. *International Journal of Environmental Research and Public Health*, 18(9), 4573. https://doi.org/10.3390/ijerph18094573

Hickman, C. (2020). We need to (find a way to) talk about … eco-anxiety. *Journal of Social Work Practice*, 34(4), 411–424. https://doi.org/10.1080/02650533.2020.1844166

Hickman, C., Marks, E., Pihkala, P., Clayton, S., Lewandowski, R. E., Mayall, E. E., … van Susteren, L. (2021). Climate anxiety in children and young people and their beliefs about government responses to climate change: A global survey. *The Lancet Planetary Health*, 5(12), E863–E873. https://doi.org/10.1016/S2542-5196(21)00278-3

Ho, L.-C., & Seow, T. (2015). Teaching controversial issues in geography: Climate change education in Singaporean schools. *Theory & Research in Social Education*, 43(3), 314–344. https://doi.org/10.1080/00933104.2015.1064842

Hollis, C., Livingstone, S., & Sonuga Barke, E. (2020). Editorial: The role of digital technology in children and young people's mental health – A triple-edged sword? *Journal of Child Psychology and Psychiatry*, 61(8), 837–841. https://doi.org/10.1111/jcpp.13302

Hunt, P. (2012). Health and well-being: The role of government. *Public Health*, 126, S19–S23. https://doi.org/10.1016/j.puhe.2012.05.017

Keim, M. E. (2008). Building human resilience: The role of public health preparedness and response as an adaptation to climate change. *American Journal of Preventive Medicine*, 35(5), 508–516. https://doi.org/10.1016/j.amepre.2008.08.022

Kessler, R. C., McLaughlin, K. A., Green, J. G., Gruber, M. J., Sampson, N. A., Zaslavsky, A. M., … Williams, D. R. (2010). Childhood adversities and adult psychopathology in the WHO world mental health surveys. *British Journal of Psychiatry*, 197(5), 378–385. https://doi.org/10.1192/bjp.bp.110.080499

Klichowski, M. (2017). *Learning in CyberParks: A theoretical and empirical study*. Adam Mickiewicz University Press. http://hdl.handle.net/10593/21250

Larson, L. R., Szczytko, R., Bowers, E. P., Stephens, L. E., Stevenson, K. T., & Floyd, M. F. (2018). Outdoor time, screen time, and connection to nature: Troubling trends among rural youth? *Environment and Behavior*, 51(8), 966–991. https://doi.org/10.1177/0013916518806686

Ma, T., Moore, J., & Cleary, A. (2022). Climate change impacts on the mental health and wellbeing of young people: A scoping review of risk and protective factors. *Social Science & Medicine*, 301, 114888. https://doi.org/10.1016/j.socscimed.2022.114888

MacKay, M., Parlee, B., & Karsgaard, C. (2020). Youth engagement in climate change action: Case study on Indigenous youth at COP24. *Sustainability*, 12(16), 6299. http://dx.doi.org/10.3390/su12166299

Massazza, A., Joffe, H., Parrott, E., & Brewin, C. R. (2022). Remembering the earthquake: Intrusive memories of disaster in a rural Italian community. *European Journal of Psychotraumatology*, 13(1), 2068909. https://doi.org/10.1080/20008198.2022.2068909

Matsuyama, Y., Aida, J., Hase, A., Sato, Y., Koyama, S., Tsuboya, T., & Osaka, K. (2016). Do community- and individual-level social relationships contribute to the mental health of disaster survivors?: A multilevel prospective study after the Great East Japan Earthquake. *Social Science & Medicine*, 151, 187–195. https://doi.org/10.1016/j.socscimed.2016.01.008

Nomura, Y., Newcorn, J. H., Ginalis, C., Heitz, C., Zaki, J., Khan, F., … Hurd, Y. L. (2022). Prenatal exposure to a natural disaster and early development of psychiatric disorders during the preschool years: Stress in pregnancy study. *Journal of Child Psychology and Psychiatry*, 64(7), 1080–1091. https://doi.org/10.1111/jcpp.13698

Ojala, M. (2011). Hope and climate change: The importance of hope for environmental engagement among young people. *Environmental Education Research*, 18(5), 625–642. https://doi.org/10.1080/13504622.2011.637157

Ojala, M., & Bengtsson, H. (2018). Young people's coping strategies concerning climate change: Relations to perceived communication with parents and friends and proenvironmental behavior. *Environment and Behavior*, 51(8), 907–935. https://doi.org/10.1177/0013916518763894

Oswald, T. K., Rumbold, A. R., Kedzior, S. G. E., & Moore, V. M. (2020). Psychological impacts of "screen time" and "green time" for children and adolescents: A systematic scoping review. *PLoS One*, 15(9), e0237725. https://doi.org/10.1371/journal.pone.0237725

Sanson, A. V., Burke, S. E. L., & Van Hoorn, J. (2018). Climate change: Implications for parents and parenting. *Parenting*, 18(3), 200–217. https://doi.org/10.1080/15295192.2018.1465307

Sanson, A. V., Van Hoorn, J., & Burke, S. E. L. (2019). Responding to the impacts of the climate crisis on children and youth. *Child Development Perspectives*, 13(4), 201–207. https://doi.org/10.1111/cdep.12342

Stevenson, K. T., Peterson, M. N., & Bondell, H. D. (2019). The influence of personal beliefs, friends, and family in building climate change concern among adolescents. *Environmental Education Research*, 25(6), 832–845. https://doi.org/10.1080/13504622.2016.1177712

Taber, F., & Taylor, N. (2009). Climate of concern: A search for effective strategies for teaching children about global warming [Yes]. *International Journal of Environmental and Science Education*, 4(2), 97–116. https://hdl.handle.net/1959.11/4483

Tidball, K. G., Metcalf, S., Bain, M., & Elmqvist, T. (2018). Community-led reforestation: Cultivating the potential of virtuous cycles to confer resilience in disaster disrupted social–ecological systems. *Sustainability Science*, 13(3), 797–813. https://doi.org/10.1007/s11625-017-0506-5

Vergunst, F., & Berry, H. L. (2021). Climate change and children's mental health: A developmental perspective. *Clinical Psychological Science*, 21677026211040787. https://doi.org/10.1177/21677026211040787

Whitchurch, G. G., & Constantine, L. L. (1993). Systems theory. In P. Boss, W. J. Doherty, R. LaRossa, W. R. Schumm, & S. K. Steinmetz (Eds.), *Sourcebook of family theories and methods: A contextual approach* (pp. 325–355). Springer US. https://doi.org/10.1007/978-0-387-85764-0_14

Wise, S. B. (2010). Climate change in the classroom: Patterns, motivations, and barriers to instruction among Colorado science teachers. *Journal of Geoscience Education*, 58(5), 297–309. https://doi.org/10.5408/1.3559695

Wood, L., Hooper, P., Foster, S., & Bull, F. (2017). Public green spaces and positive mental health – investigating the relationship between access, quantity and types of parks and mental wellbeing. *Health & Place*, 48, 63–71. https://doi.org/10.1016/j.healthplace.2017.09.002

Zhang, J., Xie, C., Morrison, A. M., & Zhang, K. (2020). Fostering resident pro-environmental behavior: The roles of destination image and Confucian culture. *Sustainability*, 12(2), 597. www.mdpi.com/2071-1050/12/2/597

CHAPTER 16

Parenting and Grandparenting Our Youth in the Climate Crisis

Judith Van Hoorn, Susie Burke, and Ann Sanson

We, Judith, Susie, and Ann, are all psychologists, parents, activists, and in the case of Judith and Ann, also grandparents. Judith and Ann have worked as developmental psychologists and researchers for many decades. We have studied children's and young people's responses to global crises, and how to support them in home, school, and community contexts. Susie, in her work as a therapist, has worked with many people who have shared stories of climate distress, and their challenges as parents and teachers raising children amidst the threat of climate change. As activists and advocates for climate, we have clocked up many years of climate action between us – campaigning, marching with our children in climate rallies and protests, writing submissions and speaking at Parliamentary inquiries on psychological aspects of the climate crisis. In recent years, we have been writing together about the psychological impacts of climate change on children and young people, and exploring how families are coping (Sanson et al., 2018, 2022).

The Challenges of Parenting in the Climate Crisis

Throughout history and across cultures, parents, grandparents, and others caring for children have tried their best to raise, protect, and prepare their children for adulthood. Today, parents have the unprecedented challenge of supporting their children to survive, cope with, and adapt to the current impacts of the climate crisis while simultaneously preparing them for an uncertain future in which the climate will continue to change rapidly in largely negative ways. At the same time, parents need to cope with their own climate distress. Given the enormity of these challenges, we understand why many of today's parents are anxious and uncertain about how to raise their children and prepare them for what lies ahead.

These tasks are particularly urgent and difficult for the majority of families who live in geographically vulnerable areas already experiencing climate-fueled emergencies such as storms, floods, and fires, or gradual climate changes such as droughts and sea level rise. The Children's Climate Risk Index (CCRI) is UNICEF's (2021) calculation of children's exposure and vulnerability to the impacts of climate change worldwide. Many countries in Africa and Asia have the highest CCRI scores, reflecting that children there are most exposed and vulnerable. This 2021 UNICEF report emphasizes that approximately half the world's children are considered high risk and extremely vulnerable, with about one-third currently exposed to four or more environment-related stressors.

In contrast, the direct impacts of climate change on young people and families in other parts of the world are not yet so noticeable. In these areas, primarily in the Global North, climate change is still largely a future or vicarious threat. Consequently, parents are challenged to help their children cope with the distress of learning about the implications of climate change for the planet and their future lives.

Theoretical Framework

This chapter draws on research and practice relating to the impacts of climate change on youth mental health, and on parenting research and practice. Climate change and youth mental health is an emerging field that involves health and mental health professionals, social scientists, climate scientists, and groups of citizens including parents and young people themselves. Similarly, parenting science is a multidisciplinary specialization drawing from psychology, medicine, social work, and related disciplines. Recognizing differences across cultures, we use the term "parents" in a broad sense to include all who take primary responsibility for raising children, and use more specific terms such as grandparents, carers, and adult relatives when appropriate.

Adults in different cultures have varied expectations of children and young people. The roles and responsibilities of parents, grandparents, and other carers differ as well. However, a universal parental responsibility is to try to ensure children's survival and well-being.

The existing literature in the field of parenting through the climate crisis is limited in two ways: (1) the great majority of research and writing focuses on young people and parents/grandparents in the Global North, whereas families most impacted by climate change typically live in the Global South; (2) there is very little research on the efficacy of different parenting approaches regarding the climate crisis. Consequently, this chapter draws on the relatively small number of studies of parenting and family responses in disaster situations related to climate change as well as clinical insights and generalizations from effective parenting practices in other difficult situations.

To discuss the developing person, we employ two frameworks we view as complementary. First, the *whole child framework* emphasizes the interrelationships of all domains of individual development, including emotional, cognitive, language, social, and physical development. Second, Bronfenbrenner's (2006) *bioecological framework* considers developing persons within their social and historical context over time.

Throughout this chapter, we discuss the great variations in individuals' experiences of the climate crisis depending on where they live and the climate-related disasters they have already experienced. We also consider the resources available in their family, community, and country to protect them or help them recover from climate impacts. A recurrent theme is that climate change exacerbates current and future social inequalities.

Helping Young People Cope with the Direct Impacts of the Climate Crisis

We begin this section by examining how parents help their children cope with the direct impacts of climate change, starting with sudden extreme weather events (EWEs) such as hurricanes/cyclones, floods, heatwaves, and wildfires that are occurring with increasing frequency and intensity around the globe, particularly in the Global South (UNICEF, 2021). Next, we turn to how parents can help their children cope with more gradual impacts of climate change measured in years and decades, such as droughts and rising sea levels. Throughout, we discuss the indirect or *flow-on* effects of climate change. For example, droughts result in loss of crops, which can lead to famine and deaths, force families to migrate and navigate significant post-migration stressors, and lead to conflicts over diminishing resources.

Additionally, specific demographics place some young people at higher risk from the impacts of climate change, thus increasing the need for parents to keep them safe and healthy. These include young people with disabilities, those with mental health or behavioral problems, young people from low-income families, Indigenous youth, and pregnant young women (Sanson et al., 2022). Clearly, parents may be at higher risk themselves if they are pregnant, disabled, or elderly. In these situations, young people often have added family responsibilities.

Sudden Direct Impacts

Research and reports on EWEs from the past few decades have found high levels of PTSD and other mental health sequelae in parents, caregivers, and young people (Byrant et al., 2021), as well as negative impacts on family relationships and parenting following climate disasters (Kosta et al., 2021). Although it is well established that children's capacity to cope with disasters is strongly influenced by their parents' coping and support, recent research has taken a broader perspective and emphasizes the importance of mutual support among family members as well as friends, schools, and the larger community (Gipps et al., 2015).

Given sufficient warning about a pending disaster, parents can model support and coping before the disaster occurs. Parents can involve their children of all ages in emergency preparedness, discussing family emergency plans, and giving them tasks that they can help with – for example, packing backpacks with cherished items for emergency evacuation. Parents can also encourage emotional expression and coping by helping children think about the sorts of feelings and thoughts they may have during the event, and how they might manage these reactions. Australian young people (aged 10–24) interviewed about disasters did not think that they were well-prepared for disasters in an increasingly unsafe world and wanted to know how to plan, prepare, and protect themselves and their communities (Australian Institute for Disaster Resilience, 2020).

Parents can also use a range of strategies to help their children manage anxieties throughout and after emergencies such as fires, floods, or hurricanes (Sanson et al., 2018). For example, parents can encourage them to notice and name uncomfortable feelings (e.g., fear), identify bodily cues that they are feeling anxious (e.g., sweating or shivering), use relaxation techniques (e.g., progressive muscle relaxation exercises), and manage anxious self-talk. Parents are also encouraged to model their own effective coping skills (even – and particularly – when distressed), seek social support, and reestablish children's routines as quickly as possible (APS, 2016), and to make time for positive activities that family members enjoy together or as individuals (Berkowitz et al., 2010).

Parents can also help their school-aged children become involved in useful activities during and after disasters, which can play a powerful part in helping young people cope. Having jobs to do can help children calm down, focus, and develop a sense of agency (e.g., a 10-year-old evacuated to a shelter could help bring snacks to younger children).

With adolescents and young adults, parents can support a broader range of active involvement. For example, in the aftermath of a major Californian fire, Judith's 16-year-old grandson volunteered for more than 12 hours daily at the local shelter, helping families, setting up cots, preparing food, and distributing clothes. He explained that he needed to feel useful at a time when "*my world and the world of my friends is burning.*"

The disaster research also emphasizes the importance of cultivating hope (Hobfoll et al., 2007). Hope increases when parents talk about some of the positive aspects arising from distressing or tragic events; for example, noticing increased prosocial behavior such as neighborly and community kindness and helpfulness in the wake of the disaster, having increased appreciation for family and friends, and planning helpful things to do for others so children feel they can make a positive difference (APS, 2016).

In the wake of disasters, families face different situations with varied flow-on effects. In better scenarios, parents and children soon return to their homes, schools, and jobs, and resume lives that seem fairly unchanged, although mental health issues may be longer lasting.

However, as disasters become more frequent and ferocious due to climate change, they create greater destruction in more communities. For instance, in 2022, Hurricane Ian created chaos in Cuba, Puerto Rico, and Florida, destroying homes, schools, and businesses, and overwhelming medical services. After such disasters, family members may be injured, unable to work, or lose employment, and families with fewer resources can lose access to housing. In worst-case scenarios, family members are killed, badly injured, or missing, and many families are forced to move, seeking refuge with relatives or migrating elsewhere. In these life-altering situations, parents and older family members can prioritize finding ways to calm themselves and others; seek support and assistance from others in the community including available health and service agencies in order to be able to care for their children; and, in the case of death of family, friends, and community members, help young people deal with grief and loss using their own cultural customs and rituals.

Finally, we also need to address the devastating scenario in which parents face the possibility that they and their families will not survive an unfolding, catastrophic weather event. Despite death being the inevitable end for every human on the planet, and the enormous numbers of lives already lost in climate-related disasters, it is rare to find advice for parents on how to support their children in this tragic situation. We turn to the literature on basic human needs – to be safe, content, and loved – for help in formulating this advice for parents and families, although of course every situation will be different. Where possible, draw on comforting family, cultural, or religious rituals, such as singing or praying. Do what you can to protect them from pain and fear. Dependent on age and circumstances, engage them in caring for others. But perhaps the most potent way to try to meet children's core needs in such critical times is simply through our reassuring presence – by cuddling and touching, using a soothing tone, loving words, and warm eye contact. We are better able to do this for our children if we can manage our own fear and panic. Of course, this sounds extraordinarily difficult, but parents' instincts to protect and nurture their children are powerful motivators. Breathe out slowly, hold your family close, tell them you love them.

Gradual Direct Impacts

Worldwide, parents try to protect their children from the more gradual impacts of climate change including increased precipitation, protracted droughts, rising sea levels, and loss of habitat. This is especially challenging in the African and Asian countries where children's risk is highest (UNICEF, 2021).

More than two-thirds of the world's population live in global monsoon regions. Many rely on monsoonal rainfall to sustain agriculture, industrial, and domestic water demands. Historically, monsoonal precipitation has led to floods, but climate-fueled changes, including longer monsoon seasons and increased precipitation, are leading to more severe and widespread floods, affecting millions (Fountain et al., 2022).

Protracted droughts are affecting each continent. In the Horn of Africa, for example, entire communities have been forced to flee in search of water and food for themselves and their livestock, often moving to refugee camps. Many families face life-threatening flow-on effects of the drought such as malnutrition, starvation, and disease, and loss of education with lifetime disadvantages. Droughts in wealthy nations with substantial resources can also have serious impacts on families that increase and perpetuate social inequalities.

Rising sea levels threaten families around the world. Most people threatened by sea-level rise live in low- and middle-income countries in Asia and the Pacific. The Small Island Developing States in Oceania (including the Solomon Islands, the Maldives, Kiribati, Samoa, Nauru, the Fiji Islands, Tuvalu, and Vanuatu) have lost land and some risk completely disappearing. Although low-lying coastal areas comprise only 2 percent of the world's landmass, eight of ten of the world's largest cities are near a coast where sea-level rise is leading to flooding, shoreline erosion, and hazards from storms (Lindsay, 2022).

Globally, many Indigenous people live in coastal communities. Climate change threatens the ecosystems they revere and depend upon, their cultural traditions, beliefs, and livelihoods passed down from generation to generation, and even the viability of continuing to live in their communities. Parents face many cultural and personal challenges in reestablishing family lives away from their homeland. Newtok, an Indigenous village in Alaska, is the first US community facing total relocation.

These direct gradual impacts of climate change confront families with the loss of their homes, fields, and livestock, leading to malnutrition and disease, loss of education, and often increased risk of violence. Frequently, climate-amplified impacts result in the family's loss of livelihoods, forcing them to move. For many in low- and middle-income countries, this may mean moving to Internally Displaced Persons (IDP) camps.

The suggestions in Textbox 16.1 are drawn from NGO resources and observations of programs to support the well-being of children and young people in refugee and IDP camps (David Morley, C.M., president and chief executive officer, UNICEF Canada, personal communication. December 12, 2022).

Textbox 16.1 Moving to refugee camps: Suggestions for parents

PLANNING TO MOVE
- When possible, increase physical and emotional support by planning to move in a group with others from family, community, or ethnic groups.
- Assess resources and risks, and learn from the experiences of others.
- Plan as a family or review plans with children.
  o Discuss what to take (pots, money, objects for barter, etc.).
  o Emphasize the invisible family and cultural resources that help keep your family strong, for example, rituals, favorite traditional songs, stories, sayings and tales from elders, family memories.
  o Anticipate challenges and responsibilities such as how to ensure that family members remain together, stay safe, and receive needed assistance.

TRAVELING TO REFUGEE CAMPS
- Travel in larger groups for greater protection.
- Try to maintain daily routines and rituals, for example, who takes care of whom and when; rituals for sleeping and waking (e.g., favorite songs and stories).

> - Try to keep yourself and others calm. Be aware that the long journey, combined with hunger and thirst, may lead to anger and discord.
>
> TRANSITIONS TO LIFE IN REFUGEE AND IDP CAMPS
>
> - If possible, find others you know and trust.
> - Learn about critical services: places and times for water and food distribution, medical services, and help from Camp Management and agencies such as the UNHCR.
> - Adapt to the rhythm of the camp.
> - Learn about possible dangers such as roving animals, violence, gangs and drug issues.
> - Consider participating in services for your children and adult family members, for example, supervised play spaces for young children, schools and recreation for school-aged children and adolescents, and programs for adults arranged by Camp Management or community groups.
> - Find continuity, comfort, and strength in family and cultural rituals and traditions that enrich your family.

Helping Young People Cope with Vicarious Impacts of the Climate Crisis

Not all children and young people have yet been directly affected by the climate crisis; however, most young people globally – whatever their experience – are aware of the threat it poses, and many express high levels of distress and concern (Hickman et al., 2021). In the following sections we explore what parents everywhere can do to support their children's coping with the knowledge that climate change will bring massive changes to their lives and to the planet.

Promoting Nature Connections

There is consensus in the literature on the importance of young people developing a deep connection to nature, both for their own well-being and the preservation of the biosphere. Chawla (2020) emphasizes the key role parents have in promoting their children's feelings of connection to nature that can endure throughout their lives. These feelings include comfort, confidence, enjoyment, exploration, challenge, and achievement. Parents foster their children's empathy for living things by giving them opportunities and time to freely explore nature at their own pace and by promoting environmental citizenship behaviors in their families. For instance, parents and their children can notice elements of their natural world such as the weather and changing seasons, flowers, birds, and butterflies. They can learn how to protect and care for plants and animals and, when older, participate in group activities to restore and protect natural habitats.

Studies suggest that promoting and honoring intergenerational relationships can promote young people's care for the environment. In their research in Mexico, Trujillo and Vázquez (2019) explored relationships between sustainable conduct and intergenerational relationships. They found that young people learn traditional knowledge from grandparents and other elders about caring for and protecting their land, thus contributing to global sustainability efforts. Van Hoorn (2021) describes the many ways that grandparents can build children's love of nature through playful interactions.

Talking with Children at Different Developmental Levels about Climate Change

Advice to parents on helping their children cope with the climate crisis often begins with how to talk with children about climate change. Of course, how to do this varies according to the child's age, personality, and developmental level. Family and community experiences are important considerations, especially for those who have already experienced dire climate-related impacts.

Conversations with children can begin with helping them build connections with nature. Parents and grandparents can use the "how" and "why" questions children ask (e.g., "why are the flowers dying?") to begin conversations about climate change. They can then give simple explanations of key climate concepts; for example, "Our planet is getting too warm because we're not treating it right," and comparing carbon dioxide to a cozy blanket which used to keep us at the right temperature. "Now there is too much carbon dioxide and, like too many blankets, it's making the planet too hot." (See Sanson et al., 2022 for further discussion.) Talking with children of all ages should involve conversations about solutions and ideas for actions to protect the planet. Books such as *Coco's Fire: Changing Climate Anxiety into Climate Action* model these conversations for younger children (Wortzel et al., 2022).

Some parents express concerns about talking with children about climate change and try to shield them from gaining knowledge about it (Global Action Plan UK & Unilever, 2021). However, research suggests that most children and adolescents already know and are worried about climate change. And, as stated in the United Nations Convention on the

Rights of the Child (1989), children have a right to learn about issues such as climate change that affect their future and be involved in addressing it. Susan Clayton, an environmental psychologist, points out that trying to conceal the truth about the climate crisis can generate fear, harm a child's ability to trust their parents, and skew their objectivity about the climate crisis (Akpan, 2019).

From about age 9, children begin to take a more global perspective, comprehend cause-and-effect relationships, and understand a timeline with interconnecting past, present, and future events. They can understand simple explanations of the science of climate change, such as the role of greenhouse gasses and ocean acidification, and the reasons why species in their local environment are stressed by the changing climate. By asking what their child is learning about climate change in school, from friends, and in the media, parents have opportunities to expand the depth of discussions and correct children's misperceptions (APS, 2018a). Parents and children can research answers to their questions together as a supportive way to learn about climate change.

Conversations with adolescents can involve more complicated questions and concepts. Parents should take care not to minimize the problem, which risks invalidating their deep concerns. Advice in a tip sheet by ReachOut Australia (2022) reminds parents that no one benefits when adolescents keep their worries to themselves. Parents need to be careful not to glibly promise that everything will be fine or that "silver bullet" technological solutions will be the answer, as these types of responses can feel invalidating. Young people who are aware of the scale of the climate crisis know that addressing it requires enormous changes at every level of society. When the adults around them seem to be relying on fantasizing or denial to cope with this reality, adolescents may feel even more helpless, hopeless, or uneasy that they're being lied to (Eklund & Nylen, 2021). Parents can also model good media literacy practices such as not following every link that pops up on a search, which risks young people feeling overwhelmed with information, some of which may be inaccurate.

Parents and grandparents can enter into mutually respectful conversations with older adolescents and young adults with the awareness that their children might know more than they know about climate change, and might be disappointed, angry, and/or cynical about the lack of action on the part of parents and other adults. In these conversations, parents might take on a listening role or discuss news relating to climate change and articles that they've found helpful (Hickman et al., 2021).

Talking with adolescents and young adults also involves discussions about who is responsible for solving the problem, especially for families living in higher income countries that produce higher percentages of greenhouse gases and therefore have greater responsibility for taking action *right now*. This can lead to supportive brainstorming about what people in their own country can do. Of course, it is important for parents to emphasize that adults have the responsibility to act now, and not pin all their hopes on young people.

Helping Children and Young People Cope with Climate Emotions

Emotional regulation and emotion-focused coping are terms psychologists and educators use to talk about how people try to cope with upsetting feelings. Emotional regulation refers to people's ability to effectively manage and respond to an emotional experience and includes calming yourself down when upset or picking your mood up when you are feeling down. Emotion-focused coping refers to the strategies we use to cope with upsetting feelings.

Strategies that parents, grandparents, and other carers can use to help young people with emotion-focused coping with the climate crisis include:

- Helping their children put words to their feelings.
- Acknowledging and validating children's feelings, letting them know that their emotions are normal and manageable – for example, "I can understand why you are angry with adults for failing to act sooner."
- Encouraging young people to brainstorm things they can do to manage challenging emotions, such as listening to uplifting or calming music, soothing themselves by cuddling a pet, expressing feelings through art, spending time in nature, being physically active, or seeking support from parents and other family and friends (e.g., talking with them or getting a hug).
- Letting your children know they can always come to you, even when it seems as if you are stressed out.
- Sharing your own feelings about environmental threats with your older children, thereby demonstrating that "it's okay to not be okay" and that you trust and respect them enough to reveal some of your vulnerability.
- Showing your children how you care for yourself emotionally (e.g., trying to go to bed earlier, regularly talking with close friends).

(For further ideas see APS, 2018b; and ReachOut Australia, 2022.)

Parents' Dealing with Their Own Feelings about the Climate Crisis

Many guides written to help parents talk with children about difficult issues such as the climate crisis address the importance of parents being able to process their own painful feelings about the crisis first, to prepare for difficult conversations with their children and make space for children's own feelings. The *Our Kids Climate* tip sheet advises parents to let themselves "feel the science" to show that they understand the severity of the situation (Shinn, 2019).

However, dealing with one's own feelings about the climate crisis can be hard (Wiseman, 2021; Australian Psychological Society, 2017). Therefore, parents need to proactively acknowledge and manage their painful feelings about the climate crisis, talk with other adults, and overcome "the conspiracy of silence." Many groups are forming to help people deal with climate distress (e.g., Moms Clean Air Force).

Cultivating Hope

There is a growing literature about the importance of building hope in the climate crisis (e.g., Stoknes, 2015; Wiseman, 2021). While mostly written for adults, understanding how children and young people can build and maintain hope in the face of survival threats is an increasing focus (e.g., Chawla, 2020; Ojala, 2012). One model, Active Hope, involves three steps: (1) taking a clear view of reality; (2) identifying a direction to move toward; and (3) taking concrete steps to change things (Macy & Johnstone, 2012).

Based on research from Ojala (2012) and a review by Chawla (2020), the following meaning-focused coping strategies (i.e., ways of thinking differently about a problem) can help children to cultivate hope:

- Putting trust in the actions of others (e.g., scientists, politicians) who are working on solutions
- Looking at how other complex problems have been solved throughout history
- Thinking about the positives of climate action
- Coming together with other young people to share concerns
- Working on shared projects, sometimes with adult activists and scientists, and being supported by adults in their ideas and projects, including personally relevant local issues.

Drawing on research about young people and the importance of hope in the face of climate change, writers and mental health providers advise parents to use the following cognitive strategies to build their children's hope:

- Point out that it is not a "done deal," and the world isn't doomed
- Emphasize that there is still time to avoid some of the worst possible outcomes through actions to reduce emissions and protect the environment
- Draw attention to the millions of people working on solutions around the world
- Explain that it will never be time to give up, that a difference can always be made.

(See other examples in APS, 2018a, 2018b; Eklund & Nylen, 2021.)

Helping to Build Young People's Agency and Efficacy
Another aspect of cultivating hope is building young people's belief that they can make a difference and take action in response to the climate crisis (Burke et al., 2018). Young people can become anxious when they are aware of a danger but feel that they don't have ideas or competencies to deal with it. Agency refers to one's personal capacity and ability to take action. Efficacy refers to the belief that one is competent to create change. When parents engage with their children's concerns about environmental issues, encourage them to explore ways to take action on the problems that distress them, and respond in solution-oriented and supportive ways, they can help build their children's sense of agency and efficacy (Ojala & Bengtsson, 2019) as well as overall self-esteem. Taking action is an example of doing something about the problem causing the stress (problem-focused coping). Parents can show their children how solutions at different levels (individual, group, and societal) are all important to reach the ultimate solution of whole-scale system change. Parents can help their children to think about what actions give "best bang for one's buck." In general, people are *not* particularly good at identifying what behaviors are most effective for addressing climate change, so discussing and researching the relative impacts of different actions in reducing greenhouse gases is valuable. These processes also teach scientific methodology and create space for processing related emotions.

A Global Action Plan study of 916 parents and children from the UK and Turkey (Global Action Plan UK & Unilever, 2021) found that the majority of parents see the benefits of teaching their children to take action as a way of empowering them to feel that they can make a difference (78 percent), get involved in issues they care about (76 percent), and speak up about their concerns (74 percent). However, fewer parents actually put this into practice, citing concerns about wanting to protect their children from world issues and not putting pressure on them. Parents' inability to translate intention into action is a dangerous gap that needs to be urgently addressed. When young people are already worried, parents' avoidance of the topic exacerbates the problem and creates further anxiety. The researchers found that young people want their parents to take action with them, as illustrated by Ellen, an adolescent: "Go with them and protest with them. See what goes on and then go from there" (Global Action Plan UK & Unilever, 2021, p. 34).

An important caveat is that parents should be mindful of not rushing straight from identification of the problem to acting on solutions. It is important for parents to give their children time to reflect – to make room for the feelings brought up by the climate crisis. Often this requires parents to expand their own capacity to handle the uncomfortable feelings of watching their children struggling with uncomfortable feelings.

Promoting Environmental Values

Values are beliefs about what is important to us in life. Studies show that parents and grandparents play a pivotal role in shaping their children's pro-environmental attitudes, behaviors, and orientations throughout childhood and adolescence (Matthies & Wallis, 2015). Parents can transmit pro-environmental attitudes and behaviors by modeling behaviors such as recycling and using public transport (and explaining why they are doing it), by praising children when they practice pro-environmental behaviors, and by speaking openly about caring for other people and the environment and why this is important to them. These conversations nurture young people's own compassionate values (Knafo & Schwartz, 2003). Furthermore, when parents ask their children about what is important to them, the children feel they have freely chosen their values rather than having them imposed upon them and are more likely to internalize these values and take them into adulthood (Barni et al., 2011).

Modeling: Parents in Action

As Eklund and Nylén (2021) argue, because adults have created the crisis, adults must lead the way in resolving it. It is equally critical to demonstrate to young people that they are not being asked to take on the whole burden for action on climate change themselves (Sanson & Bellemo, 2021).

As noted in ourkidsclimate.org:

> It's extra important to show children who are worried about the climate crisis that we are willing to pull our weight. Keep in mind that many children who learn about climate change in school can become frustrated with family behaviors that are contrary to what they learn, for instance driving fossil fuel cars, flying or eating a lot of meat. Show that you as an adult are ready to compromise and discuss how you can best make changes together (Eklund & Nylen, 2021).

Researchers in the Global Action Plan study argued that parents need to take action because children perceive adults' lack of engagement as a lack of concern. Similarly, in their study of 10,000 youth, Hickman et al. (2021) found that 85 percent of respondents believed that adults have failed to care for the planet. By taking action, parents help children and young people believe that the adults around them do care and are actually "doing something," which can build young people's sense of optimism and well-being, as well as help to foster their own compassionate values and their confidence and motivation to act themselves (Global Action Plan UK & Unilever, 2021).

To equip themselves for these tasks, parents need to educate themselves about the climate threat. Importantly, they also overcome the many psychological barriers in the way of engaging with climate change. Many social scientists have studied the psychological factors that contribute to avoidance, minimization, and denial, and being aware of these factors is an important part of overcoming them. (See the *Climate Change Empowerment Handbook* [APS, 2017] for a summary of some of this research and eight strategies to help people deal with social and psychological barriers to climate action.)

Joy, Fun, and Being in the Present Moment

Finally, but importantly, parents can help children, adolescents, and young adults to remember the importance of having fun together, feeling joyful, and being in the present moment. Everyday and special opportunities abound, whether it's joining in a favorite game, singing songs, playing catch in a neighborhood park, or celebrating a birthday with friends. This lesson was brought home to Susie, who took a break from writing this chapter to attend a public music camp with her teenage daughter and their friends, most of whom have been at the forefront of the school strike climate movement in Australia. For three days they camped, far from mobile phone reception, in a misty, forested valley, where the hills rang with the sound of their violins, guitars, ukuleles, saxophones, songs, bird calls, and laughter. The joy, connection, and optimism that they fostered among themselves lingers long after the camp ends. The adolescents and parents returned home refreshed for the final school term and the start of the students' final exams, and felt renewed energy for their ongoing climate action.

Conclusion

Parents are facing an unprecedented situation: they are tasked with managing their own concerns for their children's (and their own) future while simultaneously supporting their children both to cope in the here-and-now and to develop the capabilities to cope in an uncertain, but likely difficult, future. Awareness that urgent climate action at a global scale is needed to save future generations from a catastrophic future adds an extra dimension to the complexity of parenting.

Climate change is a threat to the well-being of families and children everywhere. The specific challenges differ greatly according to contextual, familial, and individual child characteristics; however, some general parenting strategies, drawn from theory and research on child development, parenting and mental health, and disaster research apply across direct sudden climate changes and more gradual changes:

- Attend to basic needs of food, health, shelter, safety
- Communicate in age-appropriate ways
- Restore everyday routines as quickly as possible
- Engage children in helpful activities
- Soothe, reassure, and foster children's hope for the future
- Promote social support.

Whether families are currently facing climate effects or not, parents everywhere can help their children manage the wide gamut of emotions that knowledge of climate change can engender. Here, themes of emotional regulation, community connectedness, building a sense of efficacy and agency, action, and cultivating active hope are central.

At the start of this chapter, we emphasized that the literature in the field of parenting in the climate crisis is limited. There are critical gaps in our understanding. We encourage researchers and practitioners to take up the challenge of filling these gaps in culturally appropriate ways, including:

- How parents can help children cope with impacts that may continue through their adulthood

- Models of family support in low- and middle-income countries
- Models for families living in wealthier countries
- Development and evaluations of parenting programs and services
- Develop culturally based parenting advice from NGOs and researchers for families in refugee camps
- Investigations of the many ways in which systems beyond the family affect parents' ability to support their children, for example schools, communities, health systems, social welfare systems, overall infrastructure, cultural values and attitudes, and political systems.

A central theme that emerges from this review is that climate change contributes to the perpetuation and exacerbation of social and economic inequalities and prevents many children from reaching their full potential (Sanson et al., 2022). A second theme is the crucial importance of parental modeling – not only modeling effective coping, pro-environmental values and behavior in their family lives, but also engaging in their own climate action.

Change is always difficult, but standing by and drifting towards a catastrophic future for our children because we are afraid of change is worse. This means that we, whether as practitioners, researchers, parents, grandparents, or carers, need to act as citizens and engage with political decision-making processes. We end by encouraging all of us to take action in our personal, professional, and community lives because it's the right thing to do, and "standing by" is unacceptable.

We are in a difficult place in time, but we are here together. To keep facing the tough truths and to sustain our motivation requires attention to our inner and outer world. As John Wiseman (2021) writes:

> Awareness and understanding of the fragile impermanence of our dew drop world is also a constant reminder of our shared responsibility to keep paying attention; to keep turning up; to hold the line and to keep nurturing and sustaining relationships and practices of kindness and compassion; justice, love and care. (p. 230)

References

Akpan, N. (2019). How to talk to your kids about climate change. [Radio broadcast] *PBS*, September 30. www.pbs.org/newshour/science/how-to-talk-to-your-kids-about-climate change

Australian Institute for Disaster Resilience (2020). Our world, our say: National Survey of Children and Young People on Climate Change and Disaster Risk. www.aidr.org.au/media/7946/ourworldoursay-youth-survey-report-2020.pdf

Australian Psychological Society (2016). Tips for talking with and helping children and young people cope after tragic events: Guidelines for parents, caregivers and teachers. https://psychology.org.au/getmedia/a61fcf9d-dc4c-40f3-b94d-65995c85995b/helping-children-affected-tragic-events.pdf

Australian Psychological Society (2017). The climate change empowerment handbook: Psychological strategies to tackle climate change. https://psychology.org.au/getmedia/88ee1716-2604-44ce-b87a-ca0408dfaa12/climate-change-empowerment-handbook.pdf

Australian Psychological Society (2018a). A guide for parents about the climate crisis. https://psychology.org.au/getmedia/f7d0974d-4424-4d60-a7eb-cfa0431b6860/parents-guide-climate-crisis.pdf

Australian Psychological Society (2018b). Raising children to thrive in a climate changed world. https://psychology.org.au/getmedia/e8cda6ca-ecfe-42c7-8538-492950bac8ba/raising-children-climate.pdf

Barni, D., Ranieri, S., Scabini, E., & Rosnati, R. (2011). Value transmission in the family: Do adolescents accept the values their parents want to transmit? *Journal of Moral Education*, 40(1), 105–121. https://doi.org/10.1080/03057240.2011.553797

Berkowitz, S., Bryant, R., Brymer, M., Hamblen, J., Jacobs, A., Layne, C., … & Watson, P. (2010). *Skills for psychological recovery: Field operations guide*. National Center for PTSD and National Child Traumatic Stress Network.

Bronfenbrenner, U., & Morris, P. (2006). The bioecological model of human development. In W. Damon & R. M. Lerner (Series Eds.) & R. M. Lerner (Vol. Ed.), *Handbook of child psychology: Vol. 1. Theoretical models of human development* (6th ed., pp. 793–828). Wiley. https://doi.org/10.1002/9780470147658.chpsy0114

Bryant, R. A., Gibbs, L., Gallagher, H. C., Pattison, P., Lusher, D., MacDougall, C., … & O'Donnell, M. (2021). The dynamic course of psychological outcomes following the Victorian Black Saturday bushfires. *Australian and New Zealand Journal of Psychiatry*, 55, 666–677. http://dx.doi.org/10.1177/0004867420969815

Burke, S. E. L., Sanson, A. V., & Van Hoorn, J. (2018). The psychological effects of climate change on children. *Current Psychiatry Reports*, 20(5), 1–8. https://doi.org/10.1007/s11920-018-0896-9

Chawla, L. (2020). Childhood nature connection and constructive hope: A review of research on connecting with nature and coping with environmental loss. *People and Nature*, 2(3), 619–642. https://doi.org/10.1002/pan3.10128

Eklund, F., & Nylén, K. (2021). Talk to children about the climate crisis: A guide for parents and other adults. ourkidsclimate.org. https://media.ourkidsclimate.org/2021/06/Talk-about-climate-guide-for-parents-2021-06-01.pdf

Fountain, H., Khandelwal, S., Levitt, Z., & White, J. (2022). The South Asia monsoon is becoming more extreme. *New York Times*, October 4. www.nytimes.com/interactive/2022/10/04/climate/south-asia-monsoon-climate-change.html

Gibbs, L., Block, K., Harms, L., MacDougall, C., Snowdon, E., Ireton, G., … & Waters, E. (2015). Children and young people's wellbeing post-disaster: Safety and stability are critical. *International Journal of Disaster Risk Reduction*, 14(2), 195–201. https://doi.org/10.1016/j.ijdrr.2015.06.0060

Global Action Plan UK and Unilever (2021). *Generation action: How to unleash the potential of children and young people to take positive action and create a better world for all*. Global Action Plan UK. https://doi.org/10.1016/S2542-5196(21)00278-3

Hickman, C., Marks, E., Pihkala, P., Clayton, S., Lewandowski, E. R., Mayall, E. E., ... & van Susteren, L. (2021). Young people's voices on climate anxiety, government betrayal and moral injury: A global phenomenon. *The Lancet Planetary Health*, 5(12), e863–e873. https://doi.org/10.1016/S2542-5196(21)00278-3

Hobfoll, S. E., Watson P., Bell, C. C., Bryant, R. A., Brymer, M. J, Friedman, M. J., ... & Ursano, R. J. (2007). Five essential elements of immediate and mid-term mass trauma intervention: Empirical evidence. *Psychiatry*, 70(4), 283–315; discussion 316–369. https://doi:10.1521/psyc.2007.70.4.283

Knafo, A., & Schwartz, S. H. (2003). Parenting and adolescents' accuracy in perceiving parental values. *Child Development*, 74(2), 595–611. https://doi.org/10.1111/1467-8624.7402018

Kosta, L., Harms, L., Gibbs, L., & Rose, D. (2021). Being a parent after a disaster: The new normal after the 2009 Victorian Black Saturday bushfires. *The British Journal of Social Work*, 51(5), 1759–1778.

Lindsay, R. (2022). Climate change: Global sea level. *NOAA Climate.gov*, April 19. www.climate.gov/news-features/understanding-climate/climate-change-global-sea-level

Macy, J., & Johnstone, C. (2012). *Active hope: How to face the mess we're in without going crazy*. New World Library. https://ebookcentral.proquest.com/lib/gbv/detail.action?docID=5840728

Matthies, E., & Wallis, H. (2015). Family socialization and sustainable consumption. In L. A. Reisch & J. Thørgersen (Eds.) *Handbook of research on sustainable consumption* (pp. 268–284). Edward Elgar. https://doi.org/:10.4337/9781783471270.00028

Ojala, M. (2012). Regulating worry, promoting hope: How do children, adolescents, and young adults cope with climate change? *International Journal of Environmental and Science Education*, 7(4), 537–561.

Ojala, M., & Bengtsson, H. (2019). Young people's coping strategies concerning climate change: Relations to perceived communication with parents and friends and proenvironmental behavior. *Environment and Behavior*, 51(8), 907–935. https://doi.org/10.1177/0013916518763894

ReachOut Australia (2022). Talking to your teenager about the drought. https://parents.au.reachout.com/common-concerns/coping-with-the-drought/talking-to-your-teenager-about-the-drought

Sanson, A. V., & Bellemo, M. (2021). Children and youth in the climate crisis. *BJPsych Bulletin*, 45(4), 205–209. https://doi.org/10.1192/bjb.2021.16

Sanson, A. V., Burke, S. E. L., & Van Hoorn, J. (2018). Climate change: Implications for parents and parenting. *Parenting*, 18(3), 200–217. https://doi.org/10.1080/15295192.2018.1465307

Sanson, A. V., Malca, K., Van Hoorn, J., & Burke, S. (2022). *Children and climate change* (Elements in Child Development). Cambridge University Press. https://doi.org/10.1017/9781009118705

Shinn, L. (2019). *Your guide to talking with kids of all ages about climate change.* National Resources Defense Council. www.nrdc.org/stories/your-guide-talking-kids-all-ages-about-climate-change

Stoknes, P. E. (2015). *What we think about when we try not to think about global warming: Toward a new psychology of climate action.* Chelsea Green Publishing.

Trujillo, E. P., & Vázquez, E. L. (2019). La conducta sustentable: un enfoque intergeneracional. *Revista Digital Universitaria,* 20(1).

United Nations (1989). Convention on the rights of the child. *United Nations Treaty Series,* 1577(3). www.ohchr.org/en/instruments-mechanisms/instruments/convention-rights-child

United Nations Children's Fund (2021). The climate crisis is a child rights crisis. Introducing the Children's Climate Risk Index. www.unicef.org/reports/climate-crisis-child-rights-crisis

Van Hoorn, J. (2021). *The gift of play: How grandparents enhance the lives of young children.* Judith Van Hoorn.

Wiseman, J. (2021). *Hope and courage in the climate crisis: Wisdom and action in the long emergency.* Palgrave Macmillan.

Wortzel, J. D., Champlin, L. K., Wortzel, J. R., Lewis, J., Haase, E., & Mark, B. (2022). Reframing climate change: Using children's literature as a residency training tool to address climate anxiety and model innovation. *Academic Psychiatry,* 46, 584–585. https://doi.org/10.1007/s40596-022-01651-y

CHAPTER 17

Perspectives on Addressing Young People's Climate Distress in Education

Matt Carmichael

Our schooling isn't preparing us for our climate future. The gravity of what awaits us is hidden from us, not to protect us but to deny us the opportunity to question why we're being educated in this way in the first place. School should not simply be about "study, do your exams, and pass." It should give us the tools and information to make decisions about *our* future.

Vanessa Nakate, Ugandan climate justice activist (italics hers)

So I tell you this not to scare you,
But to prepare you, to dare you
To dream a different reality

it is our hope that implores us, at our uncompromising core,
To keep rising up for an earth more than worth fighting for.

US National Youth Poet Laureate, Amanda Gorman

Introduction

I recently attended a "teach the teacher" event held in Manchester, England in which a panel of young people explained climate change to an audience of teachers. Of the educators in the audience, one geography teacher was already well informed, but most had never received any training and knew only what they'd gleaned from media and friends. Many had basic misunderstandings. An art teacher was surprised that her meticulous recycling, whilst welcomed by the panel, would not save carbon emissions; an English teacher learned that the ozone hole is a separate issue; a primary teacher who has young children of her own seemed shaken by a graph showing global carbon emissions this century – she'd assumed they were coming down by now. The panel of young people finished by talking about their feelings about climate change, mentioning anxiety, frustration, a sense of abandonment, dread, and confusion. The experienced geography teacher asked, very humbly, how he could teach the topic better, and a 17-year-old panelist suggested that he could make it more human. He said, "You called it a topic, but for us it's not a topic like a separate thing before you move on to volcanoes," and spoke about how it affects everything – whether there will be enough food and water, whether to have children, what clothes to buy and where from. He said he wanted to go traveling but also felt that would be too selfish if he did it for its own sake, so he was finding ways to justify it through volunteering. "So that's what I'm thinking about when we're looking at a picture of the carbon cycle. Give us space to talk about that."[1]

Globally, climate change education as it is currently practiced is woefully inadequate to serve young people's needs to understand and prepare well for the future they face. Very few educators have ever had the opportunity to consider the social and emotional impacts of what young people learn about climate change, or of how they learn it. While studies involving climate change abound in the field of education, few address the mental health implications that can arise from students' thorough understanding of the current global predicament. For example, from 2013–2022 the *Journal of Environmental Education* published only eight studies relating to schools or school-age young people in which mental health, an emotion, or state of mind was included in the title. Hardly any studies exist on the specific impact of school-based climate change education on young people's mental health.

Despite the lack of research and training in this area, teachers and others in education are generally motivated by a genuine desire to care for young people and contribute to their future success. A growing minority of educators are well informed about the climate crisis and are finding ways to facilitate climate change education in sensitive and empowering ways. A discourse has begun in the education community which will no doubt develop and, as the global crisis deepens, will likely inform future education-based practice on a grand scale, depending upon whether national governments opt to encourage or restrain good practice in climate change education.

An Overview of Climate Change Education

Globally, we are failing to inform young people about the basic facts of climate change. In a major study of nearly 17,500 young people from 166 countries, the United Nations Educational, Scientific and Cultural Organization

---

[1] Teach the Teacher Manchester event, December 2022.

(UNESCO, 2022) found that 70 percent of respondents knew little or nothing about climate change, and only 13 percent had been asked to consider their feelings about it. In separate research investigating the extent to which climate change education is included the National Curriculum Frameworks across 100 countries, UNESCO (2021) found that 47 percent of the National Curricula investigated made no mention of climate change. Only about half of a representative sample of twenty teachers interviewed in greater depth had any teacher training for climate change education at all, generally in geography and science. A separate global survey of over 58,000 teachers from 144 countries on their readiness to integrate climate change education into their teaching found that 95 percent of teachers rated climate change as an important or very important topic, but only 40 percent felt confident teaching about it. Similarly, roughly 40 percent of these educators felt confident in teaching the factual aspects of climate change, but only about one fifth could effectively explain how to take action. Action, which builds young people's sense of agency, is an essential pillar supporting young people's mental health in the context of climate change.

Education is a largely unrecognized domain in the formal pledges made by nations to tackle climate change. Of 140 new or updated pledges submitted since 2021, only a third mention education, and those which do are mostly from countries with high climate vulnerability (Education International, 2022). Education is, however, a key component of the Action for Climate Empowerment (ACE).[2] In 2021, ACE put forth a four-year plan mandating the UN to map and collate guidelines and good practice on climate education annually.

One country has already implemented climate education policies that include social-emotional support, providing a potential model. A key architect of New Zealand's climate change education policy, Green Party Member of Parliament James Shaw, explained to *The Guardian* newspaper (Graham-McLay, 2020) how a pilot program on climate change education led to increased emphasis on processing emotions: "By necessity … students would 'delve into the bad news' of the science explaining the climate crisis. But the resources had been bolstered with 'quite an emphasis on talking through with students how they're feeling about it.'" Concrete resources for supporting students' mental health were also provided for teachers; for example, encouraging students to keep a feelings thermometer

---

[2] ACE is a term used by the UN Framework Convention on Climate Change to represent work under Article 6 of the Convention and Article 12 of the Paris Agreement (Action for Climate Empowerment, n.d.).

to track their emotions, learning how to challenge defeatist self-talk, and considering how students' feelings could generate action. These very much reflect recommendations made by Maria Ojala (2012), who is a leading researcher on coping with climate change.

In my home nation of England, politicians generally make no mention of the emotional impacts of learning about climate change. To my knowledge, the only exception to this involved a candidate in the 2022 Conservative Party leadership contest to become prime minister, who used young people's climate distress as a reason not to teach them the truth about climate change. Campaigns to make climate change education fit for purpose in England and Wales have been led by teaching unions and, strikingly, by young people themselves. Teachers' unions agree that a comprehensive review of the National Curriculum is needed to ensure long-term sustainability, and cite eco-anxiety as a reason.

A remarkable youth-led organization, Teach the Future, has arguably been the most effective in raising the profile of climate change education policy in the UK through its innovative and eye-catching projects. In 2021 they presented their Climate Education Bill to parliament – the first Bill ever written by young people – seeking wholesale reform of school curricula and buildings. And in 2022 their "tracked changes" project added annotations to the National Curriculum in seven subject areas, explaining how these curricula would have to be changed in order to bring them into line with ten climate education principles, all of which support the inherent mental health challenges of climate education and three of which are explicit in this regard (see Appendix A for this resource).

At the school leadership level, responses to the growing pressure to address climate change occupy the full spectrum from actively hostile to progressive and innovative. The Youthstrike 4 Climate walkouts in 2019 succeeded in getting the attention of many headteachers, whose unions' advice about how to handle the situation demonstrated no awareness of the distressing emotions lending impetus to the movement. Activist teachers often highlight climate change as a safeguarding issue (i.e., relevant to the role of schools in keeping children safe), using this as a kind of trojan horse to get it on the agenda of harried school leaders.

UK-based teachers have indicated in surveys that they feel ill-equipped to deal with climate change in their classes (e.g., Teach the Future, 2021). Some high school geography and science teachers are required by the National Curriculum to deliver content about climate change, but this does not guarantee an emotionally literate approach; some textbooks are actually misleading, for instance by presenting equal benefits and drawbacks of higher concentrations of greenhouse gases, and even exam questions can trigger climate distress (Harvey, 2022).

Educators' increasing awareness of and interest in climate change means that more well-meaning educators are likely to venture onto this territory, with or without the explicit knowledge of their institutions. In the absence of adequate guidance or training, many go it alone, using their own knowledge supported by a proliferating range of online resources. While this can be done well, any approach that lacks sufficient socio-emotional supports for students risks causing climate distress that may go unacknowledged and/or unsupported.

Climate Change: It's Emotional

Climate Distress

The experience of finding out about climate change is very different for today's young people, compared with all but the youngest adults:

- It is more emotive. For the past several decades, the tone of climate discourse has become more threatening and urgent. Young people arrive in a world where threat and urgency are the norm.
- It is more chaotic. Modern society exposes young people of all ages to an unpredictable and unreliable assortment of messages about climate change.
- It is more personal. Messages about possible futures are mostly within the expected lifetime of young people.
- It is harder to deny. Conspiracy theories thrive, but the eccentricity of climate denial is increasingly clear.
- It requires more trust. The younger they are, the less agency children have, and the more trust they must necessarily place in adults for protection. (Barnwell, 2021, p. 11)

It is no wonder, then, that when young people begin to grasp the reality of the situation, a host of complex emotions follow:

> Obviously climate change is also mostly negative, but having a lesson about the upcoming apocalypse … and then moving on to algebra is not very good for my mental health. (Madeleine, Melbourne, Walker et al., 2022, p. 30)

> Even though it's like exposing us to like the truth of what's happening, it's also dampening our passion for changing climate change. It's terrifying … that's why some people may not feel empowered to take action, because it terrifies them. (Lisa, Melbourne, Walker et al., 2022, p. 32)

These quotes are consistent with research showing that young people experience a wide range of negative emotions when they learn about climate change (Ojala, 2012). Dr. Panu Pihkala provides a useful list to classify these emotions in Chapter 2, Table 2.1. For our purposes in this chapter, the term climate distress is appropriate as an umbrella term covering the full range of negative emotions young people may feel, which Dr. Pihkala defines as "various kinds of distress which are significantly shaped by the climate crisis." These often include worry, fear, shame, guilt, frustration, grief, disillusionment, inadequacy, confusion and various types of anger (see Boler's [2017] incisive distinction between moral and defensive anger).

Institutional Betrayal

Betrayal is an insidious emotion that is acknowledged far less often. As others in this volume have highlighted, young people's perceptions and feelings of betrayal receive much less attention than other climate- and eco-emotions, despite the fact that many young people report feeling betrayed (Hickman et al., 2021) and that betrayal can erode young people's sense of safety and trust in the adults and institutions who are meant to protect them.

Furthermore, there is evidence that betrayal by institutions can add a layer of trauma to the distress caused directly by the traumatic event. Smidt and Freyd (2018) examined cases of sexual assault on university campuses, in healthcare systems and in armed forces, finding that when trust in institutions was broken (due to failure to take appropriate responsibility), victims already suffering the trauma of the assault itself then experienced the secondary trauma of feeling betrayed by these institutions.

In a report on the mental health consequences of climate change in South Africa, clinical psychologist Dr. Garrett Barnwell (2021) argues that "the lack of sufficient climate action by the 'adult world' is a threat to children, youth and future generations and contributes to psychological injuries" (p. 22). In a similar vein, Dr. Karen Hopenwasser argues in Chapter 7 of this volume that failure to provide safety for our children is "institutional abuse" analogous to neglect, reflecting Smidt and Freyd's (2018) finding that "Institutional betrayal includes … acts of omission" (p. 491).

Climate change education has an institutional dimension at the level of the whole school. What is sometimes called climate's "hidden curriculum" of, for example, site management, energy use, travel policy, and procurement, has an important educational effect in shaping young people's perception of the issue. These choices can serve to undermine or enhance the gravity of what is learned in the classroom. They influence social norms. And to many young people, they are a powerful sign of how deeply the adult world really cares about their future. "Where are the solar panels? Where can you lock up your electric bike? Why is the heating on today? It's *warm*. Nothing's happening, is it? They can see the pictures of houses floating down the river [in Germany] on the news, can't they? So. Can't they make the connection? Duh" (17-year-old, personal communication, July 2021).

The institution of school also represents most young people's most direct interaction with the institution of government. During 2019's global Youthstrike 4 Climate movement, an estimated 1.6 million young people in 125 countries demonstrated a clear understanding of this by withdrawing their cooperation with the school system in order to exert political pressure. This was an expression of climate distress in its adaptive capacity; that is, frustration and worry coupled with hope turned into action. Young people's demands, displayed on numerous placards and articulated in speeches and letters, implied an underlying trust that the authorities would listen, and in their potential to change course. Vanessa Nakate's words, above (Nakate, 2020, p. 129), eloquently express a logic young people everywhere are working out for themselves: they are profoundly suspicious about what motivates existing systems, yet hopeful for better education provision.

Without change, how long can that hope last in a heating world? If entire generations in whole nations come to feel institutionally betrayed by their education, we might expect social contracts with both education systems and broader government systems to break down at a time when both are needed to facilitate social and cultural transformation towards a sustainable economy.

Challenges of Climate Distress

This emotional dimension to climate change education raises challenging fundamental issues regarding the aims of education and the responsibilities of the educator. In their study on the post-school significance of emotional aspects of climate change schooling, Jones and Davison (2021) found that, "In contrast to discourses of education as empowering, [21-year-olds] told of feeling disempowered by their educational encounters with climate change" and that "climate change schooling had ongoing significance for participants as they sought to make life choices in the shadow of a frightening future."

Some educators feel uncomfortable when negative emotions come into play (Ojala, 2021). We like to think of our learning spaces as places of curiosity, inspiration, and excitement, or perhaps of objective and empowering reason. But if we present climate change without accounting for the emotional consequences of doing so, we fail in our duty of care.

Another reason for considering the role of emotions in educational contexts is the diversity of young people's values (Ojala, 2021). Responses to climate change interact with local history, religious conviction, political allegiance, cultural practices, gender politics, racial identity, and psychogeography. Whilst climate distress may describe the emotional response of most young people, some may feel skeptical, resistant, threatened, unfazed, or even pleased. Commercial and political forces have also made climate change a socially divisive issue, for which young people are not to blame. The feelings of educators and young people are present whether or not we invite them, communicated through connotations, intonation, facial expressions, and body language. If we deny the emotional dimension, which is intrinsic to climate change education, we may unintentionally marginalize individuals and groups, further polarizing and dividing communities.

Young people need us to face these challenges. When we teach young people about climate change, climate distress responses are normal, natural, and predictable. As the climate crisis intensifies over the coming years, it is increasingly likely that climate change education will pose significant challenges for students' mental health. But as supportive adults, we can help them identify and channel their emotions in healthy, adaptive ways. To provide examples of what this can look like, the remainder of this chapter explores how several leading practitioners integrate social-emotional support into climate change education.

A Qualitative Study of Climate-Related Educational Practices

Methods

Four leading practitioners were selected and interviewed by this author to provide examples of a range of educational practice in different settings. All the interviews and the handling of data were conducted according to high ethical standards, including permission to use the words recorded here. Based on these interviews, case studies on each practitioner were created and themes were identified using thematic analysis.

Selection of Interviewees

The interviewees in this study were selected to provide depth and range of educational experience. Each interviewee has many years' experience in climate change education and has been developing methods to support young people's mental health for over three years. Across the four practitioners, the range of their experience covers: the full age-range in schools; public and private sector education; education in the Global North and South; curricular and extra-curricular contexts; and educators working as teachers, both in academia (in education) and in the third sector (voluntary and charities, such as providing educational experiences as visitors or providing training for teachers).

Data Collection and Analysis

Semi-structured individual interviews (Drever, 1995) were performed remotely with educators at home or in their place of work. The questions used as a basis for the interviews covered: how interviewees became aware of the emotional dimension of climate change education; their approach and practice now; and any advice they would give teachers. The interviews were transcribed to facilitate thematic analysis of the material. All of the interviews were conducted in English.

Interviewees' answers were reviewed carefully by this author and recurring themes were identified qualitatively using thematic analysis (Braun & Clarke, 2006). Due to the small sample size, at least three of the interviewees had to refer to a theme for it to be included. The approach was both deductive and inductive, with the identification of themes being influenced, on the one hand, by previous research about climate change education and, on the other, by an openness and responsiveness to the interview material (i.e., the specific experiences and reflections of the interviewees). Quotations were excerpted from each interview and placed under theme headings. Illustrative quotations were chosen for inclusion here.

Case Studies

Dr. Martín Bascope – Villarrica, Chile

Dr. Martín Bascope is a professor and researcher at CEDEL-UC, Pontifica Universidad Católica de Chile. A background in sociology and economics followed by a PhD in education led him to become interested in how education can encourage participation in community life. He now provides teacher training while conducting education research.

Dr. Bascope's approach focuses on real life issues in the local community. It is active, mostly outdoors, and focuses on feelings and values. In one example, "Children researched medicinal plants and herbs and worked with a medicine woman and with parents to make medicine boxes for people in care homes to help reconnect them to the environment and protect them from malaria [and other ailments]. The home had a big ceremony to [receive] the boxes." This involved collaboration, understanding the value of plants and finding or growing them, and caring for others in the community.

During Chile's COVID-19 lockdown, Dr. Bascope saw that "some teachers had doom and gloom" and realized that "feelings are something we have to take care of." He said, "I [didn't] want to scare the children." Out of this experience came a process for educating young people about climate change with "a lot of focus on feelings. We use the emotion wheel at the beginning and at the end and make the children aware of how they are feeling and then find the values behind that ... this leads to thinking ethically about how to act." (See Appendix A for the emotion wheel.)

Dr. Bascope also supports young people's self-efficacy by focusing on solutions: "We start from something that really motivates you that you want to make a difference to, and build it from there ... We can start from little, specific, very situated solutions, both inside the school and nearby in the community that give young people a sense that we can act differently." This means that teachers have to let go of an attachment to starting with curricular objectives. "We give them a guide ... the ones who were prepared to follow the guide and wait to see [how it would meet the requirements of the curriculum] were much more impressed. When we started the other way round, starting from the problem [of covering the curriculum], we found that teachers felt tied – 'where do I fit it? I don't have space. It's just more work'."

Sarah Fishwick – Leeds, England

Sarah Fishwick is a primary teacher who has also worked for a third sector education organization, the Leeds Development Education Centre (Leeds DEC), where she helped to develop its climate curriculum for Key Stages 1–4 (ages 5–16) (see Appendix A). She has now implemented this curriculum in her own classroom practice, and to a great extent has integrated it across St Matthew's Primary School where she teaches Year 4 (age 8–9). The curriculum was designed in collaboration with climate change academics and teachers, with young people's climate distress being a key consideration.

> There are 9 strands, and Feelings and Behaviours is one … We've linked [this] to ways young people might be involved in action in their schools…. There's also one on Possible Futures, and that's really important that they have that emotional investment in something positive … and learn that there are lots of co-benefits; it's not *either* we carry on and burn the world *or* we have to give everything up … They understand a range of probable outcomes so they've got a much more nuanced understanding than the kind of apocalypse stuff they may see especially as they get older on social media.

The Leeds DEC climate curriculum is designed to be taught through the existing school curriculum so that "they're hearing about it in Maths and English and Science and Art and [Modern Foreign Languages] … and in an integrated way" that is "planned and progressive and age-appropriate." For example, "One of the [climate curriculum] outcomes is understanding how people around the world are responding to the climate crisis and understanding different mindsets and viewpoints … so in [Religious Education] in Year 4 we learn about Hinduism, so … we learn about the [1970s] Chipko movement and how people today in Delhi have been inspired by it."

Sarah was worried that teaching young people about climate change would "terrify them. But it's absolutely not my experience that this happens. It never has. In fact, I recently asked all the staff in my school that question and absolutely nobody had experienced children being distressed and parents hadn't reported any either … I think that may be down to the fact that we've been aware of [the potential for distress] from the start."

Rachel Musson – Devon, England

Rachel Musson is a former high school English teacher and founding director of ThoughtBox Education, which provides resources and training for teachers and school leaders (see Appendix A). Her approach is based on what she brands "Triple WellBeing." "Every field I investigated looking for answers [to the ecological crises] you find the same three things: soil, soul, society; social, emotional, ecological … because this is what we need to flourish…. This is not an add-on, it's a way of learning, a process."

The ThoughtBox website offers free curricula for all ages – entitled *Awe and Wonder*, *Equality and Justice*, and *Changing Climates* – all of which promote emotional, social and ecological well-being. "The lessons use a facilitated discussion-based process rather than 'teaching'." They incorporate "lots of perspectives from the Global South" and include lessons on learning to see things from the perspective of nonhuman beings. "[Teachers who come back for more] like it because it's all about healthy relationships."

Rachel noted that different issues arise for different age groups. At primary, "the barrier for teachers is the instinct to protect." Here, "We need to give [young people] truth in an age-appropriate way and give them empowerment by understanding things that are happening to create a healthier world." With older students, teachers are "concerned about the limitations of the education system to be having quite political conversations … One school was talking about how a lot of the girls are very angry at the older generation … but [teachers] have to have a non-partisan view … so we spent quite a lot of time talking about the importance for the school [institution] to make clear where they stand."

Dr. Jessica Tipton – London, England

Dr. Jessica Tipton is a former secondary modern languages teacher who worked at a private girls' school in London, and until May 2023 as Head of Youth Networks for Global Action Plan, an environmental charity that mobilizes people and organizations to take action on the systems that harm people and planet. As a school sustainability coordinator she started setting up networks to link up "eco-committees" of students tasked with helping to improving environmental practice in their schools, which grew across London and provided a model for other regional networks to meet, share ideas, and coordinate their activities. Her role at Global Action Plan involves uniting these eco-committees under the umbrella organization she founded, UK Schools Sustainability Network (UKSSN), which now has connections with 300 secondary schools in England.

"I'm mostly working with groups of young people in their own time who read up on climate change for themselves. They tend to be self-motivated, aspirational, from all different backgrounds." The majority of young people in such self-selecting groups are predictably distressed about climate change, so Dr. Tipton's work is very much geared to their mental health.

High-profile visiting speakers at UKSSN online meetings are told that content must be age-appropriate "and they've all completely got that." Some schools run climate cafés where climate distress can be aired. "These are peer-to-peer without adults, you might have Year 12s taking a lead with some training and resources so the older ones help younger ones. They've ideally met up with the school counsellor…"

Educational Perspectives

Dr. Tipton emphasized the importance of supporting student expression:

> A lot of them do need to be active in pursuing the thing that they enjoy. So we have some that do art; they responded to [a trip to Glasgow for] COP26 [UN climate conference in 2021] through art and we put [their work] on social media to showcase it. There are some who like doing book reviews. There are some who like presenting at or hosting events… or being on a panel or putting on a workshop for primary pupils. Some do social media takeovers.

She also focuses on students' relationship with nature and building their connection with place. "We went to Wytham Woods [ancient woodland] to get out into nature with them. They met Oxford University researchers and had talks … and ate marshmallows round a campfire and for [the young people who don't see themselves as leaders] that's the antidote."

Thematic Analysis

Qualitative Analysis of Themes

Themes were included if they were mentioned by at least three of the four interviewees. Nine total themes were identified and grouped into four broad domains: (1) rationales for tackling emotions; (2) interviewees' understanding of underlying issues; (3) methods in common across settings; (and 4) educators' well-being (see Table 17.1). All interviewees were explicitly asked to comment on themes 1 and 2 – young people's climate-related emotions

Table 17.1 *Summary of domains and themes identified from interviews*

Domain	Theme identified	Number of interviewees who spoke about theme
1. Rationales for tackling emotions	1. Young people's emotions in relation to climate change	4
	2. Educators' influence on young people's emotions in relation to climate change	4
2. Interviewees' understanding of underlying issues	3. Disconnection and re/connection	4
	4. Systems thinking	3
	5. Young people's need to feel a sense of agency	4
3. Methods in common across settings	6. Age-appropriateness	3
	7. Outdoor learning	3
	8. Collaborating	4
4. Educators' well-being	9. Climate distress in educators	3

and educators' influence on young people's climate-related emotions. The remaining seven themes were not prompted and arose organically from the reflections and experience of the interviewees themselves.

Domain 1: Rationales for Tackling Emotions
The interviewees spoke about the emotional dimension of climate change education and how it informed their approaches to climate change education.

Theme 1: Young People's Emotions in Relation to Climate Change. When asked to explain the origins of their work with climate distress, all four interviewees referenced the emotions young people may feel when learning about, or after having learned about, climate change. The interviewees listed a range of emotions that they have witnessed in their work with young people, including: frustration; irritation; anxiety/fear; the heavy burden of a great responsibility; overwhelm, loss; grief; loneliness; powerlessness/disempowerment; and stress. Dr. Tipton also described the pressures young people who are taking action on climate change can place on themselves: "It can become quite addictive, there's a sort of guilt."

Sarah Fishwick's account of a visiting speaker to her primary school highlights the ethical demand to support young people with climate distress:

> We had … a specialist on forests to do an assembly … and her basic message was about climate change and trees and how it's very serious but if we do enough we can deal with it … And a child put their hand up and said, 'What happens if we don't?' And I suppose behind that question is potentially fear. And it's giving that question its due weight and not side-stepping it.

Theme 2: Educators' Influence on Young People's Emotions in Relation to Climate Change. All interviewees spoke about young people's emotions arising not only as a result of information or learning, but also from interactions with adults. Rachel Musson emphasized the danger of separating these considerations: "The [Climate Psychology Alliance's] foundational knowledge is that [just] giving young people information about why and how the climate change is changing is actually increasing levels of overwhelm and stress and disempowerment."

Dr. Tipton related instances of adults telling young people that everything is going to be alright: "It's very irritating, especially to a young person who really knows what's going on." Relatedly, Sarah Fishwick was concerned about a similar glibness at the institutional level: "The window-dressing [whole-school responses] are counterproductive; they actually make young people feel worse."

Dr. Bascope's aims are representative of all interviewees: "We don't say 'kids are the future and you are the ones that must really make a change'. I want to empower them, but at the same time that's a heavy burden so we try to get a balance."

Domain 2: Understanding of Underlying Issues
The interviewees shared underlying understandings of the problems and solutions which inform their practice.

Theme 3: Disconnection and Connection/reconnection. All the interviewees' work emphasized facilitating connection and/or reconnection with both nature and other people/peoples, countering the individualistic tendencies that wealthy nations have globalized. As Rachel Musson put it, "the root cause is disconnection, so the solution lies in reconnection; it's as simple, or as difficult, as recalibrating and nurturing our relationships with self, other and the more-than-human world." Dr. Bascope also linked social reconnection with the need to feel connected with nature: "We are explicit about Richard Luov's idea of Nature Deficit Disorder, that if you don't have connection with nature then it's very hard to empathize."

Theme 4: Systems Thinking. Just as the word "ecology" has come to be used far beyond its niche within biological studies, the idea of ecosystems – of understanding the world more organically in terms of systems, rather than mechanically in terms of parts – has also become central to green thinking. Interviewees felt strongly that the siloed, prescriptive educational orthodoxy of today is a barrier to meaningful change. For example, Dr. Bascope said, "Curricular thinking can be very linear. But when we open the climate box we find complexity and this requires systems thinking." Rachel Musson added, "The system is set up to want quick fixes, and tangible, neat ways of doing things. This is not that, this is systems work, it's lifelong." All four educators had risen to the challenge and were demonstrably succeeding in applying systems thinking in their work.

Theme 5: Young People's Need to Feel a Sense of Agency. Giving young people opportunities to make a difference was central to all of the approaches developed by the interviewees. For instance, Sarah Fishwick said, "it's all about agency ... on the training course we've linked the Feelings and Behaviours strand to ways young people might be involved in action." She added, "People are telling us at secondary that it does make a massive difference if they feel that they've got a voice and that feeds through into something happening in the real world…" Dr. Jessica Tipton sounded a note of caution, though: "[taking action] can become a bit addictive and you feel you've never done enough."

Domain 3: Methods in Common across Settings
The interviewees had ways of working in common.

Theme 6: Age-appropriateness. Interviewees emphasized the importance of making sure that young people's exposure to climate change content is developmentally appropriate and not too frightening for their age. See case studies above and resources for specific examples.

Theme 7: Outdoor Learning. Interviewees were aware, as Dr. Bascope said, that "There is a lot of research on the importance of green spaces … for mental health" and he saw this daily, "when you look at children's reactions." Dr. Tipton described "getting into nature," as "the antidote" to worrying in isolation. "Getting away from your devices and properly connecting with others who 'get it'. So they're together in a calm, beautiful space."

Theme 8: Collaborating. All interviewees stressed the need to collaborate with colleagues and like-minded adults. For example, Sarah Fishwick said: "Be collaborative with others in your school because one single person can't do it all on your own."

Domain 4: Educators' Well-being
The interviewees shared a concern for the educators who deliver climate change education.

Theme 9: Climate Distress in Educators. Rachel Musson pointed out that as humans, "This is an existential crisis we're living through … it's going to impact the teacher as much as it's going to impact young people." Dr. Bascope simply advised, "Practice self-care."

Conclusions

Leadership in climate-change education is coming from the grassroots. Understanding the severity of climate change inevitably causes distressing emotions, and this is especially true of young people. Ignoring this emotional dimension in our teaching about climate change is harmful. However, promising approaches which support young people's mental health can be effectively implemented across different contexts. These approaches are age-appropriate, acknowledge and validate negative emotions, balance the responsibilities of the educating institution with those of the young people, and nurture connections between young people and their social and natural worlds. In practical terms, they often involve outdoor learning, and prioritize providing opportunities for learners to build agency by making a positive difference.

References

Action for Climate Empowerment (n.d.). https://unfccc.int/ace

Barnwell, G. (2021). The psychological and mental health consequences of climate change in South Africa. Expert Report for the Centre for Environmental Rights, Cape Town. https://cer.org.za/wp-content/uploads/2021/09/CER-Expert-Report-Garret-Barnwell-31-August-2021-Public-1.pdf

Boler, M. (2017). Pedagogies of discomfort: Inviting emotions and affect into educational change. Transcript of *Discomfort Zones* conference proceedings, Vanier College, Montreal. www.vaniercollege.qc.ca/psi/files/2017/10/Discomfort-Zones_Final.pdf#page=9

Braun, V., & Clarke, V. (2006) Using thematic analysis in psychology. *Qualitative Research in Psychology*, 3(2), 77–101. http://dx.doi.org/10.1191/1478088706qp063oa

Drever, E. (1995). *Using semi-structured interviews in small-scale research: A teacher's guide.* Scottish Council for Research in Education.

Education International (2022). COP 27 is another cop out but education unions continue to build the change our planet needs. Education International, November 30. www.ei-ie.org/en/item/27111:cop-27-is-another-cop-out-but-education-unions-continue-to-build-the-change-our-planet-needs?

Gorman, A. (2018). *Earthrise*, for the Climate Reality Project. Text and video widely available online. www.sierraclub.org/los-padres/blog/2021/02/earthrise-poem-amanda-gorman

Graham-McLay, C. (2020). New Zealand schools to teach students about climate crisis, activism and 'eco anxiety.' *The Guardian*, January 13. www.theguardian.com/world/2020/jan/13/new-zealand-schools-to-teach-students-about-climate-crisis-activism-and-eco-anxiety

Harvey, F. (2022). UK pupils failed by schools' teaching of climate crisis, experts say. *The Guardian*, January 28. www.theguardian.com/education/2022/jan/28/uk-pupils-failed-by-schools-teaching-of-climate-crisis-experts-say

Hickman, C. (2020). We need to (find a way to) talk about … eco-anxiety. *Journal of Social Work Practice*, 34(4), 411–424.

Hickman, C., Marks, E., Pihkala, P., Clayton, S., Leandowski, R.E., Mayal, E.E., … & van Susteren. L. (2021). Climate anxiety in children and young people and their beliefs about government responses to climate change: A global survey. *The Lancet Planetary Health*, 5(12). https://doi.org/10.1016/S2542-5196(21)00278-3

Jones, C. A., & Davison, A. (2021). Disempowering emotions: The role of educational experiences in social responses to climate change. *Geoforum*, 118, 190–200.

Nakate, V. (2020). *A bigger picture*, Pan Macmillan.

Ojala, M. (2012). Regulating worry, promoting hope: How do children, adolescents, and young adults cope with climate change? *International Journal of Environmental Science Education*, 7(4), 537–561. https://files.eric.ed.gov/fulltext/EJ997146.pdf

Ojala, M. (2015). Hope in the face of climate change: Associations with environmental engagement and student perceptions of teachers' emotion communication style and future orientation. *Journal of Environmental Education*, 46(3), 133–148. https://doi.org/10.1080/00958964.2015.1021662

Ojala, M. (2021). Safe spaces or a pedagogy of discomfort? Senior high-school teachers' meta-emotion philosophies and climate change education. *Journal of Environmental Education*, 52(1), 40–52. https://doi.org/10.1080/00958964.2020.1845589

Pihkala, P. (2022). Toward a taxonomy of climate emotions [original research]. *Frontiers in Climate*, 3. https://doi.org/10.3389/fclim.2021.738154

Smidt, A. & Freyd, J. (2018). Government-mandated institutional betrayal. *Journal of Trauma and Dissociation*, 19, 491–499.

Teach the Future (2021). *Teaching the Future* report. www.teachthefuture.uk/teacher-research

UNESCO (2020). *Is Italy the first country to require climate change education in all schools?* International Bureau of Education. www.ibe.unesco.org/en/news/italy-first-country-require-climate-change-education-all-schools

UNESCO (2021). *Getting every school climate-ready: How countries are integrating climate change issues in education*. UNESCO. https://unesdoc.unesco.org/ark:/48223/pf0000379591

UNESCO (2022). *Youth demands for quality climate change education*. UNESCO. https://unesdoc.unesco.org/ark:/48223/pf0000383615/PDF/383615eng.pdf.multi

Walker, C., with Rackley, K. M., Summer, M., Thompson, N., & Young Researchers. (2022). Young people at a crossroads: Stories of climate education, action and adaptation from around the world. www.sci.manchester.ac.uk/research/projects/young-people-at-a-crossroads

Wals, A. E. J. (2020). Transgressing the hidden curriculum of unsustainability: Towards a relational pedagogy of hope. *Educational Philosophy and Theory*, 52(8), 825–826. https://doi.org/10.1080/00131857.2019.1676490

Wu, J., Snell, G., & Samji, H. (2020). Climate anxiety in young people: A call to action. *The Lancet Planetary Health*, 4, e435–e436. https://doi.org/10.1016/S2542-5196(20)30223-0

CHAPTER 18

Activists' Perspectives
Using Climate Activism to Heal Youth Climate Distress

Jennifer Uchendu and Elizabeth Haase

> I'm only a child and I don't have all the solutions, but I want you to realize, neither do you.
> Severn Cullis-Suzuki, 12 years old, Rio Earth Summit, 1992

What Is Activism?

This chapter discusses climate activism in young people. We review types of activism and principles that have been important for youth climate activist groups to help them be most inclusive and effective, as well as the literature on the mental health risks and benefits of activism, both generally and for youth climate activists in particular. This conceptual basis for the chapter is interwoven with the activist journey of author Jennifer Uchendu, founder of SustyVibes, in hopes that her story of resilience through eco-anxiety and burnout can help others apply the relevance of these concepts to their own experiences and feel inspired and empowered by her story.

We define activism as actions and expressions, both small and big, towards social, environmental, or political change. These actions are not limited to campaigns, political protests, and social movements, but are initiated when people challenge power and dominant narratives in any form. There are many types of activism: it can happen through art (artivism), computer hacking (hacktivism), education, judicial activity, consumer choices or brand campaigns, shareholder activity, alternative community building, guerilla tactics, peace camps, nonviolent resistance, vigils, culture jamming, and in many other and surprising unusual places – even just speaking one's truth in social settings (see Textbox 18.1). Activism is about standing for something you believe. The people who become activists often recognize that doing nothing about a situation makes things worse. They show up and make moves with a clear demand for what change they seek in our world. And our world today, in its often-repressive form, so desperately needs change. There are so many things that have come to be that should never have happened, and when the cycle of oppression, greed, and hate is allowed to go unchecked, we are presented with a society dealing with anthropogenic climate breakdown alongside deeply rooted social injustices.

A Brief History of Children and Youth Activism

The first systemic efforts to advocate for the rights and needs of children emerged from the Industrial Revolution, as harmful child labor practices that also deprived children of their education became prevalent. One significant event of youth activism recorded from that time occurred in the United States in 1903, where child textile workers organized by Mary Harris "Mother" Jones marched from Pennsylvania to New York, where they sought unsuccessfully to meet with President Theodore Roosevelt. These efforts, as well as those of many other child welfare agencies and commissions, culminated in 1990 in the adoption of the United Nations Convention on the Rights of the Child (UNCRC), a document that advocates for the provision for and protection of children's rights, including the right to participation (United Nations General Assembly, 1989). The participation aspect of this policy broadly expresses a child's right to be heard in all matters that affect them and is articulated in Article 12 of the UNCRC, protecting their right to activist activity, amplifying children's voices, and outlining the moral and civic responsibility of governments and parents to listen to and act on children's demands and perspectives. Through the lens of Article 12, there have been numerous studies and judicial and civic interventions taking steps to ensure that children's voices are heard and that their well-being is protected, especially on issues that concern their future, such as climate change.

Textbox 18.1 Selected types of activism

Marching	Educating	Uncivil obedience
Sit-ins, die-ins, walk-outs	Fundraising	Life support
Rallies and speeches	Running for office	Mass media campaigns
Community organizing	Campaigning	Slactivism
Voting	Strikes and culture jamming	Art activism
Craftivism	Supporting mutual aid	Hacktivism
Letter writing	Petitioning	Shareholder activism
Volunteering	Civil disobedience	Vigils

Four Roles for Social Activism

Child and youth climate activists often seek urgent changes in the way that society is organized and hence contributing to the climate crisis. Given that these demands involve difficult social change, it is imperative to learn about the ways activism succeeds.

As conceptualized by Bill Moyers (2001), there are four roles that activists, including young people, can play in order to achieve social and environmental change. Each role has its own distinct set of skills and styles and serves different purposes. The following is a summary of his work.

The Citizen

An effective citizen activist understands their civic responsibilities and exercises them dutifully. In seeking to promote their cause, they align themselves with positive national values such as democracy, inclusion, and obedience to the rule of law from a centrist position that places high value on the common good and a sense of community. In advocating for changes that are closely connected to core values of their particular culture, citizen activists are thought to be effective because of the natural human tendency of those petitioned to accept new ideas that are aligned with what they already believe, a cognitive process known as "confirmation bias."

Citizen activism is beneficial because it is accessible for people with a range of levels of interest in a problem, it falls within civic roles available to every person in a society, and it uses channels for effecting change that are already established and can theoretically be more easily responsive to input. The risks of being a citizen activist include naive or extreme obedience to cultural norms and values, failing to understand that institutions and those in power are often serving special interest groups (rather than these values), failing to understand the diversity of views that exist in alignment with these values, or becoming intolerant to divergent or "nonpatriotic" views.

A nuanced example of successful citizen activism is Intersectional Environmentalism, a mainstream environmentalist movement led by Leah Thomas. The movement demands that our planet and all its people, including those in discriminated groups, are both cared for and seen as interconnected. Its core approach demonstrates citizen activism by calling for greater adherence to mainstream democratic ideals such as equality and inclusion for all, individual rights, and freedom of expression. Intersectional Environmentalism has used belief in these ideals to bring attention to the fact that environmental issues disproportionately affect marginalized and discriminated communities, and has helped advocates understand and address these disparities. It has also highlighted the need for more diverse voices and perspectives in the environmental movement, which has spurred action to address these issues in a more inclusive and equitable way.

Citizens' Climate Lobby is another example of citizen activism. It is a grassroots organization that advocates for a revenue-neutral carbon fee and dividend policy, which would put a price on carbon and return the revenue to households as a dividend. The group uses a variety of established legal methods to push for this policy, including lobbying, voting, community outreach, and working with lawmakers, all based on core duties of the citizen in participatory government.

The Reformer

The reformer believes that policies and laws are essential in driving social change. Their activity also involves working within existing political and social structures to effect change, but includes changes in laws, policies, and institutions to make them more equitable and just. Reformers use mainstream official systems and institutions such as the courts and the legislature to advance the movement's goals and values through tactics such as lawsuits, lobbying, referenda, coalition building, rallies, and public opinion shaping.

A well-known and inspiring exemplar of reformer activism was Ruth Bader Ginsburg, lawyer and Supreme Court justice. She worked ceaselessly within the system to reform the laws of the United States in line with gender equality, playing a pivotal role in landmark cases that helped to advance women's rights.

The strength of reformer activism is its ability to have a long reach, integrating long-lasting changes into laws and policy. Because of this bureaucratic and top-down focus, however, reformers are vulnerable to patriarchal and hierarchical errors (e.g., using elite educated people to shape ideas and practices for others), and can be co-opted by the structures of power they seek to change. They can become overly preoccupied with organizational stability over the needs of the movement and can settle for minor reforms in the name of "being realistic." These tendencies can also alienate and disempower participants involved in their grassroots efforts.

An example of youth reformer activists can be found in Melati and Isabel Wijsen, sisters from Bali who campaigned for the reduction of plastic waste in Bali. Their main goal was to ban the use of plastic bags and to promote reusable bags instead. To achieve this goal, they started the "Bye Bye Plastics Bags" movement, which focused on education and awareness-raising campaigns and working with schools, businesses, and communities to promote sustainable practices and reduce plastic waste. The movement has also engaged in activism and advocacy, organizing protests, petition drives, and social media campaigns to raise awareness and build legislative support for their cause. Their campaign succeeded in achieving a legislative ban on single-use plastic bags, straws, and styrofoam in Bali.

Another example of reformer activism is the Movement for the Survival of the Ogoni People (MOSOP) led by Ken Saro Wiwa in the Niger Delta region of Nigeria (Ogoni Case Study, n.d.). His movement was notable for its nonviolent campaign to protect and preserve the Ogoni environment and people from the devastating impact from oil drilling on their water and land, particularly that of Shell Oil. MOSOP wrote a Bill of Rights for the Ogoni people, which was presented to the Nigerian government and the UN, where they successfully demanded economic justice, political autonomy, medical aid, and a moratorium on oil drilling and gas flaring. Despite their legislative success, Ken Saro Wiwa was later sentenced to death and hanged along with other leaders of the movement by the Nigerian ruler of that time. His family later used the American courts to achieve US$15.5 million in damages for wrongful death (Mouawad, 2009).

Reformers may engage with corporations as well as governments to encourage sustainable practices and reduce their greenhouse gas emissions. This can involve shareholder activism, where investors use their leverage to push companies to change their behavior, or corporate social responsibility campaigns, where activists pressure companies to adopt ethical and sustainable practices. The Climate Group is one such organization that works with businesses and governments to accelerate the transition to a low-carbon economy. The group works to promote policies and practices that reduce greenhouse gas emissions, and has helped to establish high-profile initiatives, such as the RE100 campaign, which encourages businesses to commit to 100 percent renewable energy.

The Rebel

The rebel activist role involves challenging the status quo and pushing for radical change. Rebels are willing to take risks and engage in direct action to disrupt existing power structures and create space for new ideas and approaches. Rebels use a variety of tactics, including civil disobedience, protest, and direct action. They may work outside of existing political and social structures to create alternative systems and communities.

There are several examples of youth rebel movements, such as the Fridays for Future movement led by Greta Thunberg. This movement has mobilized millions of people, especially students around the world to demand action on climate change. Their strikes have included disruptive actions such as school walkouts and sit-ins, blocking traffic, and occupying public spaces. The movement gave birth to the Fridays for Future organization, which is now active in various countries in the world.

The Sunrise Movement, a youth-led climate organization in the United States, has also used civil disobedience to push for policies to address climate change. Members of the organization have engaged in sit-ins at Congressional offices and disrupted events to demand climate action. Similarly, the Extinction Rebellion (XR) movement is a global activist organization that uses nonviolent civil disobedience to demand action on the climate and ecological crisis. The movement has organized mass protests, blockades, and other disruptive actions in cities around the world to draw attention to the urgency of the climate crisis and demand radical change.

Another example of rebel activism led by young people is the #EndSARS movement that started in Nigeria in 2020 as a response to protests against the Special Anti-Robbery Squad (SARS) of the Nigerian Police. This Squad was notoriously involved in human rights abuses on young people. The movement was largely led by young people, who used social media to mobilize and organize in several parts of the country. This movement had no individual leader or organized structure, but was popular for its hashtag #EndSARS, which allowed it to sustain its activity in different settings and through multiple waves of police suppression and to engage an international following of celebrity, legal, and other support. Although the movement was gruesomely suppressed by the Nigerian Army, it remains a pivotal moment in the history of Nigeria as a nation for its tenacity in pushing back against entrenched state violence.

Also in Nigeria, the Movement for the Emancipation of the Niger Delta (MEND) has used rebel action to effect change. Militancy, destruction of pipelines, kidnapping, and other violent direct action have been used to demand a greater share of the region's oil wealth and better living conditions for their people.

In Australia, the Stop Adani movement organized direct actions and blockades in an unsuccessful attempt to prevent the construction of the proposed Adani Carmichael coal mine. The mine is one of the largest in the world, and will not only contribute significantly to greenhouse gas emissions but will also deplete at least 270 billion liters of water from groundwater over its lifetime. Protesters had chained themselves to equipment, blocked access roads, and disrupted business operations to stop the mine from being built, and achieved one of the most effective and productive activist campaigns ever recorded. While the mine has moved forward, protester tactics have contributed to investor jitters and other delays in funding and profitability (Gulliver, 2022).

Rebel activism is exciting, empowered, courageous, and risky. It can be successful in putting issues and policies in the spotlight of media and public attention and represents an important part of limiting abuses of power. When ineffective, however, its strengths can become its weaknesses. The fierce stances of rebel activists can become totalitarian and arrogant, and their sometimes destructive or violent approaches make building a broad consensus of support for their work more difficult. Sources of power can use their civil disobedience to create fear and turn public opinion against the rebel's radicalism, displacing attention from their own destructiveness and marginalizing and victimizing these supposedly "dangerous" and "fringe" voices.

The Change Agent

The change agent activist works from within established systems to bring about major paradigm and power shifts. Change agents aim to influence decision-makers and create change by mass grassroot organization of networks and coalitions engaging in participatory democracy to create new social structures and mores. Change agents can be credited with advancing civilization towards more noble and democratic modes. The righteousness of their cause provides the energy that inspires their followers and creates moral discomfort in others, leading to examination of what needs to change. Martin Luther King, a civil rights activist and preacher who led a movement that significantly improved rights for people of color in the United States, is the paradigmatic example of the change agent activist.

Change agents run afoul of success when they are too utopian in their goals, promoting visions of perfected social alternatives that fail to take into account the need to grapple with and be patient with alternative views to fully transform long-held social standards. In their single-minded pursuit of their goals, they can develop tunnel vision and ignore the personal and diverse needs of their activist members as well as those of the constituencies they seek to change.

Other examples of a change agent would be a sustainability officer in a company whose role is to help the company reduce its environmental impact and promote sustainability initiatives, or a legislator who works to build support for something that is difficult for older voters or religious subgroups to embrace to create policies that promote social justice and equality.

On the international front, a prominent change agent is Malala Yousafzai, a Pakistani activist who became a change agent for girls' education, something that demanded a major social shift for her country. She was shot in the head by the Taliban for speaking out about the importance of education for girls, but survived and continued to advocate for the cause even after recovering from the attack, becoming the youngest Nobel Prize laureate.

The four roles for social activists so wonderfully delineated by Bill Moyers are just one model for understanding activism. Another particularly compelling framework comes from Terry Patten, who was a philosopher, therapist, teacher, spiritualist, and more. He proposed something he called "evolutionary activism" or "sacred activism," as a model for a just transition to more sustainable ways of living. In this form of activism – also called "Alter-Activism" or "Regenerative Activism" by other groups – external activist activities, as well as social and political engagement, are coupled with conscious community and business building, lifestyle innovation, and other changes built on inner psychological work and regenerative, spiritually informed relations with others, including the living elements of the natural world. Increasingly, many environmental activist groups incorporate the kind of psychological work built into this kind of activism to ensure that we are relating in ways that are restorative and supportive in order to combat burnout and build a new paradigm to replace the narratives of dominance and competition built into our current social structures.

Writers have also identified a number of helpful, more practical tips for engaging in activism. These include:

1. Know what you want and why you want it.
2. Be on the side of the angels – frame your argument to give your position the moral high ground, to reach across party lines, and to appeal to the best in both sides.
3. Make your opponents uncomfortable. People are biased not to act on complex problems, so you must ignite some sort of awareness and distress about the gap between the current system and what solution would be better.

4. Try to frame your position as the best solution, one that it is heartless to ignore.
5. Think about why your opponents might want to do what you ask and appeal to that reasoning in them.
6. Try to have constructive proposals to solve the problem.
7. Carefully select and groom your presenters for those who can best connect to the particular audience they will address.
8. Be polite and respectful, no matter what.
9. Stay on message: Ask for one thing, only one thing, and be happy when you get it, without immediately adding more demands.
10. Be a gracious loser and take time to replenish yourself and understand what you had not foreseen before planning new efforts.

We now turn to the activism experience of our lead author, Jennifer Uchendu.

Jennifer's Climate Activism Journey

When I was an 8-year-old, our mango tree was cut down to provide space in the compound. The mango tree had come not only to be but also to mean so many things to me and my family. Concerned and stressed, I struggled with the justification provided by the landlord who owned the property. The tree for me was a place of shade and resting place for us. It also provided us with food. It was my favorite tree in season, and I loved its thick, broad trunk all year. Although I was not exposed to the idea of environmental protection as a child, something in me felt uneasy when the environment was littered and I instantly felt relief and calm within nature. I grew up knowing that I had some form of affinity to nature, and to trees especially. I also wanted to be a medical doctor, a gynecologist in particular. I was interested in work that supported women and women's rights. Growing up in a patriarchal society in Nigeria made me very sensitive to injustice and to the cultural stereotypes placed on women and girls. Then I did not get into medical school; this was one of the many setbacks I have faced in my journey. I studied biochemistry instead, and became fascinated with biomimicry and biotransformation. Through this new interest I learnt about biofuels and renewable energy and began to explore a career in the energy sector. By the time I graduated college in 2011, I was able to secure an unpaid internship in my state government's Ministry of Energy and Mineral resources. There I was afforded the opportunity to learn about renewable energy projects, and especially to connect with young students in the classroom and tell them about the science and technology of solar panels. Through this experience, I began to notice my flare for environmentally focused education and advocacy. The power of passing scientific information to people in a way they could apply at home propelled me into my current work in sustainability.

I started to learn about sustainability when I worked at the Unilever company in Nigeria. The job was mostly part of my placements as a junior officer on the mandatory National Youth Service Corps program, a one-year service requirement for young Nigerians. At Unilever, I learned about businesses and their roles in environmental protection. I learned about the triple bottom line of people, planet, and profits, and their interconnectedness. As an activist in the making, I was always passionate for new knowledge. The more I learned, the more I realized how much I did not know. This humbling reality made me desire a master's in environmental sustainability. Year after year, I would apply to programs abroad and get accepted. But I did not have the funding to take these on. More setbacks. I took free online courses and training, attended related conferences and events in Nigeria and networked with a lot of professionals who were working on sustainability or corporate social responsibility projects. Understanding sustainability and our environment from the lens of people, livelihoods, and protection made me interested in one day building a platform that made sustainability projects possible for young people like myself.

After five years of actively trying to get into school for a masters degree, I decided to start SustyVibes – first as a blog for young people to read and learn about sustainability from a youth lens. SustyVibes was about bringing in a fun side to environmental protection and making climate action exciting, attractive, and enjoyable for young people in Nigeria. Through storytelling, I was building a community of readers who agreed that it was time to have a youth lens to environmental sustainability, and that the lens had to be fully owned by us and for us. We were the sustyvibers, and, with time, we grew from 50 to 100 to over 500 scattered across the country.

Despite this success, my journey has not been straightforward. Activism has many setbacks, and I have learned to cope by finding communities of like minds and experimenting with small steps together.

Our first logo was the head of an African woman in the shape of a tree, expressing that our community sought to incorporate women's issues in our work as environmental warriors. As an ecofeminist, in SustyVibes I could blend both of my passions, for women and for the environment, and also find like-minded comrades who believed in the importance and intersection of the two issues. As a group, our community worked on several projects for women's empowerment and environmental protection. For instance, we taught some young girls living in the Niger Delta how to use photography for environmental advocacy. We planted thousands of trees across the country. We even went into schools to discuss the UN's Sustainable Development Goals and climate action with pupils. Because pop-culture was at the core of our approach, we held parties, movie screenings and several other interesting events as part of our efforts.

People often wonder how we were able to do all these things as young people. We wrote letters to schools and government bodies – we still do – and they do not get tired of us. In these letters, we declare our intentions. When people see that we have no bankroller or adult setting our agenda behind the scenes, they genuinely welcome us into their spaces and schools. We have also been very fortunate to work with some state agencies on projects such as our street conference, where we go into the streets to discuss issues such as climate change and waste pollution with the average Nigerian.

SustyVibes has now become a training ground for young people looking to make a change in the environmental space. So many new and creative initiatives have been born since our inception seven years ago. Our work was organic and funded from our own pockets. It is a testament to what happens when young people lead on issues they care about.

Our brand of activism falls within the model of the reformer, bringing about change within the system. It involves thinking about the ways young people can intentionally change; they deepen their understanding of our relationship with the environment and then actively make changes in their lifestyles. It is about understanding the impacts of climate change on us as a people and figuring out the best ways to hold our leaders accountable while holding space for intergenerational support and action. This form of activism wants to build a community of young people who are empowered by the skills they have acquired and are going into jobs that heal, repair, and solve critical problems in the world today. We know we are doing the right thing when our numbers increase and impacts spread across the country.

Mental Health and Activism at SustyVibes

By the time we got to our third year at SustyVibes, we were starting to feel stressed and overwhelmed with our work as activists and advocates. It was not exactly burnout, because we were incorporating a lot of fun and rest into our work. Rather, it was a case of eco-anxiety or eco-distress, a weaving together of feelings that included hopelessness, fear, overwhelm, and most especially anger – anger at the sheer burden of responsibility we felt about having to continuously demand for a safe future, and anger at the injustice of climate change and the unequal burden we have to deal with in the Global South.

Young people in the group who were already dealing with mental health challenges felt added stress when they read or witnessed something triggering about climate change. It seemed as if the more we knew about the problem, the more we encountered mental blocks that made us feel small and powerless. We were also presented with power dynamics that used cultural stereotypes to make activism hard. For instance, when the #EndSARS protests were abruptly halted by the Nigerian government and our access to Twitter was banned, we felt impotent and silenced, and this strongly impacted how we felt about our work as climate activists. When we read reports such as the Intergovernmental Panel on Climate Change and tried to analyze them as a community, climate change felt too big and complex and we felt too small and powerless. These were some of the ways climate distress showed up in our work at SustyVibes.

We could not define these emotions at the time, but we made an effort to explore them. We created a physical space and invited our community members to attend and share their experiences of emotional stress related to working as climate advocates and activists, establishing that we were not alone. Something was happening to us on a psychological level, and we needed support to build up our mental resilience.

Fortunately, I secured entry into a master's program in the United Kingdom and was afforded an opportunity to attend my first ever UN Climate Conference in Madrid, Spain. Ironically, what should have been one of my most energizing opportunities left me disillusioned. I witnessed youth tokenism and a general disregard for the urgency of the climate crisis from the world leaders present. Living in Europe made me even more aware of the racial roots of climate change and the colonial linkages to climate injustice. I decided to focus my master's research on eco-anxiety. This led me to start up The Eco-anxiety Africa Project (TEAP) upon my return to Nigeria. TEAP has been focusing on inquiry into climate change and its impacts on our mental health through participatory and lived experience-based research, space making, community action, and climate-aware psychotherapy. All of these, of course, are not very familiar to Africans; however, we recognize the need to do this work and bring African perspectives and solutions that are contextual and relatable.

Our Core Values at SustyVibes

As activists, we encounter multiple emotions through our work. To be resilient through these feelings and to heal damage that occurs, it is important to develop and maintain some core values and principles. While I do not claim to have completely hacked this area, I believe we are onto something.

The first core value at SustyVibes is ***passionate***. Activism requires passion and genuine commitment towards a cause. At SustyVibes, being passionate about the environment is a first step to being part of our community. Passion fuels us on hard days and makes us ever creative and willing to lead on new ideas. The second core value is ***community***. A community-centered approach to activism, whether virtual or physical, helps to navigate feelings of individual guilt and individualism and helps members draw strength and inspiration from one another. The third core value is ***having a sense of ownership*** within the movement. Every member is allowed and encouraged to contribute to our overall decision-making; any member can step up to lead a project at any time. We talk about our community members both serving the work of others within our collective and feeling as if they founded SustyVibes and are entitled to take the lead. The fourth core value is ***knowledgeable***. We feel empowered when we have knowledge about our histories and the policies and science of climate change. We want to learn so we can teach our community members and other young people well. Finally, we have a core value of centering our work in ***fun and simplicity*** – we incorporate joy into our activity work at every stage; we also ensure that our campaigns, projects, and communication are simple to understand. This way, we are making sustainability cool, relatable, and actionable.

The Relationship of Activism, Ecoactivism, and Mental Health

Jennifer has not felt that activism is a clear fix for eco-anxiety and related climate distress. Community action does impress her, however, as having a positive impact on how we interact with the emotions of climate crisis. She is inspired by organizations such as ***Plogging***, which incorporates sports with community clean-ups, and the ***World Clean-up Day*** as a way of bringing world communities together. She has also been inspired by the use of Indigenous practices, including storytelling, to motivate people to persist in the fight against climate change. Indigenous narratives and folklores can remind people of community and shared history and keep up important traditions of caring for the natural world. For example, one Nigerian organization, Health of Mother Earth Foundation, supports community resilience by exploring narrative building and storytelling through fictional writing and roleplay in what they call healing circles.

In Jennifer's earlier research with Extinction Rebellion (XR) leadership in Brighton, XR leaders highlighted the importance of embedding resilience within their activist movement. In fact, XR describes itself not by activism but by regeneration, defined by building a culture that cares for self as well as for others and the planet in order to get us out of toxic social structures: self in action and in relationship to community, planet, and all life. XR has a list of governing concepts to support this culture:

1. A shared vision of a world that is fit for future generations
2. Mobilizing the 3.5 percent of the population necessary for a cultural shift to embody this vision
3. Leaving the practices of our toxic system and comfort zones behind
4. Reflecting, learning, and planning again
5. Welcoming everyone
6. Striving actively to break down hierarchies of power
7. Avoiding blaming and shaming
8. Emphasizing autonomy and decentralization
9. Nonviolent regenerative work that supports all members.

This form of activism has been called "Alter-Activism," similar to Patten's evolutionary activism, in which the way activists live and connect is the power of the change. Organizing groups based on interests and professions, such as doctors and parents, helps XR address the change needed within their particular group more easily and is valuable for this community building.

XR groups declare their commitment to regenerative principles as part of their meetings:

<u>XR Regenerative Declaration</u>

we slow down our yeses
we give back work that we can't do
we see ourselves as in a marathon and not a sprint
we celebrate our wins,
but we accept that there will be failures along the way.

Implicit within this pledge is an awareness that activism may be damaging to mental health as well as beneficial. Activists may be exposed to harassment, arrest, violence, and, rarely, death. Even within the most careful approach, there can be structural inequity, with those more vulnerable to unjust and brutal treatment suffering the consequences of their activism disproportionately to those whose privilege more often protects them from police brutality and discrimination by the courts (Wretched of the Earth, 2019). Activists are confronted with backlash, lack of progress, and feelings of overwhelm from trying to solve large problems. Activists may miss out on sleep, exercise, and school work, and can develop symptoms of burn-out that include depression, frequent headaches, and insomnia (Gorski & Chen, 2015). In a review of the field that includes a study of forty-two student activists of all types, (Conner et al., 2023a), 60 percent reported adverse consequences of activism for their psychological well-being – particularly stress, exhaustion, and guilt for not doing enough.

At the same time, activism has been associated with many positive effects on mental health. For racially marginalized and LGBTQ+ youth, activism can be profoundly healing, buffering the negative mental health impacts of discrimination and violence (Alexander et al., 2022; Fine et al., 2018). By providing a space to examine and challenge embedded discriminatory structures and assumptions through critical consciousness – a teaching and inquiry technique that seeks to look for embedded power narratives and biased assumptions in societal structures and knowledge – marginalized youth shake both internalized and external oppression and gain cultural authenticity and self-knowledge (French et al., 2020). The power of the collective to effect change and the concept of radical hope, that positive change is possible even without having words for it, can help youth overcome demoralization and cynicism. While activists can suffer the harm of inadequate or hostile responses to their demands, most studies have shown that activism promotes positive affect, self-actualization, vitality, hope, and meaning (Klar & Kasser, 2009). For a scale measuring the costs and benefits of activism, see Appendix B (Costs and Benefits of Activism Scale, adapted from Smith et al., 2019).

Ballard and Ozer (2016) describe five ways that activism can support young people's mental health and well-being, including through improved social capital and connections to others, increased sense of personal identity and purpose, and lessened stress through empowerment and improved coping. More recently, research has shown that activism can be an effective place for youth to practice emotional regulation, decentering from and observing their reactions to their activist experiences and the causes they care about to bring those reactions under control (Fernandez & Watts, 2022). As one study summarized, activists feel "skilled up, in it together, with power in numbers and a place to go" (Montague & Eiroa-Orosa, 2017b).

Activism not only supports emotional well-being and buffers the negative mental health impacts of adverse stressors; it can also be important for the development of skills. Studies have shown benefits of activism on youth school grades, risk behaviors, civic knowledge, communication, time management and planning skills, interpersonal knowledge, capacity for social analysis and leadership (reviewed in Conner et al., 2023b). The learning that accrues in the climate activism space is also less likely to suffer from neoliberal cultural biases that equate progress with free-market privatized economic expansion and educate students towards such goals (Sharma, 2021), rather than the more collectivist and sustainable goals of a just and care-based circular economy.

Perhaps one of the most important benefits of youth activism is its role in identity development and efficacy. "Identity achievement" is a term that refers to "commitment to a particular set of values, priorities, or interpersonal style" (Pancer et al., 2007). Activists can cultivate many areas of identity, including sociopolitical, civic, and moral aspects of the self. Harre (2007) explores the role of activism as an "identity project," a term that unifies activities done in response to psychologically salient concerns – beyond the basics of survival and reproduction – including belonging, stimulations, efficacy, and integrity. Within the enhanced personal identity gained through activist "identity projects," activists can also feel more efficacious, both at an individual and group level (see Montague & Eiroa-Orosa, 2017a; Pearce & Larson, 2006). The support and efficacy of the collective can also support the activists' identities during setbacks and increase their chances of achieving other goals (Bandura, 2000), again showing the buffering effect of activism on stress, personal development, and well-being.

When we seek an empiric understanding of the relationship between youth mental health and activism for climate change specifically, we find a much narrower literature. Godden et al. (2021) collated subjective narratives about activism from Aboriginal and West Australian youth who participate in School Strike 4 Climate, Millennium Kids Inc, Climate Justice Union WA, and Sharma versus the Minister for the Environment. These young people said they benefitted from having a space to be honest and real about their climate distress, being supported by peers, parents, and mentors, engaging in collective action, communicating with each other during climate crises, and being honest and validated about the realities of the crisis. The researchers call for more participatory action research and decolonization of the systems damaging the well-being of these young people, including research strategies that mute individual voices.

In a study involving in-depth interviews of 15 New Zealand climate strike leaders, Bright and Eames (2022) found that these leaders described a series of preliminary stages to activism, including apathy, awareness, anxiety, and anger. These findings highlight the importance of understanding what feelings are most motivational in order to provide young people with climate education experiences that will help them engage most fully in their learning, a call echoed in Sharma's description of the young people he interviewed, who felt climate education in schools had treated it as superficial, negligible, and as an "aside" (Sharma, 2021).

Schwartz et al. (2023) have provided one of the only studies that included an adequately robust assessment of environmental activism in assessing its relationship to climate anxiety in young people. In their analysis, which correlated the general anxiety and depressive (functional) subscales of the Climate Change Anxiety (CCA) scale (Clayton & Karazsia, 2020) with a scale of eighteen types of environmental activist activity (Alisat & Riemer, 2015), engaging in collective climate action significantly lessened depression associated with the severity of the climate problem and individual powerlessness to affect it. Similar to other research on activism in groups with high levels of emotional distress due to discrimination, such as LGBTQ+ and youth of color, these results confirm that activism can reduce distress about the problem.

Conclusion

Throughout this chapter, we have discussed and defined movements and activism led by youth and children from all over the world. We described the four roles of activism and provided some examples of past and current movements that use different activism strategies. We dove into a detailed personal journey of founding SustyVibes in Nigeria and how Jennifer Uchendu and her colleagues built a movement grounded in youth participation, leadership, and fun. We also discussed some core values that have made SustyVibes continue to stay active in Nigeria and beyond, building self-care, passion, fun, and community as they work towards their goals. As we conclude, we want to mention one final consideration. Not every movement has to last forever. Some movements go viral and inspire others to start other spin-off movements or develop new creative forms of climate action. Others remain small and local until their task is complete. Evolution is a chaotic process of interweaving systems that rise and fall in their interactions. Acknowledging this aspect of activism helps us understand the role of movements and appreciate the value they bring in their most active years. Finally, being creative and allowing space for the growth, diversity of ideas, and discussion that have been maintained within SustyVibes and other generative and regenerative climate activist groups allows for the flexibility that keeps activist activity vibrant, no matter what type or what size. While strategies such as space making, community action, and storytelling protect against climate distress and the emotional toll of climate activism, ultimately it is our ability to live in harmony and support each other and other beings in cycles of rest, renewal, and activity that will sustain the most regenerative world.

References

Alexander, A. C., Waring, J. J. C., Noble, B., Bradley, D., Olurotimi, O., Fronheiser, J., ..., & Kendzor, D. E. (2023). Perceptions of mental health and exploring the role of social activism among African Americans exposed to media coverage of police brutality and protests. *Journal of Racial and Ethnic Health Disparities*, 10(3), 1403–1413. https://doi.org/10.1007/s40615-022-01326-2

Alisat, S., & Riemer, M. (2015). The environmental action scale: Development and psychometric evaluation. *Journal of Environmental Psychology*, 43, 13–23. https://doi.org/10.1016/j.jenvp.2015.05.006

Anderson, J. (2013). Five principles of useful political activism. https://blogs.dcvelocity.com/policy/2013/09/five-principles-of-useful-political-activism.html

Ballard, P. J., & Ozer, E. (2016). The implications of youth activism for health and well-being. In J. O. Conner & S. M. Rosen (Eds.), *Contemporary youth activism* (pp. 223–243). ABC-CLIO.

Bandura, A. (2000). Exercise of human agency through collective efficacy. *Current Directions in Psychological Science*, 9(3), 75–78. https://doi.org/10.1111/1467-8721.00064

Bright, M. & Eames, C. (2022). From apathy through anxiety to action: Emotions as motivators for youth climate strike leaders. *Australian Journal of Environmental Education*, 38(1), 13–25. https://doi.org/10.1017/aee.2021.22

Christens, B. D., Winn, L. T., & Duke, A. M. (2016). Empowerment and critical consciousness: A conceptual cross-fertilization. *Adolescent Research Review*, 1(1), 15–27. https://doi.org/10.1007/s40894-015-0019-3

Clayton, S., & Karazsia, B. T. (2020). Development and validation of a measure of climate change anxiety. *Journal of Environmental Psychology*, 69, 101434. https://doi.org/10.1016/j.jenvp.2020.101434

Conner, J. O., Crawford, E., & Galioto, M. (2023a). The mental health effects of student activism: Persisting despite psychological costs. *Journal of Adolescent Research*, 38(1), 80–109. https://doi.org/10.1177/07435584211006789

Conner, J. O., Greytak, E., Evich, C. D., & Wray-Lake, L. (2023b). Burnout and belonging: How the costs and benefits of youth activism affect youth health and wellbeing. *Youth*, 3(1), 127–145. https://doi.org/10.3390/youth3010009

Eisenberg, N. & Fabes, R. A. (1998). Prosocial development. In N. Eisenberg (Ed.), *Handbook of child psychology: Vol. 3. Social, emotional, and personality development* (5th ed., pp. 701–778). Wiley. https://doi.org/10.1002/9780470147658.chpsy0311

Fernandez, J. & Watts, R.J. (2022). Sociopolitical development as emotional work: How young organizers engage emotions to support community organizing for transformative racial justice. *Journal of Adolescent Research*, 38(4). https://doi.org/10.1177/07435584221091497

Fernandez-Ballesteros, R., Diez-Nicolas, J., Caprara, G. V., Barbaranelli, C., & Bandura, A. (2002). Determinants and structural relation of personal efficacy to collective efficacy. *Applied Psychology*, 51(1), 107–125. https://doi.org/10.1111/1464-0597.00081

Fine, M., Torre, M. E., Frost, D. M., & Cabana, A. L. (2018). Queer solidarities: New activisms erupting at the intersection of structural precarity and radical misrecog- nition. *Journal of Social and Political Psychology*, 6(2), 608–630. https://doi.org/10.5964/jspp.v6i2.905

French, B., Lewis, J., Mosley, D., Adames, H., Chavez-Duenas, N., Chen, G., & Neville, H. (2020). Towards a psychological framework for radical healing in communities of color. *The Counseling Psychologist*, 48(1), 14–46. https://doi.org/10.1177/0011000019843506

Gilster, M. E. (2012). Comparing neighborhood-focused activism and volunteerism: Psychological well-being and social connectedness. *Journal of Community Psychology*, 40(7), 769–784. https://doi.org/10.1002/jcop.20528

Godden, N. J., Farrant, B. M., Yallup Farrant, J., Heyink, E., Carot Collins, E., Burgemeister, B., ..., & Cooper, T. (2021). Climate change, activism, and supporting the mental health of children and young people: Perspectives from Western Australia. *Journal of Paediatrics and Child Health*, 57(11), 1759–1764. https://doi.org/10.1111/jpc.15649

Gorski, P. C. & Chen, C. (2015). "Frayed all over:" The causes and consequences of activist burnout among social justice education activists. *Educational Studies (Ames)*, 51(5), 385–405. https://doi.org/10.1080/00131946.2015.1075989

Gulliver, R. (2022). Australian campaign case study: Stop Adani (2012–2022). *The Commons* Library. https://commonslibrary.org/australian-campaign-case-study-stop-adani-2012-2022/

Harré, N. (2007). Community service or activism as an identity project for youth. *Journal of Community Psychology*, 35(6), 711–724. https://doi.org/10.1002/jcop.20174

Kirshner, B. (2007). Introduction: Youth activism as a context for learning and development. *American Behavioral Scientist*, 51(3), 367–379. https://doi.org/10.1177/0002764207306065

Kirshner, B. (2009). "Power in numbers": Youth organizing as a context for exploring civic identity. *Journal of Research on Adolescence*, 19(3), 414–440. https://doi.org/10.1111/j.1532-7795.2009.00601.x

Klar, M., & Kasser, T. (2009). Some benefits of being an activist: Measuring activism and its role in psychological well-being. *Political Psychology*, 30(5), 755–777. https://doi.org/10.1111/j.1467-9221.2009.00724.x

Larson, R. W. & Hansen, D. (2005). The development of strategic thinking: Learning to impact human systems in a youth activism program. *Human Development*, 48, 327–349. https://doi.org/10.1159/000088251

Maslach, C. & Gomes, M.E. (2006). Overcoming burnout. In R. M. MacNair (Ed.), *Working for peace: A handbook of practical psychology and other tools* (pp. 43–50). Impact Publishers.

Montague, A. C. & Eiroa-Orosa, F. J. (2017a). Exploring the role of engagement on well-being and personal development: A review of adolescent and mental health activism. In N. J. L. Brown, T. Lomas, & F. J. Eiroa-Orosa (Eds.), *The Routledge international handbook of critical positive psychology* (pp. 437–446). Routledge.

Montague, A. P., & Eiroa-Orosa, F. J. (2017b). In it together: Exploring how belonging to a youth activist group enhances well-being. *Journal of Community Psychology*, 46(1), 23–43. https://doi.org/10.1002/jcop.21914

Mouawad, J. (2009). Shell to pay $15.5 million to settle Nigerian case. *New York Times*, June 9. www.nytimes.com/2009/06/09/business/global/09shell.html?ref=global

Moyer, B. (2001). *Doing democracy: The MAP model for organizing social movements*. New Society Publishers, as adopted by The Commons Library, https://commonslibrary.org/the-four-roles-of-social-activism/ (accessed May 28, 2023).

Ogoni Case Study (n.d.). The curse of oil in Ogoniland. http://websites.umich.edu/~snre492/cases_03-04/Ogoni/Ogoni_case_study.htm

Pancer, S. M., Pratt, M., Hunsberger, B., & Alisat, S. (2007). Community and political involvement in adolescence: What distinguishes the activists from the uninvolved? *Journal of Community Psychology*, 35(6), 741–759. https://doi.org/10.1002/jcop.20176

Pearce, N., & Larson, R. (2006). How teens become engaged in youth development programs: The process of motivational change in a civic activism organization. *Applied Developmental Science*, 10(3), 121–131. https://doi.org/10.1207/s1532480xads1003_2

Schwartz, S.E.O., Benoit, L., Clayton, S., Parnes, M. F., Swenson, L., & Lowe, S. R. (2023). Climate change anxiety and mental health: Environmental activism as buffer. *Current Psychology*, 42, 16708–16721. https://doi.org/10.1007/s12144-022-02735-6

Sharma, R. (2021). Learning to recycle is not enough: Youth-led climate activism and climate change education. In R. Iyengar & C. T. Kwauk (Eds.), *Curriculum and learning for climate action: Toward an SDG 4.7 roadmap for systems change* (Vol. 5). Brill. https://doi.org/10.1163/9789004471818

Smith, K.B., Hibbing, M.V., & Hibbing J.R. (2019) *Friends, relatives, sanity, and health: The costs of politics*. PLoS ONE, 14(9), e0221870. https://doi.org/10.1371/journal.pone.0221870

UN General Assembly (1989). *Convention on the Rights of the Child*, November, 20. United Nations, Treaty Series, vol. 1577, p. 3. www.refworld.org/docid/3ae6b38f0.html, accessed May 28, 2023.

Wretched of the Earth (2019). An open letter to extinction rebellion. www.redpepper.org.uk/an-open-letter-to-extinction-rebellion/

Zari (2020). Basic activism principles. https://standuptothegrownups.net/147/basic-activism-principles/

CHAPTER 19

Perspectives from Creative Spaces
Transforming Climate Distress through Creative Practice and Re-storying

Jeppe Graugaard

Introduction: Being Young in a Time of Planetary Change

In late 2008, I had an experience that changed my outlook on life for good. I was 25 years old, and my interest in politics, anthropology, cybernetics, and chaos theory had led me to enter a master's program on climate change. I remember sitting at the desk in my study, when I first came across the collection of graphs produced by Steffen et al. (2004) for the report "Global Change and the Earth System: A Planet under Pressure." The graphs show how human activities have become the main driver for change in the Earth system and illustrate trends in greenhouse gases, resource consumption, and habitat destruction between the years 1750 and 2000. Looking across all of the graphs, it was clear that all of these trends were accelerating exponentially. Extrapolating the trends to 2008, I felt physically overwhelmed. The thought that living in the twenty-first century is like riding a megatrend of accelerating destruction sent me to bed. I didn't get out until days later.

Processing the emotional shock of understanding those graphs took years. It was a very lonely process in the beginning. Speaking to my friends about it felt alienating when they told me that everything will turn out ok – or deflected the topic altogether. I needed long breaks from thinking about it so as not to reenter an emotional sphere which was overwhelming and uncontrollable. But as I began research for my PhD on grassroots innovation and societal transitions, I found a group of people with whom I could have a different kind of conversation. The Dark Mountain Project began as an endeavor to start a literary movement that could confront being "trapped inside a runaway narrative, headed for the worst kind of encounter with reality" (Kingsnorth & Hine, 2009). In the events and conversations that sprang up around the publication of the Dark Mountain manifesto – a publication that invited readers to join the Dark Mountain Project – a space emerged in which people could speak freely and openly about how they experience the climate crisis. By partaking in the conversational mode that formed within that space, something surprising happened to my feelings of despair and anxiety: they eased and, eventually, gave way to a sense of acceptance and, later, belonging.

As more and more young people become aware of the climate crisis and have to deal with the psychological consequences of facing an increasingly uncertain future, it is important that young people, those who work with young people, and those whose work affects young people, have access to a broad spectrum of approaches to help them deal with the psychological, emotional, and spiritual complications that emerge from growing up in a time of global climate crisis. Here, there is ample inspiration to draw from creative spaces – spaces where people bring their full attention and creativity to bear on whatever they are doing, individually or collectively – which explore the relationship between humans and more-than-human nature. In such spaces, people freely exercise a creative state of mind of the kind David Bohm says "is always open to learning what is new, to perceiving new differences and similarities, leading to new orders and structures, rather than always tending to impose familiar orders and structures in the field of what is seen" (Bohm, 2004, p. 21). Creative spaces can take the form of a creative practice, such as a craft, an art form, or body work, but they can also exist in collective learning environments, such as a class or a game. As such, creative spaces are not defined spatially or temporally but by the mindset of the practitioners.

In this chapter, I will outline some of the findings from my research on the transformative potential of creative spaces on the distress arising from growing awareness of the global climate crisis. I have used this approach in my work as a folk high school teacher at Ry Folk Highschool in Denmark, where I have taught a course on global ecology and alternatives to consumer society for the last six years to young people in the age group 18–25.

Making Sense of Systemic Global Crises

A seminal insight from cross-disciplinary research related to the history of human-made climate change is that global warming is best understood not just as a consequence or output of material systems but as a cultural predicament (Capra & Luisi, 2014; Graeber & Wengrow, 2021; Lent, 2017; Latour, 2018; McKibben, 2019; de Oliveira, 2021). To understand the roots of climate change it is necessary to move beyond questions that merely focus on the material and technical aspects of societal evolution and instead ask questions such as: "how do societies that normalize waste and toxic by-products emerge in the first place?" Overconsumption, pollution, and unsustainable ways of life are not the result of separate environmental, social, and economic crises but rather part of an interconnected problematic with deeper roots in the worldviews, cultural values, and social structures connected with modernity and late capitalism (Jackson, 2021; Moore, 2016). This perspective opens up and invites the opportunity to reenvision the ways in which we imagine and enact our relationship with the surrounding world as a way to ground and resituate our social roles within the places we inhabit. Transitioning towards more just, equal and sustainable societies involves transitioning the worldviews and ways of being of people living in high-consumption societies. This change can be conceptualized as a transformation of the epistemological and ontological frameworks that guide individual lives and collective action (Graugaard, 2014).

The crux of such an "onto-epistemological transition," understood as a transformation within personal and collective ways of knowing and being, is a shift in foundational beliefs and meaning-making. Beliefs about the structure of the world and how it is known guide our interactions and relationships (Larson, 2011; McIntosh, 2008). Meaning gives form to perception (Bohm, 2004) and meaning-making imbues lived reality with cognitive "patterns" and "restraints" (Bateson, 2000; McGilchrist, 2009). For example, if I understand the world to consist primarily of material objects where individuals compete to optimize their preferences and choices, I will perceive and experience life differently than if I see the world as made up of a variety of living beings who play different roles, and have different histories and functions, within integrated ecosystems and habitats. How we understand and make sense of the world, and of the global climate crisis, affects what we consider to be meaningful action. Putting *meaning-making* at the center of addressing social and environmental problems can help us understand how particular activities or interventions open up or close down new avenues for thinking and acting. To this end, it is helpful to look at the ways in which narratives of climate, nature, sustainability, and the future develop and function within interpretive communities and how mutual narration of these topics can reframe the storyline and give rise to new meanings and actions within narrators' lives.

Narratives are both "recipes for structuring experience which direct us into the future" (Bruner, 2004, p. 708) and a form of "wayfaring" where storying is in itself knowing and storytelling is bringing what is known

Table 19.1 *Examples of cultural metaphors that guide how we think about our subjectivity*

The human body:	The body is a container/The brain is a computer
Time:	Time is money/The future is approaching
Money:	Money is power/Money makes the world go around
The economy:	The economy as a market/The invisible hand creates equilibrium
Nature:	Nature as wilderness/Nature is red in tooth and claw
History:	History is a river/History progresses
Evolution:	Survival of the fittest/The selfish gene
The universe:	The universe is a clockwork/The billiard ball universe

to life (Ingold, 2011). They can be seen as integral to the "framework of people's reality structures" (McIntosh, 2012, p. 235) and this framework is partly revealed in the central metaphors that are employed to give stories their meaning: metaphors help us make sense of one thing in terms of another and thereby bring particular imageries, values, and ideas to the story. Metaphors focus attention on certain aspects of the wider movement of life and privilege certain ways of understanding over others with real social and political consequences. In his in-depth study of the role of metaphors in shaping cultural values and social relations, Brendon Larson (2011) describes how preexistent metaphysical and cultural suppositions have come to be accepted as "facts" in scientific and social discourse through the way metaphors connect, feed back, and resonate with each other. "Framing metaphors" form a web of meaning which place thought and language in living context and structure the experience of reality. For example, you are bound to think and feel differently if you take our current situation to be one of "being onboard Titanic" or see it as a phase of "humanity coming of age." See Table 19.1 for examples of some key metaphors that frame how we think about the world and our place in it within Western cultures.

In this way, narrative inquiry offers possibilities for resituating the narrator within their lifeworld and opening up new ways of thinking and acting. Ten years ago, working with the stories we tell about the systemic crises connected with global changes in the Earth's climate system – including what our role as a species has been in creating those changes and how we confront these circumstances on an individual level – seemed to provide an opening for reframing the sustainability challenge and reimagining relations between human and more-than-human worlds. Today, new concerns regarding the story of global crises have emerged – and these are perhaps even more pressing as global media (largely) have stopped sowing doubt around climate science and more and more young people become aware of the severity and scale of the crises we are dealing with. Faced with the terrible facts of climate catastrophe, mass extinction and extreme weather, how do we as parents, teachers, health workers, community activists, policymakers – from any position of authority – enable young people to become whole, healthy, and resilient human beings? How do we establish interpretive communities where young people can make sense of global crises and receive support for the cognitive and emotional processes they are going through? And how do we create spaces where young people can transform a direct experience of the regenerative force within nature into their personal lives and outlook?

Research within various disciplines which consider the effects of creative practices and nature experiences offer important insights into these questions – not just in terms of the potential of narrative inquiry as a way to engender new ways of thinking and being but also with regard to the transformative power of practicing convivial skills and relationships.

The next section outlines some of the findings from my research with the Dark Mountain Project on the ways in which this particular interpretive community helped individuals come to terms with the consequences of climate change through collective narrative inquiry and meaning-making. The research project investigated how alternative worldviews are imagined and embodied in grassroots innovations through an in-depth ethnographic study of the Dark Mountain Project.

Researching the Dark Mountain Project

In the years following the publication of "Uncivilisation – The Dark Mountain Manifesto" (Kingsnorth & Hine, 2009), I followed different offline and online conversations, talks and events curated by the Dark Mountain Project. The manifesto was authored by the British writers Paul Kingsnorth and Dougald Hine, who decided to launch their own journal in response to a perceived lack of literary and artistic expressions that grapple with the realities of interweaving ecological, social, and economic crises. The project quickly attracted a growing number of participants and initiated various public debates about environmentalism, social-ecological collapse, art, and cultural narratives. The first issue of the Dark Mountain journal was published in the summer of 2010, showcasing a range of "uncivilized" essays, short stories, poems, interviews, and images authored by "mountaineers" from across the globe. The Dark Mountain website and associated Ning platform became fora for online discussions that spilled over into the blogosphere and other virtual social networks while a series of festivals, book launches, public debates, local meetings, and artistic events became the basis for offline interactions around the ideas of the project. Local groups sprang up across Britain, America, Australia, Sweden, and a number of other countries.

The Dark Mountain manifesto presented a perspective on global systemic crises which had not yet found its way to the mainstream in 2009: we live in a time of ecological and economic collapse and the foundations of global civilization are falling apart. This outlook calls for a different kind of conversation about the crises we are facing – and how we got into them:

> And so we find ourselves, all of us together, poised trembling on the edge of a change so massive that we have no way of gauging it. None of us know where to look, but all of us know not to look down. Secretly, we all think we are doomed: even the politicians think this; even the environmentalists. Some of us deal with it by going shopping. Some deal with it by hoping it is true. Some give up in despair. Some work frantically to try and fend off the coming storm.
>
> Our question is: what would happen if we looked down? Would it be as bad as we imagine? What might we see? Could it even be good for us?
>
> We believe it is time to look down. (Kingsnorth & Hine, 2009, p. 15)

The manifesto is an open call to join the discussion and contribute words and images to the Dark Mountain journal. The ambiguity and openness about the uncertainty of what would come of the project, combined with the poetic imagery of looking at socioecological collapse as a "journey," an "expedition," or a "climb up the Dark Mountain," provided the reader with different possibilities for joining in. By opening a space for a discussion about the future with the premise that socio-environmental crises cannot be "solved" – but rather are realities we have to come to terms with – the Dark Mountain Project became a platform for a wide range of conversations about how to confront the prospect of "changes so massive that we have no way of gauging them." As one person put it to me, encountering the Dark Mountain Project "was a realization that I wasn't alone and that there is a way of being that can somehow cope with this" (Graugaard, 2014, p. 138).

The manifesto opened up a lacking perspective on the mainstream framing of the sustainability challenge. Adams (2014) has observed that the narrative of Uncivilization occupies a space between two dominant narratives about climate change: one about consequences and catastrophic loss, another about solutions and averting crisis. Drawing on Rosemary

Randall's (2009) work on the psychological cost of this "split" mainstream narrative which "projects all loss into the future making it catastrophic and unmanageable, denies the losses that have to be faced now and prevents us from dealing with them" (p. 127), Adams suggests that the Dark Mountain Project provides a new narrative framing which lies outside both business-as-usual optimism and apocalyptic defeatism. For many, "Uncivilization" presented a necessary break with mainstream narratives and, perhaps more importantly, a meaningful countermeasure: creating a different reality by finding new stories about life within civilization. Kingsnorth and Hine's (2009) critique and "questioning the foundations of civilization, the myth of human centrality" (p. 28) went hand in hand with a call for creative explorations of other ways of seeing and being in the world. The creative responses to this call became an important way for many participants to work through the overwhelming thoughts and feelings connected with climate catastrophe.

Creative Practice as a Way of Confronting Existential Uncertainties

In the gradual development of the Dark Mountain Project into a more or less coherent cultural movement, which provides a platform for a different kind of conversation about systemic global crisis, creative practice became a way not only to articulate a critique of the origins of this crisis but also to begin embodying alternate ways of seeing and being in it. This can be seen as acts of "re-storying," which is also a core theme in the manifesto:

> Words and images can change minds, hearts, even the course of history. Their makers shape the stories people carry through their lives, unearth old ones and breathe them back to life, add new twists, point to unexpected endings. It is time to pick up the threads and make the stories new, as they must always be made new, starting from where we are. (Kingsnorth & Hine, 2009, p. 12)

The various forms of practice that participants in the Dark Mountain Project engage with include writing, painting, photography, crafts, storytelling, performances, installations, game-playing, music, body practices, dialogue, theatre, improvised rituals, and contemplative exercises. The journal exhibits a wide range of creative expressions in print format while the festivals and events have included a diversity of workshops, skill shares, and performances. In many of the conversations, events and activities I took part in, there was a clear sense that engaging in creative practice is a means of inhabiting a different mindset, seeing the lifeworld differently and experimenting with new metaphors and imagery (examples of what this means and looks like in practice can be found in the Dark Mountain journal and on their website).

Besides the potential therapeutic effect of creative expression, the experimentation with different creative practices in the context of the Dark Mountain Project should be seen as an endeavor to actively re-story and reexperience human–nature relations through imaginative exercise. As McGilchrist (2009) points out, the imagination plays a central role in the process of forming personal identities: it is in the imagination that the meaning of a particular image or story falls into place within the larger web of metaphors or structures of the mind. By imagining what a story is like in lived reality, it subsequently becomes possible to enact this within the lifeworld. As one participant described it to me: "While reading stories we are not trapped in thought, we are. We exist imaginatively within an alternate set of conditions, not stuck within our present conditioning. We leave the finite limitations of what-has-been-conceived. We expand our view" (Graugaard, 2014, p. 174). In opening up a space for imagining a different kind of reality, art and creative practice can support both envisioning and enacting new worldviews. Because art springs from and is grasped through the imagination, it is a space that provides direct access to other ways of seeing. In creating a poem, a piece of writing, a painting or picture, a practitioner has to remain open to the ambiguity within what is created in order to let the work emerge and take form. And, if a work of art tells a particular story, the artist becomes familiar with the people and things that inhabit that story: in storying, we imagine how plots unfold and how people and objects relate (Ingold, 2011).

By exploring and practicing a different way of seeing or being in the imagination it becomes possible to begin to embody that different way of relating to the surrounding world and articulate what it is like. However, this process is impossible to control or force. One participant used the metaphor of "a snake shedding its skin" to describe how the shifts in perception and meaning-making are organic processes that cannot be willed. Reason can help us identify concepts or ways of thinking that (de)limit the imagination, but actually probing into what the world might be like outside of past mental constructs involves other faculties than thought. That is why *attitude* emerged as a theme in both written and live conversations during the research. Paul Kingsnorth described to me that "at the heart of Dark Mountain is an attitude … to life and an attitude to reality and to one's situation" (Graugaard, 2014, p. 141). One participant described her understanding of this attitude as "a stance of humility, navigating with uncertainty instead of the desire for security, or the even deeper desire to be right" (Graugaard, 2014, p. 143). Part of the effort to "make the stories new" involves a letting go of the old systems of meaning – and in the absence of a master narrative it is necessary to "accept the chaotic as the only way past our condition," as another participant put it (Graugaard, 2014, p. 143).

To "navigate with uncertainty" it is necessary to be attentive to the present moment and to develop the ability to respond to whatever the moment brings. These skills are honed within creative practices, play and experimentation. As a skill of unrehearsed action in the face of unanticipated circumstances, *improvisation* became another theme that ran through many of the conversations in or around the Dark Mountain Project in the first years. Many of the performances and workshops that took place at the festivals and events featured an element of improvisation. Dougald Hine has proposed that improvisation offers a radically different principle for social organization to what he calls "orchestration" because it involves learning to partake in complex relationships without continually having to arrive at an expressed agreement or consensus (Hine, 2011). For many of the participants whom I interviewed, improvisation is a life skill, which opens up new perspectives by learning to be attentive to what is going on in the moment, and getting to grips with how to respond creatively to that through detachment from outcomes, attention to means, and openness to the surrounding environment.

Creative practices, which enable the practitioner to confront uncertainty without being overwhelmed by feelings of dismay or despair, can thus be a way to learn to confront the existential uncertainties that open up in the face of climate catastrophe. But more than that, engaging creatively with existential uncertainty can help to find new ways of re-storying both individual and collective futures. There was a shared recognition among the Dark Mountain participants I interviewed that we live "in between stories" and that, in such a time of both letting go and opening up to new ways of storying a life, it is necessary to actively create alternate realities, which enable meaningful and good lives in a time of global crises.

Re-storying as the Creation of Alternate Realities

Looking at the big issues of climate change, biodiversity loss, global pollution, and social upheaval that frame our time is disconcerting and provokes existential questions both at the personal and collective level. It also invites questioning of the modern narrative of progress and development because, in the light of global crises, the future clearly does not look like an upgrade of the status quo. The dissolution of particular narratives implies a period of not knowing or "being without reason," a threshold state where clarity and meaning are absent or obscure, and identities and social positions are momentarily suspended. Anthropologists describe threshold or "liminal" states as "characterized by the dislocation of established structures, the reversal of hierarchies, and uncertainty regarding the continuity of tradition and future outcomes" (Horvath et al., 2009, p. 3). A degree of liminality is inherent to transitory situations or events where participants stand at a threshold between worldviews (Szakolczai, 2009). It is a state where social structures are temporarily interrupted and from which new relationships can emerge (Turner, 1974). Being "between stories" – conceived as a situation or time where established ideas and identities give way to new relations and ways of seeing – is implicit in many of the writings, conversations and performances inspired by the Dark Mountain Project.

In combination with the approach to creative practice, and grounded in the attitude towards uncertainty described above, working actively with renarrating or re-storying one's own lifeworld was integral to personal participation in the Dark Mountain Project among the participants I interviewed. This process involved an extended period of feeling in between stories – a state which is necessary for finding something "outside" of existing frames of reference or understanding. Here, being part of a community of interpreters was crucial in terms of both emotional support and integration of new meanings. In the gatherings I attended, there was an explicit focus on "holding the space" for the inquiry and conversation in a way that engendered trust and conviviality. Establishing a secure ground for transformative conversations is perhaps one of the most important aspects – and learnings – of the Dark Mountain Project, and it has to a large degree depended on the skills and capacities of its participants: it involves a willingness to "unlearn" habitual modes of interacting, to becoming comfortable with not constructing answers or solutions, and to being prepared to sit with the incompleteness of a broken narrative about one's lifeworld. When this approach to mutual inquiry worked, it opened up the possibility of experimenting with other ways of seeing as well as offered support and inspiration for personal practices and questioning of engrained preconceptions.

Re-storying – as a process of revisiting, reflecting, and renarrating one's own story of who we are, why we are here, and where we are going – can be seen as a way of recalibrating the meanings and metaphors that shape a life. By organizing events, characters, and plots, as well as contextualizing perspectives, relationships, and actions, narratives position narrators in relation to the wider universe and give meaning to the complex phenomena of the lifeworld. Communications theorist Walter Fisher (1987) explained how narratives are "meant to give order to human experience and to induce others to dwell in them in order to establish ways of living in common, in intellectual and spiritual communities in which there is confirmation of the story that constitutes one's life" (p. 63). Recognizing narration as a process of meaning- and identity-making in which the narrator positions herself interactively within a wider field of relationships, Bamberg (2004) describes participation in locally situated narrating practices as potentially emancipatory: by situating subjectivities differently to positions given in a cultural meta-narrative, the narrator creates a possibility for a transformation in her onto-epistemological outlook. When her role shifts within the narrative, so does her worldview and relationships. Viewing narratives as "landscapes for the perception of different possibilities," renarrating one's own life-story can be seen as a process of opening up for new realities to emerge.

From his experience with creating the campaign that led to the community buyout of the Isle of Eigg in 1997, Alastair McIntosh (2001) describes how what was initially deemed impossible became reality through "constellating an alternate reality." This involved working actively with the stories that constituted "the fabric of social reality" and "alter[ing] the co-ordinates by which reality was mapped and reset them" (p. 166). Such transformation entails a repositioning of the involved human actors within their wider social relations, allowing people to envision and enact a qualitatively different reality: "At the deepest level of the psyche this transformation has got to be cosmological. It has got to position the human person more meaningfully than before in relation to the universe" (p. 166). This approach to re-storying was implicit to many of the stories and meetings, and much of the art, that were produced in the context of the Dark Mountain Project (McIntosh is a friend of Paul Kingsnorth and Dougald Hine and a contributor to the journal). As a critique of the narrative framing of progress, the project invites participants to experiment with "constellating alternate realities." As one participant put it to me: "we don't change the meta-narrative by sitting around thinking up new stories. We do it by getting out there. By not only seeing in new ways, but living in new ways. By being the subjects for those stories. More than that – by being the stories" (Graugaard, 2014, p. 164).

Participants in the project experimented with re-storying in a variety of ways: through the various creative practices mentioned above, through contemplative practices, nature rites and experiences, dialogue and collaborative inquiry as well as a wide range of craft and DIY projects. These different experiments did not necessarily grow out of the Dark Mountain Project – the project became a place for people to converge and find support for their experimentation with establishing new relations between people and the more-than-human world. As I experienced myself, re-storying may start out feeling like something that requires a particular mindset or space but the real work is to integrate the new story into the life that is lived.

Working Creatively with the Frameworks That Delineate our Lifeworlds

At least two aspects of the creative spaces that emerged in connection with the Dark Mountain Project are particular to Dark Mountain – and the learning that has grown from the project should be seen in the context of the narrative of the manifesto and the evolution of Dark Mountain as a cultural movement. First of all, the acceptance of collapse as a framing of the present global situation can be both unsettling and disorienting; it can create a turbulence within familiar ways of thinking, which is both emotionally difficult and psychologically disconcerting. But the disruption of the narrative framing of progress allows for giving up hope or expectation – at least momentarily – and come to terms with the reality that cultures, languages, creatures, and habitats are disappearing at a rate that has very few precedents in Earth's history. While this is not an easy process, it is an important psychological experience with parallels to Randall's (2009) work on dealing with loss. In this way, the framing of collapse opens the door to grief and mourning. *Collapse* implies a dissolution of a particular imagination of the future and the gradual cessation of associated concepts, meanings, and beliefs. In this way, collapse is also a breakdown in the validity and meaning of some of the concepts and constructs that have previously made sense of reality and shaped a course of life. This also applies to the wider cultural realm where concepts and narratives framed by progress are increasingly failing to explain the course of history as well as individual lifeworlds.

Secondly, the explicit rejection of anthropocentrism and the embrace of animism and ecocentrism gives nature "centre stage, not as a receptacle for human activities, emotions, or narratives, but as itself, on its own inhuman terms," as Greer puts it in the first Dark Mountain journal (Greer, 2010, p. 7). Ecocentrism is not only an ethical outlook, it is connected with the view that stories are constitutive of reality, which, in the words of the manifesto, "remains mysterious, as incapable of being approached directly as a hunter's quarry" (Kingsnorth & Hine, 2009, p. 10). This approach supplements the narrative of collapse with a narrative of re-enchantment understood as "a reconceiving and a re-seeing and sensing of this wild-flowering world as something that cannot ever be fully objectified" (Hine & Abram, 2011, p. 64). It is this element which brings the authors of the manifesto to speak of *hope beyond hope*: "The end of the world as we know it is not the end of the world full stop. Together, we will find the hope beyond hope, the paths which lead to the unknown world ahead of us" (Kingsnorth & Hine, 2009, p. 19).

With these aspects of the research in mind, we can now consider how learnings from the Dark Mountain Project translate into suggestions for the significance of creative spaces in working with young people who experience distress in response to climate change and systemic global crises.

The Role of Creative Spaces in Learning to Respond to Climate Distress

It is important to underline that feelings of distress, fear, anxiety, and despondency in relation to climate change and global crises should not be considered wrong or unwanted but are actually healthy responses to being confronted with a predicament with no easy solutions. These seemingly negative psychological and emotional states are not the end station but important places along the way of dealing with the existential issues that arise in the wake of becoming aware of the consequences of planetary change. However, if these states are not addressed adequately – and young people who are experiencing climate distress often need help and guidance – they can present a psychological impasse, which can lead to more serious feelings of meaninglessness and depression. The climate crisis should be seen as a call for new meanings and values which will aid us in building lives that do not cost the Earth but support the continued flourishing of the community of life. In the shift towards low-consumption lifestyles, we may lose some sense of ease and comfort, but life becomes more meaningful as we build new relations between people and the more-than-human world within human-scale, post-industrial societies.

To support young people in coming to terms with climate change and finding ways to build flourishing lives, those who work with young people, or who have responsibility for young people, should look across disciplines that explore the relation between humans and more-than-human nature to find their own personal approach and resources for offering guidance, counsel, and inspiration. There are many places to look for resources of this kind: from nature writing and the literature on ecoliteracy to outdoor learning activities and contemplative practices. A focus on human–nature relations offers possibilities for working with the kind of onto-epistemological transformation that can "position the human person more meaningfully than before in relation to the universe" (McIntosh, 2001, p. 166). Enhanced eco-literacy and attention to the living world, combined with actively working with narrative inquiry and re-storying, can support each of us in redefining some of the parameters that define our life and outlook. In addition to the above descriptions, I would like to highlight some observations from my research with the Dark Mountain project, which have general cogency and may help others in establishing the ground for a personal practice or collective conversation that grapples with global crises and planetary change. I have used these insights in my own courses, which deal with global ecology, politics, and climate change. Some have to do with the framing and dynamics of the creative space and some have to do with content and relations.

In group-work it is imperative to establish a safe space where young people can be themselves without fear of being wrong. The space itself affects what kind of interactions and transformation is possible. It is important that those who are responsible for holding the space pay attention to both setting and maintaining a frame that allows the participants to feel ownership and build trust. To create a common ground that is generative for shared inquiry and dialogue, it is helpful to encourage reciprocity, respect, and openness between young people. The mode of conversation is different to a discussion or debate, so it is necessary for young people to accept whatever comes up instead of trying to push a certain viewpoint or agenda. In relation to issues that are sensitive and personal, it is crucial that all contributions to the conversation are welcome and that there is space for whatever emotions arise in the flow of the conversation. All thoughts and feelings are valid! It is essential that young people feel supported, but it can be counter-productive to "comfort away" any difficult thoughts and feelings. For such emotions to be transformed they need to be acknowledged and accepted rather than pushed aside. In general, it is the questions, not the answers, which hold the transformative potential.

As a young person, it is also important to feel part of a wider community that supports the work. The support can both be "active," as in direct feedback or interim meetings, and "imagined," as is the audience an author is writing to. But the key is *perception* and to arrange the creative space so that the young person is able to "listen at the edge of her understanding," as mythologist Martin Shaw puts it (Graugaard, 2014, p. 188). This frame of mind requires the young person to be attentive, aware, and sensitive to her inner and outer worlds. Entering this mindset can be a practice in itself, which centers on perceiving the world without preconceptions – much like practicing mindfulness or meditation. The creative expression of this encounter can be immaterial and fleeting or physical and lasting. This is where improvisation, and an attitude that embraces uncertainty, plays an important role. Whatever arises becomes the locus for renewed attention and experimentation. Examples from my own teaching are writing courses, conversational group seminars, improvisation classes, sensory training, and meditation exercises.

With the right frame of mind, and a creative space to practice within, young people can experiment with meaning-making and cognitive repositioning within their wider field of relationships. By deepening the awareness of one's personal relations with more-than-human nature, it is possible to expand the experience of reality, to become more sensitive to the mystery of existence and to realign with the living world. Such an enhanced sense of belonging provides an antidote to the alienation or separation from reality, which people can experience in the state of despair that often follows when looking at the state of the planet.

Conclusion

In describing the way meaning-making, narrative inquiry, and re-storying can affect onto-epistemological transformation through creative practices, I have suggested that this kind of experimentation can support young people in dealing with climate distress. Although the effects of this work may be therapeutic, I want to underline that I have worked with this topic as a question of learning in my work as a researcher and teacher. In holding the space for others to learn and to be creative it is important to acquire the attitude of humility described above: Embracing the uncertainty of what happens in a creative space requires the teacher to accept that she is as much a learner as the rest of those in that space. This means taking seriously that, as a person of authority, the teacher does not "have the answers" and that young people are capable of taking on responsibility for their own and our common future. The global crises in our midst are not just a socio-technical quandary, they challenge how we think about and carry out education and mental healthcare. To relieve the mental distress connected with the global perspective of climate change, it is necessary for educational and health perspectives to be integrated. These fields can help young people to approach sustainability as an integrative personal process rather than a mental abstraction of a future goal or state of the world.

The findings outlined here may transfer to other learning environments more or less easily. The participants I interviewed for my research tended to be middle class and white individuals aged 30–50, while the student cohorts I currently teach are middle class and white individuals in the age group 18–25. While some students have experienced significant climate distress, they tend to be stable characters with a strong support network. Where other personal complications enter the picture, it may not always be advisable to add further weight to the situation. It should always be assessed on an individual basis whether a young person who experiences significant mental and emotional distress is able to benefit from this kind of work. There is a strong cultural inclination to this work as it has been developed within groups of people who have become disillusioned with globalized Western culture but who tend to live relatively comfortably within Western societies. In working with other cultural groups, the conversations, practices, and framing metaphors will have to be appropriate to the culture they work within and the language they use to describe their experiences. Youth living with significant stressors, such as housing instability and poverty, may well have more pressing existential worries than climate change to attend to.

For most people who experience increasing emotional distress in the face of climate change, there is a seeming dilemma in the prospect of dealing with the affliction: Do I choose to enter deeper into distress or should I ignore or suppress these feelings so I remain functional within my everyday world? As I hope to have shown, establishing creative spaces where young people feel safe to explore different ways of seeing or being may offer new ways of creating alternate realities which enable meaningful and good lives in a time of global crises.

References

Adams, M. (2014). Inaction and environmental crisis: Narrative, defence mechanisms and the social organisation of denial. *Psychoanalysis, Culture & Society*, 19, 52–71. https://doi.org/10.1057/pcs.2013.21

Bamberg, M. G. (2004). Considering counter narratives. In M. G. W. Bamberg and M. Andrews (Eds.), *Considering counter narratives: Narrating, resisting, making sense* (pp. 351–372). John Benjamins. https://doi.org/10.1075/sin.4.43bam

Bateson, G. (2000). *Steps to an ecology of mind: Collected essays in anthropology, psychiatry, evolution, and epistemology*. University of Chicago Press. https://doi.org/10.7208/chicago/9780226924601.001.0001

Bohm, D. (2004). *On creativity*. Routledge Classics, Taylor & Francis. https://doi.org/10.4324/9780203822913
Bruner, J. (2004). Life as narrative. *Social Research: An International Quarterly*, 71(3), 691–710. https://doi.org/10.1353/sor.2004.0045
Capra, F., & Luisi, P. L. (2014). *The systems view of life*. Cambridge University Press. https://doi.org/10.1017/cbo9780511895555
de Oliveira, V. M. (2021). *Hospicing modernity: Facing humanity's wrongs and the implications for social activism*. North Atlantic Books
Fisher, W. R. (1987). *Human communication as narration: Toward a philosophy of reason, value, and action*. University of South Carolina Press. https://doi.org/10.2307/j.ctv1nwbqtk
Graber, D., & Wengrow, D. (2021). *The dawn of everything: A new history of humanity*. Allen Lane.
Graugaard, J. D. (2014). Transforming sustainabilities: Grassroots narratives in an age of transition. An ethnography of the dark mountain project. Doctoral thesis, University of East Anglia.
Greer, J. M. (2010). The falling years: An Inhumanist vision. *Dark Mountain*, 1, 6–17.
Hine, D. (2011). Remember the Future? *Dark Mountain*, 2, 260–271.
Hine, D., & Abram, D. (2011). Coming to our (animal) senses: A conversation with David Abram. *Dark Mountain*, 2, 61–73.
Horvath, A., Thomassen, B., & Wydra, H. (2009). Introduction: Liminality and cultures of change. *International Political Anthropology*, 2(1), 3–4.
Ingold, T. (2011). *Being alive: Essays on movement, knowledge and description*. Taylor & Francis. https://doi.org/10.4324/9781003196679
Jackson, T. (2021). *Post growth: Life after capitalism*. Polity Press.
Kingsnorth, P., & Hine, D. (2009). *Uncivilisation: The dark mountain manifesto*. Dark Mountain Project.
Larson, B. (2011). *Metaphors for environmental sustainability: Redefining our relationship with nature*. Yale University Press. https://doi.org/10.12987/9780300151541
Latour, B. (2018). *Down to earth: Politics in the new climatic regime*. Polity Press.
Lent, J. (2017). *The patterning instinct*. Prometheus Books.
McGilchrist, I. (2009). *The master and his emissary: The divided brain and the making of the western world*. Yale University Press. https://doi.org/10.12987/9780300247459
McIntosh, A. (2001). *Soil and soul: People versus corporate power*. Aurum Press.
McIntosh, A. (2008). *Hell and high water: Climate change, hope and the human condition*. Birlinn.
McIntosh, A. (2012). Teaching radical human ecology in the academy. In L. Williams, R. Roberts, & A. McIntosh (Eds.), *Radical human ecology : Intercultural and indigenous approaches* (pp. 235–255). Ashgate.
McKibben, B. (2019). *Falter: Has the human game begun to play itself out?* Wildfire.
Moore, J. W., ed. (2016). *Anthropocene or capitalocene? Nature, history, and the crisis of capitalism*. PM Press.

Randall, R. (2009). Loss and climate change: The cost of parallel narratives. *Ecopsychology*, 1(3), 118–129. https://doi.org/10.1089/eco.2009.0034

Steffen, W., Sanderson, W. A., Tyson, P.D., Jäger, J., Matson, P.A., Moore III, B., ... & Wasson, R.J. (2004). *Global change and the earth system: A planet under pressure*. Springer-Verlag. https://doi.org/10.1007/b137870

Szakolczai, A. (2009). Liminality and experience: Structuring transitory situations and transformative events. *International Political Anthropology*, 2(1), 141–172.

Turner, V. (1974). Liminal to liminoid in play, flow, and ritual: An essay in comparative symbology. *Rice University Studies*, 60(3), 53–92.

CHAPTER 20

Landback
Climate Justice and Indigenous Youth Mental Health in the Anthropocene

Kyle X. Hill and Lynn Mad Plume

Introduction

Climate change and associated health impacts are experienced most acutely within historically oppressed, vulnerable, marginalized, and disenfranchised groups, such as elderly, youth, Indigenous communities and those who experience disabilities (EPA, 2023; IPCC, 2022; Schramm et al., 2020; World Health Organization, 2022). The threats posed by climate change to Indigenous communities operate at the nexus of intersecting crises borne from a myriad of social, political, structural, and health inequities that correspond to a history of injustice vis-à-vis settler-colonialism. These impacts – recognized as social and ecological determinants of health – are unequivocally responsible for health inequities and undermine the resolve and sovereignty of Indigenous Peoples globally. Thus, while Indigenous communities grapple with risks associated with both direct and indirect impacts of climate change, they also continue to live according to ancestral knowledge systems that govern a spiritual kinship to Land. Given that Indigenous communities caretake as much as 80 percent of the Earth's remaining biodiversity (Redvers et al., 2023), many continue to inherit the most immediate risks and health implications of climate change due to an enduring interconnectedness with Mother Earth.

The history of settler-colonial violence and ongoing structural and systemic oppression that signifies both the colonial subjugation of Indigenous communities and the anthropogenic causes of climate change are often cited as principal causes of contemporary health disparities, trauma, grief, damage, and loss (EPA, 2023). Taken together, these conditions substantially limit the adaptive capacity of Indigenous communities as they contend with the tremendous burden of climate change. Nonetheless, the prophecy and epistemic promise of the seventh generation recognizes

Indigenous youth as the keepers of collective survival, resilience, and continuity of Indigenous community health, land stewardship, and Indigenous traditional ecological knowledge(s). These (and other) values guided resistance during the Dakota Access Pipeline (#NoDAPL) protests at Standing Rock, ND, when Mņí Wičóni (Water is life) – a Lakota way of recognizing the power and importance of water as kin and source of spirituality, as a life-giving force to Indigenous communities and a sovereign being with a right to life – was a signal of resistance efforts.

Indigenous youth are inheriting the burden of climate-driven risk factors while grappling with vulnerabilities associated with deeply rooted systems of structural and systemic racism (EPA, 2023). The cumulative nature of these risks places considerable stress on Indigenous communities, which is exacerbated by high-heat days, air quality, pollen, coastal flooding, and vector-borne illnesses, among other factors (EPA, 2023). Yet Indigenous youth are amongst the most active subpopulations pursuing climate justice and are involved in grassroots organizing and resistance efforts on the frontlines. Landback, the "bat signal" for climate justice for Indigenous communities, has served as the conceptual and ethical basis for resistance efforts from Standing Rock and the #NoDAPL movement to saving Oak Flat, stopping the Line 3 pipeline in Minnesota, and the Keystone XL pipeline, all of which invariably threaten the delicate ecosystems and waterways home to scores of Tribal Nations. In each of these resistance movements to protect Mother Earth, young Indigenous people risk their mental health and well-being to lead climate justice efforts. Many of these young people experience acute and insidious mental health conditions that are often exacerbated by ongoing resistance efforts rooted in the Indigenous struggle to exist spiritually, physically, emotionally, and mentally, according to our own epistemologies – the same struggle that shares etiological bases with intergenerational and historical loss and trauma stemming from the genocide of Indigenous Peoples.

In this chapter, we outline the intersecting crises of climate change and Indigenous youth mental health and wellness as they manifest within the context of contemporary health inequities. We provide a glimpse into the impact of climate change on Indigenous Peoples' mental health and wellness as a whole; Indigenous Peoples, by virtue of their designation as such, are communities that share an intimate relationship to land and place and that have experienced a profound social, cultural, and ecological disruption as a result of settler-colonialism (United Nations, 2015). Indigenous youth, or what many consider the seventh generation, have been recognized as among the most vulnerable subpopulation in the Anthropocene and are among those likely to shoulder the greatest burden of these crises moving forward. At the same time, as we take inventory of the strengths of Indigenous communities, particularly those communities that have ancestral land claims to Turtle Island (North America), interconnectedness and kinship to Land is regarded as central to existence and conveys a profound opportunity to steward climate adaptation movements at a global scale. Finally, we conclude with a call for climate justice that interrogates the ways in which settler-colonialism, White supremacy and capitalism have disrupted Indigenous lifeways, belief and knowledge systems, with corresponding impacts on Indigenous youth mental health and wellness.

As a matter of respect to the adaptive capacity of Indigenous traditional ecological knowledges (ITEKs), the seventh generation and the collective threats posed by climate change, we recognize that any efforts of truth and reconciliation with Indigenous Peoples are hollow until: (1) we atone for the historical and state-sanctioned systemic injustices that have disrupted cultural continuity and challenged the survival of Indigenous communities, their knowledge systems, and kinship to ancestral homelands and ecosystems; and (2) in efforts to adapt and mitigate climate change using ITEKs, we recognize the empirically supported causal attribution of anthropogenic causes to current and anticipated environmental shifts as a consequence of settler-colonialism and Eurocentric value systems (i.e., capitalism and egocentrism). It is our belief that we cannot truly convey the ideological impetus behind the calls for climate justice unless we can appropriately resource the knowledge of Indigenous communities on a global scale. As we expound on this solemn truth, we know well that this is not only a call for acknowledging or redressing the history of violence and genocide of Indigenous peoples worldwide as a residue of colonialism, but also a call to address centuries of state-sanctioned economic, political and socially mediated violence that have systematically eroded planetary health and the health of Indigenous communities (Redvers et al., 2022).

We Are the Land; the Land Is Us

Naatookyookaasii: Two Medicine

Misfortune
The buffalo no longer wandered the prairie.
The streams no longer ran full and deep.
The parched earth lay scorched.
A wave of misfortune had come to the Blackfeet Nation.

Two Medicine Lodges
Along the shore of a sacred lake, two medicine lodges had been built.
Ceremonies were held, chants were sung, and prayers were made.
Old Man, through his spirit helpers, answered the prayers.
The Blackfeet were instructed to send seven of the old and wise to Chief Mountain.
At the summit of Chief Mountain lived Wind Spirit.
It was Wind Spirit who caused the drought and must be appeased.

First Climb
The seven old and wise men traveled to Chief Mountain and its summit.
When they arrived, Wind Spirit was so terrifying.
The men fled in fear.
The drought continued and the suffering increased.
The Blackfeet needed a solution.

The Brave
Old Man sent another word.
The Blackfeet were instructed to send fourteen warriors.
The bravest warriors were selected.
The brave traveled to the summit of Chief Mountain.

A Promise
Wind Spirit waited at the door of his lodge.
Bearing no weakness, the warriors approached Wind Spirit.
Wind Spirit was pleased with the courage of the warriors.
He sent them home with a promise.

Happiness and Prosperity
Wind Spirit brought forth the rain.
The grass grew thick and green.
Waters and streams were replenished.
The buffalo returned.
Happiness and prosperity dwelt within the land of the Blackfeet.
(Lynn Mad Plume, personal communication of Blackfeet legend)

Indigenous peoples value storytelling as a way of conveying history and knowledge through their families and communities. Storytelling is a process of reclaiming and owning the story rather than being defined or storied by others (Chan, 2021). Colonizers have historically told and shaped the stories of Indigenous peoples, dispossessing Indigenous peoples of their culture and disconnecting them from their ecologies: land, language, and community (Alfred, 2009). The result was social and political alienation and turmoil. Storytelling is critical to Indigenous methodology; it is a part of healing and a means for renewed engagement with one's self-knowledge (Chan, 2021). Indigenous people have distinctive values, languages, cultures, and governance structures that should not be generalized. While views of health and well-being derive from vastly diverse Indigenous peoples from communities and cultures across the world, there is congruence around mental health as intrinsic and integrated with the health and wellness of our ecosystems. Indigenous concepts of mental health and well-being also include connectedness with ancestors, family, community, culture, spirituality, lands, and knowledge systems. Storytelling, in its many forms, has served as a resource to communicate the embeddedness and importance of ceremony, spirituality, cultural identity, and engagement to Indigeneity, sovereignty, and self-determination (O'Keefe et al., 2022).

In the era of the Anthropocene, Indigenous children and youth are experiencing increasing levels of mental health distress due to the climate crisis, characterized by feelings of sadness, guilt, changes in sleep and appetite, difficulty concentrating, solastalgia, general distress, worry, ecological grief, and loneliness that manifests from isolation, the existential dread that accompanies climate change and disconnection from land (Gislason et al., 2021). Cultural connectedness has been recognized as key to health and wellness – including mental health – for Indigenous individuals, families, and community well-being, particularly in healing historical and intergenerational trauma (Gray & Cote, 2019). Globally, Indigenous communities, leaders, mental health providers, and scholars have called for strengths-based approaches to mental health that align with Indigenous and holistic concepts of health and wellness (O'Keefe et al., 2023).

Indigenous youth development and well-being occur through strengths-based relationships across interconnected environmental levels (O'Keefe et al., 2022). The mental health impacts of climate change on children and youth are tied to Social Determinants of Health (SDoH) but also need to be understood in relation to the Ecological Determinants of Health (EDoH) (United Nations, 2023). Through an eco-social lens, these conceptual issues provide a more universal understanding of the interplay between social and ecological determinants of mental health for children and youth.

In addition to the cumulative impact and trauma imposed by a legacy of subjugation associated with settler-colonialism, Indigenous youth grapple with climate-related environmental shifts, both acute (i.e., wildfires, extreme precipitation events, increases in high-heat days) and insidious (i.e., drought related ecosystem changes, sea-level changes, sea and lake ice-extents/durations) causing further displacement from traditional homelands and loss of sense of place as a direct consequence of climate change (Cunsolo & Ellis, 2018; Ford, 2012; Hill, 2022; World Health Organization, 2022).

The scale of historical loss of traditional territories and homelands during westward expansion throughout periods of settler-colonialism in the United States was comprehensive, whereby Indigenous communities in the United States and Canada were forcibly removed from their traditional homelands and territories, and moved onto reservations or reserves, amounting to a near-total loss (98.9 percent) of co-extensive historical lands (Farrell et al., 2021). Not coincidentally, this period is often referred to as the Assimilation Era, driven by Christianity and founded on the belief that European Settlers were entitled to land claims, without regard for Indigenous Peoples' stewardship of their lands. Although a full review of the course of settler-colonialism on Turtle Island (North America) is beyond the scope of this chapter, it is important to recognize the advent of climate colonialism as starting at least with the forced removals and ethnic cleansing of Indigenous Peoples during this time period of the nineteenth and twentieth centuries (Gone & Trimble, 2012; Thornton, 1987). The vulnerability of Indigenous youth to climate change threats posed by environmental shifts – direct or indirect – must be understood relative to the cumulative impacts of settler-colonialism and the burden of contemporary social and health inequities of Indigenous communities, which, in turn, contribute to a unique risk profile among Indigenous youth. In an effort to understand and characterize this unique vulnerability of Indigenous communities to indirect climate impacts, the term *ecological grief* – the erosion of ecosystems that corresponds to a disruption of Indigenous identity, lifeways, and spirituality – has provided a way to describe this process (Cunsolo & Ellis, 2018). Furthermore, ecological grief asserts that environmental shifts substantially impact sense of identity and belonging to place among Indigenous communities, particularly as such shifts challenge traditional knowledges as well as spiritual and traditional belief systems that establish the sense of self and have stood as pillars to community health since time immemorial. Additionally, the antecedents of ecological grief (i.e., environmental shifts) undermine Indigenous communities' health and flexibility in their quest to adapt to and mitigate the effects of climate change, which are important indicators of climate resilience (Cunsolo & Ellis, 2018; Ford, 2012; Gone et al., 2019; Tobias & Richmond, 2014; Warne & Wescott, 2019).

Current Indices of Indigenous Youth Mental Health

Indigenous communities experience disproportionate rates of mental health conditions relative to other racial groups, including substance use and other disorders, although the prevalence of these conditions can differ significantly between communities. While a thorough background on psychiatric epidemiology of Indigenous youth mental health is beyond the scope of this chapter, it is important to contextualize Indigenous youth climate distress within the overall mental health status of American Indian and Canadian First Nation youth on Turtle Island (North America). The most critical and enduring public health issue for American Indian and Canadian First Nations youth has been an enduring epidemic of suicide (Gone & Trimble, 2012; Indian Health Service, 2014), with rates as high as thirteen times greater than other races (Hill et al., 2018; Mullany et al., 2009). Despite the low base rate of suicide overall, the etiological pathways of suicide within these communities, by and large, involve disconnection from lands, culture, family, and community (Alcantra & Gone, 2007; Gone & Trimble, 2012). Thus, cultural discontinuity, historical trauma as a sequela of colonization, corresponding impacts on cultural identity, and the experience of adverse childhood experiences have been cited as risk factors for Indigenous suicidal ideation as well as depression, anxiety, PTSD, alcohol misuse, and smoking (Gone & Trimble, 2012; Hill et al., 2018). Furthermore, American Indian youth substance use, particularly alcohol abuse, has proven to be a risk factor not only for morbidity and mortality associated with suicide attempts but also for unintentional injuries (Gone & Trimble, 2012; Hill et al., 2018; IHS, 2014; NCAI, 2018). Finally, there are considerable mental health inequities related to the high rates of adverse childhood experiences within American Indian and Alaska Native communities (Brockie et al., 2015; Warne et al., 2017).

The ongoing impact of climate change-related loss, damage, displacement, dispossession, and associated environmental shifts on Indigenous communities also contributes to disproportionate levels of *ecological grief* (Cunsolo & Ellis, 2018). Indigenous communities experience existential and anticipatory reactions to current and projected environmental shifts and are considered vulnerable to eco-anxiety related to the potential loss of ecosystems and environmental habitability (Coffey et al., 2021).

Following from a history of violent oppression, genocide, and historical loss, the intimate relationship of settler-colonialism to extractive industries (i.e., logging, mining, coal, gas, and petroleum) has been fundamental to the erosion of Indigenous community health while simultaneously operating as the largest anthropogenic contributor to climate change to date (Czyzewski, 2011; Ford, 2020; IPCC, 2022; Jonasson et al., 2019; Paradies, 2016). Altogether, the cultural discontinuity imposed by settler-colonialism and associated industrialization and globalization of North America on Indigenous communities has resulted in cumulative impacts of several forces, including forced land removal and land dispossession; prohibition of traditional activities; subsistence methods and spirituality; removal of children from families to boarding and residential schools via federal policies of assimilation; displacement and dispossession away from mineral-rich territories; and massacres of Indigenous communities (Cunsolo & Ellis, 2018; Ferrell et al., 2021; Gone & Trimble, 2012; National Collaborating Centre on Aboriginal Health, 2013; Warne, 2019). These traumas directly affect how Indigenous communities experience climate impacts and their accompanying psychological responses. The ethics and values that govern Western, Euro-Settler versus Indigenous relationships to our environments and ecosystems are chasmic. Importantly, the epistemic divergence between the Western and Indigenous relationship to our earth and ecosystems is representative of ongoing colonial discourse; the extractive nature of our economies is, in and of itself, unsettling and disturbing to the lifeways and cultures of Indigenous Peoples. For these reasons, Indigenous health and well-being, as well as the vitality of Indigenous epistemologies and ontologies, have been recognized as determinants of planetary health (Redvers et al., 2023).

Social and Ecological Determinants of Health

Indigenous epistemologies are relational and ecological; no single individual, or individual mind, is self-determined, separated, and autonomous from its ecology, which for us means land, community, and ancestors (Chan, 2021). Therefore, kinship or relationality is key to Indigenous methodology, which is about relationships, ceremony, and forms of cultural practice (Wilson, 2008). Indigenous methodology is formative in planetary health and climate justice discourse – "the Land is us, we are the Land." Importantly, these basic tenets provide the foundation of social determinants of health of Indigenous people, whereby circumstances and ecological environments – as well as structures, systems, and institutions – influence the development and maintenance of health for Indigenous communities (Reading & Wien, 2009).

For the purposes of this chapter, social determinants of health are categorized as *proximal* (e.g., health behaviors, physical, and social environment), *intermediate* (e.g., community infrastructure, resources, systems, and capacities), and *distal* (e.g., historic, political, social, and economic contexts) determinants of health (Reading & Wien, 2009). Individuals, communities, and nations that experience inequalities in any of these categories carry an additional burden of health problems and are often restricted from access to resources that might improve those problems, such as education, healthcare, and healthy food access (Braveman & Gottlieb, 2014). Health issues also often lead to circumstances and environments that, in turn, worsen subsequent determinants of health (Braveman & Gottlieb, 2014). For example, living in conditions of low income has been linked to increased illness and disability, which are linked to diminished opportunities to engage in gainful employment, thereby aggravating poverty and increasing illness risks (Reading & Wien, 2009). Negative social and ecological determinants, such as poverty, land dispossession, forced acculturation, underfunded systems, structural racism, and food and water insecurity strongly influence the health disparities experienced by Indigenous people (United Nations, 2023).

Proximal Determinants
Proximal determinants of health include conditions that have a direct impact on physical, emotional, mental, or spiritual health. For example, in conditions of overcrowding, children often have little room to study or play and adults have no private space to relax. These conditions increase the likelihood of behavioral and learning difficulties in children and adolescents, as well as substance abuse and other social problems among adults. Similarly, family violence directly impacts all family dimensions of health, especially women's health, with a resultant negative impact on children's physical and emotional health (Reading & Wien, 2009). Beyond the negative impact of proximal determinants on our abilities to meet basic survival needs (e.g., in poverty), unfavorable proximal determinants contribute to other stressors that in turn can generate or exacerbate health problems. Moreover, individuals acquire personal skills and resources for coping with health challenges, developing health behaviors throughout life that also help them cope with other life challenges, and vice versa. When proximal determinants of health prevent control over the basic material resources of life, choice – which is key to health – is denied (Reading & Wien, 2009). Indigenous peoples have songs, ceremonies, and stories that guide our healing and our actions. When these practices are disrupted and hindered through poverty (often leading to inaccessibility of culture, spirituality, etc.), other proximal determinants, or poor health and indices of mental health, are adversely impacted as well.

Intermediate Determinants

Indigenous peoples are stewards of the Land and recognize communities and ecosystems as extensions of personal health and well-being. When our deep-rooted cultural wounds are left untreated, ecosystems and communities are out of balance and suffer as a result. The origins of proximal determinants are rooted in colonial paradigms, such as the discouragement/dismantling/destruction of Indigenous languages. Indigenous peoples were also forced to discontinue centuries-long practices that fostered kinship, planetary health, and health and well-being. While proximal determinants represent the root of much ill health among Indigenous peoples, intermediate determinants can be thought of as their origin. For instance, poverty and deleterious physical environments are rooted in a lack of community infrastructure, resources, and capacities, as well as restricted environmental stewardship (Greenwood & de Leeuw, 2012). Likewise, inequitable health care and educational systems often act as barriers to accessing or developing health promoting behaviors, resources, and opportunities. Ecologically, the creation of an environment that inhibits Indigenous Land stewardship has ultimately created an environment where Indigenous people inherently cannot be well. Inequitable systems have been made for and by non-Indigenous people, rendering them ineffective for Indigenous communities because they are culturally irrelevant. The impact of intermediate determinants is particularly evident in the connection between cultural continuity and other intermediate determinants (Greenwood & de Leeuw, 2012). A colonial system creates a cycle that keeps Indigenous people disconnected from the Land, from their community, and their identity. Real estate, Land tenure and implications of federal-Indian policy, such as the Dawes General Allotment Act, are important considerations for Indigenous health and welfare when considering proximal determinants.

Distal Determinants

Distal determinants of health are difficult to measure, as colonialism is the most prominent distal determinant of Indigenous peoples' health. According to Kelm (1998), "colonization is a process that includes geographic incursion, socio-cultural dislocation, the establishment of external political control and economic dispossession, the provision of low-level social services and ultimately, the creation of ideological formulations around race and skin color that position the colonizer at a higher evolution level than the colonized." Distal determinants have the most profound influence on the health of populations because they represent the political, economic, and social powers of societal architecture that construct both intermediate and proximal determinants (Woolf & Braveman, 2013). Neo-colonialism continues to exert detrimental influence on the health of contemporary Indigenous peoples, and historic, successive colonial trauma continues to affect current generations, creating conditions of physical, psychological, economic, and political disadvantage for Indigenous peoples (Braveman & Gottlieb, 2014).

Indigenous youth are particularly impacted by the individual and cumulative effects of inequitable social determinants of health, which result in diminished physical, mental, and emotional health for young people (Short & Mollborn, 2015). Beginning in early childhood, social determinants establish a trajectory that is only moderately mutable in the current social and economic contexts within which many Indigenous children live (Likhar et al., 2022). Access to health resources during this critical developmental stage has implications over the entire life course, particularly when we consider the impacts of adverse childhood experiences (ACEs) on Indigenous youth mental health and well-being (Brockie et al., 2015). In the past, Indigenous kinship structures were disrupted by policies that prohibited traditional child-rearing practices Indigenous peoples need to be connected to their cultural practices, ceremonies, and community, not only so that the Earth and its people can be well, but to pass down critical Indigenous Land stewardship knowledge and restore kinship structures that can heal the family and the Land and ensure cultural perpetuity.

Climate Resilience and Well-Being of Indigenous Youth

As an Anishinaabe, Dakota and Lakota Ikče Wíčasa and scholar, both a witness and participant to this struggle for survival, four tenants become clear in resistance efforts that serve as an important ethos in the efforts to steward climate resilience and Indigenous well-being:

1. Indigenous peoples are not activists, we are beings and relatives of the Land. Therefore, protection of the Land and ecosystems is about kinship and love for all – Mítakuye Oyásiŋ (all my relations)
2. Movements are led with prayer and spirituality, recognizing the spirits and interconnectedness of the land, waters, animals, and other nonhuman relatives
3. Indigenous rights and human rights are at stake, with critical implications for Tribal/Indigenous sovereignty
4. The people cannot be healthy until the Land is healthy. Again, We are the Land, the Land is Us.

Centering planetary health while reconciling the imposition of settler-colonialism on Indigenous health will require the intentional development of economic and climate adaptation frameworks that revolve around ITEKs. Indigenous concepts of health rely on ITEK practices to support individual, family, and community well-being. In particular, cultural connectedness, language revitalization, and spirituality are critical to Indigenous youth mental health and well-being (Ullrich, 2019). This lens can reframe public concepts of identity, illness, and healing from Indigenous perspectives, nurturing youth in their attempt to navigate the active perpetuation of violence in systems and institutions that threaten not only Indigenous well-being but also planetary health (Redvers et al., 2023).

Furthermore, previous literature has demonstrated the need to develop context-specific climate health planning which recognizes the important relationship between Indigenous well-being and Land/place (Cunsolo et al., 2012; Cunsolo & Ellis, 2018; Ford, 2012). Context-specific climate adaptation and mitigation planning has centered ITEKs in the efforts to revitalize sustainability in otherwise vulnerable ecosystems, such as low-lying coastal and desert ecosystems (Ford, 2012; IPCC, 2022; Whyte, 2017). While the prospect for preventing further ecological damage is quite clear and promising with these adaptation programs, such programs are also critical to revitalizing Indigenous lifeways that have been historically marginalized and targeted in ethnic cleansing campaigns in the United States and Canada (e.g., in boarding and residential school programs) (Heid et al., 2022; Schramm et al., 2020). Today, Indigenous youth are uniquely situated to reclaim ITEKs that diverge from the Western concepts of empiricism and positivism that challenge their rights to land vis-à-vis relationship to place, while inviting epistemic pluralism as a solution to the climate crisis as we know it.

Naturally, Indigenous communities have explicitly supported calls for justice over those of resiliency, largely due to the problematic assumption that further insult and oppressive circumstances are likely to continue (i.e., structural oppression) with the expectation that Indigenous people become more "resilient" in the face of considerable violence/injury. In recognition of this problematic and inflexible assumption, climate justice can be approached as conceptually similar to the United Nations Declaration of Indigenous Peoples, which privileges the right to place (territorial homelands), culture, spirituality, Indigenous languages and the maintenance of Indigenous traditional knowledge systems (IPCC, 2022; United Nations, 2015).

Finally, concepts of climate justice and the portability of ITEKs extend to Indigenous connectedness frameworks for Indigenous youth. The Indigenous connectedness framework is one in which culture, Land, language, spirituality, and ceremony are central aspects of well-being and health for Indigenous youth (Ullrich, 2019). Similarly, Indigenous-led climate adaptation and mitigation programs have been developed that are consistent with the Indigenous youth connectedness frameworks outlined above, which provides evidence for effectively converging Indigenous youth mental health/wellness and efforts to improve the health of our most vulnerable ecosystems. More recently, concepts such as cultural connectedness and Indigenous eco-relational engagement (IERE) have begun to proliferate in academic literature in efforts to translate place-based traditional and cultural activities, as well as Indigenous languages, into Indigenous health prevention program development and climate adaptation and mitigation frameworks.

Conclusion

Youth across Indigenous Nations in the United States and Canada recognize the importance of connectedness to land as central to Indigenous well-being (Kading et al., 2019; Lines et al., 2019). One program, developed by the National Indian Health Board in collaboration with the Centers for Disease Control and Prevention (CDC), provides promising insights into how Tribal communities are developing climate adaptation programs that center ITEKs while remaining committed to Indigenous Peoples' health and well-being (Schramm, et al., 2020). "*Chemṣhúun Pe'icháachuqeli (When Our Hearts Are Happy):* A Tribal Psychosocial Climate Resilience Framework" was developed in accordance with the Tribal vulnerability assessment to help community members care for their cultural and emotional well-being when preparing for projected impacts of climate change (Schramm et al., 2020). Within this same program, the Swinomish Indian Tribal community culturally adapted an existing CDC climate adaptation framework that incorporates complex atmospheric data to provide both short- and long-range climate data projections (Schramm et al., 2020).

Climate-related loss and damages to ecosystems that have governed a spiritual kinship to place, and maintained ITEKs since time immemorial, are not only a source of distress for Indigenous communities but are also a reminder of a painful history of settler-colonialism and the abrogation of natural law (Cunsolo & Ellis, 2018; IPCC, 2022; Redvers, 2022; Schramm et al., 2020; Whyte, 2017). Indigenous youth contend with the burdens of ever-widening health inequities, navigate a history of environmental racism, and bear witness to the day-to-day stressors of structural and systemic oppression, all while grappling with the acute nature of the climate crisis in hopes of justice, to any end. While ITEKs and Indigenous concepts of health and wellness have positioned youth to be principal stewards of Mother Earth, our role, according to seventh generation prophecies, is to support our youth in all their beauty, strength, and sacredness to be able to carry out these roles in a healthy way. In a good way. If we can appreciate the Lákota belief of our children as Wakáŋyeja "sacred gift," we can begin to understand their importance to the survival of our Nations and our Earth. Therefore, as climate justice champions and stewards of future generations, we understand that both climate adaptation programming and Indigenous youth mental health and connectedness to language, spirituality, culture, and traditional activities are not mutually exclusive. In fact, these are the same – We are the Land, the Land is us.

References

Alcántara, C., & Gone, J. P. (2007). Reviewing suicide in native American communities: Situating risk and protective factors within a transactional-ecological framework. *Death Studies*, 31, 457–477.

Alfred, G. T. (2009). Colonialism and state dependency. *International Journal of Indigenous Health*, 5(2), 42–60. https://doi.org/10.3138/ijih.v5i2.28982

Braveman, P., & Gottlieb, L. (2014). The social determinants of health: It's time to consider the causes of the causes. *Public Health Reports*, 129(1)(Suppl 2), 19–31. https://doi.org/10.1177/00333549141291S206

Brockie, T. N., Dana-Sacco, G., Wallen, G. R., Wilcox, H. C., & Campbell, J. C. (2015). The relationship of adverse childhood experiences to PTSD, depression, poly-drug use and suicide attempt in reservation-based Native American adolescents and young adults. *American Journal of Community Psychology*, 55, 411–421. http://dx.doi.org/10.1007/s10464-015-9721-3

Chan, A. S. (2021). Storytelling, culture, and indigenous methodology. In A. Bainbridge, L. Formenti, & L. West (Eds.), *Discourses, dialogue and diversity in biographical research* (pp. 170–185). Brill. https://doi.org/10.1163/9789004465916_012

Clayton, S., Manning, C. M., Krygsman, K., & Speiser, M. (2017). *Mental health and our changing climate: Impacts, implications, and guidance.* American Psychological Association, and ecoAmerica.

Coffey, Y., Bhullar, N., Durkin, J., Islam, M. S., & Usher, K. (2021). Understanding eco-anxiety: A systematic scoping review of current literature and identified knowledge gaps. *Climate Change and Health*, 3, 100047, pp. 1–6. https://doi.org/10.1016/j.joclim.2021.100047

Cunsolo, A. W., & Ellis, N. R. (2018). Ecological grief as a mental health response to climate change-related loss. *Nature Climate Change*, 8, 275–281.

Cunsolo, A. W., Harper, S. L., Ford, J. D., Landman, K., Houle, K., Edge V. L., & Rigolet Inuit Community Government (2012). "From this place and of this place": Climate change, sense of place, and health in Nunatsiavut, Canada. *Social Science and Medicine*, 75, 538–547.

Czyzewski, K. (2011). Colonialism as a broader social determinant of health. *International Indigenous Policy Journal*, 2(1). doi: 10.18584/iipj.2011.2.1.5

Environmental Protection Agency (EPA) (2023). Climate change and children's health and well-being in the United States. www.epa.gov/system/files/documents/2023-04/CLiME_Final%20Report.pdf, accessed April 26, 2023.

Farrell, J., Burow, P. B., McConnell, K., Bayham, J., Whyte, K., & Koss, G. (2021). Effects of land dispossession and forced migration on Indigenous peoples in North America. *Science*, 374(6567), eabe4943. https://doi.org/10.1126/science.abe4943

Ford, J. D. (2012). Indigenous health and climate change. *American Journal of Public Health*, 102(7), 1260–1266.

Ford, J. D., Willox, A. C., Chatwood, S., Frugal, C., Harper, S., Mauro, I., & Pearce, T. (2014). Adapting to the effects of climate change on Inuit health. *American Journal of Public Health*, 104(3), 9–17.

Garcia-Olp, M. (2018). How colonization impacts identity through the generations: A closer look at historical trauma and education. *Electronic Theses and Dissertations*, 1487. https://digitalcommons.du.edu/etd/1487

Gislason, M. K., Kennedy, A. M., & Witham, S. M. (2021). The interplay between social and ecological determinants of mental health for children and youth in the climate crisis. *International Journal of Environmental Research and Public Health*, 18(9), 4573. https://doi.org/10.3390/ijerph18094573

Gone, J. P., & Calf Looking, P. E. (2011). American Indian culture as substance abuse treatment: Pursuing evidence for a local intervention. *Journal of Psychoactive Drugs*, 43(4), 291–296. doi:10.1080/02791072.2011.628915

Gone, J. P. & Trimble, J. E., (2012). American Indian and Alaska Native mental health: Diverse perspectives on enduring disparities. *Annual Review of Clinical Psychology*, 8, 131–160.

Gone, J. P., Hartmann, W. E., Pomerville, A., Wendt, D. C., Klem, S. H., & Burrage, R. L. (2019). The impact of historical trauma on health outcomes for indigenous populations in the USA and Canada: A systematic review. *American Psychologist*, 74(1), 20–35. doi:10.1037/amp0000338 [doi]

Gray, A. P., & Cote, W. (2019). Cultural connectedness protects mental health against the effect of historical trauma among Anishinabe young adults. *Public Health*, 176, 77–81. doi:S0033-3506(18)30378-0 [pii]

Greenwood, M. L., & de Leeuw, S. N. (2012). Social determinants of health and the future well-being of Aboriginal children in Canada. *Paediatrics & Child Health*, 17(7), 381–384.

Hancock, T., Spady, D. W., & Soskolne, C. L. (2016). *Global change and public health: Addressing the ecological determinants of health*. Canadian Public Health Association.

Hautala, D., & Sittner, K. (2019). Longitudinal mechanisms linking perceived racial discrimination to aggressive delinquency among North American Indigenous youth. *Journal of Research in Crime and Delinquency*, 56(5), 694–735.

Heid, O., Khalid, M., Smith, H., Kim, K., Smith, S., Wekerle, C., ..., & Thomasen, K. (2022). Indigenous youth and resilience in Canada and the USA: A scoping review. *Adversity and Resilience Science*, 3, 113–117.

Hill, K. (2022). Indigenous climate justice: Anticolonial prescriptions for the Anthropocene. *ReFrame: Mental Health and Climate Justice, The Mariwala Health Intitiative Journal*, 5, 22–25. https://reframe2022.mhi.org.in/

Hill, K., Eck, K. V., Goklish, N., Larzelere-Hinton, F., & Cwik, M. (2018). Factor structure and validity of the SIQ-JR in a Southwest American Indian Tribe. *Psychological Services*. Published online November 26, 2018.

Indian Health Service, US Department of Health and Human Services (2014). Trends in Indian Health, 2014. www.ihs.gov/dps/index.cfm/publications/trends2014/

IPCC (2022). Summary for policymakers. In H.-O. Pörtner, D. C. Roberts, E. S. Poloczanska, K. Mintenbeck, M. Tignor, A. Alegría, ... & A. Okem (eds.), *Climate change 2022: Impacts, Adaptation and Vulnerability. Contribution of Working Group II to the Sixth Assessment Report of the Intergovernmental Panel on Climate Change*.

Jonasson, M. E., Spiegel, S. J., Thomas, S., Yassi, A., Wittman, H., Takaro, T., ... & Spiegel, J. M. (2019). Oil pipelines and food sovereignty: Threat to health equity for Indigenous communities. *Journal of Public Health Policy*, 40, 504–517.

Jones, R., Macmillan, A., & Reid, P. (2020). Climate change mitigation policies and co-impacts on Indigenous health: A scoping review. *International Journal of Environmental Research and Public Health*, 17(23), 9063. doi: 10.3390/ijerph17239063.

Kading, M. L., Gonzalez, M. B., Herman, K. A., Gonzalez, J., & Walls, M. L. (2019). Living a good way of life: Perspectives from American Indian and First Nation young adults. *American Journal of Community Psychology*, 64(1–2), 21–33. doi:10.1002/ajcp.12372

Kelm, M.-E. (1998). *Colonizing bodies: Aboriginal health and healing in British Columbia, 1900–50*. UBC Press.

Likhar, A., Baghel, P., & Patil, M. (2022). Early childhood development and social determinants. *Cureus*, 14(9), e29500. https://doi.org/10.7759/cureus.29500

Lines, L. A., Yellowknives Dene First Nation Wellness Division, & Jardine, C. J. (2019). Connection to land as a youth-identified social determinant of Indigenous Peoples' health. *BMC Public Health*, 19(176), 1–13.

Mullany, B., Barlow, A., Goklish, N., Larzelere-Hinton, F., Cwik, M., Craig, M., & Walkup, J. T. (2009). Toward understanding suicide among youths: Results from the White Mountain Apache tribally mandated suicide surveillance system, 2001–2006. *American Journal of Public Health*, 99, 1840–1848. http://dx.doi.org/10.2105/AJPH.2008.154880

National Collaborating Centre for Aboriginal Health (2013). Setting the context: An overview of Aboriginal health in Canada. www.nccih.ca/495/An_Overview_of_Aboriginal_Health_in_Canada.nccih?id=101

NCAI Policy Research Center (2018). *Diabetes and behavioral health comorbidities: Advancing the tribal behavioral health agenda*. National Congress of American Indians.

O'Keefe, V. M., Fish, J., Maudrie, T. L., Hunter, A. M., Tai Rakena, H. G., Ullrich, J. S. ... & Barlow, A. (2022). Centering Indigenous knowledges and worldviews: Applying the Indigenist ecological systems model to youth mental health and wellness research and programs. *International Journal of Environmental Research and Public Health*, 19(10), 6271. https://doi.org/10.3390/ijerph19106271

O'Keefe, V. M., Maudrie, T. L., Cole, A. B., Ullrich, J. S., Fish, J., Hill, K. X. ... & Walls, M. L. (2023). Conceptualizing Indigenous strengths-based health and wellness research using group concept mapping. *Archives of Public Health*, 81, 71. https://doi.org/10.1186/s13690-023-01066-7

Ozbay, F., Johnson, D. C., Dimoulas, E., Morgan, C. A., Charney, D., & Southwick, S. (2007). Social support and resilience to stress: From neurobiology to clinical practice. *Psychiatry*, 4(5), 35–40.

Paradies, Y. (2016). Colonisation, racism and Indigenous health. *Journal of Population Research*, 33, 83–96. doi: 10.1007/s12546-016-9159-y.

Parkes, M. W., Poland, B., Allison, S., Cole, D. C., Culbert, I., Gislason, M. K., ... & Waheed, F. (2020). Preparing for the future of public health: Ecological determinants of health and the call for an eco-social approach to public health education. *Canadian Journal of Public Health*, 111(1), 60–64.

Reading, C. L. & Wien, F. (2009). *Health inequalities and social determinants of Aboriginal Peoples' health*. National Collaborating Centre for Aboriginal Health.

Redvers, N., Celidwen, Y., Schultz, C., Horn, O., Githaiga, C., Vera, M., ... & Blondin, B. (2022). The determinants of planetary health: An Indigenous concensus perspective. *The Lancet*, 6(2), E156–E163. https://doi.org/10.1016/S2542-5196(21)00354-5.

Redvers, N., Reid, P., Carroll, D., Cunningham Kain, M., Kobei, D. M., Menzel, K., ... & Roth, G. (2023). Indigenous determinants of health: A unified call for progress. *The Lancet*, published online June 21, 2023. https://doi.org/10.1016/S0140-6736(23)01183-2.

Schramm, P. J., Al Janabi, A. L., Campbell, L. W., Donatuto, J. L., & Gaughen, S. C. (2020). How Indigenous communities are adapting to climate change: Insights from the Climate-Ready Tribes Initiative. *Health Affairs*, 39(12), 2153–2159.

Short, S. E., & Mollborn, S. (2015). Social determinants and health behaviors: Conceptual frames and empirical advances. *Current Opinion in Psychology*, 5, 78–84. https://doi.org/10.1016/j.copsyc.2015.05.002

Singh, G., Xue, S., & Poukhovski-Sheremetyev, F. (2022). Climate emergency, young people and mental health: Time for justice and health professional action. *BMJ Paediatrics Open*, 6, e001375. doi:10.1136/bmjpo-2021-001375.

Sultana, F. (2022). The unbearable heaviness of climate coloniality. *Political Geography*. 99(1), 1–14. https://doi.org/10.1016/j.polgeo.2022.102638.

Thornton, R. (1987). *American Indian holocaust and survival: A population history since 1492*. University of Oklahoma Press.

Tobias, J. K., & Richmond, C. A. (2014). "That land means everything to us as Anishinaabe….": Environmental dispossession and resilience on the North Shore of Lake Superior. *Health & Place*, 29, 26–33. https://doi.org/10.1016/j.healthplace.2014.05.008

Ullrich, J. S. (2019). For the love of our children: An Indigenous connectedness framework. *AlterNative: An International Journal of Indigenous Peoples*, 15(2), 121–130. https://doi.org/10.1177/1177180119828114

United Nations (2015). United Nations Declaration on the Rights of Indigenous Peoples.

United Nations (2023). Permanent Forum on Indigenous Issues: Indigenous determinants of health in the 2030 Agenda for Sustainable Development.

Vecchio, E. A., Dickson, M., & Zhang, Y. (2022). Indigenous mental health and climate change: A systematic literature review. *Journal of Climate Change and Health*, 6, 1–8.

Warne, D., and Wescott, S. (2019). Social determinants of American Indian nutritional health. *Current Developments in Nutrition*, 3(Suppl 2), 12–18.

Warne, D., Dulacki, K., Spurlock, M., Meath, T., Davis, M. M., & McConnell, K. J. (2017). Adverse childhood experiences (ACE) among American Indians in South Dakota and associations with mental health conditions, alcohol use, and smoking. *Journal of Health Care for the Poor and Underserved*, 28, 1559–1577.

Whyte, K. (2017). Indigenous climate change studies: Indigenizing futures, decolonizing the Anthropocene. *English Language Notes*, 55, 1–2

Wilson, S. (2008). *Research is ceremony: Indigenous research methods*. Fernwood Publishing.

Woolf, S. H., & Braveman, P. (2013). The social and ecological determinants of health. In James W. Holsinger (Ed.), *Contemporary public health: Principles, practice, and policy* (pp. 25–46). University Press of Kentucky.

World Health Organization (2022). Mental health and climate change: Policy brief.

CHAPTER 21

Future Directions
Youth Climate Distress and Climate Justice
Sarah Jaquette Ray and Britt Wray

As this volume has shown, young people indisputably comprise a globally dispersed vulnerable population that is unjustly threatened by climate change-related harm. Children shoulder more than 85 percent of the global burden of disease from climate change (Sheffield & Landrigan, 2011), and while the danger this poses to physical health is well described, the injury this inflicts on young people's mental health has been much slower to gain attention. It is a ripe time for a volume such as this one to help fill that critical gap. We see the major contributions of this book as having struck the sweet spot where three areas of knowledge intersect: young people, climate justice, and mental health. It is not easy to identify climate as a sole stressor in a time of polycrisis – as young people face climate change, biodiversity loss, environmental degradation, pandemic, fraying democracies, rise of authoritarianism, war, financial crisis, structural inequality, racism, and more – but best efforts throughout this book are made. Taken together, the chapters weave expertise from family, developmental, and systems theory, psychoanalysis, psychology, psychiatry, neuroscience, pediatrics, law, activism, trauma science, ecotheories, environmental justice, Indigenous knowledge, theology, and the wide-ranging therapeutic practices derived from these fields. In doing so, they offer rich insight into research and practice at the raw bleeding edge of what is known about the youth mental health crisis within the larger climate crisis. Crucially, this includes what can be done to empower and support young people in navigating these challenges while protecting and promoting their personal and community well-being.

In concluding the collection, we would like to offer a nuanced thrust of resistance to the "mental healthification" of discourse around young people's psychological and emotional responses to our warming world. By "mental healthification" we mean a fixation on Western psychology and psychiatry, therapies, treatments, and other pathways to recovery that see difficult climate emotions as something to be "overcome," as well as a rigid loyalty to biomedical approaches to trauma and related responses. We see this approach as unfortunately deflecting attention from the political, cultural, economic, and structural systems that shape and are shaped by the mental and physical capacities and orientations of the body politic, whereby individuals are pathologized while harmful and potentially genocidal systems are perversely portrayed as innocent, neutral, and inevitable. At the same time, we recognize that the harmful complex systems in which people live that lead to climate distress and trauma have catalyzed the onset of acute pain for many people, and it is only appropriate that some individuals seek mental health care to live better with these afflictions. Climate-aware mental health professionals are increasingly organizing their communities of practice around a nonpathologizing approach to suffering in the face of climate change. This partly means experimenting with community approaches to mental health care that live beyond the biomedical model, as well as co-opting and adapting preexisting therapeutic interventions to support people who are struggling with diverse climate mental health outcomes. Seeking out a therapist when the climate crisis is a presenting feature in one's pain therefore does not necessarily mean being faced with the real dangers of a misunderstanding and pathologizing professional. The climate-aware clinician can offer radical and empowering forms of support for the unique stressors of climate trauma and distress. However, these nonpathologizing approaches are still not the norm in the mental health professions at large, and the "mental healthification" of climate distress and trauma still looms uncomfortably large in the public psyche around care and response.

While many contributions in this volume have clarified and argued for the appropriateness of framing climate mental health issues through a non-pathologizing lens, oceans of insights from contemplative practices, environmental humanities, Indigenous wisdom traditions, spiritual approaches, MAPA (most affected people and areas) perspectives, affect studies, posthumanism, new materialism, betrayal trauma, queer theory, transpersonal psychology, existential approaches, social movement studies, and critical approaches to futurity, temporality, and extinction– not to mention traditional disciplines of ecology, sociology, economics, politics, history, literature, arts, and others – remain relatively untapped in our emerging field. This volume contributes to the bridging of the mental health world and these other epistemologies and methodologies from both within and outside the academy.

There are libraries full of knowledge about how to live better with suffering that stretch far beyond the typical shelves of mental health, as well as communities of people with lived experience of suffering whose wisdom has never been jotted down. Extraordinary opportunities await for supporting young people around the world with their wisdom and practices. While climate-aware mental health professionals with biomedical approaches must be uplifted in the work of sustaining young people through climate trauma (Li et al., 2022; Woodbury, 2019), we encourage future contributions from diverse multidisciplinary perspectives that have historically been excluded from serious conversations about mental health. In this chapter, we break the ice with a few of these domains, in order to invite further investigation and strengthening of their shared purpose; that is, equitably safeguarding and fostering young people's mental health and emotional well-being in the climate and wider planetary health crisis. At the same time, we offer our reflections on issues that need remedying for researchers to be more effective in this work.

Centering Emotions in Research, Policy, and Practice

What would future research look like if it centered emotion as the primary factor in climate change mitigation and personal action? The essays in this volume move us in that direction; Cartesian dualisms in Western colonial-capitalist thought treat emotions as needing discipline from the more superior faculty of reason, as the unruly barrier to progress and human potential. In this frame, emotions are shameful, private, transgressive, undignified, and pathological – the domain of stigma and deviance, requiring medicalized intervention to assist individuals in becoming accommodated to the demands of modern life. Emotions inhibit rational thought and thwart strategic efforts to influence political reality. In the realm of power-*over* (as opposed to power-*with*, as many grassroots social movements often prefer to operate), which remains the dominant modality of politics, emotions are thought of as needing to be suppressed, or if they are valued, are far more often exploited than supported.

The vast majority of people in globalized Western societies have been enculturated in this dualistic worldview that sees emotion as a barrier to progress – whether that progress is economic or social. This means that they often suffer maladaptation to the (often traumatizing) systems they live in alone, in private, and in shame. This isolation and stigma in turn serve to make matters worse for them, and increasingly, as climate psychologists argue, they are making matters worse for the planet. The more emotionally connected we are to ourselves and others, the more connected we may be to the greater web of life on this planet. We may be better equipped to access what is required to sustain life on earth by way of mutualism and partnership, as opposed to the domination, denial, and dissonance bred from isolation. Buddhism, for example, frames this healthy response to the state of existence in terms of "interbeing." Climate and eco-psychologists add to a chorus of voices from spiritual and Indigenous perspectives saying we need more reflexive awareness and practice of interbeing, to not only survive the challenges ahead, but to honor other lifeforms and ancient lineages that still have a chance at evolving as sacred beings on their own.

This volume offers a critical corrective to some of these assumptions of Western thought by challenging the dualistic view, and posits emotions as a *source of* – not *anathema to* – political and social change. For the contributors herein, emotions, not just reason per se, are the terrain of political power. Rejecting the binary entirely, they amplify current research and the wisdom of many marginalized communities and social movements, which show there is reason to emotion, and conversely, that reason itself is based in emotion. Beyond the important work of delineating understandable and healthy climate-related emotional and psychological responses from preexisting mental health disorders (see Haase, Chapter 3), there lies a potent force field in which emotional disturbances are lifesaving instruments of political and structural change. Disturbances force movement, and difficult emotions have always been key ingredients of protest and societal transformation (Jasper, 1998). The emotional disturbances young people appropriately experience in relation to climate can constructively shape political aspirations and feed actions to build a more just and livable world.

Studies of social movements suggest that successful movements often build out from the intimacy of emotional motivation (hopes, fears, resentment, betrayal), personal stories, as well as through opportunities to voice and engage those affective phenomena as part of a wider shared community that feels the same (Ganz, 2010; Gould, 2009). This is the work of building power with others through communities of care, such that people cultivate strong social ties and connectedness with each other, and learn how to lead and follow to achieve shared goals in the face of uncertainty. Social capital and the ability to organize are born from these skills. Evidence suggests that social capital can help prevent mental disorders when disasters strike, enabling communities to rebuild faster on the far side of adversity, as well as provide ongoing psychosocial support that builds resilience for turbulent times (Berry, 2009; Wray, 2022). Therefore, with one eye, we should admire the disturbing climate thoughts and feelings young people express for their potential to galvanize connections that have a protective effect. With the other, we should keep a lookout for risk factors that any number of events can trigger to harm young people's mental health. To be a researcher or practitioner in this growing field is to be able to walk a balance beam as one's eyes dart in two different directions. As many chapters have discussed, more research that investigates protective and risk factors that shape how climate distress becomes adaptive for some individuals, yet maladaptive for others, or, how it becomes adaptive at certain times and maladaptive at others within the same individual, is crucial.

These essays inspire us to think in even more ways about how emotion can be understood and leveraged for the climate. Climate change is often framed as a problem of the natural sciences, a matter of technology or even economics and politics. But the science of emotions, including its sister domains of mood and affect, and the proximate, cultural, and political environments that shape them, which the essays in this volume explicate, are perhaps even more important to study and address. As Paul Hawken (2021) puts it, "The most complex, radical climate technology on Earth is the human heart and mind, not a solar panel." This book treats the heart and mind as critical "technologies" to address climate change, a direction we need to keep pushing forward in policy, research, and practice.

The Danger of Big Climate Emotions

One of the arguments in favor of bringing climate emotions out of the therapy room and into research, policy, education, and mainstream discourse is that in doing so, we can untangle the threads between big feelings and climate politics, or healthy and unhealthy ways of acting in response to one's emotions. Although the science of emotions tells us that we want to acknowledge nonjudgmentally, not all actions derived from those emotions are equally morally good. While intense emotions about climate change are indeed a reasonable response to what we are learning is happening all over the planet, unhealthy emotionality is always lurking in the shadows, as is reflected in extreme and often harmful behaviors on both the political right and left.

One area where this political lens on emotions is essential for the sake of climate *justice* (not just in addressing climate *change*) is in confronting eco-fascism and climate racism. People along the political spectrum, in many corners of the globe, are responding to climate forecasts with fear and urgency – emotions that are the intended consequences of climate discourse and science communication. Fear and urgency are effective orientations to motivate action, as several essays in this volume show, but not all action is good for the climate or for social justice. The line between actual, real threat and various communities' perception of risk is rarely straight, and many interests, agendas, and filters can obfuscate it further. It is difficult to get a critical mass of people to agree on a course of action around a particular threat, such as climate change, but even before that can happen, there's the challenge of getting everybody to unify around a particular threat as a priority over other threats that they perceive. (What makes a person "believe" in climate change as a threat is arguably the entire *raison-de-entre* of the field of climate communication.) The job isn't done when we get all people to *perceive* and *care* about climate change; the politics of risk perception mix with the existing landscape of cultural politics and affects, and can lead, ironically, to actions that increase rather than reduce harms to the planet and its inhabitants.

Indeed, the mass shootings of El Paso, Christchurch, and Buffalo in the past few years, as well as the rise of authoritarianism in many countries, are the tip of the iceberg of a growing movement of white supremacists who hear in climate forecasts a scientific rationale for hoarding resources, eliminating communities deemed as threats to nature and nation, controlling the reproductive power of women (Sasser and Hendrixson, 2021), and supporting policies that are less about the climate and more about social engineering and control (Hartmann et al., 2021). In Foucauldian terms, these are the biopolitical implications of climate distress, and they are not new; blood and soil ideology (most prominently espoused during the Nazi regime) has roots in Thomas Malthus's ideas about resource scarcity and human population growth, from the late 1700s, and even as far back as scientific racism and expansionism of the seventeenth century (Ray, 2013). Not only are these ideas not new, they are also not "fringe"; big climate emotions drive current reproductive, immigration, antidemocracy, and gun policy in the United States and beyond. From the survivalist fantasies of the ultra-rich (see Elon Musk and his dream to "occupy Mars," for instance, which was hilariously spoofed by the character Peter Isherwell in the 2021 film *Don't Look Up*), to the eugenicist, "great replacement theory," authoritarian, anti-abortion, "white extinction anxiety" groundswell (especially in contemporary US politics), these ideas are only growing in popularity alongside mounting climate alarmism. Essays in this collection that focus specifically on climate justice (see Chapters 11 and 18, for example) insist on emphasizing the justice dimensions of climate distress; however, we need to continue to train our critical eyes on the parallel (re)emergence of this "new" climate racism and the role of emotions in emboldening it.

When we treat emotions as private, especially ones related to planetary-scale uncertainty, it becomes difficult to address the distress, much less the propensity toward climate racism and the politics that ensue. As this volume expertly navigates, emotions are always already the domain of politics and justice. If we seek to advance climate justice, not just climate change mitigation, we will need to continue to build expertise around the role of climate emotions in these myriad and seemingly unrelated political conversations.

Positionality, Climate Risk Perception, and Justice

The growing interest in climate emotions is an understandable consequence of the mass public awakening underway, wherein even the most privileged and protected individuals may for the first time be feeling ontologically insecure due to climate change. Unfortunately, this may risk over-privileging constructs such as climate anxiety, grief, and general climate distress at the expense of other acute, subacute, or chronic stressors that can affect mental health over the life-course and over the real physical threats of climate change to the Global South. Depending on who is doing the research, there is a risk of disproportionately playing into the interests of the worried well of enfranchised communities in the Global North, which are responsible for a whopping 92 percent of excess carbon emissions (Hickel, 2020), particularly worrisome from a climate mental health justice perspective. As this volume highlights, there are significant biological mental health challenges created and exacerbated by climate change that take root in early life, which are pronounced for the most vulnerable communities, and so developmental approaches are key (see Chapters 3 and 4). Prioritizing mental health and psychosocial support for young people in disaster and conflict settings, migrants, those experiencing food and water scarcity, extreme heat, air pollution, climate-related gender-based violence, and more are all critical pieces to work on for climate mental health justice.

Climate and mental health research has a rich opportunity to take seriously the ways that emotions have everything to do with positionality, which is constantly shifting and evolving in mutual co-creation with culture and politics. Climate change is often considered an elite concern, despite the ways that it is and will continue to be experienced most intensely by those with the least power (see Chapters 4 and 20). This is because climate change is a kind of epi-phenomenon, a meta-category that includes a wide variety of threats and risks (and opportunities) that are experienced unevenly across different populations.

Climate change touches absolutely everything; this is why philosopher Timothy Morton calls it a "hyperobject" that is vastly "dispersed across space and time" (Morton 2013), and manifests like a "Whack-a-Mole" toy in so many different ways and contexts. One's mental health response to it can vary as much. One can be experiencing climate impacts (such as an infectious disease pandemic, one example of this phenomenon) and yet fail to perceive the cause of one's predicament as deeply intertwined with climate change, and vice versa. Much depends on the politics of risk perception and the stories we each disparately live within and believe. (This is where research about the psychological concepts of the availability heuristic, negativity bias, choice architecture, and confirmation bias, to name a few examples, could further bear on climate politics.) Whether any given community or individual position vis-à-vis climate change understands the risks they face *qua* climate change has everything to do with the stories circulating around them, their relative vulnerability to confirmation and negativity biases, and a whole layer of interpretative infrastructure that often goes unacknowledged in climate research (see, for example, Barrett, 2017 and Mesquita, 2022). In other words, one person in one part of the world and one point in history may be experiencing climate change as an increased incidence of wildfire, and may have access to a culturally constructed suite of emotions and cognitive concepts through which to understand the threat as such. But in order for that person to understand the threat they're experiencing as a function of climate change, much has to happen first. They have to have a particular understanding of climate change and of the risk they perceive. (This is perhaps why people who have had some kind of environmental education report feeling more climate distress, and why they are also relatively privileged.) This perspective enables them to connect the dots between what they are phenomenologically experiencing and the otherwise abstract scientific concepts of climate change.

And for them to respond with any particular emotion (such as "anxiety"), they have to have access to a particular vocabulary and cultural context where such an emotion has meaning and purchase as a response to the perceived risk, as we unpack further down. Their feelings emerge out of a complex dynamic of causes and conditions that shape their positionality, and same too of their perception of risk. Positionality not only determines how they are positioned vis-à-vis different threats caused by climate change; it also determines how they will understand their concerns within a particular frame or narrative, as well as what emotions they will feel in response to them. Put simply, if climate isn't part of that frame, they won't perceive their suffering in terms of climate change. In this way, we can see the stickiness of the questions, "who feels climate distress?" and "what are the mental health impacts of climate change on a given community?" Thus, if we want to shift climate politics, we will need to deeply query these complex matters of risk perception, threat response, positionality, and the science of emotions. This could look like doing more research on different communities' perceptions of climate change and other risks, as well as exploring the ways different emotions are culturally constructed among various communities (instead of assuming the universality of emotions). This could involve using language that a community uses for itself to identify its own stressors and recognizing why, even though climate change may be connected to those stressors, there may be suspicion that climate change diverts resources away from that community. It could mean uplifting leaders from the community and listening to them on what needs are most salient to the community in order to see their tie-in (or, as is sometimes the case, their conflict) with climate politics, and attending to other sources of suffering as a primary goal that climate change will surely make worse. Otherwise, the risk exists that communities experiencing "more immediate threats" than climate change (police brutality, food insecurity, waste siting, etc.) will continue to distance themselves from the climate movement because they do not see their interests as aligned, even though climate change is predicted to exacerbate these other problems.

One direction in which to move in order to address this issue is to reframe climate change as lots of different problems that are interconnected. Deconstructing "climate change" as the problem allows us to see it in all of its proxies and knock-on effects. That is, we can recognize that a pandemic, a fire, police brutality, environmental racism, food insecurity, abortion controls, hunger, and any number of more "immediate" threats (immediate relative to different communities across space and time, that is) are inextricably tied to climate change. We should start to connect the dots between those disparate, immediate threats to distinct communities, while also acknowledging the tensions and costs of clumping all these problems under one umbrella of "climate." For instance, a group of Black community members in New Orleans, Louisiana may not be all that energized to discuss how climate change writ-large is impacting their mental health. But when the conversation shifts to how hurricanes, floods, and tornadoes affect them personally, and how structural racism has long impacted the degree of help they receive from outside sources for dealing with the impacts of these disasters, people come alive around the topic. We are tasked to name the polycriss within the climate crisis, and know that one person's climate polycrisis may be materially different – and, crucially, *articulated* differently – from the next (Ray, 2021).

This book gestures in such a direction, but we call for even further thinking about this question: what is gained (or lost) when we get rid of climate change as the main frame through which we understand different communities' concerns? Paradoxically, perhaps, might a more robust and justice-oriented approach to climate change jettison the concept entirely? Climate communicators are demonstrating that climate frames that are most accessible across most populations are ones that emphasize health (Maibach et al., 2010); if this is true, how might the mental health frame advanced in this volume help move the conversation around climate in this health-focused direction? And in terms of youth mental health, this line of inquiry asks, whose young people's mental health are we circumscribing our concern around when we consider only those concerned about "climate change"? How might we expand our research if we understood that it takes a particular positionality to not only *experience* the threat of, but to *articulate* their experience of that threat *as* climate change? Further research on the role of positionality to threat assessment and response in climate mental health would expand the implications of this current volume for youth climate justice. However, caution should be applied to how much one dilutes the climate frame in order to make space for other connected priorities, as the further away we get from conceptualizations of climate change, the harder it is to keep the focus on the overall needed intervention to protect and promote the mental health of all: reducing the use of fossil fuels at global scale.

Gaining Clarity across Scales and Language

While exciting that the climate mental health space is gaining ground as more researchers flock to the field and the public takes interest in it, not all growth is good. Without many standardized, validated, and culturally sensitive scales for measuring relevant constructs in climate mental health, it can sometimes feel like we are adding more noise than signal to an already complex space. Furthermore, papers that measure distinct experiences such as eco-anxiety, climate anxiety, climate distress, or climate worry, are of great interest on their own, but the lack of clarity around the overlap and standardization of these constructs limits the comparison of findings across disparate regions and contexts. Future research that responds to the functionality (or not) of climate mental health constructs would be a boon to the field.

It isn't just scales that lack clarity and unity. The vocabulary we use to describe our emotional and cognitive experiences with climate change often varies, yet carries political salience and cultural specificity based on our positionality, as discussed above. There is a thumping call for shared language that can transcend our differences so that humanity can effectively meet this moment, indict the political failures and name the structural forces that are making people mentally ill and subclinically distressed, and finally, find ourselves in partnerships with each other that support the shared existential project of fostering a better future. While there are many examples of climate emotions in other languages (Schneider-Mayerson & Bellamy, 2019), research on climate psychology is concentrated on emotions experienced in the Anglosphere. What does this leave out, considering that the majority of climate impacts will be felt in non-English speaking low- and middle-income countries? How are we to make sense of the psychological and emotional impacts of climate change for communities dealing with legacies of imperialism, colonization, extraction, and poverty at the same time as climate change if we are missing the words they use to make sense of these layered impacts for themselves? Linguistically diverse investigations of climate emotions – codeveloped with community members and diverse cultural brokers – are needed that respect local context and culture. So too is a broad cross-cultural vocabulary that local findings can be (roughly) translated into, in order to make sense of political and structural forces that shape people's internal climates across disparate regions. Words are material to how we make sense of the world, and therefore how we can act in it. The lack of nuanced international vocabulary in this respect risks perpetuating the pathologizing or ignoring of young people who are impacted by any number of legitimate climate stressors.

Climate Hostages and Critical Consciousness

Young people worldwide could be understood as what the climate-aware psychologist Thomas Doherty calls "climate hostages" (Doherty et al., 2022) – given that they are being forced to adapt to the damaging effects of climate change over their entire lives, are up against a system laden with an entrenched status quo, and have inherited the burden of being "the climate generation" that will somehow fix the problem inside said system. Terms such as hostage and "institutional betrayal" helpfully evade any passivity and underscore the political nature of being restrained by powerful structures that seek to dampen young people's alarm about the destructive system in which they are living, contributing to mental health struggles. Institutional betrayal refers to wrongdoings, including moral injury, carried out by an institution upon individuals dependent on that institution, and it can lead to a number of harmful psychological consequences, including anxiety, depression, and suicidality (Smith & Freyd, 2014). In the climate context, young people are dependent upon national and global leadership to take climate actions that are in line with climate science in order to create a sustainable future and safeguard a planet in which they can grow up and thrive for generations to come. Young people may not be old enough to vote, let alone run for office or lead powerful institutions, and so are deeply dependent upon powerholders to uphold their end of the deal. When young people witness that these responsibilities are not taken seriously by powerholders over time, this violates a basic sense of right and wrong, causing mental suffering on moral grounds. Young people recognize that they are distressed not just because "the environment is not doing well," but because something wrong is being *done to them* that leads to the emergence of their critical consciousness (Freire, 2012). Critical consciousness is a key skill to support young people in cultivating, for their own agency, integrity and motivation to cause change, and future research that digs into this would be a striking contribution.

Queering Climate Anxiety

Another future direction of climate justice and mental health research that builds on what has been accomplished in this collection is to explore the impact of queer ecological theory on climate distress and other eco-emotions. Queer ecological theory attempts to expose the unacknowledged assumptions in much environmental discourse and politics that the actors and subjects are cis/straight/heteronormative people, operating within a system that assumes and rewards heteronormative nuclear family structures. It exposes the ways that ideas about how nature works are often culturally constructed from a homophobic culture, such that heterosexuality or monogamy, for example, are portrayed as "natural," and anything else as "unnatural" and therefore morally bad. "Queering" ecology helps us see the ways cultural norms are projected onto nature, and how nature is used to reinforce existing or status quo expectations. What would it mean to queer climate anxiety?

Taking the lead from thinkers such as Nicole Seymour, affect theorists such as Sara Ahmed (2014), and disability and Indigenous scholars, what would a fuller picture of climate mental health look like if it challenged heteropatriarchy, ableism, and colonial ideas of individualism and anthropocentrism at their roots? One exciting example of this direction is Vanessa Mochado de Oliveira's *Hospicing Modernity*, which brings together neuroscience, mental health, Indigenous critique, and environmental education in ways not yet seen in traditional disciplinary scholarship.

This question opens many lines of inquiry, which we cannot do justice to here. We mean to provoke the conversation to continue to develop these lines, as they are happening already in these fields, by bringing them to bear on research on youth climate mental health more fulsomely. For starters, queering climate emotions can involve expanding the range of emotions that dominant climate discourse avails. For example, queer climate activist and writer adrienne maree brown calls for *pleasure* as a central emotion for climate justice engagement (brown, 2019), while Nicole Seymour discusses *irony*, *irreverence*, and *embarrassment* as generative orientations for climate advocacy (Seymour, 2018).

Moreover, queer, Indigenous, feminist, posthumanist, and disability scholars challenge dominant models of *relationality* as it is defined as normative in mainstream psychology research and public discourse. That is, individualism, the family structure, social reproduction within capitalism, care work, kin, the role of community and "all our relations" (a term popularized by Winona LaDuke, 1999), what it means to be dependent upon and in relationship with "others," the transcorporeal nature of our bodies and cells (Alaimo, 2010) – these are all topics of central interest to disability, Indigenous, posthumanist, and queer scholars (among others) that have implications for climate mental health.

Scholars rethinking the colonial, ableist, anthropocentric, and heteronormative models of family and bodily autonomy, much less binaries such as mind/body and reason/emotion discussed above, have much to offer the study of youth mental health and climate change. These fields also expose the unsustainability, misogyny, colonialism, and state-sponsored heteronormativity of the nuclear family structure, posing the question: How might non-normative views of temporality, kinship, and definitions of what constitutes the body expand the conceptual and ethical net of climate mental health conversations? And to connect it more explicitly to this book, what do young people have to teach us about the political and climate implications of these non-normative critiques? How might these critical inquiries be enlisted to support youth engagement with the polycrisis within which they find themselves?

With reproductive refusal due to climate change at an all-time high (Wray, 2022), rather than bemoan this as tragic, as the dominant discourse does, perhaps there is an opportunity here for recognizing the failure of the dominant nuclear family heteronormative model – both in terms of its exploitation of invisible care labor and in terms of its unecological structure. What happens when we explore broader kinship models that include communities, the more-than-human, ecosystems? If isolation and ruptured relationships are at the root of both our existential and climate crises, might new models of relationality be the right medicine for both dis-eases? What does "care" mean in these conversations, and how might they dismantle the medical model to deepen our relationships and healing (Mochado de Oliveira, 2021)? These lines of inquiry only begin to scrape the surface of what queer, Indigenous, and disability theorists could offer the field of youth climate mental health studies.

Transformative and Transgressive Research

With the UN Secretary General telling the world that we are on a "highway to climate hell" (Frangoul, 2022) and that the state of the climate crisis presents a "code red for humanity" (Joly, 2021), nothing short of societal transformation is being called for at the highest levels of governance. In order to transform society, science and knowledge production itself must also be transformed in order to step away from dominant modes of thinking and doing that have historically marginalized non-Western wisdom traditions and practices that are now sorely needed (Temper et al., 2019). A key aspect of producing knowledge differently means producing it in equitable partnerships with people outside the university, who live in the communities we hope our research will serve. In the climate mental health context, this means coproducing knowledge alongside people with lived experience of climate mental health issues, with youth, with frontline communities, with disabled people, with Indigenous communities, queer communities, women, farmers, and migrants. What this looks like in practice is inviting members of disproportionately affected communities into codesigning interventions they develop shared ownership of, for the benefit of their community (such as through the global mental health model of "task-sharing"), with those from communities perpetuating the problems, and more. Sharing power so that research questions are guided through equitable partnerships will be key to enriching not only our academic outcomes, but its real-world impacts. We see climate mental health researchers as perfectly positioned to engage in this kind of transformational work, as long as we can admit to ourselves and our colleagues that what we aim to do is bring about structural change, not just observe the maladies of the moment. The tension this creates for us as scientists and researchers who have been taught to treat subjective desires and emotions around our work as artifacts that ought to be extracted signals that we are at a crossroads.

With so many "isms" shaping climate impacts, how harmful they are, and for whom, (colonialism, racism, sexism, etc.), scholars have argued for transgressive approaches that cut across the boundaries such "isms" create. Transgressive research is defined by Lotz-Sisitka et al. (2016) as "critical thinking and collective agency and praxis that directly and explicitly challenges those aspects of society that have become normalized, but which require challenging for substantive sustainability transformations to emerge (e.g., colonial practice or epistemology, gender and race relations, social exclusion, environmental injustice)." In order to maximize the ability of climate mental health researchers to achieve our shared goals of protecting and promoting mental health, climate justice, and youth well-being, we argue that it is not only appropriate but vital for climate mental health researchers to see ourselves as part of a bigger movement of scholarly activists doing transgressive and transformational work.

Conclusion

Community-based solutions that bring all of the above into view are on the rise. Mental health is part of a vast web of relationships, between individuals and each other, structures, and the more-than-human world, and conversations in books such as this one are casting this ancient truth in new, sharp relief, with a much-needed focus on youth. In coming to a close for this essential guide, we especially want to surface the ways the book opens up these possibilities, as well as for the *positive* mental health experiences activated by climate change. This book offers relationships between mental health and climate change in a series of overlapping domains and feedback loops, rather than a top-down model (as an unnuanced approach to the "mental healthification" of climate distress would have it); it is not just that climate change affects mental health; mental (and physical) health is required for its mitigation. All of these nuances and directions are advanced in this book, and it is an honor to have the opportunity to comment on its contributions. We look forward to seeing its impact on these many fields, and expect these conversations to unfold richly for years to come – hopefully, in service of us thriving together on a thriving planet.

References

Ahmed, S. (2014). *The cultural politics of emotion* (2nd ed.). Edinburgh University Press.

Alaimo, S. (2010). *Bodily natures: Science, environment, and the material self.* University of Indiana Press.

Barrett, L. F. (2017). *How emotions are made: The secret life of the brain.* Houghton Mifflin Harcourt.

Berry, H. (2009). Pearl in the oyster: Climate change as a mental health opportunity. *Australasian Psychiatry*, 17(6), 453–456. https://doi.org/10.1080/10398560903045328

brown, A. M. (2019). *Pleasure activism: The politics of feeling good.* AK Press.

Doherty, T. J., Lykins, A. D., Piotrowski, N. A., Rogers, Z., Sebree Jr, D. D., & White, K. E. (2022). 11.12-Clinical psychology responses to the climate crisis. In G. J. G. Asmundson and M. Noel (Eds.), *Comprehensive clinical psychology* (Vol. 11, pp. 167–183). Elsevier.

Don't Look Up. Dir. Adam McKay. Netflix Films, 2021.

Frangoul, A. (2022). We're on a "highway to climate hell," UN chief Guterres says, calling for a global phase-out of coal. *CNBC*, November 7. www.cnbc.com/2022/11/07/were-on-a-highway-to-climate-hell-un-chief-guterres-says.html

Freire, P., Ramos, B. M., & Macedo, D. (2012). *Pedagogy of the oppressed.* Bloomsbury.

Ganz, M. (2010). *Why David sometimes wins: Leadership, organization, and strategy in the California Farm Worker Movement.* Oxford University Press.

Gould, D. B. (2009). *Moving politics: Emotion and Act Up's fight against Aids.* University of Chicago Press.

Hartmann, B., Ray, S. J., Sasser, J., & Weston, R. (2022). When climate anxiety leans right: Eco-fascism, Buffalo, and Roe. Climate Psychology Alliance of North America, June 11. www.climatepsychology.us/recorded-talks/when-climate-anxiety-leans-right-eco-fascism-buffalo-and-roe-1

Hawken, P. (2021). *Regeneration: Ending the climate crisis in one generation.* Penguin Books.

Hickel, J. (2020). Quantifying national responsibility for climate breakdown: An equality-based attribution approach for carbon dioxide emissions in excess of the planetary boundary. *The Lancet Planetary Health*, 4(9). https://doi.org/10.1016/s2542-5196(20)30196-0

Jasper, J. (1998). The emotions of protest: Affective reactive emotions in and around social movements. *Sociological Forum* 13 (3), 397–424.

Joly, J. (2021). UN report on climate change warns of "code red for humanity." *Euronews*, October 27. www.euronews.com/green/2021/10/27/cop26-un-secretary-general-antonio-guterres-warns-of-code-red-for-humanity

LaDuke, W. (1999). *All our relations: Native struggles for land and life.* South End Press.

Li, C., Lawrance, E. L., Morgan, G., Brown, R., Greaves, N., Krzanowski, J., ..., & Belkin, G. (2022). The role of mental health professionals in the climate crisis:

An urgent call to action. *International Review of Psychiatry*, 34(5), 563–570. https://doi.org/10.1080/09540261.2022.2097005

Lotz-Sisitka, H., Ali, M. B., Mphepo, G., Chaves, M., Macintyre, T., Pesanayi, T., ... & McGarry, D. (2016). Co-designing research on transgressive learning in times of climate change. *Current Opinion in Environmental Sustainability*, 20, 50–55. https://doi.org/10.1016/j.cosust.2016.04.004

Maibach, E. W., Nisbet, M., Baldwin, P., Akerlof, K., & Diao, G. (2010). Reframing climate change as a public health issue: An exploratory study of public reactions. *BMC Public Health*, 10(1), 1–11.

Mesquita, B. (2022). *Between us: How cultures create emotions* (First ed.). W.W. Norton & Company.

Mochado de Oliveira, V. (2021). *Hospicing modernity: Facing humanity's wrongs and the implications for social activism.* North Atlantic Books.

Morton, T. (2013). *Hyperobjects: Philosophy and ecology at the end of the world.* University of Minnesota Press.

Ray, S. J. (2013). *The ecological other: Environmental exclusion in American culture.* University of Arizona Press.

Ray, S. J. (2021). Who feels climate anxiety? *Cairo Review of Global Affairs*, Fall. www.thecairoreview.com/essays/who-feels-climate-anxiety/

Sasser, J., & Hendrixson, A. (2021). Don't blame babies (or their mothers) for climate change. *Ms. Magazine*, May 28. https://msmagazine.com/2021/05/28/climate-change-population-control-covid-baby-bust/

Seymour, N. (2018). *Bad environmentalism: Irony and irreverence in the ecological age.* University of Minnesota Press,.

Schneider-Mayerson, M., & Bellamy, B. R. (2019). *An ecotopian lexicon.* University of Minnesota Press.

Sheffield, P. E., & Landrigan, P. J. (2011). Global climate change and children's health: Threats and strategies for prevention. *Environmental Health Perspectives*, 119(3), 291–298. https://doi.org/10.1289/ehp.1002233

Smith, C. P., & Freyd, J. J. (2014). Institutional betrayal. *American Psychologist*, 69(6), 575–587. https://doi.org/10.1037/a0037564

Temper, L., McGarry, D., & Weber, L. (2019). From academic to political rigour: Insights from the "tarot" of transgressive research. *Ecological Economics*, 164, 106379. https://doi.org/10.1016/j.ecolecon.2019.106379

Woodbury, Z. (2019). Climate trauma: Toward a new taxonomy of trauma. *Ecopsychology*, 11(1), 1–8. https://doi.org/10.1089/eco.2018.0021

Wray, B. (2022). *Generation dread: Finding purpose in an age of climate crisis.* Knopf-Canada.

Appendix A
Resource List for Educators

(Referenced in Chapter 17)

Climate Psychology Alliance – especially lectures for parents and teachers www.climatepsychologyalliance.org/index.php

Emotion wheel example www.phoenixperform.com/single-post/a-wheel-of-human-emotions

Force of Nature guide to discussing ecoanxiety for educators www.forceofnature.xyz/discussion-guide

Interview with Senior Lecturer in Educational Psychology Dan O'Hare www.youtube.com/watch?v=Yc3NecAtEYA

Leeds DEC climate curriculum https://leedsdec.org.uk/climate-action-resources/

Teach the Future policies – see especially Track Changes docs www.teachthefuture.uk/policy

Thoughtbox Triple Wellbeing Hub – free online community; access to Thoughtbox resources, training and more www.thoughtboxhub.com

Walker, C (2023) Young People at a Crossroads Creative Book https://documents.manchester.ac.uk/display.aspx?DocID=64151

Appendix B

Costs and Benefits of Activism Scale

(Used with permission from Conner et al., 2023)

Answer choices on a seven-point Likert scale range from strongly disagree to strongly agree. The two parts of the scale should be summed separately and can stand alone or be studied in relationship to other measures of well-being.

The Political Costs of Activism (adapted from Smith et al., 2019)

1. I have felt tired as a result of my activism.
2. I have felt depressed as a result of my activism.
3. I have lost sleep because of my activism.
4. I have felt hopeless as a result of my activism.
5. I have felt guilty for not doing enough in my activism.
6. My activism has created problems for me with my family.
7. My activism has created problems for me with my peers.
8. My activism has created problems for me with academics/school work.
9. My activism has created problems for me with the police.
10. I have experienced harassment due to my activism.
11. I have experienced identity-based discrimination due to my activism.
12. I have had traumatic experiences due to my activism.

The Political Benefits of Activism (adapted from Oosterhoff et al. [62])

1. My political and social views are an important part of who I am.
2. On occasion, I have been proud of comments I made during a political discussion.
3. I have posted or written political things online that I am proud of.
4. Activism has given me a chance to demonstrate good judgment.
5. Activism has contributed to my personal growth.

6. Engaging in activism allows me to express myself.
7. Engaging in activism makes me fulfilled.
8. Being an activist has given me a sense of purpose.
9. Being an activist has made me feel empowered.
10. Similarities in political and social views have brought my extended family closer together.
11. On occasion, activism has made my home life more pleasant.
12. Similarities in political and social views have strengthened a friendship I valued.

Reference

Conner, J. O., Greytak, E., Evich, C. D., & Wray-Lake, L. (2023). Burnout and belonging: How the costs and benefits of youth activism affect youth health and wellbeing. *Youth*, 3(1), 127–145. https://doi.org/10.3390/youth3010009

Index

#EndSARS, 352

ABC model, 152
acceptance and commitment
    therapy, xvii, 197
Action for Climate Empowerment, 331
activism, xix, 210, 274–275
    alter/regenerative activism, 354
    bringing and end to groups, 363
    change agent in, 353
    citizen activist, 349
    climate distress due to, 358
    cultivating resilience during, 359
    definition of, 347
    mental health risks of, 360
    multiple types of, 347
    positive effects of, 361
    rebel activist, 351
    reformer activist, 350
    sacred/evolutionary, 354
    stresses related to, 276
    successful practices for, 354
    SustyVibes and, 357
activists
    negative portrayals of, 30
adaptation
    policy and, 83
ADDRESSING framework, 151
adolescence, 118
    psychiatric epidemiology and, 56
    risk-taking and, 98
    self states and, 172
    ventral striatum and, 55
adolescent coping, 269
adolescent dip, 125
adverse childhood events, 140
    climate stresses as, 172
agency, 321, 331, 343
Aiken, Ann, 259
air pollution, 57
    developmental impacts of, 178

Aji P. v. State of Washington, 262
Alter-Activism, 354, 360
American Academy of Pediatrics, 231, 233, 243
amygdala, 100
Anglosphere, 413
animism, 378
ansiedad ecológica, 32
Anthropocene, 120
anthropocentrism, 378
anxiété climatique, 32
anxiety, 3, 10, 13, 22–23, 93, 96, 153, 189
    normal *versus* pathological, 4, 45, 94, 169, 404
    paralyzing, 5
    parental influence on, 49
    practical, 5, 23
    trait *versus* state, 48, 169
    treatment of, 51
    versus worry, 22
anxiety disorders, 59, 93
    avoidant behavior and, 101
    genetic heritability of, 49
    parental factors in, 49
anxiety sensitivity, 48, 105
art, 374
attachment, 343
    cultural connectedness and, 389
    to nature. *See* nature
automaton conformity, 112
autonomy *vs* shame and doubt, 117. *See also*
    Erikson, Erik

Bascope, Martin, 337
basic trust *vs* mistrust, 117. *See also* Erikson, Erik
behavior, 12. *See also* pro-environmental
    behavior
behavioral approach system, xv, 97
    anatomy of, 99
behavioral inhibition. *See* anxiety
behavioral inhibition system, 97
    anatomy of, 99
belonging, 368, 381

Index

Bendell, Jim, 121
betrayal, 115
bidirectional influences, 304
bioecological framework, 311. *See also* Bronfenbrenner, Urie
biopsychosocial model, 47
biopsychosocio-environmental model, 40, 47
Bohm, David, 368–369
Bowen's Family Systems Theory, 295
brain development. *See* neurodevelopment
breast and toilet mother, 114
Bronfenbrenner, Urie
  bioecological framework of, 311
Bronfenbrenner's social-ecological theory, 288
"Bye Bye Plastics Bags" movement, 351

case conceptualization, xvi, 148–150
case formulation, 148
causal loop diagrams, 304
CCAS. *See* Climate Change Anxiety Scale
CEE
  climate and ecological emergencies, 149
change agent activist, 353. *See also* activism
Chemṣhúun Pe'icháachuqeli (*When Our Hearts Are Happy*), 397
child abuse, 348. *See also* child neglect
child neglect, xvi, 132
  climate inaction and, 135
child welfare, 134
Children's Climate Risk Index, 310
chronosystem, 290
citizen activist, 349
Citizens' Climate Lobby, 350
climate anxiety, 7. *See also* eco-anxiety
  clinical anxiety disorders and. *See* pediatric anxiety disorders
  definition, 4
  features of, *versus* distress, 27
  psychiatric case studies of, 59
  recommended strategies for, 105
  suggested approaches for, 50
climate change
  violence against children and, 132
Climate Change Anxiety Scale, xiv, 5, 7, 29, 41
  climate anxiety scales, limitations of, 171
  clinical symptomatology in, 42
  cross-cultural validation of, 5
climate dialectics. *See* dialectics
climate distress, 22, 41, 149, 192, 287, 290, 379. *See also* climate anxiety
  adaptive elements of, 28
  assessment of, 58, 148, 196
  characteristics associated with, 41

child-bearing decisions and, 13
community and, 380
conceptualization of, 21
creative practice for, 367
definition of, xiv, 21
de-motivating effects of, 333
functional impairment in, 59
geographical effects on, 291
history of, 28
Indigenous youth and, 389
joyfulness and, 323
linguistic considerations in, 31, 120
mental healthification of, 94, 403
overlap with psychiatric disorders and, 58
parents and, 295
peer influences and, 296
personal factors influencing, 294
politicization of, 40
power-based usage of, 30
prevalence, 3, 5
psychiatric issues in relation to, xv
psychoeducation for, 176
psychotherapies for, 197
social media and, 297
strength-based approach to, 389
systemic influences on, 291
terms related to, 25
validation of, 10
climate education
  qualitative analysis of, 336
Climate Education Bill. *See* education, policy and
climate emotions, 6, 9–10, 301
  abandonment and, 10
  anger and, 6
  betrayal and, 6, 115, 194
  Cartesian and Western influences on, 405
  depression and, 6
  grief and, 6, 24, 112, 142, 223
  joy. *See* activism, cultivating resilience during
  linguistic justice and, 413
  negative emotions and, 278
  positive emotions and, 11
  pride and, 11
  shame and, 6
  types of, 45
  uncertainty, 195
The Climate Group, 351
climate hostages, 413
climate impacts, 71
climate justice, xviii, 85, 106, 385
  climate racism and, 407
  co-production of knowledge and, 416
  heteronormativity and, 415
Climate Justice Union WA, 362
climate racism, 408

Index

climate worry
  clinical depression and anxiety and, 41
Climate-Aware Therapists, 177
  therapy components and, 196
climatic stressors, 70
  disrupted development and, 74
cognitions, 11
cognitive defusion, 197
cognitive behavioral therapy, xvi, 152, 154, 197
  ABC model and, 152
  cross-cultural application of, 156
cognitive control, 102
cognitive reappraisal, 279
cognitive strategies, 12
collapse, 378
collapse psychology, 378
collective action, 84, 106, 275–276, 300
  knowledge gaps, 322
Common Threads Project, 143
communication
  developmental level and, 317
  invalidation and, 318
  literature for, 317, 320, 323, 410
  non-verbal, 190
community, 274
community action, 106
community mental health, 174
complex systems, 133
confirmation bias, 159
consensus trance, 112
containment, xvi, 113, 122
  flexible container, 123
  fragmented container, 123
  rigid container, 123
Cooper, Christi. *See Youth v. Gov*, film
coping, 4, 9, 11–12, 269
  coactivational model of, 271
  emotion-focused, 4, 174, 270, 295
  meaning-focused, xviii, 11, 121, 174, 272, 274, 277, 294, 320
  meaning focused in CBT, 161
  proactive, 271
  problem solving, 12
  problem-focused, 174, 270, 321
  solution-focused, 338
  transactional theory of, 270
core beliefs, 154. *See also* cognitive behavioral therapy
  influence of ecodistress on, 155
Costs and Benefits of Activism Scale, 361, 421
creative spaces and practice, 367–368, 371, 373, 375, 379–380
critical consciousness, 414
critical emotional awareness, 281
critical hopefulness, 281

Dakota Access Pipeline, 386
Dark Mountain Project, the, xix, 367, 371–373, 376, 378
  meaning of "attitude" and, 374
DARVO, 135
Dawes General Allotment Act, 394
death
  supporting children during, 313
Deep Adaptation, 121
default mode network, 103
defenses, 173
  immature, 113, 122
depression
  "climate depression," 28
  clinical characteristics of, 46
  normal (sadness) *versus* clinical, 46
  pediatric, 47
  pediatric depressive disorders and, 52
  risk factors for, 47
  treatment of, 51
depressive position, 114. *See also* Klein, Melanie
development
  adolescence, 78
  adolescent. *See* Erikson, Erik
  adolescent identity and, 45
  adolescent identity formation, 53
  adolescent risk-taking and, 55
  core concepts in, 73
  early childhood, 77
  eco-related, 151
  infancy. *See* Erikson, Erik
  life course model and, xv
  mentalization and. *See* mentalization
  middle childhood, 77
  Piagetian stages, 193
  prenatal, 74
  pre-pubescent. *See* Erikson, Erik
  preschool. *See* Erikson, Erik
  risk appraisal across, 101
  school age. *See* Erikson, Erik
  sociopolitical, 275
  toddlerhood. *See* Erikson, Erik
developmental psychopathology, 72
dialectics, 126, 173, 281
disasters, 141, 170, 311
  community effects of, 299
  epidemiology of pediatric disorders in, 77
  parenting in, 312
  pediatric health impacts and, 237
  PTSD and, 238
  technical, 255
disasters, youth impact of, 13
disavowal, 111
displacement, 8, 40, 74, 143, 211, 392
dissenting opinions, 261

dissociation, xvi, 130–131, 142
distress
  psychiatric definitions of, 25. *See also* climate distress
Don't Look Up, 131
drive and affect regulation, 125
DSM-5 Cultural Formulation Interview, 151
duty of care, 253, 336. *See also* child neglect

Early Teens, 118
Earth Leadership Cohorts, xvii, 211, 213
eco-action, 174
ecoansiedad, 32
éco-anxiété, 32
eco-anxiety, 23
  history of, 29
The Eco-anxiety Africa Project (TEAP). *See* activism
eco-awareness, 150
ecocentric/eco-centrism, xvii, 219, 378
eco-distress
  case conceptualization and. *See* climate distress, assessment of
  constructive, 161
  constructive, work with, 156
  existential, 157
  impairing, 159
  treating impairing levels of, 156
  value of, 155, 163
eco-fascism, 407. *See also* climate justice
eco-literacy, 380
ecological determinants of health, 389
ecological distress
  ethical issues in defining, 22
ecological grief. *See* grief; solastalgia
  Indigenous people and, 391
eco-neglect, 130
eco-nostalgia, 169
eco-paralysis, 102, 169, 174
ecopsychology, 219
eco-rage, 62
ecoterrorism, 62
education, 329
  climate curriculum and, 299
  collective action, 275–277, 300, 362, 369
  educator underpreparation and, 329
  emotional impacts of, 333
  impacts on climate mental health, 330
  interpretative communities, 371
  knowledge gaps in. *See* knowledge gaps
  policy and, 331
  resource list for, 420
  teaching the teacher and, 329
embodied awareness, 130
embodied cognition, xvi

emergence, 130
emergency preparedness, 312
emotional regulation, 319
emotion-focused coping, 319
environmental distress scale, 29
environmental doom, 24
environmental identity, 151
Environmental Identity Scale, 41
environmental justice. *See* climate justice
environmental racism
  Indigenous peoples and, 398
Erikson, Erik, 116
eustress, 28
evolutionary activism, 354. *See also* activism; Patten, Terry
exosystem
  exosystemic influences, 290, 300
Extinction Rebellion, 352, 360

fear, 140
  of abandonment, 124
  of annihilation, 124
  of nature, 124
  of one's own destructiveness, 124
  of powerlessness/loss of control, 124
felt sense, xvi, 132
Fisher, Walter, 377
Fishwick, Sarah, 338
flow on effects, 311
Fridays for Future, 352

Gendlin, Eugene, 132
Ginsburg, Ruth Bader, 350
Global North, 291
Global South, 291
good-enough mother, 122
Gorman, Amanda, 329
green exposure interventions, 177
grief, 6, 24, 112, 142, 223. *See also* climate emotions, grief and
group identity *vs* alienation. *See* Erikson, Erik

Hawken, Paul, 407
health
  climate impacts on youth and, 7
  epidemiology of pediatric and, 231
  prenatal development and climate impacts on, 8
Health of Mother Earth Foundation, 359
heat, 288
  children's health and, 236
  mental health impacts of, 57
  neuropsychiatric effects of, 177
  prenatal effects, 76, 236
  urban heat island effect, 236

Index

Held v. State of Montana, 260
hidden curriculum, 334
Hine, Dougald, 367, 371, 373
Hogg Eco-anxiety scale, 35, 42
hope, 6, 9–10, 14, 206–207, 271
   active, 212, 235, 320
   constructive, xviii, 273, 278
   critical hopefulness and, 281
   defiant, 274
   hope beyond hope and, 379
   radical, 121
   realistic, 279
   reasonable, 121
Hughes, Charles Evan, 261
human centrality
   myth of, 373
human exceptionalism, 130
Hurricane Ian, 313
hyperobject, 173, 410
hypervigilance, 159. *See also* stress

identity, 45, 53, 151, 288
   activism effects on, 362
   imagination and, 374
identity project, 362
identity *vs* role diffusion. *See* Erikson, Erik
ilmastoahdistus, 33
imagination, 374
improvisation, 375, 381
Indigenous Eco-Relational Engagement, 397
Indigenous people
   Assimilation Era, 390. *See also* displacement
   biodiversity and, 385
   epistemological systems of, 392
   kinship with land, 392
   language sovereignty and, 394, 396
   relation to extractive industry, 391
   resilience through justice, 396
   seventh generation prophecy and, 398
   storytelling and. *See* re-storying
   tenets of resilience in, 395
   terms of reconciliation with, 387
Indigenous Traditional Ecological Knowledge, xix, 133, 359, 386–387
Indigenous youth
   cultural connectedness. *See* attachment
   mental health in, 385
   place-based mental health and, 396
   substance abuse in, 391
   suicide in, 391
industry *vs* inferiority. *See* Erikson, Erik
infancy, 117
initiative *vs* guilt. *See* Erikson, Erik

institutional abuse, 132
   child labor and. *See* child abuse
institutional betrayal, 255, 334, 414. *See also* climate emotions, betrayal and
interbeing, 406
Intergovernmental Panel on Climate Change, sixth assessment, 3
internal locus of control, 49
Intersectional Environmentalism, 349
intersectionality, 172, 218
   and climate activism, 211
interventions
   systems adaptivity, 304
intimacy *vs* isolation. *See* Erikson, Erik

Jones, Mary Harris "Mother," 348
Juliana v. United States, 251, 259

Keystone XL pipeline, 386
King, Martin Luther, 353
Kingsnorth, Paul, 367, 371, 373–374
Klein, Melanie, 114
Klima-angst, 33
klimatångest, 33
knowledge gaps, 329
Krakauer, David, 132

la ansiedad climática, 32
La Rose v. Her Majesty the Queen, 252
la solastalgie. *See* solastalgia
Lalonde, Albert-Jerome, 253
landback, 385–386
legal remedy, xviii, 253, 257, 262, 301
legal right to a healthy environment, 260, 262
legal rights
   climate related, 254
   standards for children, 258
Levine, Peter, 132
liminality, 376
litigation, climate, 252
loss, 378

macrosystem, 302
   macrosystemic, 290
Macy, Joanna. *See* Work that Reconnects, the
manic defense, 114. *See also* defenses
meaning
   global meaning, 272
   situational, 272
meaning-focused coping, 273
meaninglessness, 379
meaning-making, 369, 371, 377, 381
medical specialization, 179
mental disorder
   onset of, 71

mental health, 7, 71
  acknowledging emotions and, 6
  and climate health, IPCC, 3
  climate stressors on, 70
  non-medical approaches to, 404
  pediatricians and, 231
  rigid approaches to, 403
  social capital and, 406
mental healthification, xx. *See also* climate distress
mentalization, 56
mesosystem
  mesosystemic influences, 290, 299
metaphor, 370, 374, 376
microsystem
  microsystemic influences, 288
Millennium Kids Inc, 362
mindfulness, 274
Mní Wičóni, 386
Mochado de Oliveira, Vanessa, 415
monsoon, 314
moral disengagement, 173
moral distress, 160
moral injury, 160, 414
more-than-human nature, 368, 370, 379, 381
mortality, 313. *See also* Bendell, Jim
Morton, Timothy, 410
Movement for the Emancipation of the Niger Delta (MEND), 352
Movement for the Survival of the Ogoni People (MOSOP), 351
Moyers, Bill, 349
Musson, Rachel, 339

Naatookyookaasii: Two Medicine, 387
Nakate, Vanessa, 329
Namewog, 224
narrative, 372, 375, 378
  false narratives, xvii
narrative inquiry/work, 367, 369–371, 373, 377, 380–381
  metaphor and, 370
  splits in mainstream climate narrative and, 373
National Curriculum, 331
nature
  Confucianism and, 303
  connection to, 316
  importance of, 302
  time in, 297
Nature Relatedness Scale, 41
neoliberal exceptionalism, 133
neurodevelopment, 54, 294
  air pollution, 57
  direct climate impacts on, 57
  impact of stress on, 56
  neurochemistry and, 55
  risk-perception and, 54
  sex steroids and, 55
neuron, 97
neuroplasticity, 97, 103
New York Society for the Prevention of Cruelty to Children, 134
nutrition
  psychiatric impacts of, 57
NYSCHECK, 243

Oak Flat, 386
Öko-Angste, 33
optimal stress, 57
overwhelm, 143

paranoid-schizoid position. *See* Klein, Melanie
parenting, xviii, 49, 125, 295, 309
  climate distress and, 310
  influences on climate distress outcomes, 50
  overprotection and, 322
  pro-environmental values and. *See* pro-environmental behavior
  promoting nature connectedness and. *See* nature
  styles of, 49
parents
  definition, 310
Paris Agreement/Paris Climate Accords, 256
pathway thinking, 280
Patten, Terry, 354
pediatric anxiety disorders, 52, 59
pediatric psychiatric disorders, 52
  common features of, 52
  treatment of, 51
pediatricians and youth climate anxiety, xvii, 231
  American Academy of Pediatrics and, 237, 240
  professional roles in, 233, 242
perfectionism
  impairing eco-distress and, 159, 162
periaqueductal gray matter, 100
physical health
  childrens' bodies and, 72
Piaget, 193. *See also* Development, subentry Piagetian stages
Plogging, 359
policy
  protecting youth and, 301
  research basis of, 82
politicization, 40
  psychotherapeutic work with, 206
positionality, 30, 152, 409
  climate mental health research and, 412

positive psychology, 272
positive reappraisal, 272
post-traumatic growth, 13–14, 175
power/powerlessness, 7, 10, 15, 30, 211
　disengagement and, 125
　heteropatriarchal structure and, xx
　role of emotions in, 405–406
prenatal development, 8
pre-school, 117
pre-traumatic stress disorder, 170
preventive psychiatry, 85
pro-environmental behavior, 5, 322
　climate distress and, 101
　climate worry and, 12
　relationship to climate anxiety, 7
progress, 405
　narratives supporting, 375
projection. *See* defenses, immature
psychiatric disorders
　common features of, 52
　iatrogenic fads in, 44
　onset of, 56
　youth climate distress and, 40
psychiatric trainee education, 176
psychoanalysis, xvi, 111
　psychodynamic psychotherapy and, 201
psychoeducation
　pediatricians and, 240
Psychological First Aid, 159, 239
psychotherapy
　climate informed, 196. *See also* climate distress, psychotherapies for
　developmental level and, 192
　therapeutic alliance and, 64
　therapist as role model, 191

queer ecological theory, xx, 414

Race to Resilience, 175
RE100 campaign, 351
rebel activist, 351
re-enchantment, 379
reformer activist, 350
refugee camps
　parenting in, 315
Regenerative Activism, 354
regression, 113, 192
relational trauma. *See* betrayal
reproductive refusal, 13, 415
research, xvi, 168, 412
　activism impact on climate distress and, 177
　agendas for climate mental health, 168
　challenges in climate mental health measurement, 79
　climate parenting knowledge gaps and, 324

　funding for, 179
　interventions requiring study, 175
　mapping and, 80
　mechanistic questions and, 82
　neurodevelopmental impacts of climate and, 177
　political bias and, 179
　priorities for, 83
　on psychotherapy for climate distress, 176
　study length, 82
　transgressive, 417
resilience, 13–14, 175, 304
　negative outcomes of, 142
　transformational resilience, 14
re-storying, 367, 373, 375–376, 380–381
revising goals, 272
rhythmic attunement, 133
rising sea levels
　Indigenous peoples and, 315
　small island states an, 314
risk-taking behavior, 55, 98
ritual. *See* work that reconnects, the
Robinson, Sierra Raine, 252
rumination, 12
Ruminative Responses Scale, 42

sacred activism, 354. *See also* activism; Patten, Terry
sadness, 6
Safety Seeking Behaviors, 153
salience network, 103
salience theory, 153
Sámi culture, 303
school age, 117
School Strike 4 Climate, 29, 362
Seeley, Kathy, 260
self-destructive behavior, 119
settler-colonialism, xix, 385–386, 390
Seymour, Nicole, 415
Sharma, Anjali, 136
Sharma *versus* the Minister for the Environment, 362
Siegel, Dan
　Triune Brain and Window of Tolerance, 218
social determinants of health, 47, 139, 389
　distal determinants, 394
　Indigenous groups and, 392
　intermediate determinants, 394
　proximal determinants, 393
Social GGRRAAACCEEESSS, 151
Social Graces, 151
social learning, 97

social tipping points
  youth understanding of, 162
solastalgia, 29, 169, 241
  Freud and, 96
  Indigenous youth and, 390
soliphilia, 11
Solnit, Rebecca, 132
Somatic Experiencing Therapy, 132
souffrance écologique, 32
splitting. *See* defenses, immature
St. Onge, Patricia, 217
Standing Rock, 386
Staton, Josephine, 259
Stop Adani movement, 352
stress, 57, 94, 139–140, 170. *See also* trauma, neuropsychiatric effects of
  prenatal impacts, 171
  toxic, 140
stress inoculation, 57
stress-diathesis model, 104
structural racism, 386
suicide, climate effects on, 57
Sunrise Movement, 224, 352
superego integration, 125
SustyVibes, xix, 356
Symbiocene, 120
systems theory, xviii, 287
systems thinking, xv, 80, 290, 343
  bidirectional influences, 291

Teach the Future, 332
techno-subsystem, 289, 296
telehealth
  underserved areas and climate, 174
thematic analysis. *See* education
therapeutic alliance, 64
Thomas, Leah, 349
Thunberg, Greta, 29, 33–34, 43, 191, 223, 352
Tipton, Jennifer, 340
toddlerhood, 117
trait anxiety, 294. *See also* anxiety, trait *versus* state
Trans Mountain pipeline expansion, 255
transdiagnostic treatment approach, 156
Transformational resilience, 175
transgressive research, 417
transition, onto-epistemological, 369, 380–381
  to sustainability, 369
trauma, 130
  in adolescence, 119
  creativity as healing and, 143
  dissociation and, 131
  guns/active shooter drills and, 135
  historical, 120

neuropsychiatric effects of, 139
relational, 136
transgenerational, 136
triple bottom line, 356
Triple WellBeing, 339
trust *vs* mistrust, 116
Tuckman, Bruce, 218
Turtle Island, 391

Uchendu, Jennifer, xix, 355
UK Schools Sustainability Network, 340
Umweltangst, 33
uncertainty, 195, 275
  positive valuation of and youth outcomes, 161
uncivilization, 372
Uncivilisation–The Dark Mountain Manifesto, 371
Unheimliche, 96
United Nations Convention on the Rights of the Child, 134, 258, 348
United Nations Declaration of Indigenous Peoples, 396

values, 198
  action aligned with, 161
  alignment with, 200
  meaning and, 272
Van der Voo, Lee, 263
Van Susteren, Lise, 255
ventral striatum, 55
  prosocial behavior and, 55
vicious cycle, 304
vicious flower, 153
virtuous cycle, 84, 304
vulnerability, 15, 137
  climate stressors, 72
  Indigenous youth and, 390

Wardell, Susan, 22
Weintrobe, Sally, 120, 122, 133
Weiss Functional Impairment Scale, 42
Whis.stem.men.knee, 190
white supremacy
  and climate threats, 408
  white extinction anxiety and, 408
whole child framework, 311
wicked problem, 4
Wijsen, Melati & Isabel, 350
Wilson, Mike, 256
Wiwa, Ken Saro, 351
Work that Reconnects, the, xvii, 210, 212
  The Cairn of Mourning, 222
  Earth Leadership Cohorts, 213

The Evolutionary Walk, 220
The Great Turning, 225
The Mirror Walk, 220
soil/soul sustainability practice, 221
The Spiral, 214
World Clean-up Day, 359
worry about climate change, 3–4, 9, 269
Wright, Lauren, 251

ympäristöahdistus, 33, 34
young adulthood, 118. *See also* Erikson, Erik
Yousafzai, Malala, 354

youth, 8
   concern about climate change, 3, 9
   definition of, 8
   developmental vulnerabilities of, 8
   global diversity of, 9, 15
   impacts of climate change, 9, 13–14
   trangenerational responsibility and, 13
   vulnerability to climate change, 15
Youth Leading Environmental Change. *See* Earth Leadership Cohorts
Youth v. Gov, film, 263
Youthstrike 4 Climate, 332, 335

Printed in the United States
by Baker & Taylor Publisher Services